PRAISE FOR
The Secret War by Max Hastings

"In his monumental work, *The Secret War*, Max Hastings reminds us that intelligence did not become a 'growth industry' until World War II. . . . A real page-turner."
—*New York Times*

"A compendious, crisply argued, and witty assessment."
—*Financial Times* (London)

"As gripping as any spy thriller. Hastings understands, better than any previous historian, that this is as much a story about human nature as it is about the mechanics of code-breaking or spycraft. . . . He has the novelist's eye for the telling detail. . . . This book works because Hastings is simply a very fine writer who is not afraid of making judgements. . . . Hastings's achievement is especially impressive, for he has produced the best single volume yet written on the subject."
—*Sunday Times* (London)

"This is his war and he writes with an easy assurance, scatter-gunning opinions. . . . Hastings is on form. He has set out to provide thought and discussion and, with his familiar robustness, shotgun at side, he has succeeded."
—*The Times* (London)

"Authoritative, exciting, and notably well written." —*Daily Telegraph* (London)

"A serious work of rigorous and comprehensive history . . . royally entertaining and readable."
—*Mail on Sunday*

"A well-crafted, impeccably researched, and humor-leavened account of both Allied and Axis World War II backstage intrigue." —*World War II Magazine*

"[Hastings's] massive overview is a fascinating look at the dark world of espionage and dirty tricks that are a part of warfare, with terse and readable looks at spies, communications intercepts, and guerrillas." —*Washington Times*

"I must award Mr. Hastings another 'Best' [after *Inferno*]. In a quarter century of reviewing books on intelligence . . . *The Secret War* ranks foremost. . . . Ten cloaks, ten daggers."
—Joseph Goulden, *The Intelligencer*

"Hastings (*Catastrophe 1914*) further solidifies his gift for combining scholarship and readability in this scintillating overview of intelligence operations in WWII. . . . Hastings tells it all in a book everyone interested in WWII should acquire."
—*Publishers Weekly*

"Impeccably researched. . . . Hastings understands that we're all thrilled by a good spy story, and in this masterful, gripping narrative, he delivers just that."
—*BookPage*

"Ambitious and often fascinating. . . . This wide-ranging account is filled with compelling characters. . . . A superb survey of an always interesting aspect of warfare."
—*Booklist*

"Few readers will be able to resist his version of events. . . . A masterful account of wartime skullduggery that has relevance still today." —*Kirkus Reviews*

Also by Max Hastings

REPORTAGE
America 1968: The Fire This Time
Barricades in Belfast: The Fight for Civil Rights in Northern Ireland
The Battle for the Falklands (with Simon Jenkins)

BIOGRAPHY
Montrose: The King's Champion
Yoni: Hero of Entebbe

AUTOBIOGRAPHY
Did You Really Shoot the Television?
Going to the Wars
Editor

MILITARY HISTORY
Bomber Command
The Battle of Britain (with Len Deighton)
Das Reich
Overlord: D-Day and the Battle for Normandy
Victory in Europe
The Korean War
Warriors: Portraits from the Battlefield
Armageddon: The Battle for Germany 1944–1945
Retribution: The Battle for Japan, 1944–45
Winston's War: Churchill, 1944–45
Inferno: The World at War, 1939–1945
Catastrophe 1914: Europe Goes to War

COUNTRYSIDE WRITING
Outside Days
Scattered Shots
Country Fair

ANTHOLOGY (EDITED)
The Oxford Book of Military Anecdotes

MAX HASTINGS

THE SECRET WAR

SPIES, CIPHERS, AND GUERRILLAS 1939–1945

HARPER PERENNIAL

NEW YORK • LONDON • TORONTO • SYDNEY • NEW DELHI • AUCKLAND

First published in a different form in the United Kingdom in 2015
by William Collins.

A hardcover edition of this book was published in 2016 by HarperCollins Publishers.

THE SECRET WAR. Copyright © 2016 by Max Hastings. All rights reserved. Printed in the
United States of America. No part of this book may be used or reproduced in any manner
whatsoever without written permission except in the case of brief quotations embodied
in critical articles and reviews. For information, address HarperCollins Publishers, 195
Broadway, New York, NY 10007.

HarperCollins books may be purchased for educational, business, or sales promotional
use. For information, please e-mail the Special Markets Department at SPsales@
harpercollins.com.

FIRST U.S. HARPER PERENNIAL EDITION PUBLISHED 2017.

Library of Congress Cataloging-in-Publication Data has been applied for.

ISBN 978-0-06-225928-8 (pbk.)

20 21   PC/LSC   10 9 8 7 6 5 4

For

WILLIAM and AMELIE

the next generation

Contents

Illustrations

Stewart Menzies (Evening Standard/Getty Images)

Hermann Görtz (IMAGNO/Austrian Archives (S)/Süddeutsche Zeitung Photo)

The Registration Room at Arlington Hall (From Stephen Budiansky, *Battle of Wits*)

Joe Rochefort (Photo by Carl Mydans/The LIFE Picture Collection/Getty Images)

Thomas Dyer (From Elliot Carlson, *Joe Rochefort's War*)

Stars of the US Army's Signals Intelligence Service: Frank Rowlett, Abraham Sinkov and William Friedman (From Stephen Budiansky, *Battle of Wits*)

Libertas and Harro Schulze-Boysen (Collection Megele/Süddeutsche Zeitung Photo)

Arvid and Mildred Harnack (Gedenkstätte Deutscher Widerstand/ Bundesarchiv, Plak 009-009A-020)

Alexander Foote (Jay Robert Nash Collection/CRIA Images)

Alexander Radó (The National Archives, KV2/1647)

Anatoli Gourevitch (From Anatoli Gourevitch, *Un certain monsieur Kent*)

Rudolf Rössler (dpa/Süddeutsche Zeitung Photo)

Ursula Hamburger (Jay Robert Nash Collection/CRIA Images)

Leopold Trepper (The National Archives, KV2-20741)

Italian SOE agent Paolo del Din (From Marcus Binney, *The Women Who Lived for Danger*)

Oluf Reed-Olsen (From Oluf Reed-Olsen, *Two Eggs on My Plate*)

Gilbert Renault – 'Colonel Rémy' (Rue des Archives/Tallandier/ Süddeutsche Zeitung Photo)

Elyesa Bazna – 'Cicero' (From Elyesa Bazna, *I Was Cicero*)

Nigel Clive (From Nigel Clive, *A Greek Experience*)

Ronald Seth (From Ronald Seth, *A Spy Has No Friends*)

Sterling Hayden (© John Springer Collection/CORBIS)

Hugh Trevor-Roper (By permission of the Master and Fellows of St John's College, Cambridge)

Bill Bentinck (Photo by Tony Linck/The LIFE Picture Collection/Getty Images)

A wardrobe specialist at OSS's London station dresses an American agent for a mission (Joseph E. Persico Papers, Envelope A, Hoover Institution Archives: Courtesy of Hoover Institution Library & Archives, Stanford University)

Wrens operating Colossus, 1943 (Bletchley Park Trust)
Max Newman (By permission of the Master and Fellows of St John's
    College, Cambridge)
Tommy Flowers (Courtesy of Kenneth Flowers)
The German Lorenz teleprinter (Courtesy of Steve Montana Photography)
Bill Tutte (Trinity College, Cambridge)
R.V. Jones (From R.V. Jones, *Most Secret War*)

TEXT ILLUSTRATIONS

*Every effort has been made to trace copyright holders and to obtain their
permission for the use of copyright material. The publisher apologises for any
errors or omissions in the above list and would be grateful if notified of any
corrections that should be incorporated in future editions of this book.*

Introduction

This is a book about some of the most fascinating people who participated in the Second World War. Soldiers, sailors, airmen, civilians had vastly diverse experiences, forged by fire, geography, economics and ideology. Those who killed each other were the most conspicuous, but in many ways the least interesting: outcomes were also profoundly influenced by a host of men and women who never fired a shot. While even in Russia months could elapse between big battles, all the participants waged an unceasing secret war – a struggle for knowledge of the enemy to empower their armies, navies and air forces, through espionage and codebreaking. Lt. Gen. Albert Praun, the Wehrmacht's last signals chief, wrote afterwards of the latter: 'All aspects of this modern "cold war of the air waves" were carried on constantly even when the guns were silent.' The Allies also launched guerrilla and terrorist campaigns wherever in Axis-occupied territories they had means to do so: covert operations assumed an unprecedented importance.

This book does not aspire to be a comprehensive narrative, which would fill countless volumes. It is instead a study of both sides' secret war machines and some of the characters who influenced them. It is unlikely that any more game-changing revelations will be forthcoming, save possibly from Soviet archives currently locked by Vladimir Putin. The Japanese destroyed most of their intelligence files in 1945, and what survives remains inaccessible in Tokyo, but veterans provided significant post-war testimony – a decade ago, I interviewed some of them myself.

Most books about wartime intelligence focus on the doings of a chosen nation. I have instead attempted to explore it in a global context. Some episodes in my narrative are bound to be familiar to specialists, but a new perspective seems possible by placing them on a broad canvas. Though spies and codebreakers have generated a vast literature, readers may be as astonished by some of the tales in this book as I have been on discovering them for myself. I have written extensively about the Russians, because their doings are much less familiar to Western readers than are those of Britain's Bletchley Park, America's Arlington Hall and Op-20-G. I have omitted many legends, and made no attempt to retell the most familiar tales of Resistance in Western Europe, nor of the Abwehr's agents in Britain and America, who were swiftly imprisoned or 'turned' for the famous Double Cross system. By contrast, though the facts of Richard Sorge's and 'Cicero's'* doings have been known for many decades, their significance deserves a rethink.

The achievements of some secret warriors were as breathtaking as the blunders of others. As I recount here, the British several times allowed sensitive material to be captured which could have been fatal to the Ultra secret. Meanwhile, spy writers dwell obsessively on the treachery of Britain's Cambridge Five, but relatively few recognise what we might call the Washington and Berkeley five hundred – a small army of American leftists who served as informants for Soviet intelligence. The egregious Senator Joseph McCarthy stigmatised many individuals unjustly, but he was not wrong in charging that between the 1930s and 1950s the US government and the nation's greatest institutions and corporations harboured an astonishing number of employees whose first loyalty was not to their own flag. True, between 1941 and 1945 the Russians were supposedly allies of Britain and the United States, but Stalin viewed this relationship with unremitting cynicism – as a merely temporary associa-tion, for the narrow purpose of destroying the Nazis, with nations that remained the Soviet Union's historic foes and rivals.

Many books about wartime intelligence focus on what spies or code-breakers found out. The only question that matters, however, is how far secret knowledge changed outcomes. The scale of Soviet espionage dwarfed that of every other belligerent, and yielded a rich technological harvest from Britain and the United States, but Stalin's paranoia crippled exploitation of his crop of other people's political and military secrets. The most distinguished American historian of wartime codebreaking told me in 2014 that after half a lifetime studying the subject he has decided that Allied intelligence contributed almost nothing to winning the war. This seems too extreme a verdict, but my friend's remarks show how scepti-cism, and indeed cynicism, breed and multiply in the course of decades wading in the morass of fantasy, treachery and incompetence wherein

---

* Agents' codenames in the pages that follow are given within quotation marks.

most spymasters and their servants have their being. The record suggests that official secrecy does more to protect intelligence agencies from domestic accountability for their own follies than to shield them from enemy penetration. Of what use was it – for instance – to conceal from the British public even the identities of their own spy chiefs, when for years MI6's* most secret operations were betrayed to the Russians by Kim Philby, one of its most senior officers? The US government repudiated a bilateral intelligence exchange agreed with the NKVD† by Maj. Gen. William Donovan of OSS, but official caution did little for national security when some of Donovan's top subordinates were passing secrets to Soviet agents.

Intelligence-gathering is not a science. There are no certainties, even when some of the enemy's correspondence is being read. There is a cacophony of 'noise', from which 'signals' – truths large and small – must be extracted. In August 1939, on the eve of the Nazi–Soviet Pact, a British official wrung his hands over the confused messages reaching the Foreign Office about relations between Berlin and Moscow: 'We find ourselves,' he wrote – using words that may be applied to most intelligence – 'when attempting to assess the value of these secret reports, somewhat in the position of the Captain of the Forty Thieves when, having put a chalk mark on Ali Baba's door, he found that Morgana had put similar marks on all the doors in the street and had no indication which was the true one.'

It is fruitless to study any nation's successes, its pearls of revelation, in isolation. These must be viewed in the context of hundreds of thousands of pages of trivia or outright nonsense that crossed the desks of analysts, statesmen, commanders. 'Diplomats and intelligence agents, in my experience, are even bigger liars than journalists,' wrote the British wartime spy Malcolm Muggeridge, who was familiar with all three, and something of a charlatan himself. The sterility of much espionage was nicely illustrated

---

* Britain's MI6 is often known by its other name, SIS – the Secret Intelligence Service – but for clarity it is given the former name throughout this work, even in documents quoted, partly to avoid confusion with the US Signals Intelligence Service.

† The Soviet intelligence service and its subordinate domestic and foreign branches were repeatedly reorganised and renamed between 1934 and 1954, when it became the KGB. Throughout this text 'NKVD' is used, while acknowledging also from 1943 the counter-intelligence organisation SMERSh – *Smert Shpionam* – and the parallel existence from 1926 of the Red Army's military intelligence branch, the Fourth Department or GRU, fierce rival of the NKVD at home and abroad.

by František Moravec of Czech intelligence. One day in 1936 he proudly presented his commanding officer with a report on a new piece of German military equipment, for which he had paid an informant handsomely. The general skimmed it, then said, 'I will show you something better.' He tossed across his desk a copy of the magazine *Die Wehrmacht*, pointed out an article on the same weapon, and said dryly, 'The subscription is only twenty crowns.'

In the same category fell the Abwehr transcript of a December 1944 US State Department message appointing a new economic affairs counsellor to the Polish exile government in London. This read, in part: 'His transportation expenses and per diem, Tunis to London, via Washington, DC, transportation expenses and per diem for his family and shipment effects direct authorised, subject Travel Regulations.' A page-long translation of this decrypt was stamped 'Top Secret' by its German readers. The man-hours expended by the Nazi war machine to secure this gem reflect the fashion in which intelligence services often move mountains to give birth to mice.

Trust is a bond and privilege of free societies. Yet credulity and respect for privacy are fatal flaws to analysts and agent-runners. Their work requires them to persuade citizens of other countries to abandon the traditional ideal of patriotism, whether for cash, out of conviction, or occasionally because of a personal bond between handler and informant. It will always be disputed territory, whether those who betray their society's secrets are courageous and principled heroes who identify a higher loyalty, as modern Germans perceive the anti-Hitler Resistance, or instead traitors, as most of us classify Kim Philby, Alger Hiss – and in our own times Edward Snowden. The day job of many intelligence officers is to promote treachery, which helps to explain why the trade attracts so many weird people. Malcolm Muggeridge asserted disdainfully that it 'necessarily involves such cheating, lying and betraying, that it has a deleterious effect on the character. I never met anyone professionally engaged in it whom I should care to trust in any capacity.'

Stalin said: 'A spy should be like the devil; no one can trust him, not even himself.' The growth of new ideologies, most significantly communism, caused some people to embrace loyalties that crossed frontiers and, in the eyes of zealots, transcended mere patriotism. More than a few felt exalted by discovering virtue in treason, though others preferred to betray for cash. Many wartime spymasters were uncertain which side their agents were really serving, and in some cases bewilderment persists to this day. The British petty crook Eddie Chapman, 'Agent ZigZag', had extraordinary war experiences as the plaything of British and German intelligence. At different times he put himself at the mercy of both, but it seems unlikely that his activities did much good to either. He was an intriguing but unimportant figure, one among countless loose cannon on the secret battlefield. More interesting, and scarcely known to the public, is the case of Ronald Seth, an SOE agent captured by the Germans and trained by them to serve as a 'double' in Britain. I shall describe below the puzzlement of SOE, MI5, MI6, MI9 and the Abwehr about whose side Seth ended up on.

Intelligence-gathering is inherently wasteful. I am struck by the number of secret service officers of all nationalities whose only achievement in foreign postings was to stay alive, at hefty cost to their employers, while collecting information of which not a smidgeon assisted the war effort. Perhaps one-thousandth of 1 per cent of material garnered from secret sources by all the belligerents in World War II contributed to changing battlefield outcomes. Yet that fraction was of such value that warlords grudged not a life nor a pound, rouble, dollar, Reichsmark expended in securing it. Intelligence has always influenced wars, but until the twentieth century commanders could discover their enemies' motions only through spies and direct observation – counting men, ships, guns. Then came wireless communication, which created rolling new intelligence corn prairies that grew exponentially after 1930, as technology advanced. 'There has never been anything comparable in any other period of history to the impact of radio,' wrote the great British scientific intelligence officer Dr R.V. Jones. '... It was the product of some of the most imaginative developments that have ever occurred in physics, and it was as near magic as anyone could conceive.' Not only could millions of citizens build their own sets at home, as did also many spies abroad, but in Berlin, London, Washington, Moscow, Tokyo electronic eavesdroppers were empowered to probe the deployments and sometimes the intentions of an enemy without benefit of telescopes, frigates or agents.

One of the themes in this book is that the signals intelligence war, certainly in its early stages, was less lopsided in the Allies' favour than popular mythology suggests. The Germans used secret knowledge well to plan the 1940 invasion of France and the Low Countries. At least until mid-1942, and even in some degree thereafter, they read important Allied codes both on land and at sea, with significant consequences for both the Battle of the Atlantic and the North African campaign. They were able to exploit feeble Red Army wireless security during the first year of Operation 'Barbarossa'. From late 1942 onwards, however, Hitler's codebreakers lagged ever further behind their Allied counterparts. The Abwehr's attempts at espionage abroad were pitiful.

The Japanese government and army high command planned their initial 1941–42 assaults on Pearl Harbor and the European empires of South-East Asia most efficiently, but thereafter treated intelligence with disdain, and waged war in a fog of ignorance about their enemies' doings. The Italian intelligence service and its codebreakers had some notable successes in the early war years, but by 1942 Mussolini's commanders were reduced to using Russian PoWs to do their eavesdropping on Soviet wireless traffic. Relatively little effort was expended by any nation on probing Italy's secrets, because its military capability shrank so rapidly. 'Our picture of the Italian air force was incomplete and our knowledge far from sound,' admitted RAF intelligence officer Group-Captain Harry Humphreys about the Mediterranean theatre, before adding smugly, 'So – fortunately – was the Italian air force.'

The first requirement for successful use of secret data is that commanders should be willing to analyse it honestly. Herbert Meyer, a veteran of Washington's National Intelligence Council, defined his business as the presentation of 'organized information'; he argued that ideally intelligence departments should provide a service for commanders resembling that of ship and aircraft navigation systems. Donald McLachlan, a British naval practitioner, observed: 'Intelligence has much in common with scholarship, and the standards which are demanded in scholarship are those which should be applied to intelligence.' After the war, the surviving German commanders blamed all their intelligence failures on Hitler's refusal to countenance objective assessment of evidence. Signals supremo Albert Praun said: 'Unfortunately ... throughout the war Hitler ... showed a lack of confidence in communications intelligence, especially if the reports were unfavourable [to his own views].'

Good news for the Axis cause – for instance, interceptions revealing heavy Allied losses – were given the highest priority for transmission to Berlin, because the Führer welcomed them. Meanwhile bad tidings received short shrift. Before the June 1941 invasion of Russia, Gen. Georg Thomas of the WiRuAmt – the Wehrmacht's economics department – produced estimates of Soviet weapons production which approached the reality, though still short of it, and argued that the loss of European Russia would not necessarily precipitate the collapse of Stalin's industrial base.

Hitler dismissed Thomas's numbers out of hand, because he could not reconcile their magnitude with his contempt for all things Slavonic. Field-Marshal Wilhelm Keitel eventually instructed the WiRuAmt to stop submitting intelligence that might upset the Führer.

The war effort of the Western democracies profited immensely from the relative openness of their societies and governance. Churchill sometimes indulged spasms of anger towards those around him who voiced unwelcome views, but a remarkably open debate was sustained in the Allied corridors of power, including most military headquarters. Gen. Sir Bernard Montgomery was a considerable tyrant, but those whom he trusted – including his intelligence chief Brigadier Bill Williams, a peacetime Oxford don – could speak their minds. All the United States's brilliant intelligence successes were gained through codebreaking, and were exploited most dramatically in the Pacific naval war. American ground commanders seldom showed much interest in using their knowledge to promote deceptions, as did the British. D-Day in 1944 was the only operation for which the Americans cooperated wholeheartedly on a deception plan. Even then the British were prime movers, while the Americans merely acquiesced – for instance, by allowing Gen. George Patton to masquerade as commander of the fictitious American First US Army Group supposedly destined to land in the Pas de Calais. Some senior Americans were suspicious of the British enthusiasm for misleading the enemy, which they regarded as reflecting their ally's enthusiasm for employing guile to escape hard fighting, the real business of war.

GC&CS, the so-called Government Code and Cipher School at Bletchley Park, was of course not merely the most important intelligence hub of the conflict, but from 1942 Britain's outstanding contribution to victory. Folk legend holds that Alan Turing's creation of electro-mechanical bombes exposed Germany's entire communications system to Allied eyes by breaking the Enigma's traffic. The truth is far more complex. The Germans employed dozens of different keys, many of which were read only intermittently, often out of 'real time' – meaning insufficiently rapidly to make possible an operational response – and a few not at all. The British accessed some immensely valuable Enigma material, but coverage was never remotely comprehensive, and was especially weak on army traffic. Moreover, an ever-increasing volume of the Germans' most secret signals was transmitted through a teleprinter network which employed an entirely different encryption system from that used by Enigma. The achievement of Bletchley's mathematicians and linguists in cracking the Lorenz

Schlüsselzusatz was quite distinct from, and more difficult than, breaking the Enigma, even though recipients in the field knew the products of all such activities simply as 'Ultra'.* Bill Tutte, the young Cambridge mathematician who made the critical initial discoveries, is scarcely known to posterity, yet deserves to be almost as celebrated as Turing.

Ultra enabled the Allied leadership to plan its campaigns and operations in the second half of the war with a confidence vouchsafed to no previous warlords in history. Knowing the enemy's hand did not diminish its strength, however. In 1941 and into 1942, again and again the British learned where the Axis intended to strike – as in Crete, North Africa and Malaya – but this did not save them from losing the subsequent battles. Hard power, whether on land or at sea or in the air, was indispensable to the exploitation of secret knowledge. So, too, was wisdom on the part of British and American commanders and their staffs – which proved conspicuously lacking at key moments during the 1944–45 north-west Europe campaign. Intelligence did, however, contribute importantly to mitigating some early disasters: young R.V. Jones's achievement in showing the path towards jamming the Luftwaffe's navigational beams significantly diminished the pain inflicted by the Blitz on Britain. At sea, Ultra's pinpointing of German U-boats – with an alarming nine-month interruption in 1942 – made it possible to reroute convoys to evade them, an even more important contribution to holding open the Atlantic supply line than sinking enemy submarines.

The Americans had some reason to suspect their allies of romanticism about deception. Col. Dudley Clarke – famous not least to Spanish police, who once arrested him wearing woman's clothes in a Madrid street – conducted a massive cover operation in the North African desert before the October 1942 Battle of El Alamein. Historians have celebrated Clarke's ingenuity in creating fictional forces which caused Rommel to deploy significant strength well south of the focal point of Montgomery's assault. However, such guile did not spare Eighth Army from the fortnight of hard fighting that proved necessary to break through the Afrika Korps. The Germans argued that Clarke's activities changed nothing in the end,

---

* Americans referred to their Japanese diplomatic decrypt material as 'Magic', but throughout this text for simplicity I have used 'Ultra', which became generally accepted on both sides of the Atlantic as the generic term for products of decryption of enemy high-grade codes and ciphers, although oddly enough the word was scarcely used inside Bletchley Park.

because they had time to redeploy northwards before the decisive British assault. In Burma Col. Peter Fleming, brother of the creator of James Bond, went to elaborate and hazardous lengths to leave a haversack full of deceptive 'secret papers' in a wrecked jeep where the enemy were bound to find it, but the Japanese took no notice of this haul when they got it. From 1942 onwards, British intelligence achieved an almost complete understanding of Germany's air defences and the electronic technologies they employed, but Allied bomber forces continued to suffer punitive casualties, especially before US long-range fighters wrecked the Luftwaffe in the air in the spring of 1944.

Whatever the contribution of British tactical deceptions in North Africa, Allied deceivers had two important and almost indisputable strategic successes. In 1943–44, Operation 'Zeppelin' created a fictitious British army in Egypt which induced Hitler to maintain large forces in Yugoslavia and Greece to repel an Allied Balkan landing. It was this imaginary threat, not Tito's guerrillas, that caused twenty-two Axis divisions to kick their heels in the south-east until after D-Day. The second achievement was, of course, that of Operation 'Fortitude' before and after the assault on Normandy. It bears emphasis that neither could have exercised such influence had not the Allies possessed sufficient hard power, together with command of the sea, to make it credible that they might land armies almost anywhere.

Some Russian deceptions dwarf those of the British and Americans. The story of agent 'Max', and the vast operation launched as a diversion from the Stalingrad offensive, at a cost of 70,000 Russian lives, is one of the most astonishing of the war, and almost unknown to Western readers. In 1943–44, other Soviet ruses prompted the Germans repeatedly to concentrate their forces in the wrong places in advance of onslaughts by the Red Army. Air superiority was an essential prerequisite, in the East as in the West: the ambitious deceptions of the later war years were possible only because the Germans could not carry out photographic reconnaissance to disprove the 'legends' they were sold across the airwaves and through false documents.

The Western Allies were much less successful in gathering humint than sigint.* Neither the British nor the Americans acquired a single highly placed source around the German, Japanese or Italian governments or

---

* 'Humint' is the trade term for intelligence gathered by spies, 'sigint' for the product of wireless interception.

high commands, until in 1943 OSS's Allen Dulles began to receive some good Berlin gossip. The Western Allies achieved nothing like the Russians' penetration of London, Washington, Berlin and Tokyo, the last through their agent Richard Sorge, working in the German embassy. The US got into the business of overseas espionage only after Pearl Harbor, and focused more effort on sabotage and codebreaking than on placing spies, as distinct from paramilitary groups, in enemy territory. OSS's Research and Analysis Department in Washington was more impressive than its flamboyant but unfocused field operations. Moreover, I believe that Western Allied sponsorship of guerrilla war did more to promote the post-war self-respect of occupied nations than to hasten the destruction of Nazism. Russia's partisan operations were conducted on a far more ambitious scale than the SOE/OSS campaigns, and propaganda boosted their achievements both at the time and in the post-war era. However, Soviet documents now available, of which my Russian researcher Dr Lyuba Vinogradovna has made extensive use, indicate that we should view the achievements of the Eastern guerrilla campaign, at least until 1943, with considerable scepticism.

As in all my books, I seek below to establish the 'big picture' framework, and to weave into this human stories of the spies, codebreakers and intelligence chiefs who served their respective masters – Turing at Bletchley and Nimitz's cryptanalysts in the Pacific, the Soviet 'Red Orchestra' of agents in Germany, Reinhard Gehlen of OKH, William Donovan of OSS and many more exotic characters. The foremost reason the Western Allies did intelligence best was that they brilliantly exploited civilians, to whom both the US and British governments granted discretion, influence and – where necessary – military rank, as their opponents did not. When the first volume of the British official history of wartime intelligence was published thirty years ago, I suggested to its principal author Professor Harry Hinsley, a Bletchley veteran, that it seemed to show that the amateurs contributed more than did career secret service professionals. Hinsley replied somewhat impatiently, 'Of course they did. You wouldn't want to suppose, would you, that in peacetime the best brains of our society wasted their lives in intelligence?'

I have always thought this an important point, echoed in the writings of another academic, Hugh Trevor-Roper, who served in both MI5 and MI6, and whose personal achievement makes him seem one of the more remarkable British intelligence officers of the war. In peacetime, most secret services fulfilled their functions adequately, or at least did little harm, while staffed by people of moderate abilities. Once a struggle for national survival began, however, intelligence had to become part of the guiding brain of the war effort. Clashes on the battlefield could be fought by men of relatively limited gifts, the virtues of the sports field – physical fitness, courage, grit, a little initiative and common sense. But intelligence services suddenly needed brilliance. It sounds banal to say that they had to recruit intelligent people, but – as more than a few twentieth-century sages noted – in many countries this principle was honoured mostly in the breach.

A few words about the arrangement of this book: while my approach is broadly chronological, to avoid leaping too confusingly between traitors in Washington, Soviet spies in Switzerland and the mathematicians of Bletchley Park, the narrative persists with some themes beyond their time sequence. I have drawn heavily on the most authoritative published works in this field, those of Stephen Budiansky, David Kahn and Christopher Andrew notable among them, but I have also exploited archives in Britain, Germany and the US, together with much previously untranslated Russian material. I have made no attempt to discuss the mathematics of code-breaking, which has been done by writers much more numerate than myself.

It is often said that Ian Fleming's thrillers bear no relationship to the real world of espionage. However, when reading contemporary Soviet reports and recorded conversations, together with the memoirs of Moscow's wartime intelligence officers, I am struck by how uncannily they mirror the mad, monstrous, imagined dialogue of such people in Fleming's *From Russia With Love*. And some of the plots planned and executed by the NKVD and the GRU were no less fantastic than his.

All historical narratives are necessarily tentative and speculative, but they become far more so when spies are involved. In chronicling battles, one can reliably record how many ships were sunk, aircraft shot down, men killed, how much ground was won or lost. But intelligence generates a vast, unreliable literature, some of it produced by protagonists for their own glorification or justification. One immensely popular account of Allied intelligence, *Bodyguard of Lies*, published in 1975, is largely a work of fiction. Sir William Stephenson, the Canadian who ran the British wartime intelligence coordination organisation in New York, performed a valuable liaison function, but was never much of a spymaster. This did not prevent him from assisting in the creation of a wildly fanciful 1976 biography of himself, *A Man Called Intrepid*, though there is no evidence that anybody ever called him anything of the sort. Most accounts of wartime SOE agents, particularly women and especially in France, contain large doses of romantic twaddle. Moscow's mendacity is undiminished by time: the KGB's official intelligence history, published as recently as 1997, asserts that the British Foreign Office is still concealing documentation about its secret negotiations with 'fascist' Germany, and indeed its collusion with Hitler.

Allied codebreaking operations against Germany, Italy and Japan exercised far more influence than did any spy. It is impossible to quantify their impact, however, and it is baffling that Harry Hinsley, the official historian, asserted that Ultra probably shortened the war by three years. This is as tendentious as Professor M.R.D. Foot's claim, in his official history of SOE in France, that Allied commanders considered that Resistance curtailed the global struggle by six months. Ultra was a tool of the British and Americans, who played only a subordinate role in the destruction of Nazism, which was overwhelmingly a Russian military endeavour. It is no more possible to measure the contribution of Bletchley Park to the timing of victory than that of Winston Churchill, Liberty ships or radar.

Likewise, publicists who make claims that some sensational modern book recounts 'the spy story that changed World War II' might as well cite *Mary Poppins*. One of Churchill's most profound observations was made in October 1941, in response to a demand from Sir Charles Portal, as chief of air staff, for a commitment to build 4,000 heavy bombers which, claimed the airman, would bring Germany to its knees in six months. The prime minister wrote back that, while everything possible was being done to create a large bomber force, he deplored attempts to place unbounded confidence in any one means of securing victory. 'All things are always on the move simultaneously,' he declared. This is an immensely important comment on human affairs, especially in war and above all in intelligence. It is impossible justly to attribute all credit for the success or blame for the failure of an operation to any single factor.

Yet while scepticism about the secret world is indispensable, so too is a capacity for wonder: some fabulous tales prove true. I blush to remember the day in 1974 when I was invited by a newspaper to review F.W. Winterbotham's *The Ultra Secret*. In those days, young and green and a mere casual student of 1939–45, like the rest of the world I had never heard of Bletchley Park. I glanced at the about-to-be-published book, then declined to write about it: Winterbotham made such extraordinary claims that I could not credit them. Yet of course the author, a wartime officer of

MI6, had been authorised to open a window upon one of the biggest and most fascinating secrets of the Second World War.

No other nation has ever produced an official history explicitly dedicated to wartime intelligence, and approaching in magnitude Britain's five volumes and 3,000-plus pages, published between 1978 and 1990. This lavish commitment to the historiography of the period, funded by the taxpayer, reflects British pride in its achievement, sustained into the twenty-first century by such absurd – as defined by its negligible relationship to fact – yet also hugely successful feature films as 2014's *The Imitation Game*. While most educated people today recognise how subordinate was the contribution of Britain to Allied victory alongside those of the Soviet Union and the United States, they realise that here was something Churchill's people did better than anybody else. Although there are many stories in this book about bungles and failures, in intelligence as in everything else related to conflict victory is gained not by the side that makes no mistakes, but by the one that makes fewer than the other side. By such a reckoning, the ultimate triumph of the British and Americans was as great in the secret war as it became in the collision between armies, navies and air forces. The defining reality is that the Allies won.

Finally, while some episodes described below seem comic or ridiculous, and reflect human frailties and follies, we must never forget that in every aspect of the global conflict, the stakes were life and death. Hundreds of thousands of people of many nationalities risked their lives, and many sacrificed them, often in the loneliness of dawn before a firing squad, to gather intelligence or pursue guerrilla operations. No twenty-first-century perspective on the personalities and events, successes and failures of those days should diminish our respect, even reverence, for the memory of those who paid the price for waging secret war.

MAX HASTINGS
West Berkshire & Datai, Langkawi
June 2015

1

Before the Deluge

1 SEEKERS AFTER TRUTH

The secret war started long before the shooting one did. One day in March 1937, a letter dropped onto the desk of Colonel František Moravec, addressed to 'the chief of the Czechoslovak Intelligence Service' – which was himself. It began: 'I offer you my services. First of all I shall state what my possibilities are: 1. The build-up of the German army. (a) the infantry …' and so on for three closely-typed pages. The Czechs, knowing themselves to be prospective prey of Hitler, conducted espionage with an intensity still absent elsewhere among Europe's democracies. They initially responded to this approach with scepticism, assuming a Nazi ruse, of which there had been plenty. Eventually, however, Moravec decided to risk a response. After protracted correspondence, the letter-writer whom Prague designated as agent A-54 agreed to a rendezvous in the Sudeten town of Kraslice. This was almost wrecked by a gunshot: one of Moravec's aides was so nervous that he fired the revolver in his pocket, putting a bullet through the colonel's trouser leg. Tranquillity was fortunately restored before the German visitor arrived, to be hurried to a nearby safe house. He brought with him sheaves of secret documents, which he had blithely carted through the frontier posts in a suitcase. Among the material was a copy of Czechoslovakia's defence plan which revealed to Moravec a traitor in his own ranks, subsequently hanged. A-54 departed from Kraslice still nameless, but richer by 100,000 Reichsmarks. He promised to call again, and indeed provided high-grade information for the ensuing three years. Only much later was he identified as Paul Thummel, a thirty-four-year-old officer of the Abwehr intelligence service.

Such an episode was almost everyday fare for Moravec. He was a passionate, fiercely energetic figure of middling height. A keen game-player, especially of chess, he spoke six languages fluently, and could read

some Latin and Greek. In 1914 he was an eighteen-year-old student at
Prague University, with aspirations to become a philosopher. Conscripted
into the Austro-Hungarian army, like most Czechs he was unwilling to die
for the Hapsburgs, and once at the front seized the first opportunity to
desert to the Russians. He was wounded under their flag in Bulgaria, and
finished the war with a Czech volunteer force on the Italian front. When
Czechoslovakia became an independent state he gratefully cast off these
tangled loyalties, to become an officer in its new army. He joined the intelligence branch in 1934, and took over as its chief three years later. Moravec
learned the trade mostly from spy stories bought off bookstalls, and soon
discovered that many real-life intelligence officers traffic in fiction: his
predecessor's supposed informants proved to have been figments of the
man's imagination, a cloak for embezzlement.

The colonel devoted much of his service's resources to talent-spotting in
Germany for informants, each network painstakingly ring-fenced. He set
up a payday loan company inside the Reich, targeted at military and civil
service clients. Within a year ninety of the bank's representatives were
roaming Germany, most *bona fide* employees, but some of them intelligence personnel who identified borrowers with access to information,
vulnerable to bribery or blackmail. The Czechs also pioneered new technology – microdot photography, ultra-violet rays, secret writing and state-of-
the-art wirelesses. Moravec was plentifully funded, a recognition of his role
in his nation's front line, and was thus able to pay a Luftwaffe major named
Salm 5,000 Reichsmarks – about £500 – as a retainer, and afterwards the
huge sum of a million Czech crowns – £7,500 – for Göring's air force order
of battle. Salm, however, flaunted his new-found wealth, and found himself
arrested, tried and beheaded. Meanwhile other people's spies were not idle
in Czechoslovakia: Prague's security officers arrested 2,900 suspects in 1936
alone, most of them allegedly acting for Germany or Hungary.

Every major nation probed the secrets of others in the same fashion,
using both overt and covert means. After Russia's Marshal Tukhachevsky
visited Britain in April 1934, he conveyed personally to Stalin a GRU
agent's description of the RAF's new Handley Page Hampden bomber,
detailing its Bristol and Rolls-Royce engine variants and attaching a sketch
showing its armament:

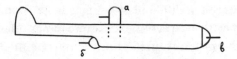

The Abwehr somehow laid hands on the 1935 fixture list of a British chemical plant's football team, which in the course of the season played at most of the company's other British factories; Berlin thus triumphantly pinpointed several chemical installations the Luftwaffe had hitherto been unaware of. The Australian aviator Sidney Cotton conducted some pioneering aerial photography over Germany at the behest of MI6's Wing-Commander Fred Winterbotham. The summer roads of Europe teemed with young couples on touring holidays, some of whom were funded by their respective intelligence services, and displayed an unromantic interest in airfields. MI6 sent an RAF officer, designated as Agent 479, together with a secretary to assist his cover, on a three-week spin around Germany, somewhat hampered by the facts that Luftwaffe station perimeters seldom adjoined autobahns, and neither visitor spoke German. The airman had originally planned to take his sister, who was fluent, but her husband refused consent.

In the Nazis' interests, in August 1935 Dr Hermann Görtz spent some weeks touring Suffolk and Kent on a Zündapp motorbike, pinpointing RAF bases with pretty young Marianne Emig riding in his sidecar. But Emig tired of the assignment, or lost her nerve, and Görtz, a forty-five-year-old lawyer from Lübeck who had learned English from his governess, felt obliged to escort her back to Germany. He then returned to collect a camera and other possessions – including plans of RAF Manston – that the couple had left behind in a rented Broadstairs bungalow. Unluckily for the aspiring masterspy, the police had already secured these incriminating items, following a tip from the spy-conscious landlord. Görtz found himself arrested at Harwich and sentenced to four years' imprisonment. He was released and deported in February 1939; more will be heard of Hermann Görtz.

For probing neighbours' secrets, every nation's skirmishers were its service officers posted to embassies abroad. Prominent among Berlin military attachés was Britain's Colonel Noel Mason-MacFarlane. 'Mason-Mac' was shrewd but bombastic. One day in 1938, he startled an English visitor to his flat by pointing out of the window to the spot where Hitler would next day view the Wehrmacht's birthday parade. 'Easy rifle shot,' said the colonel laconically. 'I could pick the bastard off from here as easy as winking, and what's more I'm thinking of doing it … With that lunatic out of the way we might be able to get some sense into things.' Mason-MacFarlane did nothing of the sort, of course. In his temperate moments he forged close friendships with German officers, and transmitted to London a stream of warnings about Nazi intentions. But the vignette provides an illustration of the role played by fantasy in the lives of intelligence officers, tottering on a tightrope between high purpose and low comedy.

The US government was said by scornful critics to possess no intelligence arm. In a narrow sense, this was so – it did not deploy secret agents abroad. At home, J. Edgar Hoover's Federal Bureau of Investigation was responsible for America's internal security. For all the FBI's trumpeted successes against gangsters and intensive surveillance of the US Communist Party and trades unions, it knew little of the army of Soviet spies roaming America, and did nothing to dissuade hi-tech corporations from booming their achievements. German military attaché Gen. Friedrich von Bötticher observed boisterously about his years of service in Washington: 'It was so easy, the Americans are so broad-minded, they print everything. You don't need any intelligence service. You have only to be industrious, to see the newspapers!' In 1936 Bötticher was able to forward to Berlin detailed reports on US rocket experiments. An American traitor sold the Germans blueprints of one of his country's most cherished technological achievements, the Norden bombsight. The general urged the Abwehr not to bother to deploy secret agents in the US, to preserve his hosts' faith in Nazi goodwill.

Intelligence agencies overvalue information gained from spies. One of the many academics conscripted into Britain's wartime secret service observed disdainfully: '[MI6] values information in proportion to its secrecy, not its accuracy. They would attach more value … to a scrap of third-rate and tendentious misinformation smuggled out of Sofia in the fly-buttons of a vagabond Rumanian pimp than to any intelligence deduced from a prudent reading of the foreign press.' American foreign correspondents and diplomats abroad provided Washington with a vision of the world no less plausible than that generated by Europe's spies. Major Truman Smith, the long-serving US military attaché in Berlin and a warm admirer of Hitler, formed a more accurate picture of the Wehrmacht's order of battle than did MI6.

America's naval attachés focused on Japan, their most likely foe, though they were often reduced to photographing its warships from passing passenger liners and swapping gossip in the Tokyo attachés' club. As secretary of state in 1929, Henry Stimson had closed down his department's 'Black Chamber' codebreaking operation, reasoning like many of his fellow-countrymen that a nation which faced no external threat could forgo such sordid instruments. Nonetheless both the army and navy, in isolation and fierce competition, sustained small codebreaking teams which exerted themselves mightily. The achievement of William Friedman, born in Russia in 1891 and educated as an agriculturalist, whose army Signals Intelligence Service team led by former mathematics teacher Frank Rowlett replicated the advanced Japanese 'Purple' diplomatic cipher machine and broke its key in September 1940, was all the more remarkable because America's crypt-analysts had shoestring resources. They made little attempt to crack German ciphers, because they lacked means to do so.

The Japanese spied energetically in China, the US and the European South-East Asian empires, which they viewed as prospective booty. Their agents were nothing if not committed: in 1935 when police in Singapore arrested a local Japanese expatriate on suspicion of espionage, such was the man's anxiety to avoid causing embarrassment to Tokyo that he swallowed prussic acid in his cell. The Chinese Nationalists headed by Chiang Kai-shek sustained an effective counter-intelligence service to protect his dictatorship from domestic critics, but across Asia Japanese spies were able to gather information almost unhindered. The British were more interested in countering internal communist agitation than in combating prospective foreign invaders. They found it impossible to take seriously 'the Wops of the East', as Churchill called the Japanese, or 'the little yellow dwarf slaves', in the words of the head of the Foreign Office.

Britain's diplomats were elaborately careless about protecting their secrets, adhering to the conventions of Victorian gentlemen. Robert Cecil, who was one of them, wrote: 'An embassy was an ambassador's house party; it was unthinkable that one of the guests could be spying on the others.' As early as 1933 the Foreign Office received a wake-up call, albeit unheeded: after one of its staff put his head in a gas oven, he was revealed to have been selling British ciphers to Moscow. Next a clerk, Captain John King, was found to have been funding an American mistress by peddling secrets. In 1937 a local employee in Britain's Rome embassy, Francesco Constantini, was able to rifle his employer's papers for the benefit of the Italian secret service, because the ambassador assumed that one could trust one's servants. At that period also, Mussolini's men read some British codes: not all Italians were the buffoons their enemies supposed. In 1939, when Japanese intelligence wanted the codebooks of the British consulate in Taipei, its officers easily arranged for a Japanese employee to become night-duty man. During the ensuing six months Tokyo's agents repeatedly accessed the consulate safe, its files and codebooks.

Yet nowhere in the world was intelligence wisely managed and assessed. Though technological secrets were always useful to rival nations, it is unlikely that much of the fevered secret political and military surveillance told governments more than they might have gleaned from a careful reading of the press. Endemic rivalries injured or crippled collaboration between intelligence agencies. In Germany and Russia, Hitler and Stalin diffused power among their secret policemen, the better to concentrate mastery in their own hands. Germany's main agency was the Abwehr, its title literally meaning 'security', though it was responsible for both intelligence-gathering abroad and counter-espionage at home. A branch of the armed forces, it was directed by Admiral Wilhelm Canaris. When Guy Liddell, counter-espionage director of MI5 and one of its ablest officers, later strove to explain the Abwehr's incompetence, he expressed a sincere belief that Canaris was in the pay of the Russians.

The Nazis also had their own security machine, the *Reichssicherheitshauptamt* or RSHA, directed by Ernst Kaltenbrunner within the empire of Himmler. This embraced the Gestapo secret police and its sister counter-intelligence branch the *Sicherheitdienst* or SD, which overlapped the Abwehr's activities in many areas. A key figure was Walter Schellenberg, Reinhard Heydrich's aide: Schellenberg later took over the RSHA's foreign intelligence-gathering service, which subsumed the Abwehr in 1944. High Command and diplomatic codebreaking activities were conducted by the *Chiffrierabteilung*, colloquially known as OKW/ Chi, and the army had a large radio intelligence branch that eventually became OKH/GdNA. Göring's Air Ministry had its own cryptographic operation, as did the Kriegsmarine. Economic intelligence was collected by the WiRuAmt, and Ribbentrop's Foreign Ministry gathered reports from embassies abroad. Guy Liddell wrote crossly: 'Under our system of government there was nothing to stop the Germans from getting any information they required.' But the elaborate Nazi intelligence and counter-espionage machines were far more effective in suppressing domestic opposition than in exploiting foreign sources, even when they heard something useful from them.

France's intelligence departments enjoyed a lowly status and correspondingly meagre budgets. Pessimism overlaid upon ignorance caused them consistently to overstate German military strength by at least 20 per cent. František Moravec believed that politics crippled French security policy as war loomed: 'Their desire to "know" seemed to decrease proportionately as the Nazi danger increased.' Moravec the Czech found his French counterparts half-hearted colleagues, though he returned from one inter-Allied conference with a present from a famous French criminologist, Professor Locarde of Lyons: a chemical developer which proved useful for exposing secret writing.

Since the beginning of time, governments had been able to intercept each other's communications only when spies or accidents of war physically diverted messages into their hands. Now, however, everything was different. Wireless communication was a science slightly older than the twentieth century, but thirty years elapsed before it became a universal phenomenon. Then, during the 1930s, technological breakthroughs prompted a global explosion of transmissions. The ether hummed, whined and crackled as messages private, commercial, military, naval, diplomatic traversed nations and oceans. It became indispensable for governments and their generals and admirals to communicate operational orders and information by radio, to every subordinate, ship and formation beyond reach of a landline. Making such exchanges secure demanded nice judgements. There was a trade-off between the speed at which a signal could be dispatched and received, and the subtlety of its encryption. It was impracticable to provide front-line army units with ciphering machines, and thus instead they employed so-called hand- or field-ciphers, of varying sophistication – the German army used a British-derived system called Double Playfair.

For the most secret messages, the only almost unbreakable code was that based upon a 'one-time pad', a name that reflected its designation: the sender employed a unique combination of letters and/or numbers which became intelligible only to a recipient pre-supplied with the identical formula. The Soviets especially favoured this method, though their clerks sometimes compromised it by using a one-time pad more than once, as the Germans found to their advantage. From the 1920s onwards, some of the major nations started to employ ciphers which were deemed impregnable if correctly used, because messages were processed through electrically-powered keyboard machines which scrambled them into multi-millions of combinations. The magnitude of the technological challenge posed by an enemy's machine-encrypted signals did not deter any nation from striving to read them. This became the most important intelligence objective of the Second World War.

The brightest star of the Deuxième Bureau, France's intelligence service, was Capitaine Gustave Bertrand, head of the cryptanalytical branch in the army's *Section des Examens*, who had risen from the ranks to occupy a post that no ambitious career officer wanted. One of his contacts was a Paris businessman named Rodolphe Lemoine, born Rudolf Stallman, son of a rich Berlin jeweller. In 1918 Stallman adopted French nationality; simply because he loved espionage as a game in its own right, he began to work for the Deuxième. In October 1931 he forwarded to Paris an offer from one Hans-Thilo Schmidt, brother of a German general, to sell France information about Enigma in order to dig himself out of a financial hole. Bertrand accepted, and in return for cash Schmidt delivered copious material about the machine, together with its key settings for October and November 1932. Thereafter he remained on the French payroll until 1938. Since the French knew that the Poles were also seeking to crack Enigma, the two nations agreed to a collaboration: Polish cryptanalysts focused on the technology, while their French counterparts addressed enciphered texts. Bertrand also approached the British, but at the outset they showed no interest.

Britain's codebreakers had acquired an early-model commercial Enigma as early as 1927, and examined it with respect. Since then, they knew that it had been rendered much more sophisticated by the inclusion of a complex wiring pattern known as a *Steckerbrett*, or plugboard. It now offered a range of possible positions for a single letter of 159 million million million. That which human ingenuity had devised, it was at least theoretically possible that human ingenuity might penetrate. In 1939, however, no one for a moment imagined that six years later intelligence snatched from the airwaves would have proved more precious to the victors, more disastrous for the losers, than every report made by all the spies of the warring nations.

2 THE BRITISH: GENTLEMEN AND PLAYERS

The reputation of MI6 was unmatched by that of any other secret service. Though Hitler, Stalin, Mussolini and Japan's generals shared a scepticism, or even scorn, about the old lion's fitness to fight, they viewed its spies with extravagant respect, indeed cherished a belief in their omniscience. British prowess in clandestine activity dated back to the sixteenth century at least. Francis Bacon wrote in his *History of the Reign of King Henry VII*: 'As for his secret Spials, which he did employ both at home and abroad, by them to discover what Practises and Conspiracies were against him, surely his

Case required it.' Queen Elizabeth I's Sir Francis Walsingham was one of history's legendary spymasters. Much later came the romances of Rudyard Kipling's *Kim*, of John Buchan's Richard Hannay, of dashing 'clubland heroes' who played chess for England with a thousand live pieces across a board that spanned continents. A wartime British secret servant observed: 'Practically every officer I met in that concern, at home and abroad, was, like me, imagining himself as Hannay.' The great Danish physicist Niels Bohr told the scientific intelligence officer R.V. Jones that he was happy to cooperate with the British secret service because 'it was run by a gentleman'.

British intelligence had enjoyed a good Great War. The Royal Navy's codebreakers, such men as Dillwyn Knox and Alastair Denniston, labouring in the Admiralty's Room 40, provided commanders with a wealth of information about the motions of the German High Seas Fleet. The decryption and public revelation of Berlin's 1917 Zimmermann Telegram, urging the Mexicans to take aggressive action against the United States, played a critical role in bringing the Americans into the war. For two years after the November 1918 Armistice, the secret service was deeply involved in the Allies' unsuccessful attempt to reverse the outcome of the Russian Revolution. Even after this was abandoned, the threat from international communism remained the foremost preoccupation of British espionage and counter-espionage.

Yet amid the inter-war slump, funding was squeezed. MI6 mouldered, to an extent little understood by either Britain's friends or foes. Hugh Trevor-Roper, the historian who became one of its wartime officers, wrote: 'Foreign intelligence services envied the British secret service; it was their idealised model ... It enjoyed the reputation of an invisible, implacable force, like the Platonic world-spirit, operating everywhere. To the Nazi government, it was at the same time a bogey and an ideal ... The reality ... was rather different.' MI6's senior officers were men of moderate abilities, drawn into the organisation by the lure of playing out a pastiche of Kipling's 'Great Game', and often after earlier careers as colonial policemen.

They masqueraded as passport control officers in embassies abroad, or shuffled paper in the service's austere – indeed, frankly squalid – headquarters beside St James's Park underground station, in Broadway Buildings, a place of threadbare carpets and unshaded lightbulbs. MI6 sustained a quirky tradition of paying its staff tax-free and in cash, but so small a pittance that a private income was almost essential for officers who aspired to an upper-middle-class lifestyle, which meant all of them. Though its budget was progressively increased from £180,000 in 1935 to £500,000 in 1939, few graduates entered the service, because its bosses did not want them. MI6, in the view of one practitioner, was designed merely to receive intelligence rather than actively to procure it. It was run by a coterie of anti-intellectual officers who saw their principal, if not sole, task as that of combating revolutionary communism. The shift of emphasis to monitoring Nazis and fascists during the late pre-war period caused great difficulties.

Some recruits of that period proved ill-suited to the essential nastiness of espionage. Lt. Cmdr Joseph Newill, a retired sailor posted to Scandinavia in 1938 on the strength of speaking Norwegian, wailed to London: 'I doubt whether I have the natural guile so essential for this work!' Newill complained that his role involved much more hard labour than he had expected. He told his station chief petulantly: 'I am 52 and I am not going to work myself to death at my time of life.' But he was kept in the job, and contrived to meet Broadway's undemanding standards. MI6's Shanghai station chief, Harry Steptoe, operated under cover as vice-consul. A jaunty little cock-sparrow figure who affected a moustache and monocle, he puzzled a foreign diplomat by his appearance at receptions in a lovat-green suit adorned with gold braid. Was this, demanded the diplomat, the full-dress uniform of the British secret service? When the Japanese interned Steptoe in 1942, they dismissed the possibility that such a comic figure could be a spymaster, and instead subjected to brutal interrogation a hapless British Council representative, whose field of knowledge was exclusively cultural.

Broadway struggled to secure intelligence from the Continent. In 1936 a new MI6 department was formed to monitor Germany and Italy. Z Section was run by Claude Dansey, a former imperial soldier who bore a haversack groaning with blimpish prejudices, among them a loathing for Americans. It became an almost independent fiefdom, which operated under commercial cover from offices in Bush House in The Strand. Its sources were mostly elderly retreads such as the Lithuanian Baron William de Ropp, who for more than a decade extracted from the British £1,000 a year – a handsome competence – in return for fragments of German polit-ical gossip. The Nazis were well aware of de Ropp's role, and fed him what they wanted London to hear. In August 1938 the Baron decided that his secret life had become too fraught, and wisely retired to Switzerland.

Naval engineer Dr Karl Kruger's story had a darker ending. From 1914 to 1939 he fed some good information to the British on a cash-and-carry basis, but vanished from sight a month before the outbreak of war. His file at Broadway was eventually marked 'Agent presumed "dead"'. This was not surprising, because Kruger – like most of MI6's German informants – was controlled by its Hague station, where one of the local staff, Folkert van Koutrik, was on the Abwehr's payroll. The service's best pre-war humint source was Wolfgang Gans Edler zu Putlitz, press attaché at the German embassy in London, an aristocrat and homosexual. He was run by Klop Ustinov – father of the actor Peter – a Russian-born journalist who lost his newspaper job in 1935 because of his Jewishness. When Putlitz was transferred to The Hague in 1938, Ustinov followed him at MI6's behest. After Folkert van Koutrik later betrayed the British operation in Holland, Putlitz hastily sought asylum in London.

The flow of intelligence from the Continent was thin. The Air Ministry complained about the paucity of material on the use of aircraft in the Spanish Civil War, an important issue for planners. Britain's ambassador in Berlin, Sir Nevile Henderson, shared with his fellow-diplomats a disdain for espionage which caused him to refuse diplomatic status to Broadway's 'Passport Control Officers'. Even where MI6 tried to provide German informants with wireless sets, most were reluctant to take them, because discovery of such equipment by the Gestapo ensured a death sentence for the possessor.

Very occasionally, among the mountain of rubbish that accumulated in Broadway's files there was a pearl. In the spring of 1939 an agent code-named 'the Baron', with good social connections in East Prussia, reported to his handler Harry Carr in Helsinki that the Germans were secretly negotiating with Stalin. He followed this up with a further missive in June, asserting that talks between Berlin and Moscow were making good progress. Yet this sensational pointer to the looming Nazi–Soviet Pact, which afterwards proved to have come from gossip among aristocrats working in the German Foreign Ministry, was dismissed in Broadway. To MI6's senior officers, a devils' pact between Stalin and Hitler seemed a fantastic notion. An authentic scoop was missed; first, because MI6, like most intelligence organisations, had an instinctive and usually prudent scepticism about its own sources; second, because what 'the Baron' reported ran contrary to his employers' expectations. At that time, and indeed throughout the war, MI6 had no internal machinery for analysing incoming intelligence, though its chiefs could point out that the Axis Powers lacked this also.

Czechoslovakia and Poland occupied the front line in the European confrontation with Hitler. MI6 showed little interest in collaboration with their intelligence services until March 1939, when the strategic picture

changed dramatically: the British and French governments gave a security
guarantee to Poland. This galvanised Broadway.

On 25 July, a British delegation composed of a naval intelligence officer
together with Alastair Denniston, director of the Government Code &
Cypher School, and Dillwyn Knox, one of its foremost codebreakers,
joined France's Gustave Bertrand – himself no cryptographer, but a notable facilitator and diplomat – at an exploratory meeting with their Polish
counterparts led by Col. Gwido Langer, held at their cryptographic centre
in the Kabackie woods near Pyry, south of Warsaw. The first day's talks,
conducted in mixed French and German, went very badly. Knox, for
reasons unknown, was in a vile temper, and highly sceptical that the Poles
had anything to tell worth hearing. He seemed unable to understand the
methods by which they claimed to have achieved the breakthrough which
had enabled them to read some German naval traffic. All the parties present were fencing, to discover each other's state of knowledge. Warsaw's
decision to involve the British was prompted by new difficulties that had
frustrated their own codebreakers since the Germans on 1 January
adopted an enhanced stecker board for their Enigmas, with ten plugs
instead of seven. On the second day, 26 July, the conference's atmosphere
was transformed for the better. In the basement of the building the Poles
showed off their 'bomby', primitive computing devices designed to test
multiple mathematical possibilities. Then they produced a *coup de théâtre*:
they presented both visiting delegations with mimicked copies of the
Enigma built by their own men. Knox's scepticism crumbled, and the
meeting ended in a mood of goodwill and mutual respect. Everybody at
Broadway recognised the importance of the Poles' gesture to their allies as
a contribution to the secret struggle against the Nazis. Marian Rejewski, a
former mathematics student at Warsaw University who had joined the
Kabackie woods team back in 1932, is today acknowledged as a pioneer
among those who laid bare the secrets of Enigma, even if it fell to others,
in Britain, to advance and exploit Rejewski's achievement.

Stewart Menzies, then deputy chief of MI6, was so impressed by the
outcome of the Polish trip that he turned up in person at Victoria station
to greet Gustave Bertrand – and to inspect the mimicked Enigma. Knox
sent the Poles a gift of scarves, decorated with images of Derby runners,
with the letter thanking his hosts for their 'co-operation and patience'. At
or around this time also, the Poles provided the British with five of the
Enigma's eight alternative rotors. A chasm still yawned, however, between
understanding how the machine worked, and achieving the ability to read

its traffic. Though a trickle of German messages were broken by human ingenuity during the winter of 1939–40, traffic was breached on an industrial scale only from 1941 onwards, following the creation of revolutionary electro-mechanical technology. Nonetheless, the assistance of the French and Poles dramatically accelerated progress at the GC&CS, now evacuated from London to a safer country home. Physical possession of the enemy's encryption instrument enabled its cryptanalysts to grasp the mountainous challenge they must overcome.

Until 1939, and in large measure for two years thereafter, British intelligence remained dependent for its view of the world upon humint – reports from informants abroad. How well did MI6 fulfil its responsibility to brief the government about the mounting threat from Nazi Germany – 'Twelveland' in Broadway parlance? It produced many reports arguing that Hitler's long-term ambitions lay in the East, and this was fundamentally correct. Unfortunately for its credibility, however, in 1940 Germany chose first to seek to dispose of the Western democracies. MI6 was in no doubt that Hitler was rearming fast, but insistently emphasised the weakness of the industrial base from which he aspired to make war. Responsibility for gathering economic data rested with the Industrial Intelligence Centre, an offshoot administered since 1934 by the Foreign Office, but run by the veteran secret service officer Major Desmond Morton. During the 'wilderness years', Morton passed to Winston Churchill – with the sanction of prime minister Stanley Baldwin – details of German rearmament which empowered the unheeded prophet to cry forth warnings to the world. Ironically, the Major wildly overstated the growth of Hitler's military machine: Morton never had much grasp of economics in general, nor of the Nazi economy in particular.

But modern historians critical of pre-war British intelligence failures miss some important points. In those days few people of any nationality understood economic analysis. The IIC was correct in judging that Germany was ill-prepared to conduct a long struggle, and was rendered vulnerable by its dependence on imported commodities and especially oil. The German economy, as Adam Tooze has shown, was not strong enough to meet the huge challenge Hitler sought to fulfil, of conquering the most advanced societies on earth. Germany's GDP was no larger than Britain's, and her people's per capita incomes were lower. In 1939, Hitler's expenditures on armaments had reduced his country's finances to a parlous condition. But it was asking too much of any intelligence service to gauge the potential of German industry under the stimulus of conflict:

to the very end of World War II, the best brains in the Allied nations failed fully to achieve this. MI6 could not be expected to predict Hitler's conquests, which dramatically enhanced his access to oil, raw materials and slave labour.

On the military side, neither MI6 nor the service departments learned much about the new technology and tactics being developed by Britain's enemies. Nor about their limitations: they wildly overrated the Luftwaffe's ability to devastate Britain's cities. In 1938, Broadway reported that the Germans had 927 first-line bombers capable of mounting 720 sorties a day and dropping 945 tons of ordnance (this was an exaggeration of 50 per cent), and projections of likely casualties were even more inflated. War Office appreciations of the German army were equally mistaken, especially in estimating its potential mobilised strength. These suggested in 1939 that Hitler was already master of the largest war machine his nation's resources could bear. Rearmament, coupled with vast public expenditure, 'had taxed the endurance of the German people and the stability of the economic system to a point where any further effort can only be achieved at the risk of a breakdown of the entire structure'.

A February 1939 Strategical Appreciation by the chiefs of staff, drafted by the Joint Planning Committee, asserted that Britain could survive a long war better than Germany. This was true, but the chiefs said nothing about the danger that it could meanwhile lose a short one. Moreover, they never pressed the cabinet to acknowledge the shocking weakness of Britain's Far East empire. The three services' intelligence branches had no contact with each other, and there were no joint staffs.

As for politics, an MI6 officer wrote in a November 1938 report for the Foreign Office: 'Not even Hitler's intimates, according to one of them, knows if he would really risk world war.' A few months later, the service's credibility was severely injured by its issue of warnings that Germany intended imminently to strike at Western Europe, starting with Holland. Embarrassment was increased by the fact that the Foreign Office forwarded this alarm call to the US government. One of the British recipients, senior civil servant Sir George Mounsey, delivered a blast against MI6 which echoed around Whitehall. The Foreign Office's standing was damaged, he said, by acting on the basis of 'a highly sensational and highly disturbing kind of information which [MI6] are unable to guarantee'. Mounsey was dismissive of all covert sources, agents whose rumour-mongering had prompted Broadway's warning: 'They have a secret mission and they must justify it … If nothing comes to hand for them to report, they must earn their pay by finding something … Are we going to remain so attached to reliance on secret reports, which tie our hands in all directions?' Mounsey had his own agenda: to sustain the policy of appeasement adopted by Neville Chamberlain and Lord Halifax, whom he admired prodigiously. His views nonetheless reflected a general scepticism in high places about Broadway's performance.

Gladwyn Jebb of the Foreign Office, often a critic of MI6, on this occasion leapt to its defence. While acknowledging the frustrations of dealing with secret organisations, he said that he could not forget that its officers 'did warn us of the September [1938 Munich] crisis, and they did not give any colour to the ridiculous optimism that prevailed up to the rape of Czechoslovakia, of which our official [diplomatic] reports did not give us much warning'. In December 1938 Broadway offered a sound character sketch of Germany's Führer, at a time when many British diplomats and politicians still deluded themselves that he was a man they could do business with. 'Among his characteristics,' asserted the MI6 report, 'are fanaticism, mysticism, ruthlessness, cunning, vanity, moods of exaltation and depression, fits of bitter and self-righteous resentment, and what can only be termed a streak of madness; but with it all there is great tenacity of purpose, which has often been combined with extraordinary clarity of vision. He has gained the reputation of being always able to choose the right moment and right method for "getting away with it". In the eyes of his disciples, and increasingly in his own, "the Führer is always right". He has unbounded self-confidence, which has grown in proportion to the strength of the machine he has created; but it is a self-confidence which has latterly been tempered less than hitherto with patience and restraint.'

It is easy to catalogue the shortcomings of MI6. Like most of its sister services on the Continent, in 1939 it commanded little respect in high places, and had small influence on policy-making. It seems necessary to go beyond this, however, and pose the question: what might its spies have usefully discovered, granted more resources and cleverer people? The likely answer is: not much. MI6's reporting was matched by a daily bombardment of newspaper headlines, both showing beyond peradventure that Germany was rearming. More accurate and detailed information about Hitler's armed forces would have been useful to the War Office and Downing Street, but the critical issue, the vital uncertainty, was not that of Germany's capabilities, but rather that of its intentions.

It seems quite misplaced to blame wrong or inadequate intelligence for the calamitous failure of Britain and France to deal effectively with the Nazis. Both nations correctly assessed the options at Hitler's disposal for onslaughts East or West. MI6 can scarcely be held responsible for failing to anticipate exactly where or when he would attack, because he himself was an opportunist who reserved his decisions until the last moment. Sir Alexander Cadogan, permanent under-secretary at the Foreign Office, wrote much later: 'We were daily inundated by all sorts of reports. It just happened that these were correct; we had no means of evaluating their reliability at the time of their receipt. (Nor was there much that we could do about it!)' Rather than a failure of intelligence, what mattered was the democracies' failure of will – the refusal to acknowledge that the Nazis constituted an irreconcilable force for evil, which the very survival of European civilisation made it essential to destroy, rather than to bargain with.

Most of Hitler's opponents inside Germany, and indeed across Europe, were communists who considered the Russians the only people both willing and able to challenge fascism. Everything said and done by the British and French governments before the outbreak of war confirmed anti-Nazis in that view. Thus, people who wished to contribute to undoing Hitler offered information to the agents of Moscow much more readily than to those of London or Paris. It was anti-Nazis' poor opinion of Neville Chamberlain that made them reluctant to look to his country as a shield against Hitler, not their perception of MI6.

It is far more plausible to argue that Britain's diplomats should have exposed the dictator's intentions than to suggest that its spies might have done so. In peacetime, good intelligence officers can assist their governments to grasp the economic, military and technological capabilities of prospective enemies, but it is unusual for a secret service to provide a reliable crib about their intentions. Top diplomats ought to have been cleverer than intelligence officers. Their training, experience and access to sources should have empowered them to assess the world with greater wisdom than Broadway's old soldiers. It seems far more discreditable that Henderson, Britain's ambassador in Berlin, was willing for so long to think well of Hitler, than that MI6 with its meagre resources was unable to tell the government what the Führer would do next. If a German anti-Nazi had turned up on Henderson's embassy doorstep, offering inside information, it is likely that he would have been sent packing.

Admiral Sir Hugh Sinclair – 'C', as the head of the secret service was always known – died suddenly in November 1939, having occupied his post for sixteen years. Winston Churchill, as First Lord of the Admiralty, pressed the claims of the obscure Gerard Muirhead-Gould, a former naval attaché in Berlin, to succeed him. Instead, however, Sinclair's deputy, forty-nine-year-old Guards officer Brigadier Stewart Menzies, convinced the Foreign Office and the prime minister that he had been anointed by the dying Sinclair as his rightful successor. He thus inherited a mantle that he was widely considered ill-fitted to wear. The ninth Duke of Buccleuch, who had known Menzies at Eton, told a friend that 'C's' contemporaries were mystified 'how so unbelievably stupid a man could have ended up in such a position'. Hugh Trevor-Roper sneered at Menzies as 'a thoughtless feudal lord, living comfortably on income produced from the labour of peasants whom he had never seen, working estates which he had never visited'.

This was hyperbolic, as were most of the historian's private judgements on his colleagues, but it was true that Menzies had learned his craft in a bad school – not so much Eton as service on the staff of Brigadier John Charteris, Field-Marshal Sir Douglas Haig's egregious intelligence chief on the Western Front. Menzies' DSO and MC showed that he did not lack courage. His social skills sufficed to win the confidence of Maj. Gen. Hastings 'Pug' Ismay, soon to become Churchill's chief of staff, and in some degree that of the prime minister himself. But 'C' knew little of the wider world he aspired to spy upon, and tolerated in Broadway a bevy of even less inspired subordinates.

Decisions were powerfully influenced by his two joint deputies, Valentine Vivian and Claude Dansey, who hated each other. Vivian was a former Indian policeman who was credited with a major role in frustrating the machinations of the Comintern – the Communist International – in South America and the Far East; he was also an office intriguer of energy and skill. Meanwhile Dansey went briefly to Bern in September 1939, to try to organise intelligence links from neutral Switzerland to Germany. A plentiful supply of fraudulent informants emerged, of whom by no means the most imaginative was a German refugee in Switzerland who used his nation's Army List to fabricate a mobilisation programme which he attempted to sell. One of the few useful sources Dansey identified was an Austrian Pole, Count Horodyski. He, in turn, introduced the British to Halina Szymańska, wife of the former Polish military attaché in Berlin, now an exile in Switzerland. She became one of MI6's most useful conduits, with connections in the Abwehr. Dansey thereafter returned to London, where he exercised a powerful influence on the wartime fortunes of MI6, mostly to its detriment.

During the years that followed, Britain's secret service recruited numbers of outstanding officers and agents, who did some useful and a few important things for the Allied cause, but its chieftains inspired only limited respect. The stimulus of war would generate an intelligence revolution, and give birth to one of Britain's most dazzling achievements. However, this did not take place in Broadway Buildings, but instead outside a dreary suburban town in Bedfordshire.

3 THE RUSSIANS: TEMPLES OF ESPIONAGE

Just before noon on 23 May 1938, Pavel Sudoplatov of the NKVD strolled into the Atlanta restaurant in Rotterdam and greeted a Ukrainian nationalist leader whom he had come to know well, in the guise of being a sympathiser with the man's cause. Sudoplatov, newly arrived on a merchant ship from Murmansk, presented the man with a handsome box of chocolates adorned with the Ukrainian crest. The two chatted for a few moments to arrange a further rendezvous, then Moscow's agent bade his companion farewell and moved on. He was a safe distance down the street by the time he heard a sharp explosion. A timing device had detonated a bomb inside the box, killing the nationalist. This was a typical Moscow Centre* operation of the period, one thrust in the relentless campaign to liquidate state enemies, real or supposed traitors. Sudoplatov's success earned him a four-hour meeting with Stalin's foremost secret policeman, Lavrenti Beria, who marked him for bigger things, such as managing the assassination of Leon Trotsky.

The Soviet Union owned the most active and best-resourced intelligence organisations in the world – the Red Army's GRU and the NKVD, the latter controlled by Beria from December 1938. The foremost purposes of Joseph Stalin, master of the Kremlin, were the promotion of socialism abroad through the Comintern and the maintenance of his own power against domestic and foreign enemies. Both required spies in profusion. Throughout the 1930s, Russia pursued a strategy more far-reaching in its means – the plantation of deep-penetration agents – and its ends – the worldwide triumph of communism – than those of any other nation. How far the funds and energy lavished on its secret war profited the Soviet Union will be considered below. Here, it suffices to say that the espionage networks it established in the US, Britain, Japan and Europe were on a

---

* Both the GRU's and NKVD's officers and agents referred to their respective headquarters as 'Centre'.

scale far beyond those of any other nation, and manifested in big things and small. When Japanese police arrested a Soviet agent carrying a Leica camera, Tokyo's intelligence officers were pathetically envious: they could not afford to equip their own spies with technology remotely so sophisticated. This was a time when tens of millions of Russians were starving, yet Stalin's agents spent whatever seemed necessary to purchase information and the deaths of enemies. From Switzerland to Mexico they left roadsides studded with corpses, and created some of the most remarkable agent networks in the history of intelligence.

The Russian addiction to espionage and conspiracy was as old as time. In 1912, when according to official figures Germany spent £80,387 on its secret service, France £40,000 and Britain £50,000, the Russians avowed a budget of £380,000, plus a further £335,000 for the tsar's secret police. Tsarist codebreakers achieved some notable coups, and their successors sustained the tradition. In the 1930s the NKVD's Fourth Department, the world's most lavishly funded signals intelligence unit, was based in the Foreign Affairs building on Moscow's Kuznetsky bridge. Its chief, Gleb Ivanovitch Bokii, achieved a reputation as a killer and sexual predator matching that of Beria. Though Bokii's team never broke wartime German Enigma messages, it enjoyed useful earlier and lesser successes, such as securing the secret protocol to the 1936 Anti-Comintern Pact between Germany and Japan, before its chief faced a firing squad the following year. Stalin personally read many decrypts; like Churchill later, he trusted the codebreakers' product as he never did humint. The Kremlin displayed as brutal a carelessness about casualties among its spies as it did towards the fate of its soldiers. In 1936 František Moravec of Czech intelligence received a Soviet proposal that his service should provide crash espionage training for a hundred Russians, who would then be dispatched into Germany. Moravec expostulated that such novices would face wholesale extinction. His Moscow contact shrugged: 'In that case, we shall send another hundred.'

The Soviet Union enjoyed a critical advantage in building its empire of espionage. While fascism gained millions of supporters in Germany, Italy and Spain, it never matched the appeal of worldwide communism during the decades before the latter's bloodstained reality was laid bare. In every nation, men and women of brains and education, lofty ideals and unbounded naïveté queued to betray their own societies' secrets for what they deemed a higher cause. From Moscow, hundreds of men and women were sent forth to direct networks in Japan and the United States, Germany,

France and other European nations. The NKVD achieved excellent penetration of the French Foreign Office, and frequently quoted its ambassadors' dispatches. Many of its informants deluded themselves that they
were passing secrets not to the Soviets, but instead to the Comintern –
which was in truth merely a postbox for the Kremlin.

Pavel Sudoplatov became one of the principal puppeteers of the
Kremlin's *danses macabres*. He was a Ukrainian miller's son, born in 1907,
who served as a cipher clerk with the Red Army before joining the
Bolshevik security service. As a teenager, Sudoplatov ran a network of
informers in his home town of Melitopol. Secret police work became a
family affair when he married in 1928, since his Jewish wife Emma was a
more senior officer than himself in the OGPU, forerunner of the NKVD.
He was trained by its foreign department before being posted to Germany
as an 'illegal', posing as a Ukrainian nationalist. He led a roving life in the
years that followed, travelling across Europe and spending a month in a
Helsinki jail. He saw his wife just once, when she turned up in Paris as a
courier. In 1938 he visited Spain, describing its civil war as 'a kindergarten
for our future operations'. At an early stage of his relationship with Beria,
Sudoplatov noted a curiosity: this most terrible of Soviet secret policemen
displayed meticulous civility to little people – junior staff – while treating
big ones – his rivals in the Kremlin hierarchy – with lacerating rudeness.
'Beria had the singular ability to inspire both fear and enthusiasm,' he
wrote.

Sudoplatov became one of the spy chief's most devoted servants, grad-
uating from field work to senior desk roles, assisted by the demise of rivals.
Between 1937 and 1939, thousands of intelligence officers of all ranks died
before firing squads or were dispatched to the gulag. Stalin lashed out at
the intelligence services during a meeting of the Soviet Military Council
in language that defied parody: 'We have defeated the bourgeoisie on all
fronts. It is only on the intelligence front that they beat us like small boys.
This is our chief weakness ... Our military intelligence service ... has been
polluted by spies. [Its chiefs] were working for Germany, for Japan, Poland,
for anyone but us ... Our task is to restore the intelligence service. It is our
eyes and ears.' In his madness, Stalin insisted upon not merely the execution of scores of senior officers of the GRU and NKVD, but also on the
severance of Moscow Centre's relations with their informants in the field,
thousands of whom were branded as fascist stool-pigeons. The chaos that
followed impacted variously upon different departments and regions, but
paralysed some networks until 1941 and beyond. After the destruction of

Nazism, in Vienna a veteran NKVD officer met an old German source, one of many with whom he had broken contact in accordance with orders back in 1938. Now, this man demanded of the Russian: 'Where on earth were you all through the war? I was General Kesselring's personal orderly!'

Among the foremost of the NKVD's overseas agent-runners was Theodore Maly, a Hungarian who in his youth had belonged to a Catholic monastic order. He was taken prisoner as a Hapsburg officer in 1916, joined the Bolsheviks and forswore God. In 1936 Maly was posted to London, where many of Moscow's British informants later testified to their respect and affection for him. Yet in 1938 he was among those recalled to Moscow and shot as a supposed traitor, along with the NKVD's equally talented Rome resident and several of its Berlin men. An obvious question persists: why did any officer with a brain obey the order to go home, when they could surely have read the runes? The most plausible answer is that even in those crazed and bloody days, adherents to the world socialist ideal, such as Maly was, cherished a lingering faith in the Soviet system, though he also professed fatalism if his death was decreed.

Many Russian knees quaked during the Purges. Thirty-nine senior GRU officers, intelligence veterans, are known to have been shot, and the NKVD suffered in proportion. Pavel Sudoplatov survived an investigation and the threat of expulsion from the Party; he believed afterwards that he might have been preserved by Stalin's personal intervention. Clambering over a mound of corpses, he acquired his own office in the Lubyanka building at 2 L Street – cosily referred to by its occupants as 'Dom Dva', 'Number Two', a place of dread for every passer-by, and for any prisoner who crossed its threshold. Like all those who prospered in Stalin's dreadful universe, Sudoplatov learned to regard the grotesque as normal, the unspeakable as familiar. During family conversations in their apartment, for instance, he and Emma never deviated from a rigidly domestic script, because they took it for granted that every word spoken was recorded by Beria's eavesdroppers. He wrote long afterwards in an apparently half-truthful memoir: 'I accepted the brutality and stern order that characterised our centralised society; it appeared the only method of preserving the country when it was surrounded by German, Polish and Japanese enemies.'

Meanwhile, elsewhere in the forest an agent of the GRU, who would later become famous, or notorious, for his association with the German Red Orchestra – the extraordinary espionage network to be described later – was putting down roots in foreign parts. Anatoli Sukolov-

Gourevitch, born at Kharkov in November 1913, was the son of Jewish parents who were both pharmacists. He started work in 1929 as an apprentice draughtsman in a factory, and hated the life. From an early stage, and like most Soviet citizens, he acquired the habit of obsessive secrecy, writing in his memoirs: 'I learned to hide my feelings and troubles from my nearest and dearest, my friends, and indeed from everyone.' Desperate to escape from the common ruck, while still very young he became a communist functionary, and somehow secured an appointment as a lecturer on military studies at a Leningrad school for Intourist guides, thereafter serving in intelligence.

In 1937 he was recruited to travel to Spain as one of the Soviet military group assisting the embattled Republican government. Gourevitch thoroughly enjoyed his subsequent Spanish adventures – as who would not, after sampling Soviet factory life? He was able to dress with an elegance unimaginable at home, and thereafter favoured a Warsaw tailor. He took a trip in a submarine, travelled in France and learned conversational French, Spanish and German. On returning to Moscow, he was selected for training as a foreign agent of the GRU. Asked much later if it had troubled him to join the Soviet Union's murderous secret services, like Sudoplatov he shrugged that his country was encircled by enemies; he then believed that its defenders did only what they had to.

His chief, the gaunt, jug-eared intelligence veteran Major Simon Gendin, enquired whether he had any marriage plans which could complicate his future career overseas. Gourevitch replied that he was indeed in love, with a girl named Lialia whom he had met when they were both working in Spain, and who was now an Intourist interpreter. Gendin told his staff to add her name to the brief list of intimates with whom Gourevitch might correspond, though that relationship perished, like so much else, during the years that followed. On graduation from the GRU's spy school, Gourevitch himself expressed doubts about his fluency as a coder and wireless-operator – he lacked a sensitive ear for Morse. Gendin reassured him: he would not need specialised radio skills, for he was destined to become an intelligence-gatherer and agent-runner.

Gourevitch was briefed to travel to Brussels to work with another Soviet agent, codenamed 'Otto', then to move on to Sweden after establishing himself and improving his language skills. He would exploit his knowledge of Spanish by adopting a cover identity as 'Vincente Sierra', a prosperous businessman with a Uruguayan passport. For the next three years, Moscow furnished him with funds to sustain an appropriately flashy lifestyle. Yet although he was instructed about the importance of dressing smartly, affecting the hat and gloves that were then badges of bourgeois respectability, Gourevitch later complained that he was untutored in social skills. When he checked into a smart Helsinki hotel on the first leg of his journey to Belgium, he was bewildered when a porter picked up his suitcase and carried it upstairs: never in his short life had he received such a personal service. He gasped on seeing an open buffet in the hotel dining-room, which at first he assumed was set for a banquet rather than for the daily fare of guests. Later, in Brussels, as he fumbled his way towards an entrée into relatively smart social circles, he was embarrassed to be taken aside one evening by an acquaintance who told him that only waiters wore white bow ties with smoking jackets. 'I was completely ignorant of these subtleties,' he wrote ruefully.

'Otto', the Soviet agent whom Gourevitch joined in Brussels, was Leopold Trepper, born in 1904 the son of a Galician shopkeeper, one of the key figures in Russia's European intelligence operations, and later a heroic Soviet legend. As a young man, Trepper ran a Paris network which was rolled up by the French in 1933. He fled first to Germany, then to Russia where he found employment with Stalin's spymasters while moonlighting as editor of a Jewish journal. Early in 1939 he was dispatched to Brussels, which was deemed a secure base from which he could forward information from the GRU's network inside Germany, of which the most important sources were: Ilse Stöbe, who worked in the press department of Ribbentrop's Foreign Ministry, and a diplomat named Rudolf Shelia. Trepper carried a Canadian passport in the name of Adam Mikler, stolen during the Spanish Civil War. He was married with two sons, but only one accompanied him to Brussels – the other, seven-year-old Michael, remained in Moscow. Trepper became known to his sources in Western Europe as 'le grand chef', while Gourevitch was 'le petit chef'. Soviet narratives lavish praise on the Trepper network for its services to the socialist cause, and it was plainly useful as a post office for the messages of Stöbe and Shelia. But it seems unlikely that Trepper recruited useful informants of his own. The foremost achievement of the GRU agents in Belgium was to stay at liberty, make some friends and create lifestyles that supported their cover stories.

Of more importance to Moscow – certainly from 1941 onwards – were the GRU's organisations based in Switzerland. These would later channel towards the Kremlin material derived from Berlin sources such as Western agent-runners could only dream of. One network had been established in 1937 by German-born Rachel Dübendorfer. A larger group, which became known as the 'Lucy' Ring, was run by Dr Alexander Radó – 'Dora' – a 'sleeper' permitted by his chiefs to slumber almost as long as Sleeping Beauty. A Hungarian, Marxist from his youth, Radó served as a commissar in Budapest's 1919 Red Terror. Obliged to flee when Admiral Horthy became Hungary's dictator, for a time he ran an émigré Resistance group in Vienna. He then decamped to Moscow, where he received intelligence training, and was deemed sufficiently significant to be introduced to Lenin. Posted to Western Europe, he served as an agent in Berlin and Paris, under cover as a correspondent for the Soviet news agency TASS. After marrying a German communist with whom he had two children, he tried to settle in Brussels, but was sent packing by the authorities, who held a thick dossier on him. Instead he went to Switzerland, where he parleyed a lifelong passion for maps into the creation of a cartographic publishing business, which quickly became profitable.

The Swiss police watched Radó for a while, then left him alone when they decided he was what he seemed – a quiet-living fellow, forty in 1939, who simply wanted to turn an honest penny. Radó was word-painted by one of his wireless-operators, an Englishman named Alexander Foote: 'With his mild eyes blinking behind glasses, he looked exactly like almost anyone to be found in any suburban train anywhere in the world.' Moscow instructed its man to do nothing until Europe erupted. Radó settled down quite happily with his maps, which enabled him to make a living without much recourse to GRU funds. When his handler was recalled to Moscow during the Purges, Radó for a time lost contact with his chiefs. But he made useful local friends, some of them communists, others not.

Radó's comrade Alexander Foote always claimed to have been an adventurer rather than a communist ideologue. A round-faced, bespectacled, mildly seedy young Englishman, in September 1938 he returned from service in Spain with the International Brigade. A few months later, one of Moscow's British recruiters offered him unspecified new employment for the workers' cause in Switzerland. Cheap melodrama was not lacking. In obedience to instructions, Foote reported to the main post office in Geneva at noon one day, wearing a white scarf and holding a leather belt. He was approached by a woman who fulfilled her side of the identification procedure by holding a string shopping bag and an orange. She asked in English where he had bought his belt, and he replied implausibly, at an ironmonger's shop in Paris. When he had then asked where he could buy an orange like hers, she introduced herself. She was 'Sonya', Ursula Hamburger* of the GRU, whom Foote was pleased to find was no squat commissar, but instead an attractive woman of thirty-one, with 'a good figure and even better legs'. This remarkable personality was the daughter of a Berlin economist. At the age of eleven she was briefly a child actress before taking up an alternative career in espionage. She was already a veteran of exploits in China for which she had been awarded the Order of the Red Banner.

Hamburger instructed Foote to travel to Munich, establish himself in the city, learn German and make friends. He was given 2,000 Swiss francs and told to meet her again in three months in Lausanne – once again, at the post office. Keeping this rendezvous after a German sojourn that was uneventful save for a chance glimpse of Hitler lunching in a restaurant, he was told that he was now on the GRU payroll as a 'collaborator', at a salary of US$150 a month plus reasonable expenses. Given the cover name 'Jim', and various means of making contact if 'Sonya' disappeared for any reason, he was then sent back to Munich with an advance of US$900 in cash. Nothing significant happened thereafter until in April 1939 he was visited by an old International Brigade comrade from Spain, Len Brewer, British-born son of German parents, whom he appears to have introduced to Hamburger, who promptly recruited him. In August he was summoned to yet another meeting, this time at Hamburger's home, a chalet at Caux-sur-Montreux where she lived in incongruous bourgeois domesticity with her two children, Maik and Janina, and an old German nurse. Foote was disconcerted by the casualness with which his hostess left components of her wireless transmitter lying around the house.

The GRU ring in Switzerland was as traumatised as many other communists around the world by the August 1939 Nazi–Soviet Pact. Foote felt that it hit Hamburger even harder than himself; that her faith in the omniscience of the Party was shattered: 'I think that from that time onwards her heart was not in the work' – this seems implausible, since she later became courier for the atomic spy Klaus Fuchs, and died an avowed Stalinist. Desperate to get out of Switzerland, she divorced her husband and married Len Brewer. Initially, according to Foote, this was merely an arrangement of convenience to secure a 'shoe' – a passport – but then the

* Hamburger, like many others in this book, used a variety of names in the course of her career, starting out as Kuczynski and ending up as Werner. To avoid confusion, only one name is used throughout for all those described.

couple fell in love. Their plans were momentarily threatened when their maid, Lisa, became disaffected and telephoned the British consulate to denounce them anonymously as communist spies. But the girl's English was so poor that nobody at the other end understood, or at least took notice.

Days before the outbreak of war, Foote boarded a train bound for Germany once more, only to find his handler suddenly pushing her way along the carriage to reach him, just before departure time. She told him to get off, fast. New orders had come from Moscow: war was imminent; he must stay in Switzerland. During the period that followed, in which the 'Lucy' Ring was temporarily dormant, while living at a small *pension* in Montreux both Foote and Len Brewer learned how to operate a shortwave radio transmitter. They practised on Hamburger's set, though its performance was not improved by being buried in her garden between transmissions – then waited to be given messages to transmit to Moscow.

Even as the GRU's Swiss networks were bedding down, Centre's German sources were already producing information of extraordinary quality. The first musician in what became known to history as the 'Red Orchestra' was recruited following an approach to the Soviet embassy one day in 1929, by an ex-Berlin policeman named Ernst Kur. He offered his services as an informant, and was promptly recruited by the local NKVD resident as agent A/70. Kur, a rackety and often drunken boor, had been dismissed from the police, but proved to have a critical contact in its counter-intelligence branch, who was soon designated by the Russians as agent A/201. On 7 September Moscow messaged its Berlin station: 'We are very interested in your new agent, A/201. Our only fear is that you have got yourselves into one of the most dangerous predicaments where the slightest indiscretion on the part of either A/201 or A/70 could lead to multiple misfortunes. We think it necessary to look into the issue of a special channel of communication with A/201.' Investigation showed that it was A/201 – an officer named Willy Lehmann, who had prompted Kur's approach to the Russians, using him as a cut-out during their exploratory dealings.

Lehmann was born in 1884, and served twelve years in the Kaiser's navy before becoming a policeman. His NKVD file spoke in the highest terms of his character, though noting the existence of a long-term mistress, Florentina Liverskaya, a thirty-eight-year-old seamstress who lived and worked at 21 Blumenstrasse. She was described, somewhat ungenerously, as a short woman with reddish hair and a plump face. When Kur started using his payments from the Soviet embassy to fund extravagant drinking sprees, Lehmann and his handler agreed that this now redundant intermediary must be got out of the way. With unusual sensitivity for Centre, instead of being pushed under a tram, in 1933 the dissolute ex-cop was rehoused in Sweden, where he passed the rest of his days as a small trader, occasionally moonlighting as an informant.

Lehmann, codenamed 'Breitenbach', thereafter became one of Moscow's most valued German agents. For some time his handler was Vasily Zarubin, an NKVD star. Born in 1894, highly intelligent and personable though largely self-educated, Zarubin served successively in China and Europe as an 'illegal', latterly under cover as a Czech engineer. A cheerfully gregarious figure, though with ample blood on his hands, he spoke several languages and forged a warm relationship with Lehmann. Although Zarubin occasionally gave the policeman modest sums of money, Lehmann never appeared greedy, and seemed keen to assist the Russians simply because he disliked his own nation's government – an animosity that became much more marked after the Nazis gained power.

Lehmann gave Moscow details about the structure and activities of Germany's various intelligence organisations, and warned of forthcoming operations against Soviet interests. He provided samples of Abwehr codes, and passed on gossip about Nazi power struggles. He himself worked latterly in the Gestapo's Department IVE, ultimately under Himmler's control, and was made responsible for security at especially sensitive defence plants. Thus in 1935 he attended some early German rocket tests at Peenemünde, and produced a report on them which reached Stalin. He also acquired considerable information about other military and naval technological developments. As the Nazis tightened their grip during the 1930s, Lehmann became increasingly nervous about meeting Zarubin, or indeed any Soviet agent. He found himself under surveillance, as a result of a bizarre coincidence. A woman quarrelled with her lover, and denounced him to the authorities as a Russian spy: this proved to be another Gestapo officer, also named Lehmann. The muddle was eventually cleared up, and the shadow was lifted from 'Breitenbach'. But in 1935 he asked for a false passport in case he had to run in a hurry, and this was duly provided. When Zarubin reported that Lehmann had fallen seriously ill, the news prompted a panic in Moscow: Centre declared that its most precious German source must be kept alive at any cost, and that the NKVD would meet his medical bills if the money could somehow be laundered. 'Breitenbach' recovered.

Later that year the GRU made a sudden decision to wind up its German networks amid the Nazis' ruthless persecution of known communists, and to make a fresh start, beginning at the top. Both the Berlin station chief and his deputy were recalled to Moscow and liquidated. Early in 1937, the NKVD's Zarubin also fell victim to the Purges. He was summoned home, and at an interview with Beria accused of treason. After interrogation, unusually he was neither executed nor cleared, but instead demoted. He remained for a time in Moscow, serving as assistant to a novice intelligence officer, Vladimir Pavlov.

Before Zarubin's abrupt departure from Berlin, he transferred the handling of 'Breitenbach' to a woman named Clemens, one of his staff. She scarcely spoke German, but there was nobody else, and he himself expected soon to return. As matters fell out, Clemens was obliged to assume ongoing responsibility for the relationship, exchanging envelopes containing orders and information, which were then passed to another NKVD illegal, Ruben, who soon found himself the sole surviving member of the Berlin station as the Purges claimed ever more victims – the GRU's Major Simon Gendin, who had sent Gourevitch to Brussels, was shot in February 1939.

Zarubin, in Moscow, contrived to send a note to 'Breitenbach', assuring him that he was not forgotten by his friends; that he should continue his intelligence activities, while exercising extreme caution. The Gestapo officer replied: 'I have no reasons to worry. I am sure that they [in Moscow Centre] also know over there that everything is being done responsibly here, everything that can be done. So far there is no great need for anyone to visit from there. I will inform you if this will become necessary.' As the NKVD's silence became protracted, however, Lehmann grew frustrated and impatient. He sent another message to Zarubin via Clemens: 'Just when I was able to make good deals, the company there stopped being interested in doing business with me, for completely unknown reasons.' Zarubin responded soothingly that 'the company' tremendously valued his work, and besought him to keep going – which he did, until November 1938. But then, as the Soviet intelligence machine became paralysed by its domestic contortions, all contact between 'Breitenbach' and Moscow was lost: the relationship was not restored until the autumn of 1940.

Willy Lehmann was by no means Moscow's only German source, nor even any longer its most important. One day in 1935 a Luftwaffe officer named Harro Schulze-Boysen, who held a senior post in Hermann

Göring's Air Ministry, contacted the Soviet embassy in Berlin with an offer of information, which was immediately accepted. He was given the code-name 'Corporal', and NKVD file 34122. Schulze-Boysen was a champagne socialist from a smart Berlin family of intellectual inclinations – Admiral Tirpitz was among his forebears. From his desk in the Air Ministry he forged contacts in army staff communications, among Abwehr officers, and also with Hans Henniger, a government inspector of Luftwaffe equipment. Göring gave away the bride at his 1936 wedding, to the beautiful and exuberant Libertas Haas-Heye, who had worked for a time as a Berlin press officer for MGM Films. She now learned to share Schulze-Boysen's political convictions and the burden of his labours for the Soviet Union, and her bed with a legion of lovers.

At about the same time, but independently, a senior civil servant in the economics ministry, Arvid Harnack, contacted the Soviet embassy, and was likewise recruited as agent 'Corsican', NKVD file 34118. Harnack was born in 1901 into a scholarly family in Darmstadt. He qualified as a lawyer and practised as an economist, spending some time in the United States. At the University of Wisconsin's Madison campus he met Mildred Fish, a strikingly handsome and serious-minded student of English. They were married in 1929, and elected to live in Germany. Both were keenly interested in Marxism – they made a tour of the Soviet Union, and in 1932 launched a political study group. When Arvid began to pass information to the Russians, and to recruit fellow-foes of Hitler to his ring, he joined the Nazi Party to improve his protective colouring. Meanwhile both he and Schulze-Boysen steadily extended their groups of like-minded intellectual foes of Hitler. Between them, by 1939 they had opened windows into some of the most influential institutions in Nazi Germany.

Moscow now made a serious security mistake: it ordered that the two networks should collaborate. Their guiding spirits had very different temperaments. Schulze-Boysen was an exuberant, impulsive extrovert; Harnack was a quiet, intense intellectual, whose impeccable middle-class background enabled himself and his friends for years to escape the attention of the Gestapo and the Abwehr. The two men nonetheless forged a close relationship, driven by shared hatred of the Nazis and romantic enthusiasm for the Soviet Union. Until June 1941 they had no need of wirelesses, merely transmitting information through the Russians' Berlin military attaché.

One of the most striking aspects of espionage is that its processes, the mere business of living a covert existence, acquire a life of their own, heedless of spies' achievements as collectors of information. Anatoli Gourevitch, in his memoirs, touches on a weakness in his own training which might be applied to the experience of many other agents. He was exhaustively instructed in techniques – secret inks, passwords for rendezvous and suchlike. No matching effort, however, was expended upon explaining the purpose of his mission: 'Why was so little heed paid to the means by which I might obtain information, to the whole organisational aspect of the business of intelligence-gathering?' In other words, and as Gourevitch's subsequent career illustrated, for many secret agents the management and perils of daily existence consumed a lion's share of their energies, often overwhelming the function that mattered – the acquisition of information of value to their service and its government.

Arrived in Brussels early in 1939, fresh from the GRU training school, Gourevitch took rooms in a lodging house, enrolled himself in a language school in his guise as a Uruguayan visitor, and reflected that his own absolute ignorance of commerce seemed likely to prove an impediment to his intended cover life, helping to run a locally based business. This concern receded, however, in the face of a more serious one: disillusionment on first meeting his boss, Leopold Trepper. Gourevitch had forged a heroic mental image of this secret agent so much esteemed by Moscow Centre, yet now he was confronted by what he afterwards claimed was a drab, unimposing reality. He had been briefed to suppose that a solid business cover had been established for 'Otto's' network in Belgium, whereas on the spot he found only a little suburban export business employing just three people and peddling 'the Foreign Excellent Trench-Coat'. Its secretary was a young Russian émigré, married to a former tsarist army officer, who was apparently completely ignorant of the real nature of the firm's operations. All the managers were Jews, which must make them instantly vulnerable in the event of a German takeover of Belgium.

Gourevitch felt more confidence in his fellow-agent 'Andre', a thirty-five-year-old Alsatian named Leon Grossvogel, who had deserted from the French army in 1925, then drifted around Germany before travelling to Palestine, where he became a communist, and forged a friendship with Trepper. After three years there he returned to Belgium, where his parents lived and ran a small trading house named 'Au Roi'. It was the presence of the Grossvogels that persuaded Trepper to come to Belgium, and to exploit their commercial contacts as a cover, when in 1938 Moscow charged him with the formation of a West European espionage organisation. His new deputy nonetheless decided that Trepper's supposed network of important intelligence contacts was nothing of the sort. While large allowance must be made for the fact that Gourevitch published his version long after he himself was denounced as a traitor, the thrust of his remarks makes sense. Whatever Trepper's tradecraft skills, together with his plausibility in composing reports which found favour in Moscow, it is hard to imagine what useful intelligence he could have acquired in low-grade Belgian and French business circles, the only society that he had access to. Centre seemed content to accept Trepper's claim to have created a system through which material could be gathered and passed to Moscow from its Berlin sources in the event of war with Germany. But Gourevitch dismissed as 'completely false' the claims of post-war Soviet historians that Trepper ran a large network of important agents extending into Scandinavia.

On the eve of war, Moscow Centre could boast that the Schulze-Boysen/Harnack groups in Germany provided excellent information from the Nazis' inner circle. The 'Lucy' Ring in Switzerland had established itself soundly, but only began to provide important intelligence from 1941 onwards. The Trepper–Gourevitch networks trod water until 1940. The extensive Soviet secret machine in the US, which will be described elsewhere, produced a steady stream of technological intelligence, which would have been more useful to the Russians in advancing their own defence base if their industries had been capable of exploiting it.

We have left to last the best of all Moscow's men – or rather, the most spectacular. Richard Sorge grips the imagination of posterity, more because of what he was than through his influence on history, which was marginal. He dispatched to Moscow a flow of privileged political and strategic information, acquired through an access to high places achieved through sheer force of personality. Much of his material was ignored, however, or merely duplicated similar reports from more authoritative Berlin sources. Some historians who selectively quote Sorge's occasional brilliant insights have ignored his misjudgements and false prophecies – 'noise'. His character and career as an agent were nonetheless extraordinary.

'Ika', as Sorge was nicknamed, was born in Baku in 1895, one of nine children of a German petroleum engineer and a Russian mother. After completing school in Germany he found himself thrust into the Kaiser's war as a young soldier. While convalescing in Königsberg after suffering a bad wound, he was indoctrinated into communist ideology, allegedly by the father of one of his nurses, though there was already a family precedent: Sorge's grandfather had been an associate of Marx and Engels. When the war ended he became a Marxist instructor, and acquired a PhD in political science. In 1921 he married Christiane Gerlach, having persuaded her to abandon a previous husband. His communist and revolutionary links attracted the unfavourable attention of the police, and he found Germany becoming too hot to hold him. In 1924 the couple moved to Moscow, where Sorge was recruited and trained as a Soviet agent. Uncertainty persists about his movements in the next five years, though it is known that he visited Britain. Christiane left him, without the formality of a divorce – his immense appeal to women made him careless about whether they stayed or went. The combination of rough-hewn good looks and a hypnotic, driven personality enabled him to attract, and often to maintain in tandem, an impressive range of lovers of all shapes and sizes. Though sceptics later condemned Sorge as a charlatan as well as a betrayer – a fundamentally shallow figure despite his intellectual pretensions – he was a strikingly successful one.

In 1929 the Red Army's Fourth Department – later the GRU – offered him an overseas assignment. He requested China, and arrived in Shanghai that November under cover as a freelance journalist, with a wireless-operator in tow. He achieved rapid social success in the European concessions, and made well-informed friends. Also agents. He himself was masquerading as an American, but dropped the pose with Agnes Smedley, the American China traveller, whom he enlisted in Moscow's service. In 1930 he met twenty-nine-year-old Hotsumi Ozaki, a struggling magazine writer with communist sympathies, whom he also recruited and who played a notable part in his subsequent career. Like almost all those who worked with him, Ozaki fell under the foreigner's spell. Long afterwards, another of his Japanese network said wonderingly of the superspy that Sorge became, 'You meet a man like him only once in a lifetime.' The GRU agent threw himself into researching every aspect of Chinese life, and his reports earned warm approval from his chiefs.

In January 1933 he returned to Moscow, where he 'married' again: a young Russian girl named Yekaterina Maximova – 'Katcha' – to whom he wrote emotional letters through the years that followed. He himself wanted to stay in Russia, but what use was a foreign spy in his employers' own country? The GRU decided to post him to Tokyo. In preparation for this assignment, Sorge travelled to Germany, now Nazi-ruled, to secure appropriate credentials, and achieved another brilliant social and professional success, while somehow evading exposure of his communist past. He met the publisher of *Zeitschrift fur Geopolitik*, an ardent National Socialist, and secured from him both a contract as a 'stringer' and a letter of introduction to the German embassy in Tokyo.

He also gained the goodwill of the magazine's founder, Karl Haushofer, a second 'stringing' arrangement with *Täglische Rundschau*, and a letter addressed to Lt. Col. Eugene Ott, a German officer serving an exchange term with a Japanese artillery regiment. The editor-in-chief urged Ott to 'trust Sorge in everything; that is, politically, personally and otherwise'. Through these sponsors the spy pulled off a further coup: he became a member of the National Socialist Party. Thus armoured, this avowed Nazi set off for Tokyo via the United States with a wireless-operator, Bruno Wendt of the Red Army, carrying in his luggage a copy of the 1933 *German Statistical Yearbook* to provide the key for his coding. Sorge was thirty-eight, and on the threshold of one of the greatest espionage careers in history.

Arrived in Japan, with remarkable speed he established a relationship with the German ambassador Herbert von Dirksen, a Prussian aristocrat; and a much closer one with Colonel Ott, who embraced another former *Frontsoldaten* as kin. Sorge, with characteristic recklessness, promptly began an affair with Ott's wife Helma, an Amazonian six-footer who was herself a former communist. This appears to have done no harm to the spy's relationship with her husband, who seemed, as he remained, mesmerised by his new friend. The colonel was an austere and unbending figure who perhaps saw qualities in Sorge which he envied, not least exuberance. The newcomer also ingratiated himself with the convivial and charming Captain Paul Wenneker, who joined the German mission in 1934 as naval attaché.

Sorge's intimacy with the embassy won him some respect and attention from the Japanese, though at this stage the Tokyo government had by no means committed itself to an alliance with Hitler – German residents were subject to police surveillance as intrusive as that imposed on other foreigners. Sorge threw himself into acquiring information of all kinds about the country, its people, history and culture, forming a library of over a thousand books, though he never learned to read Japanese, nor even to speak it well. His sexual indiscretions would have earned censure in any spy school, but his management of the relationship with the German diplomatic community at the colonnaded and handsomely gardened embassy offered a masterclass in penetration. Despite his avowed National Socialist allegiance, he was gaily critical of German government policies.

At meetings with Dirksen and Ott – who was now transferred to become military attaché – Sorge appeared to provide as much information as he received. Indeed, they recognised that the journalist knew more about Japan than they did. He started to assist in the compilation of diplomatic reports for Berlin, and forged a long-distance relationship with the editor of the Nazi Party newspaper, contributing to its columns and attending local Tokyo branch meetings. Meanwhile, patiently and skilfully, Sorge built up his network of informants for Moscow. Hotsumi Ozaki, his old friend and source from Shanghai, was now a respected journalist in Osaka, whence he was able to transfer to Tokyo. In that pre-social-media universe, for the next two years Sorge was able to prevent Ozaki from discovering his real name: the German was known to him only as 'Mr Johnson', the American cover identity he had worn in his China days.

Another recruit, Yotoku Miyagi, was a painter born in 1903, whose family had moved to California when he was a child. The American Communist Party talent-spotted Miyagi for the Comintern, and the slightly-built young man was persuaded to move back to Japan, where he proved a superb agent. In keeping with Moscow's stringent finance policies, though Miyagi received a salary from Sorge, he supplemented this through giving language lessons and selling his pictures, which commanded respectable prices. Another key Sorge subordinate was a Yugoslav-born journalist, Branko de Voukelitch. The Fourth Department peremptorily instructed Voukelitch to strengthen his cover by divorcing his wife Edith and marrying a Japanese woman. This the compliant agent duly did, confusing himself as well as his associates by falling sincerely in love with a well-born local girl, Yoshiko Yamasaki, who eventually married him.

It was a reflection of Colonel Ott's intimacy with Sorge that when he toured Manchuria in 1934, he took along the Russian spy as his courier in the Nazi interest. Sorge subsequently ghosted Ott's report to the army economic department, which won plaudits in Berlin. The following year, the Japanese police broke up another Soviet spy ring in Tokyo run by an American, John Sherman, a development which increased Moscow's dependency on Sorge. He once said, 'Spying work must be done bravely,' and indeed he became a famous figure in Tokyo's social, journalistic and diplomatic circles, careering about the city on a motorbike, drinking heroic quantities of alcohol, bedding every woman within his reach. He rented a two-storey Japanese-style house at 30 Nagasaki Machi, and Moscow kept him supplied with sufficient funds to sustain the rackety life he loved. He had a housekeeper who became devoted to him, together with a maid and a laundryman who were routinely quizzed by the police. But even the pathologically suspicious Japanese had no clue that Sorge might be a spy; they regarded him merely as an influential acolyte of the Nazis.

He performed a daily tour of newspaper offices and the German Club before making his way to the embassy, where he now spent so much time that he was provided with his own office in which to conduct research and prepare material for transmission to Berlin; privacy was also useful for photographing documents for Moscow. A German diplomat spoke later of Sorge as 'a gay, dissolute adventurer with a brilliant mind and an unassailable conceit'. The spy wrote a memorably ironic letter to his Moscow 'wife' Katcha in 1937: 'it is very hard, above all this solitude'.

It was indeed a ceaseless challenge for the Soviet agent to sustain a masquerade as a Nazi stooge while he partied and womanised. In the evenings he frequented a string of bars and clubs – Lohmeyers' restaurant in the Ginza, which had a loyal German clientèle; the seedy little Fliedermaus; and the Rheingold, whose proprietor Helmut Ketel was an ardent admirer of Hitler. It was there that Sorge met 'Agnes', one of many bar girls who fell for him. Agnes proved to have staying power. She was twenty-three, and her real name was Hanako Ishii. She became increasingly a fixture in his house, and he paid for her to take lessons to fulfil a cherished ambition to become a singer. But Sorge was no more faithful to Hanako than to any other woman: he conducted a long parallel relationship with Anita Mohr, wife of a locally based German businessman, who was described as a 'blonde bombshell'. Hanako appears to have provided a convenience rather than an object of real affection.

Sorge's priority was always service to Moscow. As the weight of GRU material increased, so did the difficulties of transmitting it. Wendt, his radioman, was incompetent, and Sorge insisted that a better man must be found. In 1935 the spy left Tokyo, supposedly on holiday, bound for the United States. From there he travelled covertly to the Soviet Union, to confer with his chiefs and sort out the communications issues. In Moscow he was rebriefed about priorities, foremost among which was to explore Japan's intentions towards the Soviet Union. Thereafter, in descending order he was ordered to study the Japanese army and industry; policies in China; positioning towards Britain and the US.

Soon after Sorge's return to Tokyo, a new wireless-operator and courier joined him from Moscow. Max Clausen held officer's rank in the Red

Gun licence issued to Richard Sorge in 1927

Army. To provide cover he established a blueprint-copying business in Tokyo, which became a notably profitable pet project. Clausen's first intelligence task was to build his own wireless set, common practice among agents in countries to which it was deemed too difficult or dangerous to dispatch a professionally constructed one. He used a domestic radio receiver, attached the transmitter to a Bakelite panel mounted on a wooden box, and wound tuning coils from copper tubing intended for motor manufacture. In the absence of instruments to measure wavelengths, Clausen transmitted on a 37–39 metre band, and received on 45–48.

Sorge persuaded a friend and fellow-journalist, Gunther Stein, to allow the Soviet operator to message Moscow from his flat. Stein initially recoiled from accepting this appalling risk, but eventually assented. Since Clausen dared not set up an external aerial, he stretched two copper-stranded wires, seven metres in length, around the room from which he transmitted. Stein also became a useful informant for the Sorge ring, exploiting friendships he had formed at the British embassy. So too did Torao Shinotsuka, owner of a small military-equipment factory in Kansai, who provided extensive material on military aircraft and naval armaments. Anna Clausen, Max's adored wife, arrived in Tokyo from Moscow to share the wireless-operator's hazardous existence.

The Soviet network's membership thus expanded at a period when Japan was entering a period of paranoia about foreign espionage, and reinforcing its domestic security agencies. In 1936 there was a bad moment when Tokyo police arrested Taikichi Kawai at the request of their Manchurian counterparts. Kawai had been an informant of 'Mr Johnson' in Shanghai. In captivity he was brutally interrogated. Unlike most agents under torture, however, he gave away nothing significant. Sorge's luck held. His work was giving the highest satisfaction to both of its beneficiaries, Moscow Centre and the Foreign Ministry in Berlin. The latter was especially delighted by a report which he compiled on the 1936 Japanese army revolt, but which he insisted should circulate among the Nazi hierarchy only under the coy initials 'RS', because he remained fearful of a Gestapo investigation of his political past.

He helped Ott and Dirksen draft a cable to Berlin, asking for information about a rumoured German–Japanese negotiation. Sorge sought to promote Moscow's agenda by urging on the German embassy team the view that such an alliance would be mistaken, and rooted in absurd rumours that Stalin's fall was imminent. He published an article on the

Japanese army in *Die Wehrmacht* magazine. His reputation with the Tokyo embassy and with Berlin soared after the fulfilment of his prediction that Japan's war in China would prove protracted. More important, however, was the mass of information about Japanese deployments on the Soviet border which Ott provided to Sorge, who swiftly forwarded it to the GRU. Moscow also professed appreciation of industrial data delivered by Hotsumi Ozaki at monthly restaurant meetings. The journalist had become influential in government circles, and correspondingly well-informed: for a time he even served in the Japanese prime minister's office as an expert on China. Even though he lost that role when the government changed in 1939, he secured a new job as a Tokyo-based researcher for Japan's Kwantung army in Manchuria.

In 1938 Herbert von Dirksen was invalided home. His successor as ambassador was none other than Colonel Ott. Sorge thenceforward found himself drafting the German embassy's dispatches for Berlin, while transmitting his own to Moscow. On his forty-third birthday he was presented with a signed photograph of Nazi foreign minister Joachim von Ribbentrop as a token of Berlin's appreciation for his services. No foreign penetration of a British diplomatic mission could be compared in significance with that achieved by Sorge of Hitler's Tokyo embassy. When a Russian general defected to Tokyo in 1938, the spy was immediately able to warn Moscow that its codes were compromised. In May 1939, when tensions on the Russo–Japanese border erupted into local clashes, thanks to Ozaki Sorge could tell Moscow authoritatively that the Japanese had no intention of escalating the 'Nomonhan Incident' into a wider war. On this issue as on many others, however, doubts persist about the use made of his material. Sorge supposedly gave the Soviets detailed Japanese order-of-battle information, but Georgi Zhukov as the Red Army's local commander complained bitterly about the absence of such data. It seems likely either that Sorge later exaggerated his own contribution, or that the GRU failed to pass on his material.

He sought to strengthen his cover by publicly taunting Soviet diplomats when he met them at international receptions, but the stress of his fantastic high-wire act increasingly told on him, and was reflected in massive infusions of alcohol. In the company of Hanako, he succumbed to morose, drink-fuelled monologues, especially when she begged him to give her a child: 'I am an old man. I am going to die soon. I can do without a baby! Oh, poor Sorge. You should study so that you can get along without Sorge …' One night he crashed his motorbike, with agonising consequences –

many days in hospital and the loss of his teeth. For the rest of his life he could swallow meat only if it was minced.

He had sense enough to abandon biking, and instead acquired a small car. He embarked on a whimsical cultural improvement programme for Hanako, persuading her to read *Gone With the Wind*, which he himself considered 'magnificent'. Several hundred pages later she said, 'I like Captain Butler.' Perhaps providing a glimpse of his self-image, Sorge demanded, 'Do you think I am like Rhett Butler?' But Clausen wrote later about him: 'He is a true communist ... He is a man who can destroy even his best friend for the sake of Communism.' He could also destroy a comrade. The spy's treatment of his wireless-operator was cavalier, even brutal. And his lifestyle was ever more at odds with the ideal of a dedicated servant of the Party. Sorge had made himself probably the best-informed secret agent in the world. Nonetheless, his rashness made an ultimate train wreck inevitable, even if in 1939 this still lay a surprising distance in the future.

By the coming of war, the Soviet Union's huge expenditure on espionage, and its access to highly placed communist sympathisers in many lands, should have made the Kremlin the best-informed centre of government on the planet. Yet those in Moscow who received and processed the reports from the field were far too fearful of offending the only audience that mattered – Joseph Stalin, master of the Kremlin – to forward any intelligence that was likely to prove unwelcome. Even when important information reached Moscow, it was seldom properly reviewed, far less exploited by policy-makers. Christopher Andrew has written: 'The Soviet capacity to understand the political and diplomatic intelligence it collected ... never approached its ability to collect the intelligence in the first place.' Stalin acted as his own analyst, preferring to drill endless wells of espionage in search of imagined conspiracies rather than to use intelligence to inform policy-making. Soviet intelligence officers feared for their lives, with good reason, if they told Stalin what he did not want to hear. He seemed to credit only reports that identified plots against himself or the state, at home and abroad. Where these did not exist, Russia's most senior intelligence officers invented them. Stalin used the product of his codebreakers to some effect where and when this was available, but entered the greatest conflict in history almost blind through his own acts of will.

After Munich, with the doom of Czechoslovakia sealed, the Czech intelligence chief František Moravec was approached by three rival bidders for his services: Admiral Wilhelm Canaris for the Germans, Colonel Louis Rivet for the French, and MI6's local man, Major Harold Gibson, for the British. Mistrusting the French, Moravec determined to throw in his lot with Britain. In anticipation of the Nazi occupation he did his utmost to reinforce links with local informants before himself leaving his country. He was able to transfer to London large sums of foreign currency, and hoped thus to ensure that he could sustain a Czech intelligence service in exile, though few of his agents were ever heard from again. On 3 March 1939 the Abwehr's Paul Thummel, Moravec's best German source, met him in Prague and reported that the city would be occupied on the 15th. 'Agent A-54' also warned that his entire staff would be seized by the Gestapo, and could expect no mercy. Moravec was amazed that Thummel declared himself willing to continue his own collaboration. The only proviso, said the Abwehr man, was that the Czechs must ensure that everything about himself in their files was destroyed. With that assurance, the two men parted. Thummel said, 'Good luck, Colonel. This is not good-bye but *Auf wiedersehen.*' The German officer took away with him two addresses for future correspondence, one in Holland, the other in Switzerland.

In Prague on the night of 13 March, Harold Gibson of MI6 – 'Gibby', as Moravec always called him, a small, slight figure with a moustache in proportion – drove a car into the Czech Intelligence Department's garage. This was loaded with hundreds of files packed in canvas bags, which were borne away to the British embassy. The following afternoon, a Dutch civilian plane chartered by Broadway landed at Ruzyn airfield outside Prague to collect passengers for England – Moravec and ten officers of his staff. He chose them unsentimentally, he wrote later, taking those who would be most valuable in London, and those who knew too much to be left to the Gestapo. He felt obliged to leave behind his own wife and two daughters, and indeed to conceal from them his intended destination: he said he was merely making an overnight trip to Moravia.

The plane took off with difficulty amidst a snowstorm, which for a time threatened to force them down into the path of the approaching Germans. Moravec carried a briefcase containing 200,000 Reichsmarks and 100,000 Dutch guilders in cash – about £32,000 – to provide his little team with further seed money for future operations. As the plane passed over the mountains where lay Czechoslovakia's frontier, the colonel buried his head in his hands and sobbed unashamedly at the prospect of exile. After a brief stop in Amsterdam, the party landed safely at Croydon. When former

Czech prime minister Edvard Beneš later arrived in London, Moravec reported to his Putney residence to offer his services and those of his officers, which were readily accepted – his role was formalised the following year, when Beneš formed a government in exile. The colonel's wife and children escaped from Prague and walked to safety in Poland, from whence they joined him in Britain.

In June 1939 Moravec was delighted to receive a letter, forwarded from a Zürich cover address, which began, 'Dear Uncle, I think I am in love. I have met a girl.' On the same page was a secret ink message, appointing a rendezvous in The Hague. It was from agent A-54, the Abwehr colonel Paul Thummel. The Czech officer who duly met him early in August warned Thummel that Moravec's shrunken organisation no longer had cash to lavish upon him as generously as in the past, but the German responded dismissively that 'more important matters than money are at stake'. He told the Czech that an invasion of Poland was planned for 1 September, and provided details of the latest Wehrmacht order of battle. He also handed over a list of Polish traitors working for the Germans. Thummel subsequently provided the Nazis' amended timetable, including on 27 August a final date for the Polish invasion of 3 September 1939. For the people of Czechoslovakia, Poland, and now of all Western Europe, the sparring was over: the death struggle had begun.

2

The Storm Breaks

1 THE 'FICTION FLOOD'

The first significant excitement of the British secret service's war came in November 1939. A document later known as the 'Oslo Report' was sent anonymously to the British legation in Norway, then forwarded to London by its naval attaché. The parcel that reached Broadway contained several pages of German typescript and a small cardboard box. It represented the outcome of an earlier 'feeler' message to the legation, saying that if the British wanted to receive details of new scientific developments in Germany, they should make a minor change in the wording of a BBC broadcast to Germany: instead of starting, 'Hello, this is London calling', it was to say, 'Hello, hello, this is …' This was duly done, and after a short delay the 'Oslo Report' was submitted.

Its narrative covered a remarkable range of enemy activities. The anonymous author asserted that the Germans were developing acoustic and radio-controlled torpedoes; detailed the wavelengths on which German radar stations were operating; suggested bombing the Luftwaffe research station at Rechlin; and much else. The box contained a trigger tube, to be employed for new anti-aircraft shell proximity fuses. But the credibility of the whole document was undermined by the inclusion of two nonsenses: a claim that the Luftwaffe's Ju-88 bombers were being produced at the impossible rate of 5,000 a month; and that a German aircraft-carrier, the *Franken*, was approaching completion at Kiel. These mistakes contributed to a verdict by Whitehall that the document should be dismissed as a German plant.

But the report was also read by Dr Reginald Jones, the outspoken, combative, twenty-eight-year-old assistant director of Air Ministry scientific intelligence. Jones shines forth as an authentic star in the wartime secret firmament. He was a social hybrid, son of a sergeant in the Grenadier

Guards who displayed precocious brilliance at his south London school, and later proved as much at ease holding forth at grand country-house parties as fighting his corner in meetings chaired by the prime minister. Having had a notable early career in physics and astronomy at Oxford, where for a time he worked under Frederick Lindemann – later Lord Cherwell – he became fascinated by the possibilities of exploiting infra-red technology for the detection of aircraft, and in 1936 went to work for the Air Ministry. He was intolerant of slow-mindedness or bureaucracy wherever he encountered it, and there was plenty of both at Broadway Buildings, where after a brief stint at Bletchley Park he was invited to share an office with Fred Winterbotham.

In the course of the war Reg Jones became one of the foremost British investigators of German air technology. In November 1939, however, his achievements still lay in the future, and he was seen in Whitehall simply as a pushy young 'boffin' who seemed too free with his opinions in the presence of senior officers. Jones, almost alone, elected to believe that the Oslo document was authentic. His instinct became a near-certainty in the summer of 1940, when the Luftwaffe began to use the Wotan naviga-tional beam to guide its bombers over Britain, exploiting principles mentioned by Oslo's author. R.V. Jones, as he is known to posterity, found the information invaluable in devising counter-measures during the 'Battle of the Beams' that influenced the Blitz – which gained him the ear and the admiration of Winston Churchill. Again and again through the years that followed, when the British gained hints about new German weapons – the acoustic torpedo, for example – Jones was able to point out to service chiefs that Oslo had warned of them. After the war, in a retro-spective on his own intelligence career, the scientist used the example of the 1939 document to urge that 'casual sources should not be treated flip-pantly. It was probably the best single [scientific intelligence] report received from any source during the war.'

Only after an interval of almost forty years did Jones establish the docu-ment's authorship. It was the work of a forty-five-year-old German physi-cist named Hans Ferdinand Mayer, who adopted a scientific career after being badly wounded on his first day in action as a conscript in 1914. He had been employed by Siemens since 1922, doing work that resulted in the award of eighty-two patents and the publication of forty-seven papers, and also spent four years as professor of signals technique at America's Cornell University. During the inter-war years he formed a warm friendship with an Englishman working for GEC named Cobden Turner, who became godfather to Mayer's second son. The German was especially impressed by a good deed: when he told Turner about the tragic case of a Jewish school-child disowned by her Nazi father, the Englishman arranged for the little girl to come to England, where for eight years she lived as a member of his own family.

When the international horizon darkened, on what proved Turner's final visit to Germany Mayer told him that if war came, he would try to supply Britain with information about German scientific and technologi-cal progress. In late 1939 the scientist exploited a chance business trip to Norway to make good on his promise. He borrowed an old typewriter from the porter at the Hotel Bristol and composed the 'Oslo Report', which was dispatched in two parts to the British embassy on 1 and 2 November. Mayer also wrote directly to Cobden Turner, suggesting further contact through an intermediary in neutral Denmark. But although this letter caused two British security officers to visit and question the GEC man, for reasons unknown nothing was done to open communication with Mayer – MI6's official history makes no mention of this courageous German. In August 1943 Mayer was arrested by the Gestapo in his office at Siemens, and charged with listening to the BBC. He was confined in Dachau, but was fortunate enough to be employed in a technical plant, where he survived the war. His brave gesture was prompted by admiration for Cobden Turner, whom he liked to regard as a representative Englishman. Recognition of Mayer's contribution, however, came only from Reg Jones.

Among the reasons the 'Oslo Report' received such a chilly reception is that it was debated in Whitehall just as the British secret community reeled in the wake of a successful German ruse. On 9 November 1939, during the first, passive phase of the war that became derisively known as the 'sitzkrieg', the two senior MI6 officers in the neutral Netherlands, Captain Sigismund Payne Best and Major Richard Stevens, drove with a Dutch officer in Best's Lincoln Zephyr car to a rendezvous at the Café Backus, situated between the Dutch and German border customs barriers at Venlo. Within minutes of their arrival, they were seized by armed men. When the Dutchman drew a pistol and fired at one assailant, he was himself shot dead. Best, Stevens and their local driver were then hustled 150 yards to the frontier: their kidnappers were Nazi counter-intelligence officers of the SD, led by the branch's later boss, Walter Schellenberg, who was narrowly missed by the Dutch officer's bullet. The British spies were fortunate enough to keep their lives, but spent most of the rest of the war in Sachsenhausen concentration camp. In contradiction of myths about heroic silence under interrogation, Stevens and Best told their abductors what they knew about MI6, which was plenty: its Continental operations were chiefly conducted from their own Hague station.

'The Venlo incident', as it became known in Whitehall, derived from an approach some weeks earlier by supposedly anti-Nazi German generals eager to negotiate with Britain. MI6 became much excited by the prospect of brokering a deal, though the Foreign Office was prudently sceptical. Sir Alexander Cadogan wrote in his diary on 23 October: 'I think they [the German "plotters"] are Hitler agents.' The war cabinet was informed a week later, and Winston Churchill, then still First Lord of the Admiralty, expressed violent objections to any parley. But the government authorised MI6 to continue discussions, provided – as Cadogan strictly instructed – nothing was put in writing to the supposed dissidents. The British ignored the danger that their interlocutors would play not merely a diplomatic game with them, but a rougher one. They should have been alert to such an outcome, because the Nazis had previous form as cross-border kidnappers.

In November 1939, it was symptomatic of MI6's institutional weakness that its Hague station employed Folkert van Koutrik, an Abwehr inform-ant. The supposed representative of the disaffected German generals, 'Major Schaemmel', was in truth the RSHA's Schellenberg, whom the British officers obligingly supplied with a wireless transmitter. Either Hitler or Himmler personally authorised the kidnapping, which the British at first sought to keep secret. When an official asked Cadogan what was to be said about 'the brawl in Holland', the subject of fevered rumour and speculation, the permanent under-secretary ordered the issue of a 'D' Notice, forbidding mention of it in the British press. Amazingly, for a fort-night after Venlo the German 'conspirators' sustained a dialogue with MI6, until on 22 November Himmler lost interest and the Germans shut down the exchange after sending a last derisive message to Broadway. The Nazis then publicly announced that Best and Stevens had been engaged in an assassination plot against Hitler. Meanwhile van Koutrik's betrayal went so far undetected that he secured employment with MI5 in London, and it was very fortunate that he broke off contact with the Abwehr – perhaps for lack of means of communication – because it was within his later knowledge to have betrayed elements of the Double Cross system to them.

Inside Whitehall, MI6 sought to talk down Venlo, arguing that the Germans had behaved crassly by grabbing the two officers instead of sustaining a double-cross game with them. It is hard to overstate the episode's significance, however, for the future course of the secret war. British espionage activities on the Continent, such as they were, suffered a devastating blow: the Germans were able to relieve Best of a list of his station's contacts, which he had taken in his pocket to the rendezvous. The reputation of the secret service within the British government, not high before the débâcle, afterwards sagged low indeed. Guy Liddell of MI5 speculated in his diary that Best, a preposterous figure who affected a monocle, might have been a double agent – 'the real nigger in the wood-pile. [He] had apparently been in fairly low water and it was noticeable that after he became associated with [Dr Franz] Fischer [a Nazi double agent in Holland] he seemed to be very well in funds.' There is no reason to think Liddell's suspicions justified. Mere bungling was responsible for the fiasco, though Walter Schellenberg asserted later that Best was willing to be 'turned'. Meanwhile, the Dutch were embarrassed by the revelation that one of their own intelligence officers had been complicit in a British plot, which strengthened the Nazis' propaganda hand by compromising Holland's proclaimed neutrality.

A further consequence of Venlo was that the British became morbidly suspicious of any approach – and there were several, later in the war – by Germans professing to represent an 'anti-Hitler Resistance'. In one sense their caution was prudent, because most of the aristocrats and army officers who became engaged in plots against the Nazis cherished absurd fantasies about the Germany they might preserve through a negotiation with the Western Allies. Former Leipzig mayor Karl Gördeler, for instance, was a nationalist with views on German territorial rights in Europe that were not far short of Hitler's. Even had the Führer perished, there would have been nothing plausible for Germany's enemies to discuss with his domestic foes. At the very least, however, British paranoia about suffering a repeat of the Venlo humiliation permanently excluded MI6 from some useful sources, which the Russians and later the Americans were left to exploit. Moreover, for the rest of the war Broadway's chiefs maintained an exaggerated respect for their German adversaries, derived from the memory of having been fooled by them in November 1939.

Through the icy winter months of the 'Phoney War', the GC&CS at Bletchley struggled with the intractable Enigma problem, while Broadway's spies produced little or no useful information about the enemy and his intentions. Kenneth Strong of War Office Intelligence wrote: 'We had a continuous stream of callers from the Services with an extraordinary variety of queries and requests. What were the most profitable targets for air attacks in this or that area, and what effect would these attacks have on the German Army? Was our information about these targets adequate and accurate? How was the German Army reacting to our propaganda campaigns? I found some quite fantastic optimism regarding the effects from propaganda. The dropping of leaflets was considered almost a major military victory.'

Some MI6 officers went to elaborate lengths to conceal their lack of agent networks. Reg Jones cited the example of Wilfred 'Biffy' Dunderdale, who was responsible for France, and fed to Jones's branch a succession of tasty titbits on the German Ju-88 bomber, allegedly collected by spies. First there was information about its engines; then its electrics; and somewhat later its armament. Jones teased Dunderdale that he must have secured a copy of the aircraft's operating handbook, then fed extracts to Broadway, to create an impression of multiple sources. The hapless officer admitted that Jones was right, but begged him to keep his mouth shut. He could keep his bosses much more interested, he said, by drip-feeding the data. This was not the only occasion when Dunderdale – like officers of all intelligence services – sought to 'sex up' the means by which his material had been acquired. He also produced details of German troop movements supposedly secured by agent networks, which in reality derived from French intercepts.

Much could be learned from an enemy's wireless transmissions, even without breaking his codes, through 'traffic analysis' – the study of signal origins, volume and callsigns to pinpoint units, ships, squadrons. Useful information was also gleaned by the 'Y Service', which was responsible for eavesdropping on enemy voice transmissions, and by breaking simple enemy codes used for passing low-grade messages. The French forward cryptographical unit was based at 'Station Bruno', in the Château de Vignobles located at Gretz-Armainvilliers, fifteen miles east of Paris. Bruno received an important reinforcement following the fall of Poland. Guy Liddell of MI5 recorded on 10 October 1939 that seventeen Polish cryptanalysts were seeking asylum in Britain. Bletchley Park shrugged dismissively that it had no use for them, even though its chief Alastair Denniston had met some of the same men in Warsaw a few months earlier, and knew that their claims to have penetrated Russian and German ciphers 'can to some extent be maintained'.

Denniston suggested that they would be more useful at the Château de Vignobles, working with Gustave Bertrand, which was where they were sent – though Bletchley later changed its mind and tried in vain to get them back. It was at Bruno, on 17 January 1940, that the ex-Warsaw group broke its first wartime Enigma signal. By 11 March Col. Louis Rivet, head of the French secret service, was writing in his diary: 'The decrypts of the Enigma machine are becoming interesting and numerous.' During the months that followed, however, material was read far too slowly – out of 'real time' – to influence events on the battlefield. Instead, Allied intelligence officers strove to make sense of a jumble of humint warnings, of varying degrees of plausibility, about when Hitler intended to strike in the West.

The first of these had come in the previous November when Major Gijsbert Sas, Dutch military attaché in Berlin, received a dramatic tip-off from his friend Colonel Hans Oster of the Abwehr: the Wehrmacht, said Oster, would launch a full-scale offensive against the British and French armies on the 12th of that month. This coincided with several other identical or similar warnings – including an important one from Col. Moravec's Czechs in London, relayed by their man in Switzerland from Agent A-54, the Abwehr's Paul Thummel. When nothing happened on 12 November, the British and French chiefs of staff assumed that they were the victims of Nazi disinformation. The Dutch already suspected Sas of being a double agent, and the credibility of the other sources, including A-54, suffered accordingly. Yet the warnings were correct. Hitler had indeed intended to strike in November. He was enraged that his generals insisted upon a last-minute postponement until spring, because the army was unready to move. Here was a vivid illustration of a precept later advanced by a British Army intelligence officer: 'Perfect intelligence in war must of necessity be out-of-date and therefore ceases to be perfect ... We deal not with the true, but with the likely.'

The next excitement took place one day in January 1940: thick fog caused a German courier aircraft flown by Major Erich Hönmanns to forced-land in neutral Belgium. Local police arrested the pilot and his passenger, an officer named Reinberger, interrupting them as they attempted to burn papers they carried, and retrieved the charred sheets from a stove. Within forty-eight hours the French and British high commands were reading the Wehrmacht's plan for its intended invasion of France and the Low Countries, focused on a thrust through Holland and Belgium. Here was a textbook example of a genuine intelligence coup, with wholly unhelpful consequences. The French were confirmed in their conviction that the Germans would attack through Belgium as they had done in 1914, and as all France's deployments anticipated. The British suspected an enemy deception: the material seemed too good to be true. Guy Liddell of MI5 wrote wearily on 14 January: 'A German aeroplane came down in Belgium ... with certain papers found on the pilot indicating projected attack by the Germans on Belgium and Holland. It looks rather as if this may have been part of the scheme for the war of nerves.' Cadogan at the Foreign Office described receiving 'complete plan of German invasion of the Low Countries. Very odd. But one can't ignore these things, and all precautions taken.'

Kenneth Strong wrote ruefully afterwards: 'So often I have heard it said that if we only had the plans of the other side things would be simple: when they actually came our way we found great difficulty in persuading ourselves that they were genuine.' Most important, however, the capture immediately forfeited all virtue, because the German proprietors of the plan knew that the Allies had it. Thus, Hitler insisted on changing the invasion concept, to thrust instead through the Ardennes, which proved the one authentic strategic inspiration of his life. Here was another critical lesson about intelligence, especially important for codebreakers: captured material became worthless if its originators discovered that it was in enemy hands.

Alexander Cadogan noted in his diary for 19 January 1940 that Stewart Menzies now seemed to expect the Germans to attack soon after 25 January, and added dismissively, 'but he's rather mercurial, and rather hasty and superficial (like myself!)'. If this remark somewhat short-changed the diarist, it was scarcely a ringing endorsement of 'C'. There was one further strand: low-grade Abwehr messages decrypted by MI5's Radio Intelligence Service offered indications about the looming onslaught. At that time, however, machinery was lacking to analyse such material, to feed it into the military command system and ensure that notice was taken by commanders. In that pre-Ultra universe, politicians, diplomats and generals were chronically sceptical about intelligence of all kinds. When a new warning reached MI6 via Moravec's 'London Czechs' – that Abwehr officer Paul Thummel expected a great Wehrmacht thrust on 10 May, it vanished in the welter of 'noise' that spring.

The 9 April German invasion of Norway caught the Western Allies totally by surprise. Though no decrypts were available, the Admiralty ignored or misread plentiful clues about Hitler's intentions. When the Wehrmacht's amphibious forces began to land on the Norwegian coast, the Royal Navy's major units were far away, awaiting an anticipated breakout into the Atlantic by German battleships. Through the weeks that followed, Wehrmacht eavesdroppers easily tracked the British brigades struggling to aid the little Norwegian army, while intelligence learned little or nothing about the invaders' lightning movements.

On 10 May 1940, Hitler launched his Blitzkrieg in the West. The panzers swept through the Ardennes, across the Meuse, and thence to the Channel coast and into the heart of France. Much of the information sent back from the front by French units was so fanciful that a headquarters intelligence officer, André Beaufre, dismissed it contemptuously as a 'fiction flood'. Gen. Maurice Gamelin, the Allied commander-in-chief, rejected every report that contradicted his obsessive belief that the Germans still planned to make their main attack through Belgium.

The campaign proved a triumph for the German army's intelligence department, as well as for its generals. An anglophile and *bon viveur*, Lt. Col. Ulrich Liss, headed Foreign Armies West – FHW, the Wehrmacht's principal intelligence evaluation department. Liss, who was exceptionally able and energetic, called sigint 'the darling of all intelligence chiefs', because it could be trusted as spies could not – and in May 1940 the best of it was in the hands of his own staff. During the long, static winter, German interceptors had identified the locations of most of the Allies' formations, much assisted by the insecurity of the French army's wireless-operators and headquarters staffs, who often discussed plans and deployments in plain language. Col. Handeeming, radio intelligence's interception chief with Army Group A, was explicitly commissioned to monitor the French Seventh Army's advance into Belgium, which he did with notable efficiency.

Liss's men also benefited from securing vast numbers of Allied prisoners. All armies gleaned much from PoW interrogation. Throughout the war, even if few prisoners knowingly betrayed secrets, amid the shock of capture most gave their captors more than the regulation 'name, rank and number'. Rommel's intelligence staff found that British prisoners talked freely until a late stage of the North African campaign. One of Montgomery's officers enthused to the Germans, with almost insane indiscretion, that Eighth Army's radio monitoring service was 'brilliant in every respect'. A German wrote that British officers were repeatedly captured 'carrying important lists, codes and maps'. It was a standard technique for intelligence officers to engage PoWs in apparently innocent conversation about non-military subjects. The Wehrmacht's 'Guidelines for the interrogation of English prisoners of war', dated Berlin, 16 April

1940, urged commanders whenever possible to use interrogators familiar with Britain and the British. 'If cordially addressed,' said the briefing note, 'every Englishman will at once answer all questions entirely frankly.' Beyond immediate tactical issues, the Intelligence Department advised:

Special value is set on probing prevailing economic and social circumstances in England. Answers to the following questions are useful:

a) What are you told about Hitler?
b) What are you told about the Nazis?
c) What are you told about the Gestapo?
d) What are you told about the Jews?
e) What are you told about food conditions in Germany?
f) What are you told about military successes?
g) How do you make propaganda?
h) How are women and children cared for?
i) Do you take care of elderly parents no longer able to work, whose sons are soldiers? …
k) What is the food situation – especially meat, vegetables, eggs, butter, and bread?
l) What do you think of the black-out?
m) Who is currently the most popular man in England?
n) Who do you consider the most forceful personality in the British cabinet?
o) Do you listen to German radio?
p) Do you like [Lord] Haw-Haw [the Nazi propaganda broadcaster William Joyce]?
q) How are your relations with the French?
r) Do you believe that Germany is bent on world conquest?
s) Would you make peace tomorrow?

The behaviour of most PoWs was strongly influenced by their own nation's immediate circumstances. At this time, when Allied fortunes were plumbing the depths, a report on the handful of German PoWs in British hands recorded gloomily: 'The officers (and most of the men) were quite immune to propaganda, think Hitler is a god and refuse to believe a single word of the British news.' By contrast, a South African RAF pilot named Sgt Edward Wunsch provided his German captors with a highly sympathetic view of the Nazi cause, as recorded by his interrogator: 'Like all South Africans who have entered Dulag Luft, Wunsch is an unashamed anti-Semite … [He says] There is no hatred towards Germany in South Africa, no enthusiasm for the war at all. Most people believe the nonsense press and propaganda tell them about German atrocities but … W. thinks it possible that one day South Africa could agree to a separate peace, *if Germany continues to be militarily successful* [author's italics].'

The Allies lost the 1940 battle for France for many reasons. It has been a source of fierce controversy ever since, whether the French army's defeat resulted from a failure of judgement by Maurice Gamelin, Allied commander-in-chief, or instead from a national moral collapse. It is unlikely that any amount of intelligence or advance warning could have changed 1940 outcomes. The German army showed itself an incomparably more effective fighting force than the Allies', and there would be no victories until that changed. If British and French intelligence was poor in 1940, so was everything else.

As the Continent was evacuated, there was a late flurry of buccaneering by secret service officers and freelances: MI6's Major Monty Chidson, a former head of the Hague station, rescued a priceless haul of industrial diamonds from Amsterdam. Peter Wilkinson got most of the Polish general staff out of France. Tommy Davies, a peacetime director of the Courtaulds textile business, escaped from its Calais plant with a load of platinum hours before the Germans arrived. But these little coups were fleabites in the great scheme of affairs. MI6 had made no contingency plans for stay-behind agents, to report from France in the event of its occupation by the Nazis, and Broadway would probably have been accused of defeatism had it done so. Through many months that followed, Britain's intelligence services were thus almost blind to events on the Continent, to the frustration of the prime minister. Beleaguered on their island, they became dependent for knowledge of Hitler's doings on the vagaries of air reconnaissance, and reports from neutral diplomats and correspondents.

The security service explored the limits of the possible and the acceptable in handling a stream of Abwehr agents who descended on Britain, and were promptly captured. MI5 spurned torture as a means of interrogation, but in September 1940 at Camp 020, the service's interrogation centre at Latchmere House near Ham Common, one of its officers assaulted and battered the captured Abwehr agent 'Tate' – Harry Williamson – until he was dragged off him. Guy Liddell deplored this episode, saying that he objected to 'Gestapo methods' on both moral and professional grounds. Col. Alexander Scotland was likewise prevented from injecting Williamson with drugs. Naval Intelligence Division interrogators tested drugs on each other as a means of extracting information, and concluded that it was a waste of time. Skilled questioning, they decided, was not merely more ethical, but more effective.

As the next act of the great global drama unfolded – Hitler's air assault on Britain – neither Broadway nor Bletchley Park had much to contribute. The most significant aid to Fighter Command in its epic struggle to repel Göring's air fleets was wireless traffic analysis of the flood of Morse from the Germans' new French, Belgian, Dutch and Norwegian bases, together with monitoring of Luftwaffe cockpit chatter by the German linguists of the RAF's infant Y Service, most of them women.

The prime minister and the chiefs of staff were for many months preoccupied, even obsessed, by two questions: would the Germans invade; and if so, when? In the mad mood prevailing in London in the autumn of 1940, a blend of heroic defiance and absurdity, the War Office's director of military intelligence suggested exploiting captured Abwehr agents to try to provoke the Germans into hastening an invasion, which he felt sure could be defeated by the Royal Navy and the British Army. This proposal found no favour in Whitehall. Meanwhile the disaster in France had endowed the Wehrmacht with almost magical powers in the minds of the generals, many of whom convinced themselves that Hitler might launch an amphibious assault on Britain with only a few weeks' preparation, offering no notice to the defenders.

The Royal Navy's Commander Geoffrey Colpoys was responsible for delivering to Downing Street each day at 1 p.m. a report from the Special Invasion Warning Committee, which for most of the autumn took it for granted that a German assault was imminent, and concerned itself chiefly with the timing. The Joint Intelligence Committee, chaired by the Foreign Office's Victor 'Bill' Cavendish-Bentinck, only once sounded the alarm to suggest that invasion was imminent, on 7 September, when, as Bentinck himself noted sardonically later, he himself was briefly absent and the army's somewhat unstable director of intelligence – the same man who advocated inciting the Wehrmacht to land – temporarily held the chair. Churchill himself was always sceptical about an invasion, but he deemed it politically imperative to sustain the British people's belief in the threat not only in 1940, but throughout the following year also, to promote their vigilance and sense of purpose. On 31 July Sir Alexander Cadogan expressed his own conviction that the Germans would not come, but would instead thrust at Gibraltar and Egypt, then added, 'our "intelligence" gives nothing to corroborate this theory. But then they're awfully bad.' Nowhere in the world were British agents providing information of much assistance to the war effort. The British C-in-C in Singapore, Air-Marshal Sir Robert Brooke-Popham, wrote in frustration: 'Little or no reliance is placed upon MI6 information by any authorities here and little valuable information appears to be obtained.' The same was true nearer home.

For many months after the German occupation of Western Europe, the only nation still able to exploit secret sources on a large scale was the neutral Soviet Union, through its networks in Belgium, Germany and Switzerland. In those days its agents did not even need to trouble with wireless: they simply passed reports to their nearest Soviet diplomatic mission. In May 1940 the GRU's Leopold Trepper moved from Brussels to Paris, taking with him his mistress, the exotically named Georgie de Winter, a twenty-year-old American, and leaving his deputy Anatoli Gourevitch to arrange the Trepper family's return to Moscow. Gourevitch's own personal affairs were scarcely uncomplicated. Under his cover as a 'Uruguayan businessman' he had a succession of girlfriends, but felt obliged to break off relations with the prettiest when she revealed that her father knew South America well. 'In other circumstances,' he wrote wistfully, 'I could probably have loved her, but such good fortune is denied to a secret agent.' Thereafter, however, he formed a friendship with a neighbouring family named Barcza, whose elderly Hungarian husband was married to Margaret, a much younger Belgian blonde with an eight-year-old son. Following her husband's sudden death, Gourevitch began an intense affair with her. Mikhail Makarov, the other GRU career officer in Belgium, was also leading what Gourevitch described primly as 'an excessively dissipated life', in which prostitutes played a conspicuous role.

The German invasion of Belgium gave Gourevitch some bad moments: Brussels police arrested his supposed English friend and language teacher, who turned out to be an Abwehr agent; the man was promptly liberated when his compatriots overran the capital. The GRU network's cover company 'Au Roi' collapsed when its Jewish frontmen fled and the business was sequestered. Moscow ordered Gourevitch to take over control of the Belgian operation. He entered Margaret Barcza on Centre's books – allegedly without her knowledge – as a source unimaginatively codenamed 'the Blonde'. The most believable aspect of his own later account of the whole saga is its emphasis on the rickety, rackety nature of a spy ring that history – especially Soviet history – has dignified as one of the great secret operations of all time. Gourevitch asserted that Leopold Trepper's much-vaunted intelligence network in France and Belgium 'was composed almost entirely of his old Palestinian friends', and provided Moscow with no usable intelligence about Germany's descents on Poland, Scandinavia or Western Europe. It seems unlikely that the Russians learned much more from its activities during the year that followed than Churchill and his generals gleaned from their morning papers.

In the absence of serious British military operations save in North Africa, secret war became a massive growth activity, impelled by the prime minister himself. Special Operations Executive was created in July 1940, to 'set Europe ablaze', while the armed forces spawned commandos, paratroopers and a string of 'private armies', notably in the Middle East. New recruits of all kinds flooded into Broadway, some of them exotic. 'Writers of thrillers,' wrote the supremely cynical Malcolm Muggeridge, 'tend to gravitate to the secret service as surely as the mentally unstable become psychiatrists, or the impotent pornographers.' Thus was Graham Greene dispatched to Freetown, Sierra Leone, Muggeridge himself – a veteran foreign correspondent – to Lourenço Marques, in Portuguese Mozambique, and the journalist Kim Philby welcomed into Broadway. It became a source of dismay to career intelligence officers, protective of MI6's reputation, that its wartime recruits who later commanded most public attention were all either mavericks or traitors.

Lacking its own agents on the Continent, Broadway turned to the European exile governments in London for assistance in identifying sources. The Poles began to build impressive networks in their own country, though they suffered grievously from the fact – then of course unknown to them – that the Germans read the ciphers in which they communicated with their agents. František Moravec and his Czech group achieved formal recognition as the intelligence arm of their government; MI6 provided them with wireless facilities and documents. The Czechs established a new base in three little adjoining suburban houses in Rosendale Road, West Dulwich, until these were destroyed by the Luftwaffe, then late in 1940 moved to a new building in Bayswater. MI6 did not, however, give them money. Moravec, after spending the last of the cash he had brought out of Prague, was obliged to negotiate a loan of £50,000, to pay his network's outgoings of £3,000 a month. For some time he continued to receive East European material via Zürich – Captain Karel Sedlacek had served as Moravec's station chief there since 1934, under cover as a newspaper correspondent; since he lacked any literary gifts he was obliged to pay a ghost to write copy in his name. The Abwehr's Paul Thummel used the Czech officer as his link to London; when he was arrested by the Gestapo in March 1942, Moravec's little group ran out of sources.

The British enjoyed one immense piece of good fortune following their eviction from the Continent: nowhere did the Germans capture people or documents that betrayed Allied progress in cracking Enigma. Between 1940 and 1944 many Frenchmen, including hundreds of thousands of servants of the Vichy puppet regime, collaborated with their occupiers. But Vichy's military intelligence officers, and several Poles attached to them who were privy to the pioneering Enigma codebreaking operation, revealed nothing even later in the war, when they were exposed to enemy interrogation. The capacious nets cast across Europe by the Nazis focused overwhelmingly on hunting dissenters, not machines. In the early years of occupation, when most people in the conquered societies acquiesced in their fate, Berlin's spies and policemen uncovered little to ruffle their masters' complacency, and mercifully nothing that caused them to doubt the security of their own communications.

In the winter of 1940–41, none of the principal belligerents knew much more about each other's affairs than they learned from studying the international press and watching such movements as they could see of the rival armies, navies and air fleets. Most of the successful codebreaking that was taking place was being done by the Germans, and especially by the Kriegsmarine's B-Dienst. The British lacked power to accomplish anything save the feeding of their own people. Hitler prepared to launch the most dramatic and ambitious lunge of his career, the assault on the Soviet Union, an act that could only have been undertaken by a man either bereft of accurate intelligence about the economic strength of his intended victim, or recklessly indifferent to it.

2 SHADOWING CANARIS

The Germans had made themselves masters of Europe, and shown the Wehrmacht to be the most formidable fighting force in the world. By contrast, whatever the limitations of the British and other Allied intelligence services, those of Hitler's Abwehr were incomparably worse. In the summer of 1940 the chiefs of the Nazis' information-gathering machine toyed with a scheme to plant an agent on a wrecked ship off the English south coast, though they never came up with a credible notion of what such a hapless castaway might achieve there. They also discussed landing agents in Kent, who would be invited to scale the white cliffs, a plan that was frustrated by a shortage of spies with mountaineering skills. Meanwhile the Luftwaffe's intelligence department misjudged every aspect of the Battle of Britain, from respective aircraft strengths and losses to target selection. In September 1940, following the interrogations of the first enemy spies landed in Britain, Kenneth Strong of War Office intelligence professed himself baffled. He could not reconcile his lifelong respect for German efficiency with the risible management of the Nazis' espionage activities.

The Abwehr bungled the selection, training, briefing and equipment of agents for service abroad; seldom were they even provided with decent forged passports. It is hard to distinguish between reality and fantasy in the doings of its operational section, Abwehr II, because its war diary was compiled to impress higher authority, and thus included reports from agents who never existed, about operations that never took place. Its chief, Admiral Wilhelm Canaris, who was regarded for decades after the war as an important personality and even as a hero of the Resistance to Hitler, was in reality a temporiser who lacked both the moral courage to challenge the Nazis whom he despised, and the skills to run an effective secret service in their interests.

The first man to grasp this was not a German, but a young English historian with a disdain for mankind in general, and professional secret service officers in particular. The manner in which Hugh Trevor-Roper became not the nemesis of Canaris, but instead his shadow, is one of the more remarkable stories of the secret war. The brilliant, testy, supremely arrogant Oxford don who, while not homosexual, professed a deep dislike of women, had just written his first book, a study of Archbishop Laud which he often reread during the war years: 'I am forever discovering yet more exquisite beauties, lurking unsuspected among yet profounder truths.' He spent the years between 1940 and 1945 monitoring the wireless traffic of the Abwehr, first for MI5 then for MI6. Trevor-Roper lived and breathed Canaris and his organisation, except on days when he went foxhunting. In growing degree, and comprehensively from 1943 onwards, the English academic learned more about Germany's intelligence services than any man in the Nazi high command knew – certainly more than

Canaris himself, because Trevor-Roper could identify the Abwehr's many
false informants, controlled by the so-called 'Twenty Committee' of intelligence officers in London chaired by MI5's Jack Masterman.

In December 1939 Hugh Trevor-Roper, then twenty-five, was
summoned from Merton College to work alongside Walter Gill, a lecturer
in electricity who had achieved celebrity as college bursar by installing
lighting in Merton's quadrangles. During World War I 'Gilly' had served
in an army wireless section in Egypt, where he ran an aerial up the Great
Pyramid. He listed his recreations in *Who's Who* as riding, wireless
research and 'rebuking sin'. Now he and Trevor-Roper formed the nucleus
of the Radio Security Service, a branch of MI5 initially quartered in the
cells at Wormwood Scrubs jail in west London. Day after day, Post Office
operators, previously employed to catch unlicensed private wireless
transmissions, scoured the airwaves for signals from enemy agents transmitting from Britain, whom it would then be the role of the Merton pair
to scotch.

Gill and Trevor-Roper found themselves frustrated by the emptiness of
the ether, or rather by the absence of such traffic as they sought. They were
failing, so it seemed. Only slowly did they come to understand that this
was not because their own eavesdroppers were incompetent, but because
no German spies were signalling home. Finding their original function
redundant, on their own initiative the two dons widened their researches:
they began to gather intercepts from stations in Europe that used known
Abwehr callsigns. One evening, in the flat they shared in the west London
suburb of Ealing, over tea and biscuits they cracked an Abwehr hand-
cipher – a lower encryption system used by Canaris's bases for
communications with out-stations and agents lacking Enigma machines.
Trevor-Roper, a fluent German linguist, started to read its messages.

When this came to the notice of Alastair Denniston, chief of Bletchley
Park, he was not amused. The RSS's amateurs were told that they were
meddling in matters of no proper concern to them. Denniston added
crossly that the Abwehr material was unimportant anyway. In fairness, his
dismay about the RSS's freelancing reflected more than petty jealousy.
Months, indeed years, lay ahead before Bletchley's codebreaking operations achieved maturity, but from the outset it was obvious that if the
Germans gained an inkling of what was being achieved, the game would
be over. The more diffused was British cryptographic activity, the greater
the risk of a leak. Broadway stepped in, to vent its own justified anger,
when it was learned that Trevor-Roper's report on Abwehr activities in

North Africa was circulated to a distribution list that included the Post Office wireless section.

Gill and Trevor-Roper, stubborn and mischievous men both, persisted nonetheless; they were soon reading much of the Abwehr's traffic with its out-stations. To the dons' glee, even when Bletchley established its own cell to monitor the same Canaris links, it was RSS and not GC&CS which broke the next four hand-ciphers. In the spring of 1941 RSS acquired a new interception centre with American equipment at Hanslope Park in Buckinghamshire, and began to establish its own out-stations abroad. In the course of the war, the little service passed on a million signals to Bletchley.

MI6 eventually made a successful takeover bid for RSS, which was logical, given Broadway's suzerainty over signals intelligence. Trevor-Roper found himself working with Stewart Menzies' communications supremo, one of the secret service's more exotic figures, Colonel Richard Gambier-Parry. The colonel was one of many luminaries of 'secret shows' who was able to exploit to his own advantage their freedom from accountability to a service hierarchy. Gambier-Parry established MI6's communications centre at Whaddon Hall in Buckinghamshire, which he also made his personal residence. A keen horseman, he took over the pre-war owner's pack of hounds and placed the huntsmen on Broadway's payroll; on one notable occasion, the hounds in hot pursuit streamed through the security gate of Bletchley Park, arousing in the mind of a mounted spectator in the know about its activities an idyllic vision of the brutes gorging on half-digested decrypts. Gambier-Parry lived like a medieval baron. Trevor-Roper, who knew him as a fellow-foxhunter, marvelled: 'In the world of neurotic policemen and timid placemen who rule the secret service, he moves like Falstaff, or some figure from Balzac, if not Rabelais.' It should be added that for the rest of the war Gambier-Parry ran MI6's communications with energy and flair.

Hugh Trevor-Roper became head of the intelligence section of MI6's Radio Analysis Bureau, run by Felix Cowgill, a former Indian policeman. Cowgill intensely disliked his new junior, whom he deemed guilty of 'irreverent thoughts and dangerous contacts'. The Oxford historian took it upon himself to go well beyond the production of raw intelligence, conducting evaluation and analysis in a fashion MI6 had always spurned, because it lacked officers clever enough to do such work. The RAB began to produce 'purple primers', local guides to Abwehr personalities and agents around the world, which soon ran to many pages. The bureau noted that the Italians, who before the war had enjoyed some notable intelligence successes, were now almost entirely dependent for material on the Germans, and thus acquired their weaknesses.

In the summer of 1941 Trevor-Roper acquired an assistant, twenty-one-year-old Charles Stuart, who had just left Christ Church with a First in history, and the two were joined by another Oxford man, Gilbert Ryle. Patrick Reilly, a gifted young diplomat who became Stewart Menzies' personal assistant, thought their little cell 'a team of a brilliance unparalleled anywhere in the Intelligence machine'. Trevor-Roper began to serve as secretary of the joint MI5–MI6 Wireless Committee, in which role he came to know almost everyone significant in the secret world. The peering, bespectacled historian became one of the outstanding British intelligence officers of the war. His mastery of German operations increased steadily, especially after Bletchley's Dillwyn Knox broke into the principal Abwehr machine cipher in December 1941. While the chiefs of Broadway believed – more so following the Venlo fiasco – that their enemies' intelligence officers were wizards of guile, from an early stage Trevor-Roper became convinced of the Germans' institutional incompetence. As for the Abwehr's chief, he said, far from being a masterspy Canaris was a lost little man drifting on the tides of fate.

Admiral Wilhelm Canaris came from a family of Rhineland industrialists. After service as a U-boat officer in World War I he became engaged in right-wing politics, while playing a role in rebuilding the German navy. A senior officer's 1926 personal report extolled his skills at the military-political interface: 'With the finest feel for foreign psychology and mentality, together with uncommon linguistic ability, he knows in exemplary fashion how to deal with foreigners (from the lowest to the prominent).' Interestingly, however, other naval officers, including Erich Raeder and Karl Dönitz, disliked Canaris, thinking him sly.

During the early years of Hitler's rule he ingratiated himself enthusiastically and successfully with the foremost Nazis. In 1935, aged forty-eight, he was appointed chief of Germany's intelligence service, controlling both espionage abroad and counter-espionage at home, though Himmler ran his own domestic security service, the RSHA, under Ernst Kaltenbrunner, with the Gestapo as its enforcement arm. As Trevor-Roper noted, 'All German politicians of consequence sought to set up their own information bureaus (just as they also sought to establish private armies) as additional supports for their personal authority; and it was essential to the purpose of these bureaus that their results should be the private property of their chiefs.'

The RSHA was no more efficient than the Abwehr, but it wielded more influence through its direct subordination to Himmler. MI6 noted that it achieved good penetration of neutral embassies in Berlin, which yielded useful information. Meanwhile, Canaris's service had stations around the world and intelligence cells within every formation of the Wehrmacht. The admiral's early years of office saw a dramatic expansion of his empire; he achieved a reputation for administrative efficiency and diplomatic skills, both in his handling of the Nazi hierarchy and in dealing with prominent foreigners. Until at least 1942, the service's prestige stood high both inside Germany and abroad.

Canaris was instinctively secretive, even before he became a spymaster, and more so thereafter. Within the rambling warren of offices in a row of converted mansions on Berlin's Tirpitzüfer, where the Abwehr had its headquarters until it was bombed out in 1943, he seemed to glide almost invisibly from one room to another. So he did too on his frequent travels to other countries, especially Spain: a signed portrait of Franco, its dictator, adorned his office wall. He seldom wore uniform – an oddity in Nazi society, which was obsessed with fancy dress. He was elaborately courteous, not least to subordinates, and something of a hypochondriac who took too many pills. He relaxed by riding regularly and playing a smart game of tennis. His passion for animals was much remarked: he was followed around Abwehr headquarters by two dachshunds, to which he talked constantly. One of them once fell ill while Canaris was visiting Italy, and he telephoned at length to Berlin to discuss its condition. His Italian companions assumed that he was speaking in code about great issues of state, but his obsession with the dog was authentic. He often said that he trusted animals more than people; it was probably more accurate to say that he liked them better. In conversation, whether professional or social, he was a master of equivocation. Few people were ever sure what Canaris really thought, which was supposed by contemporaries to reflect his depth of character. More likely, it masked chronic indecision.

Although technically a branch of OKW, the Abwehr quickly became Canaris's personal fiefdom. Throughout the war his men achieved considerable success in suppressing dissent and capturing Western Allied agents operating in Hitler's empire, which did much to sustain the admiral's standing in Nazi high places: Col. Franz von Bentevegni, who ran counter-espionage, was one of Canaris's few impressive subordinate appointments. Yet the Russians were able to sustain their astonishing espionage activities inside Germany until 1942, and military leakages persisted until 1945, even if the huge matter of Germany's broken codes lay beyond Canaris's remit.

The agents his officers dispatched to gather information abroad were almost all unfit for the role. It is odd that Berlin never attempted to recruit spies to dispatch to Britain who might have passed for gentlemen. Even in 1940, the accent and manners of the upper class remained a passport to social acceptance in Churchill's embattled island. The writer Cyril Connolly wrote an angry letter to the *New Statesman* complaining that when he himself was detained as a possible spy, he was immediately released when it was discovered that he had been educated at Eton. The experience of the Cambridge Spies, deemed beyond suspicion as members of the upper-middle class, suggests that if the Abwehr had dispatched to Britain a few Nazis with passable table manners and some skill as fly-casters or grouse-shooters, they would have been asked to all the best houses.

As it was, however, when two of Canaris's key men, Col. Hans Pieckenbrock, the head of intelligence, and Col. Erwin Lahousen, head of sabotage, were sacked in 1943, this was no gesture of Nazi spite, made for political reasons; it was the consequence of their obvious incompetence and of their departments' failure. German secret operations abroad deployed immense labour for negligible results. One of the Abwehr's most notable recruits was naval lieutenant Heinrich Garbers. He was a vegetable farmer's son, a passionate Nazi, who in 1938 had sailed across the Atlantic in a thirty-foot yacht, the *Windspiel*, which he constructed himself. Amid the Allied naval blockade, the Germans devised the notion of dispatching agents to far-flung places in sailing boats too humble to attract the attention of the enemy. In 1941 and 1942 Garbers made epic forays to South Africa and Namibia respectively. Thereafter he captained the little schooner *Passim*, which made two immense voyages at an average speed of six knots. The boat sailed under the name of the *Santa Maria*, and flew successively French, Spanish and Portuguese colours as Garbers deemed appropriate. In 1943 he carried three Abwehr men, codenamed 'Walter', 'Fred' and 'Jim', to Argentina, in what he afterwards described laconically as 'an uneventful voyage of 65 days'.

In a nautical sense it may be true that nothing much happened, but relations on board were poisoned by the mutual loathing of Walter and Fred, while Jim was perpetually prostrate with sea-sickness, which cost him a drastic weight loss. The passengers were successfully delivered to a reception committee of Argentine sympathisers at Rio de la Plata, who presented the *Passim*'s crew with coffee and oranges before the little vessel turned about and sailed home. Garbers, plainly a man of iron, seemed wholly untroubled by his experiences. He returned safely to Europe and received the Ritterkreuz. There is no evidence, however, that his passengers contributed anything to the Nazi war effort. Likewise, the Hungarian air force officer Count László Almásy crossed 2,000 miles of North African desert to deliver two agents to Egypt in May 1942, a remarkable achievement, and Almásy later inspired the novel and film *The English Patient*, though its version of this enthusiastic Nazi was fanciful. His passengers, however, did nothing on arrival to justify their epic journey. Nearer home, it became increasingly clear to the British monitoring the Abwehr's wirelessed reports that its network of overseas stations and informants produced almost nothing that was both new and true.

As Trevor-Roper pursued his researches through the ever-growing harvest of Bletchley decrypts, 'We soon became aware that "the little Admiral" was a far more complex and controversial character than we had supposed. As the incompetence of his organisation was progressively revealed to us, we discovered, or deduced, something of the politics in which he was involved, and we noted his feverish travels, in every direction, but especially to Spain, which distinguished him sharply from our own more sedentary chief' – Stewart Menzies. For several decades after the war, Canaris was treated as a major figure of the era, the subject of several weighty biographies. The foremost element in the Canaris mythology was a claim that he had been a secret crusader against Hitler, who had given active assistance to the Allied cause. Several German writers energetically promoted this view, because their post-war society was desperate to identify virtuous men who had dared to raise their hands against the vast evil of Nazism, and suffered martyrdom in consequence.

It is now plain that such claims were unfounded. Until 1938 Canaris was an ardent supporter of the Nazis, and for years thereafter Hitler frequently used him as a personal emissary abroad. The admiral worked amicably with Reinhard Heydrich of the RSHA. The two families socialised: Frau Canaris and the executive planner of the Holocaust sometimes played the violin together. From 1939 onwards, the admiral became increasingly gloomy and nervous – colleagues noted him drinking heavily. Trevor-Roper regarded it as an absurd delusion that Canaris was the directing brain of 'the other Germany'. The Abwehr's chief, in his view, was a man of limited gifts, who confined his anti-Nazi activities to making his organisation a haven for officers who shared his rising distaste for Hitler and his supporters, and who resisted active complicity in the Nazis' atrocities. Canaris's fastidious nature recoiled from the coarseness of their conduct, perhaps more than from its insensate barbarity.

The only Abwehr officer known to have been a source for MI6 was Hans-Berndt Gisevius in Switzerland, a Prussian lawyer of giant physical proportions who served five years in the Gestapo and hated it, before transferring to the Ministry of Internal Affairs in 1938 and thence to the Abwehr. Canaris sent him to Zürich under diplomatic cover as vice-consul, and thereafter he passed information to Halina Szymańska, whom he knew was an informant for both British and Polish intelligence. Gisevius provided material for twenty-five reports dispatched from Bern to Broadway between August 1940 and December 1942, some of them citing Canaris's professed opinions; also among his sources was Hitler's finance minister, Hjalmar Schacht.

Szymańska, the conduit, was the formidable and beautiful wife of the former Polish military attaché in Berlin, and once dined with Canaris in Bern. Much of Gisevius's material was accurate: in January 1941 Szymańska passed on his report about German aircraft stocks, together with the Abwehr man's opinion that an invasion of Britain was 'off'. In April she quoted Gisevius's view, based on information from Schacht, that Hitler would invade Russia during the following month – which indeed was then his intention. But, as usual with intelligence, the German also passed on some rubbish: on 28 March 1941 he told Szymańska that German forces would not take the offensive in Libya – two days before Rommel launched a major onslaught.

Gisevius's contribution, and those of a handful of his colleagues, scarcely made the Abwehr a pillar of Resistance against the Nazis. Its wartime shortcomings were the product of indolence and incompetence rather than of considered treachery. Canaris was a poor delegator, who chose weak subordinates. German intelligence had one notable success abroad, in suborning Yugoslav officers ahead of their army's 1941 emergency mobilisation, in time to sabotage the process, but thereafter its espionage operations were uniformly unsuccessful. The admiral was nonetheless too much a German patriot actively to assist his country's enemies. Like many such people of the time, he harboured muddled political views. A monarchist and a conservative, Franco's Spain was his spiritual home; he travelled there as often as he could, not merely to visit the large Madrid Abwehr HQ at Calle Claudio Coello 151, but also to commune with like-minded Spanish politicians and grandees. The Abwehr's ship-watching service in Spain, the *Unternehmen Bodden*, monitoring Allied movements through the Straits of Gibraltar with the aid of advanced infra-red technology, and reporting them to the Kriegsmarine and the Luftwaffe's Air Fleet 1 in Italy formed the most impressive element in the organisation's overseas operations.

Yet if Canaris bears much responsibility for the shortcomings of Germany's 'big picture' intelligence, he could never have run an honest operation under the dead hand of Hitler, any more than Moscow Centre could do so in the shadow of Stalin. Reports on the condition and prospects of the enemy were permitted to reach conclusions only within parameters acceptable to the Führer. This crippling constraint was symbolised by Hitler's annotation on an important intelligence report about Russian agricultural conditions: 'This cannot be.' Kurt Zeitzler, chief of the army general staff, wrote on 23 October 1942, the eve of Stalingrad: 'The Russians no longer have any reserves worth mentioning and are not capable of launching large-scale offensives.' Himmler in 1944 declared without embarrassment that his first requirement from Germany's intelligence services was not truth, but loyalty to the Führer. This was an important statement, the most vivid expression of the huge weakness of the Abwehr and the RSHA throughout the Second World War.

Historian Michael Handel has written: 'Leaders in a democratic system are generally more inclined to consider a wide variety of options than those who have always functioned within authoritarian or totalitarian political systems. In authoritarian countries, where the climb to the top is an unrelenting struggle for power, habits of cooperation and openness are usually less developed … Tolerance for ideas that deviate from the "party line" … are seen as personal criticism.' These features of almost all dictatorships crippled German intelligence activities beyond the battlefield, and sometimes also within it. Himmler's deputy Reinhard Heydrich, for instance, was far more interested in using the RSHA as a weapon against the Nazi empire's internal enemies than as a means of securing information about its foreign foes. Hitler never wished to use intelligence as a planning or policy-making tool. He recognised its utility only at a tactical level: the Nazis were strikingly incurious about Abroad.

Yet the fact that the Abwehr was an unsuccessful intelligence-gathering organisation did not mean that Hitler's armed forces were blind on the battlefield: their access to tactical intelligence was generally good. In the first half of the war Germany's wireless interceptors and codebreakers enjoyed successes which would today seem impressive, were they not measured against those of the British and Americans. The Wehrmacht had excellent voice-monitoring units, which in every theatre of war provided important information. 'The Y Service was the best source of intelligence,' said Hans-Otto Behrendt, one of Rommel's staff in North Africa. In August 1941, aided by an Italian employee, two agents of the *Sezione Prelevamento* – the 'extraction section' of Italian intelligence – opened the safe of the military attaché's office at the US embassy in Rome. They removed his codebook – Military Intelligence Code No. 11 – and photographed it. This enabled the Axis to read substantial traffic through the ensuing ten months, and proved a seriously significant intelligence break. In 1942 it had especially grievous consequences for Eighth Army in the desert, since the US military attaché in Cairo, Col. Bonner Fellers, reported in detail to Washington on British plans and intentions. A German intelligence officer paid generous tribute to 'this incomparable source of authentic and reliable information, which ... contributed so decisively during the first half of 1942 to our victories in North Africa'.

At sea, some of the Royal Navy's ciphers were found aboard the British submarine *Seal*, captured off the German coast on 5 May 1940, owing to an extraordinary and culpable failure by the minelayer's officers to destroy its confidential papers. The Kriegsmarine was able to read much of the Royal Navy's North Sea traffic until August 1940, and some warship communications until September 1941. Throughout the first half of the war, the Kriegsmarine's B-Dienst read the Royal Navy's convoy codes, with grievous consequences for Allied shipping losses. Even where signals could not be decrypted, radio-traffic analysis enabled Axis intelligence staffs to judge enemy deployments remarkably effectively, at least until the second half of the war, when Allied commanders became more astute and security-conscious. Patrolling, air reconnaissance and PoW interrogations all provided streams of useful data to German operational commanders, as did open-source information – enemy newspaper and broadcast monitoring.

In the first phase of the war until 1942, while the Wehrmacht was triumphant on battlefields across Europe, these sources sufficed to tell its commanders all that they felt they needed to know about the world, and about their enemies. Victories masked the abject humint failures of the Abwehr. As long as Germany was winning, why should anyone make trouble about imperfections in the war machine? It was only when Hitler's armies started losing that hard questions began to be asked about the Reich's abysmal political and strategic intelligence. Hitler himself was, of course, much to blame, but Canaris exercised operational responsibility.

The admiral fell from grace, though it was by then far too late – probably impossible, for reasons institutionalised in the Nazi system – to repair his corrupt and ineffective espionage organisation.

While anxious not to be a bad man, Canaris lacked the courage to be a good one. Far from being a substantial historical figure, he was a small one, grappling with dilemmas and difficulties far beyond his capabilities. Trevor-Roper professed to see a close resemblance between the admiral and Menzies, his British counterpart. Both men were conservative, honourable – and weak. By a trifling coincidence, Canaris had a mistress in Vienna whose sister was married to Menzies' brother. Trevor-Roper came to regard the Abwehr as 'a mirror image of [MI6], with many of the same weaknesses and absurdities ... I recognised, across the intervening fog of war, old friends of Broadway and Whaddon Hall transmuted into German uniform in the Tirpitz Ufer or at Wansee.' The admiral did little to merit his eventual fate at the hands of Hitler's executioners: he frequently talked treason, but did nothing to further it. Far from becoming a martyr to the cause of a 'good Germany', he was merely an incompetent servant of an evil one.

3

Miracles Take a Little Longer: Bletchley

1 'TIPS' AND 'CILLIS'

In the winter of 1939, MI6 came under scrutiny and fierce criticism within Whitehall, intensified by the Venlo fiasco. Stewart Menzies, knowing the precariousness of his position as 'C', compiled a twenty-six-page document defending his service, in which he risked playing one card which might – and did – save his bacon. He promised his masters that the country was 'about to reap the fruits' of MI6's liaison with Allied secret services in a fashion 'which should be of inestimable benefits to the Air Ministry within a few weeks, and probably to the Admiralty within a month or two'. The significance of this vaguely expressed claim was that Menzies believed that Bletchley Park, with the help of the French and Poles, was close to cracking some German ciphers. Such successes could go far indeed towards compensating for MI6's humint failure. His expectations would remain unfulfilled for much of the year that followed. Few even within the intelligence community dared to hope that Britain could emulate, far less surpass, the 1914–18 codebreaking triumphs of the Admiralty's Room 40. Admiral Godfrey, head of naval intelligence, wrote to Menzies on 18 November, saying that 'whether or not Cryptanalysis will ever again give us the knowledge we had of German movements in the late war', MI6 should exert itself to plant agents in enemy ports to report shipping movements. Godfrey did not seem to expect much from the codebreakers.

In peacetime, few nations commit their finest brains to national security. Brilliant people seldom choose careers in intelligence – or, for that matter, in the armed forces. A struggle for national survival alone makes it possible for a government to mobilise genius, or people possessing something close to it, in the interests of the war effort. The British, and latterly the Americans, did this more effectively than any other participants in World War II. A remarkable proportion of their nations' brightest and best sooner or later found themselves performing tasks worthy of their talents – in scientific or technical research; and especially in intelligence, which absorbed thousands of outstanding intellects from many walks of life. The outbreak of war enabled the German section of British military intelligence, for instance, to recruit writers and academics. One of them, Noel Annan, a Cambridge don who had only a passable acquaintance with German and French, observed wonderingly: 'Within a week I was piecing together the reports of agents in the Balkans and the early stutterings of Ultra.'

Donald McLachlan, a journalist who served under Godfrey at the Admiralty, afterwards argued that all wartime intelligence departments should be run by civilians in uniform, because they are unburdened by the lifetime prejudices of career soldiers, sailors and airmen: 'It is the lawyer, the scholar, the traveller, the banker, even the journalist who shows the ability to resist where the career men tend to bend. Career officers and politicians have a strong interest in cooking raw intelligence to make their masters' favourite dishes.' MI6 remained until 1945 under the leadership of its old hands, but most of Britain's secret war machine passed into the hands of able civilians in uniform who – after an interval of months or in some cases years while they were trained and their skills recognised – progressively improved the quality of intelligence analysis. The Admiralty's Submarine Tracking Room was directed by Rodger Winn, a barrister and future judge. Gen. Sir Bernard Montgomery's chief of intelligence from Alamein to Luneburg Heath was the Oxford don Edgar 'Bill' Williams, latterly a brigadier. Reg Jones made himself a legend in scientific intelligence.

These men, and a few hundred others throughout the armed forces, spent much of the war exploiting and assessing information derived overwhelmingly from interception and decryption of the enemy's wireless traffic. Bill Williams, who served in the Mediterranean until 1943 and in Europe thereafter, stated in an important 1945 report: 'It must be made quite clear that Ultra and Ultra only put intelligence on the map.' Until decrypts began to become available in bulk in 1942, 'Intelligence was the Cinderella of the staff ... Information about the enemy was frequently treated as interesting rather than valuable [though] of course this attitude varied according to the commander.'

Scepticism was often merited, because much material was downright specious. The 1940 war diary of the army's Middle East intelligence section in Cairo included comically frivolous snippets: 'All Hungarian cabaret artistes have been ordered to leave the country by the end of May.' Data about the Italian army was scanty, so that on 9 August the section recorded: 'The present location and organisation of Libyan troops in Eastern Cyrenaica is obscure.' A despondent staff officer added a week later: 'There has been no further reliable information of fresh [Italian] ground units or formations arriving in Libya from overseas.' On 27 September, the British high command's weekly intelligence summary included a paragraph on domestic conditions in Germany: 'A neutral traveller to the Leipsic fair, whose personal observations are believed reliable, reports that relations between the [Nazi] Party and the Army are not good.' Three months later, the head of MI6's Political Section wrung his hands: 'It is piteous to find ourselves in this state of ignorance' about both Germany's internal condition and economy.

Only when Allied warlords were empowered to read the messages being exchanged between enemy generals in the field and their higher headquarters was scepticism about the value of 'intelligence' replaced by increasingly fervent belief. Ultra forced commanders-in-chief, not to mention the prime minister, to treat senior intelligence officers with a respect they had seldom received in the pre-Bletchley universe. Brigadier Ian Jacob of the war cabinet secretariat said: 'My impression is that once the Ultra business got well-established, Churchill didn't look at anything else.' Eisenhower's intelligence chief Kenneth Strong wrote in 1943, in a memorandum on training staff officers: 'We no longer depend on agents and cloak-and-dagger sources for our information. Modern methods have completely transformed intelligence.'

He meant codebreaking, of course, and in Britain the fountainhead of such activity was the Government Code & Cypher School at Bletchley. In the months following the outbreak of war, GC&CS expanded dramatically with the arrival of a stream of academics, many of them earmarked by its recruiters before the war. Though some were seconded from the armed forces, it was understood that there was no need to train the universities' contingent to march, blanco webbing, and name the parts of a rifle. They remained their sallow, tweedy, pipe-smoking young selves when housed in lodgings around the dreary suburban town, and enlisted on the government payroll without uniform or ceremony. Twenty-year-old mathematician Keith Batey found his landlady demanding an assurance from his employer that he was not a despised 'conchy' – conscientious objector – before he joined the growing body of academics working on a task of supreme importance to their country, fulfilment of which might do something to assuage its shocking vulnerability. What was the task? Bletchley's little band, 169 strong in 1939 including support staff, understood only that the nation's enemies communicated in a multitude of codes and ciphers, vulnerable to interception. If even a portion of these combinations of numbers and letters could be rendered intelligible, information might be gained of priceless value to the war effort.

Nobody knew, in the beginning, whether a given message hijacked from the airwaves might be an order from Hitler for his armies to march on Warsaw, or a request from a Luftwaffe airfield in eastern Germany for a delivery of filing cabinets. Ahead of the codebreakers lay a mammoth menu of requirements which could only be addressed as mobilisation sluggishly made available ears, brains and hands to monitor the enemy's frequencies around the clock, log some of his vast output of messages, fix the locations and possible identities of the senders – diplomatic, police, military, naval or air force. Then came the much greater challenge, of discovering what the messages meant.

All radio communications involved a trade-off between speed and security. At the simplest level, battlefield direction by land, sea and air required some voice linkage. This enabled the instantaneous passage of orders and information, at the cost of being overheard by anybody else who cared to tune to a given frequency. Crude security could be introduced by using coded callsigns in place of names and suchlike – during the Battle of Britain fighter controllers added 5,000 feet to indicated altitudes, to confuse eavesdroppers. But voice messaging was inherently insecure: sensitive information should never be passed verbally, though it often was.

Most military messages were instead wirelessed by Morse key. Low-level material could be rapidly encrypted under battlefield conditions by relatively unsophisticated personnel using so-called hand- or field-ciphers, usually involving groups of two or three letters or numbers – the Kriegsmarine employed twenty-seven variants. More sensitive traffic, issuing from higher echelons, was translated by machine-generated or manual ciphers, usually involving combinations of four or five letters or numbers. The British thought justifiably highly of the security of their Type-X machines, though they never had enough of them.* The Americans rightly trusted their Sigaba, a fifteen-rotor system.

For substantial periods between 1939 and 1943 the Germans broke

---

* The Type-X was developed in 1934 by Wing-Commander O.C. Lywood and Ernest Smith of Air Ministry Signals, improving upon a borrowed commercial Enigma, and entered British service three years later.

some Allied codes, including those of the US State Department and military attachés, along with the traffic of several exile governments, notably the Poles and Free French. They sometimes also accessed messages of all three British services, including the RAF's four-character cipher, and later had successes in attacking products of the US Army's M-209 field-ciphering machine. It deserves emphasis that Allied code-security weaknesses, and enemy achievements in exploiting them, gave the Germans much more operational assistance than some Western historians acknowledge, especially in the Battle of the Atlantic. However, higher British, American and Russian communications defied enemy scrutiny: Nazi eavesdropping on transatlantic telephone conversations between Churchill and Roosevelt told Berlin little of value. Modern claims that the Germans broke into Russian higher ciphers deserve to be treated with caution: certainly from 1942 onwards, there is no evidence that Hitler's generals profited from any such insights; if they had, they would have been less often deluded by Soviet deceptions.

Most German senior officers – though by no means all their crypto-graphers – were confident that Enigma ciphering machines, which scrambled messages by means of shifting rotors and a plugboard, and rendered them comprehensible only by a matching machine with identical settings, were immune to the attention of any enemy, and indeed to the workings of the human brain. It is unsurprising that in 1939 they discounted the possibility that electro-mechanical technology might dramatically accelerate exposure of the Enigma's secrets, because it did not then exist. It is extraordinary, however, that such serene confidence persisted through six years that followed, even following the discovery that the Poles had broken some pre-war Enigma traffic, and several warn-ings from their own experts. Amazing hubris was expressed by the Wehrmacht's last signals chief, Lt. Gen. Albert Praun, who preened himself before his Allied captors after the war ended: 'The achievements of German communications intelligence ... may speak in favour of the German type of intelligence organisation.' His organisation, he said, 'gave German commanders a hitherto unattained degree of [signal] security'.

The British breaking of the Enigma, then subsequently and separately of German teleprinter traffic, was a progressive, incremental operation which attained maturity only between 1943 and 1945, and was never unin-terrupted or comprehensive: even at peaks, only about half of all intercepts were read, many of them too late to provide practical assistance 'at the sharp end'. What was done at Bletchley Park was indeed miraculous, but the codebreakers were never able to walk on all of the water, all of the time.

The 1939–40 Phoney War conferred few benefits on Britain, but it granted GC&CS precious time to bolster its strength and refine its methods. Without mechanical aids Bletchley's brainstormers made modest and delayed breaches in a small number of enemy ciphers. The Germans employed acronyms and codenames which took weeks or months for their enemies to interpret. The importance of what happened at Bletchley in the first two years of war was not that it enabled Britain's generals to avert or arrest a disastrous run of defeats, which it certainly did not, but that it lit a candle of hope about what the codebreakers and their embryo technology might accomplish in the future. It enabled the directors of the war effort to lay upon the board a few scattered pieces of a vast jigsaw, which would be filled only during the Allies' years of victory.

Bletchley Park – Station X, Box 111 c/o The Foreign Office – was a notably ugly Victorian pile of bastard architectural origins surrounded by fifty-five acres of trees and grassland, located fifty miles from London. It was purchased in 1938 to house GC&CS at a safe distance from German bombs by Admiral Sir Hugh Sinclair, then head of MI6; as legend has it, he used £7,500 out of his own pocket, but more plausibly he paid with secret funds under his control. Whatever MI6's humint weaknesses, the service's chiefs, especially Sinclair, deserve full credit for backing the establishment of Bletchley at a time when resources were desperately constrained. Work began at once on laying direct phone and teleprinter lines to London, and in the following year MI6's skeleton team of cryptanalysts moved from Broadway to the Park, where they came under the orders of Alastair Denniston. One of his colleagues from the old Admiralty days, Dillwyn Knox, an expert on ancient Egyptian papyri, became an early Bletchley stalwart. The most prominent of the younger recruits were Gordon Welchman of Sidney Sussex College, Cambridge, Hugh Alexander, Stuart Milner-Barry, John Jeffreys – and Alan Turing.

This last, the twenty-seven-year-old son of an Indian civil servant and the product of an austere and emotionally arid childhood, had just returned from a stint at Princeton clutching one of his own creations, a so-called electric multiplier machine mounted on a breadboard. His headmaster at Sherborne had once written: 'If he is to stay at a public school, he must aim at becoming *educated*. If he is to be solely a *Scientific Specialist*, then he is wasting his time.' In the headmaster's terms, Turing had indeed been 'wasting his time': he had evolved into a shy, narrow, obsessive. Noel

Annan wrote: 'I liked his sly, secret humour ... His inner life was more real to him than actuality. He disliked authority wherever he was ... [and] enjoyed games and treasure hunts and silliness ... Turing was the purest type of homosexual, longing for affection and love that lasted.' More even than by his sexuality and his often childlike immaturity, however, his tragedy was to be afflicted by the exquisitely painful loneliness of genius.

Other drafts of young academics followed, variously codebreakers and linguists, together with the first of what became successive waves of young women, who would play a vital role in the operations of 'BP'. The first two of these were daughters of golfing partners of Denniston, reflecting the importance of personal connections in Bletchley's recruitment process in the early days, before industrialisation became inescapable. Indeed, the whole wartime intelligence machine emphasised the cosiness of the upper reaches of British life. Oxford University Press was entrusted with responsibility for printing vast quantities of codes, maps and reports, because of its pre-war experience producing examination papers under secure conditions. The Admiralty's liaison with OUP was handled by Margaret Godfrey, wife of the director of naval intelligence. The Royal Navy's Topographical Photographic Library was housed in the basement of the nearby Bodleian Library, which eventually dispatched 300,000 images a month to operational areas. The World War I intelligence veteran Admiral Sir William 'Blinker' Hall introduced Godfrey, his modern successor, to the City of London banking giants Montagu Norman, Olaf Hambro and the Rothschilds, who helped to identify suitable recruits for the NID.

Candidates being scrutinised for Bletchley were often asked: 'Do you have religious scruples about reading other people's correspondence?' Twenty-year-old Harry Hinsley was interviewed at St John's College, Cambridge, by Alastair Denniston and Col. John Tiltman, the senior codebreaker. They said: 'You've travelled a bit, we understand. You've done quite well in your Tripos. What do you think of government service? Would you rather have that than be conscripted?' Hinsley would indeed, and joined the Naval Section located in Bletchley's Hut 4. Through the icy winter of 1939–40, such men and women wrestled with Enigma traffic. Working conditions were dismal, with staff muffled in overcoats and mittens. The first break into a Luftwaffe Enigma key – designated 'Green' – is thought to have been made on 25 October 1939. In December, by unaided intellectual effort Alan Turing is believed to have broken five days' worth of old naval messages. By the end of March, the French – or rather, the Poles working at France's Station Bruno – had broken twenty days' worth of old signals and BP about thirty, all Luftwaffe traffic.

Turing was much more importantly engaged. He compiled a 150-page treatise on Enigma, studded with schoolboyish blots, deletions and illegibilities. While most codebreakers addressed each other by first names or nicknames, heedless of age and status, almost everyone knew Turing as 'Prof' rather than as Alan. When his Enigma study was circulated later in 1940, it became known as 'the Prof's book'. He also set about fulfilling his concept for a 'bombe', a primitive but revolutionary electro-mechanical device for exploring multiple mathematical combinations. This borrowed its name, though not its design, from the Polish '*bomby*', and would be capable of examining the 17,576 possible wheel deployments for a three-rotor Enigma in about twenty minutes: the order for the first machine was placed in October 1939, and the prototype became operational six months later. Meanwhile, outside in the park, workmen sawed and hammered at an ever-widening array of low wooden buildings which housed the growing staff. Eventually, only administrators worked in the main building, where the telephone switchboard was established in the ballroom. In the huts, signals were shifted from one section to another on a small trolley pushed along a makeshift wooden tunnel.

Hut 8 attacked German naval traffic, which was then passed to Hut 4 for translation and processing. Hut 3 performed the same function for Wehrmacht and Luftwaffe traffic decrypted by Hut 6. The former would eventually play a pivotal role in Allied wartime intelligence, but in its early incarnation it had a staff of just four. Frank Lucas, who was one of them, wrote: 'On a snowy January morning of 1940, in a small bleak wooden room with nothing but a table and three chairs, the first bundle of Enigma decodes appeared. [We] had no idea what they were about to disclose.' A few score yards away, Hut 6 run by Gordon Welchman wrestled with army-Luftwaffe 'Red' key traffic, which was the first to be broken in bulk.

From the outset, pains were taken to disguise from all but the most senior operational commanders the fact that information was being gained from codebreaking. This gave an unintended boost to the prestige of MI6, and to that of Stewart Menzies in particular. When Reg Jones gave a disguised report based on an Ultra decrypt to the RAF's director of signals, Air Commodore Nutting, the airman professed astonished admiration for the courage of the presumed spies who had provided the information, saying, 'By Jove, you've got some brave chaps working for you!' The ever-growing scale of the enemy traffic to be trawled was intimidating.

Bletchley Park, 1944

It is a measure of the expansion of communications as a branch of warfare that by August 1943, 305,000 personnel among the Luftwaffe's total strength of 2.3 million were employed on signals duties – transmitting, receiving or processing – and the same was true on both sides of the war, and of all armed forces.

At GC&CS there were inevitable personality clashes. Gordon Welchman, whose creative contribution became second only to that of Turing, and whose organisational skills were also priceless, found it hard to work with the highly strung and fractious Dillwyn Knox, a contender for the hotly contested title of Bletchley's star eccentric. A notoriously awful driver, Knox giggled: 'It's amazing how people smile, and apologise to you, when you knock them over.' He sustained a stream of intemperate complaints and demands to Denniston, his old comrade from Room 40, about staff shortages, working conditions, low pay, together with the intrusion of and excessive authority conceded to non-cryptanalysts: service intelligence officers 'who maul and conceal our results'. Knox was seriously ill with the cancer that would kill him in February 1943, but meanwhile he and Welchman bickered: the older man accused the younger of exceeding his narrow initial brief, and was also impatient of Turing, writing, 'He is very difficult to anchor down. He is very clever but quite irresponsible and throws out a mass of suggestions of all degrees of merit. I have just, but only just, enough authority and ability to keep him and his ideas in some sort of order and discipline. But he is very nice about it all.' Turing prompted mirth by joining Bletchley's Home Guard because he was seized by an impulse to learn to shoot, then provoked the apoplectic rage of its colonel by absenting himself from parades once he had fulfilled this private purpose. His unworldliness could provoke real exasperation among those under relentless pressure to produce results. A colleague spoke of Turing's 'almost total inability to make himself understood'.

There were plenty of minor tantrums lower down the hierarchy, unsurprising when staff were performing stressful tasks through long hours in bleak working conditions. Angus Wilson, the later novelist, once vented such a storm of rage that a colleague said wearily, 'Do stop it, Angus, otherwise we'll put you in the lake!' Wilson retorted defiantly, 'Don't worry, I'll do it myself,' and duly plunged into the water in front of the house; on another such occasion he hurled a bottle of ink at a Wren. Many wartime codebreakers suffered temporary or permanent physical or mental collapses, brought on by their work: William Friedman, one of America's pioneer practitioners, underwent a nervous breakdown in January 1941 which incapacitated him for three months. Hugh Trevor-Roper languished for several months at about the same time, and others regularly succumbed.

German signals were at first intercepted by a battery of army wireless-operators stationed in an old naval fort at Chatham, a role later assumed by Gambier-Parry's organisation at Whaddon Hall. In the early war years there were never enough operators, and both the RAF and the army were reluctant to acknowledge the priority of meeting GC&CS's demands. Signals were brought in batches to Bletchley's guardroom by motorcycle couriers, at all hours and often in dreadful weather, then distributed between the relevant huts. From an early stage, the codebreakers learned to identify German senders by the unencrypted preamble to their message texts, none of which was longer than 250 words. It was then a matter of sitting hunched over a deal table through the hours of a shift, pondering a jumble of numbers and letters from which only men – and

Bletchley's handful of women – with remarkable logical or mathematical powers might hope to extract fragments of meaning. 'The ideal crypt-analyst,' Stephen Budiansky has written, 'was Beethoven with the soul of an accountant.' When Christopher Morris was a new recruit to Bletchley he heard one of his senior colleagues, asked the requirements for the job, respond laconically, 'Oh, I suppose a sharp pencil and a piece of squared paper.' Morris himself thought that the main requisites – except at the exalted level of Knox, Turing, Welchman and later Max Newman – were 'patience, accuracy, stamina, a reasonably clear head, some experience and an ability to work with others'.

They opened what became vast card indexes, stacked in shoeboxes along the sides of the huts, cataloguing enemy units, personnel, code-names, locations, abbreviations and military hardware; different Enigma keys were distinguished by colour – for instance, yellow, green, red and blue, respectively indicating Norway, Wehrmacht, army-Luftwaffe and air training codes. 'When a new word came up in the message you were trans-lating,' wrote Hugh Skillen, 'a new type of jet fuel, or machine part – you looked for it, and if it was not there, the indexer put it in with a reference time and date stamp.' Bletchley's meticulous record-keeping became a crit-ical element in its triumphs.

For security reasons, the Park's operations were rigidly compartmental-ised, and there was little exchange of information or gossip between sections. Even Welchman remarked years later how little he knew about what colleagues were doing a few yards away from his own Hut. As the staff grew from hundreds into thousands, facilities lagged behind: a section head complained that two hundred men and women enjoyed the use of just one lavatory. The food in the Bletchley canteen was poor even by wartime standards. Former debutante Sarah Norton one night found a cooked cockroach in her meat: 'I was about to return it to the catering manageress when my friend Osla, who had the appetite of a lioness with cubs, snatched the plate and said: "What a waste – I'll eat it!"' The nearest available delicacies outside the wire were to be found at the Station Inn in Bletchley town, which offered ox heart. Welchman recalled having to provide his own newspaper to wrap fish and chips at the local shop. The codebreakers worked around the clock in three rotating shifts, starting with 8 a.m. to 4 p.m. When the exhausted men and women cycled or took a bus through the blackout to their lodgings, they found few comforts: dim lighting, hot baths often rationed to one a week, draconian rules about inter-sex visiting.

It is deeply impressive that those who worked at Bletchley sustained such dedication while working day after day, month after month, in a drab world devoid of glamour, excitement, variety, glory and decorations. In Hut 3, the watch sat around a horseshoe table, translating deciphered signals, each one resembling a telegraph flimsy, forwarded from Hut 6. Ideally, decrypts were composed of complete German words, but often there were interruptions and corruptions in the texts, which demanded leaps of imagination from the linguists. William Millward recalled with shame a night when he invented a place named 'Senke', near Qatara in the North African desert – having forgotten that *Senke* was the German word for a geographical depression. Schoolmasters proved ideal as watch chiefs, wrote Peter Calvocoressi, because they were naturally meticulous: 'If not satisfied, they would throw back a translation at even an eminent professor. It reminded me of Chief Examiners at "A" Level who would send back scripts to an Assistant Examiner to re-mark.' No one could work at GC&CS who did not love brain games. There were dreary, idle yet sleepless lulls, when no traffic arrived for the watches to work on. Peter Hilton once used such a doodle time to compose a palindrome: 'DOC NOTE, I DISSENT, A FAST NEVER PREVENTS A FATNESS. I DIET ON COD'.

Although Alan Turing was acknowledged as the highest intellect at Bletchley, its achievement was supremely a team effort; the creative input of some others, Welchman prominent among them, was almost as important as that of Turing. One night in February 1940, several months before the arrival of the first bombe, twenty-one-year-old Cambridge mathematician John Herivel was smoking a pipe before the fire in his billet, and concentrating furiously on encoded messages even as he drifted in and out of a doze. An inspiration struck him as he gazed with the mind's eye at a German Enigma operator. He perceived such a man starting his morning's work bored or weary or hungover, and thus not troubling to change the previous day's ring setting on his machine before starting to cipher messages. Herivel scarcely slept that night, as he went on to deduce how such an act of carelessness might be detected, then exploited to break a message.

Welchman, who had supervised him at Cambridge, immediately saw the importance of this flash of insight, a marriage of mathematical brilliance to a grasp of human weakness. He told the young man fervently that he 'would not be forgotten', and indeed his inspiration became known as 'the Herivel tip'. Dillwyn Knox had already identified another entry point to messages, rooted in operator errors and text settings – what the codebreakers christened 'Cillis' or 'Sillies'. Welchman wrote later that Bletchley remained 'entirely dependent on Herivel tips and Cillis from the invasion of France to the end of the Battle of Britain'. In other words, until the arrival of the bombes, codebreaking was being done by raw brainpower, without significant mechanical assistance: at this early stage, the British lagged behind their American counterparts in exploiting technology – both the US Army and US Navy codebreaking teams used Hollerith punched-card sorters, of a kind that only began to appear at Bletchley in May 1940, because chief codebreaker Col. John Tiltman had been sceptical about them. Ultra provided no important material during the summer of 1940, but several indications about the postponement of 'Sealion', the Nazi invasion of Britain, notable among them a September Luftwaffe message ordering the dismantling of air transport equipment at Dutch airfields.

Fred Winterbotham, the MI6 officer who eventually became overseer of the 'Special Liaison Unit' network which fed Ultra decrypts to commanders in the field, described the first bombe – christened 'Agnus', corrupted to 'Agnes' – as resembling 'some Eastern goddess who was destined to become the oracle of Bletchley'. It was installed in Hut 11 on 14 March 1940, but suffered substantial teething troubles. Gordon Welchman made an important contribution to Turing's creation by devising a 'diagonal board', an element introduced into the first really effective model, which came into service in mid-August. Agnes and its many successors were not computers, because they had no memory. They were instead electro-mechanical key-finding aids, six and a half feet high and seven wide, mounted in bronze-coloured cabinets, and containing thirty-six banks of high-speed electrically-driven Enigma replicas. Each bombe contained eleven miles of wiring and a million soldered contacts. Built by the British Tabulating Machine Company at Letchworth, they depended partly on components assembled in scores of local village halls, by casual workers who had no clue of the importance to the war effort of the twenty-six-way cables and other small electrical parts they contributed.

With the assistance of a clue or 'crib' – a vital identifying link, usually a codebreaker's guess about the nature of part of a given signal – a bombe could test millions of mathematical possibilities for the settings of three Enigma rotors. Figuratively, Agnes and her kin were bloodhounds needing a slipper or handkerchief to take up a scent. If there was no 'crib', the bombe could not solve the key – but mercifully often, there was one. Subsequent machines, miracles of reliability given their continuous operation, were given their own names by the Wrens who manned them around the clock, usually those of warships – *Warspite*, *Victory* and suchlike. The bombes did not take in enemy cipher messages and disgorge them in fluent German. They were instead priceless accelerators, once the codebreakers secured an insight into the nature of a given signal or traffic stream. Also useful was a battery of British Type-X cipher machines, modified to match the behaviour of Enigmas, on which Wren operators tested speculative message solutions. One of the principal constraints on codebreaking, especially between 1940 and 1942, was that access to the scarce technology had to be apportioned between competing claimants of the three services, and there was never enough 'bombe time' to go around.

Throughout 1940, human brainpower remained the dominant element in Bletchley's successes, which increased with every passing week. It was 'the Herivel tip', not bombes, that enabled the team to crack the army-Luftwaffe 'Red' key in May. The overwhelming bulk of enemy traffic read through the rest of the year – around a thousand messages a day – was that of the Luftwaffe, and until the end of the war air force material was accessed more swiftly than that of the other services. An important requirement for success was what the codebreakers called 'depth' – possession of sufficient messages in a given key to give them playing space for calculations and speculations.

Luftwaffe signals provided many clues to the Wehrmacht's parallel activities, but in the early days interpretation was impeded by lack of understanding of German terminology and abbreviations. In September 1940, Bletchley broke some traffic from Göring's pathfinder unit, KGr100, which enabled it to forecast the targets of several bomber raids. But warning was of little practical usefulness to the defenders when hard power, in the form of radar-guided RAF night-fighters, was lacking in both numbers and effectiveness.

As more bombes were built – by 1945 there were 211 of them – they were dispersed around the London suburbs as a precaution against an enemy air attack on Bletchley. The operators, chiefly young women of the WRNS, found long hours beside the hot, smelly, clattering machines extraordinarily gruelling, especially when they were obliged to use tweezers to adjust the delicate electrical wiring. Some girls were unnerved by the monotonous racket. One of them said: 'It was like a lot of knitting machines working – a kind of tickety-clickety noise.' They went home with their shirt cuffs blackened by a fine spray of oil from the bombes' revolving drums.

Naval Enigma remained for many months impenetrable. This was partly because its system of eight rotors, of which three were used at any one time, posed greater difficulties than the army's five, and partly also because the Kriegsmarine's operators were more disciplined than their Luftwaffe counterparts, and committed fewer errors to provide openings for Bletchley. There was a brief spasm of success in late April 1940, when five days' traffic was read, but thereafter more than a year elapsed – an eternity in the minds of those who wrestled vainly with the problem day after day, week upon week – before the big breakthrough. Denniston said gloomily to Frank Birch, a 1918 veteran of Room 40 who now headed the naval section: 'You know, the Germans don't mean you to read their stuff, and I don't suppose you ever will.' Alan Turing himself had been dallying with the Kriegsmarine's traffic almost since his arrival at Bletchley. A colleague, Hugh Alexander, observed that he became engaged because nobody else seemed to be making headway, and in his remote fashion he was fascinated by the abstract challenge.

It was Turing who devised a new method christened 'Banburismus', employing long punched paper sheets manufactured in the town of Banbury, which assisted the first important breaks into Kriegsmarine messages by reducing the number of possible Enigma rotor orders to be tested from 336 to around eighteen. This system was introduced in the spring of 1941, just as British losses to U-boats began to become alarming. On land, the British in those days lacked power and opportunity to do much with such knowledge of the Wehrmacht's movements as they secured, and there was a large element of luck about what messages were broken. In North Africa in early 1941, the British Army profited from some good sigint derived from eavesdropping on the Italians, but few Enigma messages were broken quickly enough to assist decision-making on the battlefield. At sea, by contrast, there was an early golden prize for GC&CS's labours.

The impetus towards success was provided by a series of captures far out on the ocean, which dramatically increased Bletchley's knowledge of the enemy's naval communications. On 23 February 1941, British commandos raiding the Lofoten Islands seized the German armed trawler *Krebs*, from which spare rotors for a naval Enigma were recovered, though the machine itself had been thrown overboard. This 'pinch' prompted the Royal Navy to launch an operation explicitly designed to capture more Enigma material, targeting German weather-reporting trawlers between Iceland and Jan Mayen Island. On 7 May, a sweep by three cruisers located and seized the *München* – but too late to save its Enigma and associated coding data from the Arctic deep. On 25 June the navy caught its sister vessel the *Lauenburg*, again minus its Enigma, but with a useful haul of cipher material.

Hut 8 now had enough information to read some U-boat signals, but the seizure which opened the traffic to fluent decryption was the fruit of chance and high courage, rather than of design. On 9 May 1941 a convoy escort group attacked and forced to the surface Julius Lempe's U-110. A boarding party from HMS *Bulldog* commanded by Sub-Lieutenant David Balme secured the submarine, prevented its sinking, and brought back to his destroyer pearls beyond price: documentation for current Enigma. Though U-110 later sank under tow – fortunately so, from a security viewpoint – the short signal book, officer ciphering instructions and other material reached Bletchley safely, and the secret of the submarine's capture was preserved beyond the war's end. An Enigma machine was also recovered, but perversely this was the least useful element of the booty, because Bletchley had one already, together with assorted rotors seized in other 'pinches'. Within days, Hut 8 was reading a steady stream of German naval messages. Ralph Erskine, one of the foremost experts on codebreaking at Bletchley, believes that the Park was already close to reading the Kriegsmarine traffic, even without the U-110 haul. What is for certain, however, is that it was impossible to break the U-boat ciphers without the assistance of captured material, which would again become a vital issue later in the war.

The breakthrough into the Kriegsmarine ciphers came just too late to influence the pursuit of the *Bismarck* in the latter days of May 1941. Conventional direction-finding on the behemoth's wireless transmissions, supported by air reconnaissance, were the key factors in enabling the Royal Navy to intercept and sink it on the morning of the 27th, though assisted in the last stage by decryption of a Luftwaffe signal revealing Brest as *Bismarck*'s destination. Thereafter, Bletchley produced a steady stream of messages that revealed U-boat positions and intended courses. The so-called Hydra cipher was laid bare, and other keys were progressively broken: the more the Park knew, the more it was able to discover. The flow of decrypts was never assured, however, and disturbing delays sometimes took place. 'Huff-Duff' – High-Frequency Direction-Finding – played an important secondary role in the location of U-boats. The outcome was a relentless shift in the balance of advantage in the Battle of the Atlantic through 1941 and into 1942. Here was a case where intelligence indisputably and importantly influenced events.

Bletchley was also reading a significant portion of Italian naval traffic. On 25 March 1941, one of the small number of women decrypters, nineteen-year-old mathematician Mavis Lever in Dillwyn Knox's team – he was famously supportive of talented girls in a male-dominated institution – played a critical role in breaking a message which revealed that the Italian fleet would shortly put to sea to attack British convoys. The warning enabled the Mediterranean C-in-C Admiral Sir Andrew Cunningham to contrive an encounter off Cape Matapan during the afternoon and night of 28 March which ended in a striking victory for the Royal Navy. By dawn on the 29th, three cruisers and two destroyers had been sunk, while the battleship *Vittorio Veneto* was damaged, an outcome that deterred the Italian surface fleet from making any further attempt to interdict British troop movements to Greece.

Spring brought an increasing flow of decrypts about Wehrmacht operations in the Eastern Mediterranean. Senior officers strove to streamline the transfer of information from Bletchley to battlefields, so that material reached commanders in real time. One of the most significant intercepts, detailing German plans for the May 1941 invasion of Crete, reported 'probable date of ending preparations: 17/5. Proposed course of operation … Sharp attack against enemy air force, military camps and A/A positions … Troops of Fliegerkorps XI: parachute landing to occupy Maleme, Candia and Retiomo; transfer of dive-bombers and fighters to Maleme and Candia; air-landing operations by remainder of Fliegerkorps XI; sea-transport of flak units, further army elements and supplies.' Churchill personally annotated the flimsy: 'In view of the gt importance of this I shd like the actual text transmitted by MOST SECRET together with warnings about absolute secrecy.' This information was passed to Wavell and Freyberg, the relevant commanders, at 2340 on 6 May. The loss of the subsequent Battle of Crete, following the German invasion which began on the morning of the 20th, emphasised a fundamental reality about Enigma decrypts: they could change outcomes only when British commanders and troops on the ground were sufficiently strong, competent and courageous effectively to exploit them. Stuart Milner-Barry of Hut 6 said that he and his colleagues looked back on Crete as 'the greatest disappointment of the war. It seemed a near certainty that, with … every detail of the operation spelt out for us in advance … the attack would be ignominiously thrown back.'

The Cretan signal, informing British generals of German intentions in time to respond, was an exception rather than a commonplace in 1941.

Bletchley was able to provide an ever-growing flow of information about the deployments of the enemy, not least in Eastern Europe, most of it derived from Luftwaffe and army-Luftwaffe decrypts. Wehrmacht traffic stubbornly resisted penetration, but German railway codes provided information about – for instance – troop movements to Yugoslavia, Greece and Eastern Europe in the summer of 1941. Hitler's looming invasion of the Soviet Union, the towering event of the war, was also the first great strategic development for which Ultra intelligence provided explicit warning. While Britain had no power to influence or impede Hitler's Operation 'Barbarossa', it was clearly of the highest importance to Churchill and his generals to be able to monitor its unfolding.

It became a source of increasing frustration to the prime minister that British troops in North Africa failed to frustrate or defeat Rommel when they had not only superiority in men, tanks and guns, but also an ever-growing stream of information about German deployments and movements, for instance at Halfaya Pass in May. Churchill pored intently over his own daily file of Ultra material. When he read a decrypt reporting petrol stocks at various Luftwaffe airfields in Libya, he scrawled on it in his red ink: 'CAS [Chief of Air Staff] How many hours flying can their a/c do on this – about? WSC.' Air Chief Marshal Sir Charles Portal responded testily: 'Unfortunately it is not possible to make any general deduction since the figures only relate to the stock at Benghazi. We do not possess complete figures for the supply and consumption of oil and petrol throughout Libya. All we know is that there are indications of an overall shortage which is limiting operations in the forward area.' This problem was endemic when decrypts were fragmentary. Stewart Menzies performed an important service by dissuading the prime minister from fulfilling his frequent desire to dispatch raw Ultra direct to commanders-in-chief in the field, as he had done in the case of Crete. 'C' was surely correct, on security grounds, and also because decrypts that lacked the context of other intelligence could be highly misleading to untrained eyes.

On land, in 1941 Bletchley provided more guidance to strategy than to tactics: it gave Churchill's high command an authoritative, though never comprehensive, picture of German deployments in every theatre of war. Ultra could do little to assist the RAF's ongoing struggle with the Luftwaffe for mastery of the skies. Only the Royal Navy gained immediate advantage, both in the Mediterranean and the Atlantic. Nothing altered the fact that, until the worldwide balance of strength began to shift in the Allies' favour in the latter part of 1942, the operational superiority of German and Japanese forces enabled them to keep winning victories. Bletchley was an increasingly important weapon, but it was not a magic sword.

The practices and disciplines of GC&CS evolved progressively, with many wrangles and turf wars along the way. Deputy director Nigel de Grey complained about the 'very low standards of military behaviour' prevailing in what was supposed to be a military establishment. But how could it be otherwise? Noel Annan wrote: 'Many of the cryptanalysts who produced Ultra were agnostic, heterodox dons who did not set much store by the normal interpretations of patriotism and democracy.' It was not easy to combine the discipline essential to the operation's smooth functioning with sensitivity to the wayward and frankly eccentric character of some of its resident geniuses. Col. Tiltman wrote ruefully on 2 March 1941: 'Cryptanalysts have to be handled delicately and do not take kindly to service methods of control, which are essential to the good working of signals.' When the director of the Royal Navy's women personnel visited the Park, she demanded indignantly: 'Why are my Wrens working with civilians?' WAAFs in the teleprinter room expressed resentment about taking orders from civilians. In December 1940 the War Office's director of military intelligence staged a grab for Bletchley's military output. Until 1941, the Admiralty tried to continue some cryptographic work under its own roof. In Hut 3, rows erupted between representatives of the three armed services. Stewart Menzies received a constant stream of complaints from rival interests, while Bletchley staff referred to Broadway without enthusiasm as 'the other side'. One of the most durable criticisms of 'C' is that he was ever eager to accept credit for the achievements of the Park, while declining to engage with its chronic resource problems, which eventually prompted the October 1941 letter to Churchill signed by Turing and his colleagues pleading for more staff, that caused Churchill to send his famous 'Action This Day' message: 'Make sure they have all they want on extreme priority.' It is a serious charge against Menzies, that he was an absentee landlord of GC&CS.

Yet all this made mercifully little impact on the work of the codebreakers. Edward Thomas, a naval officer who worked at the Park, was impressed by the absence of hierarchical distinctions: 'Despite the high tension of much of the work ... anyone of whatever rank or degree could approach anyone else, however venerable, with any idea or suggestion, however crazy.' Few people of any rank or status felt denied a voice – an unusually rare and privileged state of affairs in the wartime institutions of any nation.

From 1941, the Cambridge scientist and novelist C.P. Snow became a key Whitehall intermediary, responsible for channelling suitable mathematicians and other scholars to Bletchley. GC&CS also employed thousands of humbler folk, recruited chiefly for their language skills. Its files record details of some RAF personnel interviewed, such as Leading Aircraftsman Berry, aged twenty-three, who had started training as a pilot but remustered owing to his conscientious objections to dropping bombs. His German language skills were graded only 'B', and the recruiters noted: 'if interested in work might do well, but needs careful handling'.

LAC Gray was also ex-aircrew, 'grounded as result of crash', had 'B' grade Spanish. Cpl Hodges, aged twenty-six, was unfit for aircrew, 'anxious to use his German "A"', in civil life worked in architect's office'. AC1 Tew, a twenty-eight-year-old clerk, had German 'A', as well as some Spanish, French and Danish, acquired while working in his father's leather-trading business. There was much snapping between Bletchley and the Air Ministry about the latter's reluctance to grant commissioned rank to RAF men seconded to cipher or wireless interception duties. Group-Captain Blandy of the Y Service complained that such people were 'picked individuals having considerable linguistic qualifications and a high standard of education … [Mere Aircraftsmen] and NCOs lack the necessary authority required to carry out their duties efficiently'.

Not all the personnel posted to Bletchley proved suited to its demands. A March 1941 report on an RAF officer returned to general duties after a spell at BP noted: 'Although an excellent linguist, he does not appear to me to have any aptitude or inclination for the research side of the work. He had been relegated to clerical tasks, but did not seem thus to justify his pay'. There were equally bleak verdicts on the performance of some women staffers lower down the hierarchy: 'Wren Kenwick is inaccurate, very slow and not a bit keen on her work, not very intelligent. Wrens Buchanan and Ford are unintelligent and slow and seem unable to learn. Wren Rogers suffers from mild claustrophobia and cannot work in a windowless room'. The report concluded: 'The remainder … are doing most excellent work', but the selectors were urged to recognise the importance of the jobs the women were required to fulfil, 'and not to send us too many of the Cook and Messenger type'.

Enfolded within their oppressive security blanket, Bletchley's people lived, loved and largely played within their own community. Almost all were paid a pittance: nineteen-year-old mathematician Mavis Lever, one of 'Dilly' Knox's team, initially received thirty shillings a week, of which she paid twenty-one shillings for her lodgings. When staff did escape into the world beyond the perimeter fence, the civilian status of the young men incurred dark suspicions among the uninitiated about their absence from any battlefield. The dramas and pantomimes performed by the Park's amateur dramatic society became high spots in the annual calendar: Frank Birch, formerly of King's College, Cambridge, and now head of Hut 4, was celebrated for his appearances as the Widow Twankey in productions of the pantomime *Aladdin*.

By 1942, common sense had achieved some important successes in the Park's management. Each section worked to its appointed head, irrespective of rank or lack of it. Cryptanalysis for all Britain's armed forces was handled entirely at Bletchley and its Indian out-stations, a concentration of effort that neither Germany nor the United States ever matched. Gordon Welchman emerged as the foremost lubricator, curbing feuding; several notoriously stupid service officers were transferred out; the popular Eric Jones was appointed to head Hut 3. It was acknowledged that the civilian codebreakers must be ridden on the lightest possible rein, though the director was prone to occasional surges of authoritarianism.

On 1 February 1942, Admiral Karl Dönitz introduced a reflector or fourth rotor into the Atlantic U-boat service's Enigma, with immediate and calamitous results for Allied fortunes in the Battle of the Atlantic: this imposed a twenty-six-fold increase in the range of possible settings, and blinded Bletchley. Sinkings soared. At sea, the Royal Navy was obliged to rely upon 'Huff-Duff' to locate enemy submarines until these approached within range of underwater detection by the Asdics of convoy escorts, which were impotent against night surface attackers. Breaking what was now designated the 'Shark' submarine key became the Park's foremost priority, a challenge unresolved for nine frightening months, by far the most stressful period of the war for those engaged in the task. They knew, as they sat hunched over their labours in those austere huts, that at sea men were dying every day because of their failure – though no rational person would have called it such.

Also on 1 February, coincidentally, Alastair Denniston was pushed aside into a subordinate London role, to be replaced by his deputy, Edward Travis. In some measure this development reflected a clash of personalities – Denniston and Stewart Menzies disliked each other – together with the infighting characteristic of any large bureaucracy. But it was widely felt at Bletchley that its operational head was being overwhelmed by the strains of running an establishment that since the outbreak of war had increased fourfold in size, and many times that much in its importance to the war effort. Power struggles were unavoidable. Denniston was a good and kind man who had done many things well, but Bletchley had outgrown him. Travis, whose edicts were issued in a curious trademark brown ink, was generally considered a success in his new role, not least by such influential creative figures as Welchman. When another codebreaker, Ralph Bennett, returned that summer from detached duty in the Middle East, he found that the atmosphere had changed markedly: 'I had left as one of a group of enthusiastic amateurs. I returned to a professional organisation with standards and an acknowledged reputation to maintain. Success was no longer an occasional prize, but the natural reward of relentless attention to detail.'

Throughout 1942, Bletchley's activities were hampered by a desperate shortage of bombes, and thus by argument about their best employment. In January the army-Luftwaffe Hut 6 was receiving 1,400 intercepts a day, of which an average of 580 were broken, a proportion that slowly increased, reaching about 50 per cent by May 1943. Often no more than one three-wheel bombe was available at any given time to work on the Shark U-boat cipher, because the others of what was still only a handful of machines were committed to breaking army and air traffic. The codebreakers said later that they would have needed ten four-wheel bombes – which did not then exist – significantly to accelerate their progress. By November, a note of desperation had entered the Admiralty's pleas to the Park about Shark. The Battle of the Atlantic, said the navy's Operational Intelligence Centre, was 'the one campaign which BP are not at present influencing to any marked extent – and it is the only one in which the war can be lost unless BP do help'. A critical breakthrough was imminent, however. On 30 October in the Eastern Mediterranean U-559 was attacked by an escort group, and forced to the surface by depth-charging. Tony Fasson, thirty-year-old first lieutenant of the destroyer *Petard*, along with Able Seaman Colin Grazier, hastily stripped naked and swam sixty yards to the stricken submarine, then hauled themselves into the conning tower. The crew had opened the seacocks before abandoning their boat, and the sea was flooding in even as the two men searched the control room with desperate urgency.

They found treasure: the second edition of the *Wetterkurzschlussel*, or weather short signal book, for its Enigma. Having wrapped this and other documents in waterproofing, Fasson and Grazier handed them up the hatch to sixteen-year-old NAAFI canteen assistant Tommy Brown, who had followed in swimming to the U-boat. He in turn passed the packages to the crew of a whaleboat, which arrived alongside in the nick of time. Brown, a civilian, lived to receive a George Medal for his daring, but the two supremely dedicated British sailors pushed their luck by plunging once more into the submarine's control room, possibly in the belief that that they might retrieve a cipher machine. Bletchley did not need this, for it had already reconstructed the wiring of a four-rotor Enigma: it was the signal books that mattered. U-559 suddenly vanished into the Mediterranean, taking with it Fasson and Grazier, both of whom received posthumous George Crosses. The captured documents reached Bletchley on 24 November, and made possible the critical break into the Shark key on 13 December, assisted by data from weather decrypts secured by Hut 10.

That day, the codebreakers teleprinted to the Admiralty's Operational Intelligence Centre locations for twelve Atlantic U-boats. Their positions were by now a week out of date, but they sufficed to provide critical guidance about the Germans' likely courses. Thereafter, Shark signals were frequently broken within twenty-four hours, though the delay sometimes extended to forty-eight. This was one of the indisputably decisive moments of the intelligence war. Once regular Shark decrypts began to flow through to the Royal Navy, the balance in the war at sea shifted dramatically. Though Hut 8 later suffered more delays and difficulties with Shark, never thereafter was British control of the Atlantic sea route seriously threatened, and U-boat sinkings soared.

Among much else remarkable about Bletchley were not its periodic rows and tantrums, but that the front-line codebreakers, whose average age was twenty-three, sustained such a degree of fellowship. Derek Taunt described how they felt 'devoted to the task of outwitting the enemy and happy to be part of a complicated organization designed to do just that'. Rolf Noskwith paid tribute to what he described as the Huts' 'exemplary leadership'. The integrity of the decoding operation was much assisted by the personal friendship between Stuart Milner-Barry of Hut 6 and Hugh Alexander of Hut 8. But tranquillity could never be attainable when thousands of men and women were working under appalling pressure around the clock, month upon month, year after year, knowing that lives depended upon their efforts. On 15 May 1943 Welchman wrote to Nigel de Grey, apologising for an explosion of rage during a discussion about organisation and shortage of resources, an ongoing bugbear. 'My touchiness,' he wrote, 'is probably due to the fact that I always have the extreme value and urgency of our work very much on my mind. Throughout the whole history of Hut 6 there has never been a time at which I felt that we were being as efficient as we could be and you can imagine that this has been a heavy and continual strain ... The present situation is an absolute scandal, but there is nothing we lack now that has not been asked for again and again. So please forgive me for being somewhat bitter and ill-tempered.'

He added: 'A great deal of the work is terribly monotonous and deadly dull, and this has a very serious effect on morale over a long period. Some of the girls are almost physically sick at the sight of a Type-X machine. Now, if our girls crack up as many have done, we are absolutely sunk, and no amount of belated assistance will save us ... Incidentally, could you possibly persuade Travis to get [Air-Marshal Charles] Medhurst [RAF director of intelligence] and [the CIGS Gen. Sir Alan] Brooke to spend even one minute telling the girls that their work is important? Yours ever Gordon.' But difficulties persisted in securing qualified personnel, not least because so few people in Whitehall had any inkling of the supreme priority of GC&CS's work. When BP needed personnel to operate punch-card machines, its recruiters turned to employees of the John Lewis Partnership, the department-store chain which had personnel trained to use them. Astoundingly, after ten women had been selected, the Ministry of Labour insisted that they should instead be dispatched to do land work. An internal memo at the Park seethed: 'The John Lewis episode is a disgrace.' The girls were eventually released to GC&CS, but only after a bitter wrangle with the civil bureaucracy.

From the war's first day to its last, security was an obsession of every Allied officer privy to the Ultra secret. In 1941 a certain Col. Gribble, who had served as an air liaison officer with the RAF in France in 1940, published a book entitled *Diary of a Staff Officer*, which caused near-hysteria when Whitehall noticed, because it contained references to unidentified 'secret sources'. Gribble's work had been passed by a censor who knew nothing of Bletchley Park. What if somebody in Berlin read it, and drew lethal inferences about the vulnerability of Germany's ciphers? MI5 bought up and pulped 7,000 unsold copies of the book, trusting to luck that none of its existing buyers had German friends. Before the fall of Singapore in February 1942, the key local Ultra and Y Service personnel received priority for evacuation, as did their American counterparts on Corregidor two months later. Had they fallen into captivity, not only would they have suffered a ghastly fate alongside other British and

Australian prisoners, and their rare skills have been lost, but the risk to Allied codebreaking was frightening if they were exposed to interrogation and torture.

Most of Bletchley's staff displayed marvellous conscientiousness about secrecy, all the more remarkable among young men and women – Station X's footsoldiers – performing humdrum functions. In 1941 a civilian doctor in Nottingham wrote to the GC&CS authorities, reporting that one of his patients, a Wren named Adele Moloney, was in bed with a high temperature, having overstayed her leave with symptoms of acute exhaustion. He wrote: 'Miss Moloney has hypertrophy of the conscience to such an extent that she will not divulge the smallest detail of what she does, even though it is against her interests. As I find it difficult to believe that this young girl is on work which is so important that her doctor must have his hands tied by lack of knowledge, I thought I would write to ask for your comments.' Bletchley responded blandly that 'there is in the ordinary way nothing that we know of in the work that she does that is in any way likely to be prejudicial to her health. The same work is done by a large number of other girls, none of whom so far as we know have suffered in any way.' But BP told the doctor that Miss Moloney's discretion was not merely correct, but 'highly commendable', and so indeed it was.

There was much unease among the administrators about the security risk posed by the rolling population of cooks, cleaners and workmen who serviced Station X. A 1941 report reflected uneasily: 'New faces are being sent daily from the Labour Exchange to Bletchley Park.' A series of flagrant breaches in the spring of 1942 prompted a magisterial memorandum to all personnel from the Park's senior security officer: 'There have been recent instances among you of a spirit of such reckless disregard for the conse-quences of indiscretion as would seem to argue not only a condition of ignorance or folly, but a contempt for the laws by which each one of us knows himself to be bound. In one instance [a BP staffer] disclosed the nature of their duties within her family circle ... [this] was repeated by one of its members in mixed company, actually at a cocktail party, whence it was duly reported to me. In another instance one of the most vital tasks in which the organisation is engaged was disclosed, possibly in a spirit of pride or ostentation, in an after-dinner conversation to the Seniors of this person's old College, whence a report reached me ... It would be a reflec-tion on your intelligence to suppose that you do not realise ... that an idle piece of boasting or gossip ... may be passed to the enemy and cause, not only the breakdown of our successful efforts here, but the sacrifice of the lives of our sailors, soldiers and airmen, perhaps your own brothers, and may even prejudice our ultimate hopes of victory.'

If this broadside was fiercely worded, it was not in the smallest degree extravagant. Bletchley Park was the jewel in the crown of Britain's war effort, one of its principal assets in the struggle to save the nation from Nazi enslavement. Alan Brooke wrote in his diary after visiting GC&CS in April 1942: 'A wonderful set of professors and genii! I marvel at the work they succeed in doing.' Betrayal of its secrets could overnight have crippled the cause of freedom – most immediately by denying to the Royal Navy its key to the locations of Dönitz's U-boats. Well before the Soviet Union became a supposed ally in June 1941, British traitors were passing to NKVD agents whatever pearls of Ultra they thought might be of interest to Moscow; it was fortunate that Stalin did not inform Hitler of Bletchley's doings – in the months before 'Barbarossa', he was desperate to appease Berlin.

It was an even larger stroke of fortune that Germany's commanders sustained their dogged belief in Enigma's inviolability. Early in the 1930s the head cryptanalyst of Göring's Forschungsamt cipher unit, Dr Georg Schröder, asserted passionately: 'the whole Enigma is garbage!' No heed was taken of his warning, which was deemed only relevant to the commercial machine, which lacked a plugboard. In October 1939 Lt. Col. Ruzek, former head of Czech cryptanalysis, revealed to German interrogators that the Poles had been working with the French to break Enigma traffic. In captured Polish files, the Nazis discovered three 1938 plain-language translations of signals from a German cruiser in Spanish waters. Polish PoWs were exhaustively interrogated in attempts to discover how these messages had been decrypted, but the Abwehr drew a blank: almost all the men who knew the answers were at that time beyond their reach. OKW/Chi's cryptanalysts in Berlin felt intensely frustrated that, while they were supposedly responsible for ensuring the security of the Wehrmacht's communications, they were expressly forbidden to conduct tests on breaking Enigma traffic. They nonetheless believed the system institutionally safe, and argued that occasional signals could only be broken if dispatched by careless operators who neglected procedure. Even in 1946 the Wehrmacht's chief cryptanalyst, Wilhelm Fenner, maintained stubbornly: 'The Enigma was regarded as antiquated, but it was secure when properly used.'

It is possible to identify several moments of the war at which British blunders could have enabled the Germans to recognise that their ciphers were compromised, and plug the gusher of intelligence flowing from Bletchley Park. On 24 August 1941, Churchill made a BBC broadcast in which he alluded to explicit numbers of Jews known to have been murdered by the SS behind the Eastern Front. The Germans noticed, and within days Oberstgruppenführer Kurt Daluege issued an order that details of such killings should no longer be mentioned in radio traffic: 'The danger of enemy decryption of wireless messages is great. For this reason only non-sensitive information should be transmitted.' One consequence of Churchill's slip was that when in October 1942 the Foreign Office compiled a report on known German atrocities, especially those committed against Jews, this was not publicly released, to avoid any new risk of compromising intelligence sources.

It was remarkable that the German high command failed to draw far-reaching conclusions from Churchill's August 1941 words, and likewise a year later when German interrogation of Allied prisoners revealed that Montgomery's Eighth Army had been expecting the Afrika Korps' attack at Alam Halfa in North Africa. Early in 1942 also, Dönitz became acutely suspicious that the Allies were monitoring his communications with U-boats. He was persuaded that his fears were groundless by British carelessness with their own convoy codes, which were being broken by the Kriegsmarine's decryption service, the B-Dienst. If Enigma was indeed insecure, the admiral reasoned, the British would have learned about this yawning chasm in their own security: a nation clever enough to crack U-boat signals would employ better codes of its own. The U-boat chief was careful enough to introduce the four-rotor Enigma, but insufficiently so to question the fundamental basis of the system.

Potentially the most dangerous threat to the Ultra secret also came in 1942. On 5 May the Australian freighter *Nankin* sailed from Fremantle for Calcutta with a cargo of explosives, 180 crew and 162 passengers. In the Indian Ocean early on the morning of 10 May, a small floatplane circled the ship. Soon afterwards its parent, the German raiding cruiser *Thor*, closed in and opened fire. *Nankin* signalled 'Raider sighted,' and her captain jettisoned the confidential books before surrendering an hour after the first shot. The passengers and crew were transferred to *Thor* and its accompanying supply ship, along with hundreds of sacks of mail. Among these, the Germans identified a consignment from the Combined Operations Intelligence Centre at Wellington, New Zealand. Its contents included a 'Most Secret' summary for the period 21 March to 20 April, largely based on Ultra material, which gave the positions of every known

Allied and enemy warship and merchant vessel in the Pacific and Indian Oceans. With criminal carelessness, these documents had been dispatched not by hand of *Nankin*'s captain, but instead with the general mail.

Even though the COIC data was well out of real time, imaginative analysis of the intelligence summary by the Abwehr would have shown the Germans that some at least of their ciphers, as well as those of the Japanese, were compromised. Such scrutiny appears never to have taken place. The *Thor*'s captain saw no special urgency about sending the captured documents to Berlin. Only at the end of July, after the raiding cruiser's supply ship docked at Yokohama, did Germany's naval attaché in Tokyo receive the COIC papers. A further month elapsed before Berlin authorised him to pass the documents to its Asian ally. Thereafter, the Japanese navy changed its main code, so that the US Navy lacked 'real time' decrypts to empower its operations during the 11–12 October Battle of Cape Esperance, the 26 October Battle of Santa Cruz, and the 13–15 November Guadalcanal actions.

It would be fanciful to suggest that the *Nankin* captures thus altered the course of the naval war, because the code alteration was part of a regular routine: the Japanese still doggedly refused to acknowledge that their entire communications system was vulnerable. But if they had read the Allied COIC documents soon after the Germans got their hands on them, and had possessed a more sophisticated capability for assessing intelligence, they would have changed their ciphers weeks, instead of days, before launching their June assault on Midway, with momentous consequences. The British do not appear to have told the Americans about the *Nankin* loss. This may have been because they suffered an attack of well-deserved embarrassment about a major breach of security. It was the same story when the second of two copies of the Japanese Purple cipher machine, presented to the British by their American creators, was dispatched to the Ultra team in Singapore by freighter. It is known to have left Durban in December 1941, but thereafter vanished without trace, its fate unknown from that day to this.

No Whitehall correspondence concerning the *Nankin* has thus far been found in British archives, and it would be unjustified to build too high a tower of speculation around its story. The Allies escaped significant consequences from their blunder – and from the others cited above – because the intelligence systems of Germany and Japan lacked the coherence and imagination to profit as they should have done from their haul of Allied secrets. One further critically dangerous moment should be mentioned:

in November 1942 the Germans swept across unoccupied France. Among those whom they took into custody in Vichy were three Poles who had served in Gustave Bertrand's codebreaking department since 1940, and before that had been engaged in Poland's own cryptographic operation. In March 1943, two such prisoners were interrogated by German sigint experts in the presence of an Abwehr officer. Had the men told what they knew, or could have surmised, about the Allies' progress in cracking Enigma, the worst could have happened. Fortunately, before being questioned the Poles were briefly alone together, and coordinated explanations which were accepted: that while some traffic had been briefly broken in 1938, improved German systems thereafter closed the breach. Here were two more people to whom the Allies owed a debt for their role preserving the Ultra secret. Cleverer men in Berlin and Tokyo might have made much of the material and prisoners that fell into their hands, and abruptly halted the music for the Allies' wondrous dance across the ether.

2 FLIRTING WITH AMERICA

From the day Winston Churchill became prime minister until Pearl Harbor nineteen months later, his foremost political purpose was to drag the United States into the war, because only thus could the embattled island hope to accomplish more than its own survival. To that end, the British sought the closest cooperation the Americans would countenance. They professed to wish to extend this to intelligence, but in truth sought a notably one-sided relationship, which protected most of Britain's secrets. In the spring of 1940, Stewart Menzies asked the Canadian businessman Sir William Stephenson to try to open a link to J. Edgar Hoover, director of the FBI. Stephenson, eager for a top-table role for himself, set about this mission with a will, using an unlikely mutual acquaintance, the former world heavyweight boxing champion Gene Tunney, with whom he had sparred in France back in 1918. In those days the Canadian had been a fighter pilot, who went on to make a fortune before creating his own industrial intelligence network in the 1930s, from which he offered material to the British government. This opened a relationship with Desmond Morton and Dick Ellis of Broadway, which continued after the outbreak of war. Hoover, before meeting the ebullient Canadian, took care to secure White House approval. Stephenson reported back to London that the FBI chief was keen to cooperate with MI6, and had suggested that his visitor should secure some official title to formalise his status in the US.

Menzies promptly gave Stephenson a modest cover role as Passport Control Officer in New York, where he set up shop on 21 June 1940. Thereafter the Canadian built a substantial organisation which in January 1941 acquired the title of British Security Coordination. BSC, quartered on the 35th and 36th floors of the Rockefeller Center on Fifth Avenue, was charged with sabotaging Axis operations, liaising with the Americans and gathering intelligence about enemy activity. It also managed anti-Axis propaganda throughout the Americas. In its role as a flag-carrier for Britain and its spies, it enjoyed considerable success until the respective national intelligence services began to bypass BSC in favour of doing business with each other direct, in the spring of 1942 after the US came into the war.

New York became MI6's most important out-station, from which its agents set forth to try to penetrate Axis-run companies and foreign embassies. BSC could claim credit for such coups as tipping off the FBI in November 1940, when a Mexico City informant revealed that four German ships intended to run the British blockade across the Gulf of Mexico: the US Navy stopped the ships. Likewise, J. Edgar Hoover warned BSC that the Italians intended to transfer to South America almost $4 million in cash, which might be used to bankroll sabotage. Two-thirds of the money got through, but a BSC agent alerted police in Mexico City about the smuggling operation: they opened the bags and confiscated $1.4 million. On the debit side, however, Stephenson was alleged to have recruited some frankly disreputable officers. Guy Liddell of MI5 fumed about one in particular, Ingram Fraser, who was alleged to have been 'running a mistress in Washington DC who was supposed to be acting as an agent on the Finns. She was getting $500 a month for her flat and $500 for her services, all paid out of office funds.' BSC wasted as much energy on absurdities as every other intelligence organisation: three of its cleverest officers – Oxford dons Freddie Ayer, Bill Deakin and Gilbert Hignet – spent weeks planning a response to a possible Japanese invasion of South America.

What mattered most, however, was Stephenson's liaison role: he forged close personal relations with many prominent administration figures, and especially with Colonel William Donovan, who would become the most influential single personality in America's wartime foreign intelligence operations. Donovan was a natural showman, where the other belligerents' spymasters were men of the shadows or – in the case of Stalin's intelligence chiefs – creatures of the night. Born in 1883, 'Wild Bill' rose from

a poor Irish background in upstate New York to become a classmate of
Franklin Roosevelt at Columbia Law School; he later became an influential friend of the president. He fought with Pershing against Pancho Villa,
then commanded the New York Irish 69th Regiment on the Western Front
in 1917–18, returning home as his nation's most decorated soldier, a colonel with the Medal of Honor and a reasonably authentic reputation as a
hero. Thereafter he fulfilled several fact-finding missions for the White
House. Following the first of these, to the new Soviet Union in 1919,
Donovan urged Washington against supporting White Russia, describing
workers in Siberia as 'yearning for Bolshevism'. As US Attorney for the
Western District of New York, he became famous – or notorious – for his
energetic enforcement of Prohibition. Later, though himself a Republican,
he visited Abyssinia and Spain as an emissary for Roosevelt the Democrat.
He returned home an implacable foe of Hitler, and advocate of US engagement in Europe.

In 1940 and 1941, Donovan made trips to London during which
Stephenson ensured that he received red-carpet treatment, including
lunch with the prime minister. Some British officers recoiled from the
visitor's brashness. Maj. Gen. John Kennedy, director of military operations, wrote in his diary: 'Donovan … is extremely friendly to us & a
shrewd and pleasant fellow and good talker. But I could not but feel that
this fat & prosperous lawyer, a citizen of a country not in the war …
possessed very great assurance to be able to lay down the law so glibly
about what we and other threatened nations should & sh[oul]d not do.'

Donovan's influence at the White House nonetheless ensured continuing British gratitude and goodwill. In September 1940 he persuaded
Roosevelt to commit the US to a policy of intelligence collaboration with
Churchill's nation. When Godfrey, the director of naval intelligence,
visited the US in May 1941 with his personal assistant Commander Ian
Fleming, in New York the two men stayed at Donovan's apartment. The
admiral's trip was not an unqualified success: he was shocked by the depth
of hostility between the US Army and US Navy, and got little change out
of Hoover, who was less interested in joining the war against the Axis than
in securing the FBI's monopoly control of the nation's intelligence activities. In this, Hoover was unsuccessful. While his Bureau retained responsibility for counter-espionage – the role of MI5 in Britain – Godfrey and
Stephenson played some part in convincing the Roosevelt administration
that the country needed a new intelligence organisation, and that Donovan
was the man to run it. From July 1941 he held the title of Coordinator of

Information, though in reality his new Office of War Information was an embryo secret service, and he set about supervising its birth and precocious growth with energy and exuberance.

Donovan and Stephenson – the latter known in the US as 'Little Bill' rather than 'Intrepid', which was merely his telegraphic address – were buccaneers both, who shared credit for securing a reasonably free hand for British intelligence operations in the Americas, against the wishes of the FBI and the State Department. Their rapport did not, however, change an overarching reality: the wartime relationship between Britain and the United States was characterised by tensions and suspicions, merely painted over by the magnificent rhetoric of Churchill and Roosevelt. In 1940–41 the British were fighting for their lives while Americans were not, and indeed operated a cash-and-carry policy for the modest quota of weapons and supplies they sold to Churchill's people. Most of America's defence community had some respect for Britain, but little affection.

The British officers privy to the Ultra secret knew that they were custodians of one of their country's most precious assets, which would become instantly forfeit if any hint of their growing successes reached Berlin. American security was poor, as might be expected of a people not yet committed to the struggle, who were anyway constitutionally ill-suited to keeping secrets. British intelligence chiefs were eager for American goodwill, but doubtful how much of practical value their US counterparts could tell them. Pending evidence that a two-way traffic could benefit their embattled island, they determined to give away as little as possible. Moreover, as an anguished Whitehall hand scribbled during the 1941 debate about how much to tell a visiting US delegation: 'What will they think if they find we have been reading their own stuff?' – a mild embarrassment about which Churchill came clean to Roosevelt on 25 February 1942, with the assurance that decryption of US material had stopped immediately after Pearl Harbor.

The sparse 1940–41 meetings and exchanges between the two nation's codebreakers and intelligence officers took place in a climate of mutual wariness, and it was the Americans who displayed greater frankness. On 31 August 1940 the British were told that the Signals Intelligence Service had broken the Japanese Purple key. This revelation prompted no immediate invitation to Bletchley: when the Tizard mission visited the US in September to show off such revolutionary technology as the cavity magnetron – a tempting morsel, key to new-age tactical radar, and intended to promote American reciprocity – information about Ultra was explicitly excluded. On the American side, Laurance Safford of the US Navy's Op-20-G codebreaking team was likewise opposed to sharing its secrets with the British. In December 1940 the two nations reached an agreement to pool information about codebreaking, but both were slow to bring this into effect. Only on Japanese material was there immediate close collaboration: in February 1941 the British cryptanalysis team in Singapore and its American counterpart in the Philippines exchanged liaison officers, who discovered that both were in about the same place with Tokyo's codes. In the early war years the British did better than the Americans in monitoring some low-level Japanese armed forces traffic, though they failed to break into their higher ciphers. Nonetheless, when British forces in 1941 requested urgent American assistance in securing high-altitude photographs of Japan's naval bases, Washington vetoed the proposal.

At the height of the Luftwaffe Blitz on Britain two FBI agents, Hugh Clegg and Clarence Hince, visited London to study 'law enforcement in time of war'. Guy Liddell of MI5 thought that while the visitors looked somewhat thuggish, Clegg seemed 'a very good fellow'. Such warmth was not reciprocated. On their return, the two men delivered to Hoover a report depicting the British, explicitly MI5 and the Metropolitan Police, in terms of withering scorn. They complained that it was difficult to arrange meetings before 10 a.m. or after 4 p.m. because 'the transport situation is very difficult, you know'. They said that 'The fact "exploratory luncheons" were usually two hours in length made our working day rather limited, particularly when compared to the customary hours that officials of the FBI are engaged in official business.' They concluded that the British 'might win the war if they find it convenient'. This report set the tone for the FBI's view of the British for decades thereafter.

In January 1941, when an American codebreaking team – two army, two navy – paid a pioneering visit to Britain, they brought with them a remarkably generous gift: a mimicked Purple machine, of which a second copy was handed over later. The British, however, reciprocated cautiously. With Winston Churchill's explicit sanction they admitted the visitors to Bletchley, and explained the Hut system. They revealed the bombes, GC&CS's most critical innovation, but thereafter prevaricated about fulfilling American requests to be given an example of what Washington described as 'a cypher-solving machine'. There were very good reasons for this – the US was not in the war, and the bombes were scarce pearls. The Americans recognised that they had seen in action a system way ahead of anything the US armed forces were doing. Alfred McCormack, who became the secretary for war's special assistant on comint, said later of Bletchley: 'It's not good – it's superb.'

Some people in Washington, however, were irked by apparent British pusillanimity. They themselves made little serious headway in reading Enigma traffic until floodgates opened in 1943, and – in the words of an exasperated British officer – 'showed no appreciation of the extent of the problems facing Bletchley Park and Britain'. The Park's Washington representative, Captain Edward Hastings, reported in November 1941 that 'there is grave unrest and dissatisfaction about free exchange of special intelligence'. Some Americans were doggedly convinced that the British were holding out on them. As late as December 1942, when Alan Turing visited the US, he was denied admission to the Bell Laboratories in revenge for alleged British foot-dragging about collaboration, and was finally allowed inside only after a huge and protracted transatlantic row. Although William Friedman later forged warm personal relations with BP's senior personnel, he himself made his first visit to Britain only in May 1943, about the time a formal and indeed historic intelligence-sharing pact was agreed between the two nations. Meanwhile collaboration remained wary and incomplete. Even after Pearl Harbor, Bletchley and its owners remained fearful not only about American security shortcomings, but also about the danger that this brightest jewel in the imperial crown might somehow be snatched from them by the boundlessly rich, irresistibly dominant new partner in the Grand Alliance. Alastair Denniston wrote that for Britain Ultra was 'almost lifeblood', whereas the Americans seemed to view Enigma, with the detachment of distance and freedom from mortal peril, merely as 'a new and very interesting problem'.

The War Office's deputy director of military intelligence wrote on 17 February 1942, ten weeks after Pearl Harbor, that in talking to the Americans, 'the general policy is to be as frank as possible but no information will be given regarding our own future operations, or sources of information, nor will any information be passed which emanates from special most secret sources [Ultra]'. On 16 March the cabinet secretary Sir Edward Bridges wrote a memorandum warning that telephone conversations between London and Washington 'still reveal instances of gross [American] lack of discretion'. Stewart Menzies and his officers at MI6 remained reluctant to open their hearts and files to their new brothers-in-arms.

Unfortunately, the British obfuscation which persisted through much of 1942 prompted misunderstandings and mounting anger among some Americans. These crystallised around a belief – entirely mistaken – that Bletchley had broken into the U-boat Shark key, but was refusing to tell the US Navy about it. Op-20-G's eventual exasperated riposte to Bletchley's unwillingness to surrender a bombe was to announce in September 1942 – and to begin to fulfil in August the following year – its own commitment to build four-rotor models by the hundred. This was a time when the British had just thirty-two. The American machines proved technically superior to the British models, and also more reliable: in October 1943 thirty-nine were operational and by December seventy-five, though by the time these became operational much of their capacity proved superfluous to US Navy needs.

In the early war years, British intelligence collaboration with the US was cautious; only from 1943 onwards did it become wholehearted. As with so much else about Anglo–American relations, however, it is less surprising that there was so much squabbling at the outset, in the years of Allied defeat, than that the partnership eventually achieved the intimacy that it did, in the years of victory.

4

The Dogs That Barked

1 'LUCY'S' PEOPLE

The extraordinary incident of the Kremlin's dogs in the night was that they barked, and barked. Operation 'Barbarossa', the June 1941 Nazi invasion of the Soviet Union, was the defining event of the Second World War – and its most baffling, because it achieved surprise when its imminence was manifest. It was a tribute to the length and strength of Stalin's arm that humint   agents of influence abroad – provided him with comprehensive warnings. As early as July 1940, NKVD men operating in German-occupied Poland were reporting intense Wehrmacht activity, barrack-building and troop movements. That autumn, he instructed Centre to open a special file on Hitler's intentions codenamed '*Zateya*' – 'Venture'. In September this showed massive German redeployments close to the Russian border, together with continuing construction of troop accommodation. The Germans' Moscow embassy was reported by a Soviet agent within its walls to be striving to recruit White Russians and intellectual dissidents for the Abwehr. In November 1940 Stalin was told that eighty-five divisions, comprising more than two-thirds of Hitler's infantry, were deployed along the Russian frontier.

During the months that followed, however, some of these troops were shifted to threaten, and then to occupy, Romania and Greece. Neither in 1941 nor since have most Westerners grasped the intensity of Stalin's conviction that Hitler's ambitions were focused on the Balkans, where Russia also had vital interests. Nor do they acknowledge the depth of his hatred and distrust of Britain. It was barely twenty years since Winston Churchill had led a crusade to reverse the Bolshevik Revolution by force of arms. Stalin saw himself, by no means mistakenly, as the object of a sustained Churchillian campaign to drive a wedge into his pact with Hitler and force him to fight Germany, against Russia's interests and in pursuit of those of the British Empire.

The master of the Kremlin recognised that war between the Nazis and the Soviet Union might ultimately prove unavoidable. An August 1940 GRU report, quoting Hitler's ambassador in Belgrade, showed that this was certainly the other party's view: 'For Germany the Balkans are the most significant asset and ought to be included in the [Nazi-controlled] new order of Europe; but since the USSR would never agree to that, a war with her is inevitable.' Stalin, however, remained convinced that it was overwhelmingly against Hitler's interests to break the Nazi–Soviet Pact that was delivering huge supplies of oil and commodities to Germany. He believed it was in the Kremlin's gift to appoint the hour for a showdown, which was not yet. He clung to the view, slavishly endorsed by Beria, that Hitler was engaged in a massive bluff, designed to cow Russia into letting Germany have its way in the Balkans. Augusto Rosso, the Italian ambassador in Moscow, wrote on 21 September 1940: 'The Germans have raised a barrier [against the Russians]: the march to the south has been stopped, the oil is at the disposal of the Germans ... The Danube is a German river. This is the first diplomatic defeat of Comrade Stalin ... and the defeat is even more humiliating because it explodes the dream which throughout the centuries has occupied a special place in the Russian soul: [dominance] of the southern meridian.'

Friedrich von der Schulenberg, Germany's ambassador, helped to assuage Moscow's fears about Berlin's intentions, because his own honesty and sincerity were manifest, and directed towards preserving peace. Beria told Stalin that once Vichy France and Spain had joined the Axis as expected, Hitler planned to induce him to join a pact that would close a steel ring around Britain: 'Pressure was to be exerted on Russia,' the Soviet intelligence supremo wrote on 24 October 1940, 'to reach a political agreement with Germany which would demonstrate to the entire world that the Soviet Union will not hold aloof, and actively join the struggle against Britain, to secure a new European order.' In November Molotov was dispatched to Berlin, to discover 'the real intentions of Germany's proposals for the New Europe'. The foreign minister made plain that Stalin still sought control of the mouth of the Danube, which Hitler had no intention of conceding, and the visit confirmed Germany's leader in his commitment to war.

The NKVD's informants in London asserted, correctly, that many of Britain's businessmen and bankers favoured a compromise peace.

Moscow was appalled by such a prospect, which would make Hitler unstoppable. The Kremlin aspired to see Germany weakened, to make Hitler more biddable. Thus, for all Stalin's disdain for Churchill and his people, he was delighted by British successes against the Luftwaffe at home and the Italians in North Africa. Ivan Maisky, the Soviet ambassador in London, waxed lyrical about the prospects, writing on 3 November 1940: 'England has not merely survived, but has strengthened its position compared with that which prevailed after the fall of France ... in the "Battle of Britain". Hitler, like Napoleon 135 years earlier, has suffered a defeat, his first serious setback of this war; the consequences are impossible to foresee.'

Through the winter of 1940–41, Stalin was battered by contrary winds and fears. The NKVD and GRU reported insistently and accurately, on the authority of its secret Whitehall informants, that the British were considering a bomber assault on his Baku oil wells, which were supplying Russian fuel to the Luftwaffe. The Kremlin was even more dismayed by Axis preparations to invade Greece, which could presage seizure of the Dardanelles, a centuries-old Russian nightmare. If Turkey came into the war on either side, Stalin thought its army liable to invade the Caucasus, of which the Ottomans had been dispossessed barely seventy years earlier. Vsevolod Merkulov, Beria's deputy, reported intense Turkish intelligence activity on the Russian border. Meanwhile the Turks, for their part, were fearful of Nazi aggression, and in January 1941 their embassies began to brief the Russians about the German build-up in Romania. The GRU asserted on 27 January 1941 that the Balkans 'remained the decisive focus of political events, particularly since a headlong clash of German and Soviet vital interests has arisen there'.

But although Stalin was receiving a stream of intelligence about the Nazi threat to the Balkans, there was a torrent about the direct menace to the Soviet Union. On 5 December 1940 Vladimir Dekanozov, Soviet ambassador in Berlin and a veteran intelligence officer, received an anonymous letter: 'To Comrades Stalin and Molotov, very urgent. Russia, please be alert, as Hitler is soon going to attack you. It will soon be too late, but Russia is asleep now. Can't you see what is happening on the borders, from Memel to the Black Sea? East Prussia is filled with troops, new units are arriving day and night ...' Moscow was informed by its Berlin military attaché just eleven days after Hitler signed his Directive 21 on 18 December, calling on the Wehrmacht 'to crush Soviet Russia in a rapid campaign'. In mid-March 1941 the Soviet military attaché in Bucharest reported a German officer telling a friend: 'We have completely altered our plans. We aim at the East, at the USSR. We shall seize the Soviets' grain, coal and oil. We shall then be invincible and will be able to continue the war against England and the United States.'

Beria and Stalin nonetheless agreed that there was alternative evidence to show this to be mere sabre-rattling: Hitler was making a show of force on Russia's border to advance his Balkan purposes. A 20 March 1941 GRU assessment by Gen. Filip Golikov stated what he knew his readership wished to hear: 'The majority of the intelligence reports which indicate the likelihood of war with the Soviet Union in spring 1941 are derived from Anglo-American sources, whose immediate objective is undoubtedly to promote the worsening of relations between the USSR and Germany.' The Swedish minister in Moscow, Vilhelm Assarasson, was consistently well informed about Nazi decision-making, and knew about the commitment to 'Barbarossa'. But Assarasson's tip was discounted, because it was forwarded to the Kremlin by Stafford Cripps, the British envoy. The NKVD intercepted the dispatches of Turkish ambassador Haydar Aktay, who also cited Assarasson's information, along with reports of Hitler's indiscretions to Prince Paul of Yugoslavia, predicting war. Aktay's view was also dismissed.

In March Soviet intelligence suffered a shock. Moscow considered it an important interest to keep Yugoslavia out of Hitler's grasp. When it became aware that Prince Paul, the ruling regent, intended to throw in his lot with the Axis, Gen. Solomon Milshtein and a band of GRU 'illegals' were dispatched to Belgrade to organise a coup against him. They were confounded when Britain's SOE pre-empted them, launching its own coup to install King Peter II. Moscow was even more appalled a few days later, when the Wehrmacht swept across Yugoslavia in the face of negligible resistance. Yet even though the Russians sympathised with its people, as fellow-Slavs, Stalin dismissed their pleas for military assistance. He remained stubbornly determined not to be provoked by the British – as he saw it – into an armed struggle against Germany over Yugoslavia. He merely signed a meaningless non-aggression agreement with Belgrade, shortly before German troops swept its new government aside. He had set a course – to buy time before confronting Hitler – and was determined nothing should deflect him from it, least of all the intelligence reports that swamped Moscow Centre between September 1940 and June 1941.

*   *   *

It is hard to assess the contribution of Soviet agents in Switzerland at this time, because modern knowledge is almost entirely dependent on the principals' later memoirs. All were compulsive liars, bent upon inflating their own roles. Thus, what follows is even more speculative than most accounts of Russian activities. The onset of war had created financial and logistical difficulties for Alexander Radó. There was no Soviet legation in Bern through which cash could be channelled to him, and his cartographic business languished. He was left with little money to fund himself and his family, far less a spy network. Alexander Foote, trained by Ursula Hamburger to serve as Radó's wireless-operator, was striving with equally meagre funds to sustain a masquerade as a British gentleman of leisure, hoping to sit out the war in the comfort of Lausanne. Wireless assumed a new importance for the network after the fall of France, because Radó could no longer use couriers to shift paper reports via Paris. To provide greater security for the Ring's communications, he opened a second trans-mitter operated by a Geneva electrical engineer named Edmond Hamel, who was trained by Foote. Hamel inspired mockery because he was a very small man married to a very large wife, Olga, but he cherished an idealistic enthusiasm for the Soviet Union.

In March 1940, Moscow ordered Anatoli Gourevitch – 'Monsieur Kent' – to travel from Brussels to Geneva to hand over a new code to 'Dora' – Radó. This was a breach of every rule of espionage, barring contact and thus the risk of contamination between networks, but the GRU man was pleased to be given such an opportunity to spread his wings. As a supposed rich young 'Uruguayan tourist', Vincente Sierra commissioned Thomas Cook to make his arrangements, and took a fat book of travellers' cheques to support his cover. On the train from Paris to Geneva, a man who looked familiar took the seat opposite him. Gourevitch was amazed when his companion introduced himself as Jean Gabin, greatest French film star of the age, on his way to Geneva to see his son make his debut as a circus performer. The two exchanged visiting cards. The enchanted young Russian decided that being a secret agent had many compensations.

Installed in Geneva's Hôtel Russie, he divided his time between tour-ism, nightclub visits to support his cover, and a cautious reconnaissance of 113, Rue de Lausanne, the address Centre had given him for Radó. He called the Hungarian's number from a telephone box, then went to a cinema and left in the middle of the film, to walk to Radó's house. He was welcomed warmly, but with surprise, according to Gourevitch. The visitor later claimed that he had been bemused by Radó's 'careless air', and by the agent's claim that, despite the depredations inflicted by war, he still had some money because his map business was not doing badly. Radó introduced his wife Lena, then the two men closeted themselves in his study. Gourevitch handed over a French novel which provided the new key for coding messages. Over the course of the next few hours they practised the routine repeatedly, until both were satisfied that Radó had mastered it. Then they parted, agreeing to meet again in Lausanne, which was conveniently near Montreux, where the 'Uruguayan tourist' had booked a stay of several days. Following this second meeting they lunched together in a restaurant, then wandered the streets.

Most Russians abroad suffered severely from homesickness. When Soviet agents met and had leisure enough to gossip, the first question to a man or woman fresh from Moscow was almost always 'What news from "the village"?', as they called their own country. Though Radó was Hungarian, according to Gourevitch they talked indiscreetly about each other's experiences of Centre. Radó allegedly begged his contact to emphasise to Moscow the lofty nature of his sources in Berlin. The Geneva agent also told him the Germans were planning to attack the Soviet Union. Yet it is implausible that in April 1940 Radó should have said Germany was preparing to invade Russia, because at that time Hitler had made no such decision, nor even come near to it. What seems certain, however, is that Centre was rash in sending Gourevitch to Geneva, and that its spies told each other things they should not have done, dangerous to both networks.

At the end of December 1940 Ursula Hamburger left Switzerland for England, where her German communist brother was already living in exile. She was soon followed by her husband Len Brewer. Her set – a 'musical box' in their jargon, just as a forger was a 'cobbler' and police 'the doctor' – was taken to Geneva. Alexander Foote moved back to Lausanne with his own transmitter. It was too dangerous to install an external aerial on his apartment building. Instead, he persuaded a nearby wireless shop to supply the deficiency, saying that he wanted to listen to the BBC. For months, however, he proved unable to raise Moscow. Despite passing countless hours hunched over a Morse key in the kitchen, his urgent pulses vanished into a void. Then on 12 March 1941 came an electrifying moment: into his earphones flickered a response 'NDA, NDA, OK, QRK5.' He was in touch with Centre.

Swiss intelligence must have been aware of the Radó group's transmissions, but at that stage they made no attempt to interfere, even when the Gestapo protested fiercely to Bern about the flood of signals its operators monitored from across the border. The spies now boasted a third transmitter: Radó had met a young woman named Margrit Bolli, daughter of strongly socialistic parents, who said that she was eager to help the communist cause. The Ring trained the twenty-three-year-old girl in Morse technique. Initially she transmitted from the family home in Basle, but when her parents not unreasonably baulked, she moved to Geneva. The Gestapo, listening in frustration to the signals – still unintelligible to them – flooding across the ether from Bolli, Foote and the Hamels christened them '*Die Rote Drei*' – 'The Red Trio'.

Who was giving Radó the information from Germany which was forwarded to Moscow in an average of five messages a day? The activities of 'Cissie', Rachel Dübendorfer, had now been merged into those of his group. Colleagues described her as a charmless woman of Balkan origins. She lived with Paul Böttcher, a former German communist illegally resident in Switzerland: Dübendorfer more than once used her nominal Swiss husband's identity documents to preserve Böttcher's neck. It is alleged that one of her sources provided an explicit warning of 'Barbarossa'. Meanwhile one of Radó's messages, dated 21 February 1941, quoted a Swiss intelligence officer, Mayr von Baldegg or 'Luise', predicting a German invasion at the end of May, a forecast perhaps secured by the Swiss Viking intelligence network inside Germany, and endorsed by a prominent Japanese diplomat. The network also became a conduit through which some Czech intelligence was passed to Moscow, most of it ultimately derived from the Abwehr's Paul Thummel. At the end of May Radó cited a French diplomat, Louis Suss, predicting an invasion on 22 June – this message provoked an icy response from Moscow. So did another report to the same effect from Rudolf Rössler, who would henceforward become the foremost source for the Radó network. His codename 'Lucy' has passed into history, since the GRU's Swiss operation became familiarly known as the 'Lucy' Ring.

Rössler, a small, grey, bespectacled German émigré born in 1897, was an impregnably enigmatic figure, of a kind that populates many spy sagas. A socialist journalist, he fled from the Nazis in 1935 and set up a little publishing business in Lucerne – the city that prompted his codename. He began writing under the name of R.A. Hermes, describing the Nazi persecution of Jews and warning that the Nazis would reoccupy the Rhineland. Berlin identified 'Hermes', and in 1937 deprived Rössler of his German citizenship. He nonetheless retained many connections in his homeland, especially within the Wehrmacht. Short of both friends and cash in Switzerland, he began to provide information to a private intelligence agency called Buro Ha, based at the Villa Stutz south of Lucerne, and run by an ardent anti-Nazi named Captain Hans Hausamann. Buro Ha had informal links to Swiss intelligence, which for a season thereafter provided some protection for Rössler.

He secured a steady flow of information from Germany, and apportioned varying quotas to Swiss, British, Czech and Soviet purchasers. Though his anti-Nazi credentials were not in doubt, he was principally and of necessity a mercenary – all his customers had to pay cash. By 1942 he had become by far the GRU's most important Swiss source, the key figure in the Radó network. Moscow Centre, mistrustful of this shadowy figure, insistently demanded that Radó should make Rössler identify his sources, and the journalist equally stubbornly refused to do so. For all his later importance, it remains unclear how much intelligence he provided in 1941. Rössler went to his post-war grave still silent about the identity of the Germans who had provided him with useful, even sensational material. Subsequent speculation has focused on Col. Hans Oster, deputy head of the Abwehr; Hans Gisevius; former Leipzig mayor Gördeler; and two unnamed Wehrmacht generals.

Uncertainty also persists about the timing and wording of some of the Swiss Ring's messages and their supposed warnings to Moscow, both before and after 'Barbarossa'. All that can confidently be said is that the GRU received a stream of messages from Switzerland in the spring of 1941, some of which strongly indicated that Hitler intended to attack Russia. Equally significant for the strategic debate in Moscow, Centre learned that Rudolf Rössler had been, and probably continued to be, an informant of MI6's Bern station. It was only one step from this knowledge to a belief inside the Kremlin that the 'Lucy' Ring had become an instrument of Churchill, peddling false information to drag Russia into the war.

2 SORGE'S WARNINGS

Stalin's Japanese sources told much the same story as his Swiss ones, though since the outbreak of war in Europe the strain of sustaining twin lives, occupying a much higher profile than the 'Lucy' spies, had exacted an ever worsening toll on its principal agent. Richard Sorge strove to use his influence to dissuade the Germans from war with Russia. He told the Tokyo embassy that Nomonhan – the summer 1939 Russo–Japanese border clashes – had been a disaster for the Japanese, and that Berlin should notice the effectiveness of the Red Army and of Zhukov, its local commander. Then came the huge shock of the Nazi–Soviet Pact, which stunned the Japanese government.

And Sorge. The spy reported on 12 August 1939 the movement of twelve Japanese divisions to Korea and Manchuria – the real total was twenty – in case the government decided on war, but he expressed his own conviction that Japan would hold back, and indeed on 4 September Tokyo formally announced a policy of non-intervention. Sorge told Moscow, on Hotsumi Ozaki's authority, that the country would enter the war only when it was confident that it had identified the winner. He added that the German embassy expected the Japanese to remain neutral, and was even nervous they might join the Allied camp.

Sorge's surreal relationship with Col. Ott's mission took a new twist when he was offered a staff post as its press attaché. He declined, as usual because he was fearful of the security checks into his past that acceptance would have provoked, but he worked four hours a day in the embassy building, while assuming a new journalistic role as a stringer for *Frankfurter Zeitung*. It was scarcely surprising that in October the Japanese police foreign section, the Tokko, committed an agent – twenty-eight-year-old Harutsugu Saito – to shadow Sorge. They suspected that he was spying … for Germany. Saito noticed Max Clausen and began to take an interest in him, too.

During the months that followed, stresses on the network intensified. Branko de Voukelitch disclosed his work for the Soviets to his adored Japanese lover Yoshiko. In 1940 the couple were married, and she never betrayed him, but his indiscretion was appallingly risky. Max Clausen became grossly overweight, and his health deteriorated. Bedridden for some time, he had to get his wife Anna to assemble the transmitter before tapping out messages to Moscow from his sickroom. His employers were unsympathetic. Clausen was peremptorily informed by the Fourth Department that funding was tight: pay was being reduced. His little blueprint reproduction company employed fourteen people, had opened a branch in Mukden and was fulfilling assignments for the Japanese War and Navy Ministries. Moscow said that he must henceforth subsidise himself out of its profits. In a farcical twist, Clausen became increasingly admiring of Hitler – who was, after all, now supposedly Stalin's friend.

But the radioman kept sending: in 1940 he transmitted sixty times, sending 29,179 words of Sorge's wisdom. Prominent among the spy's scoops was the draft of a proposed Japan–China peace treaty. It was deemed a vital Soviet interest to keep the China war going, because its termination would free the Japanese army to strike at Russia. When the treaty leaked and the draft was torn up, Sorge was also able to supply the substitute version – though this, too, remained unsigned. From the German embassy he secured data on the Mitsubishi and Nakajima aircraft factories. He provided accurate forecasts on Japan's aggressive intentions towards French Indochina. He was not infallible, however, and gave Moscow some cause for scepticism. He predicted, for instance, that the British would reject Tokyo's demand for closure of the Burma Road supply route to China shortly before they did so for three months. As is so often the case with intelligence, Sorge's original report was not mistaken: Churchill simply changed his mind.

By the end of 1940, Sorge's standing was higher in Berlin than in the Kremlin. Indeed, the excellence of his reports for the Nazis almost caused his undoing: Schellenberg of the RSHA ran a security check which revealed his communist past. The Gestapo's Joseph Meisinger was posted to Tokyo as embassy security officer, with orders to look closely at Sorge, though as yet the Nazis had no suspicion of his supreme duplicity. Meisinger was ill-equipped for his task: a creature of Reinhard Heydrich, he was a thug whose reputation rested upon a few months of orchestrating brutality in Warsaw. Much more serious for the spy ring was the fact that some of its principal members were breaking down. Though Sorge sustained his journalistic career, penning fifty-one articles for *Frankfurter Zeitung* in the first six months of 1941, his nerves were shredded. His drinking worsened, and Hanako found him an increasingly violent lover. When she sobbed and begged him to explain himself, he responded sullenly, 'I am lonely.' She said, 'How can this be, when you have so many German friends here in Tokyo?' He muttered, 'They are not my true friends.' In a September 1940 signal to Moscow, he said that he was forty-four years old and desperately tired. He yearned to be allowed to go 'home' to Russia, though he must have known that Centre would never countenance this until the war ended.

Max Clausen became too sick to keep pace with transmission of Sorge's flood of material, and began secretly to destroy unsent a substantial proportion, arbitrarily selected. Thus, while it is known what information Sorge claimed to have passed on to the Fourth Department, it is unclear what actually reached them in 1941: Russian releases of some of his material in the 1990s must be treated with caution, because selective. From the end of 1940 onwards, Sorge was personally convinced that Germany and the Soviet Union would go to war. He was deeply troubled by the prospect, and by its implications for himself. During the early months of 1941 he reported an increasing Japanese focus on a 'Strike south' strategy against the European Asian empires. On 10 March he wrote of German pressure on Japan 'to invigorate her role in the Tripartite Pact' by attacking the Soviet Union. But Sorge added that this war would only start 'once the present one is over'.

In May he asserted that Hitler was resolved 'to crush the Soviet Union and keep the European parts ... in his hands', but suggested that there was still scope for diplomacy to prevent war. Later that month he said that his German contacts expected an invasion to be launched before June, but then added that some important visitors from Berlin believed that the prospect of such action taking place in 1941 had receded. Both these signals probably reflected Sorge's conversations with Lt. Col. Schol, a Wehrmacht officer passing through Tokyo en route to taking up the post of military attaché in Bangkok. On 30 May he wirelessed: 'Berlin has informed Ambassador Ott that the German offensive against the USSR will begin in the second half of June. Ott is 95 per cent sure that the war will begin. The indirect proofs that I see at the present are as follows: The Luftwaffe technical delegation in [Tokyo] has been ordered home. Ott has requested the military attaché to halt the transmission of important documents via the USSR. The shipment of rubber via the USSR has been reduced to a minimum.'

Sorge's reports were as good as any government at any moment in history could ask from a secret agent, but he was one among many voices that cried in the wilderness surrounding the Kremlin. Stalin was no more willing to trust the word of his Tokyo man than that of any other source. He once described Sorge, about whom he had been briefed, as 'a lying shit who has set himself up with some small factories and brothels in Japan'. Although the Soviet warlord was notoriously wrong about 'Barbarossa', few national leaders have lost empires by declining to accept the unsupported word of secret agents. Historians carve spies' coups in letters of gold, but seldom detail the vastly larger volume of humint that has been partially or wholly misleading. Molotov said in old age: 'I think that one can never trust the intelligence ... The intelligence people can lead to dangerous situations that it is impossible to get out of. There were endless provocateurs on both sides ... People are so naïve and gullible, indulging themselves and quoting memoirs: spies said so and so, defectors crossed the lines ...' Stalin would have been more likely to believe Sorge had the spy reported that the Germans' posturings formed part of a plot concocted by the faraway British.

3 THE ORCHESTRA PLAYS

The most authoritative intelligence sent to Moscow in advance of 'Barbarossa' came from the Russians' Berlin networks. What became known as the *Rote Kapelle* – the Red Orchestra – was not a single entity, though supposed to be such by the Germans. It was a cluster of separate GRU and NKVD networks, which only careless tradecraft and operational emergencies caused to become entwined. The *Rote Kapelle* was less important for its impact on the war, which proved slight, than for the fact of its existence. The Western Allies secured extraordinary military intelligence through Ultra, but never had humint sources of any significance inside Germany – unless we include a product of Purple, described later – until some members of the anti-Hitler Resistance contacted Allen Dulles of the OSS in 1943. The Russians, by contrast, controlled a shaft to a goldmine.

The Harnack/Schulze-Boysen network supplied Moscow with information from an ever-widening circle hostile to the Nazi regime. Although they themselves were people of the left, they appear to have forged links with some conservative Resistance figures such as Dietrich Bonhöffer, and also to have had contact with the White Rose group in Munich. Given the number of informants involved, and their reckless insouciance about security, the group's survival until 1942 was a reflection of Abwehr and Gestapo blindness rather than of the *Rote Kapelle*'s guile. Arvid Harnack was so passionate in his commitment to the cause that he involved his group in printing anti-Nazi pamphlets and even acted personally as a watcher while other group members pasted wall posters by night. Such grandstanding was courageous, but endangered his much more important intelligence work.

Throughout the first twenty-two months of the war, while the British strove to pierce the fog obscuring their view of the Continent, the Russians were able to continue spying almost unimpeded. As neutrals, in semi-alliance with Hitler, they channelled to Moscow through their diplomatic missions agent reports from all over the world, without need for using hazardous wireless links. In Berlin, the Gestapo's Willy Lehmann had languished since Moscow shut down contact to him in the wake of the 1939 Nazi–Soviet Pact. Lehmann was a loner, and his self-purpose had come to revolve around his intelligence activities for the Russians.

Why had they abandoned him? In September 1940, season of the Battle of Britain, he risked slipping a letter into the Soviet embassy mailbox, addressed to 'the military attaché or his deputy'. In it, 'Breitenbach' pleaded for a resumption of relations. He said that unless he could serve the NKVD once more, 'my work at the Gestapo will become pointless', and provided a password for telephone contact.

This letter, and the question of whether to reactivate Lehmann, were referred to Moscow. Draconian instructions from the Kremlin decreed that the Berlin NKVD should neither offer nor respond to any provocation that might help to justify German aggression. Nonetheless, after a debate Centre dispatched an able young officer, Alexander Korotkov, codename 'Stepanov', to become deputy station chief. He contacted Lehmann, and reported back after a long meeting: the man seemed sincerely desperate to reopen his line to Centre. On 9 September 1940, a personal order from Beria reached Berlin: 'No special assignments should be given to "Breitenbach". [But] you should accept all material that falls within his direct sphere of knowledge, and also any information he can offer about the operations of various [German] intelligence services against the USSR.' 'Breitenbach's' extravagant enthusiasm kept alive Beria's suspicion that he was a Gestapo plant, testing the sincerity of the Kremlin's commitment to the Nazi–Soviet Pact. Hence the security chief emphasised that the Berlin informant should be pressed to provide documentary evidence for every assertion he made. So impoverished was the NKVD's staff in the wake of the Purges that a complete novice was dispatched to act as Lehmann's courier: Boris Zhuravlev scarcely spoke any German, and after arriving in Berlin his first step was to hire a language tutor. The young man also bought a bicycle, in order to start learning his way around the city. From the outset he was almost overwhelmed by the flow of documents Lehmann delivered at evening meetings, which had to be copied overnight, then returned before the informant set off for his office.

Meanwhile Alexander Korotkov was also charged by Moscow to reopen contact with the Harnack/Schulze-Boysen groups. To achieve this, in mid-September he risked repeatedly calling on Harnack at his home. On several occasions he was informed by a housekeeper that Herr Harnack was out. Only on the 16th did Korotkov at last meet his man. Their interview was initially tense, for Harnack was wary. When at last he was convinced of his visitor's *bona fides* – if that is not a contradictory term for an NKVD officer – he had plenty to say about his own range of contacts. Most significantly, he told the Russian that he and his friends were convinced that Hitler intended to invade the Soviet Union in the following year, 1941. Back at the embassy, Korotkov messaged Lt. Gen. Pavel Fitin, head of the foreign section of the NKVD in Moscow, under the signature of his nominal boss, Amayak Kobulov, 'Zakhar':

> Top secret
> To comrade Viktor
> 'Corporal' has learned from 'Albanian' who has spoken to a top
> Wehrmacht officer, that Germany intends to initiate a war against the
> Soviet Union early next year …
> 16 September 1940
> Zakhar

Yet Moscow had reason to be sceptical about these sensational tidings. History shows that they were correct, but on 16 September 1940 Hitler had not yet committed himself. An invasion of Russia was being feverishly debated by prominent Nazis and the army high command. But Operation 'Barbarossa' remained a controversial option rather than a settled decision. The fact that Arvid Harnack's prediction was ultimately fulfilled does not alter the important fact that it remained speculative at a moment when he asserted its finality, as did the earlier report of the 'Lucy' Ring's Alexander Radó. Only in November did Hitler decide.

The affairs of the Berlin NKVD were much complicated by the fact that Korotkov, their best man, was hated and resented by his station chief. The Czech František Moravec, who had extensive dealings with the Russians before the war, has testified to the brutish personalities of most of their intelligence officers. One such, Amayak Kobulov, now ran the NKVD's Berlin station, where he proved a blunderer more inept than MI6's Best and Stevens. Kobulov's only claim on rank was a slavish devotion to the Party hierarchy. Born into a family of Armenian small traders in Tbilisi, he worked as a bookkeeper before joining the security forces in 1927. He owed his survival, and indeed rapid advancement, to his elder brother Bogdan, an intimate of Beria. Kobulov served as a notoriously murderous deputy commissar for Ukraine, and was then appointed to Berlin despite not speaking a word of German. On arrival, he told his staff that he required their absolute subservience. When a young intelligence officer protested about being obliged to serve as the chief's domestic valet rather than to run agents, his boss threatened to dispatch him to rot in the dungeons of the Lubyanka.

Kobulov also took violent exception to Korotkov, and seized an excuse to return him to Moscow with a highly adverse personal report. Beria, receiving this, summarily sacked the young officer in January 1941. He soon retracted this decision, but for some months Korotkov was confined to desk work in the Lubyanka. Meanwhile Kobulov arranged a personal meeting with Harnack. This encounter went unnoticed by the Gestapo, but could easily have been fatal to the network. At the turn of the year, Centre acknowledged that only Korotkov was competent to handle liaison with its Berlin informants. He was sent back to Germany, with a new brief to pass on to Harnack. The NKVD wanted the German informant's group to concentrate on economics, not strategy. The NKVD Fifth Department's orders instructed Korotkov to explore the extent of the German domestic opposition, and how far it might be exploited. Nothing was said about probing Germany's military intentions towards the Soviet Union – from residual caution lest Harnack prove a Gestapo plant, or find himself under torture.

The order was endorsed in red pencil: 'Approved by the People's Commissar. [Pavel] Sudoplatov. 26.12.40.' Korotkov counter-signed the last page: 'Read, learned and received as an order. "Stepanov", 26.12.40.' He duly passed on the message to the Berlin group, bypassing Kobulov, his nominal chief. Through the months that followed, the Germans delivered a steady flow of intelligence. On 29 January 1941, Harnack reported that the Economics Ministry had been ordered to compile industrial targeting maps of the USSR, similar to those which had been made before the Blitz on Britain. He told Moscow that the head of the Russian Department in Berlin's Bureau for Foreign Literary Exchanges had been warned for possible duty as a military translator and interpreter; and that the Russian Department of the Economics Ministry was complaining bitterly about shortfalls in promised deliveries of commodities from the USSR, under the terms of the Nazi–Soviet Pact.

Harnack provided an ongoing stream of evidence to show that Hitler was preparing to invade Russia. He also provided copious details on Germany's economic situation – coal, iron and steel production; synthetic rubber consumption; industrial manpower difficulties, together with German plans to make these good by recruiting workers from occupied Europe – information MI6 would have given rubies to access. Harnack concluded, in terms that weakened his credibility in Moscow, by reverting to gossip: 'According to Hitler's circle, he is now in a very unbalanced state, suddenly runs to watch a film during the night, or – as has happened more than once, tore down the curtains in a fit of fury.' The NKVD's Berlin station reported to Moscow on 26 February 1941:

> Top Secret
> To Comrade Viktor
> According to information that Harnack obtained from Ernst von Arnim, [Dr Karl] Gördeler's [anti-Hitler opposition] group has made an attempt to achieve an agreement with the army leadership to form a new German government ... The negotiations had a negative result due to the negative reaction from the military leadership. However, according to Ernst, some top generals sympathise with Gördeler's plan ...
> Zakhar

The Berlin station was not alone in dispatching warnings to Moscow about the invasion threat: on 7 February 1941 the NKVD's Third Department cited its source 'Teffi' in Ankara as discussing 'rumours about a possible German offensive against the USSR. According to one version this will only happen after the Germans defeat England. According to another version, which is regarded as more probable, Germany will attack the USSR before striking at England in order to secure its supplies.' Next day came another report from Harnack, declaring a widespread belief at OKW headquarters that full German occupation of Romania would become a preliminary to an invasion of the USSR. This was followed by a further message early in March, claiming that the worsening food situation in Germany was intensifying the pressure on the Nazi leadership to attack Russia. Col. Gen. Franz Halder, said the Berlin informants, was planning a lightning strike similar to the 1940 French campaign to occupy Ukraine, before the Wehrmacht drove south to seize Stalin's oilfields. Harnack also described concerns in high places that Germany, instead of profiting economically from invading Russia, would find such a war draining. In another report a few days later, he described intensive Luftwaffe aerial reconnaissance activity over Russia, and operational planning for an offensive that would reach the Urals in forty-five days.

Merkulov, Beria's deputy, read the 11 March report from Berlin. Like all Soviet officials who wished to survive, he was supremely cautious. Born in 1895, he had worked with Beria in the trans-Caucasian region, and rose yapping at his heels through the Soviet hierarchy; his most recent triumph had been to preside over the massacre of 25,000 Polish officers at Katyn.

Now, he demanded of Fitin, 'Aren't there other sources on this except Harnack? How can we check the information without letting any informants know what it is? The task should be presented to them in a general and cautious form.' The March reports from Harnack were correct, though Moscow Centre also received plenty of nonsense. 'Breitenbach' reported that the British were preparing to unleash chemical warfare against Germany, and that the Germans intended to use poison gas on the Russians in the event of war. Schulze-Boysen claimed that he 'knows for sure' that the American air force attaché in Moscow 'is a German agent. He passes to the Germans the intelligence data which he, in turn, receives from his contacts in the USSR.'

On 15 March Centre increased the risk level for its Berlin informants by ordering Korotkov to establish a direct link with Schulze-Boysen, cutting out couriers, so as to hasten evaluation of his reports. Their first meeting took place in Harnack's flat, where Schulze-Boysen gave the Russian a momentary fright by turning up in his Luftwaffe uniform. 'I didn't have time to change,' he explained. Korotkov reported to Moscow: 'We talked exclusively about the information on anti-Soviet plans that was available to him. He is absolutely conscious of the fact that he is dealing with a representative of the Soviet Union [as distinct from the Comintern]. My impression is that he is happy to tell us everything he knows. He answered our questions without equivocation or any attempt to obfuscate. Moreover, it was obvious that he had prepared for this meeting, by writing down some questions for us on a scrap of paper … We hope to establish a close connection with Schulze-Boysen. However, at present he is confined to barracks and is only occasionally and unpredictably free to travel into town, often while it is still light and even in his uniform, as happened when I met him. Any rendezvous must be flexible.'

On the evening of 19 April, in Harnack's flat Korotkov met Adam Kuckhoff, a writer and theatre director, who was promptly recruited with the codename 'Old Man'. Korotkov messaged Moscow about him in frankly condescending terms: 'Kuckhoff strikes one as a cultured and educated man whose views have been influenced by reading the works of Lenin. He still keeps some of Lenin's works and thinks himself a communist.' In Moscow the Comintern checked its files on Kuckhoff and endorsed his credentials. They told Korotkov that 'Old Man' 'was deeply affected by the general crisis of the bourgeois culture and became close to the "union of Intellectuals"'. The writer now became a prominent member of the Harnack group.

The insistent theme of all the reporting to Moscow was that of looming Nazi onslaught. On 8 May 1941 'Zakhar' reported: 'rumours about Germany's attack on the Soviet Union are constantly increasing … War is going to be declared in mid-May.' A.S. Panyushkin, who unusually combined the role of Soviet ambassador to the Chinese government in Chongqing with that of NKVD station chief, reported to Moscow early in May that Hitler was expected to invade. The Chinese military attaché in Berlin even told the Russians of the Germans' intended axes of advance.

The NKVD team in Berlin was fortunate to escape disaster, living through this uniquely sensitive period in Russo–German relations with an oaf as its station chief. Kobulov's fall from grace began with a drunken row at a May 1941 embassy banquet for a visiting Soviet delegation: he publicly slapped the face of the deputy trade representative. This episode prompted the ambassador to demand the NKVD officer's recall. Kobulov counterattacked by asking Beria to bring him home; he claimed to dislike the feuding inside the embassy as much as the British bombing of Berlin. Beria felt obliged to report the banquet episode to Stalin and Molotov, but rejected the demand for his man's recall in return for Kobulov's maudlin promise of future good behaviour; he was ordered by Moscow to risk no further personal contact with Harnack.

The NKVD man attempted to redeem himself as a spymaster by recruiting as an informant a Latvian journalist codenamed 'Lycée student', who, he assured Moscow, was 'most reliable'. This man, Oreste Berlings, was already on the Gestapo's books as agent 'Peter', a double of whom Ribbentrop said complacently, 'We can pump whatever information we want into him.' This foolishness would have been trivial had it not taken place in the last weeks before the Germans launched 'Barbarossa', when intelligence from Berlin should have been of critical importance to Soviet decision-making. Kobulov's blundering contributed to the Kremlin's stubborn scepticism about NKVD reporting.

On 18 April 1941, heedless of Stalin's insistence that no clash with Germany was imminent, Russia's intelligence services formally shifted to a war footing: the GRU and NKVD warned their networks across Europe, and strengthened their stations in Switzerland and Berlin. But they did little to improve the management of informants in the field, chiefly because experienced handlers were in such short supply. Even more serious, they failed to provide agents with means of long-range communications. Russian-built wirelesses were of poor quality: NKVD communications improved only later in the war, when the Lubyanka secured American sets.

In the protracted meanwhile, contact between Moscow and its overseas agents remained precarious. On 1 May 1941 the Berlin station urgently requested transmitters for the Harnack group, in case contact through the embassy was lost. Harnack himself was reluctant to accept such equipment; he said that while he knew nothing about wireless, he was acutely conscious of the ubiquity of the Abwehr's and Gestapo's direction-finders. Eventually, however, he acquiesced in a step which merely reflected the logic of his convictions: that war was imminent, and he wished to continue to work against Hitler. After several weeks' delay, in mid-June his handlers presented him with two sets. The first was a portable D-6, with a range not much over five hundred miles and batteries with two hours' life. The NKVD man promised more batteries, but these were never forthcoming. The second set was a little more powerful, but required mains electricity.

Korotkov explained that coding procedure was easy: the spies needed only remember the number 38745 and the keyword 'Schraube'. He urged Harnack to make Karl Behrens his second wireless-operator, but the German baulked. This was a hugely risky assignment, he pointed out, and Behrens had three small children. He would never forgive himself if the man was caught, and paid the price. Behrens was anyway under Gestapo surveillance, having provided false papers for a Jewish brother-in-law. A second possible candidate, Kurt Schumacher, was called up for military duty. Eventually the second wireless set was placed in the hands of a man named Hans Koppi, suggested by Schulze-Boysen. Within weeks, however, Hitler had launched 'Barbarossa' and his hosts had swept across Russia, driving the Soviets many miles back, beyond reach of Berlin's feeble signals. The sets given to Harnack fell silent. He continued industriously to gather intelligence, but lacked means to pass it on. This impasse persisted through the first five months of the Eastern war.

Meanwhile Willy Lehmann's material also began to include evidence of Germany's commitment to war with Russia. On 28 May he told his handler that he had been ordered for undisclosed reasons to organise a twenty-four-hour duty roster for his section. A few days later his health collapsed, and he was obliged to take sick leave, from which he returned only on 19 June. What he then learned in his office caused him to discard tradecraft and call an immediate meeting with Zhuravlev, his courier: the Gestapo had been formally informed of an order to initiate military operations against the Soviet Union. This report was immediately forwarded to Moscow, but it seems unlikely that Beria showed it to Stalin until the last hours before the German invasion.

Another significant NKVD German source was Captain Walter Maria Stennes, once an enthusiastic Nazi stormtrooper and friend of Hitler. Stennes – 'Friend' in Moscow Centre's books – had since experienced a dramatic change of heart, becoming an ardent foe of the regime. Having survived a brief term of imprisonment, he departed for China where he became Chiang Kai-shek's air adviser and was recruited by the Russians. On 9 June 1941, following a conversation with a high-ranking Wehrmacht visitor, he informed Vasily Zarubin that the invasion had been planned for May, then postponed, and that a three-month campaign was now sched-uled to start on 20 June. Zarubin also told Moscow that Stennes had met Sorge in Shanghai, who had heard the same story.

Schulze-Boysen wrote to his NKVD bosses on 11 June, warning the Russians to 'prepare for a surprise attack'. He urged Moscow to bomb the Romanian oilfields and rail junctions at Königsberg, Stettin and Berlin, as well as to launch a thrust into Hungary, to cut off Germany from the Balkans. This was an extraordinary step for a German officer to take, even one as disaffected from his own government as Schulze-Boysen – explic-itly to urge a foreign power to bomb his own country. But to such a pass had matters come. In all, between September 1940 and June 1941, Harnack and Schulze-Boysen provided forty-two reports which remain extant – and perhaps more which have been lost or never reached Moscow – offer-ing ever more circumstantial detail about Hitler's preparations and operational planning. Moreover, on 20 June a Rome source informed Centre that the Italian ambassador in Berlin had sent his Foreign Ministry a coded telegram reporting that the German invasion of the Soviet Union would start between 20 and 25 June.

4 THE DEAF MAN IN THE KREMLIN

Thus, from early 1941 onwards a flood of intelligence reached Moscow, conveying a common message: Hitler was on the brink, though there were many divergences of opinion about when he would attack – unsurprising, since the Wehrmacht's timetable was repeatedly pushed back by opera-tional delays. In those days, however, the Soviet Union was better protected against its own people than against foreign foes. Russia's intelligence chiefs were preoccupied with enemies within. There were fears about rising Ukrainian nationalism. Beria reported subversive activity by Jewish and Zionist organisations – he advanced the implausible claim that these were acting on behalf of the Nazis. Merkulov described successful purges of 'anti-Soviet elements' in the Baltic republics, with 14,467 people arrested and 25,711 exiled to Siberia.

The man chiefly responsible for analysing incoming intelligence was Lt. Gen. Pavel Fitin, who had headed the foreign section of the NKVD since 1939, when he ascended to office in the wake of the Purges. He was an unlikely appointment, selected for political reliability. A former Komsomol leader and Party official, he had studied at Moscow's agricultural mechanisation school before working for some years at a farming advice service. Only then was he selected to attend SHON, the foreign intelligence training school established at Balashikha, fifteen miles east of Moscow. Students – 120 in the first three years, just four of them women – were perfunctorily introduced to bourgeois Western living: teachers with European experience lectured them on dress, manners, 'good taste'. Trainees spent four hours a day studying languages, two on intelligence tradecraft. Fitin was already thirty-nine in 1938, when he started work at the NKVD. A visiting American, gazing at his long fair hair and blue eyes which conveyed an illusion of innocence, suggested that he looked more like a cruise director than a spymaster. Although no fool, Fitin would never present to his superiors Merkulov, Beria and beyond them Stalin anything likely to incur their anger. When in mid-June 1941 an NKVD agent in Helsinki reported large-scale Finnish troop movements, a nervous Fitin scribbled to his deputy, 'Please process carefully for *Hozyain*' – 'the Master', as Stalin was always described.

The last link in the foreign intelligence chain before 'Barbarossa' was Winston Churchill. British perceptions of the Soviet Union, and of the potential of the Red Army, were coloured by the loathing of most soldiers, diplomats and Tory politicians for everything to do with the bloodstained Bolsheviks. Moreover, their expectations of German strategy were distorted by a nationalistic conviction that Hitler saw victory over Britain as his foremost objective. When Sir Victor Mallet, Britain's ambassador in Stockholm, reported in March that 'all military circles in Berlin are convinced of conflict with Russia this spring and consider success certain', the Foreign Office dismissed his dispatch as reflecting 'the usual contradictory rumours'. On 24 March 1941, Stafford Cripps cabled from Moscow, reporting his Swedish counterpart's information: 'German plan is as follows: the attack on England will be continued with U-boats and from the air, but there will be no invasion. At the same time a drive against

СОВ СЕКРЕТНО
ВЕСЬМА СРОЧНО
ЛИЧНО.

1 УПРАВЛЕНИЕ
ОТД. "А"
25 июня   41
2/А/12577

ЗАМ НАЧ 5 УПРАВЛЕНИЯ НКО СССР
ГЕНЕРАЛ-МАЙОРУ

товарищу ПАНФИЛОВУ

Прошу Вашего распоряжения установить
связь с нашей нелегальной радиостанцией, на-
ходящейся в *Берлине* (наш шифр этой
станции (" Д-5 ").

Пунктом связи желательно иметь город
Минск

Все материалы по радиообмену, которые
будут приняты от этой рации прошу пересылат
нам.-

коп. Козликов
отд. - отд. "А"

НАЧАЛЬНИК 1 УПРАВЛЕНИЯ НКГБ СССР
СТ МАЙОР ГОСБЕЗОПАСНОСТИ

(ФИТИН)

Memorandum from Pavel Fitin, head of the foreign section of
the NKVD, concerning radio contact with Soviet spies in
Berlin

Russia will take place. This drive will be by three large armies: the first based at Warsaw under von Bock, the second based at Konigsberg, the third based at Cracow under List.'

The Joint Intelligence Committee rejected this warning. In early April the JIC's assessment was not dissimilar from that of Stalin: '1. These reports may be put out by Germans as part of the war of nerves 2. German invasion would probably result in such chaos throughout Soviet Union that the Germans would have to reorganise everything in the occupied territory and would meanwhile lose supplies which they are now drawing from the Soviet Union at any rate for a long time to come 3. Germany's resources, though immense, would not permit her to continue her campaign in the Balkans, to maintain the present scale of air attack against this country, to continue her offensive against Egypt, and at the same time to invade, occupy and reorganise a large part of the Soviet Union ... 5. There have been indications that German General Staff are opposed to war on two fronts and in favour of disposing of Great Britain before attacking Soviet Union.'

Here was a manifestation of the foremost sin in intelligence analysis: the JIC reached conclusions founded upon British and not Nazi logic. The prime minister, however, had long nursed a hunch that Hitler would turn East. On 21 April he dispatched a personal warning to Stalin, inspired by Cripps's message and some Ultra indications. This was received with derision. Maisky, the Soviet ambassador, taunted Brendan Bracken: 'Since when does Churchill tend to take the interests of the Soviet Union so closely to his heart?' He told Bracken, Churchill's intimate, that such missives from London had entirely the opposite effect to that which was intended. He did not add a vital corollary: that Whitehall's traitors had briefed the Kremlin about the JIC's disbelief that Hitler would invade. As late as 23 May, the Committee reported that a new agreement between Germany and Russia might be imminent. Foolish though such speculation sounds today, it was then less than two years since just such a satanic pact had been signed. If the two tyrants had struck a bargain before, why should they not do so again? Nor was Moscow the only place where Churchill's sincerity was questioned. Bjorn Prytz, the Swedish ambassador in London, told Maisky he thought Britain's prime minister had no idea how to win the war, save by trying to drag the Russians in. Cripps told the American ambassador in Moscow that he could well imagine the British acquiescing in a German invasion of Russia, if Hitler made a compromise peace offer to Britain.

When informed and influential foreigners clung to such opinions, Stalin's cynicism about war warnings from Churchill, whom he knew to be defying the views of his own advisers, becomes less baffling. In April, *Hozyain* ordered the Red Army and the intelligence services to ignore both alleged German military preparations beyond the border, and repeated Luftwaffe violations of Soviet airspace. At the end of the month Merkulov submitted a report designed to silence the 'warmongers' and talk up prospects for a diplomatic rapprochement with Berlin. He said that German successes in North Africa had encouraged Hitler to finish off Britain before opening any new front. Much was made of the dissension between Hitler and his generals, which was real enough. The NKVD also suggested – a travesty of the truth – that the Luftwaffe was unwilling to fight Russia because of the Red Air Force's recognised superiority. Stalin briefed his intelligence chiefs that their first objective was now diplomatic: to clarify Hitler's demands – the price he would seek to extract from Moscow for keeping the peace. They responded that Berlin was likely to want an increased flow of grain, oil and other commodities. Von der Schulenberg's diplomacy played its part in feeding Stalin's delusions: as late as mid-May, the German ambassador urged the Soviet dictator to write to Hitler, exploring common ground. Meanwhile Russia's Neutrality Pact with Japan, signed on 13 April 1941, represented a sincere and desperate Soviet attempt to avert war between the two countries, and thus to reduce the range of threats facing the Soviet Union. When foreign minister Yōsuke Matsuoka left Moscow bearing the signed treaty, in an almost unprecedented gesture Stalin went to the station to see him off.

Soviet embassies and intelligence stations adhered rigidly to orders from Molotov and Beria to report nothing which suggested the inevitability of war. On 24 May, when the Finnish ambassador in Istanbul gave his Soviet counterpart details of German formations deployed on the Soviet border, Stalin's man asked contemptuously whether the Finn had counted the soldiers himself. A week later, Timoshenko and Zhukov were summoned to the Kremlin, and arrived expecting orders to put Soviet defences on full alert. Instead they were handed Stalin's acceptance of a transparently fraudulent request from Berlin that squads of Germans should be allowed to roam inside Russia's border in search of 1914–18 war dead. The generals were obliged to fume in impotence while Hitler's scouts surveyed their chosen battlefields, protected by spades and *Hozyain*'s orders.

The British government's clumsy handling of the 10 May parachute descent on Scotland by Deputy Führer Rudolf Hess converted what should have been a propaganda disaster for Hitler – one of his most intimate associates' demented solo attempt to parley with the British – into a major embarrassment for his enemy. It persuaded Stalin that both the Germans and the British were toying with him, while preparing to make a separate peace with each other. Lord Beaverbrook, a supreme mischief-maker whose interventions were all the more damaging because he was a known intimate of Churchill, told Maisky in London, 'Of course Hess is an emissary of Hitler.' The press lord claimed, rightly enough, that Hess sought to promote a common front against Bolshevik barbarism. Maisky deduced that Britain's future conduct depended not – as he had hitherto supposed – on Churchillian resolution, but instead on the acceptability of the German terms he assumed Hess to have brought with him from Hitler.

In the late spring of 1941 Stalin daily expected to receive details of an Anglo–German compromise peace, followed by a demand from Berlin that Russia should join the Axis and accelerate its economic support for Germany. As late as October 1942 Stalin wrote to Maisky: 'All of us in Moscow have gained the impression that Churchill is aiming at the defeat of the USSR, in order then to come to terms with the Germany of Hitler or Bruning at the expense of our country.' With breathtaking hypocrisy, he chose to forget that in the mood of panic that overtook the Kremlin after 'Barbarossa' began, the NKVD's Pavel Sudoplatov had been ordered to pass to the Bulgarian ambassador, for forwarding to Berlin, a secret Kremlin message inviting a compromise Russo–German peace. Only because Hitler was uninterested did that approach go nowhere. At an October 1944 dinner in the Kremlin Stalin could still offer a mocking but at least semi-serious toast to 'the British intelligence service which had inveigled Hess into coming to England'.

In June 1941 the NKVD dragged from a cell in the Lubyanka Captain Aleksandr Nelidov, an erstwhile Abwehr man in Warsaw, to invite his opinion of Hess's flight to Britain. The old soldier responded immediately: 'This means war, without any doubt. Hess is recruiting England as an ally against the USSR ...' Nelidov, born in 1893, was a former tsarist gunner officer who had roamed Turkey, France and Germany following the White Army's defeat in Russia's civil war. He struck up friendships in the German general staff, and attended several of their 1930s war games. Early in 1939 he was foolish enough to accept from Canaris an assignment to Warsaw, where he was promptly seized by the Poles. When the Russians overran eastern Poland and found him languishing in Lvov prison, as a known Nazi intelligence agent he was dispatched to Moscow.

By the time Zoya Rybkina, the tall, strikingly attractive senior operations officer of the German section of the NKVD, was handed his file in mid-1940, Nelidov was a broken man. Rybkina wrote contemptuously in her 1998 memoirs: 'His behaviour was servile ... I felt amused by him but also ashamed of him, as an officer of the old school.' The wretched captain was repeatedly summoned from his cell to be quizzed about the Wehrmacht through the day and far into the night: 'His lunch was brought from our canteen, and when he saw a knife and fork for the first time, he pushed them away and said in terrorised tones: "But I am not supposed to have these."'

Rybkina set Nelidov to work composing a narrative of the German war games he had attended, complete with maps and order-of-battle details. He told the NKVD officer that the German plan for invading Russia assumed that Minsk would fall on the fifth day. Rybkina wrote: 'I burst out laughing. "How come, on the fifth day?!" He was embarrassed and swore by every god that this was what [Gen. Wilhelm] Keitel [chief of OKW] reckoned on.' She passed on the joke to Fitin, who snarled, 'This bastard is such a liar. Just think about it, Minsk on the fifth day!' Golikov, the Red Army's chief of intelligence, laughed even louder: 'So they have decided to drive wedges forward. And imagine – they plan to take Minsk on the fifth day! Well done, Keitel, you are a strong man, such a strong man! ...' But Nelidov also told his jailers that Gen. Hans von Seekt, the hoary old former army chief of staff, predicted disaster for a German invasion of the Soviet Union, because the logistics were unsustainable.

Doubts persist, unlikely ever to be resolved, as to what precisely the Red Army knew before 'Barbarossa'. Marshal Zhukov insisted to the end of his days that he was kept in ignorance of much of the foreign intelligence that went to the Kremlin. If the Germans invaded, he himself expected them to drive south-westwards to secure Ukraine and its immense natural resources, though he thought possible an alternative attack on an axis Riga–Dvinsk. Soviet military attachés, especially those in the Balkans, provided detailed and broadly accurate information about German deployments. Russian frontier-watchers contributed substantially more than the NKVD's or GRU's foreign agents to the Stavka's – armed forces high command – grasp of the Wehrmacht's order of battle. By April Zhukov realised the importance of the central front in German planning – large forces were concentrated in East Prussia and Poland. But conflicting evidence reflected continuing arguments between Hitler and his generals.

It is often stated that the Red Army was wholly surprised when the Germans attacked. This is less than true. In the weeks before war, despite Stalin's scepticism he allowed large forces to be redeployed in the West and brought to a relatively high state of readiness. The disasters subsequently suffered by the Russians were overwhelmingly attributable to the rotten condition of the armed forces and their leadership, rather than to lack of immediate preparedness. Stalin deserves most of the blame for what befell the Soviet Union in 1941, but surprise was the least of the reasons for catastrophe. The Red Army was outfought by the Wehrmacht at every level, save that some of its units displayed an animal sacrificial courage that astonished their foes. Before the invasion, on 12 May Zhukov had moved into forward positions four Soviet armies, 800,000 men. On 2 June Beria told Stalin that the Germans were at a high state of readiness along the entire border. On the 12th a further report on German deployments went to Stalin, noting a high level of hostile intelligence activity: the Wehrmacht had some two hundred 'line-crossers' scouting in the Soviet border region. In response, Stalin grudgingly agreed that war readiness should be reduced to two hours for rifle divisions, three for motorised and artillery divisions. This scarcely constituted absolute passivity in the face of the threat.

Both the Russians and the British were naïve enough to expect an ultimatum to precede hostilities. On 11 June, Sir Stafford Cripps returned home 'for consultations'. The purpose of his recall was exactly as stated – to enable the British government to discuss with him the bewildering and momentous developments that were unfolding. London was dismayed by a German propaganda campaign, designed to persuade the world that a new Russo–German rapprochement was imminent. The Kremlin was shocked by Cripps's journey, for the opposite reason: Stalin assumed that the British were preparing some byzantine diplomatic stroke, which would leave the Soviet Union isolated. On 16 June Maisky was summoned to Britain's Foreign Office and given a cool recital of its latest intelligence on German deployments, based on Ultra. The Wehrmacht was thought to have eighty divisions in Poland, thirty in Romania, five in Finland and north Norway, 115 in all. This was little more than half the reality, substantially fewer than the GRU had already identified. It was a reflection of the limitations of Ultra in 1941, and of the War Office's poor analytical capability at this stage, that they got the numbers so badly wrong. But even former sceptics on the JIC no longer doubted the overarching reality: Hitler was about to invade the Soviet Union.

In Moscow, the NKVD adopted a desperate last-minute ploy: its operatives intercepted two German diplomatic couriers, about to leave Moscow
for Berlin with the German embassy's dispatches. One man was trapped
in a hotel lift, while the other was locked in the bathroom of his suite. In
the five minutes before the lift-bound courier was freed, the NKVD photographed the German ambassador's correspondence before restoring it to
its briefcase. The contents, when examined in the Lubyanka, proved equivocal: Schulenberg reported that he was confident Soviet intentions
remained peaceful. But he also stated that he had obeyed instructions
from Berlin to reduce his staff to an absolute minimum, an obvious
preliminary to war.

On Cripps's way back from London he stopped in Stockholm, where he
told the director of the Foreign Ministry about rumours of a new Russo–
German agreement. Rubbish, said the Swede. His country's intelligence
service had intercepted orders to German forces in Norway, which made
plain that they would attack between 20 and 25 June. The Swedish ambassador in Moscow, doyen of the diplomatic community, reported: 'The only
certain thing is that we face either a battle of global significance between
the Third Reich and the Soviet Empire or the most gigantic case of blackmail in world history.' Zoya Rybkina, key NKVD analyst of Germany,
described how on 17 June she prepared a situation report for Pavel Fitin
to present to Stalin, based chiefly, but not entirely, on the Red Orchestra's
messages – Sorge, of course, reported to the GRU. She later professed to
have concluded that war was inevitable: 'All of Germany's military preparations for armed aggression are complete, and an attack can be expected
at any time.' In reality, however, the document was more equivocal than its
drafters afterwards tried to claim. To cover themselves, they repeatedly
used such phrases as 'It is not indicated on what data the source has
reached his conclusions … Harnack does not know where, when, or in
what connection Halder had expressed this point of view … Harnack does
not take at face value the statement of Göring, and refers to his notorious
bragging.' Knowing that the Kremlin still stubbornly rejected their own
near-certainty, they felt obliged to assert doubts they did not have.

Merkulov and Fitin went together to the Kremlin at noon on 17 June.
The latter, who had seldom met Stalin, afterwards acknowledged his own
trepidation, which might more justly be called terror. The two grey, bleak,
merciless heroes of so many state killings agreed their line before entering
Hozyain's presence: they would describe their own intelligence assessment
as merely 'likely to be true', rather than certain. They found Stalin calm,

pacing the room as was his custom. Fitin saw the most recent decrypt from Berlin lying on his desk. 'I have read your report,' murmured Stalin in his accustomed slow, understated fashion. 'So Germany is getting ready to attack the Soviet Union?' And he stared at both Fitin and Merkulov.

They had not been expecting him to address the issue so baldly, and felt lost. 'We were silent,' recalled Fitin. 'Only three days before, on 14 June, newspapers had published the TASS statement saying that Germany was still unwaveringly adhering to the conditions of the Soviet-German pact.' Both he and Merkulov preserved the stone-faced silence that seemed to offer their most plausible path to survival. Stalin fired a string of contemptuous questions about the NKVD's sources. Fitin described the Schulze-Boysen/Harnack networks, then Stalin said: 'Listen, intelligence chief, there are no Germans that can be trusted, except Wilhelm Pieck' – the Comintern's secretary, now exiled in Moscow. Then followed a silence that seemed to the visitors interminable before Stalin once more looked up, gazed hard at them and barked, 'Misinformation! You may go.' In another version of the conversation, he instructed the intelligence chiefs to go back to the sources, check their information and once more review the NKVD assessment. What is certain is that Stalin rejected the war warning.

Rybkina wrote later: 'It is hard to describe the state of our team while we awaited Fitin's return from the Kremlin. He called to his office me and [Pavel] Zhuravlev' – the veteran director of the German section, much admired by colleagues. Fitin tossed the stapled document onto the coffee table at which his two subordinates sat. 'I've reported to the Boss,' he said. 'Iosif Vissarionovich studied your report and threw it back at me. "This is bluff!" he said irritably. "Don't start panic. Don't deal with nonsense. You'd better go back and get a clearer picture."' Fitin told the nonplussed intelligence officers: 'Check this one more time and report to me.' Once alone together, Zhuravlev said to Rybkina, with the parade of conviction indispensable to survival in the Soviet universe: 'Stalin can see further from his bell-tower. Apart from our reports he is being briefed by the GRU, ambassadors, trade missions, journalists.' Rybkina professed to agree, but added: 'This means that our agents, who have been tested over years, must be considered untrustworthy.' Zhuravlev shrugged, with authentic Russian fatalism, 'We shall live, we shall see.' Beria, in grovelling anticipation of *Hozyain*'s wishes, ordered that forty NKVD officers who had passed on warnings of war should be 'ground into labour camp dust'. He wrote to Stalin on 21 June: 'I again insist on recalling and punishing our ambassador to Berlin, Dekanozov, who keeps bombarding me with "reports" on

Hitler's alleged preparations to attack the USSR. He has reported that this attack will start tomorrow ... But I and my people, Iosif Vissarionovich, have firmly embedded in our memory your wise conclusion. Hitler is not going to attack us in 1941.'

Much ink has been expended by historians on attempts to determine what proportion of the intelligence garnered by Russia's secret services reached the Kremlin, rather than remaining in the desk drawers of Beria, Merkulov and Fitin. This controversy seems spurious. Beyond doubt, Stalin was provided with overwhelming evidence about the German military build-up on the Soviet border. The Homeric blunder lay in his analysis of its significance. Posterity derides Stalin for rejecting obvious truth. But he merely chose to share the strategic view held by the British, and especially their Joint Intelligence Committee, with the sole exception of Churchill, until the last days before 'Barbarossa'. This seems important in comprehending the tyrant's conduct. Thanks to Whitehall traitors, the Kremlin knew that Bletchley Park had begun to read German wireless traffic on a substantial scale, which increased Stalin's belief in London's omniscience. A perversely exaggerated respect for the skill of Britain's secret services and the guile of its diplomacy thus caused him to accept Whitehall's view of Hitler's intentions in preference to that of his own marvellous networks of spies. He could never believe that Churchill's personal judgement about Hitler's intention to attack Russia was both honestly expressed, and superior to that of Britain's intelligence apparatus – until the JIC changed its mind, thanks to Ultra, just before Hitler struck.

Here was the most remarkable aspect of Kremlin behaviour in advance of the invasion: 'Barbarossa' did not represent a failure by the Soviet intelligence-gathering machine. Few military operations in history have been so comprehensively flagged. There was, instead, simply a historic misjudgement by the head of state. Stalin's deafness during the overture to 'Barbarossa' emphasised the indissolubility of the links between intelligence, diplomacy and governance. Unless all three did their parts, each one was useless.

In the early hours of 22 June 1941, the Lubyanka was almost silent. The NKVD's heads of department customarily went home at 8 p.m., though never without a nod from Beria or Merkulov. Pavel Sudoplatov was among the building's few occupants above cell level when, at 3 a.m., the telephone rang. It was Merkulov, who announced that a German invasion of the Soviet Union had begun. Sudoplatov began hastily calling staff into the building, including his wife Emma, who had abandoned operational work to become an agent trainer. Leonid Eitingon, his deputy, almost invariably cracked a joke or two on arrival in the office; but like every other Russian that fateful morning he found nothing to justify breaching the building's mood of stunned near-paralysis.

The memoirs of Soviet intelligence officers sometimes convey an illusion that life within the Lubyanka was little different from that in Broadway, but glimpses nonetheless break through of the institutionalised terror. The White Russian officer Aleksandr Nelidov, one of those who had predicted 'Barbarossa', was told nothing of its occurrence until on 22 July 1941 he was dragged from his cell into the office of Zoya Rybkina. He grew wide-eyed when he found her sitting behind black-out curtains amid the crump of falling bombs and anti-aircraft fire. 'Zoya Ivanovna!' he exclaimed. 'They are firing real shells. This is war!' She nodded and said, 'Today is exactly a month since it started. And Minsk did fall, not on the fifth day as you said that the Germans predicted, but on the sixth ...' A guard came running, out of breath, to take Nelidov back to his subterranean quarters. The old tsarist said gloomily, 'Farewell, Zoya Ivanovna. You can trust all that I have written here, in this room.' He crossed himself and bowed as he departed, plainly expecting to be shot.

Two days later, however, he was returned to Rybkina's office, abruptly handed a suitcase of clothes to replace his prison rags, and ordered to go into an adjacent room and change into them. The guard returned a few minutes later and reported that Nelidov was sitting sobbing, paralysed by fear. The prisoner kept asking why they needed to dress him so smartly before killing him. Rybkina marched next door and told the wretched man to pull himself together. 'Come on, Aleksandr Sergeevich, how could you let yourself go like this? You need to get a grip. I am taking you to meet my bosses.' They proceeded first to the offices of Pavel Zhuravlev and his deputy Pavel Sudoplatov, then all together presented themselves before Pavel Fitin. The general invited the astounded Nelidov to become an NKVD agent in Turkey, a country he knew well.

Nelidov said with a choked, hysterical giggle, 'But first of all I should be ... executed ...' Fitin responded impatiently, 'I am asking whether you would agree to work in Turkey. Turkey, as you know, is neutral.' Nelidov muttered, 'Whatever you want.' Rybkina stared reproachfully at her ungracious protégé, who simply muttered again and again, 'Whatever you want ...' She took the stupefied man back her office, where he asked why all the chiefs he met were introduced as Pavel; was this a common codename?

No, no, said his new employer irritably, merely a matter of chance. She led him out of the building to a nearby restaurant called the Aragvi, where they sat among tables occupied by Red Army officers, and she recommended the kebab.

Her guest remained too traumatised to eat. When she ordered wine, fearful of being poisoned he begged to be allowed to swap glasses. At last he took a cautious sip, then asked, 'So when are they coming for me?' Rybkina responded wearily, 'Didn't you hear the order for your release being read?' Her guest persisted: 'I don't understand. How can I be forgiven?' After lunch she suggested that she show him around a nearby agricultural exhibition, and they drove down Gorky Street, where every shop window was sandbagged and the traffic policemen carried gas masks. She left her man that evening at the Moskva hotel, telling him that Vasily Zarubin had been appointed as his case officer.

Rybkina's narrative of these events is shot through with merciless contempt for the weakness of Nelidov. For all her striking looks, she was not a woman to whom any prudent man would offer his back, far less his lips. Nelidov never went to Turkey. When Zarubin knocked on his door next morning, it remained unopened. On breaking in, he found his new recruit suspended from a rope made of torn sheets. The transition from doomed prisoner to favoured protégé of the Lubyanka was too much for his broken spirit. Who can say that Nelidov's last decision was ill-judged?

5

Divine Winds

1 MRS FERGUSON'S TEA SET

The Japanese made less effective use of intelligence than any other warring nation between 1942 and 1945. But in the months before they went to war, their decisions were significantly influenced by an extraordinary British indiscretion. It would be an exaggeration to say that Mrs Violet Ferguson's tea set, scarcely a masterpiece of the potter's art, caused Japan to attack the British Empire. But the incident in which it played a part was an example of an intelligence coup that helped to decide the fate of nations.

On 11 November 1940 SS *Automedon*, a humble 7,528-ton British merchant ship of the Blue Funnel Line, exotically named for Achilles' charioteer, was ploughing a lonely course for Penang, in a stretch of the Indian Ocean west of Sumatra far from any active theatre of war. Nonetheless, at 7 a.m. when the officer of the watch spotted a distant ship, he woke his sleeping captain. 'The old man', veteran seafarer William Ewan, quickly made his way to the bridge, just forward of the ship's spindly funnel. Ewan peered hard through his binoculars, decided that the stranger was a Dutch liner, and held course. At 8.03 the other vessel was less than a mile distant when it broke out the international flag hoists 'Do not raise the alarm' and 'Stop', then fired a warning shot across the bows of the freighter, which had left Liverpool on 24 September, just as the Battle of Britain gave way to the Blitz, carrying a mixed cargo of aircraft, cars, machine parts, microscopes, military uniforms, cameras, sewing machines, beer, 550 cases of whisky, 2.5 million Chesterfield cigarettes, and six million dollars in newly printed Straits currency.

The interloper was the disguised German armed merchant-cruiser *Atlantis*, one of the most successful commerce raiders of the war, which had already captured and sunk twelve Allied vessels since leaving Bremen on 31 March. The ships' 11 November meeting was not a matter of chance.

The *Atlantis*'s captain, forty-one-year-old Bernhard Rogge, had captured a set of British Merchant Navy codes aboard the freighter *City of Baghdad* on 11 July, which assisted him in intercepting other vessels thereafter. Moreover, an Italian intelligence unit in the Mediterranean forwarded decrypts which helped to pinpoint the freighter. *Automedon*'s bridge crew failed to read the German flag hoist, and the ship's radio-operator began tapping out an 'RRR' emergency signal. The doughty Captain Ewan shouted 'Hard on the wheel!' and his ship began to sheer away. He then said, 'Come on everyone, let's do it – we're going to fight.' On the stern deck of the merchantman was mounted a single elderly 4-inch gun. Unfortunately for the British, however, *Atlantis* carried five 5.9-inch guns and a sophisticated fire-control system. Having intercepted the British ship's distress call, the Germans started shooting in earnest. The first shell of *Atlantis*'s opening salvo, fired at point-blank range, smashed into the bridge, followed by a further succession of hammer blows which brought down the wireless antenna, killed or wounded almost a score of men and transformed *Automedon*'s upperworks into a tangle of twisted steel inter-rupted by gaping holes. By now *Atlantis* was so close that when a British seaman ran aft, a German officer called through a loudhailer in English, 'Do not approach the gun, or we will blow you out of the water!'

Second Officer Donald Stewart regained consciousness on the bridge to find his captain lying dead beside him. First Officer Peter Evan, know-ing that protracted resistance was impossible, had dashed for the ship's safe to destroy the confidential papers as soon as the enemy opened fire, but fell victim to the same shell that killed Ewan: Evan collapsed seriously wounded on the threshold of the captain's cabin where the safe key was kept. In all, six crew members were now dead and twelve others wounded. Both ships stopped. Stewart and the deckhands watched grimly as a launch bore a boarding party from *Atlantis* to *Automedon*. A stream of shocked and scalded Chinese firemen emerged from a hatchway leading to the freighter's engine room, where blast had caused steam leaks.

The Germans had planned to commandeer *Automedon* as a supply ship, but on seeing the scale of damage caused by their shells, instead they began to set scuttling charges. Lt. Ulrich Mohr, *Atlantis*'s adjutant, made a hasty tour of the capture during which he blew open its safe, removing cash and confidential papers along with a weighted green canvas bag found in the chartroom, which *Automedon*'s dead officers had been tasked to throw overboard in any emergency. The Germans enlisted the aid of British seamen to shift frozen meat, whisky and cigarettes to *Atlantis*, before the crew was transferred to the German ship. Personal money was confiscated, though their captors issued receipts for the contents of each man's wallet. Captain Rogge was not only an excellent seaman and tactician, but a man of honour who took pains for the welfare of prisoners from the ships he seized on his remarkable eight-month cruise. Among the British personnel transferred to *Atlantis* were three passengers, including a chief engineer of the Straits Steamship Company named Alan Ferguson, and his thirty-three-year-old wife Violet, on passage to Singapore. Encountering the *Atlantis* was only the latest of several unfortunate adventures that had befallen Mrs Ferguson since her marriage in 1936, including a miscarriage and an enforced flight from France in June 1940 aboard the last ferry out of Bordeaux. Now, intensely emotional, she went to Captain Rogge and pleaded with him through tears to save her luggage – two trunks which contained almost all her worldly possessions, including a prized tea set. The German took pity. He signalled Mohr, still on the doomed *Automedon*, to make a quick search for the Fergusons' luggage.

Donald Stewart, the only British officer remaining aboard, did his best to deflect Mohr from the locked strongroom below the bridge where the luggage was held, but the *Atlantis*'s adjutant would brook no distraction. Seeing a door that answered Mrs Ferguson's description of the baggage space, he had it blown open. Beyond, as well as her trunks he found sack upon sack of mailbags, some of them prominently labelled as containing official communications. The launch that bore Mohr, Stewart and the boarding party to *Atlantis*'s side soon afterwards repeated the trip heaped with mailbags, as well as Mrs Ferguson's luggage.

The freighter was dispatched to the bottom a few hours after its fateful encounter with *Atlantis*. As the German raider hastened to put distance between itself and *Automedon*'s last known position, Rogge and Mohr set to work on the treasure trove of documents brought across from the British ship. The Merchant Navy's codes and sailing orders were familiar stuff. But then the two Germans found themselves scanning much more interesting material – a mass of reports and correspondence destined for British military and intelligence outposts in Singapore, Shanghai, Hong Kong. The most secret papers of all included correspondence addressed to Air-Marshal Sir Robert Brooke-Popham, British commander-in-chief in the Far East. This gave details of a war cabinet meeting to discuss the strategic situation in Asia, held at Downing Street on 8 August 1940, presided over by Winston Churchill. Appended to this was a highly detailed report on the defences of Britain's Far Eastern empire, prepared for the government by the chiefs of staff.

Rogge immediately realised the urgency of landing his catch. The British official mail was placed aboard the captured Norwegian freighter *Ole Jacob*, which sailed with most of *Atlantis*'s prisoners and a small prize crew to Kobe, in neutral Japan, where it arrived on 5 December. The British documents, now reposing in a locked chest, were forwarded under escort to the German embassy in Tokyo, where naval attaché Paul Wenneker studied them with all the attention they deserved – it is unknown whether he shared their secrets with Richard Sorge. He cabled a digest of the highlights to Berlin, then sent home copies of the key material via the Trans-Siberian railway, in the hands of Lt. Paul Kamenz, Captain Rogge's prize officer. Five days later, Wenneker was given orders, personally endorsed by Hitler, to pass the documents to the Japanese government, with one stipulation: the Abwehr wanted the credit. The embassy was told to say nothing about the papers having been removed from a British freighter – perhaps partly because this might suggest to the Japanese that Churchill's government did not much value the material. Instead, Wenneker was told to convey an impression that the prize had been secured by brilliant German secret service work.

On 12 December Wenneker took the documents and translations personally to the offices of the Japanese naval staff, placed them without comment on the desk of Vice-Admiral Nobutake Kondo, Yamamoto's vice-chief, and sat in silence while they were read. Kondo was appropriately stunned – and grateful. That evening he entertained Wenneker to the best dinner Tokyo could provide, expressing repeated thanks and saying wonderingly, 'such significant weaknesses in the British Empire could not be detected from outward appearances'. What did the documents contain, that caused Kondo such amazement? By far the most important revelation was a fifteen-page British chiefs of staff report, presented to the war cabinet on 8 August, entitled 'The Situation in the Far East in the Event of Japanese Intervention Against Us'. It was headed:

SECRET COPY 72
COS (40) 302 (also W.P. (40) 302)
TO BE KEPT UNDER LOCK AND KEY
It is requested that special care be taken to ensure the secrecy of this document.

The British chiefs correctly predicted the likelihood of deeper Japanese incursions into French Indochina, threatening Malaya. Churchill's government asserted its unwillingness, founded on avowed military weakness, to go to war with Japan over Indochina. It acknowledged that Hong Kong, pearl of the British Empire on the China coast, was indefensible: in the event of war, only token resistance could be offered to a Japanese assault on the colony. The Royal Navy was pathetically weak in Far Eastern waters, but until the tide of war had turned in the Mediterranean, the British acknowledged their inability to send major reinforcements. At best – or rather, in dire emergency – only a battlecruiser and a single aircraft-carrier could be spared for the Indian Ocean. If Japan attacked Australia or New Zealand the only credible response would be an appeal to the United States to send forces to their aid. The dominant theme of the chiefs of staff's report to government was an assertion of Britain's strategic weakness: 'The forces in Malaya are still far short of requirements, particularly in the air … Our own commitments in Europe are so great that our policy must be directed towards the avoidance of an open clash with Japan … Our general policy should be to play for time; to cede nothing until we must; and to build up our defences as soon as we can.' The paper also showed that the British were unaware of Japan's formidable strength in naval torpedo-bombers, among the deadliest weapons in its armoury.

This, then, was the thrust of the documents handed over by the Germans in December 1940, at a moment when Berlin's foremost foreign policy objective was to drag Japan into the war. The haul was passed to the army's newly established Asia Development Agency, headed by Lt. Col. Yoshimasa Okada, which was explicitly tasked to study the defences of Britain's Asian empire. His first instinctive reaction was to assume that the papers must be a German plant, fabricated for political purposes – the Japanese rightly declined to believe that any mere spy could have secured such material. But as Okada and his colleagues studied the British order of battle, they found that this closely matched assessments made by the intelligence staffs of both the Japanese army and navy. Belief grew, and finally became absolute, that the papers were authentic. They were passed to Japan's prime minister, who was as impressed as had been Admiral Kondo and Col. Okada.

It would be as absurd to suggest that the *Automedon* papers determined Japan to risk war in December 1941 as it is to attribute any other decisive event in history to a single cause. But the evidence is plain that the captured documents accelerated the sea change in Japanese thinking that took place during the winter of 1940–41. Having been allowed to discover that the British themselves believed their South-East Asian empire to be acutely vulnerable, the Japanese army and navy became increasingly persuaded that the 'southern strategy' of assaulting the West's overseas empires offered a more attractive option than the alternative 'northern strategy' of engaging the Soviet Union. As is the way of warlords, because the *Automedon* material encouraged them towards a course they were minded to take anyway, Japan's leaders wilfully neglected other intelligence from Europe, especially reports from their naval attachés, which cast doubt upon the prospect of German victory, and especially upon its imminence. Tokyo adhered stubbornly to a belief that Hitler was destined to triumph. Conviction grew upon the generals that if they wished to share in the spoils of looming Axis victory, to avoid 'missing the bus' they must strike soon against the Western Powers.

Atlantis was scuttled by her own crew south of St Helena on 22 November 1940, after receiving a first salvo from the 8-inch guns of the British cruiser *Devonshire*. The German raider thus became itself a victim of secret intelligence: it had been ordered to make a refuelling rendezvous with U-126, at a position in the South Atlantic revealed to the Royal Navy by Bletchley Park. Bernhard Rogge and his crew took to the boats, escaped capture, and survived the war. The *Automedon* documents were recognised in Tokyo as the captain's notable contribution to Japan's 1941–42 triumph: after the fall of Singapore Rogge was presented with a samurai sword by a grateful Japanese Emperor – Göring and Rommel were the only other German recipients of this wartime honour.

Alan Ferguson and his wife Violet came through the war, after enduring years of internment. So too, remarkably, did her tea set. The trunk in which it reposed accompanied her to Germany, then was recovered intact by British forces in 1945. It was dispatched to Singapore, where Ferguson resumed his career as an engineering officer, while enjoying his wife's genteel afternoon entertaining ashore. As for the British government's priceless documents, their capture with *Automedon* reflected a notable and by no means unique carelessness with secret papers. Whitehall went to elaborate lengths to conceal the blunder from the world until it was revealed accidentally many decades later, by discovery of some of Wenneker's messages in a German archive. The saga vividly illustrates the fact that some remarkable intelligence coups are the fruits of raw luck, rather than of inspired espionage.

2 THE JAPANESE

The *Automedon* documents contributed to Tokyo's impressively comprehensive local intelligence picture before its forces attacked Pearl Harbor and the Western European Asian empires in December 1941. The Japanese took more trouble to inform themselves about their immediate objectives ahead of the outbreak of war than ever they did afterwards. For months their agents cycled across Malaya, explored the US Pacific Fleet's Hawaii anchorages, parleyed with the Hong Kong Triads. This, although the bulk of the Japanese army's attention and resources remained focused on China, where its men had been fighting and dying since 1937, and where intelligence – *joho* – was easily secured and Nationalist codes readily broken. In May 1940, during the Yichang offensive, army codebreakers enabled Tokyo's armies to anticipate the movements of almost every Chinese division. In the summer 1941 Battle of South Shanxi, thanks to decrypts they inflicted 80,000 casualties on much larger Chinese forces, while themselves losing only 3,300 men. Captain Katsuhiko Kudo was hailed as Japan's ace cryptanalyst, and became the first intelligence officer to be awarded the *Kinshi Kunsho* – 'Golden Kite' – decoration for his achievements in China.

The Japanese army's 'China hands' were known as *Shina-tsu*, of whom the most celebrated was Gen. Kenji Doihara, dubbed 'Lawrence of Manchuria' for his espionage activities. In July 1940 Kioya Izaki, the Shanghai intelligence centre's deputy chief, spent a month visiting Hong Kong, Canton and Taipei under cover as a trader. The station ran covert operations with codenames like '*Sakura*' ('Cherry Tree'), '*Take Bambo*', '*Fuji-Wisteria*'. One of these, in 1941, flooded China with forged currency, printed by the Army Institute for Scientific Research on specially imported German high-speed presses. Meanwhile the Shanghai counter-intelligence branch boasted a strength of 1,500 men. The navy's Special Duties Section used disguised fishing boats for offshore surveillance of freight movements to the Nationalists, especially by the British, and opened a private trading company as a cover for agent-running.

Yet Tokyo learned little about the communists, partly because Mao Zhedong's forces used intractable Soviet codes. And despite all the activity described above, an ingrained sense of cultural superiority – which also caused them to condescend to Anglo-Saxons – made the Japanese unwilling seriously to engage with China for intelligence purposes. A staff officer acknowledged after the war: 'We failed to realise that we were fighting the Chinese not only in the military field but also in the political, economic and cultural fields. We were almost blind in the latter.' One Japanese agent in Shanghai was reduced to forwarding to Tokyo as source material Agnes Smedley's bestselling book *China's Red Army Marches*.

Until at least 1942 the Russians, across the border in Manchuria, were the targets of much more ambitious Japanese covert operations than the Western Powers. Tokyo was morbidly fearful of its communist neighbours, and after its drubbing at Nomohan in 1939 the Imperial Army sustained a profound respect for their military abilities. Most of the 22,000 Kempeitai military police deployed overseas were either performing security duties in China or watching the Russians. So primitive was their training that Japanese spies were taught to measure the length of bridges in the Soviet Union from inside closed trains by counting the number of bumps as wheels passed over rail joins. At the Manchurian post of Hsinking, 320 listeners tapped phones and monitored voice radio communication. Eight sigint sites monitored Russian wireless transmissions, and the Japanese sometimes changed border guards at Sakhalin just to provoke the Russians into sending signals, in the hope that these could be decrypted. In 1940 a former Polish army codebreaker assisted the Japanese to crack some low-grade Red Air Force and diplomatic codes. Three hundred Japanese officers a year attended the Russian language school in Harbin.

Seven hundred soldiers were continuously employed peering through binoculars across the border from Manchuria into the Soviet Union, recording the movements of every man, horse and vehicle, together with all ship traffic in and out of Vladivostok. Several ex-tsarist officers scraped a living in Harbin scanning *Pravda*, *Izvestia* and other Soviet publications for Tokyo's benefit. A ceaseless pingpong game was played, wherein the Japanese recruited Russian expatriates, dispatched them across the Manchurian border only for the Soviets to 'turn' them: the average Japanese agent survived at liberty for just a week. In 1938 Gen. Genrikh Lyushov of the NKVD's Far Eastern Directorate escaped a firing squad by fleeing into Manchuria. He spent the ensuing seven years under house arrest in Tokyo, but his hosts found that their prize had frustratingly little to tell of practical value. In the wake of 'Barbarossa', a steady stream of Russian deserters – 130 of them by the end of 1941 – crossed into Japanese territory, but many proved to be NKVD plants.

Some Japanese initiatives were spectacularly unprofitable: the Intelligence Department enlisted the aid of the Army Institute for Scientific Research at Noborito to devise a chemical to paralyse Russian guard dogs' power of scent and stimulate their sexual appetite, to make them less manageable; both dogs and handlers remained unmoved. Attempts to use as sources Japanese businessmen visiting Russia achieved little, for whenever such visitors left their hotels they were dogged by NKVD watchers, as were attachés in Moscow. An intelligence officer, Lt. Col. Saburo Hayashi, complained that probing Soviet secrets was 'like searching for very fine gold dust in mud'.

Japan's ideas about gathering foreign intelligence focused overwhelmingly upon espionage. Its agents penetrated the Soviet embassy in Beijing, and in 1941 one concealed himself in a cupboard of the library of the British consulate in Taipei, where the safe was located. The man collapsed unconscious in his stifling confinement, but he revived in time to watch the consul open the safe and to memorise its combination, which eventually yielded a few crumbs. Japanese agent networks operated in California and Mexico under cover as fishermen, dentists and barbers; there was a chain of Japanese barber/agents in the Panama Canal Zone. Some British and American renegades were recruited as sources: former Royal Navy submariner Lt. Cmdr Collin Mayers provided information for cash until his arrest in 1927. An ex-US Navy yeoman named Harry Thompson received $200 a month from his Japanese handler until sentenced to fifteen years' imprisonment in 1935.

Cmdr Fred Rutland was a decorated British airman who made his living after retirement by briefing the Japanese and promoting dud companies at their expense – for a time they maintained him in a mansion in Beverly Hills. Both MI5 and the FBI were well aware of his activities. The latter decided that he was Japan's principal agent in the US, though a May 1935 report to Tokyo from Rutland in California was a fair sample of his unimpressive wares: 'The [US] Army and Navy want war and in my view this might be put off for a few years ... Everyone I have met in America thinks a war with Japan is inevitable.' Lt. Cmdr Arata Oka, Japan's naval attaché in London, argued that 'it would be wrong to rely on Rutland alone in case of war', which was an understatement. The Japanese nonetheless liked their tame traitor sufficiently to give him another £4,000 when he revisited Japan in 1938. The ungrateful Rutland then sailed to America and approached Captain Ellis Zacharias, the US Navy's Asian intelligence specialist, to propose a sale of Japanese secrets. This left the FBI bewildered about which side Rutland was on, but he was plainly a troublemaker, and was finally arrested on 6 June 1941. London's anxiety to avoid a public scandal caused him to be deported to Britain, where he was interned. Four years after his release at the end of the war, Rutland killed himself.

Cmdr Oka did no better when he hired Herbert Greene, a nephew of William Greene, a senior Admiralty official and brother of the novelist Graham. Oka codenamed him '*Midorikawa*' – 'Green River' – paid him £800 and cherished hopes that Greene had an entrée to the smart London clubland where secrets were discussed. Instead, in December 1937 Greene proclaimed his half-hearted treachery to the *Daily Worker*, which blazoned all over its front page his announcement that he was a Japanese spy. In July 1941, when Japan was still a neutral, its naval attaché formally requested from the British government details of the national electricity grid. Guy Liddell of MI5 branded this 'characteristic impertinence', since British surveillance officers had just seen a member of the Japanese embassy staff pass German cash to an Abwehr agent operating under Double Cross control. The only advantage enjoyed by Japanese spies, said Liddell, was that they were very hard to watch 'as to a European they all look alike and there is the additional difficulty of the blackout and four exits from the military attaché's office'. The Japanese navy's most useful intelligence connection in London was Rear-Admiral Lord Sempill, an enthusiastic Nazi sympathiser. When it was found that he had been selling classified information to Tokyo, in 1941 he was permitted to resign quietly from the Royal Navy and retire to his Scottish castle; Churchill flinched from a treason trial at the heart of the old aristocracy.

The last significant Japanese spy in America – if she can be dignified as such – was Velvalee Dickinson, who passed childishly simple information on naval matters based on tidbits about the activity of West Coast defence facilities through a friend in Buenos Aires. Born in Sacramento in 1893, a Stanford graduate, she worked for some years in a San Francisco bank, then assisted her husband Lee in a brokerage business that failed. Thereafter she found work in New York City as a doll saleswoman at Bloomingdale's, before starting a modestly successful doll store of her own on Madison Avenue. Her association with Tokyo began with her husband's membership of a Japanese-American society before his death in 1943. As an informant for Japanese intelligence she received $25,000, at the cost of also receiving a ten-year jail sentence from a federal court for violation of censorship statutes when arrested and convicted in 1944. Other clumsy Japanese espionage efforts on both sides of the Atlantic, including the extensive Californian Tachibana network, were curtailed without much difficulty, and with negligible loss of Allied secrets.

The leaders of Japan's armed forces disagreed about almost everything else, but were of one mind in regarding intelligence-gathering as a mechanical process which could readily be carried out by junior officers – their view was even more myopic than that of Hitler's OKW. Analysis, such as it was, was conducted by the army's 2nd Department and the navy's 3rd. The navy designated sigint as *Toku-jo* – special information; codebreaking as *A-jo*; telephone taps as *B-jo*; DF direction-finding as *C-jo*. It identified four levels of reliability for information: *Ko* – certain; *Otsu* – almost certain; *Hei* – a little uncertain; *Tei* – uncertain. As with other nations, in the Japanese army and navy a posting to intelligence was a career dead-end. Even when war came and clever university graduates were conscripted into uniform, almost all were dispatched to become cannon fodder, rather than assigned to military or naval roles – intelligence in particular – where their brains might have been useful.

Japan's naval codebreakers achieved little success in breaking higher British and American ciphers, and thus concentrated instead on radio direction-finding and traffic analysis. So bitter was the rivalry between the services that when the army broke some low-grade American strip codes, the soldiers concealed their knowledge from the sailors until 1945. At no time before 1943 did Japan devote anything like the personnel and resources necessary to make eavesdropping and codebreaking major sources of intelligence against the Western Powers, nor did their commanders seem much to care about this weakness.

With nationalistic complacency, Japan took for granted the security of its own codes, diplomatic, military and naval. Captain Risaburo Ito warned the navy that its traffic was vulnerable, but was ignored. Japan's Type 91 and 97 *Shiki O-bun Injiki* cipher machines, created by naval engineer Kazuo Tanabe and known to the Americans as 'Red' and 'Purple' respectively, were deemed impregnable – the Foreign Ministry used the latter, and the navy's 'Coral' and 'Jade' employed similar technology, differing from Enigma because it employed telephone stepping-switches instead of rotors. The army's 'Green' machine alone used the latter. Supremely fortunately for the Allies, Tokyo ignored an April 1941 warning from the German embassy in Washington, derived from an American traitor's tip to the Soviets, that US codebreakers had cracked Purple. When Berlin presented the Japanese with several Enigmas and urged them to manufacture copies for their own use, the machines were left to rust; Japan persisted with its home-grown models. Given the difficulties experienced by American and British codebreakers in reading the Japanese army's traffic, they may well have been better off doing so.

Japan's military counter-espionage organisation was bizarrely named

TOP SECRET

From: Washington (Nomura)
To: Tokyo
May 20, 1941
Purple (CA)

#327

   INTELLIGENCE:

    Though I do not know which ones, I have
discovered that the United States is reading some of our
codes.

    As for how I got the intelligence, I will
inform you by courier or another safe way.

ᵁther cpy is classified SECRET only

Carbon contained these entries:

    Found in Minckler safe
          E.

17424 - - -This is not thre 17424 in SIS Bulletin file. F.

TOP SECRET

ARMY JD-1:2636 SECRET   Trans. 5/21/41 (7)

This was originally given SIS #17424
but was then withdrawn from Bulletin
file and another message (Wash → Tok 13 may 41 Purple-(A) substi
             F.

US transcript of a potentially momentous intercepted and
decoded cable from ambassador Nomura in Washington to
Japanese foreign minister Matsuoka containing a warning,
thought to have come from the Soviets via their then allies
the Nazis, that the Americans had broken Purple. The date
given refers to its decryption, not its transmission

TOP SECRET

From: Tokyo (Matsuoka)
To : Washington (Nomura)
7 May 1941
(Purple - CA)

#198

or "rather"
or "pretty"

Regarding your #267:*

    _ This matter was told very confidentially
to Ambassador Oshima** by the Germans as having been
reported to them by a fairly reliable intelligence
medium; but to our inquiry they are said to have refused
to divulge the basis on which they deemed it to be
practically certain.

*JD-1:2367   Nomura requests further details of the
               basis for the report that his code msgs
               are being read by the U.S. government.

**General Ōshima, the Japanese Ambassador to Berlin.

Note: Two copies of this were prepared:
      (1) Admiral Noyes
      (2) General Mauborgne

Notation on other copy:

    Found in Minckler's safe F.

TOP SECRET

JD-1:2388   (F) Navy trans. 7 May 1941 (S-TT)

Not in SIS Bulletin file

The decrypt of a related message to Tokyo confirms the
Japanese ambassador in Berlin as the source of the warning,
which was fortunately ignored

the 'Conspiracy Section', devoted to rooting out plots against the nation.
In December 1937 an intelligence training centre was opened, later known
as the Nagano School. This offered the usual tradecraft courses, with
optional extras in lock-picking, ninja martial arts and '*Kokutai-gaku*' –
'Study for National Structure and Mind', ideological indoctrination.
Nagano's teaching was unusual: it encouraged officers to stay alive, rather
than to conduct *banzai* charges and commit ritual suicide in the event of
failure. A weakness of the counter-espionage service persisted, however:
it lavished extravagant energy on monitoring Japan's own civilian politicians, not for evidence of treason, but to ensure that they did not deviate
from their own army's foreign policy objectives. In July 1937, when Prince
Konoye as prime minister dispatched envoys to Nankin to discuss possible
peace negotiations with the Chinese Nationalists, the army decrypted
cables about the talks, and promptly sent military police to arrest Konoye's
couriers.

Hachiro Arita, a pre-war foreign minister, moaned: 'In Japan we are in
a very difficult position for conducting real diplomacy, because Japanese
politicians are always watched by the military. I cannot make good use of
flattering or diplomatic language … If I say something wrong in a telegram, the Japanese army and navy intercept it and immediately criticise
me … The situation is so awkward.' Japan had a Cabinet Intelligence
Department, intended to brief the prime minister, but the navy and army
insisted on sustaining monopoly influence over the nation's inner councils, and secured its emasculation: the CID became a mere propaganda
organ.

The War Ministry had its own counter-intelligence organisation, with
a fifty-strong staff charged with concealing Japan's preparations for war. In
Mitsubishi's Nagasaki shipyard, work on the new battleship *Musashi* was
carried on behind vast hemp curtains, screening it from view. The luggage
of foreign rail travellers was routinely examined. The Kempeitai's 6th
Section maintained RDF surveillance for illegal wireless transmissions by
foreign agents in Japan. Almost all foreigners' correspondence was intercepted at Tokyo's Central Post Office and photographed before onward
dispatch. Outside the US embassy Japanese secret policemen, stripped to
their underpants against the heat, maintained 24/7 surveillance from
behind curtains in a supposedly broken-down car – 'the spy wagon', as it
was known to diplomats. In July 1940, military police chanced on a letter
in English, signed only 'Jimmy' and posted at the Teikoku hotel in Tokyo;
it gave details of the refitting of the battleship *Nagato*. An investigation

swiftly pinned authorship on local Reuters correspondent and MI6 informant James Cox. He was arrested, and three days later died after being thrown or throwing himself from the fourth floor of the Tokyo police headquarters.

It was never established whether Cox committed suicide or was murdered – the latter seems more plausible, given the brutality of the Kempeitai. The British Foreign Office gave his widow a £5,000 pay-off, said to be paid in compensation by the Japanese. Nor was her husband's the only mysterious death of an Englishman: in October 1938 a Royal Navy lieutenant named Peacocke also vanished without trace. In July 1940 alone, fifteen British citizens were arrested on suspicion of espionage, though most were later released. If these cases represented supposed successes for Japanese counter-intelligence, it remains striking to behold that, for all Japan's increasingly feverish xenophobia and intensive surveillance of foreigners, the Sorge spy ring functioned for eight years at the heart of Axis strategy-making.

Japan's intelligence-gathering machine failed miserably where it mattered most: in providing the nation's rulers with an understanding of the principal enemy whom they proposed to attack – the United States, most powerful industrial nation on earth. After Japan's defeat Col. Shinobu Takayama of the army's Operations Department acknowledged ruefully that it would have been prudent to research America's actual and potential warmaking powers before embarking on a conflict with it. The most striking characteristic of Japan's leadership was its refusal to examine, far less to act upon, unpalatable information. No single branch of government was responsible for making and coordinating grand strategy. The chief of army intelligence, Major-General Yuichi Tsuchihashi, was not consulted about the implications of joining an alliance with Germany and Italy, because he was known to oppose it. The army paid little attention to American matters, which its generals considered the business of the navy and the Foreign Ministry. They read some low-grade diplomatic wireless traffic, and gained a little intelligence from *niseis* – immigrants living in the US – but mostly relied on open sources, which meant attachés reading newspapers. Several officers explored the Philippines and its garrison, but there was no serious analysis of the US Army's actual and potential strength. Once the war began, some officers who had spent their entire previous careers studying the Soviet Union were arbitrarily transferred to monitor America. Japan's South Area Army eventually abolished its US and British intelligence sections, because its senior officers decided that they were producing nothing of practical value. Operations departments despised intelligence officers as old women who raised objections to intended courses of action, and themselves preferred to rely upon front-line eyeball observation by soldiers in the field. When the army moved into Indochina in 1940, its Operations Department summarily appropriated all intelligence responsibilities to itself, and ran the invasion as if the intelligence staff did not exist.

The attitude of the Japanese navy before Pearl Harbor reflected a profound contradiction: those of its senior officers who used their brains recognised their own nation's strategic vulnerability, because of its dependence on imported oil and commodities, but made little attempt to impose their views upon the Tokyo government. They knew that it would be easy to annihilate the Royal Navy's small forces in the Far East, but recognised the immense power of the US Navy. Operations chief Captain Tasuku Nakazawa wrote before hostilities began: 'We have no chance to win a war [with Britain and the US]. War games resulted in heavy losses in shipping and loss of control of overseas shipping lanes and lines of communication.' Admiral Isoroku Yamamoto was foremost among those who, while disliking and resenting the United States' policies, recognised its economic and industrial supremacy. He and his cleverest subordinates knew that if they failed to secure victory fast, they would not get it at all. A February 1941 assessment concluded: 'After 1944, the US Navy would be confident of victory.'

In 1941 also, a new National Institute for Total War Studies carried out exhaustive war gaming, presuming an advance into South-East Asia. This concluded that within two years Japan would be on its knees, with Soviet entry into the war delivering a *coup de grâce*. Gen. Hideki Tojo, soon to become prime minister, read the Institute's report, then commented: 'You did a good job, but your report is based on a kind of armchair theory, not a real war … War is not always carried out as planned. We shall face unpredicted developments.' Tojo chose insistently to believe that these would operate in favour of the Axis. In September 1941 the Economic Planning Section of the War Ministry reached the same conclusion as the War Studies Institute, but once again the findings were rejected by the high command. The Imperial Japanese Army's chief of staff declared that 'the report is against our national policy', and ordered it to be burnt.

The army's iron men almost always prevailed, reciting their mantra that the government and people of the United States would succumb to a moral collapse after suffering the early defeats and humiliations that Japan was rightly confident of being able to inflict upon them. The soldiers were also convinced of German invincibility, and spurned doubters. In 1940 Japan's naval attaché in London and military attaché in Stockholm emphasised British successes in resisting the German onslaught on their island, and the scale of Luftwaffe losses. On 25 July the army's monthly intelligence report expressed respect for the strength of Britain's resistance in the air battle over the island: 'The UK is maintaining the fight against Germany with great determination ... British public opinion continues to support the government's hard-line policy.' The report highlighted the postponement of Hitler's invasion, Operation 'Sealion', because of German lack of amphibious capability, and failure to achieve air superiority.

IJA headquarters dismissed the authors of these reports as having succumbed to British propaganda, and instead embraced the supremely optimistic dispatches of Baron Ōshima, the Japanese ambassador in Berlin. Until June 1941 the Foreign Ministry made policy on an assumption that following Britain's defeat, the Nazis would forge an alliance with the Soviet Union to divide the spoils. Japan's generals succumbed to euphoria following the signing of the 13 April 1941 Soviet–Japanese neutrality pact, which they convinced themselves made the nation safe from a two-front war. When Ōshima reported that Hitler planned to invade the Soviet Union – his warnings became explicit on 18 April 1941 and were reinforced on 4 June – the Japanese government simply refused to consider this new and unwelcome scenario. Only a fortnight before the German onslaught, foreign minister Matsuoka doggedly insisted that there was only a 40 per cent prospect of such an event. War minister Tojo said: 'I do not think it is an urgent matter.' The cabinet deferred discussion of the implications of a Russo–German war, clinging blindly to its policy of supporting the Nazis more or less whatever they did. Without reference to the civilian politicians, the army dispatched large reinforcements to Manchuria in case a decision was made to join Hitler's assault on Stalin.

Before 'Barbarossa' was launched, intelligence officer Lt. Col. Saburo Hayashi suggested that if the Russians could get through winter undefeated, their armies could regroup and sustain a long struggle, but the Operations Department and higher commanders dismissed this assessment out of hand. Hayashi wrote again in August: 'It is expected that the Germans will occupy Moscow, but have no more success within 1941. When winter comes the Soviet Army will have an opportunity to catch its breath, and will never surrender. The Communist Party is strong and solid. Following the fall of Moscow, the Germans will be obliged to continue the war, while maintaining control of huge captured territories. To summarise: the war will not end quickly.' Yet the all-powerful Operations Department instead predicted Stalin's looming overthrow by his own generals. In Japan as in Nazi Germany, it had become an institutional precept that no intelligence assessment could be countenanced by policy-makers which ran contrary to a desired national course. Again and again between the 1930s and 1945, strategy was distorted to conform with the visceral inclinations and ambitions of commanders, rather than with realities, of which by far the most important were America's economic superiority and Germany's precarious strategic predicament.

The most penetrating appreciation of Japan's prospects before Pearl Harbor was presented to Tokyo not by its own analysts, but by Winston Churchill. In April 1941 he dispatched a memorandum to the Japanese foreign minister which was designed to deter war. 'I venture to ask a few questions,' wrote the British prime minister,

> which it seems to me deserve the attention of the Imperial Japanese Government and people.
>
> 1. Will Germany, without the command of the sea or the command of the British daylight air, be able to invade and conquer Great Britain in the spring, summer or autumn of 1941? Will Germany try to do so? Would it not be in the interests of Japan to wait until these questions have answered themselves?
> 2. Will the German attack on British shipping be strong enough to prevent American aid from reaching British shores, with Great Britain and the United States transforming their whole industry to war purposes?
> 3. Did Japan's accession to the Triple Pact [with Germany and Italy] make it more likely or less likely that the United States would come into the present war?
> 4. If the United States entered the war at the side of Great Britain, and Japan ranged herself with the Axis Powers, would not the naval superiority of the two English-speaking nations enable them to dispose of the Axis Powers in Europe before turning their united strength upon Japan?
> 5. Is Italy a strength or a burden to Germany? Is the Italian Fleet as good at sea as on paper? Is it as good as it used to be?

6. Will the British Air Force be stronger than the German Air Force before the end of 1941, and far stronger before the end of 1942?

7. Will the many countries which are being held down by the German army and Gestapo learn to like the Germans more, or will they like them less as the years pass by?

8. Is it true that the production of steel in the United States during 1941 will be 75 million tons and in Great Britain about 12½, making a total of nearly 90 million tons? If Germany should happen to be defeated, as she was last time, would not the 7 million tons steel production of Japan be inadequate for a single-handed war?

From the answers to these questions may spring the avoidance by Japan of a serious catastrophe, and a marked improvement in the relations between Japan and the two great Sea-Powers of the West.

Tokyo's anodyne reply was inevitable: 'The foreign policy of Japan is determined upon after an unbiased examination of all the facts and a very careful weighing of all the elements of the situation she confronts.' Yet such a process never took place in Tokyo. Japan's rejection of strategic intelligence assessment, and of rational decision-making, was responsible for its commitment to a path to catastrophe on 7 December 1941.

The only species of intelligence the Japanese high command treated seriously was that which concerned immediate objectives. Thus, in the months before the army and navy went to war, both energetically probed the defences of the European South-East Asian empires, the Philippines and Pearl Harbor. Tokyo's appetite for an advance into Indochina was sharpened by the July 1940 decryption of a telegram to Washington from the American consul in Saigon, saying that the British would make no military response to such a Japanese initiative without a promise of US support, which would not be forthcoming. Further decrypts of diplomatic messages in August, notably including those of the Vichy French authorities in Indochina, confirmed the inability or unwillingness of the Western Powers to resist a Japanese takeover. Thus, on 22 September, the Japanese forced a French signature on an agreement which admitted their troops next day. Here was a case where intelligence played a significant role, albeit in confirming Japan's commitment to a course its rulers favoured anyway.

The army's South-East Asia Group, established in 1939, was responsible for exploring the defences of the European empires. Because Thailand was the only independent country in the region, the Japanese made it the hub of their intelligence-gathering, directed by military attaché Col. Hiroshi Tamura, who focused especially on identifying Malayan invasion routes. His soldiers measured every road and bridge from Indochina and Thailand into Malaya. Agents explored the huge Dutch oil refineries at Palembang so diligently that when Japanese paratroops later descended upon them, each man knew every detail of the target. The Japanese acknowledged that the British had some formidable codebreaking talent, focused in their Far East Combined Bureau in Singapore, which worked closely with Bletchley Park. A naval codebreaker who monitored its traffic, Commander Monotono Samejima, decrypted material which showed that the British had been reading some low-grade Japanese signals within twenty-four hours of transmission. Samejima recalled later: 'I became aware of the tremendous capability of UK intelligence.' His superiors, however, cared only about counting their enemies' soldiers. By the end of 1940 a thousand Japanese 'tourists', all graduates of the army intelligence school, were working out of Thailand. British troops exercising in Malaya found themselves followed everywhere by bicycling Japanese equipped with pencils and notebooks. Their findings were circulated throughout the army as an 'Intelligence record of British Malaya', which included maps of the Singapore garrison's installations. The general staff concluded from such agents' reports that the ethnic diversity of British imperial forces was a weakness. It was dismissive of the Australians: 'Their quality is bad. The troops are composed chiefly of jobless men and rough individuals. They are not a well-disciplined army. Their valour in battle is famous, but their training and equipment are not adequate.' Tokyo asserted that many Indian soldiers were both ill-trained and anti-British; they could fight bravely in a head-on positional clash, but were vulnerable to rapid flanking movements – a shrewd assessment, vindicated by events in the subsequent campaign.

In the course of 1941 Japanese agents made contacts with Indian, Malayan and Burmese nationalist groups, offering covert support for their ambitions for independence, which many found an attractive proposition. A January 1941 telegram from Tokyo to Japan's consul-general in Singapore ordered him to accelerate 'agitation, political plots, propaganda and intelligence'. In May, Japan's Foreign Service cabled all its missions in the region, urging them to hasten the expansion of clandestine networks on the periphery of the Indian Ocean, because war was obviously looming. The Indians, especially, were urged to promote disaffection among soldiers of the Raj, and began to do so in 1939; when the assault on Malaya was unleashed, the poor performance of several Indian regiments suggested that the Japanese propaganda offensive had achieved some success: the 1st Hyderabads, for instance, are believed to have shot their own British colonel and adjutant at an early stage of the battalion's disintegration on the battlefield.

Tokyo thought British aircrew green, and it was true that most of the pilots deployed in Malaya and Burma were less experienced than their enemy counterparts. The Japanese probably received some information from a traitor in the British ranks: for several months during 1941 Captain Patrick Heenan of 300 Air Intelligence Liaison Section appears to have wirelessed information about RAF dispositions from a secret transmitter. Thirty-one, born in New Zealand, Heenan had inherited from his father a warm sympathy for the Irish Republican Army. He was recruited by Tokyo during a 1938 leave spent in Japan, and ended his espionage career by being shot against a harbour wall in Singapore just before its fall.

As for Pearl Harbor, in August 1941 twenty-eight-year-old Ensign Takeo Yoshikawa of the US & British section of Japanese naval intelligence arrived in Hawaii with diplomatic cover, and spent the months that followed exploring every accessible area of interest to the planners back at home, while conducting an uncommonly energetic off-duty love life. He reported three times a week by Purple cipher, and though his messages were routinely intercepted, the US Signals Intelligence Service in Washington was often three weeks in arrears decrypting them, not least because it had only two fluent and accurate Japanese linguists. In October, Yoshikawa's boss Lt. Cmdr Minato Nakajima made a personal visit on a Japanese liner, and received the ensign's written report on the US Navy's local strengths, deployments and defences. Though Yoshikawa was interned after Pearl Harbor, he was subsequently allowed to return home under the agreement on exchange of diplomatic personnel.

Further information was acquired by the local consular staff, assisted by the large Japanese expatriate colony on Hawaii – 41,346 of them. Their data confirmed the navy in its determination to strike at Pearl Harbor rather than against the alternative American anchorage at Lahaina Port. Neither the army nor the Ministry of Foreign Affairs was informed about the agreed objectives, and Pearl was never explicitly mentioned in naval radio traffic. The critical mistake in the planning of the onslaught was not one of intelligence collection, but of analysis: the admirals back in Japan failed to recognise the importance of Pearl's huge oil-tank farms and repair facilities, and never included these in their target programme. As for Japanese perceptions of the US Army, they assessed American troops – especially the Philippines garrison – as individualists who lacked staying power and fighting spirit for a protracted struggle. Japan's generals planned for a victorious termination of the Pacific war in the spring of 1942, where-upon they would launch a major assault on the Soviet Union.

Thus Japan went to war knowing much about its immediate objectives, but wilfully ignorant and naïve about what would follow. Yamamoto's air squadrons took off for Pearl Harbor on 7 December 1941 at just the moment when German failure before Moscow was becoming apparent in Berlin. The only success of the advocates of caution in Tokyo was to persuade Japan's rulers to confine themselves to assaulting the US and Western European empires, and to avoid joining hostilities with the Soviet Union until German victory seemed imminent. The judgements on which the Japanese based their decision to fight – to shackle themselves to a tottering giant – were fantastically ill-informed. They overvalued German might, underrated that of the United States. Moreover, they persuaded themselves that they could conduct a limited war, which they could termi-nate by negotiation at a moment of their own choice. Instead, of course, they found themselves engaged in an existential struggle in which they must either achieve total victory or face almost annihilatory defeat.

3 THE MAN WHO WON MIDWAY

The surprise suffered by the United States at Pearl Harbor was as great as that which the Soviet Union incurred at the launch of 'Barbarossa', and equally inexcusable. Its army codebreakers led by Frank Rowlett had achieved an extraordinary feat by cracking Japan's 'Purple' diplomatic cipher in August 1940. During the weeks and days before the Japanese attack on Hawaii, almost as much information became available to the US govern-ment to indicate the imminence of war as Stalin received before Hitler attacked him. But the US administration's response was as supine as had been that of the Kremlin. Just as the British required many months under the stimulus of war before they developed effective machinery for managing and exploiting intelligence, so the American armed forces began to do so only amid the wreckage of the battleships of its Pacific Fleet.

Admiral John Godfrey's July 1941 British report on US intelligence concluded that 'cooperation between the various organisations is inadequate and sources are not coordinated to the mutual benefit of the departments concerned. There is little contact between the intelligence officers of the different departments and the desire to obtain a "scoop" is fairly general ... The value of the material obtained by the US intelligence organisations from Europe is not considerable, though information on the Pacific area and South America is ... on the whole, high-grade ... The Office of Naval Intelligence is in danger of degenerating into a graveyard for statistics because it is inclined to regard intelligence as an end in itself ... Many of the faults which have been enumerated will be recognised as similar to those from which British Intelligence suffered before the war.' Godfrey concluded that once William Donovan's new intelligence-gathering organisation got going, many good things might be possible, 'but it would be prudent to conclude that US Intelligence is unlikely to be of much assistance to the joint war effort for many months to come'.

This proved to be true. The US Army and US Navy contributed nothing significant to Allied knowledge of Axis motions for months after Pearl Harbor. But then, in June 1942, from out of a dank basement in the Navy Yard on Oahu came a single piercing shaft of light that illuminated the entire Pacific theatre. It made possible the US Navy's victory at Midway, which inside forty-eight hours transformed the course of the war against Japan. It was arguably the most influential single intelligence achievement of the global conflict.

While the British even before the war deployed brilliant civilians to spearhead their codebreaking, the US Navy chose to rely instead upon an almost randomly selected group of career officers, among the least valued of their service. With pitifully slender resources, their achievement could not match in scale that of Bletchley Park, nor did it save the US from humiliation on the December 1941 'Day of Infamy'. But the officer who made the greatest single contribution to subsequent triumph at Midway retired from his service with little honour, and went to his grave known only to historians.

Joseph Rochefort cut an awkward figure: he was a poor seaman, with no talent for making important friends. Without his gifts, however, it is unlikely that a decisive battle would have been fought in the Pacific between 4 and 7 June 1942, and even less plausible that it would have been won by the United States. What happened that day was the outcome not of a sudden flash of inspiration, but of two decades of weary, thankless labour.

Rochefort was born in 1900, youngest son of Irish parents; his father was an Ohio rug salesman. An untidy child, in high school he excelled only at maths. At seventeen he enlisted in the US Navy as an electrician 3rd class, then scraped a commission as a reservist and became an engineer. At twenty-one he married Elma Fay, his childhood sweetheart, though he was Catholic and she a Baptist. In 1921 he managed to transfer to the regular navy, but his career languished: he narrowly escaped court-martial when a tanker on which he was duty officer dragged its anchor in San Francisco Bay amid six destroyers. In 1925 he was detached from service on the battleship *Arizona* to study cryptanalysis, for which skill at bridge and crosswords seemed to fit him. He worked in the Navy Department on Washington's Constitution Avenue, but the assignment did not represent promotion: though codebreakers affected the communications of Japan, America's most plausible enemy, intelligence ranked low on the service's totem pole. The US Navy had thus far achieved nothing to match the achievement of the army's codebreaking department, the 'Black Chamber' established in 1917 under Herbert Yardley, which broke a Japanese diplomatic cipher as early as 1921.

The navy was learning, however. Rochefort started by reading the book *Elements of Cryptanalysis*, written by the War Department's William Friedman. He worked under the brilliant Lt. Laurance Safford, a former chief yeoman in the US Naval Reserve, who became his tutor and mentor. They were assisted by a civilian, Agnes Meyer Driscoll, who also made a notable contribution. Rochefort found himself enjoying the work. Breaking a code, he said later, 'makes you feel pretty good, because you have defied these people who have attempted to use a system they thought was secure … It was always somewhat of a pleasure to defeat them.' In February 1925 Safford departed for an almost mandatory spell of sea duty, leaving Rochefort in charge of the research desk. This consisted of only three full-timers: himself; an ex-actor named Claus Bogel, who did little to justify his rations; and Driscoll, dubbed 'Madame X', who cursed fluently, despised make-up, but rubbed along pretty well with Rochefort. Japan's secrets were always the principal targets. In 1920 the Office of Naval Intelligence had run a 'black bag job', photographing a copy of the Japanese Red Code from the New York consulate. It became obvious that higher language skills were indispensable if the codebreakers were to make serious headway: Lt. Cmdr Ellis Zacharias, a career intelligence officer and fluent Japanese speaker, was drafted into the section to work alongside Rochefort.

Zacharias wrote later: 'The few persons who were assigned to this section were taciturn, secretive people who refused to discuss their jobs … Hours went by without any of us saying a word, just sitting in front of piles of indexed sheets on which a mumbo-jumbo of figures or letters was displayed in chaotic disorder.' Given that the United States was at peace and determined to stay that way, the intensity with which a handful of naval officers laboured at their arcane craft seems extraordinary, and far removed from the lazy tempo that prevailed elsewhere in the US Navy. Those men and that one remarkable woman were obsessives, who worked all hours and ignored Sundays. The office was permanently shrouded in tobacco smoke: Rochefort chain-smoked cigarettes, a pipe, the odd cigar. They sometimes went home too tired to eat until they had unwound for several hours. All lost weight.

Safford had established a chain of intercept stations in Shanghai, Hawaii and elsewhere, which lifted Japan's signals from the ether. Once the messages reached Rochefort's office, the section worked together to crack them, with Agnes Driscoll probably the ablest analyst. Occasionally, new officers were sent to them, to test their suitability as codebreakers. Most were washed out: they lacked the peculiar, indispensable sense for the rhythm of puzzles.

After two years, Rochefort had had enough – not of codebreaking, but of Navy Department politics. His section's activities came under Communications, but Intelligence waged constant war to take it over. Still a lieutenant, Rochefort became executive officer of a destroyer. At sea his tactlessness, carried to the point of boorishness, exasperated superiors. In his spare time he checked out the US Navy's codes, and told the commander-in-chief that the communications system was clogged with trivial messages that should never have been encrypted. This was poorly received.

In 1929 his old colleague Ellis Zacharias arranged for him to be posted to Japan, to learn the language. While serving there for three years, Rochefort became a close friend of another American naval officer, Edwin Layton; it is a measure of his almost morbid sense of discretion that in all their hours together, he told Layton nothing about his background in cryptanalysis. Thereafter, Rochefort spent most of the 1930s at sea, successively as a gunnery, intelligence and navigation officer. In October 1939 he was posted to Pearl Harbor, where he was appalled by the casual routines, but shared the delusions of his superiors that no enemy would dare to attack Hawaii or the Philippines.

Laurance Safford now headed Op-20-G, the navy's codebreaking operation. With half the world at war this was modestly expanding, while Japanese relations with the US deteriorated. Between 1934 and 1939 the US government and armed forces had faithfully respected domestic law – explicitly Section 605 of the 1934 Federal Communications Act, which barred interception of messages between the US and foreign countries, radio or cable. Thereafter, George Marshall granted some latitude to the various codebreaking agencies and their eavesdroppers, which made possible the small miracle of Purple. Safford's activities, like Friedman's, nonetheless represented lawbreaking. He asked for Rochefort to head up the Pearl station, known as COM 14. Rochefort accepted the posting reluctantly, because of his memories of the departmental struggles. But where else was he to go, at forty-one, with nobody clamouring for his services? In June 1941 he took up his new responsibilities, reporting direct to Admiral Husband Kimmel, Pacific Fleet C-in-C. Only belatedly, four months later, did he receive a long-delayed promotion to commander.

COM 14 – 'Station Hypo' – where Rochefort and his team were to make history, was quartered in the echoing, unlovely basement of the Navy Yard administration building, entered through a time-locked unmarked door guarded by marines. 'The Dungeon', as it was dubbed by inmates, looked like a small-town pool hall, even unto the chronic smoke haze, because everybody worked with a cigarette stuck in his mouth. A chief petty officer, Tex Rorie, sat at a desk by the door, screening visitors. The floor was undressed concrete, the walls were painted with mud-coloured sealant, and the primitive ventilation system recycled stale air. When Rochefort first joined, much of the basement's hundred feet by fifty was emptiness, but through the months that followed, it filled rapidly. A battery of IBM Hollerith punch-card tabulating machines clattered relentlessly: their contribution to Hypo's successes, as indeed to all US codebreaking, deserves emphasis. In September, five Japanese-language officers joined the section. Soon there were twenty-three men, working in four sectors: the language team, traffic analysts, ship-plotters, cryptanalysts. Lt. Cmdr Thomas Dyer, a short, dark officer with heavy spectacles who looked more like an eccentric professor than a naval officer, was considered the best of the latter, and became a hero of America's cryptographic war. Others included Lt. Ham Wright, who bore a passing resemblance to the actor Wallace Beery; and Lt. Cmdr Jack Holtwick. Rochefort no longer thought of himself as a cryptanalyst; instead, he said, '[I] fancied myself a translator.'

They worked in the atmosphere of a university library – there was no chatter or loud talk, instead a fierce earnestness. When Jasper Holmes, an ex-submariner invalided out of the service, joined the team, he was awed by the intensity of its labours: 'Had I not witnessed it I never would have believed that any group of men was capable of such sustained mental effort under such constant pressure for such a length of time.' But he added: 'the results they achieved did not appear proportionate to their efforts'. In 1941–42, when Bletchley Park was already operating a dozen bombes, the tools most used by Rochefort's team were paper, pencil and the IBM tabulators, though Holtwick experimented with another crude mechanical aid. The cryptanalysts used mathematical skills to expose the code groups in a message – if they could get that far – then turned it over to the linguists. The introductory briefing for novices was simple: 'Gentlemen, here are your desks. Start breaking Japanese codes.' The Dungeon's personnel worked in an atmosphere of almost defiant informality. They addressed each other by name, not rank, and cared nothing for dress. Rochefort affected slippers and a maroon smoking jacket, which he claimed protected him from the chronic chill. Jasper Holmes found nothing companionable about his chief, but immediately recognised his strength of leadership. They worked an eight-day week: six on, then two off. A painted sign was affixed to a pillar near the desks: 'We can accomplish anything … provided … no one cares who gets the credit.' Rochefort, always obsessed with security, caused Hypo to be officially designated as 'Navy Communications Supplementary Activity'. Those personnel in the Navy Yard who knew what the team was doing regarded them with condescension in those days; they commanded no respect, because they had done nothing to earn it. As at Bletchley in the beginning, only the codebreakers themselves understood what they might be able to achieve, and how vast could be the significance of success.

Pearl's listening stations were located at Wahiawa and Lualuale, with a direction-finding facility at the latter, some thirty miles from the Navy Yard. Operators recorded messages transmitted in the Japanese version of Morse: this customarily used a blend of the *kana* syllabary and *romanjii* transliterated characters, superimposed on a telegraphic code – 'JN-25' messages contained only numbers. In the late autumn of 1941, a startling lack of urgency characterised the logistics of the codebreaking operation. Although both the intercept operators and Hypo had begun to maintain watches around the clock, there was no secure teleprinter link between the receiving stations and the Dungeon, only a party phone line. Once every twenty-four hours, the latest crop of messages was collected by jeep for the forty-minute trip to the Navy Yard. US Navy codebreakers around the world could communicate with each other by private cipher system, using an ECMII machine with fifteen rotors in three rows, but liaison between them was criminally poor. Rochefort's team was not informed that the army in Washington was breaking the Japanese Purple cipher, nor about the ONI's May 'pinch' of the Orange code from a Japanese freighter in San Francisco harbour. Indeed, Hypo was told nothing about where its own labours fitted into a bigger picture. At Pearl, the office of Fleet Intelligence Officer Edwin Layton – Rochefort's old comrade in Tokyo – was located a mile from the Navy Yard, at the Fleet submarine base.

Most of the weaknesses of US Navy intelligence, matching those of the US Army, were rooted in Washington, founded in the inability of senior officers to grasp the proper nature of information-gathering and management, which they understood little better than did their Japanese counterparts. They underrated Japan's air power – when Tokyo naval attaché Stephen Juricka saw a Zero on the ground at an air show and sent home a detailed report, he was rebuked for taking the plane so seriously. In 1940 a friendly informant in Japan gave the US embassy details of the new Type 93 'Long Lance', an oxygen-fuelled torpedo that was the best of its kind in the world. The Bureau of Ordnance dismissed this report, declaring such a weapon to be impossible. Here was a reflection of the tribalism of many nations' armed forces: if We have not created such a weapon, how could They have done so? It was astounding yet characteristic that Brigadier-General Hayer Kroner, head of the army's intelligence division, told a Pearl Harbor inquiry in 1942 that he had not been privy to his own service's Japanese decrypts. Meanwhile within the signals departments, a childish inter-service agreement had been reached in 1940, whereby the army and navy read Purple on alternate days, and delivered its output to the White House in alternate months. The dysfunction between the navy's operations and intelligence divisions was not improved by the fact that in 1941 the latter had three successive directors. Only brutal war experience caused the US armed forces slowly to learn to treat intelligence, and especially codebreaking, with the seriousness and sensitivity it merited.

In December 1941, Hypo had not come close to breaking the Japanese Flag Officers' Code, not least because there was too little traffic to work on, but it was enjoying some success with secondary systems. For most of 1941, just ten members of Op-20-G were working on the Japanese navy's JN-25. At that stage the most important weapon in Rochefort's armoury for producing radio intelligence was traffic analysis – locating Japanese warships through their wireless messaging, even though the content was unreadable. Even for achieving this, the US Navy lacked the technology the British had developed and employed in their Far East Combined Bureau in Singapore: 'radio fingerprinting' through cine-camera records of the oscilloscope images of each unique signal pattern, enabling interceptors to identify individual ships.

In the days before Pearl Harbor, it was evident to the team in the Dungeon that the Japanese were planning something big, though they had no notion what it might be. They detected an unprecedented concentration of naval air power, but Admiral Yamamoto put down a dense electronic smokescreen to mask its purpose. For months Rochefort had been tracking the movements of major units of the Japanese fleet, but in mid-November he lost its six carriers. His counterparts at the Cast station in the Philippines said they were confident the flat-tops were still in home waters. No thought of an assault on Pearl crossed Rochefort's mind: knowing Japan as he did, and as a doggedly logical man, he thought it implausible that Hirohito's nation would start a war with the US which it was certain to lose. So poor was intelligence liaison that Rochefort was told nothing of the 24 September message from Tokyo to its Hawaii consulate, asking for the precise locations of US battleships inside Pearl Harbor. This was sent in the Japanese consular code, designated 'J-19', which was deemed a low priority for breaking, and thus the coded message was not flown to Washington until 6 October, amid a mass of other material. Even when the signal was read, neither the US Army nor US Navy intelligence directorates thought it significant enough to replay to Hypo.

But Rochefort was sufficiently sure of the imminence of some major Japanese initiative that on 29 November he dispatched four officers to the intercept station to maintain a listening watch for a 'Winds' action message that they knew must be coming. Next day, the Japanese changed all their ships' identification callsigns for the second time in a month – yet another indication that a big operation was imminent. On 3 December, Washington at last condescended to inform Pearl – and Rochefort – that the Japanese had ordered all their diplomatic missions to destroy codes and ciphers. An FBI tap on the Japanese consul in Honolulu confirmed that he too had been told to burn his codes. But still no 'execute' order to the Japanese fleet was intercepted on Hawaii. In the week before the storm broke, Rochefort pleaded guilty to neglecting one message to a Japanese submarine that was not broken until 12 December. But even had this been read, given the

institutionalised passivity of the US government and armed forces, it is
hard to suppose that it would have changed anything. On Saturday, 6
December, an exhausted Rochefort went home at lunchtime. That afternoon a last coded cable from the Japanese consulate, detailing the positions of barrage balloons and torpedo nets around the Pearl anchorage,
was handed in at the RCA office for dispatch. But the copy earmarked for
America's codebreakers went uncollected until much later.

The legend of the Day of Infamy began at Bainbridge Island in Puget
Sound early on 7 December, when a US Navy listening post intercepted
cipher messages dispatched from Tokyo to Washington on the commercial circuit of the Mackay Radio & Telegraph Company. Bainbridge
re-transmitted them to the Navy Department's 20-GY, where they were
received by Lt. (Junior Grade) Francis Brotherhood as he approached the
end of his night shift. Brotherhood had already seen thirteen parts of the
Japanese message to its embassy, in response to the US diplomatic note
demanding Japan's withdrawal from China. Now, a short final decrypt
clattered off the printer – in Japanese. It was just after 5 a.m. Lt. Cmdr
Alwin Kramer, chief USN translator, arrived 150 minutes later, at 7.30
a.m., and within minutes recognised that the last message, breaking off
negotiations, must mean war. An army messenger set forth with a copy
destined for the War Department, while others were sent to the White
House and the Navy Department. At 9 a.m. – 3.30 a.m. in Hawaii – Rufus
Bratton, chief of the Far Eastern section of military intelligence, read the
decrypt, four hours before the Japanese ambassador was instructed to
deliver his momentous message to the State Department. Bratton
attempted to contact Gen. George Marshall, and was told that he was out
riding. An aide who went in search of the chief of staff failed to find him.
At 10.30, Bratton at last spoke to Marshall, stressed the urgency of the
news, and offered to dash out to his quarters at Fort Myer. Marshall
instead drove to the War Department, where he insisted on reading all
fourteen pages of the Japanese message in sequence, though Kramer
urged him to go straight to the end. At 11 a.m., with two hours still to go
before Pearl was hit, the chief of staff vetoed use of the scrambler phone
to contact Hawaii, on the bizarre grounds that it was insecure. Instead he
sent a warning cable via the War Department's message centre, which
reached Honolulu via RCA at 7.33 a.m. It was finally delivered to Gen.
Walter Short, local army C-in-C, at 2.40 p.m., as fires raged around the
fleet anchorage.

In Hawaii at 7.55 on Sunday morning, Joe Rochefort was packing up his car for a family picnic when the first Japanese aircraft streaked across the sky above Pearl Harbor. Moments later, Dyer called him to proclaim emotionally, 'We're at war.' One of Rochefort's men said much later, '[All] of us felt the remorse of participating in a tremendous intelligence failure.' This sentiment was quite unjustified. What took place represented a political and operational failure, matching that of the Kremlin less than six months earlier. Rowlett's achievement in breaking Purple was entirely wasted when its revelations mattered most. Thanks to the Signals Intelligence Service, overwhelming evidence was in the hands of the nation's executive branch and armed forces chiefs to indicate that the Japanese stood poised on the brink of offensive action. While there was a case for supposing that the British and other European colonial powers in Asia might be Tokyo's targets, rather than the United States, failure to place the nation's defences in the maximum state of readiness reflected negligence at the highest level. It was only because General George C. Marshall commanded such affection and respect that he escaped devastating and deserved personal censure for the blow that fell upon his country on 7 December. The same might be said about the president and his departmental heads. Instead, however, blame was allowed to stop with the service commanders-in-chief on Hawaii, and with the US Navy's chief of operations, an outcome justified on pragmatic grounds, though not on principled ones.

What mattered now was to strike back. Rochefort said laconically to his team, 'Forget Pearl Harbor and get on with the war.' In the first days of January 1942, the new Pacific C-in-C Admiral Chester Nimitz visited the Dungeon. It was not a happy occasion. Rochefort, preoccupied with a Japanese signal he was working on, gave a perfunctory reception to this new arbiter of his destiny. Nimitz was anyway in no mood to be impressed, because he regarded the 7 December catastrophe as representing a culpable failure by the navy's signals intelligence officers. From Washington, Laurance Safford warned Rochefort that the Navy Department shared Nimitz's view. It considered that Hypo was blameworthy, because it had been fooled by Japanese deceptions. In the following month Safford himself joined the casualties of the Day of Infamy, being removed and replaced by Commander Joseph Redman, an officer more skilled in self-promotion than cryptanalysis. Redman had one significant talent: he understood the importance of radio deception in modern war, and had written a paper about it for the chief of naval operations. But he was no fan of Rochefort, who would probably have lost his own job but for the support of Edwin Layton, whom Nimitz retained as fleet intelligence officer.

Hypo was now inundated with work, created by a continuous torrent of intercepts. One morning Jasper Holmes was talking to a naval friend outside the intelligence loop, who saw Thomas Dyer emerge from the Dungeon unshaven, dishevelled, utterly exhausted after hours of toil. The other officer gazed at Dyer without enthusiasm and said, 'Now, there goes a bird who should be sent to sea to get straightened out.' One reason the codebreakers held lowly ranks was that they had spent insufficient time afloat to qualify for promotions. Holmes, ever mindful of Rochefort's insistence on security, merely mumbled as they watched Dyer walk away, 'Oh, he's all right.' Afterwards, however, he felt that he had let down Hypo's most brilliant cryptanalyst, 'like Peter when he betrayed the Lord'.

The challenge was to crack the enemy's new JN-25b Fleet Code. Dyer, Wright and Holtwick were at the forefront here – Rochefort focused on trying to analyse the significance of the fragmentary traffic they read. Now that the importance of mechanical assistance was recognised, more men were needed to run the IBM sorters which constituted Hypo's memory bank; each intercept required some two hundred punch cards. The only hands available were bandsmen from the wrecked battleship *California*. When the FBI set about screening the men for high-security duty, several with foreign names were marked for exclusion, but Rochefort took them anyway; Layton got a nod from Nimitz.

In the weeks that followed, the Dungeon's standing with the commander-in-chief remained low. He repeatedly demanded information from Rochefort about the movements of Japan's carriers, and again and again traffic analysis produced the wrong answers. But then Rochefort and his men noted the build-up of Japanese forces at Truk, and correctly guessed that they were heading for Rabaul. His stock rose. He highlighted Japanese weakness in the Marshalls and the Gilbert Islands, which prompted strikes there by Halsey's and Fletcher's task forces. Hypo began passing intelligence about prospective targets to Fleet submarine headquarters, though this yielded meagre results because American torpedoes failed – as they continued to do until the end of 1943. Nimitz transferred some of Rochefort's Japanese linguists to the US carriers at sea, to monitor the voice traffic of enemy pilots. This was a significant loss to the codebreakers, but probably a valid switch of a desperately scarce resource.

From mid-January 1942 onwards, Hypo was reading fragments of JN-25b messages, albeit with many words missing. On 2 March Rochefort predicted an air raid on Hawaii on the 4th. Sure enough, two big flying-boats attacked at night – the Japanese enjoyed the assistance of being able to read American weather reports. Some bombs fell harmlessly in the mountains ten miles from Pearl, others in the sea; US fighters failed to intercept the attackers. But Rochefort had produced an accurate prediction, and did so again when he warned of a March air raid on Midway island. The most important aspect of this last break was that it gave Hypo the Japanese code designation for Midway: 'AF'. By the end of March the Americans were reading a substantial number of JN-25b messages.

The unrelenting stress afflicting the inmates of the Dungeon was now intensified by overcrowding – forty officers and a hundred enlisted men were crammed into the basement, where Jasper Holmes compared the atmosphere to that of an operational submarine. He and other supporting staff felt guilty that they could do nothing to alleviate the strain on the handful of cryptanalysts, who carried so much of the load. Rochefort and Dyer started a new routine of their own, each alternating twenty-four hours on, twenty-four off. Hypo's chief, scarcely a sunny soul nor an enthusiast for small talk, seemed never to relax. He spoke less and less about anything save the Japanese signal of the moment. He worked twenty hours a day and sometimes more, breaking off only to snatch a little sleep on a cot in a corner of the Dungeon. Dyer, meanwhile, subsisted on a diet of Benzedrine in the morning, Phenobarbital at night. Even those of their staff who managed longer breaks found themselves bored and lonely, existing in a sweat-stained, subterranean, monastically masculine world. Ham Wright's quarters near the submarine base became a lounge where officers could listen to his opera records and take a drink if they left a quarter behind.

Rochefort's record at this time was patchy, though no less so than was that of Bletchley in its early days. Between December 1941 and June 1942, while Op-20-G in Washington recovered 16,000 Japanese code additives, Hypo recovered 25,000 – the IBM machines played an important role here, using two to three million punch cards a month. On 8 April 1942, its chief correctly predicted that the Japanese were heading for Port Moresby in Papua New Guinea, having identified 'RZP' as its code designation. But many other locations remained obscure, and Rochefort proved mistaken in supposing five Japanese carriers to be at sea – at that time there were only three. He made an accurate appreciation of Japanese intentions ahead of the 7–8 May Battle of the Coral Sea, but misjudged two critical Japanese carrier movements. The outcome of the clash was a draw, but a strategic success for the Americans, because the Japanese abandoned their thrust against Port Moresby.

Early in May, Rochefort informed Nimitz that it was plain the Japanese were planning a major new initiative, though he was unsure what. Among his virtues was a fabulous memory for places, words, callsigns. The Navy Department decreed that the three codebreaking groups in Washington, Melbourne and Hawaii should each address enemy messages relating to designated geographical areas. Rochefort ignored this clumsy constraint, and strove to grasp the strategic big picture. Hypo was now receiving between five hundred and a thousand intercepts a day, about 60 per cent of all Japanese transmissions, of which its officers managed to read fragments of some 40 per cent. By 9 May, Rochefort was able to tell Nimitz that the Japanese fleet would sail for a major operation on the 21st, but added: 'Destination of the above force is unknown.'

The C-in-C speculated that the Japanese might intend a new assault on Pearl, or even against the US West Coast. Hypo, aware that Yamamoto was interested in the US base in the Aleutians, pondered the possibility that he might launch not just one major operation, but two. 13 May was a critical day: decrypts made plain that Pearl and the Aleutians were not the foremost Japanese priority. Instead, this was to be Midway, the most forward of all American Pacific bases, 1,200 miles north-west of Hawaii. An intercepted message instructed the supply ship *Goshu Maru* to load stores at Saipan, then proceed to 'Affirm Fox' – AF. Rochefort recalled signals back in March which identified AF as Midway. He picked up the secure phone to Layton, telling him, 'It's not cut and dried, but it's hot!' The intelligence officer said, 'The man with the blue eyes will want to know your opinion of it.'

Nimitz was assuredly interested, but preoccupied with other business. On the morning of 14 May he sent Captain Lynde McCormick, his new war plans officer, to discuss the possible threat to Midway. On ply sheets laid upon trestles in the Dungeon, Rochefort and his team set out their exhibits – a succession of key intercepts, together with equally important traffic-analysis data, and talked McCormick through them. This proved a fiercely intense, protracted conversation, which continued for most of the day. At the end of it, McCormick returned to Nimitz's office and reported that he believed Rochefort had got the story right. Though Hypo had no indication of the full Japanese order of battle, it seemed plain that Yamamoto intended to commit four carriers in support of an amphibious assault on Midway.

This was a debate of supreme importance and delicacy, of which Washington was informed. The US strategic position in the Pacific was still relatively weak, the Japanese fleet very strong. Amid the ocean's millions of square miles, most warships took twenty-four hours to traverse six or seven hundred miles. With only two, or at best three, operational carriers of his own, Nimitz could not divide his forces. If he wished to engage the enemy, he must bet the ranch on a single rendezvous. A misjudgement about the intended destination of the bulk of Japan's naval air force would be almost impossible to undo in time to avert a new disaster for American arms. Admiral Ernest King, chief of naval operations, gave his Pacific C-in-C little help with the decision-making. While King professed to favour engaging the Japanese wherever possible, he was wary of any course of action that might inflict further attrition on America's dangerously small carrier and cruiser force.

The Office of Naval Intelligence still thought the most likely enemy objective was Johnston Island, an atoll 720 miles west of Pearl; it was a further reflection on the navy's lamentable coordination that the ONI did not know that Rochefort had already identified Johnston as Japanese designation 'AG'. Meanwhile the Cast station in Melbourne thought Yamamoto would commit his main force against an island in the Marshalls. Layton clung to a belief that Pearl could be a target. Redman in Washington, no admirer of Rochefort's view about anything, simply rejected this one. By Saturday, 16 May, however, the man who mattered was increasingly convinced that Rochefort was right. Nimitz accepted that the Japanese were headed for Midway, and his judgement was confirmed by an important new intercept that day, giving the fly-off position for the Japanese carriers. Yet this too failed to convince Washington that Midway was their target. Rochefort, exasperated, dismissed Redman and his comrades as 'those clowns' – but they were also his superior officers.

Early on 19 May an impromptu conference took place in the basement, around the desk of Jasper Holmes. How could the doubts about Midway be dispelled? It was Holmes who conceived a solution, which was immediately adopted: the naval air station on Midway was sent a ciphered message by undersea cable, instructing its operators to send a plain-language wireless signal to Pearl, reporting difficulties with its distillation plant and requesting supplies of fresh water. An American not in on the secret exclaimed furiously, 'Those stupid bastards on Midway, what do they mean by sending out a message like this in plain language?' Holmes's ruse was brilliantly judged, however: the water issue was just trifling enough to be credibly flagged in a plain-language signal, yet its substance was sufficiently interesting to Japanese eyes to merit forwarding to naval headquarters. Sure enough, there was the message winging its way across the enemy's wireless net, containing the key reference to 'AF' – Midway.

On 20 May the Dungeon's Red Lasswell broke the Japanese operation order for the assault; though unknown to the Americans, this disclosed only a part of Yamamoto's plan: they had no hint of the fact that his main force of battleships would trail six hundred miles behind the carrier group, poised to close in and finish off the US Pacific Fleet when this appeared on the Midway battlefield – as Tokyo anticipated that it belatedly would. Nimitz now launched an effective little deception: the seaplane tender *Tangier* was sent to fly off planes to stage a token air raid on Tulagi; this perfectly served its purpose, convincing the Japanese that a US carrier group must be within range, and thus thousands of miles from Midway.

Next day the Cast team in Melbourne declared that it was now persuaded Rochefort was right. On 22 May the British Far East Combined Bureau also concluded from its own decrypt activities that Midway was the Japanese objective. But in Washington, Redman and Op-20-G were furious that Rochefort had persuaded Nimitz to undertake the water-signal ruse without reference to them. Stimson, at the War Department, said the US Army still doubted Rochefort's assessment, and feared Hypo was falling victim to an elaborate Japanese deception. Nimitz wrote uneasily in his own assessment on 26 May: 'our sole source of information is [sigint] … The enemy may be deceiving us.'

It is hard to overstate the personal strain on Rochefort in those days. This unloved, awkward man was making a case against the judgement of most of his peers, especially in Washington. Seldom in history has so much hung upon the word of a single junior officer. If he was wrong, the United States could suffer a strategic disaster in the Pacific. On the morning of 27 May, Rochefort donned a clean uniform: he was scheduled to brief Nimitz and his staff. Just as he was about to leave the basement for the C-in-C's office, Joe Finnegan and Ham Wright broke a signal that identified the dates of the Japanese strikes: 3 June against the Aleutians, the 4th for Midway. This caused Rochefort to arrive half an hour late for Nimitz's meeting, to a correspondingly stony reception. He was told to describe what he thought he knew, without mentioning in the presence of officers not in on Hypo's secret the means by which the information had been secured.

He outlined the Japanese plan for twin strikes, though mistakenly suggesting that the Aleutians thrust was a mere diversion: in reality, it was much more substantial. In consequence of that wrong call, Nimitz sent only cruisers and destroyers northwards. But the Pacific C-in-C made the pivotal decision to commit all his three carriers to meet the enemy at Midway, just before a bitter blow struck the Americans. The Japanese changed their codes, introducing JN-25c. This development had been expected, but the consequence was to slam shut, for a period of several weeks, Hypo's peephole on the motions of their foes. Rochefort and his team, during the days of electric tension before 4 June, were obliged once more to rely solely upon traffic analysis of enemy transmissions, and there were precious few of these: Yamamoto had imposed wireless silence on his attacking forces.

American carelessness jeopardised Nimitz's trap. As his ships set forth to meet the enemy, they talked too much: there was a sharp increase in US Navy wireless traffic, and the Japanese noticed. But Yamamoto scented only a mouse when he should have smelt a giant rat. In one of his major misjudgements of the war, he decided not to break wireless silence to inform Vice-Admiral Chuichi Nagumo, commanding his carrier group, that the Americans might be up to something, perhaps even heading for Midway. Here was a moment when a commander's fear of the consequences of dispatching a stream of Morse across the ether precipitated a worse outcome than had he done so. At Pearl, tension rose to an almost unbearable level through the long hours of 3 June, as Midway's reconnaissance aircraft gained no glimpse of the expected enemy flat-tops. Then, at 5.30 a.m. next day, exactly in accordance with Rochefort's prediction, at last a Catalina flying-boat sent a momentous signal: the enemy's principal carrier force was in sight.

The American triumph that followed was anything but ordained. Destruction of Nagumo's four carriers, the transformation of the balance of the war in the Pacific, was achieved by phenomenal luck as well as the skill and courage of the US Navy's dive-bomber pilots. While Nimitz had gambled courageously to bring about the clash, the outcome could have gone disastrously the other way. Only on 5 June did Hypo discover Yamamoto's battleships closing in on the scene, which prompted the American carrier groups to beat a hasty and prudent retreat. But Midway was above all else an intelligence victory, sharing with Bletchley's breach of the German U-boat codes the status of most influential Western Allied intelligence achievements of the war. Nimitz recognised this when he sent a car to bring Rochefort to attend his own celebration party. The Hypo chief's luck was as lousy as ever: he arrived only after the guests had dispersed. But Nimitz, in the midst of conducting a staff conference, used the opportunity to pay tribute to the codebreaker: 'This officer deserves a major share of the credit for the victory at Midway.'

Those words were to be Rochefort's only reward. When he was proposed for a Distinguished Service Medal, the citation was quashed by Rear-Admiral Russell Willson, the CNO's chief of staff: 'I do not concur in the recommendation ... he has merely efficiently used the tools previously prepared for his use. It would be inappropriate to award a medal only to the officer who happened to be in a position to reap the benefits, at a particular time, unless in actual combat with the enemy.' Jasper Holmes wrote of the post-Midway mood in the Dungeon: 'there was no great moment of exhilaration'. Rochefort enjoyed one more important success as chief of Hypo: he revealed the Japanese landing on Guadalcanal on 5 July, which precipitated a dramatic and ultimately triumphant American riposte with land, sea and air forces. He was also able to alert MacArthur's command to the Japanese attempt to cross the Owen Stanley range and fall on Port Moresby.

So far as Washington was concerned, however, far from Rochefort being dubbed the hero of Midway, he was simply an insubordinate cuss whom nobody liked. On 14 October 1942 he was relieved of his post and assigned to command a floating dry dock in San Francisco. He was succeeded by Captain William Goggins, an officer with no previous experience of cryptanalysis, who was deemed a competent administrator. Although all hierarchies commit some arbitrary injustices, this was an exceptionally brutal and mean-spirited one. In the autumn of 1944 Rochefort gained sufficient rehabilitation to be put in command of the Pacific Strategic Intelligence Unit, but he died undecorated in 1976. Only in 1985 was he posthumously awarded the Distinguished Service Medal that had been denied him in 1942.

It was a sort of miracle that Rochefort and his team achieved what they did, with the makeshift resources available. The army–navy feud which caused the US for so long to divide its codebreaking operations was worsened by the low priority accorded to intelligence. By 1942, Bletchley and the British service intelligence departments deployed hundreds of the finest civilian brains in the country alongside a handful of career professional soldiers, sailors and airmen, together with technology in advance of anything being used by Hypo or Cast. Rochefort was merely a highly experienced, not personally brilliant crypto-linguist and analyst, and his team was a group of hitherto lowly regarded naval officers.

The post-war narrative of the US Navy's Pacific Combat Intelligence Center stated bluntly: 'In the defensive stages of the war [1941–43] radio intelligence was not only the most important source of intelligence in the Central Pacific, it was practically the only source. There were very few captured documents or prisoners of war. There were no photographs of enemy positions … Excluding the Solomons and New Britain, spies and coast-watchers' reports never supplied any important intelligence.' The operational diary of the Japanese navy general staff recorded bitterly after Midway: 'the enemy had grasped our intentions beforehand'. But not for a moment did Yamamoto or his officers consider the possibility that their ciphers were compromised; they attributed the disaster merely to the mischance that their carriers had been spotted by American reconnaissance aircraft or submarines.

Joe Rochefort was not personally indispensable. After his departure the US Navy's intelligence and codebreaking operations became ever more sophisticated and effective, although the difficulties of breaking JN-25's variants persisted until 1944, and sometimes even beyond. The cottage industry of 1941–42 became FRUPAC – Fleet Intelligence Radio Unit Pacific – a department employing five hundred men, a formidable tool in Nimitz's hand. But Rochefort deserves to be remembered as a man who changed history, while the honour of the US Navy was tarnished by the scurvy ingratitude with which its chiefs rewarded him.

6

Muddling and Groping:
The Russians at War

1 CENTRE MOBILISES

No one who cherishes illusions about the skill and omniscience of Russia's secret services could sustain these after studying their wartime record. It was certainly no better, and in most respects worse, than that of the Western democracies. Hitler's invasion on 22 June 1941 precipitated a crisis for Stalin's intelligence organisations, which like the Red Army had been crippled by the Purges. Pavel Sudoplatov's reward for organising Trotsky's killing in August 1940, together with his unflinching participation in many other liquidations, was an appointment a month after the start of 'Barbarossa' to head the NKVD's 'Administration for Special Tasks', officially responsible for 'sabotage, kidnapping and assassination of enemies', a job description worthy of Ian Fleming's novels. Sudoplatov handed Beria a list of 140 intelligence officers confined in prisons or the gulag for political offences whose services were now vitally needed by the state, either to spy or to run spies. He noted that the files showed all those named to have been detained on the personal orders of either Stalin or Molotov. Now, Beria asked no questions about the prisoners' guilt or innocence, merely demanding, 'Are you sure we need them?' The new head of special tasks responded, 'Yes, I am absolutely certain,' and was ordered to arrange their release. Unfortunately, as Sudoplatov observed unemotionally in his memoirs, three of the best men proved already to have been executed. The remainder returned to intelligence duties, in varying conditions of relief and trauma.

If the lives of the NKVD's officers were precarious, they also enjoyed the perquisites that accrued to favoured servants of the Soviet state – for instance, the children of 'illegals' operating abroad were admitted to universities without being required to pass entrance exams. Sudoplatov occupied a relatively spacious apartment above the Dynamo sports store on Gorky Street, in a block exclusively tenanted by the Kremlin's secret soldiers, including foreign intelligence chief Vsevolod Merkulov. After the June 1941 mass release of political suspects to resume intelligence work, several moved in temporarily with Sudoplatov, their deliverer. One night Merkulov suddenly telephoned to announce that he was coming down to talk. The newly liberated officers were hastily herded into hiding in the bedroom, lest their presence prompt embarrassment. Sudoplatov had sufficient sense of self-preservation to have taken care not to sign their rehabilitation documents personally. Instead he got Fitin to do so – which, he said, probably saved his life in 1946, when his own survival hung by a thread.

The intelligence officers rescued from the gulag rejoiced in their freedom, in some cases too soon. One of them, Ivan Kavinsky, danced about Sudoplatov's flat in the three-piece suit with which he had been issued in place of prison denims. How wonderful it was, Kavinsky exulted, to be acknowledged at last as a patriot. Hours later, he was dispatched to serve as a stay-behind agent in Zhitomir, deep in Ukraine, which was about to be overrun by the Germans. There, he was almost immediately betrayed by Ukrainians, as many other servants of Moscow were betrayed. Arriving at a rendezvous and sensing a trap, Kavinsky shot himself. The remainder of his cell perished in a subsequent gun battle with the Gestapo. In the same fashion several other important NKVD residents were swiftly eliminated by the Germans. One of Beria's most cynical ruses was carried out in August 1941: NKVD agents disguised as Nazi parachutists were dropped into the Volga German autonomous region, to test the loyalty of its citizens. Villages where the new arrivals were offered shelter were liquidated wholesale; the entire region's surviving population was eventually deported to Siberia and Kazakhstan.

Some intelligence officers liberated for war service had suffered unimaginable horrors in jails of the kind to which they had been accustomed to dispatch others. Dmitri Bystroletov, a pre-war agent-handler in Berlin, was tortured with a ball-bearing swung on a steel cable. After signing a confession, in 1939 he was sentenced to twenty years' imprisonment. His wife Shelmatova was sent to the gulag, where she slit her throat with a kitchen knife; Bystroletov's elderly mother meanwhile poisoned herself. It is hard to suppose that rehabilitation now secured him much happiness. Another such figure was Pyotr Zubov, who had been disgraced for failing to carry through an attempted coup in Yugoslavia. Since 1939 Sudoplatov had been urging Zubov's qualities as an intelligence officer – without mentioning the man's important role in Beria's ascent to power. In prison he refused to confess to non-existent crimes against the state, even after his knees were smashed with a hammer, rendering him a lifelong cripple. Zubov was confined in the same Lubyanka cell as Col. Stanislas Sosnowski, former head of Polish intelligence in Berlin, and his compatriot Prince Janusz Radziwiłł. The NKVD set about turning both for their own purposes, and Zubov's role in achieving this enabled Sudoplatov to secure his release. Zubov became one of his section heads, limping and shuffling around the Lubyanka.

Sosnowski started working for the Russians, who sought to exploit his old sources in Berlin, most of them women. His old network had been broken up by the Nazis back in 1935, when he himself was imprisoned for espionage, then obliged to witness the guillotining of his agents at Plötzensee jail. He was eventually exchanged for the leader of the German minority community in Poland, but was sacked following a financial scandal. He was living in retirement when the Russians scooped him up during their 1939 invasion. He claimed just two surviving German sources, and reactivated these at the NKVD's bidding. Sudoplatov asserted that he provided some value for his jailers until 1942, and thereafter was kept in the Lubyanka for the usual Soviet reason: 'He was a man who knew too much.'

Even more so than the plots of most intelligence services, those of the NKVD lurched between the imaginative and the ridiculous. In the winter of 1941, at Stalin's personal behest a plan was devised for the killing of Hitler. The principal assassin was to be an NKVD 'illegal' named Igor Miklashevsky, a former boxing champion. In December 1941 he succeeded in gaining access to Germany, posing as a defector. His authenticity in this role was attested by his uncle, a genuine exiled opponent of Stalin.

Miklashevsky's subsequent career almost defies belief. He fought a bout with Germany's hero Max Schmeling, which he contrived to win. He reported to Moscow that while it seemed impossible to reach Hitler, it would be easy to assassinate Göring. Centre rejected this proposal, for Göring's removal seemed more likely to assist the Nazi war effort than the Soviet one. Miklashevsky remained in Germany until 1944, when he murdered his uncle and escaped to France. Stalin meanwhile withdrew his order for Hitler's assassination, fearing his removal would prompt the Western Allies to seek a separate peace with a successor German leadership. After the liberation of France Miklashevsky spent two years in the West hunting down Ukrainian renegades of Hitler's wartime 'Vlasov army', then returned to Moscow, where he boxed until his retirement.

As the Germans closed in on Moscow, the NKVD struggled to organise stay-behind espionage groups against the eventuality of the capital's fall. They prepared key installations for demolition, including Politburo members' dachas. So many NKVD staff had quit the Lubyanka that Sudoplatov's Special Tasks group took over some offices for the saboteurs. Zoya Rybkina, who was one of them, described how safes were cleared of secret files and instead crammed with weapons, ammunition, compasses, explosives, fuses and even Molotov cocktails. During the hours of darkness, teams set forth to bury arms dumps in the city's parks. 'We did not go home for a hundred days,' wrote Rybkina, 'sleeping instead in air raid shelters with a gas mask case in place of a pillow.' Each stay-behind group was organised as a 'family', with a 'grandpa' or 'grandma' as its head – usually an old Bolshevik chosen by the veteran Colonel Georgy Mordinov; some were veterans of the International Brigade in Spain, though most of these were former spies now too old for military service. Radio-operators and cipher clerks were appointed as their 'grandsons' and 'granddaughters'. Rybkina once called at Mordinov's apartment in Begovaya, and found the old revolutionary asleep on a bed composed of trotyl explosive blocks.

Senior officers despaired of amassing sufficient charges to mine the largest structures, for instance the Dynamo stadium and rail stations. Sudoplatov claimed in his memoirs that Special Tasks could call upon the services of a motorised brigade of 20,000 men and women, including two hundred foreigners of many nationalities – Germans, Austrians, Spaniards, Americans, Chinese, Vietnamese, Poles, Czechs, Bulgarians, Romanians. He also boasted of a paratroop unit on permanent standby to counterattack any German commando attack – for instance, against the Kremlin – with its own squadron of transport aircraft. Some of the USSR's finest athletes had been drafted into service, and some of these were promptly designated for partisan operations, working in places and circumstances where supreme fitness and hardiness were needed.

Sudoplatov fails to acknowledge, however, that most of these elite units became available only later in the war: in the winter of 1941 the NKVD was reduced to pitiful improvisations. A Russian officer recorded the case of one of thousands of 'line-crossers' deployed at this time, a pretty young Ukrainian girl named Oksana. The Soviet Twelfth Army several times dispatched her through the enemy front in the Don basin. She was eventually denounced, however, as having gone over to the Axis. After interrogation she admitted that she had been caught, and chose to save her own life by 'accepting the protection' of an Italian officer. The Soviet tribunal which tried her allegedly waived the death penalty and instead gave her a long prison sentence, but almost all such people of both sexes were summarily executed. It is hard to credit that mercy was shown in this case, at this worst of all times for Soviet fortunes.

With the new importance of special forces, Sudoplatov rose in the Soviet hierarchy. In February 1942 he became a commissar of state security and lieutenant-general, and in August travelled with Beria and Merkulov at the head of an NKVD mission to the Caucasus, flying in American-supplied C-47s to arrange the blockage of mountain passes and stay-behind sabotage operations. The Special Tasks chief admitted later that having no military training, he felt out of his depth at a war front. So did his followers, who had been chosen for their skills as mountaineers rather than as soldiers: those who stayed to fight in the Caucasus suffered heavy losses. Beria suggested that Professor Konstantin Gamsakhurdia, a prominent local intellectual, should be designated to head the Caucasus groups. Sudoplatov thought this was a terrible idea: Gamsakhurdia was only on the NKVD's books because he had been blackmailed into service as an informer years earlier, through a rash attachment to the Georgian nationalist movement. Now he met the professor at Tbilisi's Intourist hotel, and was unimpressed: 'He appeared to me unreliable, and besides his experience as an agent was not in inspiring people, only informing on them. He was too preoccupied with writing verses and what he believed to be great novels in the Georgian language such as *Abduction of the Moon*, a mediaeval saga.'

Sudoplatov preferred for the leadership role a local playwright named Georgi Machivariani, who was entrusted with a small fortune in gold and silver to finance partisan operations. In the event Tbilisi was never taken by the Germans. After the tide of war had turned, the NKVD chief described his amazement when Machivariani refunded his treasure undiminished, though he does not speculate about whether his conduct reflected honesty or terror. When Beria and his deputies returned to Moscow, Stalin reprimanded them for having ventured into a combat zone. He needed his spymasters closer to home.

2 THE END OF SORGE

Japan assumed a pivotal importance after Germany invaded the Soviet Union, a development which deeply distressed Richard Sorge, as all those around him observed. Moscow needed the answer to a critical strategic question: would the Japanese seize the opportunity to strike at Russia from the east, forcing the Red Army to fight on two fronts? Sorge's informant Hotsumi Ozaki wielded significant influence through his membership of two government advisory groups, upon both of which he urged that Japan should move south, against the Europeans, rather than against the Russians. On 29 June Max Clausen wirelessed to Moscow a Sorge message reporting that Japan was staging a test mobilisation for war with Russia, but that prime minister Konoye remained opposed to belligerence. The operator's mental health cannot have been improved by a routine visit from the Kempeitai military police during this transmission.

On 10 July, Sorge told Moscow that while Japan would continue contingency preparations for war with the USSR, the main thrust of its policy would be to pursue negotiations with the United States and to plan for war with the European empires. Tokyo would attack the Soviet Union only if its collapse seemed imminent. Nonetheless, it is important to note that the wording of his dispatches remained equivocal and inconclusive. They reflected the fact that while Sorge and Wenneker, the German naval attaché, thought Japan would not fight Russia in 1941, Ott and his military attaché disagreed, believing that Tokyo would become a belligerent by autumn. Sorge several times asserted that Japan would probably be tipped into attacking the Soviet Union by the fall of Leningrad and Moscow, but at no time did he explicitly and uncompromisingly assure Moscow that Russia was safe from any Japanese threat. Contrarily, he reported the high command's conviction that the Wehrmacht would enter Russia's capital within weeks – which would almost certainly prompt the Japanese to attack the reeling Soviets from the east.

For years it was claimed that Sorge's intelligence changed the course of history, by enabling Stalin to shift major formations from the East, to check the Nazi onslaught in the autumn and winter of 1941. In truth, such a redeployment began as early as May. A modern Russian source asserts that Moscow Centre received information from many foreign sources in the latter part of 1941 confirming that Japan had no intention of attacking Russia, allegedly on the basis of documents in the Moscow intelligence archive. On 17 July, the NKVD in London sent the text of a Bletchley decrypt of a telegram from the Japanese Foreign Ministry, announcing the decision of an imperial conference not to join Hitler's attack on the Soviet Union. The Tokyo spy's dispatches may have increased the Stavka's willingness to reduce the Red Army's Asian forces, but as in all matters relating to intelligence, many sources and factors influenced Stalin's decision, and the codebreaking operation described below may also have played a part. The reports of spies, however well placed and however romantic their stories, can never offer national leaders certainty, nor even probability. Jack Masterman, orchestral conductor of the British Double Cross system, has written: 'It is a mistake to suppose that the well-placed person, friendly, let us say, with a Cabinet minister or an official in the Foreign Office or a highly placed staff officer is necessarily in the highest grade of agents. The individual remarks of ministers or generals do not carry much conviction, and it is a truism of historical research that when dealing with diplomatic conversations and the rumours of embassies, we are in the very realm of lies.'

No more than any other agent could Sorge complete strategic jigsaw puzzles, nor even provide pieces in the same fashion as did signal decrypts or captured enemy documents. He could merely offer clues and pointers, for instance about the dispositions of the Japanese army, though Ozaki achieved an important coup by securing details of Japan's petroleum reserves. In July, Ott dispatched Sorge to Shanghai to investigate the prospects of a mediated Japan–China peace. On his return, Hanako said that she had been questioned about him by the police. When an officer visited the house again shortly afterwards, Sorge was angry enough to hit the man. He escaped arrest for the assault, but it is plain that he was close to a nervous breakdown.

He reported to Moscow that the Japanese had been reinforcing their troops in Manchuria, but ever more of his material was failing to reach the GRU – for instance, a significant message about shrinking Japanese petrol stocks – because Clausen could not handle the stack of messages awaiting encryption and transmission. On 20 August, however, a signal did get to its destination, saying that Japan's military leadership was still unwilling to enter the war, pending decisive German success in the West, but this ended – again, inconclusively – 'Japan might not join the war this year, although the decision has not yet been taken.' In August also, Ozaki visited Manchuria in his role as an important adviser to the railway management. On 14 September this yielded a report to the Russians that the Japanese were reducing their immediate military commitment in Manchuria, but were building a new strategic road to the frontier in preparation for a possible war with the Soviet Union in 1942. On Saturday, 4 October, a further message stated that an early Japanese attack on Russia was now highly unlikely. This proved to be the last transmission Max Clausen ever made.

On 10 October 1941 the Tokko security police arrested first Tomo Kitabayashi, then Yotoku Miyagi, both former members of the American Communist Party. In the latter's room searchers found a report on Japan's oil stocks, unlikely reading material for a professional artist. During his interrogation, Miyagi suddenly sprang to his feet and leapt out of a window, in a suicide bid. He fell two storeys, as did a police officer who jumped in pursuit. Both men survived. Under further questioning Miyagi told all he knew, revealing the names of Clausen, Voukelitch, Ozaki – and Sorge. At first the Tokko flatly declined to consider arresting the last of these, because of his status as a prominent member of the German embassy community. On 15 October, however, Ozaki was arrested at his home, and at Meguro police station began to talk almost immediately. He became outspoken to his inquisitors, declaring confidently on the 18th when the Tojo government succeeded that of Prince Konoye: 'This cabinet is the one which is going to war against the United States.' Clausen, Voukelitch and Sorge were all arrested in their homes on that same day. The wireless-operator made no attempt to destroy his codes, and had preserved copies of scores of messages he had transmitted. Instead of killing themselves, as their captors expected, most of the prisoners talked their heads off. It remains disputed whether this was a consequence of torture or – quite plausibly – because they were morally exhausted. All were questioned in English.

Sorge, alone, initially held out. He was visited by Eugene Ott, who was not merely furiously angry with the Japanese police, but also stubbornly disbelieving of his friend's guilt – as he remained into old age. On 24 October, however, the spy suddenly broke. He wrote with a pencil: 'I have been an international Communist since 1925,' then burst into tears. His interrogators, overwhelmed by the compulsive flood of disclosures that followed, provided him with a typewriter. He set about composing a detailed narrative of his experiences, most of which was subsequently destroyed in the 1945 Tokyo fire-bombing. He asked his jailers to contact the Russians and attempt to arrange an exchange, a proposal which elicited a stony response from the Soviet embassy. The German mission succumbed to a sustained trauma, shock waves from which reached Berlin. The Gestapo's Joseph Meisinger was disgraced for his egregious failure as security officer, and Walter Schellenberg was reprimanded by Himmler. Ott was summarily recalled, and Hitler informed. Yet in accordance with the erratic conduct of tyrannies, the Führer chose not to exact drastic penalties. The ambassador suffered dismissal, but escaped the executioners who would surely have awaited him in Moscow, had he been Stalin's servant.

The spies meanwhile languished in Tokyo prisons. During the Second World War the Japanese behaved with institutionalised barbarity towards vast numbers of enemies in their power. It is bizarre, therefore, that the Tokko and the justice system appear to have treated Richard Sorge and most of the members of his ring relatively humanely, though they spent the ensuing three years in prison cells. While all were repeatedly and sometimes harshly interrogated, there is no evidence that they were tortured, as Tokyo's prisoners were so often tortured; none of their family members or associates were persecuted or killed. Japanese restraint was probably prompted by a reluctance gratuitously to provoke Moscow, at a time when Tokyo was increasingly desperate to avoid war on a new front. Voukelitch died in prison on Hokkaido on 13 January 1945, but Clausen survived the war and was released on 8 October that year. He flew to Moscow, and thereafter lived in retirement with his wife in East Germany.

The trials of Sorge and Ozaki dragged on until September 1943, when the two men became the only members of the ring to receive capital sentences. These were carried out on 7 November 1944, at Tokyo's Sugamo prison. Its governor, Kikuyasa Ichijima, attended in dress uniform. Ozaki chose to don a black ceremonial kimono and black *tabi* before he was hooded and bound. Four executioners sprang the trap together, so that no one man bore the responsibility for killing another – this, in the midst of a war in which tens of millions were being slaughtered. Sorge was then summoned, wearing dark trousers, an open-necked shirt and loose jacket. The governor demanded formally: 'Are you Richard Sorge?' and the condemned man assented. Then he asked, 'Is it today?' and it was the governor's turn to nod. Sorge stated that he wished his property to go to Anna Clausen, wife of his wireless-operator, and she duly received the yen equivalent of some US$4,000 – Hanako's slavish loyalty to him was not reciprocated. He was offered the ritual tea and cakes, which he declined, asking instead for a cigarette. The governor said this was against the rules. The attending Tokko officer urged allowing this last request, but Ichijima was firm.

Sorge remained calm as he was bound, then cried out in halting Japanese, '*Sakigun!*' – the Red Army; '*Kokusai Kyosanto!*' – the International Communist Party; '*Soviet Kyosanto!*' – the Soviet Communist Party. The Tokko witness said later that he spoke like a man uttering a prayer. Other versions of Sorge's last words have been suggested, but this one seems the most credible: he sought to dignify the labours of his life at its ending, and spoke in the language which would ensure that he was understood. At 10.20 a.m. the trap was sprung, and after nineteen minutes he was pronounced dead. Neither the German nor the Soviet embassy wanted anything to do with his body, and thus it was committed to the prison graveyard.

Like most secret agents, Richard Sorge was an abnormal human being, who gained an emotional charge from his complex existence and multiple deceits. He had more than a little in common with Kim Philby – charm and a streak of recklessness which rendered astonishing the longevity of both men in their roles. Sorge retains celebrity because he was a remarkable personality, and also because very few spies, and certainly no wartime British, American or German agent, gained such access to high places. It is much more doubtful, however, that he alone changed any history: 'All things are always on the move simultaneously.'

3 THE SECOND SOURCE

The arrest of Richard Sorge and the break-up of his network is often supposed to have marked the end of Soviet penetration of wartime Japan. Yet this was not the case. Centre had another important source on Tokyo's affairs – and possibly also access to some of its codes. Captain Sergei Tolstoy, the Japanese specialist in the NKVD's Fifth (Cipher) Directorate, became the most decorated Soviet cryptanalyst of the war, closely followed by Boris Aronsky. Some modern Russian writers suggest that Tolstoy's team thus provided the Kremlin with information about Tokyo's intentions based on better authorities than Sorge offered. In October and November 1941 eight Soviet rifle divisions, a thousand tanks and a thousand aircraft were moved to the Western Front. The Russians claim to have read a 27 November instruction from Tokyo to Baron Ōshima in Berlin: 'see Hitler and Ribbentrop, and explain to them in secret our relations with the United States … Explain to Hitler that the main Japanese efforts will be concentrated in the south and that we propose to refrain from deliberate operations in north [against the Soviet Union].' This signal was allegedly forwarded to Moscow by Kim Philby, via the NKVD's London station. All that seems certain is that in the months following the onset of 'Barbarossa' the Russians had plenty of informants other than Sorge telling them that their eastern flank was safe.

They never remotely matched the achievements of Bletchley, Arlington

Hall and Op-20-G, because they were incapable of building bombes, and would never have licensed the sort of young iconoclasts who led the British operation. Western cryptographic experts also argue that, to have read Purple consistently, they would need to have matched the American achievement in building a replica of the machine, for which Soviet technological skills were almost certainly inadequate, and for which the Russians have never produced evidence – the Germans' OKW/Chi failed to break Purple. It is not unlikely that Tokyo's cable to Ōshima was passed to Moscow from Washington or London by an American or British traitor, rather than broken by the Fifth Directorate.

Yet the Russians had more success in reading at least lower enemy wireless traffic than is sometimes recognised. There is now no doubt that valuable coding material was provided to Centre by a Japanese informant, Izumi Kozo, whose story deserves to be better known. He was an unusually gifted linguist who spoke both Russian and English. At the age of thirty-three in 1925, he was posted to his country's newly opened Moscow embassy. He rented a room from a general's widow named Elizaveta Perskaya, whose daughter Elena was a literature graduate who worked in the library of the Internal Affairs Ministry. Kozo fell in love with Elena, and they were married two years later. The whole family was, inevitably, on the books of the secret police, not least because Elizaveta's son had been executed for anti-Bolshevik activities.

It seems almost certain that Elena was ordered by a case officer to start a relationship with Kozo. When he was reposted to the Japanese consulate in Harbin, his wife, mother-in-law and a baby boy accompanied him. Thereafter, however, Elena broke off contact with the NKVD and was deprived of her Soviet citizenship. When her mother Elizaveta was rash enough to return to Moscow, she was promptly arrested and sentenced to ten years' imprisonment for espionage. A second daughter, Vera, was shot along with her husband, though the family was told that she was confined in a psychiatric hospital. It is hard to believe that the Kozo family discovered many causes for mirth in their lives.

In 1935 Izumi became third secretary at the Japanese embassy in Prague. Two years later, Elena presented herself at the local Soviet embassy to deliver a formal request for her citizenship to be restored so she could return home and bring up her son in Moscow. The boy was not, she said, the son of Kozo, though the diplomat had adopted him as such. Moscow Centre considered this proposal. The troubled woman was asked if her husband worked in intelligence; she said she only knew that he had been learning French and German, and spent a lot of time reading the Russian émigré press. The NKVD's verdict was that its handlers should reopen contact with Elena, in hopes of securing access to Japan's diplomatic codes. They had two levers: whatever Elena felt about her husband, he was passionately committed to both her and the boy; moreover, he deplored Japan's aggressive foreign policy.

Cash provided a further motive to Mrs Izumi, if not to her husband: at a meeting in Prague on 3 May 1938, Elena offered seven Japanese code-books for £10,000, and when this deal was rejected she took the material back to the embassy. In September she renewed the negotiation, this time asking for £5,000 and £100 a month. It remains uncertain how much she finally received, but the NKVD's Prague resident duly received seven codebooks and assorted secret telegrams which were welcomed in Moscow, and appear to have enabled the Soviets to read some Tokyo diplomatic traffic. Amid the post-Munich crisis, Japanese embassy families were evacuated to Finland, but Kozo remained in Prague until late October. Though not a professional intelligence officer, he was performing some intelligence tasks, and was soon able to divert to his NKVD case officer telegrams and details of Tokyo's local agents. On 4 October he delivered a batch of twenty-five messages from Berlin, twenty-nine from London, thirteen from Rome and fifteen from Moscow. A week later he provided a memorandum on the organisation of Japanese intelligence abroad. The NKVD remained cautious about Kozo, however, and decided to work chiefly through his wife, whom they were confident they could control. The veteran intelligence officer Zoya Rybkina was posted to Helsinki to handle her.

At their first meeting, Elena besought Rybkina to be allowed to return home, but Moscow decided this was unacceptable, because her departure would be bound to rouse Tokyo's suspicion of Kozo. Through much of 1939 the Japanese diplomat – codenamed 'Nero' – channelled a stream of reports to the NKVD via Elena, about Japan's intentions to seek a military alliance with Germany, including details of a conference in Berlin about a joint intelligence assault on Russia. Kozo had just been asked for details of the Japanese War Ministry's new code when the Russo–Finnish war erupted, and contact was lost until the spring of 1940. The diplomat was then posted to Sofia, where one fine morning Elena arrived unannounced at the Soviet embassy, and demanded to see the NKVD resident. She told him her husband was happy to resume his activities on behalf of Moscow, but that she herself wanted to divorce him and to come home. Once again, Centre prevaricated, while welcoming the material from Kozo. In November 1940 he handed over the latest Japanese diplomatic codes – by now, of course, Purple was in force – followed by other material, climaxing in April 1941 with another batch of cipher telegrams – 302 pages in all – which appears to have enabled Moscow through the summer to read some traffic between Tokyo's embassies.

In May 1941, after domestic scenes which can be imagined between the lovelorn Japanese and his bitterly alienated Russian wife, Elena was at last granted her wish to return to Moscow with her son. After her departure Kozo continued to forward information, but never again sought cash; he asked that payments should go to Elena, though it is unknown whether this was done. His subsequent offerings included a 21 May report describing German–Japanese discussions in Berlin about an attack on the Soviet Union intended to start within two months. On 22 June, following the onset of 'Barbarossa', Tokyo changed all its diplomatic codes, but Kozo was quickly able to provide the new ones for Europe, the more easily because he himself was promoted to acting chargé d'affaires in Sofia. He went on passing Moscow important coding information until 1944, when amid the general turmoil of Europe contact with him was broken.

After the war he resumed his work for the NKVD, which continued until 1952. Nothing is known of the later fortunes of Elena or her mother. As long as the intelligence files of the NKVD and GRU remain closed to researchers, it is impossible to know how much Japanese diplomatic traffic was read in Moscow. As Bletchley's experience showed, it was not enough to secure details of the enemy's ciphering technology and codebooks: immense intellectual input and electro-mechanical aids were also required in order to read enemy signals quickly enough to be of operational use to the Red Army. But, given Kozo's undoubted role as an informant, it seems plausible that his material enabled the Russians to access at least some of the same information as Sorge sent from Tokyo about Japan's decision not to attack Stalin until the Soviet Union's doom was assured. And unlike the spy, he continued to pass coding secrets until the last stage of the war.

4 GOUREVITCH TAKES A TRAIN

A wireless message from Centre to Moscow's foreign stations confirmed the news of 22 June 1941: 'Fascist beasts have invaded the motherland of the working classes. You are called upon to carry out your tasks in Germany to the best of your ability (signed) Director.' The agents of the vast Soviet spy networks in Europe were profoundly shaken, as well they might be, by early German successes, and discussed them feverishly whenever they met. In Switzerland, the 'Lucy' Ring intensified its efforts and its reporting. On 2 July, Alexander Radó reported that Moscow was Hitler's main objective, and that his armies' other thrusts were diversionary. Germany's generals certainly wished that this was true, which may help to explain the information passed to Radó from Berlin. In reality, however, to the general staff's fury Hitler had insisted on striking south with equal vigour, towards the oil of the Caucasus. On 7 August Radó cited an assurance by the Japanese ambassador in Bern that there was no question of his country attacking the Soviet Union until Germany was victorious. Before 'Barbarossa', Alexander Foote transmitted to Moscow only twice a week, at 1 a.m. Now he was dispatching messages almost daily, some of them containing detailed German order-of-battle material.

Funding became a problem for the spies once Russia became a belligerent, since cash could no longer be channelled through its diplomatic missions. Money was the lifeblood of the Ring, not least because 'Lutzi' – Rudolf Rössler, the mercenary – would not sing without it. Once, absurdly, Centre instructed Alexander Foote to travel to Vichy to receive a payment, as if an Englishman could stroll at will into alien territory. Eventually Moscow devised a system whereby money was paid into a US bank, which was then credited to its Geneva branch. This suited the Americans, who made a 100 per cent profit on every transaction by employing the official dollar–franc exchange rate, rather than the real black-market one. Hundreds of thousands of dollars were eventually transferred in this way, though Centre never entrusted an agent with more than $10,000 at a time, lest the temptation to 'go private' became irresistible.

Rössler was repeatedly pressed by Moscow, through Radó, to reveal his sources, and equally insistently he declined to do so. Dr Christian Schneider, a German émigré codenamed 'Taylor', joined Rössler's business. As a test of his worth he was invited to identify German formations deployed on the Southern Front in Russia, together with the number of Wehrmacht PoWs in Soviet hands. When he responded correctly to both questions, Moscow was suitably impressed. Wehrmacht chief of staff Gen. Franz Halder later raged about the leakiness of OKW and OKH: 'Almost every offensive operation of ours was betrayed to the enemy even before it appeared on my desk.' Speculation has persisted into the twenty-first century about the source of Rössler's extraordinary information stream. He himself indicated that he had a range of contacts in the German high command. Eastern Front intelligence chief Reinhard Gehlen later claimed, absurdly, that Martin Bormann was in Rössler's pay.

Radó revealed after the war that the sources he and Rössler had guarded so zealously for so long were … strips of punched paper. Each day of the war, more than 3,000 teleprinter messages were dispatched from OKW's communications centre to the Führerquartier, unencrypted since the link was a secure landline. One of Rössler's agents persuaded two female teleprinter operators to pass to him 'spent' ribbons, intended for destruction. By this means the spy received copies of some 4,500 top secret messages and eight hundred special reports, which were subsequently carried by courier to Switzerland. If this version of events is accurate, then Rössler's notional sub-agents – codenamed 'Olga', 'Werther', 'Teddi', 'Anna', 'Ferdinand' – were in reality mere paper creations.

The truth will never be known. All that is certain is that Rössler supplied to Radó for onward transmission to Moscow an astonishing volume of highly classified information, of which fragments intercepted by the Abwehr have been published. He warned in March 1943 of the German intention to attack at Kursk. On 15 April he passed on Hitler's operational order for the offensive, then on 20 and 29 April flagged successive delays, finally reporting that Operation 'Citadel' was scheduled for 12 June. On 17 April he catalogued new tank and infantry formations being created, with their locations and identifications; a 28 June signal detailed the Luftwaffe's order of battle, while another summarised Panther tank production. On 25 September he provided minutes of an economic conference held at Hitler's headquarters. If Radó's story of the stolen teleprinter tapes seems implausible, only that or another equally astonishing narrative can explain the quality of his material. Though the Swiss ring's intelligence did not match the volume and precision of that which the British garnered through Bletchley Park, it provided the Russians with incomparably better material than the Germans secured about Allied military operations.

The evidence suggests, however, that Moscow appreciated the 'Lucy' Ring's output below its true worth. In particular, instead of recognising inconsistencies and inaccuracies as reflections of changes of plan in Berlin, the familiar, corrosive Soviet paranoia prompted a rising conviction in the minds of the NKVD – which persisted to the war's end – that Rössler and Radó of the GRU were consciously or unconsciously involved in a Nazi deception. The most fantastic twist here was that Soviet suspicions soared when they found that some German material being passed to them by British traitors matched that emerging from Switzerland. Could 'Lutzi' and her friends be part of an elaborate British plot? Nobody in Moscow, as far as can be discovered, hit upon the real and simple explanation – that the GRU's Swiss agents were forwarding some of the same German signals being intercepted by GC&CS at Bletchley Park.

Communication between the Red Orchestra and Moscow was lost from June to November 1941, when the Wehrmacht swept eastwards into Russia, driving the NKVD's wireless receivers beyond range of their Berlin agents' weak transmitters. It became a matter of urgency for the Russians to regain contact with Harnack, Schulze-Boysen and 'Breitenbach', and if possible to discover the fate of their network in Prague, which had also gone silent. In consequence Centre broke every rule of espionage by ordering the GRU's Leopold Trepper to find means to contact the NKVD networks in Hitler's capital. Though the spies' wirelesses were out of reach of Moscow, if provided with the necessary codes and schedules they could transmit messages to Belgium, for forwarding to Centre. In September, Trepper returned to Brussels from Paris to discuss this assignment with Anatoli Gourevitch, 'Monsieur Kent'.

Gourevitch's most notable achievement since 1940 had been to create in Belgium, with Moscow's money and loans from friends, an entirely new trading company, christened 'Simexco' and based in elegant rented offices on the Rue Royale, to provide cover for the network – and, eventually, amazingly substantial profits. He bought a company car and hired a chauffeur. He worked energetically at creating relationships with the new German masters of Brussels, most of whom proved eminently corruptible, especially Major Kranzbühler, a prominent figure in the Nazi administration who cheerfully provided passes, curfew laissez-passers and letters of introduction for the company's director-general, who was so pleasingly eager to collaborate. Gourevitch cemented Kranzbühler's goodwill by procuring an abortion for the German's local mistress. With his own lover Margaret Barcza acting as hostess, the GRU agent began to provide lavish entertainments for Germans and fellow-collaborators, who basked in Centre's largesse. He acquired on the black market petrol coupons which enabled him to drive with Margaret into the countryside to buy hams, chickens, butter and suchlike delicacies now denied to ordinary Belgians.

He forged business relationships with German companies eager to break into the profitable markets of occupied Europe, and especially with the Nazis' Todt Organisation. From the latter he secured and fulfilled a large order for cheap spoons and forks to be issued to Germany's multitude of prisoners, political and military. A Paris branch of Simexco, called Simex, opened an office above the famous Lido restaurant, from which it serviced many of Trepper's agents. While this remarkable and expensive operation was useful for sustaining the GRU networks' cover, there is no doubt that Gourevitch, the pharmacist's son from Kharkov and former stalwart of the Young Communist movement, also hugely enjoyed his masquerade as a rich businessman, playboy and patron of the black market.

He provided no testimony about the attitude adopted towards himself and his circle by ordinary Belgians, who hated the occupation and lived in terror of the Nazis, but it is easy to guess. There is little evidence about what intelligence 'Kent's' informants collected for Moscow, though he professed that his Todt Organisation contacts enabled him to join the 'Lucy' Ring in warning of the forthcoming invasion of Russia. What is certain is that Centre's funding of the networks stopped abruptly in June 1941, with the expulsion of Soviet diplomats from Western Europe. Thereafter, Gourevitch and Trepper were dependent for cash upon the profits of Simexco and Simex. It was a droll twist that the two agents were thus obliged to become energetic and notably successful capitalist entrepreneurs as well as communist intelligence-gatherers.

Now, in September 1941, here was Trepper asking Gourevitch if somebody from Simexco could find a credible excuse to visit Prague and Berlin. 'Kent' said that he himself was the only person with the cover and connections to secure the necessary authorisations. He began by throwing a lavish rural picnic, followed by a dinner at home, for his foremost German friends, at which he told Kranzbühler of the business trip he wanted to make. The Nazi officer responded without hesitation that 'Vincente Sierra' had always been helpful to German interests; he was sure the necessary documents could be provided. And so they were. In October 1941 Gourevitch travelled without hindrance through Germany to occupied Prague, where he set about reconnoitring the addresses supplied to him by Moscow. He disliked what he found. The premises echoed empty. He felt an instinctive unease – and walked away. His hunch was right: the Germans had rolled up the GRU's Prague group months earlier.

Gourevitch moved on to Berlin, where he checked into the city's grand Excelsior hotel. He then addressed the contacts named by Centre: Ilse Stöbe, Harro Schulze-Boysen, Arvid Harnack and others. In response to a phone call, Stöbe's mother told him that Ilse was in Dresden, and uncontactable. Next he tried Kurt Schulze, the former taxi-driver who acted as the Stöbe network's wireless-operator – and met with more success. He visited Schulze's house and spent several hours briefing him on new radio schedules, also supplying the book phrase necessary to encode messages.

Then Gourevitch set off to reconnoitre 19 Alternburger Allee, which he described as 'a big, imposing house' – the Schulze-Boysens' home. He returned to the Excelsior without approaching it, having merely satisfied himself that he was not being followed, then filled the following morning with business meetings on behalf of Simexco. That evening, at last he telephoned the Schulze-Boysens, and gave an agreed password to Harro's wife Libertas. She cheerfully urged him to come on over; her husband was at work in the Air Ministry, but she would be happy to see him. Gourevitch suggested that instead they should meet at a nearby U-Bahn station and take a walk. He would be readily identifiable by the cigar he was smoking and the crocodile briefcase he carried. Fifteen minutes later 'an elegant young woman', walking rapidly, approached him without hesitation and extended her hand. 'Call me Libertas,' she said. Her friendliness dispelled the Russian's apprehension. He was impressed by her professionalism: no watcher, he said, would guess that they were meeting for the first time. 'I never forget that I am acting a part,' she said. She added that her husband had long awaited 'Kent's' arrival – he wanted the GRU man to meet some of their friends. The network was in fine shape, she said – 'we are all safe and sound' – working hard and absolutely committed to their common ideals. To be sure, life was not easy, 'but the future looks brighter today than it did yesterday' – because of the Soviet agent's arrival.

She warned him not to telephone again, because they assumed that their line was tapped; for all his fluency in German, Gourevitch's accent was obviously foreign. She asked his name, which momentarily embarrassed him, because he was unable to reciprocate her frankness. 'Call me Valdes,' he said. They both laughed. Libertas talked about her work for the Propaganda Ministry, producing cartoon films for the regime. She warned him that his clothes, in which the GRU man took such pride, marked him out as a foreigner. Then they parted, and the Russian returned to the Excelsior.

The following evening, amid a heavy snowfall, he approached an agreed rendezvous, at which he almost suffered heart failure when approached by a uniformed officer. Then Harro Schulze-Boysen of the Luftwaffe introduced himself, saying eagerly, 'I'm thrilled to see you.' He led Gourevitch to his home, where they donned slippers as they came in out of the whiteness. The visitor was shown into a handsome library, in which he noticed Russian books alongside German ones, some of them Soviet publications. Schulze-Boysen could scarcely be described as security conscious, though he said that he could explain away such reading matter to the Gestapo as necessary for his work at the Air Ministry. He told Gourevitch that not only did he love poetry, he also wrote verse himself, though he now found the times unsympathetic to his muse. He proffered a glass of vodka, observing laconically, 'spoils of war'. Then they sat down to dinner.

As they talked, Gourevitch reflected later, 'I could not rid myself of a sense of unreality. It seemed completely incredible that, amid a reign of terror, when everybody was spying upon everybody else, a group of men could have successfully penetrated the organs of state and the armed forces at risk of their lives, so that Germany could regain its honour and the German people their freedom.' He suffered a difficult moment when Schulze-Boysen asked him directly how it was possible that Russia was surprised in June 1941, when his own group had warned repeatedly of 'Barbarossa's' imminence. Neither 'Kent' nor any man save Stalin could provide an answer.

Gourevitch recorded that, in conversation alone with Schulze-Boysen when Libertas left them after dinner, they agreed that there was no purpose in his meeting other members of the group; it sufficed that the visitor had given the vital communications instructions to Kurt Schulze. They parted after warm embraces, and the Russian returned to his hotel. He then spent hours composing a detailed report for Moscow on the conversation, written in secret ink in a pocket notebook. By yet another of the black comic chances inseparable from espionage, on reaching Brussels in the first days of November 1941 he found that his 'invisible' notes were perfectly legible, probably exposed by the heat in the railway carriage from Berlin – 'Kent' would have been at the mercy of any inquisitive border policeman. But no such figure intervened, and he survived his perilous journey unscathed. He dispatched a long report to Moscow, detailing the German armed forces' predicament in Russia as described by Schulze-Boysen. This was supposedly shown to Stalin, though it included one false and highly damaging piece of information: a claim that Canaris had successfully recruited to the Axis cause André Dewavrin, 'Colonel Passy', General de Gaulle's chief of intelligence in London.

The Berlin networks now began to relay reports to Moscow via the Trepper group's transmitters. It was during the months that followed that the Germans picked up their signals. While still ignorant of the identities of Harnack, Schulze-Boysen or any of their contacts, they deduced that these were communist agents, addressing Moscow, and christened the network *Die Rote Kapelle* – the Red Orchestra. This name distinguished it from the regime's other important secret enemy – *Die Schwartz Kapelle*, the Black Orchestra, the name given to those striving to encompass Hitler's death.

Among early fruits of the Orchestra's renewed labours, as relayed to Stalin's State Defence Committee on 2 December 1941, was a report on the Wehrmacht's fuel state, showing reserves adequate until February or March; thereafter, the Germans were pinning their hopes on exploiting the Soviet oil wells at Maikop. Moscow was told that the Luftwaffe had suffered severe losses, especially in Crete, and was reduced to a serviceable strength of 2,500 aircraft. A further December report warned of a new Messerschmitt variant armed with two cannon and two machine-guns, capable of 600kph; a proximity-fused anti-aircraft shell; development work on hydrogen-peroxide-fuelled aircraft. Army Group B, said the *Rote Kapelle*, would attack on an axis through Voronezh in the spring – as indeed it did. Berlin intended its troop concentrations to be completed by 1 May for the advance on the Caucasus. On 17 January the Stavka – also received an intercepted Italian cipher telegram from Bucharest, reporting a block on Romanian rail traffic, to allow through hundreds of German troop trains, headed for southern Russia.

The Russians were warned of a German deception plan codenamed 'Kremlin', designed to promote expectations that Hitler's forces would renew their winter assault on Moscow – conspicuous Luftwaffe reconnaissance of the city approaches, a fake attack order dated 29 May 1942, signed by Field-Marshal Kluge of Army Group Centre. By 23 March the GRU was asserting: 'This summer the Germans will attempt not merely to reach the Volga and Caspian, but also to carry out major operations against Moscow and Leningrad.' The Red Orchestra remained insistent that Moscow was a secondary objective – that Stalingrad and the Caucasus were Hitler's prime targets. The Stavka, however, chose to ignore its agents; Stalin deployed his armies for the 1942 fighting season on the assumption that the threat to the capital was the most serious. The information garnered by the Red Orchestra and the 'Lucy' Ring, at such risk to so many lives, altered little in the Kremlin's decision-making, but would soon sweep away the spies: Germany's counter-intelligence agencies began to fumble their way towards exposure of the networks led by Harnack and Schulze-Boysen.

7

Britain's Secret War Machine

1 THE SHARP END

Britain's intelligence machinery worked better than that of any other nation at war, and exercised an especially critical influence on the war at sea. A case history: just after the fall of darkness on 8 November 1941, a squadron of the Royal Navy, Force K, led by the light cruisers *Aurora* and *Penelope*, sailed from Malta's Grand Harbour, then steamed north at high speed, thrashing the sea. At 4 a.m., 140 miles east of Syracuse, the British warships met an Italian supply convoy bound for North Africa. Having worked up-moon without their presence being detected, the cruisers trained their six-inch guns and opened fire, bursting open the night with starshell before raining high explosive on the hapless enemy. For half an hour they wrought devastation: seven merchantmen totalling 39,000 tons were left sinking or sunk, together with one of the six destroyers of the Italian close escort. From *Aurora*'s bridge, Captain William Agnew's only signal of the action was a warning to his ships, 'do not waste ammunition', because stocks at Malta were low. An enemy covering force of two heavy cruisers and four more destroyers, lacking radar, failed to intervene. At 1 p.m. the triumphant British squadron reached its Maltese anchorage unscathed, to receive the congratulations of Admiral Sir Andrew Cunningham, C-in-C Mediterranean, on an action that he described as 'a brilliant example of leadership and forethought'. Mussolini's foreign minister Count Ciano fumed in his diary about the engagement, 'the results of which are inexplicable. All, I mean *all*, our merchant ships were sunk.' The Royal Navy had fallen on them 'as wolves among the sheep'.

On 24 November, Force K repeated this success. Its crews were enjoying a roistering shore leave when news reached Valletta of another Axis convoy in transit. The sailors were hastily herded back on board, then the sleek cruisers set forth to sea. After hours of manoeuvring to deceive enemy reconnaissance aircraft about their course, at 3.45 p.m. they caught two German freighters, *Maritza* and *Procida*, carrying fuel to the Luftwaffe at Benghazi in jerrycans stacked as deck cargo. Escorting torpedo boats fled. The British cruisers launched a dramatic attack during which their anti-aircraft guns fought off Luftwaffe Ju-88 bombers, while the main armament ranged by radar on the merchantmen. The crews hastily abandoned ship as the fuel cargoes erupted in flames. The destroyer *Lively* picked up German and Italian survivors before the squadron retired to Malta at twenty-eight knots.

These successes, and others in the same season, were not the fruits of mere 'forethought' by naval officers, as Cunningham's congratulatory signal suggested – they represented early achievements of Ultra in the war at sea. From June 1941 Bletchley was reading not merely the Luftwaffe's traffic, which highlighted its chronically poor fuel position in North Africa, but also an increasing stream of signals – six hundred in July 1941, rising to 4,000 a year later – reporting enemy Mediterranean convoy movements, and Rommel's logistical difficulties ashore. It was true that the Germans also had significant wireless intelligence successes in the Mediterranean war – the B-Dienst was breaking and reporting British messages which revealed some of their own convoy movements, and the Afrika Korps enjoyed the fruits of excellent sigint about Britain's Eighth Army. But Ultra's contribution was critical in enabling Cunningham's warships to interdict Axis supply traffic until early 1942, when British naval losses and German dominance, especially of the air, for several months made it impossible to exploit decrypts, in the absence of warships to mount attacks and fighters to cover them.

Here, as everywhere, the unchanging reality was that intelligence alone was useless, unless sufficient force was available at sea, in the sky, or on the ground to use secret knowledge effectively. Ultra never provided forewarning of all German movements. Until the very end of the war, there were periods in which the enemy's imposition of wireless silence, delays or interruptions in the delivery of decrypts, prevented the Allies from putting them to practical use. Churchill demanded testily of Auchinleck, then his Middle East C-in-C: 'Are you getting these priceless messages (which have never erred) in good time?' The response acknowledged that Ultra was 'of great value', but added, 'some arrive in time to be operationally of use, others not so'. Even the combination of spies, air reconnaissance and Ultra failed to prevent one of the notable British humiliations of 1942, the passage up-Channel of the *Scharnhorst*, *Gneisenau* and *Prinz*

Eugen, pride of Hitler's fleet, within twenty miles of the cliffs ʊ.
was an event that shocked Parliament and Churchill's people in thɑ
of heavy defeats in the desert and the Far East.

The ships had been deployed to Brest in the spring of 1941, at a high-
water mark of Nazi expansionism, but it had since become plain to Berlin
that they served no useful purpose on the Atlantic coast save to provide
targets for the RAF's Bomber Command, which had damaged all three. The
destruction of the *Bismarck* in May showed that Hitler's big ships could no
longer hope to venture into the Atlantic shipping lanes. He thus determined
that they should return to a German port – which became known to the
British. French agents of MI6 maintained a harbour watch at Brest, while
RAF photographic reconnaissance aircraft daily monitored the ships' condition. On 24 December the Admiralty informed RAF Commands that a
German breakout eastward could take place at any time. Late in January
1942, Ultra revealed *Scharnhorst*'s gun crews exercising aboard the heavy
cruiser *Scheer* in the Baltic. Multiple intelligence sources reported all three
big ships slipping out of Brest for night steaming trials, then returning before
dawn. They also noted the reinforcement of German light forces in the
Channel, and intensive minesweeping activity. The First Sea Lord, Admiral
Sir Dudley Pound, told the chiefs of staff on 3 February that a concentration
of Luftwaffe fighters on the Channel coast suggested that *Scharnhorst* and its
consorts intended to brave the passage, though he was unaware that Hitler
had given orders for them to tackle the Narrows in daylight, when German
air superiority would be most effective, and would almost certainly deter the
Royal Navy from committing its own heavy metal.

How did the British propose to deal with the German run for home? A
critical point was that no capital ships of the Home Fleet were deployed
anywhere within range. It was indeed deemed unthinkable to risk them
within easy reach of the Luftwaffe, especially a few weeks after the destruction of *Prince of Wales* and *Repulse* by Japanese torpedo-bombers.
Responsibility for stopping Vice-Admiral Otto Ciliax's squadron would
rest with destroyer and torpedo-boat flotillas stationed along the English
south coast, and even more with the RAF and Fleet Air Arm, whose
squadrons were brought to short notice in accordance with a plan for this
contingency, codenamed 'Fuller'. Just two British submarines were also
available, to patrol off Brest.

On 5 February, Ultra revealed Ciliax hoisting his flag aboard
Scharnhorst. Three days later, AOC Coastal Command warned RAF
Fighter and Bomber Commands that a breakout was likely 'any time after

Tuesday 10th February'. On the 10th, however, C-in-C Bomber Command stood down half of his modest Fuller force, without informing the Admiralty. This may not have been in keeping with the spirit of effective air–sea cooperation, but it reflected the RAF's cavalier mindset, which resisted any responsibility to assist the navy, when its own overriding priority was to bomb Germany. A stream of Ultra intercepts showed the Kriegsmarine conducting intensive minesweeping operations in Heligoland Bight, which removed the last lingering doubts about the German ships' destination.

Admiral Ciliax's squadron sailed from Brest at 10.45 p.m. on 11 February, and from that moment everything that could go wrong for the British did so. Bletchley Park encountered unusual difficulties breaking into naval Enigma: messages for 10, 11 and 12 February were not decrypted until the 15th. The submarine *Sealion*, having braved immense risks to penetrate Brest approaches on the afternoon of the 11th, withdrew to recharge its batteries having seen nothing unusual. Had the Germans set forth as planned at 5.30 p.m., *Sealion* must have seen them, but Ciliax's sailing time was put back two hours because of an RAF bombing raid. Three Coastal Command night-reconnaissance aircraft were aloft, monitoring the track taken by the German squadron, but the ASV radar of that period was primitive. Amid the darkness, one crew saw nothing on its screen; a second found its set unserviceable; a third was recalled early because of fog at base, before the German ships reached its search area. Even when daylight came and a photographic reconnaissance aircraft overflew Brest, low cloud and a German smokescreen prevented its crew from seeing that the big ships were gone. British coastal radar stations failed to draw appropriate conclusions from concentrations of enemy fighters in the air and attempts to jam their own wavelengths.

Two Spitfire pilots were first to sight the German squadron, at 10.42 a.m., just west of Le Touquet. They observed standard operating procedure, however, which meant wireless silence, and reported the sensational news only after landing at 11.09 a.m. Sixteen minutes later their tidings were broadcast to all British commands, precipitating a succession of futile assaults. Lt. Cmdr Edward Esmond received a posthumous VC for leading a low-level attack by six pitifully old, slow Swordfish torpedo biplanes from Manston in Kent, all of which plunged into the Channel amid a hail of anti-aircraft fire. The Germans were already through the Narrows when the 'Stringbags' made their runs at 12.42 p.m., and all of 825 Squadron's torpedoes missed. Five MTBs dashed out from Dover harbour, of which one quickly broke down. The leader of the other four, on sighting the German ships, decided that it was impossible for his boats to penetrate the escorting screen. They thus launched their torpedoes at extreme range, without effect. Another three boats, bounding forth from Ramsgate in worsening weather, failed to find the *Scharnhorst* and its consorts.

In the course of the afternoon of the 12th, a succession of naval twin-engined Beauforts and Hudsons staged piecemeal torpedo and bomb attacks on the receding Germans, without effect and with the loss of several aircraft. At 3.43 p.m. five destroyers from Harwich, under fierce German gunfire, launched a torpedo attack at a range of 3,000 yards, again without effect. Meanwhile 242 British bombers were launched against Ciliax's squadron, of which just thirty-nine dropped their loads in the vicinity without scoring a hit, and fifteen were shot down. The RAF also lost seventeen of 398 fighters committed.

The German dash up-Channel had proved a triumph for the Kriegsmarine's planning, skill, daring and luck. Or had it? *Scharnhorst* struck one British air-dropped mine at 2.31 p.m., without much effect, as did *Gneisenau* at 7.55 p.m. At 9.34 p.m., however, off Terschelling close to home, *Scharnhorst* hit a second mine, which inflicted grave damage. The ship eventually crept into Wilhelmshaven early on 13 February with its port engines unserviceable, its consorts following at 7 o'clock the same morning. The British people knew nothing, however, of the late disaster which befell the Germans, causing Hitler's naval staff to characterise the episode as 'a tactical victory, but a strategic defeat'. Churchill's countrymen saw only that an enemy squadron had defied the might of the Royal Navy in broad daylight, within sight of the white cliffs. *The Times* thundered that Admiral Ciliax had succeeded where the Spanish Armada had failed. A judicial inquiry was held, of which the findings reflected poorly on all the British force commanders involved.

In truth, though the Channel Dash caused the British government deep embarrassment at a bad time, it was unimportant. Ultra informed the Admiralty of the damage to *Scharnhorst*, which was restored to operational fitness only in January 1943, when it joined *Tirpitz* in the Norwegian fjords. Meanwhile, on 26 February 1942, RAF bombers hit *Gneisenau* in dock at Kiel, crippling the cruiser so severely that it never sailed again. It was deemed impossible, however, to broadcast any of this good news to the British people without compromising Bletchley's security. The German ships were thus generally supposed to have escaped scot-free. Public bitterness lingered for years about yet another presumed defeat.

Blame for failure to destroy the ships in the Channel Narrows certainly did not lie with intelligence, which provided commanders with the best information they could conceivably have expected about the enemy's intentions, up to the moment of sailing. Commanders drew appropriate deductions, and were alert to Ciliax's likely course, save that they expected him to close the English coast by night rather than by day. The problem, as so often, lay with lack of appropriate forces to challenge the German squadron. Anti-shipping capability was a chronic weakness of both the Fleet Air Arm and the RAF. It is often suggested that, if the British had known earlier that Ciliax had put to sea, the outcome could have been different. This seems unlikely. In the course of the conflict, many British air attacks against enemy surface ships failed. As ever, knowledge was not enough, unless matched by power.

2 THE BRAIN

The war yielded plenty of failures and disappointments to match that of February 1942 in the Channel Narrows, but they do not diminish the achievement of Britain's 'brain', the command structure and bureaucracy wherein the collection, analysis and distribution of intelligence were integrated. Bletchley Park's codebreakers would have achieved much less, but for the existence of a threshing machine for their golden harvest. This could have been created only under the hand of a wise prime minister, who thoroughly understood the making of war.

Churchill dominated his nation's decision-making much more than did Roosevelt that of the United States. Although he often baulked at assessments which did not conform to his own views, unlike the dictators he never questioned the right and duty of the chiefs of staff and their intelligence officers to speak their minds. He was a critical force in making Britain's secret services the least ineffective in the world. Because he himself respected intelligence, he ensured that its agencies, and especially Bletchley Park, were adequately resourced.

The prime minister used decrypts as often as weapons in argument with his own chiefs of staff, as against the enemy. 'Churchill had a tendency to create his own intelligence,' said the Joint Intelligence Committee's chairman Victor 'Bill' Cavendish-Bentinck, somewhat delphically. But the chiefs seldom deviated from the principle of attempting to analyse evidence objectively. 'The best arrangement,' wrote a later chairman of the JIC, Percy Cradock, 'is intelligence and policy in separate but adjoining rooms, with communicating doors and thin partition walls, as in cheap hotels.' This is what happened in Whitehall. At least in the second half of the struggle, as Britain's war effort became more coherent, an impressively robust yet sensitive system collated and examined information, then transferred it from the secret departments to operational commanders.

Bill Bentinck thought the RAF's Air Chief Marshal Sir Charles Portal the cleverest of Britain's three service chiefs, while being irked by CIGS Gen. Sir Alan Brooke's surges of stubbornness in pursuit of his own hobby-horses. In late 1941, for example, against the firm opinion of the JIC and all the evidence from Bletchley, Brooke persuaded himself that the Germans retained a 'mass of manoeuvre', uncommitted to the Eastern Front, which might still invade Britain. It was widely thought that successive War Office directors of intelligence were too eager to tell the highly opinionated army chief what he wanted to hear. The JIC, by contrast, did nothing of the sort: its reporting was almost unfailingly honest, even when it was wrong.

The Joint Intelligence Sub-Committee of the chiefs of staff – to give the JIC its full title – assumed unprecedented importance after the 1940 ascent of Churchill and the fall of France. It met in a house owned by Bill Bentinck's uncle in Richmond Terrace, a brisk walk from the war cabinet offices. The chairman enjoyed impeccably aristocratic origins, and himself ended life as the last Duke of Portland, but he had an unusual and unenviable personal history. Born in 1897, he was educated at Wellington College, where he was unhappy. In 1918 he served briefly in the army without reaching the front, then joined the diplomatic service, where good looks, easy manners and an air of benign wisdom might have sped him to the top had he not made a disastrous 1924 marriage to an American named Clothilde Quigley, with whom he had two children. As a younger son Bentinck was relatively poor – more so, after some rash stock exchange speculations. His wife nonetheless spent lavishly and quarrelled spectacularly with other diplomatic wives wherever her husband was posted. Bentinck was transferred from the prestigious Paris embassy first to Athens, then to Santiago, leaving everywhere a trail of acrimony laid by Clothilde. Back in London in 1939, he was appointed chairman of the JIC while it was still in its embryo phase, because nobody could think what else to do with him, as long as he remained encumbered by his termagant of a spouse.

Soon after war began, he received at his office an almost incomprehensible telephone call from the family's Hungarian maid, who eventually made him understand that Mrs Bentinck had packed her bags and departed with the children, apparently for Glasgow to catch a boat to America. 'It was like a French farce,' said the JIC chairman dryly long afterwards. Bentinck adopted a mask of patrician stoicism to conceal the trauma this event must have caused him. Thereafter, though his wife made trouble until they were messily divorced in 1948, he devoted himself single-mindedly to his job, and most observers thought him well suited to it. Noel Annan found Bentinck 'very impressive ... He had a temperament of extreme scepticism, yet total belief that the Allies were going to win.' For a time when Menzies' throne tottered, Bentinck was touted as his possible successor at MI6.

The chairman was no brainbox, but he had a native shrewdness, impeccable manners and a relaxed charm which enabled him for six years to manage the passions that often swirled at JIC meetings. The Committee's cleverest and most assertive service representative was John Godfrey, director of naval intelligence, but the admiral's arrogance exasperated those who had to work with him. Meanwhile Godfrey's army and air force counterparts were unimpressive officers, and the Ministry of Economic Warfare's representative only began to exert real influence later in the war, when Sir Geoffrey Vickers was appointed to the role. Though a lawyer, he was a World War I VC who had once commanded an infantry battalion: the service representatives would have found it hard to snub Vickers.

The range of issues addressed by the JIC was extraordinary. In addition to the big strategic questions, in July and August 1941 its staff produced reports on such matters as 'Military Preparations by Vichy France against Chad', 'Rumours Designed to Mislead the Enemy' – a running theme, 'Madagascar', 'Press, Cinema and Broadcasting Correspondents in Iceland', 'An advance by the Axis into Sudan and Arabia'. Every Tuesday morning at 10.30, the Committee's members reported to the chiefs of staff in the Cabinet War Rooms beneath Great George Street – what Bentinck referred to wryly as 'leading my choir'. Their assessments might, or might not, influence the chiefs' decisions, which were passed to the Joint Planning Staff for translation into operational proposals and orders. The JPS's officers, famously clever, often worked all night to prepare appreciations for the chiefs' next 8 a.m. meeting. Churchill grumbled to Alan Brooke, 'These damned planners of yours plan nothing but difficulties.' Utterly unlike Hitler, however, the prime minister acknowledged that this was their job – even if it afterwards became their duty to identify solutions.

The most important element of the JIC was its supporting body, the Joint Intelligence Staff, which was created in 1941 and thereafter provided the Committee with in-house analysis of material from all sources before members debated it. The new age of technology provided an almost infinitely wide field for exploration, as well as means of addressing this: the trick was to focus attention where it mattered. Group-Captain Peter Stewart, who ran the RAF's photo-reconnaissance operations, was exasperated by a senior officer who asked for 'all available cover' of one European country. Stewart responded that he could only provide helpful information if he knew roughly what intelligence the suppliant wanted – 'naval, military, air or ecclesiastical'. R.V. Jones made the point that, especially when technology was involved, it was essential to make a clear decision about what commanders needed to know, then to exploit an appropriate mix of aerial reconnaissance, PoW interrogation and signal decrypts, 'rather as an army commander might use his various arms in a balanced attack with artillery, tanks and infantry. The specific objective to be attacked might be suggested by what we knew was being developed by our own side, and which therefore might also be under development by the enemy, radar and atomic bombs being two such examples.'

The JIS recruited some outstandingly able civilians in uniform. Once a week Bentinck assembled its thirty-odd officers for a 'brains trust', an open discussion about the enemy's dispositions and activities. Junior members were encouraged to speak their minds – which they did, about for instance the man-for-man superiority of the Wehrmacht to their own troops. Noel Annan put it bluntly: 'The British armies and the new American armies were not the match of the German armies in professionalism and perhaps bravery.' The JIC's judgement was far from perfect, but more often right than wrong. It opposed the ill-fated September 1940 descent on Dakar, arguing that the Free French were far too optimistic about their likely reception from Vichy forces. It deserves credit for acknowledging in its reports throughout 1940–41 that much of the world expected Churchill's people to lose the war, though it was sufficiently nationalistic never to waver from the assumption that Britain was Germany's principal enemy. Thus in mid-June 1941 the Committee viewed the looming Nazi invasion of the Soviet Union as a mere gambit in Hitler's campaign against Britain. The JIS argued that one of his key objectives would be 'to use the Soviet [front] to embarrass and extend us in every way, thereby helping to achieve his supreme objective, the defeat of the British Empire'.

Throughout the summer and winter of 1941, the British assumed Soviet defeat to be inevitable. A 28 July report by the JIS mitigated its own gloom only by expressing gratitude for the breathing space granted to Britain by

'Barbarossa': 'Assuming that the campaign against Russia results in a military success for Germany, there must be some pause for regrouping and refitting before the German Army can embark on major operations elsewhere.' The JIC displayed better judgement in monitoring increasing Japanese aggression in Asia. On 25 June 1941 it weighed the prospects of Japan seizing the opportunity to strike at Russia, then concluded: 'We think her inclination will be to abstain from intervention against Soviet Union at present stage and to continue policy of Southward expansion in which case next move will probably be intensified pressure on Indo-China for bases and facilities ... It is agreed that German attack on the Soviet Union does not in any way lessen the need to press on with our own preparations for resisting Japan or aiding China.' Thereafter, the JIC assessed with notable shrewdness likely Japanese behaviour up to their December attack on the European empires.

In July 1941 the JIC discussed an approach through a 'most secret source' by Dr Carl Gördeler, ex-mayor of Leipzig, 'a German in touch with army elements in Germany who was in favour of a compromise with this country before the outbreak of war'. The JIS commented disdainfully: 'He is not, however, regarded as reliable, and it may be that he is being used consciously or unconsciously by the German government.' Gördeler had told his contact, accurately enough, that Gen. Franz Halder and other senior members of the general staff had opposed the launching of 'Barbarossa'. But the JIS commented primly that such a claim did not accord with 'other reliable information' reaching London.

Moreover, Gördeler and his friends proposed conditions for discussions which were bound to be unacceptable to the British government: 'as a preliminary ... they required a guarantee that Great Britain would agree to an armistice and that she would, with the United States, force the Russians to come to reasonable terms with Germany over the demarcation of the Polish frontier'. This approach was rebuffed as coolly as were others later in the war by prominent members of the anti-Hitler opposition, for instance the letter sent to London via Stockholm in March 1943 by Helmuth von Moltke of the Abwehr. The consequence of this fastidious policy was that the Russians, and later the Americans through Allen Dulles in Bern, enjoyed a near-monopoly of wartime 'humint' from inside Germany, though this did little to influence their policies.

The intelligence machine sometimes reached conclusions which were then rejected by the prime minister or one of the chiefs of staff. In the spring of 1942 a succession of reports highlighted the failure of Axis air forces' attempts to destroy the British submarine flotilla based at Malta, and emphasised the difficulties of penetrating the vast concrete U-boat pens at Brest and Lorient. The Royal Navy nonetheless insisted that the RAF should persist with its costly and futile attacks on the bases. As First Sea Lord in July 1942, Admiral Sir Dudley Pound overruled his own intelligence staff to make a disastrous personal judgement that Arctic convoy PQ17 was threatened by German capital ships, and must scatter, a blunder which precipitated its piecemeal destruction, and for which he should have been sacked. Intelligence could achieve nothing if it was thus ignored. Yet, while such follies have incurred just censure from historians, it is important to emphasise that unlike their enemy counterparts, Britain's leaders relatively seldom defied the counsel of their intelligence and operational staffs.

This did not prevent argument about the significance of contradictory evidence. In 1944, for example, the Ministry of Economic Warfare argued that Germany's manpower situation was deteriorating, while the War Office saw an alarming growth in the Wehrmacht's strength, as recorded in the JIC's twice-yearly *Enemy Strengths & Dispositions* report. Only belatedly was it discovered that Hitler was manipulating his armies' divisional numbers to inflate their apparent might. In the same way, in the summer of 1944 the JIC allowed itself to be persuaded by Geoffrey Vickers of MEW that lack of oil would precipitate an early German collapse. The Committee was correct in acknowledging the importance of oil, and Hitler's dire shortage of it, but was over-optimistic about the speed at which his armies' resistance would become unsustainable. There was another notorious JIC misjudgement on 5 September 1944, in the wake of the liberation of France, when the Committee allowed itself to succumb to euphoria: 'Whereas the Germans have at the moment an organised front between the Russians and the German frontier, in the West they have nothing but disorganised remnants incapable of holding the Allied advance in strength into Germany itself.' The prime minister flatly disagreed with this view, arguing that Hitler's people were still far from beaten. His own instinct proved sounder than the JIS analysis.

Every intelligence practitioner was aware of the distinction between secrets, which were knowable, and mysteries, which were usually not. Once a date was set for a given operation it became a *secret*, vulnerable to discovery by the other side. But how the enemy would behave in as-yet-unrealised circumstances was often a *mystery*, because he had not made up his own mind. The JIS made some important misjudgements in predicting

German strategic responses to Allied initiatives – for instance, the November 1942 'Torch' landings in North Africa, and the June 1943 invasion of Sicily. One of the JIS staff wrote after the war: 'Our failures lay really in our inability to appreciate the extreme obstinacy of Hitler. More than once we forecast that he would withdraw to shorter lines either in Italy or Russia or the Balkans in order to economise on divisions.' He added wryly: 'I still believe that he would have done better if he had followed our advice.' The consequences of the JIC's 1941 scepticism about a German invasion of Russia have been discussed above – it made more impact in Moscow than in London, by feeding Stalin's expectation of Churchillian conspiracies against himself. But if the difficulties of intelligence assessment in wartime are accepted, even with the assistance of Ultra, the JIC's record seems impressive. The historian G.M. Trevelyan once wrote of a sixteenth-century English queen's relationship with her intelligence chief: 'If Elizabeth had taken Walsingham's advice on every occasion she would have been ruined. If she had never taken it she would have been ruined no less.' The same might be said of the relationship between Churchill and the JIC.

The British command structure was much more centralised than that of the US: while Churchill's generals in the field were in no doubt that they took their orders from London, across the Atlantic in Washington intelligence staffs became dispirited by consciousness that local theatre commanders, and especially Gen. Douglas MacArthur in the South-West Pacific, made decisions almost heedless of Pentagon or Navy Department opinions. Moreover, although among the British there were frequent inter-service disputes, the principle of 'jointery' was sincerely embraced, as it was not between the US Army and US Navy. Meanwhile, President Roosevelt rarely became engaged in operational debates, and seems seldom to have bothered to read much of the Ultra material delivered to him.

It was much easier to achieve inter-service cooperation on Britain's side of the Atlantic because its ruling village was such a small place. The senior naval representative on the JIS was an able sailor named Charles Drake. The prime minister approached him one day at his office in Great George Street: 'I think, Captain,' said Churchill in that familiar slow-march drawl, 'we must be kin.' Drake replied, 'I think we are,' which prompted Churchill to test him by asking, 'Why do you say that?' The naval officer achieved a triumph by responding that he had read both volumes of the statesman's *Life of Marlborough*, in which Churchill recorded the first duke's pedigree, as son of the seventeenth-century Sir Winston Churchill – and his wife

Elizabeth Drake. The prime minister quizzed the naval officer further: 'And you believe it?' Yes, indeed. 'Good, Captain, then we're kin.' This anecdote helps to explain why Britain's supremely whimsical prime minister was so beloved; and how its bureaucratic brain functioned amid an intimacy unmatched by any other warring power.

From 1942 onwards Ultra dominated the JIC's and JIS's activities. Although thousands of pages of paper were also generated by MI6 and MI5, few, if any, could match the authority of decrypts. It is remarkable that the hierarchies of both services survived the war unreformed. At MI5, the 1940–41 acting director-general was the incompetent Brigadier Oswald 'Jasper' Harker, replaced by the slightly more effective Sir David Petrie, formerly of MI6, whose deputy he then became. Kathleen Sissman, one of the security service's few women and an intelligence officer of the highest gifts, fiercely denounced Harker's unfitness for his duties, and in consequence found herself sacked and obliged to transfer to MI6. Fortunately for MI5, Harker and Petrie had several outstanding subordinates, such as Guy Liddell and Lt. Col. Tom Robertson, together with some of the civilians who joined for wartime service. The same was true at MI6, though Stewart Menzies and his senior men – Dansey, Vivian, Cowgill – sustained an uneasy relationship with their 'hostilities only' staff, Hugh Trevor-Roper prominent among them. 'When I looked coolly at the world in which I found myself,' the don wrote, 'I sometimes thought that, if this was our intelligence service, we were doomed to defeat.' The historian considered Menzies an honest and decent man, as his most senior subordinates were not, but 'I do not think he ever understood the war in which he was engaged.'

Trevor-Roper had little trouble collaborating with such fellow-amateurs as the army's Brian Melland, his own cousin; the RAF's John Pope-Hennessy, an art historian; barrister Ewen Montagu at the Admiralty. He had the highest respect for the Bletchley staff, and for Liddell at MI5. But he complained to Lord Swinton, chairman of Whitehall's oversight body the Security Executive, about the failings of MI6, and wrote in equally savage terms to the prime minister's intimate, Lord Cherwell, whom he knew well from Christ Church, throwing in for good measure a denunciation of Gambier-Parry, his own superior. These interventions quickly became known in Broadway, and earned Trevor-Roper a formal reprimand from Menzies and Vivian.

Quite unperturbed, following Bletchley's Christmas 1941 breaking of the Abwehr's principal Enigma cipher Trevor-Roper demanded that a new

MI6 section should be created to study Canaris's organisation by exploiting the flow of new Ultra. Finding little enthusiasm for this proposal inside
Broadway, he took it instead to Cherwell. It is scarcely surprising that this
sort of high-handedness incurred the rage of Trevor-Roper's bosses. Nigel
de Grey, deputy chief of Bletchley, wrote crossly, 'Is it necessary to argue
with a junior officer? ... Personally if he were in my employ I should tell
him to shut up – if he persisted I should sack him.' For some time de Grey
declined to allow Trevor-Roper access to the Park, asserting that he was
'not a suitable person'. Internecine warfare escalated in 1942. Trevor-Roper
found himself in trouble after a holiday in Ireland during which Frank
Pakenham precipitated his arrest by Irish police as a British spy, an episode
which did not amuse Broadway. Then Trevor-Roper leaked to Guy Liddell's
staff the fact that MI6 was withholding from MI5 intercepts about British
agents abroad whom the Germans had identified or suspected. Vivian and
Cowgill, learning of Trevor-Roper's responsibility for the disclosure, clamoured for his sacking, though Liddell warned them that they would be
depriving British intelligence of a huge talent. Amazingly, and to the credit
of Menzies, Trevor-Roper got his way, becoming chief of a new Abwehr
section, with eventual promotion to major.

'C' kept his own job partly because Desmond Morton and other
Whitehall critics lacked the clout to unstick him. More important, Menzies
exploited his supervisory role over Bletchley Park to deliver personally to
the prime minister choice specimens of Ultra intelligence, codenamed
'Boniface', which went far to obscure the deficiencies of MI6's humint
activities. In secret services more than most institutions, in the words of
R.V. Jones, 'If good work results in success, the credit will tend to fall on
those officers who present the results to the forum where they are made
known to the operational or political staffs.' Likewise Bill Bentinck: 'Only
Bletchley kept [Menzies] in his job. He was not a very strong man and not
a very intelligent one.' Whereas many British institutions were turned on
their heads and remade in the course of the war, Broadway Buildings
escaped such a fate. But, given that no national security apparatus is
perfect, what seems remarkable is not that Menzies and his subordinates
constituted a weak link, but that other parts of the machine worked well.

Arthur Schlesinger of OSS wrote: 'Intelligence is only as effective as its
dissemination ... even the best-designed dissemination system cannot
persuade busy people to read political analysis unless it affects the decisions they are about to make.' The prime minister and chiefs of staff were

far more likely to take heed of Ultra decrypts, filling at most one side of a flimsy, than long JIS analytical papers, however ably drafted. It would be mistaken to pretend that because Churchill created an admirable system, this always worked smooth as silk. How could it be so, when he himself was a unique human being, whose attitudes and demands were never predictable? It became a familiar moan throughout Whitehall, the chiefs of staffs' offices and the secret war community that Churchill abused snippets of intelligence which reached him, to make foolish or ill-informed interventions. Sir Alexander Cadogan complained to his diary one day in 1941: 'It's hopeless conducting business like this. Anthony Eden [the foreign secretary] sees no papers, he is dragged up to London for 24 hours, dines with P.M. They both happen to see an [Ultra] intercept which makes it look as if we might get Germans out of Afghanistan. So they get on the hop, and I get messages to say that it must be done *at once*. But there are considerations of which they are blissfully unaware, poor children.'

On the credit side of the ledger, however, the system for distributing Ultra decrypts to commanders-in-chief in the field became ever more refined. On 5 March 1941, Bletchley Park sent a momentous signal to the director of military intelligence in Cairo, announcing that thenceforward decrypts containing operational data about German forces would be sent to him direct, so that hours would no longer be wasted in transit via service ministries in London. Such messages would be prefixed 'OL': 'They are to be regarded as absolutely reliable, but must receive utmost security … Source of this information though known to you is never to be mentioned. Endeavour to check any laxity of security and drastically confine personnel who see signals to absolute minimum.' The system of Special Liaison Units was created: cells at main headquarters, whose members – MI6 personnel in uniform – lived and worked entirely separately from the local army intelligence staff, and were alone responsible for receiving and processing incoming Enigma decrypts. These were then passed to senior officers with appropriate warnings about how best to disguise their contents before any part was passed down the command chain. The organisation, and its security arrangements, worked well, though only in the latter half of 1942 did Ultra flow sufficiently regularly and speedily to secure the full confidence of British generals in the desert. Moreover, it remained forever a long march to translate knowledge of the enemy's deployments into victory over his forces on the battlefield.

The British service which used intelligence least imaginatively was the

R.A.F. For all the undoubted cleverness of Portal, from October 1940 chief of the air staff, its intelligence department was weak. It was harder to measure the enemy's operational air strength than to count his ships or tanks. Throughout the war, all air forces wildly overstated their pilots' combat successes, and thus the number of enemy aircraft destroyed. Perhaps the worst Allied intelligence failure of the war was misjudgement of the German economy. This was partly because Ultra provided far less assistance in informing the Allies about the enemy's industries, which exchanged information on paper or by telephone landline more than by wireless. The weakness was well illustrated by the report of the Lloyd Committee on German oil resources, which estimated that RAF bombing had by December 1940 already achieved a cut of 15 per cent in enemy fuel availability, at a moment when Berlin was unaware that the British were even engaged in a systematic air attack.

Matters did not much improve later in the war. Sir Geoffrey Vickers wrote in a retrospective 5 February 1945 report on economic intelligence: 'The science of destroying organised war industry ... an infinitely complex social and material organism, was unborn when this war began ... Service commanders, when attacking industry, are even less professionally quali- fied than their service advisers ... The choice of industrial objectives depends on an analysis of factors far more complex than those which determine the strategy of a campaign and can rely less on science or on experience ... The correction of appreciations is verified by events much more closely and much less certainly than those which determine strategy in the field ... Economic intelligence in this war has suffered continuously from inadequate contact with those who were planning and organising our own war economy.'

A combination of meagre evidence and poor analysis, based on mistaken assumptions about the Nazi industrial machine, together with obsessive wishful thinking by the RAF's 'bomber barons', caused the airmen consistently to overstate what air bombardment might achieve, was achieving and had achieved, especially against Germany. There was also the problem that Ultra provided much less industrial data than mili- tary and naval information. In general, this book argues that what distin- guished the Western Allies' wartime intelligence processes from those of the Axis was that they strove for honesty and objectivity, even if they were not always successful. In the course of the air war, however, this principle was breached. So fixated were senior RAF and USAAF officers with their determination to demonstrate that strategic air bombardment could win the war, that the history of the bomber commands' intelligence departments shows an institutionalised commitment to fantasy, of a kind more usual in the German and Japanese high commands.

The USAAF, like the RAF, was for years more resistant to intelligence input from outside agencies than the Allied armies or navies, preferring to employ its own airmen to make their own assessments, especially about bombing targets. In 1939, Gen. 'Hap' Arnold convened a board of four officers to study bombing targets. In the summer of 1941 Gen. Heywood Hansell returned from a visit to Britain with a ton weight of RAF target folders, and his own opinion that Americans knew more about Germany's oil and power systems than did the British, though the RAF seemed quite well informed about enemy aircraft production and transport systems. Arnold told Hansell to set up his own organisation to scour civilian sources for intelligence about economic targets, and an office was duly established in New York City. This recruited a band of civilian academics, some of them very able: Wilma Brun, who taught German at Columbia; Marvin Dickey, a German professor at Cornell; a businessman named Malcolm Moss, who proved highly effective – it was he who suggested hiring a friend named McKittrick, who had studied German and Austrian power stations for American banks. McKittrick, according to Hansell, proved a 'gold mine'. By autumn, a long target list had been compiled, dominated by economic rather than military objectives. Implausibly, some were located in South America, where Washington had some fears of a German descent. Yet, until 1944, the results of all this energetic delving were meagre. The USAAF joined the RAF in conducting bomber operations against Germany that represented, in Churchill's phrase, 'a bludgeon rather than a rapier'.

Scientists and statisticians who sought to conduct objective analysis of what air attack was, or was not, achieving, such as Freeman Dyson of RAF Bomber Command's Operational Research Department – a famous figure in the US after the war – found themselves marginalised, their counsel dismissed. Only in the last fifteen months of the war did the American air staffs do somewhat better, assisted by an ever more formidable increase in hard power – bomber and fighter numbers. The USAAF achieved the destruction of the Luftwaffe in the air, and correctly identified synthetic oil plants as the weakest link in Hitler's war effort. It is striking to notice that Bletchley Park's Air Section considered the USAAF, and not Britain's own airmen, its closest partners and most enthusiastic consumers of intelligence. The Air Ministry could claim no matching access of wisdom.

3 AT SEA

The Royal Navy's intelligence department, indeed the entire Admiralty, fulfilled a very different role from the War Office and Air Ministry, which merely set policy and administered their respective services. The occupants of the magnificent eighteenth-century brick complex on the north side of Horse Guards Parade – the first purpose-designed office building in Britain – not merely administered Britain's fleet, but also acted as its operational headquarters, daily directing the motions of hundreds of ships patrolling, oiling, convoying, repairing, fighting. From the dawn of naval warfare, the foremost challenge for commanders had been to locate the vessels of their foes: Nelson spent years of his life ploughing the seas at the head of a fleet, merely seeking to find the French. In the twentieth century, however, wireless transformed the story: it enabled commanders ashore at a moment's notice to give orders to change the course of warships thousands of miles distant, and also made possible the detection and location of those of the enemy.

Two thousand men and women served in the Naval Intelligence Division, among whom Admiral John Godfrey's personal staff of fifteen clustered in the Admiralty's Room 39. This was formally known as 'NID17', flag bridge of the intelligence war at sea, with its big westerly windows looking down on the Downing Street garden, the Foreign Office, the lake in St James's Park, and Horse Guards Parade, the last disfigured by wartime clutter – barrage balloons, vehicles, temporary hutments. Donald McLachlan, one of Godfrey's wartime staff, admired his chief, but understood why others were galled by him: 'Like the driver of a sports car in a traffic queue, he saw no danger or discourtesy in acceleration.' Godfrey's impatience and irascibility prompted his replacement at the end of 1942, though the machine he created remained almost unchanged until the end of the war.

Outside the admiral's green baize door sat his personal assistant, the dashing former journalist Commander Ian Fleming. McLachlan again: 'if not the wisest of the staff in Room 39, the most vivid … His gift was much less for the analysis and weighing of intelligence than for running things and for drafting. He was a skilled fixer and a vigorous showman … a giant among name-droppers.' The NID also employed writers and historians including Hilary Saunders, William Plomer and Charles Morgan; an art historian who handled PoW interrogation reports, Charles Mitchell; and the former head of Thomas Cook's West End office, who ran the

Scandinavian section. Room 39 was known to the 'secret ladies' and typists as 'the Zoo'.

McLachlan itemised in order of importance the material from seventeen sources which was collated and reviewed by Godfrey's staff. Unsurprisingly, the list was headed by decrypted enemy wireless traffic: until the end of 1943 Admiral Karl Dönitz and his subordinates ashore sought to micro-manage Germany's U-boat campaign, and thus constantly exchanged signals with captains at sea, much to the advantage of the British. Thereafter in the roll call of intelligence sources followed captured documents; bearings on enemy shipping secured by 'Huff-Duff'; intercepted voice messages; air photographs; ship sightings by aircraft; information from agents or friendly secret services; PoW interrogations; wireless traffic analysis; enemy communiqués; hints from intercepted civilian correspondence; topographical and technical information from open sources; friendly and neutral observers; tactical information gathered during operations at sea; sightings by merchant ships and coast-watchers; intelligence forwarded from other services; instructions from enemy intelligence organisations to double agents under British control. All material was graded in reliability and importance, from 'A1' to 'D5'.

There was incessant, fractious and sometimes fierce argument about how far protection of the Ultra secret should be allowed to constrain operations against the enemy. On 11 March 1942 C-in-C Plymouth wrote to Godfrey, as DNI, complaining that information about an enemy vessel that was being towed to Cherbourg, and about an escorted German tanker on passage, had been in British hands in time to attack them, but reached operational commanders ten days late. Admiral of the Fleet Sir Charles Forbes – known to his own service as 'Wrong Way' Forbes since he shifted the Home Fleet beyond reach of Norwegian waters just before the April 1940 German invasion – fulminated: 'The intense secrecy which shrouds all information conveyed by "Ultra" messages has been found to militate against the useful employment of this information for operational purposes. There is, indeed, a tendency to place the claims of security before the claims of offensive action … I do not think it can be too strongly emphasised that however secret may be the sources from which intelligence is obtained, such intelligence can never be an end in itself, and if it does not lead to action it is valueless.'

Forbes's letter is significant, because it highlights the daily dilemmas faced by the guardians of Ultra. Moreover, it illustrates how wisely and well British and most – though by no means all – American officers served the Allied war effort, by resisting many temptations to exploit decrypts, in order that they might protect the Allies' wider interests in the secret war. In the latter half of 1942, when air interdiction of Rommel's Mediterranean supply lines attained devastating effectiveness, guided by Ultra, almost every RAF attack was preceded by a reconnaissance overflight, to mask the source of British knowledge.

If Bletchley's output was the most important source of intelligence, supplementary aids were indispensable. Sigint could not be relied upon to provide – for instance – warning of sailings of German capital ships, often screened by wireless silence. Norwegian agents monitoring the fjord anchorages of *Tirpitz* and its kind provided vital alerts about whether they were preparing to put to sea or had done so. A naval intelligence officer wrote: 'So reliable was this service ... that the OIC in London had complete faith in [the agents'] accuracy and regularity.' Here was something MI6 did well. Meanwhile, aerial reconnaissance was invaluable when the weather made this practicable, though it remained an inexact science, especially if naval intelligence officers were obliged to rely on a pilot's remembered glimpses, rather than on photographs which could be subjected to expert interpretation. It was hard for aircrew, thousands of feet up, to distinguish between a battleship, a heavy cruiser and a big destroyer. In July 1942 a Luftwaffe pilot's sighting of a single British plane in the sky off Norway deterred the Germans from dispatching *Tirpitz* against PQ17. The airman reported seeing a carrier aircraft. In reality this had been a mere floatplane, but the Kriegsmarine declined the risk that a Royal Navy carrier group might be within range of their precious monster.

In the early war years British technical knowledge about U-boats was poor, partly because the NID lacked sophisticated interrogators who knew what questions to ask prisoners. By 1942, matters had improved: U-boat crewmen in British camps revealed the existence of the *Pillenwerfer*, the bubble-ejection technique for foxing Asdic detectors; also details of German torpedoes and search-receivers for radar transmissions. Interrogators learned – as did their Luftwaffe counterparts quizzing Allied airmen – to confound prisoners by showing off knowledge of their domestic affairs, for instance the charms of the red-haired waitress at Lorient's Café de Rennes. A problem persisted, that the Royal Navy was unwilling to believe that technology its own ships lacked might work for the enemy – several U-boat refinements, and big 5.9-inch guns mounted on destroyers.

Some interrogators favoured offering relatively lavish hospitality to celebrity prisoners who might provide important information. In October

1944 the director of intelligence threw up his hands in horror when he learned that his officers had spent £2 on wining and dining a U-boat captain. The DNI issued a formal warning against 'entertaining at the Ritz and the purchase of considerable quantities of gin. If these facts became known, there might be good cause for scandal. Furthermore, I and many others are quite unable to enjoy these luxuries, and it is out of all proportion that our enemies should.' The interrogator responded impenitently that it seemed worth £2 of taxpayers' money to convince a sceptical Nazi that the Ritz was still standing.

Perversely, even as the tide of war turned decisively against the Germans, some of Dönitz's crewmen in Allied hands became stubbornly security-conscious. On 12 March 1944 the DNI briefed the First Sea Lord on recent PoW interrogations. Some 70 per cent of U-boat crews by then accepted that the war was lost, and 25 per cent would frankly avow this to a British officer. But crews were better trained to resist interrogation; even at this late hour for the Nazi empire, 'there is a general belief that those who divulge information will be punished after the war'. When censors discovered that captured U-boat crewmen were using a simple code to convey sensitive material in letters home to Germany, the traffic was allowed to continue, in hopes that the NID would find uses for such disclosures.

Next door to the Admiralty, the Operational Intelligence Centre was located in the new Citadel building, a dank concrete mass, much overcrowded, whose inmates suffered from chronic colds and viral infections. The OIC's surface-ship section, run by Commander Norman Denning, took centre stage in British naval operations during such crises as the pursuit of the *Bismarck*, the 'Channel Dash' and the Arctic agony of Convoy PQ17. During hours and days of intense debate and harsh decision-making, the First Sea Lord and his acolytes became frequent visitors to the OIC. In the early war years there were persistent delays in implementing operational decisions following the receipt of decrypts. The Far East Combined Bureau, Bletchley's Singapore out-station thereafter evacuated to Colombo, broke Japanese signals reporting the sighting of *Prince of Wales* and *Repulse*, as well as the enemy's attack orders, four hours before the first bombs and torpedoes struck the great warships. But Admiral Tom Phillips, on *Prince of Wales*'s flag bridge, learned of this only when the Japanese were already overhead and his doom was sealed. Fortunately for the Royal Navy, the transmission of such urgent material was much accelerated thereafter.

The tactical war at sea was more powerfully influenced by sigint than the land campaigns, partly because convoys and submarines travelled more slowly than tanks. Given that decryption of enemy signals required at best hours, and sometimes days, its fruits were more likely to reach commanders in time to trigger an operational response on the ocean than was usually possible on a land battlefield. On many days between 1941 and 1945, the most important place in British naval headquarters was its Submarine Tracking Room. There, Commander Richard Hall – son of 'Blinker' – gave orders to reroute convoys, in accordance with the latest appreciations of U-boat positions made by the Room's overlord, the immensely respected Commander Rodger Winn. The Room's wry but deadly earnest motto was 'Never the twain shall meet.' Winn himself, cursed since childhood polio by a limp and a twisted spine, was a remarkable personality, who treated senior officers with suitable respect, like the former barrister he was, in the company of a judge, such as he later became. Yet he never failed to assert his own convictions. His most striking characteristic, which distinguished him from many peers on both sides of the war, was moral courage. He drove his staff hard, rebuked mistakes with a biting tongue, and insisted that the Tracking Room delivered a single collective view on every issue.

Informality nonetheless prevailed: colleagues were treated as equals, heedless of rank. Civilian watchkeepers and researchers maintained the Room's signal log and compiled its records and statistics. On the walls, graphs recorded peaks and troughs of merchant-ship and U-boat sinkings, together with the progress of new construction. The Room's hub was an 8ft x 8ft table, on which was mounted a chart of the North Atlantic. Here, for up to fourteen hours a day, Winn or his deputy sat chin in hand, plotting distances and calculating speeds and angles, with one eye on the teleprinter that spasmodically clattered into life, disgorging flashes from Bletchley. On the plot, the limits of Allied air cover were shown by red arc lines painted across the ocean. U-boat positions were indicated by coloured pins: red for a firm fix, white for a sighting, blue for a DF bearing.

Sometimes during a U-boat wolf-pack attack, the Royal Navy's escorts might secure up to forty DF 'fixes' in an hour on Dönitz's submarines. To secure a reasonably accurate bearing, a ship needed to be within forty and fifty miles of the U-boat's transmissions; to get a precise one, ten to fifteen miles. In good weather, a convoy might average a speed of seven to nine knots. Though a surfaced U-boat could manage eleven knots, its submerged speed slowed to just two or three. Thus it was that Allied aircraft exercised a critical influence as long as convoys sailed within their sweep radius, by forcing submarines to dive even if air-dropped depth-charges failed to sink them. Since these naval battles took place in relatively slow motion, diverting the course of a convoy could render it impossible for Dönitz's hunters to catch up.

Every morning Winn or his deputy held a telephone conference with the C-in-C Western Approaches in Liverpool, and the chief of staff to the C-in-C of RAF Coastal Command, during which Winn described the main events of the preceding night. At midday Hall dispatched a four-page situation report to Churchill's War Room. Once a week, the entire table plot from the Tracking Room was transferred to new chart sheets, as the old ones became pepper-potted with pinpricks. A colleague wrote of Winn's 'uncanny flair for guessing a U-boat's behaviour'. During running convoy battles that persisted through several days and nights, 'the intense intellectual labour that went into this battle of tactics was tolerable to the human beings engaged only if it became for them virtually like a game of chess or bridge … they had to keep in check any leap of imagination which would have pictured in terms of appalling human suffering their failure say, to extricate a tanker convoy from the assailing pack. Otherwise the strain would have been too great.' Thus, they were once obliged to preserve an icy calm while one of their own former colleagues in the Tracking Room, a certain Commander Boyle, led a convoy from Trinidad of which eleven tankers were sunk one by one, until just one ship reached port.

In December 1942, Winn came under immense pressure to detach from a southbound Atlantic convoy the White Star liner *Ceramic*, carrying airfield specialists, because these men were urgently needed at Takoradi in West Africa. For four days he refused, asserting his conviction that the Germans were tracking the convoy and would soon attack. Then he yielded to the insistence of the Ministry of Shipping. *Ceramic* raced ahead – and was sunk with only a single survivor. By 1943, so great was respect for Winn's judgement that an Admiralty standing order was introduced that no ship or convoy should be routed against his advice. Yet so great was the strain imposed by his responsibilities that for a month the Commander had to quit his post, after succumbing to nervous exhaustion.

So much has been written about Bletchley's triumph in breaking the U-boat codes – which was real enough – that the story of the Battle of the Atlantic has become distorted. The matching achievement of the Kriegsmarine's B-Dienst intelligence service deserves more notice. For about a year, from July 1942 to June 1943, though with some intermissions and delays, Dönitz's codebreakers provided the U-boat command with an extraordinary wealth of information about convoy movements, which made almost as important a contribution to soaring Allied shipping losses as did the deadly coincidence of BP's inability to break the Shark cipher for much of the same period.

U-boat operations were controlled by a tightly knit group of five staff officers around Dönitz, at BdU headquarters located successively in Lorient, Paris, and – from January 1943 – Berlin. Among the most important personalities was the signals specialist Kapitän zur See Hans Meckel. The loss of every submarine was subjected to meticulous inquiry, not least to consider whether any breach of security might have contributed to an Allied sinking. The B-Dienst, headed by Kapitän zur See Heinz Bonatz, was based in naval headquarters, situated like the Abwehr in Berlin's Tirpitzüfer, and grew to a strength of 6,000 men and women. Teleprinters disgorged signals from listening stations all over Europe, of which the largest was in Holland. Its codebreakers, led by the veteran former naval wireless-operator Wilhelm Tranow, benefited from the fact that Dönitz was one of the few German senior officers of any service to take intelligence seriously. Like his Allied counterparts, he recognised that the first imperative of the war at sea was to locate the enemy.

During the spring and summer of 1940, the B-Dienst reckoned to read around 2,000 British messages a month, though this declined steeply in August after the Royal Navy changed its codes. From 1940 until 1944, Bonatz's men achieved reasonably regular breaks into the Merchant Navy code. After capturing its latest version, 'Mersigs II', in March 1942, they consistently penetrated convoy signals, allotting names to different varieties of British traffic in the same fashion as did Bletchley to German ones: *Köln*, *Frankfurt*, *München Blau*, *München Rot*. At this time also they began to make effective use of IBM-type punch-card technology.

One of the most serious wartime failures of Bletchley Park was that its small cipher security section failed for many months to recognise and alert the Admiralty to the vulnerability of some of its codes, despite several requests for advice and assistance from the naval officer responsible. The Germans read the signals of New York's harbour captain, who gave the composition and often course updates of eastbound convoys, even when rerouted by Rodger Winn. The B-Dienst's break into the Royal Navy's Cypher No. 3 was not comprehensive: many messages were read only after an interval of days, and only about one in ten became available fast enough to concentrate U-boats. But thanks to sigint, Dönitz's general view of Allied operations was strikingly well informed.

The post-war American study of German naval communications intelligence, based on exhaustive interrogations of personnel and study of captured documents, in this case the B-Dienst's, concluded: 'The enemy possessed at all times a reasonably clear picture of Atlantic convoys with varying degrees of accuracy as to the routes and day-by-day plotting … Convoy diversions were sometimes learned from decryption in time to re-arrange U-boat patrol lines accordingly … The most complete single statement of German convoy intelligence ever seen here in German naval traffic came in a series of messages … in December 1943 and January 1944. These messages apparently reproduced the [Allies'] current convoy chart for the North Atlantic … The convoys then at sea were correctly identified both by designators and numbers, and accurate information given on convoy cycles, speeds and general routing.'

The American study makes abundantly clear that the wireless war at sea was by no means one-sided. British sins of omission and commission both at the Admiralty and Bletchley cost ships and lives. The B-Dienst had codebreakers of considerable skill, if not quite in the class of Hut 8's people. In the ten days 9–19 March 1943, during the period when the Kriegsmarine was winning the sigint war against the Royal Navy, four convoys – SC121, HX228, SC122 and HX229 – each lost one in five of its ships, a disastrous attrition rate. Yet actions or lapses sometimes had perverse consequences. This very failure of the Royal Navy's code security conferred a priceless boon on the Allied cause, albeit at heavy cost. At intervals throughout the war, and initially as early as 1941, Dönitz entertained serious suspicions that Enigma had been penetrated. On 28 September, a British submarine ambushed U-67 and U-111 at a rendezvous near the Cape Verde islands, off Senegal. Its torpedoes missed, and it was itself rammed by a third U-boat on the scene, but the admiral said when told of this dramatic incident: 'A British submarine does not appear by chance in such a remote place,' and launched a major inquiry. Yet this concluded that 'the more important ciphers do not appear to have been compromised'. A second investigation in February 1943 reached the same conclusion, once again reassured by the vulnerability of British codes, which persisted until June. If the Royal Navy had the power to read the German hand, its chiefs would surely have closed this costly hole.

Meanwhile the U-boat command ignored the urgings of Wilhelm Tranow to use a codebook rather than a cipher machine for its wireless traffic, such as gravely inconvenienced US codebreakers when the Japanese army did so. Later, in August 1943, an informant in Swiss intelligence* told an officer of the local Abwehr station that the Allies were breaking U-boat codes, a warning promptly passed to submarine command in Berlin. Dönitz ordered yet another investigation into cipher security. Yet at its conclusion, amazingly, he allowed himself to be reassured.

The admiral wrote after the war: 'Whether and to what extent the enemy reacted to radio transmissions was something which, try as we might, we were never able to ascertain with any certainty. In a number of cases drastic alterations in the course of the convoy led us to assume that he did. On the other hand, many cases occurred in which, in spite of U-boat radio activity in the area, enemy ships sailing independently, and convoys as well, were allowed to sail straight on and into the same area.' Having satisfied himself about Enigma's security, Dönitz chose also to ignore a warning of its vulnerability from Lt. Hans-Joachim Frowein, based on his own researches using punch-card technology. If the Allies' conduct of the Battle of the Atlantic had suggested omniscience rather than fallibility, however, it is overwhelmingly likely that Dönitz would have guessed the Ultra secret.

On 1 June 1943 the Royal Navy abandoned Naval Cyphers No. 3 and No. 4, introducing Naval Cypher No. 5, also adopted by the Americans and Canadians for Atlantic operations on 10 June, which the B-Dienst proved unable to break. Bletchley was furious that the switch took so long, having warned eight months earlier of the previous ciphers' vulnerability, but the Admiralty pleaded the huge administrative challenge of issuing new codes to thousands of ships. Moreover, GC&CS's Cipher Security section had also been blameworthy.

While the war at sea was far more decisively influenced by codebreaking than was any land campaign, it is quite mistaken to view the Battle of the Atlantic exclusively as a struggle between Bletchley and the B-Dienst – here, as everywhere else, hard power was vital. In 1943, beyond GC&CS's triumph in breaking the Shark cipher, the Allies enjoyed a surge of naval and air strength that embraced new escort groups, escort carriers and Very Long Range Aircraft, mostly Liberators, together with improved technology. This prompted a policy shift away from rerouting convoys in favour of going head to head with attacking U-boats. By the winter, while the

---

* See below, p.474.

B-Dienst was once again achieving good breaks into the British Merchant Ship code, Dönitz's force lacked the capability effectively to exploit them. The Germans launched spasmodic attacks on convoys until the last days of the war, but their campaign was long lost. The principal reason that Dönitz failed to strangle the Atlantic supply route was that he lacked U-boats in sufficient numbers to achieve such a feat. Ultra much assisted the Allies' slaughter of enemy submarines in the summer of 1943, especially in providing targets for the air wings of US Navy escort carriers, but to revisit Churchill: 'All things are always on the move simultaneously.'

After the war Donald McLachlan catalogued what he and his colleagues considered the Royal Navy's Intelligence Department's principal wartime blunders and lapses. Foremost was failure to realise that the Kriegsmarine was reading important British wireless traffic. The *Scharnhorst*'s Channel Dash, and indeed several other forays by German big ships, remained lasting sources of embarrassment. The Admiralty underrated the threat from Italian frogmen, who inflicted some crippling losses in 1941, and responded too little and too late to revelations of the chronic vulnerability of warships to air attack. It failed to revive useful lessons about German U-boat tactics from World War I, and for many months refused to believe that Dönitz's craft were attacking on the surface at night. Before the war, the Admiralty's director of signals opposed an extension of the DF wireless network for fixing warship positions by direction-finding: he declared that such equipment would be a waste of resources, because in operational conditions the enemy would maintain wireless silence. All the above represented cases in which the British acquired sufficient information to counter or forestall the enemy's moves, had the Admiralty made imaginative use of this. Yet the NID was the best of the three British services' intelligence departments, and its wartime record was more impressive than that of its foes. Dönitz never acknowledged the gaping hole in his most sensitive communications, while the British plugged their own in time to secure victory.

8

'Mars': The Bloodiest Deception

1 GEHLEN

How can the incompetence and myopia of German intelligence be explained? Here was a nation of the highest cultural, technological and scientific achievements. Hitler's army showed itself for a time to be the finest fighting force the world has ever seen, albeit in a ghastly cause. It is no longer supposed by responsible historians that Admiral Canaris assisted the Allied cause – in other words, that he was explicitly a traitor. The Abwehr and Gestapo were proficient in suppressing Resistance activity and capturing Allied agents in occupied territories, even if the Red Orchestra escaped their attention for seven years. Canaris was risibly unsuccessful, however, in conducting intelligence-gathering activities abroad. Beyond losing every spy dispatched to Britain, his agents fared no better in the United States. The admiral's June 1942 Operation 'Pastorius' landed eight would-be saboteurs, who fell into FBI hands within a fortnight. Six of them went to the electric chair, and German operations elsewhere were similarly bungled. Part of the explanation for this institutional failure, banal as it seems, is that most of the Abwehr's officers did not try very hard. A large proportion of those posted abroad were content merely to enjoy an existence much more comfortable than was available in the Reich, to fiddle their expenses and transmit to Germany any hotchpotch of information fertile imaginations could contrive, assisted by input from double agents controlled by MI5. Nobody in Berlin sought to impose purpose and rigour.

The Germans invaded Russia with such a recklessly arrogant mindset that for some weeks they made no serious attempt to break the Red Army's codes, because they were confident of victory whatever their foes did. This mood changed dramatically as Soviet resistance hardened. Hitler's forces received the shock of their lives after occupying Kiev: a series of massive

Soviet demolitions erupted around them, triggered by radio control. The Wehrmacht began to acknowledge the necessity of monitoring the airwaves. In the winter of 1941, the most disturbing intimation of the vast residual strength of the Red Army came from German interception of messages from divisions with numbers in a '400' series – this, when at the outset Berlin dismissed any notion that Stalin could muster such vast forces. The distances of Russia created chronic sigint problems: even when a hundred Wehrmacht interception stations were deployed on the Eastern Front, these never sufficed for comprehensive monitoring.

The Germans learned much about Soviet wireless procedures after capturing Col. Kurmin, signals chief of the Russian Twelfth Army. The British were alarmed when Bletchley intercepted signals suggesting that much Soviet communications traffic was vulnerable: 'the Germans can read important Russian naval, military and air force codes with promptitude … [Yet] this grave handicap is not in the least realised by the Russians.' There is no doubt of the vulnerability of lower Red Army codes in 1941–42, nor that German radio intelligence read at least some command messages sent by operators who re-used one-time pads. But, in order to believe that the Germans achieved useful and consistent penetration of Soviet higher ciphers, evidence would be necessary that this was exploited by Hitler's army commanders. Instead, there is only a thin patchwork of decrypted Stavka messages, none of much significance, together with obvious signs that some intercepts derived from Russian deceptions. The dominant facts of the first year of the campaign on the Eastern Front were that, with or without breaks into Soviet codes, the Germans failed to secure Moscow and Leningrad, their principal strategic objectives. The flow of decrypts slowed greatly after 1 April 1942, when the Red Army introduced new codes and callsigns.

Lt. Col. Reinhard Gehlen, senior intelligence officer of the Wehrmacht on the Eastern Front from that time almost until the end, nonetheless achieved the highest wartime reputation of any German in his field. He was born in Erfurt in 1902, son of a bookseller. He joined the army in 1920, served in the artillery and married a descendant of a distinguished Prussian military family, Herat von Seydlitz-Kurzback. He graduated to the general staff in 1935, and in the early war years won golden opinions as an operations officer. In July 1941 he was promoted lieutenant-colonel and attached to the Fremde Heere Ost, or FHO, the intelligence section of the high command, of which he became chief in April 1942, after his predecessor was sacked for poor performance during the winter battles around Moscow, one among many scapegoats for the Wehrmacht's failure.

Gehlen was an austere figure, taciturn and physically undistinguished, who skilfully ingratiated himself with his superiors, at the same time masking from his comrades ruthless ambition. He brought to his work a new energy and imagination: while most of his counterparts throughout the army recruited conventional staff officers, Gehlen instead hired clever men heedless of their military accomplishments. He combed the Wehrmacht for linguists, geographers, anthropologists and lawyers, who dramatically raised the quantity, if not the quality, of reporting and analysis. He made good use of patrols, together with interception of low-grade Russian signals and voice traffic. Gehlen also focused energetically on PoW interrogation, exploiting the many senior Russian officers in German hands. He ran a 'celebrity camp' in East Prussia, known as *Feste Boyen*, which held an average of eighty 'guests', of whom the most important were accorded single rooms. All prisoners received full Wehrmacht rations, and the most cooperative stayed indefinitely, to provide instant responses to questions FHO needed answering from day to day and week to week.

Some PoWs stubbornly refused to talk to Gehlen's officers, who noted an oddity: better-educated men often collaborated, while humbler ones stayed mute. Much depended on prevailing battlefield conditions. When the Russians seemed to be losing and morale was low, as on every front prisoners were more willing to give information. When the tide of war turned, cooperation declined, because prisoners who aided the Nazis feared their fate – with good reason – if Stalin prevailed. The chief impediment to getting intelligence out of Russian soldiers was that they served the most secretive society in the world: few even among senior officers knew much about anything beyond their own unit.

Gehlen was no fool, and more of a realist than many of his colleagues, but he was also a skilled waffler. Consider, for instance, his 29 August 1942 analysis of Russia's condition, and of Moscow's options into the winter. This was a critical moment of the war, the eve of Stalingrad. FHO's chief offered the German high command an extensive menu of alternative scenarios. This deserves attention, because it was typical of the material produced by the Wehrmacht's most celebrated intelligence officer. Gehlen assumed, he said, that Leningrad, Stalingrad and the north Caucasus would be overrun by German forces, and a continuous front established between Persia and the Arctic. Russian actions thereafter would be determined by 'the results of the summer–autumn campaign; relative resources available to Germany and Russia; the evolving views of the Russian leadership; Russian objectives'. The Russians wanted to husband resources and fighting room for a winter campaign, said Gehlen.

'They seem willing to accept the loss of Leningrad, Stalingrad, the north and perhaps also southern Caucasus, and even Moscow. Russian losses in 1942 have been lower than in 1941. They seem content to have inflicted not insignificant German losses, and are themselves achieving manpower gains by cutting exemptions from military service, mobilising 1.4 million men born in 1925, and reducing the strength of divisions. It must be anticipated that this winter the enemy will again commit a large number of new formations to the battlefield. On the whole, there is no sign that, in the foreseeable future, the German–Russian balance of strength will shift decisively to the disadvantage of the Russians' – here was a circumlocution worthy of the NKVD.

Gehlen suggested that British-supplied war material could become a significant factor, especially in the Caucasus. The Russians, he said, were learning fast, and had adopted many German tactics: air force close support for the Red Army, aggressive patrolling, deployment of tanks in defence only behind a forward infantry screen. However, Russian middle and junior leadership had declined. 'All in all,' wrote the intelligence chief, 'it must be expected that the enemy will keep moving on his autumn and winter axes, using tried and tested methods, especially with guerrillas and airborne forces. The Russians will seek to achieve disruption of the German front at as many points as possible, shifting to major offensives where opportunity permits ... This possibility seems to exist especially on Army Group B's front (Stalingrad) and that of AG Centre at Smolensk ... On AG A's front, after the loss of the North Caucasus the enemy has convenient defensive facilities in the Caucasus mountains where it must be anticipated that he will progress to heavy counter-attacks where the ground seems suitable, aimed especially at disrupting German oil production.'

Gehlen concluded that the Soviet armies would approach winter 'enfeebled but not yet destroyed, and thus with an option to initiate new operations ... Depending on the forces available to the Russian leadership and the front positions following the summer–autumn campaign, heavy Russian offensives will be likely at a) Stalingrad and west of Stalingrad. b) Weak sections of the Allied [Axis] front, especially where the Russians hold bridgeheads. c) Voronezh. d) Mtsensk – Orel. e) Sukhinichi. f) Rzhev. g) In the gap between Army Groups Centre and North. h) Leningrad ...

Only if the Russians fail to achieve substantial successes in the winter of 1942/43; if a second front in [Western] Europe becomes less likely; and if the economic consequences of this year's losses of territory (including Baku) make a real impact, can we reckon on finally breaking Russian resistance. This will presumably not take place before the summer of 1943.'

This was not a stupid document: it reviewed perfectly rationally the options open to the Russians. It mentioned Stalingrad, though only in the context of six other possible objectives for Soviet offensives. A sceptical reader might be tempted to compare its equivocations to a prediction that, if a man turns over the fifty-two cards in a deck, he will find four aces. But during the months and years that followed, Gehlen gravely misjudged most of the big moments on the Eastern Front. He first insisted that the Russians' Operation 'Mars', their northern offensive against Army Group Centre, was Stalin's big push, to which 'Uranus' – the Stalingrad pincer movement, turning point of the war – was merely opportunistic and subsidiary.

On 25 July 1943, a fortnight after the acknowledged failure of Germany's great offensive at Kursk, Gehlen assured the high command that the Russians had no plans for a big assault of their own – only local attacks; nine days later, the Red Army drove west a hundred miles. On 30 March 1944, Gehlen's assessment of the front showed him oblivious of the looming Soviet offensive against Crimea, which brought new disaster upon the Wehrmacht. Before the Russians' summer Operation 'Bagration', greatest Allied offensive of the war, he dismissed Soviet preparations on Army Group Centre's front as 'apparently a deception', and predicted that Stalin would instead strike south, into the Balkans.

Yet Col. Gehlen retained his job, and the respect of Germany's generals, almost to the end of the war. This was partly because of his unflagging plausibility and palace political skills, but chiefly because of his success in running agents behind the Soviet front who provided information of extraordinary quality, reports that made a real impact on German deployments, and thus on the fate of the Eastern Front. Gehlen may thus be considered one of the most influential intelligence officers to serve on either side in the Second World War. But whose interests did he serve? The latest evidence suggests that he was the victim of Soviet manipulation – *maskirovka* – on an astounding scale; that far from being the wizard of his self-created legend, Gehlen was a supremely gullible dupe.

2 AGENT 'MAX'

Early in 1942, during the disastrous phase when Stalin still insisted upon exercising personal control of Russia's military operations, he decreed a wholesale reorganisation of military intelligence, dissolving its machinery for handling battlefield information, which prompted chaos in its activities through the first half of that year. Igor Damaskin, one of the more credible modern Russian historians of the period, has written: 'The chaos in the GRU during this period blighted operations and was responsible for heavy losses, as field headquarters were desperately short of information about the enemy.' Stalin rejected all reports that flew in the face of his own instincts: in March 1942, for instance, the GRU correctly predicted Hitler's Operation 'Blue': 'Preparations for a spring offensive are confirmed by the movement of German troops and materials ... The central axis of [the enemy's] spring advance will shift to the southern sector of the front with an additional thrust in the north and a simultaneous demonstration at the Central front against Moscow ... The most likely date of the offensive is mid-April to early May 1942.' Stalin castigated military intelligence for succumbing to what he described as obvious German deceptions. He insisted on launching the May offensive at Kharkov, which precipitated a new disaster for Soviet arms. Even as late as 19 June, when documents found in a shot-down German aircraft confirmed Hitler's emphasis on the southern thrusts against Stalingrad and the Caucasus, *Hozyain* dismissed them as an obvious German plant.

Within weeks, however, he was forced to acknowledge the terrific strength of Paulus's Sixth Army, driving east for Stalingrad. At last, the master of the Kremlin bowed to reality: the summer of 1942 witnessed a seismic shift in the manner in which the Soviet Union made war. Stalin implicitly acknowledged his own failure as a strategist and director of Russia's hosts. He delegated authority to his generals, at least up to army group level, and allowed intelligence departments once again to function in a coherent and professional manner. From the autumn, when the battle for Stalingrad began, the Russians began to do remarkable things in the field of strategic deception. Their Operation 'Monastery' became one of the greatest such schemes of the war, at least as important as the Anglo-American 'Fortitude', which broadcast confusion about D-Day.

'Monastery' was originally conceived in July 1941, with the limited objective of penetrating the enemy's intelligence apparatus and identifying traitors collaborating with the Nazis. It seems remarkable that such a plan could have been initiated in those dark days, when the Red Army was falling back eastwards in headlong retreat, but so it was. The NKVD and GRU worked together to create a mythical anti-Soviet, pro-German Resistance movement operating at the heart of the Russian high command, codenamed 'Throne'. It was founded upon a network of double agents among the old Russian noble class – those left alive after decades of persecution. 'Monastery' mobilised historic Russian conspiratorial skills. An old man named Glebov, whose wife had served at the court of Alexandra, the last tsarina, was designated as the 'Resistance movement's' figurehead. He lived almost as a beggar in Novodevichy monastery, but was well known in White Russian émigré circles. However, the principal active NKVD participant, or at least glove puppet, was an agent named Alexander Demyanov, who was assigned the most perilous role. Born in 1911, his background was impeccably aristocratic. His grandfather founded the Kuban Cossacks; his father was killed fighting for the tsar in 1915; his mother was a famous Moscow beauty. The family lived in poverty after the Revolution, and Alexander's origins debarred him from higher education. He was obliged to scratch a living as an electrician, and in 1929 was arrested on a charge of spreading anti-Soviet propaganda. He escaped exile or execution by the usual means – agreeing to serve as an informer, for which purpose he was given a job in the electrical branch of the Central Cinema Studio, Moscow's Hollywood. A cheerful extrovert, Demyanov became a popular figure among the stars and literati. The NKVD paid for him to acquire a horse, to ride out not only with the film-makers but also with foreign diplomats and businessmen, including a good many Germans. He married a girl named Tatiana Beresantsov, a respected technician at Mosfilms, whose father was a physician permitted the extraordinary privilege of maintaining a private practice.

Centre decided that Demyanov was so promising a deep-penetration agent that he should not be thrown away on mere informant tasks. He became well known and trusted in anti-Soviet and nationalist circles. The NKVD's glee knew no bounds when, shortly before 'Barbarossa', the young man reported an approach from a member of a German trade mission, who was obviously working for the Abwehr. Demyanov's handler instructed him to show no interest, lest over-eagerness frighten off the recruiter. Berlin anyway opened a file on Demyanov. When war broke out he enlisted in a Red Army cavalry regiment, but was quickly retrieved by Pavel Sudoplatov, who regarded him as an ideal Special Tasks agent, with

Soldiers of Hitler's Wehrmacht use an Enigma cipher machine to encrypt secret signals. Breach of Enigma by the codebreakers of Bletchley Park became one of the greatest British achievements of the Second World War.

Above: A charming snapshot of evil out of hours – Lavrenti Beria, Stalin's foremost secret policeman, holds Stalin's daughter Svetlana, while in the background the master of the Kremlin relaxes with his pipe. Beria proved better at guarding Stalin from the Russian people than from his foreign enemies. *Right*: Vasily and Elizabeth Zarubin, two of Russia's most successful agent-runners in Europe and the United States.

Richard Sorge of the
GRU, greatest secret
agent of his time, though
his influence on Kremlin
policy is more doubtful.

THE CODEBREAKERS

Above: A scene in Bletchley Park's Hut 3, probably in the latter half of the war, because conditions look less primitive than they were at the outset. *Below*: Bombes, created by Alan Turing in 1940, were revolutionary electro-mechanical aids, here tended by Wrens. They did not decrypt Enigma signals, but provided vital accelerators for doing so.

KEY PLAYERS at GC&CS
Left: Welchman, pictured in his Cambridge days. *Above*: Alexander, who played chess for England.

Above: Milner-Barry. *Right*: Turing in youthful incarnation as a Cambridge athlete as well as mathematician.

THE WAR AT SEA was more dramatically influenced by Ultra intelligence than the land struggle. *Above*: A convoy escort depth-charges a U-boat. *Left*: A German survivor pleads for rescue. *Right*: A remarkable sequence of pictures of the November 1940 German scuttling of the British merchantman SS *Automedon*, after its capture by the commerce-raider *Atlantis* while carrying cabinet documents that detailed for the Japanese British military weakness in the Far East.

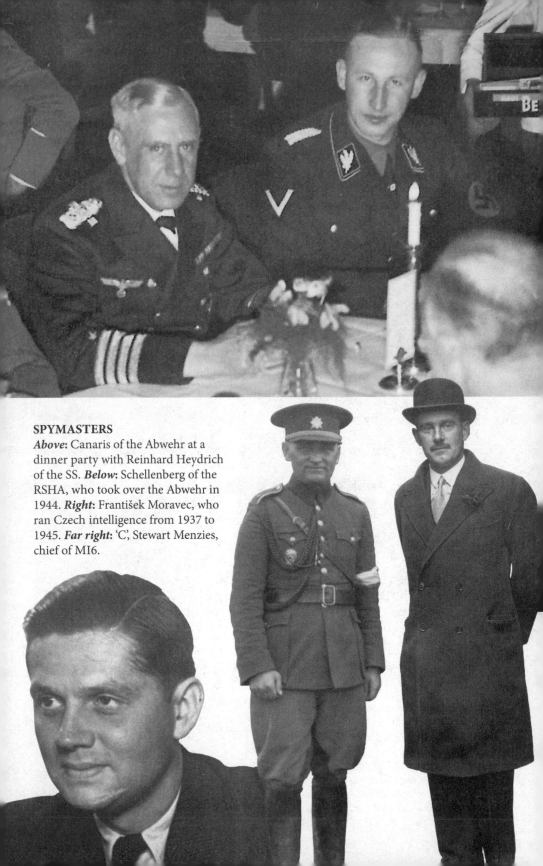

SPYMASTERS
Above: Canaris of the Abwehr at a dinner party with Reinhard Heydrich of the SS. *Below*: Schellenberg of the RSHA, who took over the Abwehr in 1944. *Right*: František Moravec, who ran Czech intelligence from 1937 to 1945. *Far right*: 'C', Stewart Menzies, chief of MI6.

ONE OF CANARIS'S MEN
Hermann Görtz, who spied for the Abwehr with heroic incompetence, here enjoying harmonica accompaniment from Marianne Emig, who accompanied him on a 1935 tour of English airfields which took him to Brixton prison. In 1940, he parachuted into Ireland from a Heinkel bomber.

AMERICA'S CODEBREAKERS
Above: The Registration Room of the US Army's monitoring unit at Avon Tyrell, part of the out-station of Arlington Hall in Britain. *Below*: Joe Rochefort of the US Navy, the man who made possible American victory at Midway in June 1942, wags a finger at fellow domino-players aboard the cruiser USS *Indianapolis*, in a fashion that helps to explain senior officers' disdain for him.

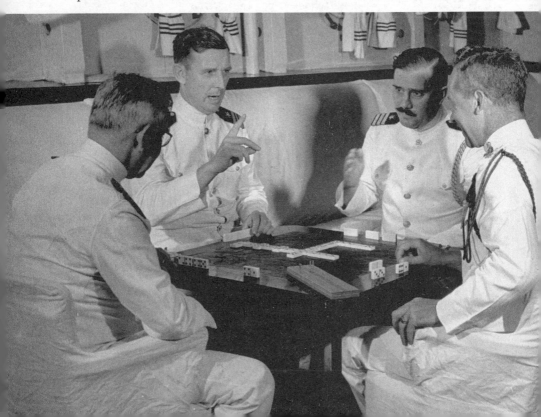

Left: Tommy Dyer, most brilliant cryptanalyst of Rochefort's team in 'the Dungeon' at Pearl Harbor. *Below*: Stars of the US Army's Signals Intelligence Service. In the centre, standing, is Frank Rowlett, credited as 'the man who broke Purple', with Abraham Sinkov to his left and below, in civilian clothes, the pioneer William Friedman.

LEADERS OF THE RED ORCHESTRA
Above: Libertas and Harro Schulze-Boysen. *Right*: Arvid and Mildred Harnack. All four suffered dreadful deaths in Nazi hands.

SOVIET SPIES IN EUROPE
Clockwise from top left: Foote, Radó, Gourevitch, Rössler, Hamburger, Trepper.

SECRET WARRIORS
Right: Italian SOE agent Paolo del Din in parachute kit, an image that captures the terrific emotional charge many agents gained from their roles. *Below*: Oluf Reed-Olsen stands on the right in a photograph of two carbine-wielding Norwegians. *Below right*: French agent-runner 'Colonel Rémy'.

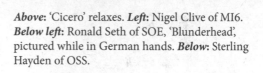

Above: 'Cicero' relaxes. *Left*: Nigel Clive of MI6.
Below left: Ronald Seth of SOE, 'Blunderhead',
pictured while in German hands. *Below*: Sterling
Hayden of OSS.

Hugh Trevor-Roper of MI6, who by 1945 knew far more about the operations of the Abwehr than any German, and (*below*) Bill Bentinck, chairman of Britain's Joint Intelligence Committee.

a decade's experience of role-playing. In the late summer of 1941 Sudoplatov told Beria this was just the man to take a lead in Operation 'Monastery'.

Thus it was that one day in December that year, during the darkest days of the struggle for Moscow, Alexander Demyanov – later codenamed 'Heine' – set off on skis from the Red Army's lines near Gzhatsk, 120 miles south-west of the capital, to defect to the Germans. His extraordinarily perilous mission almost collapsed at the outset: when he reached the Wehrmacht positions and announced himself as a Nazi sympathiser, nobody believed him, partly because he claimed to have crossed the lines by a route that traversed a German minefield. Demyanov later told the NKVD he had been subjected to a mock execution to induce him to talk. Whether or not this was true, he obviously came close to being shot out of hand. Instead, however, he was handed over to the Abwehr. Its officers proved uninterested in his tale about the 'Throne' Resistance group, but immediately enlisted him as an agent – one among thousands of such people who were perfunctorily trained, deployed and expended.

The Germans became more excited, however, when a check with their files showed that Demyanov had been earmarked as a prospective agent before 'Barbarossa'. His background among 'former people' – aristocrats – was such that he could pass muster in émigré circles as an anti-Soviet zealot. Though the Abwehr still showed no enthusiasm for following the original NKVD script – supporting a phoney counter-revolution inside Russia – its handlers thought Demyanov sufficiently smart and well connected to become an important spy. His main problem, during the training that followed, was to hide the fact that he was already – for instance – an accomplished wireless-operator. One night in February 1942, a Luftwaffe aircraft crossed the lines to a grid reference west of Moscow, where Demyanov and two other agents tasked to assist him hurled themselves into darkness over Soviet territory.

They made their parachute descents in terrible weather, and lost contact with each other as they stumbled through a snowstorm near Yaroslavl. Demyanov promptly reported to the nearest NKVD headquarters, and a day or two later his assistants were picked up. During the weeks and months that followed Centre's operation, overseen by Sudoplatov, became ever more byzantine. Demyanov's Moscow flat, where he lived with his wife and father-in-law, became the focus of the supposed Resistance group – the whole family was made privy to the scheme. A succession of Abwehr couriers reported there, some of whom were for a time left at liberty, to see whom they met. Others were 'turned', others again were jailed and presumably shot. A few were permitted to return to the German lines to report.

For Demyanov himself, the supremely perilous part of the operation was over: he was back with his own side. It almost defies belief that any man, however highly developed his sense of adventure and taste for the secret life, could have done as he did, exposing himself to the power and wrath of Nazi Germany in a game of such subtlety and deadliness, but MI5 deployed the British Eddie Chapman in the same fashion, though to much less advantage. Demyanov was thereafter required only to play out a part under the eyes of his own spymasters. The Germans had equipped him with a wireless set. Centre's 'William Fisher' was deputed to manage the subsequent radio operation – this was none other than Rudolf Abel, born to Russian parents in Newcastle upon Tyne, who after the war became a Soviet agent in the US.

The challenge was for Sudoplatov and his colleagues to play out the hand against the Abwehr. Beria warned the Special Tasks chief that he would be held personally responsible if any act of sabotage was committed on Soviet territory in the course of the 'Monastery' operation. At the outset, the Russians had no conception that they had started something that would continue for years – most radio games were detected by the enemy within weeks. The NKVD's first objective was to build up the credibility of what the Germans called the 'Max' material, emanating from Demyanov and other members of his network. He reported to them that the 'Throne' group was conducting railway sabotage near Gorky, and Soviet newspapers dutifully carried reports of train accidents to support the story; the British occasionally used the same ruse, using double agents to carry out alleged demolitions in Britain.

In the latter part of 1942, Demyanov reported to the Abwehr, and thence to Reinhard Gehlen and FHO, that he had been assigned as a junior communications officer at the Soviet high command headquarters in Moscow, a posting which explained how, thereafter, he appeared to enjoy extraordinary access to Russian secrets. Through the months and years that followed, he signalled to Gehlen's staff a mass of material about the Red Army's order of battle and strategic intentions, which reached Berlin and FHO via Sofia. The German army in the East – in the person of Gehlen – became convinced that it was receiving intelligence of the highest quality, and increasingly eager to acknowledge its authenticity. A stream of FHO signals waxed euphoric about its man's product.

Moscow now saw opportunities to exploit 'Max's' reports in support of a major deception operation, for which the NKVD and GRU collaborated. The latter's chief, Col. Gen. Fedor Kuznetsov, fulfilled the role occupied by Col. Johnny Bevan as head of the London Controlling Section and Bill Bentinck of the JIC – overseeing the scheme and supplying menus of mingled information and disinformation for presentation to the Germans. By far the most important and historically controversial development of 'Monastery' came in November 1942, a pivotal moment of the Second World War. On the 19th, the Red Army launched Operation 'Uranus', its historic double envelopment behind the German Sixth Army at Stalingrad. Four days later, however, a second thrust by six armies was unleashed on the Kalinin front at Rzhev a hundred miles north-west of Moscow – Operation 'Mars'. This engaged large German forces, but ended in a costly repulse, with all four thrusts being smashed by the Wehrmacht at a cost of 70,000 Russian dead. Marshal Georgi Zhukov later acknowledged 'Mars' as one of his own failures.

More than half a century later, however, Pavel Sudoplatov asserted in his memoirs that 'Mars' was betrayed in advance to the Germans, without Zhukov's knowledge and on the explicit orders of Stalin, as part of the deception operation to divert German forces from the critical 'Uranus' at Stalingrad. Alexander Demyanov was the instrument by which the information was conveyed to the enemy's high command. This version of events remains disputed among historians, but is largely accepted by Russian ones. Some Westerners find it inconceivable that even Stalin could have knowingly consigned hundreds of thousands of his own people to death or disablement merely to support a *ruse de guerre*, albeit for huge stakes. But the evidence seems strong, indeed almost conclusive, that Sudoplatov told the truth. There is no doubt that Demyanov was an NKVD operative, working under Moscow's control. It is also certain that the Germans regarded him as their outstanding Soviet source: Reinhard Gehlen went to his grave in 1979 still proudly asserting the brilliance of his own handling of the 'Max' material. Most significant, 'Max's' voluminous reports are readily accessible in the German military archive in Freiburg.

Among the most striking messages is one dated 6 November 1942 and headed 'Foreign Armies East – Important Intelligence Reports'. This reads:

Agent (Max): On 4 November, council of war in Moscow, chaired by Stalin. Present 12 marshals and generals. At this meeting, the following principles were laid down: a) Careful approach to all operations, avoiding major losses. b) Losses of territory are unimportant. c) Preservation of industrial and supply sites by early removal [of plant] from endangered areas is vital, on this account: directive to remove refineries and machine factories from Grozny and Makhachkala to New-Baku, Orsk, and Tashkent. d) Rely on own forces, not on assistance from allies. e) Severe measures against desertion, that is on the one hand by execution and intensified control by the State Political Directorate, on the other by stronger propaganda and improved rations. f) Execution of all planned offensive operations, if possible before 15 November, as far as weather conditions permit ['Mars' was eventually delayed by poor weather].

Chiefly:

– from Grozny towards Mozdok
– close to Nizhny and Werchny-Mamon in the Don area
– close to Voronezh
– close to Rzhev
– south of Lake Ilmen and Leningrad.

Necessary forces should be brought forward from the reserve to the front.

This signal, while some of its content is general and vague rather than explicit about 'Mars', seems to provide conclusive evidence that under orders from Moscow Centre Demyanov gave the Germans good warning, ornamented with circumstantial detail, about a looming Soviet thrust against Army Group Centre, contemporaneous with the Russian encirclement of Hitler's Sixth Army at Stalingrad. The 6 November report should be read in the context of frequent order-of-battle dispatches from 'Max' during the run-up to 'Mars', such as the samples below, which deserve quotation because they illustrate the creative effort in Moscow that was expended on compiling them:

Important Intelligence Reports: 1.) 8 October, agent (Max): 1 cavalry brigade, 1 horsed artillery regiment, and 1 pioneer battalion, all from the front, arrived in Tuapse. They will remain there in reserve. 2.) 8 October, agent (Max): 1 rifle division, 3 tank battalions, and artillery as well as several special divisions conducting demolitions in the course of retreats, all from Makhachkala, arrived in Grozny. 3.) 8 October, agent (Max): 120 English and 70 American tanks with 60 English and American instructors arrived in Zarev, assigned to the Stalingrad front. 4.) 8 October, agent

(Max): 1 cavalry division, 4 mixed tank battalions, 2 artillery regiments, and 40 anti-tank guns arrived in Kaluga. They are assigned to the western section of the Kaluga front. 5.) 9 October, agent (Max): In Mischina (45 OW Rzhev), combat groups are being assembled from tank battalions. Many anti-tank guns and a fuel depot [are located] in Mischina. 6.) 8 October, agent (Max): A military delegation consisting of 2 infantry generals, 1 tank group general, 1 air force general, 2 admirals and 2 military engineers, left Moscow for London by air.

The Germans loved it all. It was priceless to the self-esteem of the Abwehr and FHO to believe that their chiefs were successfully running agents inside the Soviet corridors of power. As far as is known, only one senior Abwehr officer, Dr Wagner Delius, head of the Abwehr station in Sofia, questioned the authenticity of the 'Max' material. But an inquiry had scarcely begun before FHO – a furious Reinhard Gehlen – intervened. The 'Max' reports were 'indispensable', he said, 'and must on no account be jeopardised'. The investigation stopped. The NKVD, knowing that Demyanov's standing stood sky-high after the failure of 'Mars', continued to feed a steady stream of intelligence to the enemy, such as this 3 December report:

> From agent (Max): Conference in Moscow, chaired by Stalin with Zhukov, Timoshenko, and Kosslow: In the northern section of the Rzhev front [where 'Mars' had taken place] [sacking] of 5 division commanders. They were replaced by 5 majors, who were appointed colonels. Stalin is dissatisfied with the course of the operations between Rzhev and Velikiye Luki. Zhukov asks for armoured and infantry reinforcements. Stalin [says that he] is sure that there have to be treacherous informants at the top, since the Germans are so well-informed about Soviet movements, plans, and troop strengths. He orders a State Political Directorate committee to be created, for strict control and investigation [of possible traitors].

There is a fascinating cross-bearing on this story: in the autumn of 1942 the British, in the person of Hugh Trevor-Roper, began to ponder decrypts of this traffic which was causing so much excitement in the enemy camp. Trevor-Roper recognised that the 'Max' material, forwarded to the FHO and Abwehr by its key Eastern Front conduit and analyst Richard Kauder – 'Klatt' – in Sofia, was 'very highly valued by the Germans'. He and his section puzzled endlessly over whether 'Max' and his alleged sub-agents inside the Soviet Union were doubles controlled by Moscow. At first this seemed highly likely – especially so when London warned the Russians about the leaks, and they showed no interest in stopping them. On 31 July 1943, however, the Radio Security Service said its former view – that the 'Max' reports were Russian plants – must be reviewed in the light of the fact that recent dispatches 'appeared to contain accurate predictions of Russian tactical moves'.

'Max' had forecast impending Soviet initiatives in the critical Kursk–Orel sector. The War Office MI14's Major Brian Melland commented: 'The possibility of "MAX" reports being, perhaps in part, planted material must, we feel, be discarded … There is ample evidence that German intelligence and Operations consider "MAX" reports to be of great value; and it is quite possible, in fact, that these reports form the best field intelligence obtained by the enemy.' By August the British were convinced – temporarily at least – that 'Max' and his friends were genuine articles – or rather, authentic traitors in the Soviet camp: 'A recent examination has shown them to have been singularly accurate in forecasting Russian operations.' Guy Liddell of MI5 wrote on 12 August: 'MAX must be regarded as a success [for the Abwehr] … reports have been singularly accurate in forecasting Russian operations and the theory that it is a Russian double-cross rather goes by the board.'

Trevor-Roper was still uncertain about 'Max' when he wrote his April 1945 valedictory report on the Abwehr. He said that the material seemed to his team 'suspiciously free from the administrative hitches to which most spy-systems are liable'. Information was transmitted to the Germans punctually and in bulk not only from 'Max' himself in Moscow, but also from alleged sub-agents in Leningrad, Kuibishev, Novorossiysk. 'Although we informed the Russians of the facts, and the names of the persons involved, no action was taken by them to suppress this apparent dangerous leakage. After a variety of other hypotheses had been found untenable, it was considered in this office (although it could never be conclusively proved) that the evidence should only be satisfactorily explained by the assumption that "Klatt", at least in respect of the "Max" Reports, was a Russian-controlled deception agent (although it is possible that he himself may have been unconscious of the fact).' The British, in short, never entirely fathomed 'Monastery', partly because it was beyond the imagination of their intelligence officers, even the supremely cynical Trevor-Roper, that the Russians should surrender so much authentic information, at a price paid in torrents of blood, to promote strategic deceptions.

The Soviet intelligence services were a strange combination of brutish incompetence, exemplified by their 1939–42 mismanagement of the Red Orchestra in Berlin, contrasted with superb sophistication, of which Operation 'Monastery' was perhaps the masterstroke. Only in Stalin's dreadful world could 70,000 lives have been sacrificed, without sentiment or scruple, to serve the higher purposes of the state. The betrayal of 'Mars' to the Germans may help to explain why, until the last years of the twentieth century, the Rzhev battle received so little attention in Soviet histories. Alexander Demyanov's double career continued until the end of the war – later Soviet deception operations through Agent 'Max' will be described below. He received the Order of the Red Banner from the NKVD for his services – and the Iron Cross from Reinhard Gehlen. His wife and father-in-law also received medals, in appreciation of their supporting roles in the web of deceit woven around the family.

It should not be supposed, however, that the triumphant management of Demyanov sufficed to win bouquets all round in Moscow. Viktor Ilyin, his personal handler in the Lubyanka, suffered a dreadful fate in one of the endemic power struggles within Soviet intelligence. It suited Stalin to sustain Viktor Abakumov as a counterweight and rival to Beria. In 1943, he made Abakumov head of SMERSh, charged with the detection and liquidation of traitors, and deputy to himself as minister of defence. In an early exercise of power in this role, Abakumov trumped up charges against Ilyin, director of the NKVD's Secret Political Department. Ilyin had run 'Heine' for five years, and was regarded by the likes of Pavel Sudoplatov as one of the few honest men in the upper reaches of Soviet intelligence. He was a friend of Maj. Gen. Boris Teplinsky, designated to become chief of the headquarters department of the Red Air Force. Abakumov denounced Teplinsky as an enemy of the people, and asserted that Ilyin had conspired to prevent his exposure. Stalin authorised the arrest of both men. Abakumov personally conducted Teplinsky's interrogation, breaking two of his front teeth on the first night. Battered into a wreck, the wretched man confessed that he had told Ilyin years before of his sympathy for men executed in the Purges, and that Ilyin had coached him about how to escape exposure.

When the general was confronted with Ilyin in the basement of the Lubyanka and repeated his farrago of nonsense, the NKVD man slapped him and told him to behave like a man. Ilyin resolutely refused to confess to anything. Defiance did not save him, however. He was held in solitary confinement, repeatedly interrogated and beaten for four years, between

1943 and 1947. Through it all he retained a gallows humour, once demanding of one of his torturers the nature of the ribbon on his chest. When the
man answered 'the Order of Lenin', Ilyin said that he was glad his own case
was deemed so important. Even when the interrogations were abandoned
in 1947 he was held in jail for a further five years, until – in the demented
fashion of higher Soviet affairs – he was suddenly brought forth to testify
against Abakumov, now himself disgraced and imprisoned. Teplinsky
remained a prisoner until 1955.

Pavel Sudoplatov is too modest to mention several Soviet deception operations that failed to fool the Germans – for instance, when the Red Army
launched attacks in the Donbas in July 1943, and in the Chernyov–Pripyat
region during August and September. Poor Russian radio security enabled
German eavesdroppers correctly to predict the Soviet axis of attack. In
general, however, the Stavka's strategic deceptions in the second half of the
war were notably successful. A second major operation, 'Couriers', also
required Stalin's endorsement, to protect its participants from firing
squads: no man dared create even a fictional anti-Soviet movement without his personal authority.

Fifty-four-year-old Bishop Vasily Ratmirov of the Russian Orthodox
Church worked in Kalinin under the control of the NKVD's Zoya Rybkina
when it was occupied by the Germans. Having thus established his patriotic
Soviet credentials, Moscow Centre turned to him to provide cover for
'Couriers'. As the Germans were pushed westwards in 1943, the bishop was
installed in Samara, in the Volga region. He dispatched two clerical novices
to Pskov monastery, south-west of Leningrad, in German-controlled territory, supposedly bearing information for its chief, who was collaborating
with the enemy. These men were in reality NKVD agents, one of them,
Vasily Ivanov, trained by Emma Sudoplatov. The mission's planning was not
without difficulties. The bishop asked for an assurance that the men would
not 'commit the sacrilege of bloodshed in God's sanctuary'. In the course of
training the agents to pass as priests, he lost patience with a coarse, brash
ex-Komsomol wireless-operator who mocked the sacrament, saying, 'Oh
Father, butter the pancakes in heaven. Bring the pancakes to the table!' This
man was replaced by twenty-two-year-old Sergeant Ivan Kulikov, who was
baffled to be quizzed in advance by an NKVD officer about his own history
of church attendance, and only accepted when he displayed an appropriate
respect for the vestments he was required to wear.

They set forth in August, first for Kalinin and thereafter for Pskov, appropriately heavily bearded, supposedly as representatives of a Church-based anti-Soviet Resistance group, and presented themselves to the Germans in this role. The Abwehr provided them with wireless-operators, Soviet PoWs, who proved readily convinced in private conversation with the two 'novices' that it was in their best interests to follow Centre's orders, rather than Canaris's. Thereafter, the Germans complacently supposed that they were in regular communication with a clerical network far behind the Red Army's lines, which was in reality controlled by the NKVD. When the Russians at last overran their location, Bishop Ratmirov and his two novices were denounced by local people as German collaborators; they were threatened with execution by SMERSh until the NKVD intervened, to garland them as heroes.

One consequence of the mission's success was to persuade Stalin that the Orthodox Church was loyal; he amazed his subordinates when he rewarded the priesthood by allowing its members once more to elect a patriarch in 1943, a ceremony attended by Pavel and Emma Sudoplatov. After the war, Ratmirov became an archbishop and was awarded a gold watch and a medal in recognition of his contribution. Ivan Kulikov, promoted to captain, married a girl he had met in his congregation in Kalinin.

Beyond 'Monastery' and 'Couriers', Sudoplatov testifies that the Russians ran a further forty wartime radio deception operations, which were controlled by SMERSh rather than the NKVD. Russian wireless security, and tactical penetration of German communications, were improved dramatically following the capture of Paulus's Sixth Army headquarters at Stalingrad on 2 February 1943, despite its staff's attempts to destroy secret documents and cipher material. *Maskirovka* achieved its greatest triumph in the summer of 1944, when the Russians successfully persuaded the Wehrmacht to expect their main assault in south-east Poland rather than Belorussia, then having smashed three German armies switched axis to Poland in the autumn. Though Reinhard Gehlen kept his job as Germany's Eastern chief of intelligence until the last days of the war, the modern evidence suggests that he was bear-led by the Stavka in Moscow even more effectively than were OKW's Western intelligence officers by the British and Americans in 1944. Argument persists between historians about which material in the 'Monastery' deception emanated from Alexander Demyanov and which from other 'Klatt' sources, but the fundamental reality is not in dispute, that the Germans were repeatedly fooled by Moscow's disinformation. Whatever the limitations of Soviet wartime intelligence, its deception operations were masterpieces of conspiracy.

9

The Orchestra's Last Concert

From the autumn of 1941, all the Russians' European spy networks operated on the brink of a precipice, rendered mortally vulnerable by the exposure of the identities of the main players in both the NKVD's 'Lucy' Ring and the Red Orchestra to Leopold Trepper and Anatoli Gourevitch, together with the reckless conduct of Moscow Centre and of the German dissidents themselves. Too many people all over Europe now knew too many names, so that a single initial arrest precipitated a vast and terrible unravelling. The Orchestra's doom was sealed by the Germans' capture through direction-finding of the wireless-operator Mikhail Makarov – 'Carlos Alamo' or 'Chemnitz' – in the Rue des Atrebates, Brussels, in the early hours of 13 December 1941.

On the previous day Trepper made a sudden, unheralded reappearance in Brussels. Relations between himself and Gourevitch, already shadowed by mutual suspicion and jealousy, thereafter deteriorated rapidly. Two days after 'Otto's' arrival, Gourevitch was at Simexco's offices, dealing with the astonishingly profitable business issues entwined with its chiefs' espionage activities, when he was summoned by phone to an urgent meeting with Trepper at his apartment. When he arrived there, he found his visitor in a state of alarm. Trepper said that he had just been questioned by the Germans, and proposed to return to France by the first train. Gourevitch was appalled that the chief should have called at his home when already under suspicion. He ran a mental eye over the entire network for weak links and fixed his attention on 'Chemnitz', who embraced louche tastes and an extravagant lifestyle, though Gourevitch himself scarcely practised austerity. The wireless-operator knew Margaret Barcza, Gourevitch's lover, and many of the group's other contacts. Suddenly the doorbell rang, and the Russian was disconcerted to open it to a Belgian acquaintance who worked for the German Kommandatur. This man invited himself in, and asked for a loan. Gourevitch handed over some cash to get rid of him, then accompanied Trepper to the station to catch a Paris train. Gourevitch now told Barcza that Brussels was becoming too warm for comfort. He himself proposed to decamp to France, and he urged her to try to reach her parents, refugees in the United States. She promptly burst into tears and insisted on accompanying him wherever he went, with her young son René. Gourevitch acceded, though he knew that Centre was bound to be enraged by their relationship, which was no less dangerous to his duties than Trepper's liaison with Georgie de Winter.

They quit their flat immediately, and took temporary shelter in a big house occupied by the 'front' director of Simexco, which he rented from the nephew of Belgium's foreign minister. Gourevitch gave his servants several months' wages – the young GRU agent had certainly risen in the world – to support the pretence that he would be coming back. He occupied the next few days 'putting to sleep' the agents of his network. Then he boarded a train to Paris, followed two days later by Margaret and René. They took up quarters in a house near the Bois de Boulogne which Gourevitch had used on previous visits to the French capital. As soon as he met Trepper, it was 'le Grand Chef's' turn to vent violent dismay. Gourevitch's arrival, he said, could compromise his French cover company, as well as the intelligence network. He insisted that his deputy should leave, fast. They decided he should head for Marseilles in unoccupied Vichy France, where Simex had a branch office. Margaret and René Barcza left first, travelling south without difficulty, using the Trepper group's contacts and taking up lodgings in Marseilles with a Czech family.

Meanwhile, Gourevitch met Hersch and Myra Sokol, two young Polish communists who acted as Trepper's Paris wireless-operators. The fugitive afterwards claimed that he used the Sokols to send a message to Centre to report the threatened collapse of his network, and his own flight from Brussels. But his warnings, he said, were transmitted at a moment in December when the GRU had evacuated its headquarters in the face of the German assault on Moscow, and lacked his code. Thus his employers learned of the Brussels crisis only much later, in February 1942, a delay which, he believed, contributed to his 1945 indictment for treason. Gourevitch reached Marseilles in January 1942, after a journey without incident. He remained there in not uncomfortable hiding for the ensuing ten months, making no pretence of conducting any espionage, and chiefly amusing himself with Margaret. Thanks to Centre's remittances and Simexco's handsome profits, they had ample money. This idyll – as Margaret afterwards recalled it – continued until 9 November; on that day,

Gourevitch, his lover and an impressive cache of cigars and silk stockings were abruptly seized in their flat by French police. The two prisoners were handed over to the Germans, then sweeping across the Vichy zone to complete their occupation of France. The Germans had at last broken into the Red Orchestra, and each successive revelation from a captured agent produced reverberations throughout Europe.

Moscow's contribution to what became a dreadful débâcle dated back to the spring of 1942, when the fortunes of the NKVD's Alexander Korotkov were once more ascendant within the Lubyanka. He took a gamble. Given the difficulties and upsets in Belgium and France, he sought to re-establish direct contact between Berlin and Centre, by providing the Orchestra with new codes and crystals, and thereafter with more powerful transmitters. Zoya Rybkina describes in her memoirs how she and her husband 'Kin', who now ran the NKVD station in Stockholm, were instructed to identify a courier who could make a delivery to Schulze-Boysen in Berlin. After considerable difficulties, they found a Swedish businessman who was persuaded to do the job. She sewed the codes and instructions into a tie, and put the crystals into a cufflink box, to be left in a cemetery for the Luftwaffe officer. The Swede returned from his next visit to Germany to confess failure: he had been too terrified to fulfil the mission, he said – everyone on the Berlin plane seemed to be staring at his tie. After a second trip the following week, however, he reported success; he claimed – truthfully or otherwise – that he had left the codes and crystals at the designated 'dead drop'.

Meanwhile Korotkov in Moscow selected two agents to travel to Germany, carrying new wireless sets to the *Rote Kapelle*, and with further orders to contact 'Breitenbach', the Gestapo officer whose existence was unknown to the Orchestra. The messengers were veteran German communists, Albert Hessler and Robert Bart, both in their early thirties. Hessler had commanded a company of the International Brigade in Spain, where he was badly wounded. He had since married a Russian girl, and after volunteering for the Red Army was trained as a wireless-operator. Bart was a printer by trade, who served a spell in Plötzensee jail during the early Nazi years before being conscripted into the Wehrmacht, with which he earned an Iron Cross during the 1940 French campaign. Soon after being posted to the Eastern Front, he defected to the Russians.

Both men took a fantastic risk by agreeing now to travel to Berlin, allegedly willingly, though this deserves to be doubted. They were provided with false identities, respectively as a lieutenant and sergeant-major on leave, then dispatched aboard a C-47 of No. 1 Long-Range Aviation Division from Podlipki near Moscow, and parachuted to a partisan reception committee between Bryansk and Gomel in occupied Belorussia during the night of 5 August 1942. Guides led them to a rail station from which, after a week-long journey via Bialystok, Warsaw and Poznan, they reached Berlin with their two radio sets, in itself a considerable achievement.

They went initially to the apartment of a *Rote Kapelle* contact, Kurt Schumacher, who received them, then separated the visitors to take refuge in the homes of sympathisers. Hessler initially transmitted from the studio of an exotic dancer named Oda Schotmüller, afterwards from the apartment of Countess Erika von Brokdorf. In mid-August he told Moscow: 'everything is going well. The group has expanded considerably thanks to the strength of the anti-fascist movement, and is working actively. I will send additional information from Harnack and Schulze-Boysen when I receive an acknowledgement of this message. Am presently busy finding lodgings.' From an early stage, both NKVD men appear to have been under Gestapo surveillance. Leopold Trepper's Brussels wireless-operator, a German named Johann Wenzel, had been seized on 30 June 1942, again after his transmissions were tracked by direction-finders. Though the truth will never be conclusively established about who gave away whom and when, under interrogation both Makarov and Wenzel seem to have told all they knew, which was a great deal. Rippling waves of arrests followed across Europe. The Gestapo formed a special *Sonderkommando*, headed by Haupsturmführer Horst Kopkow, to investigate the Soviet ring. Its officers were appalled by what they discovered: penetration of some of the highest headquarters of the Third Reich; systematic betrayal of Germany by hundreds of Germans. In August, the Gestapo net began to close on Harnack and Schulze-Boysen and their groups. The NKVD's Albert Hessler was arrested in mid-September, along with those who had sheltered him. He made his last apparently genuine transmission on 3 September; although he messaged again on the 21st, by then he was almost certainly acting under Gestapo control.

Moscow was slow to realise what had happened. Centre's first detailed account of the disaster was delayed until April 1943, and then arrived by a tortuous route: Wolfgang Havemann, a nephew of Harnack, was interrogated by the Gestapo, then released for lack of evidence. He was sent to the Eastern Front, where at the first opportunity he gave himself up to the Red Army. He confirmed to the NKVD the total destruction of the Berlin ring, accompanied by forty-eight executions. Among those seized were a married couple, Hans and Hilda Coppi. He, a radio-operator, was killed almost immediately. She, however, heavily pregnant, was kept alive until her son had been born and attained the age of eight months. She was then decapitated in August 1943, and her child handed over to his grandparents, with whom he survived to pursue a career as a historian of German Resistance.

Robert Bart was trapped because he could not resist seeing his wife and son. Unbeknown to Moscow, the Gestapo kept the families of all missing political suspects under surveillance: Bart's desertion to the Russians had been assumed. His wife fell sick, and in August 1942 languished in a clinic on Berlin's Nollenstrasse. The Soviet agent took the understandable but insane risk of visiting her. He was betrayed by a nurse, and arrested at the clinic on 9 September. Almost immediately thereafter he began to transmit to Moscow under SD control. He later claimed to have given an agreed Morse warning on 14 October, which an inexperienced Centre operator failed to notice – exactly as happened when SOE wirelesses in Holland became part of another Abwehr radio game. Centre obligingly responded by providing details of the procedure for meeting 'Breitenbach'. In mid-December 1942 Willy Lehmann, now fifty-eight years old and surely a weary man after his protracted secret service, was telephoned at home one night to hear Moscow's coded introduction of the caller as 'college Preuss' – 'colleague Preuss'. Lehmann presumably gave the appropriate response: 'Come and see me in my office.' This signified a rendezvous at 5 p.m. next day on the pavement of Kantstrasse, between two cinemas of which one was named the Olympia. The contact procedure was to approach Lehmann and ask directions to his street. He was supposed to reply that he lived there, and would walk the man to it.

The rendezvous was duly made by a young Gestapo man named Olenhorst. Lehmann was arrested and interrogated, no doubt exhaustively, then secretly executed a fortnight later, and his body cremated. His wife, who knew nothing of his work for the Soviets, was told that he had perished while on a mission; the Gestapo was probably anxious to conceal the fact that one of its own had been a traitor. Lehmann's fate was confirmed only in May 1945, when an NKVD team found documentation mentioning his demise in the ruins of Gestapo headquarters in Berlin's Prinz-Albrecht-Strasse. Bart survived the war and surrendered to the Americans, who promptly handed him over to the Russians. He was executed by firing squad on 23 November 1945, though he enjoyed the doubtful satisfaction of being rehabilitated by the Red Army's chief military prosecutor in 1996.

Zoya Rybkina records that she and her husband in Stockholm were subjected to bitter recriminations from Centre following the collapse of the Orchestra; in the course of a trawl for scapegoats that straddled half Europe, it was suggested that Schulze-Boysen and the rest had been betrayed by the Swedish businessman whom they had recruited to carry codes to Berlin. 'Kin' was recalled to Moscow in the summer of 1943, and for months his wife was obliged to continue serving the NKVD's Stockholm station while ignorant of whether he had been shot. She wrote: 'Centre kept sending telegrams enquiring about cases that "Kin" had been in charge of, and I couldn't understand why.' She herself returned to Moscow in March 1944, where she found that her husband's entire Jewish family, save one younger brother, had perished at German hands. After protracted investigations and months under fantastic suspicion of having thrown in their lot with British intelligence, both Rybkin and his wife were rehabilitated and restored to favour as colonels in the Lubyanka.

Exposure of the *Rote Kapelle* had two important consequences for Hitler's regime. First, it represented a victory for the RSHA, whose men closed the net while the Abwehr remained oblivious. Second, it severely damaged the standing of Göring, whose ministry was shown to be riddled with communist traitors: the Reichsmarschall had given away the bride at the Schulze-Boysens' wedding. If the failure of the Luftwaffe in the air was a more important cause of Göring's fall from grace, the *Rote Kapelle* affair was a subordinate one. In Russia, 'the fat man' would have been shot. As for the Allied cause, much has been made of the Abwehr's destruction of SOE's and MI6's Dutch networks,* but the fate of Moscow's Red Orchestra was a far graver matter, because its sources had access to more important secrets. Between them the *Rote Kapelle*, 'Lucy' Ring and Trepper networks claimed 117 informants: forty-eight in Germany, thirty-five in France, seventeen in Belgium, seventeen in Switzerland. Leopold Trepper himself for some months escaped arrest, though his informants in France, Belgium and Holland were swept up. The veteran spy was seized only on 24 November, in a Paris dentist's waiting-room. Thereafter he appears to have talked freely to the Germans, apparently without need for recourse to violent methods; he even dispatched invitations for informants to attend rendezvouses at which they were arrested. All the Russians' codes fell into the hands of the SD.

---

* Described below – see pp.267–69.

271/46.

Reichskriegsgericht   21 Abdrucke
  2. Senat
StPL (HLS) II 129/42
StPL (RKA) III 495/42
        III 496/42
        III 497/42

Geheime Kommandosache!   Ausf.   6. Jan. 1943

S M. geh.1943 Nr. 55

Im Namen

des Deutschen Volkes! Admiral

v.

F e l d u r t e i l .

In der Strafsache gegen

     1.) den Oberleutnant Harro S c h u l z e - B o y s e n ,
     2.) die Ehefrau Libertas S c h u l z e - B o y s e n ,
     3.) den Oberregierungsrat Dr. Arwid H a r n a c k ,
     4.) die Ehefrau Mildred H a r n a c k ,
     5.) den Oberleutnant Herbert G o l l n o w ,
     6.) den Funker Horst H e i l m a n n ,
     7.) den Soldat Kurt S c h u m a c h e r ,
     8.) die Ehefrau Elisabeth S c h u m a c h e r ,
     9.) den Dreher Hans C o p p i ,
    10.) den Kraftfahrer Kurt S c h u l z e ,
    11.) die Gräfin Erika von B r o c k d o r f f ,
    12.) den Handelsvertreter Johannes G r a u d e n z

wegen Hochverrats u.a.

hat das Reichskriegsgericht, 2. Senat, in der Sitzung vom 19. Dezember
1942 auf Grund der mündlichen Hauptverhandlung vom 15. - 19. Dezember 1942
an der teilgenommen haben

     als Richter:
        Senatspräsident Dr. Kraell, Verhandlungsleiter,
        General Mußhoff,
        Vizeadmiral Arps,
        Generalmajor Stutzer,
        Reichskriegsgerichtsrat Dr. Schmitt,
    als Vertreter der Anklage:
        Oberstkriegsgerichtsrat Dr. Roeder,
    als Urkundsbeamter:

                          Heeresjustizinspektor

Gestapo list of captured members of the Red Orchestra

The victorious Germans dealt swiftly and ruthlessly with their home-grown traitors. Harro Schulze-Boysen had been arrested at the Air Ministry on 31 August 1942. A week later, Harnack and his wife Mildred were seized while on holiday. The condemned prisoner Florestan sings in Beethoven's *Fidelio*, 'My heart is at peace for I have done what is right,' and Harnack seems to have cherished the same sentiment. While Florestan was saved at the last, however, the Berlin spies were not. On 22 December 1942, six men and three women, members of the Red Orchestra, were guillotined at Plötzensee jail. On the same day Schulze-Boysen and Harnack, together with the former's wife Libertas, suffered contrivedly lingering deaths by hanging. Harnack wrote in a last letter to Mildred that 'despite everything', he looked back on a life 'in which the darkness was outweighed by the light'. All their bodies were dispatched for anatomical dissection, in order that the remains should be unidentifiable.

The Gestapo retained 116 other *Rote Kapelle* prisoners, of whom almost half were executed once protracted interrogations had been completed. Among these was the American Mildred Harnack. She was initially sentenced to a mere six years' hard labour, but Hitler intervened person-

The last letter from Harro Schulze-Boysen, written on the day
of his execution

ally to insist upon a retrial at which she was condemned to death. She
spent some of her last hours with Pastor Harald Pölchau, a prison chaplain
who solaced hundreds of Hitler's political victims; she asked him to recite
the 'Prologue in Heaven' from *Faust*, before herself singing, 'I pray to the
power of love'. Her last, wondering words before being beheaded on 16
February 1943 were: 'And I have loved Germany so much.' She was just
forty, and her fair hair had turned white during her months of confinement. She must have felt a far, far journey from Wisconsin.

So much sentiment has been lavished upon the men and women of the
Red Orchestra that it deserves to be noticed that their espionage activities
rendered them equally liable to capital punishment under British or
American jurisdiction. But the courage with which they worked against
Hitler commands the respect of posterity, for all their illusions about the
Soviet Union they sought to serve instead. Cynics may ask: what rendered
Harnack, Schulze-Boysen and their comrades morally superior to such
British and American traitors as Kim Philby and Alger Hiss? To be sure,
they resisted one tyranny, but they chose to serve another that was equally
repellent. Any answer to that question must be subjective, but it seems
incomparably easier to justify treason against a murderous dictatorship
than against a democracy governed by the rule of law.

Anatoli Gourevitch wrote in his memoirs about the days following his
arrest in November 1942: 'Then opened the darkest period of my life, and
that of Margaret.' The Germans at first treated the couple with remarkable
courtesy as they travelled north from Marseilles. They were fed in restaurants and generously plied with wine. Initial exchanges with their captors
took the form of conversations rather than interrogations. At night during
the long car journey they were allowed to share a bedroom, though their
clothes were removed and they were denied knives and forks at the breakfast table. They gave the escort money to buy the cigarettes Gourevitch
smoked incessantly as he strove to decide what to confess or to deny. After
three days on the road the little party found themselves once more in
Belgium, at the fort of Breendonk, where Gourevitch and Margaret were
placed in separate cells. Their food continued to be excellent, however, and
the questioning was civil. Hans Giering, leader of the Red Orchestra investigation, was joined by an Abwehr officer, Harry Pipe, whom the Russian
found thoroughly informed about his activities. Gourevitch persuaded the
Germans that he needed translation of their questions, to buy time to

devise responses. He later admitted that he was disorientated by his captors' affable demeanour and considerate conduct.

While parts of the GRU man's memoir of his experiences seem credible, the narrative of events following his arrest contains irreconcilable inconsistencies and obvious implausibilities. He, and afterwards Trepper, were treated generously not because the Gestapo discovered virtue in humanity, but because torture proved unnecessary. It will never be known how far their revelations, as distinct from those of other GRU agents and wireless-operators, were responsible for the Gestapo's round-up of their informants. All later blamed each other. The Germans told Gourevitch that Makarov – 'Chemnitz' – had named him as chief of Soviet intelligence in Belgium. When the GRU man denied this, Giering ordered guards to fetch another captured Moscow agent, 'Bob' – Hermann Isbutski – who was brought forth from his cell a broken man, plainly the victim of torture. He immediately identified Gourevitch, who was stunned by the encounter. The interrogations continued for hours on end, though Giering provided plentiful food, coffee and even brandy. After about a week, the German produced two devastating documents: first, Moscow's instruction for 'Kent' to travel to Berlin to meet Harro Schulze-Boysen; second, his subsequent report to Centre. It was plain, said the Russian, that the Gestapo held decrypts of some of his wireless messages, retrieved from one of the operators.

He was allowed a meeting with Margaret, late at night, and found her shattered by her experiences, which is unsurprising since Gourevitch claimed that she had no previous knowledge of his espionage activities, nor even that he was not the Uruguayan 'Vincente Sierra'. An order arrived at Breendonk: Gourevitch and Barcza were to be taken forthwith to Berlin. Next day they set off at high speed, the two prisoners seated between armed guards. The car scarcely halted until it drew up outside a huge, grey building in Hitler's capital: this was 8 Prinz-Albrecht-Strasse, Gestapo headquarters. The Russian was taken to a cell, while his companion was removed to a women's prison on Alexanderplatz. Although Gourevitch's memoirs say nothing about his terrors, the weeks that followed must have been replete with them. He met Gestapo chief Heinrich Muller, and was shown the evidence of his dealings with the Red Orchestra. He was confronted with Ilse Stöbe, whom he had failed to meet on his earlier trip to Berlin, but who was now ravaged by torture, her appearance 'terrifying'. An interrogator sought to suggest that the

Schulze-Boysens were sexually depraved, and produced photographs of
Libertas naked to support his case. Gourevitch was told that Leopold
Trepper was now held in Fresnes prison, and was cooperating. He himself
remained in solitary confinement in the cells of Prinz-Albrecht-Strasse
for more than a month. One morning as he was being escorted to the
latrine he passed Harro Schulze-Boysen. Neither man gave any hint of
recognition. The Russian said that his former dining companion showed
no visible signs of having been tortured: 'I did not know that he had only
a few days to live.'

At the end of December 1942, Gourevitch was taken back to Paris. He
was to become a participant with Trepper in a Gestapo radio game with
Moscow, which continued through many months that followed. He
himself was briefly held in Fresnes, then transferred to Hans Giering's
headquarters in the Rue des Saussaies. Gourevitch afterwards claimed that
he resisted for some months German blandishments actively to join the
Funkspiel. It is a matter of record that Trepper's transmitter began to operate under German control on Christmas Day 1942, while that of
Gourevitch came to life on 3 March 1943, but the latter can only have been
allowed to leave Berlin for Paris once the Germans were confident of their
dominion over him.

A few months later the entire 'turned' Soviet team was moved into a
spacious house on the Boulevard Victor Hugo in Neuilly, outside Paris.
Trepper and Gourevitch alike occupied spacious quarters with the best of
food, able to wash and iron their own clothes. In July 1943, advanced
throat cancer obliged Giering – who died in the following month – to
resign his post in favour of Heinz Pannwitz. In September Trepper escaped
while on an escorted shopping trip into Paris, without apparently causing
much concern to his jailers, who had by then extracted from him all they
were ever going to. He successfully resumed contact with Georgie de
Winter, and the two remained in hiding with the assistance of the so-called
'Spaak' Resistance group. The Germans so far relaxed Gourevitch's captivity that he returned to Paris, where he was permitted to cohabit with
Margaret Barcza; she produced a son named Sacha in mid-April 1944.

It will never be known how far Pannwitz's indulgence towards
Gourevitch reflected the depth of the latter's collaboration, or the former's
concern for his own future. According to the GRU man, the Gestapo
officer recognised that the war was lost, and had become desperate to
avoid Western Allied captivity because he had led Nazi retribution for the
1942 murder by SOE-trained Czechs of Reinhard Heydrich, including the

massacre of the inhabitants of Lidice. Gourevitch persuaded the German that he would receive a warm welcome in Moscow, and no doubt believed that he could improve his own prospects by returning home with a senior Gestapo officer as a personal trophy. Gourevitch sustained a close relationship with Pannwitz until they retreated to Germany before Paris was liberated, returning only in May 1945. Meanwhile Leopold Trepper remained safely in hiding until the Allies overran his refuge in September 1944.

After the break-up of the Red Orchestra, the 'Lucy' Ring became Moscow's only means of access to Berlin's high places. Unfortunately, however, just as unauthorised sexual passions had caused complications for Trepper and Gourevitch, so they did also for the Swiss spies. Alexander Radó suddenly decided that he was in love with the wireless-operator Margrit Bolli, who was half his age. With almost insane indiscretion, he began visiting her every day. To facilitate their meetings he himself stayed in Geneva while renting a flat for his family in Bern.

This story descended into black farce when the girl decided that she was in love with someone else – a handsome young hairdresser named Hans Peter, who was a plant codenamed 'Romeo', controlled from the German consulate by Abwehr officer Hermann Hensler. The Trepper network's men in German hands had identified Radó, and the Germans set about closing down both the agent and his contacts. Bolli was so bewitched by her 'Romeo' that she invited him to dally in the flat where she kept her transmitter. The Swiss police had hitherto shown a stubborn reluctance to act against the 'Lucy' Ring, but its activities had now become too conspicuous to remain ignored. On 27 October 1942, Edmond and Olga Hamel were arrested. They managed to hide their transmitter, and were eventually released, but their days in Moscow's service were ended. The Abwehr succeeded in reading some of the GRU's Swiss messages during 1942, which revealed a string of agents' codenames. On 16 March 1943 the besotted Bolli sent an *en clair* wireless signal to 'Romeo', which further assisted German intelligence. The Abwehr now had Radó and most of the Ring under intensive surveillance, and exerted immense diplomatic pressure on the Swiss to arrest them.

From June 1943 onwards, Alexander Foote knew that he too was being watched by 'the doctor' – local police. He told Moscow that he could not safely transmit more than twice a week, but the GRU with characteristic ruthlessness insisted that he should maintain a much more intensive schedule, which made the direction-finders' task easy. Early on the morning of 20 November there was a dramatic rush of men into his flat. One of them presented a pistol and cried in German, '*Hände hoch!*' For a ghastly moment Foote feared that his visitors were from the Abwehr. It usually suited the warring nations that there should be no violence between their respective agents in Switzerland, but there could always be a first time. The Englishman was one of the few local spies who carried a gun, a .32 automatic: 'it gave me moral comfort at some of my more difficult rendezvous'. But now that Foote was cornered, it never occurred to him to try to shoot his way out.

He experienced a surge of relief when he found that he was merely in the hands of the Swiss police, whose interceptors had pinpointed his transmitter. Before being taken away he managed to swallow some messages and names concealed inside a torch. He afterwards claimed not to have disliked the prison to which he was committed: 'For the first time for years I was able to relax completely'. He was permitted to wear his own clothes and eat food brought in from outside. On 8 September 1944 he was released, though his role in the 'Lucy' Ring was at an end.

One by one, Moscow's other agents in Switzerland were removed from circulation. Among them was Anna Mueller, a veteran Soviet informant whom Alexander Foote described as 'a motherly old soul who looked – and I have little doubt, in the past, had acted as – a superior charwoman'. Mueller was the cut-out between the network and a corrupt official in the Swiss passport office. She was lured to Germany by a phoney message saying that her sister-in-law in Freiburg was sick, discovered too late that it was sent by the Gestapo, and spent the rest of the war in a concentration camp. Foote noted dryly that the GRU never paid her a single mark or franc in recompense for her sufferings for the socialist cause.

Rachel Düberndorfer – 'Sisi' – after being arrested by the Swiss and charged with espionage claimed at her trial that she was working for the British secret service, in hopes that this would secure more generous treatment from the local authorities. Although sentenced to two years' imprisonment, she was indeed soon bailed and allowed to disappear. But the claim fuelled the NKVD's darkest suspicions, and caused her arrest and confinement in the Lubyanka on arrival in Moscow in 1945. Alexander Radó went into hiding following the arrests of his wireless-operators, and eventually crossed secretly into France, where he lived underground until the liberation. Rudolf Rössler was arrested by the Swiss police in May 1944 and remained in custody until September. He was then released, but the 'Lucy' Ring's game was played out.

The Russians afterwards claimed that in early 1944 they had ninety-seven agents operating inside Germany, of whom ten were Germans. Among the most active (said Moscow) was 'Ian' – Ferenz Pataki, a Hungarian who had once worked for the Cheka, who was eventually betrayed and executed. 'Dozen', Hermann Salinger, was a former International Brigade fighter who was dropped into Germany in January 1944 – with British help, according to the Russians, though there is no record of 'Dozen' in Western files. 'Sharp', Heinz Glodjai, was parachuted into East Prussia in 1943, and provided intelligence until he was killed in the RAF's August 1944 bombing of Königsberg.

Nonetheless, it is one thing to boast, as do the modern official chroniclers of Russian intelligence, about the NKVD's and GRU's German sources in the latter phases of the war, and another to show that these produced useful, usable information, which seems unlikely. Following the break-up of the Red Orchestra, Abwehr interceptors failed to find any further evidence of Allied agents transmitting out of Germany, and it seems reasonable to discount suggestions that the NKVD and GRU deployed substantial numbers of active agents inside the Reich between 1943 and 1945. Certainly no Russian covert source in Germany generated intelligence remotely as authoritative as that produced earlier by the Red Orchestra and the 'Lucy' Ring. In the last years of the war, however, strategic intelligence had become much less important, because Russian dominance of the battlefield was overwhelming. Moreover, despite the Soviets' conviction that the Western Allies denied them important material, the British and Americans routinely informed Moscow about all German military activity revealed by Ultra which threatened their interests, or might assist Soviet operations. Centre did not, of course, return the courtesy.

10

Guerrilla

1 RESISTERS AND RAIDERS

Very occasionally in the course of the war, a marriage between intelligence and military action proved perfectly arranged. At his Paris flat in the avenue de la Motte-Picquet, on the night of 24 January 1942, Gilbert Renault – the Gaullist Resistance network chief 'Colonel Rémy' – decrypted a radio message from London. It delivered a request which constituted a very tall order indeed: to obtain, at utmost speed, details of conditions prevailing around a German Channel coastal installation at Saint-Bruneval, near Cap d'Antifer in Normandy; and meanwhile 'to deceive boches in event your agent taken be ready to reply to same question not only for place chosen, but for three or four other similar places on coast'. Renault, thirty-seven years old, lean and intensely patriotic but rejected as over-age for military service in 1939, was one of the more remarkable figures of the secret war. His Catholicism was a significant motivational force in his work as an agent, and he wrote fervently later: 'I would never have been able to carry out this assignment in a foreign country or for a less righteous cause.' He described his Resistance role as 'putting living tile upon living tile', and recruited informants from a remarkable range of backgrounds: ex-military men and architects, peasants and aristocrats. Though himself an extreme conservative, in the sacred cause of France he supped with communists. He was viewed in London as too careless about security and tradecraft to be a great spymaster, but he enjoyed a remarkable run before these weaknesses undid him. Now he dispatched Roger Dumont, a former air force officer codenamed 'Pol' – for Pol Roger champagne – to reconnoitre Bruneval.

At the end of January another 'Rémy' contact, a Le Havre garage proprietor named Charles Chauveau, drove to Paris in his Simca 5 to pick up Dumont, adopting false numberplates for the last kilometres into the capital. The two men then returned to Le Havre – amid German surveillance that mere car journey was a dangerous venture. At the port the agent took a room in a shabby hotel so cold that he could not sleep, but instead shivered through the night, fully dressed on a chair. Next morning he and Chauveau rattled twelve miles north to Bruneval, with chains on the Simca's tyres to contend with a fresh snowfall. The owner of the little Hôtel Beauminet in the hamlet, Paul Vennier, was a friend of Chauveau, a man whom the *garagiste* endorsed as 'one of the best'. Vennier was able to enumerate the Luftwaffe crew billeted in the big farm compound at Theuville, and to tell them about a guard post at a villa by the beach, 'Stella Maris'. He reported that the local Wehrmacht garrison, a platoon strong commanded by an efficient and energetic *Feldwebel*, was lodged in the Beauminet. Vennier knew nothing about what was happening at the lonely house and neighbouring 'radio station' half a mile away on the clifftop, but at Dumont's urging he led him down to the German wire entanglement just short of the seaside to see for themselves. A conversation with a friendly sentry revealed to the spy that a supposed minefield above the beach was a fiction, to deter intruders. Having explored the area as well as any man could, Dumont returned to Le Havre, and thence to Paris. On the night of 9 February, Gilbert Renault's SOE-trained wireless-operator 'Bob' – Robert Delattre – Morsed to London the agent's report on Bruneval. The fact that the mission had succeeded without incident should not for a moment mask the fact that it had involved all the parties concerned in mortal risk. Dumont's account of Bruneval made plain that it was garrisoned, but not in great strength.

The quest for technical intelligence about the enemy's weapons systems was an untiring preoccupation of every participant in the war. It was pursued through spies, photographic reconnaissance, patrolling and prisoner interrogation. If soldiers, sailors and airmen were sometimes sceptical, indeed cynical, about strategic and political intelligence, they could all grasp the importance of securing data about technology being employed by the enemy, so that means could be devised to counter it. The air war over Europe engaged the most sophisticated equipment available to both sides, and inspired correspondingly fevered efforts to understand each other's. The Germans had the easier task, because they could explore the wreckage of British and American aircraft shot down over Europe, fitted with the latest devices to aid navigation and bomb-aiming. The British, however, separated from the air battlefield by the Channel, depended on the brainpower of their intelligence officers and scientists to penetrate the Luftwaffe's secrets.

In the winter of 1941 they realised that German night-fighters were guided from the ground by two linked radar systems, codenamed 'Freya' and 'Würzburg'. R.V. Jones, the twenty-nine-year-old assistant director of scientific intelligence at the Air Ministry and adviser to MI6, together with the 'boffins' of the Telecommunications Research Establishment then at Swanage, identified these as key elements in the so-called 'Kammhuber Line', a network of guidance stations that enabled the Luftwaffe to inflict punitive losses on the RAF's Bomber Command. They knew that Freyas, with their huge aerial arrays, monitored British bombers. They guessed that Würzburgs guided the fighters, but hungered for an opportunity to dissect a specimen. On 5 December 1941, a young Spitfire pilot of the RAF's Photographic Reconnaissance Unit, Tony Hill, carried out a low-level sweep of the lonely clifftop château at Bruneval, from which 53-cm radar transmissions had been detected in Britain. Jones pored over Hill's pictures, which showed a Freya set a short distance from the house, and what the pilot described as a 'bowl heater' some ten feet in diameter – obviously a parabolic receiver which was surely that of a Würzburg – some four hundred yards southwards.

The site was only a stone's throw from the sea, less than a quarter of a mile from a beach. It was protected by no visible obstacles, such as wire entanglements. Surely it should be possible for a daring raiding party to get in – then more important, out, having secured priceless booty. Jones had already achieved an entrée to the innermost councils of the British war machine by his brilliant 1940 work on the Luftwaffe's electronic night-bombing guidance systems. Now, his proposal for a descent on Bruneval was enthusiastically accepted by the Air Staff, Downing Street and Combined Operations HQ. It was decided that the attackers must land from the air, then escape by sea.

A company of the newly formed Parachute Regiment, the 'Red Berets', commanded by Major John Frost, was briefed and trained to land just east of the house and its nearby installation, then seize both in a swift *coup de main*. A section of engineers led by Lt. Denis Vernon was detailed to dismantle the set and remove its key components, aided by an RAF radar mechanic, Flight-Sergeant Charles Cox. Cox was rushed through the jump school at Ringway, then he and Vernon were briefed by Jones and set to practising their role on a British gun-laying radar set. All the raiders spent hours mastering the topography on a detailed scale model of

Bruneval. Training on the Dorset coast was dogged by vile weather and repeated mishaps, whereby both dropping aircraft and ships made the wrong rendezvous. The last exercise, on the night of Sunday, 22 February, ended with the paratroopers struggling in chest-deep freezing water as sailors laboured to extricate the landing-craft from sandbanks. All this augured ill for the mission, as also did the gloom overhanging the Royal Navy and the British people after the Channel escape the previous week of *Scharnhorst* and *Gneisenau.*

The raid must take place within the five nights of a full moon, to provide light for the RAF and Frost's men to see their objectives. On the first three possible dates the weather was unsuitable, dampening the spirits of the raiders. Friday the 27th offered the last possible window; it was a vast relief when, at 5 p.m., word came that the operation was 'on'. The assault ship *Prins Albert*, carrying the seaborne element, set forth under motor gunboat escort. At 9.52 p.m. six landing-craft were lowered, each carrying Commando bren-gunners as well as naval crews. By coincidence, even as twelve Whitley bombers of the RAF's 51 Squadron flew south across the Channel that night, bearing Frost's paratroopers, a Lysander light aircraft passed them heading north, taking 'Colonel Rémy' from France for a meeting in London with de Gaulle's intelligence chief. Rémy's part in Operation 'Biteback' was done, even as that of the raiders began.

Just before take-off from Thruxton in Wiltshire, the party learned of a fresh snowfall in northern France. The white coveralls prepared for this eventuality had been left behind in their temporary barracks at Tilney, but on balance Frost thought the snow a bonus, because it would give his men more light. A bagpiper played a wailing pibroch as the parachutists boarded the aircraft, which pleased the Scots among them. The weather was suddenly clear and fine, after a wild week, and the raiders took off warmed by mugs of tea laced with rum. Once airborne they sang old favourites – 'Annie Laurie', 'The Rose of Tralee', 'Lulu'. After two hours, at a few minutes past midnight the first 'stick' plunged in succession through holes in the floors of the Whitleys, and a minute later most found themselves making perfect landings in soft snow: Bruneval's proximity to the coast made possible uncommonly accurate navigation. Most of the men urinated before doing anything else – in the air, Thruxton's tea had wreaked havoc with bladders. As Frost assembled his men, he reflected ruefully that on this clear night they must already have lost surprise. Yet a wonderful silence persisted, and there was only one piece of bad news: two sections, twenty men in all, were missing, having obviously landed off-target.

There was no time to waste, no question of searching for absent friends. Within ten minutes of landing, Frost led his assault party at a fast trot towards 'Lone House' – the château where the Würzburg was installed – while a second group set forth to secure the beach for their retreat. Reaching the building, the major was astonished to find its door open. He blew his whistle and charged in, finding only one German, whom they killed as he fired at them from up the stairs. Meanwhile Lt. Peter Young's party had overrun the Würzburg position, whose occupants fled, bewildered by the crackle of small arms. Flight-Sergeant Cox tore aside the curtain masking the entrance to the cabin in the radar pit, and found the set still warm – it had obviously been tracking a German fighter not many minutes earlier. Lt. Vernon, leader of the Royal Engineers team, began taking flashlight photographs, which provoked German gunfire from somewhere out in the darkness.

The British found that the Würzburg occupied a rotating platform on a flatbed truck, protected by thick stacks of sandbags. One sapper attacked the casing with a hammer and chisel, removing Telefunken labels and serial numbers. Cox was obliged to use a crowbar to prise off the transmitter's fascia. Then, amid increasingly heavy though ill-directed gunfire from Germans a few hundred metres away, the British loaded key components onto a trolley they had brought for the purpose. One of Frost's men was killed by a stray bullet, but Vernon, Cox and the others remained unscathed. The plan called for the sappers to be given thirty minutes to gut the German set. After only ten, however, truck headlights showed enemy reinforcements approaching. The major told Vernon to settle for what he and his men had got – which included all the elements that mattered to Reg Jones and his colleagues – and get moving.

The party tasked to clear the beach found themselves briefly pinned down by the Germans; machine-gun fire seriously wounded Company Sergeant-Major Strachan. As Frost, Cox and the others began to move towards the coast, they saw that the Germans had already reoccupied the château. Suddenly there was an outburst of heavy firing from the southeast: the two sections dropped off-target had doubled towards Bruneval, and now attacked the Germans from the rear, a lucky diversion which enabled their comrades to clear the way to the beach. A few minutes of acute tension followed: Frost's radio beacon, summoning the navy, failed to elicit a response. Only after the British fired a succession of green flares did the landing-craft hasten in upon the rendezvous, to the intense relief of the waiting paratroopers. Shortly before 3 a.m. the raiders, together with Flight-Sergeant Cox and his precious cargo, were loaded aboard. Once offshore the Würzburg's components were transferred to an MGB which dashed for Portsmouth at twenty knots, leaving Frost's men to follow at a more sedate pace in the landing-craft, towed by other gunboats. The attackers left behind only two men killed and six missing, who spent the rest of the war in captivity; the Germans lost five, and three more were brought back to Britain as PoWs. At 6 o'clock that evening of 28 February the entire party boarded the *Prins Albert*, where a triumphant press conference was held. In that chill season of defeats, here was a tiny but infinitely precious triumph to warm the hearts of the British people.

The Bruneval raid was the most successful such operation of the war. Through a small investment of resources, and at negligible cost, Major Frost's paratroopers and Flight-Sergeant Cox brought home for Britain the intimate secrets of the Würzburg radar: its aerial, receiver, receiver amplifier, modulator and transmitter. These sufficed to enable R.V. Jones and his colleagues to grasp the system on which the Kammhuber line was based – a chain of 'boxes', within each of which Freya and Würzburg radar sets guided a night-fighter onto the track of a bomber. Once this was understood, the RAF's response became obvious: to push aircraft through the night sky over the line at maximum density, swamping the electronic defences. 'Streaming' worked, and rendered Kammhuber's system obsolete. Although bomber losses remained severe, Bruneval provided a precious intelligence break to the Allies. Moreover, in its wake the Germans felt obliged to fortify their coastal radar chain so heavily that thereafter every station was easily pinpointed by photographic reconnaissance.

The attack represented a textbook collaboration between the 'boffins', led by Jones, who identified what they needed to know; spies on the ground – 'Colonel Rémy's' men – who reconnoitred the target for MI6; planners, who married the agent reports to data secured by air photography; and special forces, which executed 'Biteback'. In addition to the decorations awarded to the airborne force, Jones was made a CBE. The attackers were aided by the fact that a coastal target was relatively easy for the RAF and navy to find and reach. In February 1942 the French coast was defended much less heavily than it became two years later. Perhaps most important, the British had luck on their side. 'Rémy's' agents were not caught, as so many spies were caught; the parachute drop was relatively accurate, as many drops were not; the Germans put up little effective resistance; and Cox was able to carry away the treasure. Many times between 1940 and 1945, British planners had cause to lament that the course of secret war seldom ran so smooth.

2 SOE

Following the fall of France in June 1940, for almost four years Winston Churchill waged war with the conviction that Britain, even after the accession of Russia and the United States as fellow-foes of Hitler, lacked power to confront the Nazis' military might on the Continent. This made it essential to challenge the enemy by other means – the strategic bomber offensive against Germany and guerrilla campaigns in the occupied countries. The creation of Britain's SOE and the Political Warfare Executive, followed later by that of the American OSS and Office of War Information, was encouraged by a delusion that Hitler's 1939–41 Blitzkriegs had succeeded partly by exploitation of a 'Fifth Column' of secret supporters within the victim nations. Many people, the prime minister notable among them, believed this had played the same role in the enemy's onslaughts as sappers in sieges of old, who tunnelled beneath city walls before storming parties attacked. He thus sought to create his own Fifth Column to serve the Allied cause. He feared that if the peoples of occupied Europe were left to their own devices they would remain sunk in passivity, acquiescence, collaboration – and he was probably right.

In promoting raids and Resistance, the prime minister had four objectives. The first, and least important, was to fulfil military purposes, wherein there were many fiascos such as Operation 'Colossus', a 1941 Combined Operations parachute drop to destroy a Calabrian rail viaduct, the August 1942 Dieppe raid, and some early sabotage attempts in Norway. The second purpose was to promote among British people and across the world a belief – ill-founded until at least late 1942 – that the war was being energetically and effectively carried on; what this author has elsewhere dubbed 'military theatre'. A third objective was to oblige Hitler to expend resources on the internal security of his empire. The fourth, and most important, was to stimulate tension, recrimination, hatred between the Nazis and their subject peoples. Far from acknowledging that acts of repression should prompt a curb on Resistance activity, Churchill saw Nazi savagery as furthering his aims. 'The blood of the martyrs,' he told a meeting of the Cabinet Defence Committee on 2 August 1943, 'was the

seed of the Church.' The fact that by the war's end most of Europe's occupied peoples loathed the Germans was partly a consequence of policies
Hitler anyway adopted; but it was also attributable to the insurgencies
sponsored by Britain and later the US. The military achievements of
Resistance were very modest, the moral ones immense.

Operations by armed civilians behind enemy lines were far remote
from the doings of bespectacled mathematicians and chess players
huddled over cryptograms at Bletchley Park, Arlington Hall and the
NKVD's sigint centre in the old Select hotel on Dzerzhinsky Street.
Nonetheless, guerrilla campaigns became critical elements of the secret
war, eventually commanding resources as large as those expended on
intelligence-gathering, and often overlapping with it. In July 1940 Special
Operations Executive received the prime minister's mandate to 'set Europe
ablaze'. In his determination to wage a new kind of war with new men and
new means, he entrusted his brainchild to Hugh Dalton, the raffish minister of economic warfare and a Labour MP, rather than to the chiefs of staff
or Broadway. A cabinet colleague told the foreign secretary, Lord Halifax,
'You should never be consulted because you would never consent to
everything; you will never make a gangster.' Though the old secret service
fought as fiercely against its upstart rival as it did against the Germans,
SOE eventually became a more effective body than MI6, and was run by
abler people.

Between 1940 and 1943, however, its operations were dogged by the
fact of the Axis Powers' domination of the struggle. Germany and Japan
were seen by most inhabitants of occupied territories as winners, whom it
was madness to challenge. Bentinck of the JIC told Dalton he was thoroughly opposed to rousing the civilian populations of Europe: 'The time
is not ripe, and a lot of unfortunate people will be shot.' Dalton shrugged:
'These are the prime minister's orders, and must be carried out.' The minister, an ambitious and indiscreet man mistrusted by most of his colleagues,
yearned for a livelier role in the war effort than his arid responsibility for
administering blockade: stewardship of Britain's guerrilla operations
promised to provide this. An SOE officer wrote later that Dalton, who
aspired to supplant Anthony Eden as foreign secretary, 'tended to give
Churchill and other cabinet ministers forecasts of Resistance activities
based on assumptions of a will to resist in excess of any realistic views,
until the accession of the Soviet Union and United States to the Allied
cause gave the peoples of occupied Europe a real hope for an Allied
victory'.

Until 1944, when it became plain that Hitler would soon be defeated, most of the Continental societies wanted to have nothing to do with revolt, the frightful perils to their own homes and families of assisting the distant allies. Jean Cocteau, among the more notorious French intellectual collaborators with the Nazis, said scornfully to a young poet who told him that he intended to join the Resistance, '*Vous avez tort. La vie est plus grave que ça*' – 'You are wrong. Life is more serious than that.' Posterity is confident that it was Cocteau who was wrong, but especially in the early war years his view was widely shared among the social and political elites of the European nations. In the days before the Germans occupied Yugoslavia in 1941, SOE distributed seven wireless sets to prospective local stay-behind operators, but none ever transmitted. The handful of extraordinarily brave inhabitants of the occupied nations who started Resistance networks in those early days, such people as Michel Hollard and Marie-Madeleine Fourcade in France – in their cases working with MI6 –deserve the highest admiration for breaking ranks with their cowed fellow-countrymen long before the Allied cause became fashionable.

Robert Bruce Lockhart, director-general of the Political Warfare Executive and a veteran of British secret service operations in Russia after the Bolshevik Revolution, spoke to the chiefs of staff on 29 May 1942 about

False identity card provided to French Resistance agent
Marie-Madeleine Fourcade

the limitations of Resistance. Enthusiasts, he said, sometimes forgot that local support must ebb and flow with the Allies' perceived military success or failure. British prestige had been grievously damaged by years of defeats. Moreover, a ruthless occupier enjoyed great advantages over civilian Resisters: 'In the Russian revolution of 1905–6 workers with rifles could still get behind barricades and put up a show against troops,' read Bruce Lockhart's notes of the meeting. 'Today no chance against a few tanks and a dive-bomber or two. Task of controlling much easier … Gestapo, anti-sabotage units very ruthless.' He concluded: 'I don't think much hope of stimulating resistance to a more active stage until there is some considerable measure of Anglo-American military success. Propaganda can't replace military success … We should not try to promote a premature revolt which can be easily crushed.' The German policy of repression was highly effective in stifling revolt among most of the occupied peoples.

SOE's chiefs attributed the slow growth of Resistance, especially in France, to lack of arms: the RAF declined to divert bombers in significant numbers to supply partisans until 1944, when Downing Street insisted. However, the only likely consequence of arming Resisters earlier in the war would have been that the Germans killed more of them. Untrained civilians given guns were capable of assassinations and nuisance attacks, but large-scale clashes with the Wehrmacht and SS could have only one outcome – bloody defeat – as was repeatedly proven as late as 1944–45. An OSS officer, Macdonald Austin, said of the *maquis*: 'Sometimes they would do marvellous things, but one had to realise that on the next operation they could have forgotten to crank up the *gazogènes*' – the charcoal-fuelled cars on which occupied France depended for mobility. A British SHAEF intelligence officer said: 'You could never make any military plan dependent on the participation of guerrillas, because you could never be sure they would turn up.'

From 1938 until the establishment of SOE, MI6 maintained a small sabotage unit known as 'Section D', run by a tall, lanky, absurd sapper major named Laurence Grand, who affected a long cigarette-holder and a carnation in his buttonhole. Grand was a fount of exotic ideas, none of which came to much. In the early days of the war he promoted such stunts as paying Slovenian gangs to pour sand into the axle-boxes of rolling stock bound for Germany. A new assistant who joined Grand was disbelieving when ordered to fund some East European sabotage groups by sending them cash through the post. Nobody believed in Grand. The Foreign Office's Gladwyn Jebb pressed for his removal, writing contemptuously to

Cadogan: 'The only good point that I have been able to discover is that he is generous & liked by his staff, which includes one or two able persons. But to pit such a man against the German General Staff & the German Military Intelligence Service is like arranging an attack on a Panzer division by an actor mounted on a donkey.'

Hearing all this, the prime minister intervened to insist that a new organisation should be established to make mayhem across Europe, the Balkans and later the Far East. Special Operations Executive was initially run by Sir Frank Nelson, a former imperial merchant, MP and 1914–18 intelligence officer. Nelson was replaced in May 1942 by the banker Sir Charles Hambro, of whom de Gaulle's intelligence chief André Dewavrin said: 'A charming fellow, but almost invisible because of his innumerable responsibilities elsewhere.' From an early stage SOE's most effective personality proved to be Colin Gubbins, its director of operations, a Highland soldier with a background in military intelligence who had served at the War Office under the famously imaginative irregular warrior Col. John Holland. In September 1943 Gubbins became a major-general and succeeded Hambro as head of the organisation.

SOE – 'the racket', as many of its staff irreverently referred to it – started life at 64 Baker Street, with a cover name as the Inter-Service Research Bureau. By 1945 it had expanded to occupy six acres of office space between Baker Street tube station and Portman Square. It recruited staff variously among service personnel, civilians with specialist knowledge of occupied countries, refugees, and adventurers who fitted in nowhere else. It established training schools in sabotage at Stevenage, black propaganda at Watford, fieldcraft at Loch Ailort and guerrilla techniques at Arisaig. The most celebrated instructors at the school for subversion, based in Aston House near Knebworth, were two ex-Shanghai policemen, Captains Fairbairn and Sykes, who were alleged to conclude all lessons in unarmed combat with the words, 'and then kick him in the balls'. A notable failing of MI6 was that it made little attempt to train its personnel, who were expected to learn on the job, in its gentleman-amateur tradition. Even Broadway's official historian acknowledges that SOE provided good instruction: several of its training schools were incorporated into the post-war secret service.

Field duty with SOE demanded almost entirely different skills from those of MI6's people. 'The man who is interested in obtaining intelligence must have peace and quiet, and the agents he employs must never if possible be found out,' wrote Bickham Sweet-Escott, who served in both organ-

BURGLARY

1. ### DEFINITION.

   The secret entry by an agent into premises for the purpose of:

   a). Examining, photographing, stealing documents or articles profitable to your organization.

   b). Reconnoitring interior of a building for any subversive purpose - E.g. assassination.

2. ### GENERAL WARNINGS.

   a). If possible, above objectives should be attained without incurring enemy's knowledge or suspicion.

   b). Burglary with subversive intent is best not carried out by leader himself but by subordinates - preferably local people who, if caught, can use cover of "normal" burglary. (Where necessary, objects of value may be removed to substantiate this cover.)

   c). If a genuine burglar is hired or recruited for the job, greatest care must be taken that he will not give away organization to enemy.

3. ### METHOD.

   The following information has been obtained from police and very reliable criminal sources:

   a). INFORMATION NEEDED.

      i). Number of occupants.

      ii). Habits of occupants.

         - Meal-times (Especially evening.)
         - Normal times of departure and return.

      iii). Silent and covert lines of approach and retreat.

         - Use lawns and grass-borders.
         - Avoid gravel, flower-beds, dust, dirt and mud.

      iv). If dog present, discover situation of kennel.

         - Naturally noisy dog not so dangerous as normally silent one.
         - Use of aniseed for decoy, or poisoned-meat for killing.

      v). Situation and state of windows, doors (impression of key) and ladders.

   b). HOW OBTAINED.

      i). Best obtained from "insider" - E.g. maid, gardener, janitor, clerk. But risk of subsequent interrogation by police.

      ii). "Outsider" can be useful - E.g. tradesman, plumber, carpenter.

      iii). If no informants available, watching by a stranger should not exceed 48 hours.

Instructions in burglary, from a 1943 SOE training course

isations. By contrast, the agent sent into the field to promote guerrilla war is bound to make a noise, 'and it is only too likely that some of the men he uses will not escape'. In the early days, SOE made many mistakes that emphasised its inexperience. Jack Beevor, a lawyer and World War I gunner officer, was posted to its station in neutral Lisbon, where he rented a flat in his own name. He then allowed his MI6 counterparts to use it for a meeting with informants, which the landlord reported to the Portuguese authorities, who promptly expelled the SOE representative. In the spring of 1942 a member of an SOE landing party was captured by the Italians on the Mediterranean island of Antiparos; he proved to be carrying a list of British contacts in Athens, an act of carelessness which cost those hapless Greeks their lives. In Istanbul harbour, SOE planted limpet mines which failed to explode on tankers carrying Romanian oil for the Axis.

Sweet-Escott described how, in the worst early days, he shared the widespread Whitehall belief that the new organisation was 'nothing more than a wicked waste of time, effort, and money ... Our record of achievement ... was negligible. But our success or failure depended in the last resort on the willingness of men and women in enemy-occupied territory to risk their lives in the Allied cause ... Their readiness to do so was tempered by doubts as to our final victory. This attitude on their part limited the scope for successful operations on ours.' In 1941–42, SOE was besieged with requests to attack targets deep in enemy territory – for instance, the Luftwaffe's Condor long-range maritime reconnaissance aircraft, based at airfields around Brest – but its French section lacked any local supporters to undertake sabotage. The Abwehr was bemused that the British did not attack Germany's vital Romanian oilfields, as they had done in World War I, but there again Baker Street lacked means.

Among SOE's early assignments was to organise demolition parties to destroy vital installations in the wake of a German invasion of Britain. Thereafter, it set about training young men and women to be landed in occupied countries wherever contact could be made with local sympathisers – no easy task – and whenever the RAF would provide aircraft, an even bigger constraint. Baker Street's first big success was Operation 'Rubble' in March 1941, wherein George Binney stage-managed the escape from Gothenburg of a convoy of eight freighters laden with scarce commodities and industrial materials, a mission that uniformed personnel could not undertake, because it breached Swedish neutrality; a second similar coup was staged later in the year. Meanwhile the flamboyant Gus March-Phillips led a West African raid to 'cut out' the 7,600-ton Italian liner *Duchessa d'Aosta*, which was enjoying Portuguese sanctuary off Fernando Pó. He severed the ship's cable before towing it into international waters, where the Royal Navy took over. Operation 'Postmaster', as March-Phillips' raid was christened, made useful propaganda, because it showed the length of Britain's reach.

Some SOE schemes explored the wilder shores of fantasy in a fashion worthy of the Abwehr. A January 1942 Baker Street paper proposed that agents should be dispatched to rally Afghan tribes – Barakzais, Fopalzais and Alizais – on a prospective German line of advance to India. There was also a plan to launch biological warfare against Japan by parachuting hostile insects onto its crops. An officer who discussed ways and means with one of the Natural History Museum's experts in London reported afterwards: 'He tells me that boll weevil is not the best insect. A far more serious threat would be the pink boll worm, *platyedra Gossypiella Saunders*, which does ten million pounds' worth of damage annually in Egypt.' Unlike the Japanese, however, who did indeed launch biological warfare in China, Baker Street neither experimented on human guinea pigs, nor implemented the boll worm plan.

SOE had many critics. A scornful 1941 cable to London from the British embassy in Belgrade denounced such young officers as Julian Amery, committed to 'action for action's sake'. This was a widespread complaint by diplomats who failed to understand that 'action for action's sake' was exactly what the prime minister wanted. While the European governments in exile in London favoured a low-profile policy towards Resistance until the day of liberation was at hand, Churchill sought immediate, conspicuous acts of armed defiance. There were further criticisms about the real usefulness of SOE's proclaimed achievements. The destruction of the Gorgopotamos viaduct in Greece was a notable feat of arms, but the long-intended demolition did not take place until the end of November 1942, when Britain's Eighth Army was already advancing westwards from Egypt, and thus the German supply line through Greece had become irrelevant to the North African campaign.

Even Baker Street's own men considered that some operations did more to fulfil the fantasies of its adventurous young officers in the field than to hasten Allied victory. Bickham Sweet-Escott opposed one of the organisation's most famous coups, the Cretan kidnapping of a German divisional commander, because of the inevitability of local reprisals. 'The sacrifice might possibly have been worthwhile in the black winter of 1941 when things were going badly,' he later wrote. By April 1944, however, when

SOE's intrepid buccaneers carried out the operation which brought them fame, the murderous Gen. Friedrich Müller had been replaced by a 'comparatively harmless general called [Heinrich] Kreipe … The result of carrying it out in 1944, when everyone knew that victory was merely a matter of months would, I thought, hardly justify the cost.'

Many local peoples in all occupied countries were more interested in their own factional struggles than in accepting orders from London about how to serve the Allied cause. Bold, brash young men and a few women from SOE and OSS arrived on their thresholds demanding that they should set aside local differences to pursue the supreme purpose of defeating the Axis. But many Frenchmen, Greeks, Yugoslavs, Italians, Albanians, Malays and Burmese spurned such arguments. It might suit foreigners' interests to fight the Germans, Italians, Japanese to the exclusion of all else, but it did not suit many partisans. None of these British or US officers planned to live in their countries after the war; the visitors had no stake, beyond their own lives, which they held cheap as the young and unattached do, in the societies on which they so eagerly urged revolt.

Nigel Clive of MI6 signalled a report from Greece in April 1944 which emphasised the popular expectation of liberation by mid-summer, and offered a shrewd forecast: 'What matters most is what will happen thereafter. There is universal apprehension of the immediate aftermath of liberation when it looks as if the towns will become the battlefields of what is now a mountain civil war. Public clamour is for the following things in this order: food, freedom from the German occupation and a minimum of security so that a semblance of democratic life may begin again. No political movement in free Greece is capable of meeting the last requirement. All armed political mountain parties engender different degrees of mistrust.' The same was true in Yugoslavia, where unorthodox local rules of the game prevailed: the Germans were infuriated to discover from a wireless intercept that an Italian general captured by Gen. Mihailović and his Cetniks had subsequently been freed in exchange for the surrender of a field gun and ammunition to the partisans.

In January 1943 Stewart Menzies staged one of his frequent explosions of wrath about SOE to Robert Bruce Lockhart, who recorded the conversation: 'Could nothing be done about this show, which was bogus through and through?' 'C' demanded. 'They never achieved anything, they compromised all his agents, and they were amateurs in political matters … [Menzies] reckoned that if they could be suppressed our Intelligence would benefit enormously.' Guy Liddell of MI5 wrote on 3 April 1943:

'Lack of unity between ourselves, [MI6] and SOE is a serious menace.' Fractious horse-trading, as well as bitter squabbles, some of them comic, dogged the relationships. In November 1941 there was a negotiation about codenames which resulted in Air Commodore Archie Boyle of SOE minuting Claude Dansey at Broadway: 'The Greek Alphabet, together with names of motor cars, big game, fruit and colours are reserved for [MI6] ... I have abandoned fruits for SOE purposes ... I understand that you will suggest to [MI6] as additional categories, musicians and poets, and I shall therefore keep off them.' Childish rivalry caused Broadway and Baker Street to run separate wireless organisations. Differences in the field could become extreme: SOE officer Spike Moran shot dead Costa Lawrence of MI6, an unhinged Greek who became so fanatically enthusiastic about the communist ELAS faction that he tried to betray to the Germans the British team attached to the rival EDES.

SOE almost precipitated its own demise by a succession of follies that cost lives, together with massive embarrassment when they were revealed. By far the worst took place in Holland, and also involved MI6. In the summer of 1941 one of Broadway's agents was captured with a large pile of back messages – a common sin of commission by secret wireless operators – which enabled the Abwehr, with the aid of a German cipher expert named Sergeant May, to break its traffic. On 13 February 1942 two more MI6 agents were captured, one of whom talked freely.

Meanwhile two Dutch SOE agents were dropped under circumstances which suggested fantastic carelessness in Baker Street: both were issued with forged identity cards on which the royal arms of Holland were represented by two lions which both faced the same way, instead of addressing each other. Even more incredible, Hubertus Lauwers and Thys Taconis were issued with identical civilian clothes. When they remonstrated with their conducting officer in the briefing shed at Newmarket before being dropped on the night of 6–7 November 1941, he waved aside their concerns, saying that no one would notice. They arrived safely nonetheless, and went to work respectively in The Hague and Arnhem. Taconis received assistance from a local man named Ridderhof, who was a secret V-Mann – a Vertrauensmänner, or German informer, of which Holland had many in 1941. Everything Taconis did was reported to the Abwehr's effective and ingenious Maj. Herman Giskes. On 6 March 1942 Lauwers was seized in mid-transmission at a flat in The Hague, carrying copies of several old messages. When he resumed transmission, the receiving operator failed to notice that he gave the agreed security warning that he was under enemy control. Thereafter, agent after agent was parachuted into Holland to be received by Giskes' men. Amid their shock, and bitterness at betrayal, most of the prisoners talked, so that each new subject for interrogation was disorientated by the discovery of how much the Germans already knew. Lauwers inserted further warnings in subsequent transmissions, including the word 'CAUGHT', but the N Section in London blithely ignored them.

The rapid expansion of SOE meant that many agents, and especially wireless-operators, were dispatched into the field hastily trained, as were most of their Whaddon Hall counterparts. An Abwehr interception specialist later captured by the British expressed scepticism about SOE radio discipline in France. Alois Schwarze, a twenty-four-year-old NCO, said that many Allied agents transmitted very slowly; they reported the intended timings of their next schedule in plain language or very simple code; their three-letter callsigns were easy to pick up, as were their 'hellos' and 'goodbyes'. He and his colleagues were amazed how often captured wireless-operators had failed to notice that they were being monitored by German direction-finders. They were also often caught in possession of copies of old signals, in the fashion of the Dutchmen. Much of this lack of professionalism was inevitable when civilians were rushed through training as spies and dispatched into the field, but more than a few men and women paid for it with their lives.

It is a myth, vividly exposed by the Dutch experience, that Allied agents and Resistance workers who fell into German hands seldom talked. Almost every prisoner of any nationality gave away a little or much, with or without undergoing torture. Controllers expected only that their field officers and agents should withhold names for a minimum of twenty-four or forty-eight hours, to enable meetings to be cancelled, contacts to flee. The Gestapo in Paris employed Latvian, Dutch and indeed French collaborators to conduct the torture of prisoners, while German officers asked the questions. Captured agents were usually offered a 50 per cent chance of life if they talked, and such bargains were sometimes kept. An SD interpreter named Corporal Weigel, who took part in many 'extreme interrogations' at Versailles, recalled the names of just two prisoners who remained silent: one was a Madame Ziegler, whom he believed to be Alsatian, the other a Captain Tinchebray, taken in June 1944 at Saint-Marcelle. Those were exceptions to a harsh generality, recognised alike by occupiers, Resisters and their London sponsors. The broad truth about spies of all nationalities who fell into enemy hands was that they were kept alive as long as they could serve a purpose, and shot when their usefulness expired. The emotive word 'murdered' is often used by post-war writers when mentioning SOE agents, and especially women, killed by the Germans. In truth, all of them knew that if taken death would almost certainly be their fate, legitimised by the laws of war. Every captured agent who wanted to live struggled to decide how much he or she might reveal without becoming a traitor, and some misjudged the answer.

Giskes eventually operated fourteen British wireless sets in his *Englandspiel*, which continued for more than two years, with successive consignments of arms and explosives, together with saboteurs and wireless-operators, parachuted directly into German custody. Fifty-one men from SOE, nine from MI6 and one woman from MI9 were eventually taken, of whom all but a handful were shot. When five made an escape in August 1943 and sent a message to London warning of the disaster, all unknowing they entrusted it to a *V-Mann*, and thus it was never forwarded. While two of the escapers were on their way to Britain the Abwehr signalled to SOE on one of its own sets, reporting the men to be under Gestapo control, with the result that when they arrived they were confined for some weeks in Brixton prison. It was Giskes himself who decided that he had exhausted the possibilities of his Operation 'North Pole', and on All Fools' Day 1944 sent a final mocking signal to SOE: 'WHENEVER YOU WILL COME TO PAY A VISIT TO THE CONTINENT YOU MAY BE ASSURED THAT YOU WILL BE RECEIVED WITH THE SAME CARE AND RESULT AS ALL THOSE YOU SENT US BEFORE STOP SO LONG.' Beyond the MI6 and SOE agents who were lost, hundreds of local Resistance workers perished as a result of the gross misconduct of SOE's Netherlands section by Major Charles Blizard and Major Seymour Bingham. Hugh Trevor-Roper wrote on 19 June 1944, acknowledging that for all his disdain for German intelligence-gathering, its officers displayed formidable effectiveness in countering Resistance: 'Whatever the RSHA's deficiencies in the evaluation of intelligence, its competence in counter-espionage cannot be questioned.'

Those who mock the Germans for having swallowed for so long the productions of the British Double Cross system should take heed of the gullibility of SOE and MI6 in their Dutch operations. All that was different was that while the intelligence transmitted by the Abwehr double agents under British control addressed issues of high strategic importance to Germany, the Dutch connection had only local significance for the Allied war effort. The scandal – for such it was – so enraged the Netherlands government that for a time after the war they believed Major Bingham to have been a double, serving the Nazis. In truth he was merely incompetent, but he wisely emigrated to Australia, to start a new life in a continent where his shame was unknown. SOE narrowly survived Whitehall demands that it should be wound up after the fiasco in Holland was revealed, because Churchill rejected any wholesale reorganisation of the secret services until the war ended.

An anonymous post-war critic, obviously familiar with the secret world and perhaps himself a veteran of the rival MI6, wrote that many of SOE's senior personnel 'displayed an enthusiasm quite unrestrained by experience, some had [communist] political backgrounds which deserved a rather closer scrutiny than they ever got, and a few could only charitably be described as nutcases'. Yet Bill Bentinck, who knew all the secret services' top men intimately, in his old age offered warm praise for SOE, asserting that it had 'good people, very good people'. If Colin Gubbins was not brilliant, he was a capable organiser supported by some able civilians in uniform. Bentinck emphasised MI6's weakness, by contrast: 'There were a lot of old boys, people who'd been there from World War I and had been hanging on … They fancied themselves as spy-masters.' Nigel Clive, himself an MI6 field agent, said 'SOE was unquestionably the best.'

Both at the time and since, some extravagant claims have been made about the ability of Resistance movements to influence the main course of the war. R. Harris Smith, an admiring chronicler of the American Office of Strategic Services, wrote: 'Partisan warfare was a viable alternative to frontal assault, but SOE and OSS officers sent to establish links with the Resistance were hampered by anti-partisan prejudice at Allied headquarters.' British and American senior soldiers were indeed sceptical about the usefulness of guerrillas, but there were excellent reasons for their caution. Partisans made a marginal contribution to the war effort in several theatres, but even in Yugoslavia and Russia they could not provide a substitute for the might and mass of regular armies. Resistance in many societies, especially within the Balkans, had much more influence on post-war events than on the defeat of the Axis.

From 1943 onwards, Yugoslavia became the focus for SOE's most ambitious operations in support of Tito's partisan army, which received vastly more weapons than any other national guerrilla force; but France remained Baker Street's most celebrated theatre. It proved relatively easy to insert agents by light aircraft in the north, and by parachute further afield. Between 1941 and 1944 the RAF flew 320 Lysander sorties, of which 210 were successful, landing 440 passengers and evacuating 630, at a cost of only six pilots killed. In the countryside, many British agents and wireless-operators survived at liberty for long periods. But in French cities, in a society ruled by collaborators and riddled with informers, the rate of attrition was horrific. On 5 June 1943, Sir David Petrie, chief of MI5, noted in a general broadside to Menzies that both MI6 and SOE had 'for months past been suffering serious losses of agents on the continent' because of German penetration – and that was before the Dutch disaster was revealed.

A majority of all Allied agents captured by the Germans in Europe were victims of betrayal. Oluf Reed-Olsen wrote of his experience as a British spy in Norway: 'One was most afraid of one's own people; I think all agents, saboteurs and other "visitors" in Norway will agree this was so. And there were many who stood aside, from hate and fear of Russia, when even the smallest contribution to the cause was asked of them, because they considered the Allied cause to be too much affected by Communism.' Olsen's strictures applied equally in France, where a few British traitors also did terrible harm. The escape-line leader 'Pat O'Leary' – Captain Albert Guerisse of the Belgian army – used as one of his helpers in the north during the winter of 1941 a man who called himself Captain Harold Cole, supposedly an evader left behind after the BEF's 1940 evacuation. MI9 – the secret escapers' branch of the War Office – found no officer of that name on the British Army's books, but instead a Sergeant Harold Cole who had deserted from his unit, taking with him its mess funds. Guerisse was already suspicious that Cole was squandering his Line's cash on extravagant living. After a tense meeting, he dispatched the man to Lille in disgrace.

Within a few days of his arrival in the city in December 1941, Cole had assisted the Germans to arrest one of the Line's most devoted helpers, the Abbé Carpentier, who had been printing documents for escapers on a private press. Long afterwards, it was discovered that the Abwehr had been using the Englishman for months, under various aliases. An order went out to Resisters to shoot him on sight. In May 1942, however, Cole was arrested by Vichy police in the unoccupied zone of France and given a long prison sentence, which removed him from Resistance view. He reappeared only in 1945, when arrested in the American Zone of Germany, again masquerading as a British captain. He escaped from detention and fled to Paris, where he was eventually killed in a shoot-out with the police. MI9 considered him responsible for fifty deaths of members of the 'Pat' Line and their connections.

*   *   *

For much of the war a fundamental division persisted between the British and Free French visions of Resistance. Churchill was eager to stimulate and hasten armed revolt, to assist the Allied armies in achieving the defeat of Nazism. Gen. Charles de Gaulle, by contrast, cherished a political concept – salvation of the soul of France from the slough of humiliation into which it had been plunged by surrender in 1940. He defined Resistance as 'a national expression'. Free French intelligence, which depended on SOE for operational facilities, was directed from London by André Dewavrin, 'Colonel Passy', an engineer officer born in 1911, a graduate of the Paris École Polytechnique and a former instructor at Saint-Cyr military academy. Dewavrin's cleverness was never in doubt, nor his considerable personal presence – tall, with thinning fair hair and a deceptively soft voice. He proved a skilled political infighter, as was indispensable in the snakepit of London exile politics. He customarily wore civilian clothes, and SOE officers noted that when he appeared in uniform, it was a sure weather warning that there was to be a row with somebody. His department, the *Bureau Central de Renseignements et d'Action militaire*, or BCRA, was housed at 3 St James's Square, just across Pall Mall from de Gaulle's main headquarters in Carlton Gardens. Dewavrin recruited some remarkable personalities, prominent among whom was 'Rémy', Gilbert Renault, who was originally commissioned to organise an escape line through Spain, with the slender credentials that he had once directed a movie about Christopher Columbus. His organisation, the *Confrérie Notre-Dame*, became justly celebrated, respect enhanced by its contribution to the Bruneval coup.

For the most part, however, de Gaulle and Dewavrin viewed their agents in the field more as emissaries of 'their' France than as instruments of Allied victory. Free French prestige slumped when the first BCRA man dispatched into the field, late in 1940, reached his dropping zone in an RAF aircraft, but then refused to jump and spent the rest of the war as a staff officer in Carlton Gardens. In the summer of 1941 the BCRA controlled just two wirelesses in occupied France, one of which was shut down in August. SOE appropriated the most promising recruits for secret service among the refugees who arrived in Britain from France, to receive protracted interrogation and screening at the Queen Victoria Patriotic School in Wandsworth, 'a tower of Babel'. Moreover, de Gaulle's political design for a highly centralised national movement rendered the BCRA's networks especially vulnerable to German penetration.

The general professed to be insulted by the unwillingness of the British to confide their secrets to his people – who were rigorously excluded from the Ultra loop. MI6 described relations with the Free French as 'like trying to live amicably with a jealous, touchy and domineering wife'. British code-breaking revealed – for instance – de Gaulle's men conducting secret talks with the Chinese about securing their assistance to regain Indochina. A sum of £5,000 had to be paid from British secret funds in May 1944 to silence a Frenchman named Dufours, who brought a legal action against the London Gaullists to secure redress for his own unlawful imprisonment and torture by them. Carlton Gardens was indifferent to what the British regarded as a scandal. Its chiefs took the view that they had the right to treat their own nationals however they saw fit, even in the heart of London.

The BCRA inherited from the French army a reckless attitude to signal security, using codes which the Germans broke even after MI6 warned Carlton Gardens of their vulnerability. The Wehrmacht had captured a trainload of French intelligence documents during the Blitzkrieg which took lackadaisical Abwehr analysts two years to work through. In 1942 they discovered that among this haul was a list of all French sources in Germany, together with the sums of money paid to them. By far the largest recipient was known as 'Asché', or simply 'He', whom the Germans belat-edly identified as Hans-Thilo Schmidt, the Allies' pre-war informant about Enigma, who was arrested in April 1943 and perished in September, though it is uncertain whether he was executed or committed suicide.

That spring, André Dewavrin made a personal tour of France, to explore for himself occupation conditions. This was certainly courageous, and 'Passy' returned safely, but it represented a grotesque risk when he was privy to all his organisation's secrets and contacts. Flamboyance was immensely dangerous in secret agents. De Gaulle and Churchill were alike attracted to such Resisters as Emmanuel d'Astier de la Vigerie, a child of privilege who became one of the general's most prominent supporters. De la Vigerie, however, was considered by many of those who met him to be an unstable fantasist. On a tour of America he once gave a press confer-ence with a sack over his head, supposedly to mask his identity, which was well known from Berlin to Washington, DC. At a meeting at the Foreign Office, 'C' and SOE's chief expressed their shared view 'that the leaders of the French Resistance movements, including M. Emmanuel d'Astier himself, were not nearly so interested in fighting the Germans as in build-ing up an organisation which would seize power when the Germans were driven out'. There was truth in this. MI6 and SOE assembled most of the important humint to come out of France, especially in advance of D-Day. Dewavrin was embarrassed to discover that Henri Frenay, leader of the

'Combat' Resistance group, was selling intelligence for handsome sums of cash to Allen Dulles of OSS, rather than donating it to the Free French cause.

British apprehension about the elaborate Gaullist political structure inside France, and its vulnerability to informers, was vindicated in the spring and summer of 1943, when the Gestapo conducted mass arrests. Victims included Jean Moulin, principal standard-bearer of the 'London French', who was tortured and executed, and Gen. Charles de Lestraint, a sixty-three-year-old nominated by de Gaulle as leader of his so-called *Armée Secrète*. Lestraint possessed no aptitude for secret war, nor indeed much merit save his opposition to France's Vichy rulers. His arrest on 6 June 1943 was no loss to the Allied war effort. Though propaganda made de Gaulle a giant in his country by the time of D-Day, cynics asserted that the BCRA created more martyrs than useful Resisters.

It was hard for citizens of democracies to adapt to the iron disciplines of intelligence work – life in a secret universe in which trust in one's fellow man or woman was a dangerous self-indulgence. It meant much to people who nursed the shame of defeat and occupation to confide in others about the work they were doing for the cause of freedom, so that they might walk a little taller in their streets, but this was mortally perilous. Oluf Reed-Olsen avowed the habitual indiscretion of his own people: 'it was not exclusively a Norwegian weakness … and in our case the reason may have been that there had been no war in our country for about 125 years. Loquacity was our great difficulty … It was hard to get fellow-workers who could resist the temptation to tell their friends and relations what they were doing.' An overwhelming majority of dedicated Resisters were drawn from the humbler sections of society. The official historians of MI9 wrote: 'Escapers and evaders found almost uniformly … every sort of readiness to help them among the poorer sorts of people and every sort of reserve among most of the rich.' The same was true of all branches of secret activity: it may confidently be said that those with most materially to lose did least to oppose the German occupiers, while those with least property did most.

George Hiller, who served as an SOE agent in rural France in 1943–44, later gave a thoughtful and moving account of his experiences. There could be no closer bond, he said, than that between the hider and the hidden in such circumstances as those in which he found himself in the Lot: he, a British agent, daily placed his life in the hands of local Frenchmen and their families – almost invariably little people, peasants or teachers or trades unionists – whom he had never met before, from whom in peacetime he would have been separated by an unbridgeable social and cultural divide. They, meanwhile, harboured him in the knowledge that if their hospitality was ever revealed, conceivably by himself as a prisoner under torture, their lives and all that they owned would be forfeit.

Civilian bystanders who suddenly chanced on manifestations of secret operations were chiefly concerned to save themselves from being swept away in the recriminations or reprisals of the occupiers. One day Reed-Olsen found himself travelling on a Norwegian train which was subjected to a surprise search. He threw open a window and hurled out into the countryside three passports, a revolver and whirling wads of cash, while nearby passengers watched in terror, as well they might. James Langley of MI9 suggested after the war that one Resistance worker forfeited his or her life for every Allied soldier or airman who used a secret escape line. When the famous 'Comet' network was eventually penetrated and many of its members lay imprisoned and awaiting death, Langley delivered an emotional plea to MI6 to try to save some of them. Claude Dansey responded with a harshness worthy of Moscow Centre: 'Your trouble, Jimmy, is that you love your agents.'

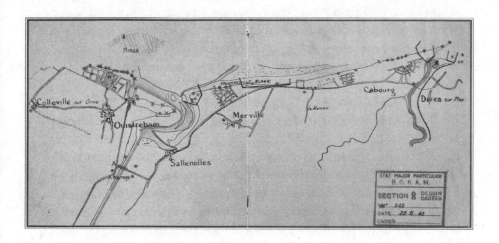

Map of the côte du Calvados hand-drawn by a French
Resistance worker

The Mediterranean became the foremost happy hunting ground of SOE, scene of some of its agents' most dramatic exploits. Critics thought that the wrong tone was set by Grey Pillars, Baker Street's Cairo headquarters, which seemed too comfortable for the hub of a military operation. In 1941–42 the building's atmosphere was poisoned by feuds and mutual suspicions: one colonel tried to get a listening device fitted to his phone, so that his conversations with colleagues could be recorded. In 1943 there was a major purge of the organisation, but SOE Cairo never became a happy ship, not least because of tensions between communist sympathisers and indeed promoters among its British officers, and colleagues of more conservative mien.

There was lasting bitterness about the manner in which SOE transferred its support from the royalist Gen. Mihailović to the communist Tito in Yugoslavia, causing the incidental deaths of several British agents. Personalities powerfully influenced this outcome: the men operating with Mihailović were lacklustre reporters, while the dispatches of Churchill's former historical researcher Major William Deakin, and later of Tory MP Col. Fitzroy Maclean, were drafted in scintillating and inspirational terms, tempered by a monumental naïveté about Tito's character, political objectives and dalliances with the Germans. Deakin and Maclean became two of the most influential secret agents of the war; their reports were decisive in persuading the prime minister to throw British support, manifested in huge deliveries of arms and equipment, behind the communist cause.

From 1943, as resources became freely available, SOE Cairo evolved into a massive operation. By October it was handling eighty field missions in the Balkans, with air transport movements organised by an ex-Nottingham Tramways manager named Wigginton, who gained a reputation for formidable efficiency. Meanwhile 'Skipper' Poole ran the superbly named Levantine Fishing Patrol, transporting supplies to Greece. Factional strife was an occupational hazard of liaison with Resistance groups in every target nation. When Nigel Clive of MI6 was parachuted into Greece in December 1943, he spent his first hour on the ground listening to a litany of complaints from SOE's Fred Wright about the frustration of being unable to do much sabotage, because 'all his energies had been concentrated on the political assignment of trying to prevent an extension of the civil war between EDES and ELAS'. Clive wrote: 'Political rather than technical or standard military qualifications were what would be required of those who [organised] the Greek resistance.'

A problem besetting SOE until the 1944 eve of D-Day in France was that it lacked a clear, overarching strategic directive, setting out the ultimate purpose of stimulating Resistance. 'Set Europe ablaze' did not amount to a coherent programme. Was Baker Street seeking to create guerrilla armies to conduct pitched battles with the Germans? To gather intelligence? To sabotage the Axis war effort? Colin Gubbins wrote about the difficulty 'of carrying out two broad tasks simultaneously, which were themselves hardly compatible, that is action, day by day and week after week, in specific attacks against selected targets in occupied countries, and at the same time the creation of secret armies, equipped, organised and trained, ready to come into action as ordered when invasion should come. Every attack carried out naturally alerted the Gestapo.' Churchill's romantic vision never attracted his own service chiefs of staff, who disliked and even deplored the pirates of SOE. They were right, in a narrowly military sense, that the Continent would not have been freed from Nazi tyranny a single day later had Resistance never existed. But posterity may choose to see its sponsorship as a significant element in Churchill's genius as a war leader, because he understood its immense moral value.

As the tide of the war turned, from 1943 onwards, in Sweet-Escott's words 'there were many more men and women prepared to take risks in the Allied cause than there had been a year before'. By the middle of 1944, SOE's operations in Western Europe were supported by a thousand air sorties a month, flown by five squadrons of RAF bombers. During 1944–45, German interceptors identified hundreds of Allied agent- or partisan-operated wireless transmitters operating in territories the Nazis were still striving to control, or where they had important interests. They detected twenty in Poland, six in Czechoslovakia, seventeen in Norway, four in Denmark, twenty-two in Holland, twenty-seven in Belgium, thirty-five in Paris, twenty in western France, sixty-one in southern France, fifteen in Normandy and Brittany, ten in Spain, four in Switzerland, twenty-five in northern Italy, eight in southern Italy, thirty in Yugoslavia – and 140 in Russia. The Abwehr's direction-finders prompted thirty arrests in 1941, ninety in 1942, 160 in 1943 and 130 in 1944; these figures illustrated not so much German vigilance as the ever-increasing energy of Resistance.

As the story drew to an end, with the progressive 1944–45 liberation of German-occupied societies, there was fierce debate about whether the outcome of SOE's activities justified their cost. Baker Street could point to such notable achievements as the February 1943 sabotage of the Rjukan heavy-water plant in Norway, and the sinking a year later of the ferry carrying to Germany rail tanker wagons laden with 15,000 litres of precious product from the plant. Three Norwegian agents, Knut Haulkelid, Knut Lier-Hansen and Rolf Sorlie, boarded the ferry disguised as greasers, and laid delayed-action charges which exploded, sinking the vessel, in the midst of Lake Tinnjo. Only after the war did it become known that Nazi atomic research had made far too little progress for the consignment to contribute anything to their war effort; but this did not negate either the wisdom of launching the mission, or the marvellous courage and ingenuity of the agents who carried it out. In France, before and after D-Day, Resistance groups launched widespread attacks on the German lines of communication which, though much less strategically influential than Allied bombing, caused the occupiers intense annoyance.

Sceptics persisted, especially in the Balkans, where communist influence was strongest, most ruthless and pernicious. David Wallace, an SOE officer killed in action on 19 August 1944, reported savagely to Cairo shortly before his death: 'Our effort in Greece, in men and money, has not only been out of all proportion to the results we have achieved against the Germans, but also to the value of the Greek people, who are not capable of being saved from themselves, nor are themselves worth it. This is also the unanimous opinion of all British liaison officers, who have been long in this country.' Wallace was quite wrong to suggest that his cynical assessment was shared by all his British comrades in Greece, or elsewhere in Western Europe. Nigel Clive described an exuberant party in the community in which he served, held to celebrate the 1944 German withdrawal from Greece. He used the sort of emotional language often adopted by British and American officers who shared secret life in occupied lands: 'I enjoyed one of those rare moments of pride, that I had lived, worked, struggled and fought with the kind of people who had shared this evening's celebration. To have gone some way to being accepted as one of them seemed to have made the whole of the adventure worthwhile … Before these people, whose titles were not in their military ranks but in their Christian names, I could only bow my head. They had no great claims on life. They were not dreaming of marble halls and the gleaming tinsel of victory. Their simple village lives had been disrupted by foreign invasions and their consequences. In response they had given all that was best within them: their courage and instinctive guile, their refusal to submit, their intelligent and critical reserve about the motive of some of their leaders … There was an unquestioned acceptance of the value of the British connection.'

This was a romantic perception. The record shows that in many countries the weapons provided to Resistance by the Allies were used more energetically to promote factional interests – mostly communist – following liberation, than to fight the Axis during the occupation. An OSS major dropped into north-west Italy reported that the partisans were '20 per cent for Liberation and 80 per cent for Russia. We soon found that they were burying the German arms they had captured.' Since 1945, many fanciful accounts have been published, which exaggerate the material damage inflicted on Axis forces by Allied agents and Resistance, especially in the wake of D-Day. It is salutary to compare these with German war diaries, which show how relatively small were the casualties imposed by guerrillas: for instance, the 2nd SS Panzer Division, which travelled from Montauban to Normandy in June 1944, shedding rivers of innocent blood on its way, lost just thirty-five killed out of 15,000 men.

Sabotage and local attacks often required acceptance of higher risks and losses than targets merited in narrowly military terms. Col. Dick Barry, Gubbins's very able chief of staff at Baker Street, said long afterwards about its wartime contribution: 'It was only just worth it.' Yet SOE's operations were important then, and seem justified now, by their moral impact and contribution to fomenting insecurity, tension, sometimes murderous hysteria among German occupying forces. It was chiefly thanks to the aid provided to local opposition movements by SOE and OSS that a legend of popular insurrection was created, which contributed immensely to reviving the self-respect of Europe's occupied societies after 1945. Never could enemies of democracy claim that Britain and the United States had abandoned the occupied nations to their fate.

Across Europe – the Asian story will be discussed below – the men and women who served as SOE's field agents offered a sacrifice to the cause of freedom which became evident to the people of most occupied societies after the war, even if they knew nothing of it during their years of trial. Moreover none of the follies, failures and embarrassments described above should be allowed to mask the towering historical reality that some hundreds of thousands of fine and brave people in the occupied countries risked everything in the cause of Resistance. Only SOE's support – with money, arms, wirelesses – empowered them to make that choice. Too much post-war attention and admiration has focused upon the deeds of the foreigners, SOE's British agents, who hazarded only their own young lives in the cause of a great and indisputably romantic adventure; too little upon the peoples of Europe, of all ages and both sexes, who joined one of hundreds of Resistance networks. Their contribution should be judged much more by the magnitude of their stakes and their sacrifices than by the military achievements, or lack of them. For all SOE's extravagances and follies, it became the most effective British secret operations organisation of the war, and justified the Churchillian leap of imagination that inspired its creation.

11

Hoover's G-Men, Donovan's Wild Men

1 ADVENTURERS

'Wild Bill' Donovan's new-born foreign intelligence service, the Office of Strategic Services, encountered most of the same difficulties, dramas and criticisms as SOE, and more of them. One day early in 1945, deep in eastern France a US Army divisional staff officer held forth to colleagues in front of one of Donovan's men: 'Gentlemen, I am going to tell you about the OSS ... the most fantastic damned organization in all our armed forces. Its people do incredible things. They seduce German spies, they parachute into Sicily one day and two days later they're dancing on the St Regis roof. They dynamite aqueducts, urinate in Luftwaffe gas tanks, and play games with IG Farben and Krupp, but' – throwing up his hands – '90 per cent of this has not a goddamned thing to do with the war.'

The staff officer's rant may have been influenced by the fact that the visitor who provoked it was a Hollywood film star, thinly disguised as one of Donovan's men. But it was the actor who recorded the story, and himself half-accepted the cynical view of OSS adopted by many uniformed soldiers: the US War Department in Washington refused to open its files to Donovan's people, or indeed to include him on the Ultra distribution list. Maj. Gen. George V. Strong, George Marshall's intelligence chief, regarded Donovan's activities with unremitting scorn, as did his 1944 successor, Clayton Bissell. OSS was exuberant, ill-disciplined, unfocused and wildly extravagant, in keeping with the personality of its founder. A cooler figure might have built a more measured service. But the United States faced an extraordinary challenge, to create from a standing start in the midst of a world war an organisation with global responsibilities for intelligence, sabotage and guerrilla operations, a range of missions that every other belligerent used several services to fulfil.

An SOE man visiting Washington in 1942 was enchanted to observe a sign in a side street near the White House: 'NO PARKING: U.S. SECRET SERVICE ONLY'. America's not-very-'secret service' officers were responsible only for guarding the president and suppressing forgery of the dollar. OSS's follies and failures were many and various, but little worse than those of its Allied and Axis counterparts. All that was different was that where other nations afterwards sought to bury their excesses and failures, the Americans characteristically avowed them. Moreover, OSS could claim to have created the most impressive research and analysis arm of any intelligence service in the world.

During the months before and after Pearl Harbor, the British were fearful that Donovan's ascent to power would be frustrated by anglophobes, because the colonel was so conspicuously enthusiastic about Churchill's people. Many of his early struggles were not against the Germans, but against J. Edgar Hoover of the Federal Bureau of Investigation. In common with the security services of every other nation, the FBI expanded dramatically during the war years, its 1941 strength of 2,280 rising by 1945 to 15,000, including 5,000 special agents – the 'G-men', as tabloid slang dubbed them. By a directive of 23 December 1941, the White House agreed that the FBI should extend its remit to cover counter-intelligence activities throughout the Americas. This empowered Hoover to create a new corporation – Importers and Exporters Services, with quarters in New York's Rockefeller Center – as a cover for its agents overseas. Later, the Bureau persuaded bona fide companies to do their patriotic duty by providing credentials for its men – Reader's Digest, Twentieth Century-Fox, Paramount, Procter & Gamble, H.J. Heinz. Special Agent Richard Auerbach, who travelled to Bogotá as a supposed representative of Wall Street's Merrill Lynch, claimed to have sold $100 million worth of stocks and bonds down there.

Hoover hurried to pre-empt Donovan by deploying his own men in South America, but the logistical difficulties of wartime foreign travel were immense, even for US secret servants, and far from any combat zone. When Special Agent Richard Crow was assigned to La Paz, he started out by plane, then became stranded in Panama for ten days before catching a flight to Colombia, where he kicked his heels for a further week before flying to Lima. After five days there, he abandoned hope of getting another plane seat and instead rented a car to southern Peru before catching a train ride to Lake Titicaca. He crossed the water in a native boat, then got a train to the Bolivian capital. What he did when he got there is unrecorded, and was perhaps less interesting.

While the FBI could claim success in protecting the United States from Axis intelligence – a relatively easy task, given the clumsiness of Abwehr and Japanese attempts at penetration – its chief quarrelled with every branch of the armed forces because of his refusal to collaborate, to share information or informants that fell into his clutches. The Office of Naval Intelligence was especially exasperated by Hoover's intransigence. On 13 August 1942 one of its officers, Commander W.S. Hogg, launched a fierce attack on the Bureau's 'inability to fit into a place in any coordinated military activity. [The] FBI is a civilian organisation with a background of peace. It has been built on its publicity, its favour with the public and Congress and its reputation as a protector of the people. It is ambitious, properly so in peacetime, perhaps, but questionably so in time of war … Ex-agents of FBI have said that every Agent owes his allegiance first to Hoover and second to the United States.'

A characteristic episode took place when an escaped German airman, Peter Krug, was arrested in San Antonio: armed forces intelligence branches were not informed until after the FBI had held a triumphant press conference. Meanwhile Laurance Safford of Op-20-G had a major row with the Bureau over ownership of some German diplomatic codes that FBI agents seized in San Francisco. Hoover launched a bitter offensive against the infant OSS's early ventures in South America, denouncing Donovan's alleged 'interference with the Bureau's responsibility for handling and controlling operations of enemy espionage agents in the Western Hemisphere'. The director was even more hostile to Churchill's nation and its intelligence services. The FBI's internal history complains: 'The British MI6 displayed its uncooperative attitude to such a degree that on Feb 4, 1944, the Bureau found it necessary to make a vigorous protest to the British Security representative in New York and to the London headquarters.' For its own part, MI6 abandoned early and unsuccessful efforts to work with the FBI's men on the ground in South America, and collaborated instead with the US Army's G-2 department.

All intelligence services seek to promote factional interests and inflate their own achievements, but the wartime FBI carried this practice to manic lengths. The British were exasperated that Hoover preferred to snatch headline credit for high-profile captures, rather than privily track or turn enemy spies. They were especially annoyed when their own prize double agent, 'Tricycle' (Dusko Popov), spent some months of 1941 in the US, and the FBI mismanaged him so grossly that he was almost blown. Moreover the Bureau had the *chutzpah* to boast that it was itself responsible for the creation and management of the Double Cross system which helped to confuse the Germans about D-Day: the FBI Espionage Section's quarterly summary of 'outstanding accomplishments', composed on 1 May 1944 for circulation throughout the higher echelons of the Roosevelt administration, recorded: 'On March 17 the first message calculated to deceive the Germans as to the date of the European invasion by the Allies was sent through the [FBI's] double agent Pat J by radio. This message was followed by similar messages for the same purpose ... The operation of double agents during this quarter continued to add to the Bureau's knowledge of the modus operandi and personnel employed by the German intelligence service.' In the winter of 1944 the FBI circulated a memorandum which concluded magisterially: 'Consideration is being given to continuing some of our double agents to penetrate the [German] underground after cessation of hostilities.' To a greater degree than any other intelligence and security organisation the FBI – or, more explicitly, Hoover its chieftain – chose to view the war as providing a theatre for the extension of his own power and prestige, rather than as a mission to defeat the Axis.

While the FBI waged a successful expansionist campaign in the Americas, elsewhere in the world Donovan triumphed, and soon presided over a large empire. Bill Bentinck of the British JIC never wavered in his view that the prime minister's creation of SOE as a separate service and rival to MI6 had been a mistake. He urged Donovan to keep 'skulduggery' and intelligence-gathering under one roof, and so indeed the Americans did. In June 1942, by executive order the Office of War Information became the Office of Strategic Services. It was housed mostly in buildings vacated by the Public Health Service, and soon comprised four branches: Secret Intelligence (SI); Secret Operations (SO); psychological warfare or 'Morale Operations' (MO); counter-espionage (X-2).

Washington bulged with people – 70,000 new arrivals in the first year after Pearl Harbor – and 5,000 more federal workers arrived each month thereafter, many bringing their families with them. The telephone system struggled to grapple with increased demand, especially for long-distance calls. The government spent – and wasted – cash on such a scale as the world had never seen. 'Tempos', buildings rushed up in a couple of months to house new departments, appeared on every green space around the city centre. Paper, filing cabinets and typewriters were in desperately short supply; amid a national appeal for used machines, radio stations played a jingle: 'An idle typewriter is a help to Hitler.' The capital was transformed over a decade from a quiet backwater into a noisy, crowded, expensive city boasting a mushroom growth of acronyms, each one signifying a new organisation: WPB, OPA, WMC, BEW, NWLB, ODT – and now OSS.

The British were delighted, except Claude Dansey of MI6, who expressed disgust. Hating both the United States and SOE, he was appalled that the latter was now to have an American counterpart, bent on pursuing the same 'noisy paths', and run by a flamboyant officer who, in Dansey's view, was 'completely sold on publicity'. Broadway judged that Donovan was more interested in the thrills and spills of sponsoring paramilitary operations in enemy territory than in intelligence-gathering. One key area of US secret activities was ring-fenced beyond OSS's remit: the colonel had no influence over the US Army's and US Navy's codebreakers, who represented by far the most important elements of America's wartime intelligence effort. Moreover, in 1942, and to Donovan's chagrin, propaganda was hived off to Elmer Davis's Office of War Information. His own men were to be spies, saboteurs and sponsors of guerrilla campaigns.

Under the stimulus of its manically energetic founder, OSS expanded like a giant party balloon. Donovan promised FDR an organisation based on men who were 'calculatingly reckless', with 'disciplined daring', and 'trained for aggressive action'. Its New York facility struck one officer as resembling a pantomime repertory company: 'Everyone was working up a scheme. Everything shimmered in secrecy, and it was a rare man who knew what his fellows were doing. Brooks Brothers was the unofficial costume-maker while Abercrombie & Fitch functioned as an uptown Quartermaster Corps, supplying air mattresses and sleeping bags and all the paraphernalia so dear to the hearts of small boys and civilians turned semi-guerrillas.' When Arthur Schlesinger joined the organisation in 1943, he wrote to his parents that nobody seemed to work too hard, the material was interesting, and there were nice perquisites such as private screenings of Hollywood new releases for Donovan's intimate circle. But the young academic deplored the remoteness from reality, as he saw it, of the new organisation: 'For all the deathly secrecy of much of the material, there is an ivory-tower serenity about the place.'

OSS eventually employed over 13,000 Americans together with many more foreigners, and enjoyed almost unlimited funding for weapons, planes, cars, office equipment, houses. Malcolm Muggeridge, MI6's man in Lourenço Marques, complained that the arrival there of an OSS representative prompted soaring inflation in the local bribe market. A US officer dispatched to the Mediterranean wrote: 'The chiefs of the various OSS headquarters overseas had a spectacular talent for living in style. The Cairo villa looked like a bastard version of the Taj Mahal. The high wall around it was pierced by a tall iron gate; there were broad verandas of inlaid tile and a profusion of shade trees above vast stretches of lawn. A platoon of servants glided in endless circles, the punkahs revolved overhead and through a leafy crevasse you could gaze each dawn on a pair of young Egyptian girls as they combed each other's hair.' OSS set up its Indian headquarters at 32 Ferozshah Road, in Delhi's smartest neighbourhood, with an implausible sign on the gate proclaiming it to be the residence of 'Dr L.L. Smith, American Dentist'.

Donovan had no patience with administration, and less with accountancy, which enabled some OSS officers to steal substantial sums of cash. Major William Holohan, a forty-year-old Harvard-educated former lawyer for the Securities & Exchange Commission, was parachuted into northern Italy for OSS in September 1944 with $16,000 in operational funds and an Italian-American interpreter, Lt. Aldo Icardi. Icardi thereafter reported his chief killed in a German ambush. After the war, however, an Italian court found *in absentia* that Icardi and his sergeant, a New York factory worker of Sicilian extraction, had poisoned then shot Holohan, dumped his body in a lake and seized his priceless dollars for the benefit of a communist partisan group. The truth of that episode remains disputed, but OSS cheerfully acknowledged employment of some bloodstained characters, including accredited members of the Mafia.

Although most of Donovan's men wore uniform, there was no saluting nor dress code. Where every other wartime intelligence chief was a creature of his respective government, he was entirely his own man, possessed of a cheek founded on a personal mandate from the president. This was a source of exasperation to the British; for the rest of the war their intelligence chiefs were torn between condescension towards Donovan, whom they regarded as a charlatan, and grudging acknowledgement of his clout in Washington. Bruce Lockhart wrote after a meeting in London in June 1942: 'The colonel has aged and is not very impressive. According to Desmond Morton ... The President likes Colonel Donovan, says he must be helped down, but that he is no organiser and is a child in political matters.'

Within the United States the new service acquired instant glamour, and a reputation as the place for any well-connected warrior who wished to serve his country on more congenial terms than line duty could offer.

American infantry leadership was as much weakened as was that of the British Army by the diversion of officers and NCOs to 'private armies', of which Donovan's was the most conspicuous example. All manner of clever, upmarket Americans gravitated to OSS who had courage in plenty, but no appetite for displaying it in foxholes. Few of Donovan's recruits had military experience; most were, instead, former corporate executives. The Madison Avenue advertising agency J. Walter Thompson provided OSS's chief of planning, Cairo's executive officer and Casablanca's black-propaganda specialist. There were many rich Ivy Leaguers, including both of J.P. Morgan's sons; in Washington a DuPont handled French intelligence activities; Andrew Mellon's son Paul was London administrative officer of Special Operations, and his brother-in-law David Bruce became head of station. Only Rockefellers were lacking: Nelson, who served as the government's Coordinator of Inter-American Affairs, got into a turf row with Donovan, as a result of which the two men were no longer on speaking terms. OSS also recruited many White Russians, including 'Prince' Serge Obolensky.

Then there were the humbler personnel, many of them women, pioneers whose previous experience of the world outside their own state, never mind the US, could be described on a postage stamp. The files record thousands of clerical staff such as Cecilia Chapman Justice, twenty-four, just five feet two inches tall, from Grosse Pointe, Michigan: she had been an airline ticket agent, then spent a few months as a cryptanalyst for Air Transport Command before she joined OSS, and was posted to India. She wrote in her own submission for suitability: 'The training I have received since I have been with OSS gives me confidence that the assignment I am to have abroad will be one I can handle with assurance. Because of the knowledge I have acquired of the politics of this organisation, I am sure I can comply with them. For the time I was employed by ATC I lived completely independent of my family, and I feel sure that I shall be competent to take care of myself while overseas. I am a Protestant and I do not belong to any organisation which advocates the overthrow of the US Government.'

The archives catalogue hundreds of other such little personal odysseys. Posterity may wonder what Martha Belle Kershaw made of Ceylon, Laura Wolcott Tuckerman of Cairo, or Thelma Stone Carson of London. What was for sure was that American diplomats had no more time for Donovan's pushy people than did their British counterparts for SOE. The US ambassador in Ankara protested furiously against demands that OSS personnel should be granted diplomatic cover. His office wrote to Washington: 'He feels very *strongly* that the Embassy must *not* be used to give cover to OSS … He himself believes that the entire idea of "cover" for OSS is ridiculous.' The US ambassador in Chongqing likewise opposed accrediting Donovan's personnel unless he was granted some authority over their activities, which the general would never countenance.

The US consul in Tangier resisted a plan to send OSS's Colonel Harry Wanvig into Spanish Morocco disguised as a civilian, pointing out that he was already known to the Spanish authorities as an army officer, and that 'his presence here would serve no useful purpose and would furthermore be undesirable from security point of view'. There were almost ceaseless State Department protests against the ballooning scale of OSS offices and staffing, as a stream of its personnel of all ages and both sexes descended on every major city where the Allies had a footing. Donovan and his subordinates, however, waved aside the nay-sayers and – at least until the autumn of 1944, when his influence in the White House began to decline precipitously – got away with plenty more than murder.

Even those OSS field officers not recruited from the social elite were often exotic personalities. Prominent among them was Sterling 'Buzz' Hayden, who became one of Donovan's stars. He was born in 1916, son of an improvident New Jersey newspaper-space salesman who died when he was nine. Exposure to New England harbours bred into his roving and rackety childhood a passion for the sea which proved lifelong. At sixteen he ran away to join a sailing schooner, and thereafter served on a Banks fishing trawler before skippering an eighty-nine-foot brigantine through a hurricane to Tahiti. He fell in love with a lot of girls, and plenty of them succumbed to his rugged good looks and venturesome spirit. He spent everything he had saved to buy Kaiser Wilhelm II's old yacht, only to have it wrecked under him in a storm. In 1939 his godfather, a New York businessman, said, 'Gollys, young feller, you've had quite a time for yourself, haven't you? Don't you think it's about time you settled down and made something of yourself?'

In a fashion, so he did. His six-foot-four, 220-pound figure caught the eye of a Hollywood talent scout. In 1940 he started work at Paramount on a $600-a-month contract, and was promptly cast opposite Madeleine Carroll, the British-born Birmingham University graduate and former schoolteacher who had become the most highly paid female star in the world. They made the movie *Virginia* together, and fell in love. She was ten years older, but somebody once described the couple as 'the two most beautiful human beings in the world.' Hayden met Roosevelt at the White House before rejecting the lead in *For Whom the Bell Tolls* to join the war. He hated Hollywood, and struck up an acquaintance with Bill Donovan. In November 1941 he sailed to England, completing commando and parachute courses there before injuring himself on a jump in March 1942 and returning to America, where he married Carroll.

Hayden was refused a US Navy commission, on the grounds that he was almost uneducated. Instead he joined the Marine Corps by way of Parris Island boot camp, then transferred to OSS. He was bent upon shedding the Hollywood fame he despised, and changed his name for operational purposes to 'John Hamilton'. His wife's sister had been killed in the London Blitz; this prompted Carroll, too, to quit the film business: for the rest of the war she served with the Red Cross in Europe. 'Lt. Hamilton' became one of the small army of OSS personnel who crossed the Atlantic to play a picaresque bit-part in that biggest blockbuster melodrama of all: *The War*.

OSS London station chief William Phillips described his own mission in terms echoed by his counterparts around the world: 'My duty was to pursue Donovan's goal of a global US intelligence service, while resisting all efforts of the British Secret Information [sic] to gobble us up.' The OSS's London base on Brook Street, a few blocks from the US embassy, eventually boasted fourteen outlying branches, and grew to a strength of 2,000 people, including a stellar constellation of academics such as Walt Rostow, Crane Brinton, Chandler Morse. Most of Donovan's men were anti-colonialist, which sustained chronic tensions with the British and French. Colonel Harold Hoskins planned a 1942 expedition through Arab countries which he hoped to persuade to expel the British. Unsurprisingly, this trip was blocked in London; the Foreign Office and SOE strove, albeit without success, to exclude OSS from the entire Middle and Far East, and especially India. There was an early Donovan plot to overthrow the pro-Vichy prime minister of Tunisia, for which the colonel established a $50,000 war chest. Robert Murphy of the State Department vetoed the scheme because it must enrage Vichy and frustrate any hopes of recruiting its armed forces to the Allies. Amid the contortions of American policy towards the French after the December 1942 assassination of Admiral Darlan, a new OSS pro-Gaullist commando unit was formed under the direction of a Harvard anthropologist and Arabist impossibly named Carleton Coon.

State aborted a succession of other OSS projects which it considered likely to 'upset colonial relationships with local native populations'. Many of Donovan's men began to work on the principle that 'in intelligence, the British are just as much the enemy as the Germans'. From every corner of the globe American officers fired off a stream of complaints about lack of cooperation from their Anglo-Saxon allies. When ten OSS men perished after planes flown by inexperienced USAAF crews crashed while carrying them to Norway, it was alleged that the mishap occurred because the British refused to allow the agents to be dispatched in RAF aircraft piloted by Norwegians.

Mistrust and disdain were mutual. Hugh Trevor-Roper wrote with characteristic scorn in January 1943 about his American counterparts: 'these callow, touchy, boastful, flatulent invaders, who seem to think themselves, as politicians, a match for the case-hardened double-crossers of struggling, tortured Europe. Will they never see ... that they are only great children, pampered children of the rich, among experienced and desperate sharpers?' When a joint OSS/SOE headquarters was established in Algiers, the two nations' officers concealed information and plans from each other, and the British took lunch an hour after the Americans' 12–1 break, in order to do their most secret business in the absence of their allies. Bickham Sweet-Escott of SOE was back-handedly delighted when a distinguished Indian major with a DSO won in the desert turned up in Washington on a tour to recover from his wounds, and was refused access to a bar because of his colour. After that episode, the British officer said that he felt much less embarrassed when OSS men fulminated in his presence about 'British imperialism'.

As US chargé d'affaires in Lisbon, George Kennan had to intervene to stop the OSS fomenting a revolt against Portuguese rule in the Azores: Donovan's agents viewed President de Oliveira Salazar simply as one more fascist dictator whose removal must represent a good deed in the world, and were mortally displeased to be prevented from performing it. Meanwhile, Eisenhower's staff in North Africa quashed another project to assassinate German generals in their headquarters, though British commandos had already tried unsuccessfully to kill Rommel. In 1942 an OSS officer quizzed Adolphe Berle of the State Department about US policy towards Thailand. Berle turned up his palms: 'We haven't got any policy yet.' This vacuum in Washington, which extended to many parts of the globe, enabled Donovan's field men to invent their own party line in the name of the United States. Dr Walter Cline of the OSS Rabat station told the pasha of Marrakech, 'The French have nothing to do [in Morocco]

... except to leave it,' a remark that naturally outraged the colonial power. Donovan wrote dismissively to Foggy Bottom, saying that Cline was doing work of 'great value', and authorised him to carry on regardless.

An 11 January 1944 meeting at the Foreign Office in London discussed with alarm Donovan's assertion to journalists that he was determined to create a US secret service regardless of opposition from any quarter. Menzies said 'he assumed this reference to opposition was directed against MI6 and SOE ... In his view there was no possibility of preventing General Donovan [as he had now become] from proceeding as he wished, and the only possible course was to fight a rearguard action with a view to preventing him from causing unnecessary mischief.' SOE and MI6 agreed about almost nothing else, but were at one in their fears of the havoc that might be wreaked by OSS officers in the field, especially in the Mediterranean and South-East Asia. In July 1945, US planes dropped OSS leaflets on Tonkin, drafted by Donovan's fanatically anti-colonialist officer in Hanoi, Captain Archimedes Patti. These proclaimed to the Vietnamese on behalf of the US: 'We are shortly coming to Indo-China to free you, but we do not act like the French who are only coming to oppress you, we are your true liberators.'

One of the most extraordinary OSS missions – though of no significance whatsoever to the war effort – was that of Brooke Dolan and Ilya Tolstoy, exiled grandson of the novelist, who were dispatched from China in September 1942 to visit the ten-year-old Dalai Lama in Lhasa. The overland journey took them three months. They were greeted amiably enough by the Tibetans, who requested a radio transmitter. The State Department objected that this would upset the Chinese, who had claims on Tibet, but in November 1943 the set was duly delivered to Lhasa, without much visible impact on the war. The two Americans got back to Chongqing in July, after a seven-month odyssey, and were hastily dispatched home in case they met with an 'accident' at the hands of Chiang Kai-shek's secret police as the price of their impudence in having trafficked with the Tibetans, whom China regarded as its own subjects.

By 1944 OSS special operations personnel were operating in every theatre of war – indeed, the size and conspicuousness of some American parties rendered them especially vulnerable. A twenty-strong team parachuted into the lower Tatra mountains on 25 September 1943 to contact guerrillas in the far east of Czechoslovakia spent weeks in hiding as its supplies dwindled, then was betrayed to the Germans by a Slovakian; only two men escaped to the Russian lines. Fifteen who landed north of Anzio in March 1944 to sabotage the La Spezia–Genoa rail link were promptly captured and shot by the Germans, in accordance with Hitler's 1942 Commando Order. Col. Florimond Duke and his fellow-members of a March 1944 OSS mission to the Hungarian government were handed over to the Germans as soon as they landed, though they were fortunate enough to survive the war. In February 1945, Berlin announced that a seven-teen-strong OSS and SOE party captured in Czechoslovakia had been shot at Mauthausen concentration camp – this included Joe Morton of Associated Press, the only war correspondent to be executed in the course of the conflict.

The left-wing enthusiasms of many OSS officers led to special difficul-ties in Greece, where they threw their full support behind the communists. George Voumas, a Washington attorney in Donovan's Cairo station, charged that Churchill's officers 'were not interested in Greek liberation or even effective prosecution of the war, but in naked [imperialist] political interest'. British policy towards the fantastically complex Greek imbroglio was indeed often fumbled, but the OSS's men were naïve in supposing that the communists of EAM-ELAS would impose a benign polity if they gained control of the country. In Greece as in neighbouring Yugoslavia, all the political options before the Allies were unpalatable, but it proved mistaken to allow young, idealistic and usually ignorant OSS and SOE officers on the spot to make judgements which influenced the fate of nations. Many saw their own role in understandably romantic terms, as latter-day Lawrences, and some managed to create no less trouble than he did.

'Here, I was America,' an OSS officer who served in Yugoslavia wrote wonderingly. 'I had a message, perhaps merely words, of course, of encour-agement to a long-suffering people.' Sterling Hayden said of a year he spent working with the Yugoslavs: 'We established a tremendously close personal feeling with these people. We had enormous, I would say unlimited respect for the way they were fighting. We got quite steamed up by it. I myself was steamed up considerably by it. I had never experienced anything quite like that, and it made a tremendous impression on me.' He was first posted to run an operations base on the Italian coast at Monopoli, south of Bari, shipping arms to the partisans. This lifelong adventurer found himself directing a shuttle service of fourteen schooners, six ketches and two brig-antines, running eighty miles across the Adriatic at an average speed of seven knots.

He fell in love with the experience, and with the four hundred Yugoslavs working the vessels. He wrote in the third person that he 'found himself committed in a way he had never known before ... He had never known such men. There was a ferocity about them ... straining and sweating for hours on end, refusing to pause or accept relief until ordered to do so.' Like more than a few left-wing American and British personnel serving in the theatre, he came to idealise Tito's men, writing to a friend in the US on 22 January 1944: 'I told you in earlier letters how reluctant some of the local British are to really go all out for the Yugoslavs. My eyes are being opened to a lot of things ... I know now that my entire life before this was one endless search for pleasure. Well, maybe it isn't too late to make up for the wasted years.'

Who could blame junior officers for succumbing to romanticism, when their chief was the foremost romantic of all? Donovan flew over Japanese-held territory in a Tiger Moth biplane to visit an OSS camp in Burma, and appeared at Roosevelt and Churchill's November 1943 Cairo summit to propose a 'Unity' plan for the partition of Yugoslavia between rival factions, which FDR endorsed. The general announced an intention himself to parachute into the wilderness, to stage-manage a reconciliation between Tito and Mihailović. This plan got nowhere because none of the Yugoslavs were interested; the Americans afterwards blamed Churchill for throwing his support behind Tito. Both Western Allies misread Yugoslavia, and it is unlikely that any peaceful non-communist outcome was achievable. In May 1944 Donovan burst into London, inspected the OSS station and accused its staff of doing too much planning, not enough fighting. He exhorted them: 'Throw your plans out of the window!' Confusion, supposedly creative, was restored. Donovan was so keen for even his chairbound operatives to smell powder that that October he caused two academics from OSS's Research & Analysis division, David Colin and George Peck, to be parachuted into the Po valley with only rudimentary special forces training. They were promptly captured by the Germans, which caused an OSS officer to express somewhat heartless concern that their experience of conducting PhD oral examinations might have left them ill-prepared to resist 'unusual methods of interrogation'.

OSS personnel were famous spenders, as attested by innumerable payment dockets in the archives, together with accompanying protests from the State Department. A truck driver could earn 200,000 francs – the equivalent of $US4,000 or £1,000 – by carrying a box of documents across France to the Spanish border, with a further 50,000 francs on offer to anybody who would take such a cargo on the last leg of the journey, across the border into Spain. A characteristic signal to the US embassy in Madrid demanded: 'Please turn over to OSS representative against his receipt one million pesetas from funds to your credit under authorisation 37 ... You are authorised to pay $2000 repeat two thousand dollars to Colonel W.A. Eddy ... You are authorised to pay to Colonel Robert A. Solborg in one or several payments a total of $100,000 ... I have arranged free dollar credit for purchase by you of one million Algerian francs with further purchase later ... You are authorised to pay Colonel W.A. Eddy on behalf of the OSS the sum of $50,000 ...'

The above-mentioned Colonel William Eddy was born in Syria to missionary parents, served as an intelligence officer in World War I, then headed the English department at Cairo's American university, where he introduced Egyptians to baseball. In April 1942, in Tangier during Donovan's pre-OSS incarnation, he demanded half a million dollars in operational funds to subvert and then arm Vichy French forces in North Africa. When the chiefs of staff baulked, Eddy messaged crossly: 'If [Robert] Murphy and I cannot be trusted with a few million francs in an emergency then I should be called back and somebody who can be trusted sent. We are desperately hoping and waiting.' One of Donovan's men in Washington commented histrionically: 'The war may be won or lost by Colonel Eddy, and certainly the day of victory will be indefinitely advanced or retarded.' The chiefs of staff remained doggedly unsympathetic, and Eddy failed to get his money.

Some swaggering initiatives by Donovan's agents alarmed Allied code-breakers, among them an OSS raid on the Japanese consulate in Lisbon. Arlington Hall and Bletchley were appalled when they heard that the Americans had stolen codebooks. The last thing they wanted was action that might prompt the enemy to believe that his communications were compromised. Towards the end of 1944 Finnish intelligence approached the OSS in Stockholm, offering 1,500 pages of Soviet codes, including keys. Donovan hastened to accept, and gleefully informed the White House of the windfall. President Roosevelt, however, at the urging of Edward Stettinius, his new secretary of state, ordered that the codebooks should be handed over to the Russians without copies being made. Donovan defied the White House by photographing the books before surrendering them, but this can have given the Americans little advantage, when so many OSS staffers were secretly briefing the NKVD.

Even by the standards of the secret war, some OSS message traffic was outlandish, for instance this on 3 October 1944 from Caserta, in Italy, to

Washington: 'We learn that King Michael of Rumania has urgently requested OSS representatives in Bucharest that 4,000 rounds of .45 caliber ammunition and 3,000 of 30 millimeter carbine ammunition be sent by plane for the Royal Palace.' In China, the OSS's Alghan Lusey, a former UPI correspondent in Shanghai, requested a delivery of sawn-off shotguns for the use of Chiang Kai-shek's agents in occupied territories, whom he described as 'a swell bunch of hard-hitting, honest men, good gunmen'. Lusey was recalled to Washington in July 1942. Donovan's station head later came to believe that Tai Li, Chiang's secret police chief – the man who wanted the shotguns – was responsible for the liquidation of several of the OSS's Chinese informants.

David Bruce, an early OSS recruit and latterly a distinguished head of its intelligence branch, wrote: 'Woe to the officer who turned down a project because, on its face, it seemed ridiculous, or at least unusual.' Although South America was notionally FBI turf, Donovan plunged enthusiastically into the continent anyway. Breckinridge Long of the State Department complained that Donovan 'is into everyone's business – knows no bounds of jurisdiction – tries to fill the shoes of each agency charged with responsibility for a war activity … has had almost unlimited money and a regular army at work and agents all over the world'.

The US ambassador to Spain, Carlton Hayes, shared with his British counterpart Sir Samuel Hoare a horror of special operations and their perpetrators, which caused frequent embarrassments in the Allies' relations with the fascist dictatorship of Gen. Francisco Franco. Frank Schoonmaker, author of a successful series of European travel guides, was caught by Spanish police in the spring of 1943 passing OSS cash to a French Resistance contact, and languished for six months in a Spanish jail before being sprung. In June that year, the British naval attaché Captain Alan Hillgarth, who liaised closely with MI6, persuaded OSS's Col. Solborg of the merits of launching a joint operation to depose Franco and replace him with a military junta. London wisely vetoed this scheme, on the grounds that it was by then obvious that Franco had no intention of entering the war.

The frustration of that scheme did not deter Donovan's men from almost immediately starting another, organised from North Africa by Donald Downes in support of the anti-Franco Spanish Resistance. He dispatched OSS-trained Spanish agents to make contact with the Republicans in Malaga. The outcome was spectacularly messy: Franco's men trapped them all. Some of Downes's men were captured, along with their American weapons. The prisoners talked, and named Downes and his colleague Arthur Goldberg as their sponsors. When the State Department confronted the OSS with this considerable embarrassment, Goldberg and Donovan pleaded ignorance. The US nonetheless made a formal apology in Madrid. The OSS-sponsored Spaniards were executed. Thereafter Donovan bowed to the US ambassador's insistence that there should be no more operations against Franco.

Some of the cooler heads within Donovan's organisation recognised that its excesses were squandering resources and injuring its reputation, to scant purpose. In the summer of 1943, while the brigadier-general – Donovan's new rank – was off roaming the world, a clutch of internal reports expressed alarm about OSS's condition. One senior officer, George Platt, compiled a memorandum in August which was forwarded to Donovan. Platt wrote of 'a deterioration of morale'. Nobody except a few people closest to the general, he said, 'can put his finger on anything concrete that the organisation has accomplished'. Another senior figure, Ellery Huntington, warned of 'a dangerous lack of cohesion'. Donovan returned to Washington in October to find a six-page memorandum from a group of senior staffers, which stated brutally: 'OSS has grown too big and is engaged in too many diverse activities.' The group concluded by proposing that Donovan should relinquish executive control of the organisation, effectively becoming 'chairman of the board' while departmental chiefs ran its operations. It was plain that these views were shared by some of the ablest and best-informed of OSS's senior staffers. The critics hit a brick wall, or rather Donovan. He dismissed their proposals out of hand, and until the war ended held OSS on the course he had set for it. He himself remained a defiantly free spirit, serving as ringmaster for a host of like-minded individualists and adventurers.

OSS earned a reputation as controversial as that of SOE for promoting communist interests in occupied Europe and the Balkans. Donovan was warned that he had recruited many known 'Reds', of whom more below. He shrugged in response, 'In that kind of game, if you're afraid of wolves, you have to stay out of the forest.' Gen. Albert Wedermeyer, one of America's more ruthless proconsuls in China, wrote sourly after the war: 'We were very much in the position of being in a football contest, going out to win the game, and then with victory achieved, proposing only to return home to celebrate the victory. We were just that naïve. We did not seem to understand that in fighting wars with the Germans and the Italians in Europe, and with the Japanese in the Far East, we should strive to create

the conditions which would bring a realistic and enduring peace.' Yet it
was asking too much of most Western Allied soldiers, politicians and
secret agents to conduct operations against the Axis with an eye over their
shoulders to what would follow victory. Even Winston Churchill only
began to do so late in 1944, when the war's outcome was assured. Stalin
alone among the Allied warlords conducted policy and strategy in iron-
clad accordance with his own post-war purposes, in which his American
and British admirers strove manfully to assist him.

2 IVORY TOWERS

It is as easy to mock OSS's 'track and field stars' and their exotic operations
as it is to deride SOE's wilder activities. In Washington, however, Donovan
created something very different and more impressive. The Research &
Analysis division recruited some of the finest brains in US academe, which
between 1942 and 1945 produced an extraordinary range of reports, most
of them interesting, a few outstanding. No warring nation's intelligence
services matched the quality – and quantity – of R&A's studies. The division was headed by James Finney Baxter, president of Williams College,
and drew its analysts – some of them later Nobel Prize-winners – from
thirty-five campuses across the nation. Bickham Sweet-Escott of SOE
toured the department while visiting the US, and came home lamenting
the lack of anything comparable in London. Britain's Joint Intelligence
Staff had only a handful of men undertaking research to which R&A
committed hundreds.

The department started its life in the annexe of the Library of Congress,
then moved to a building at 23rd and E Street which eventually housed
nine hundred analysts, covering every corner of the globe, together with
clerical and support staff. The academics who dominated the payroll
included a dozen enemy aliens and forty historians, seven of them past or
future presidents of the American Historical Association. When Donovan
quizzed one recruit, Paul Sweezy, following warnings that he was a notorious Stalinist, Sweezy soothed the colonel without much difficulty, saying
that he was a mere socialist, 'more or less like [Britain's Harold] Laski and
Nye Bevan. The only thing [Donovan] was interested in was whether I was
in favour of throwing bombs and street rioting. I assured him I was not,
which seemed to satisfy him.' R&A also hired such well-known Marxists
as Franz Neumann, Herbert Marcuse – OSS's leading analyst on Germany
– and Otto Kirchheimer.

They read press reports, transcripts of enemy broadcasts monitored by the Federal Communications Commission, PoW interrogations and cables from OSS stations. In the last year of the war they also addressed likely post-war problems. R&A produced reports on subjects as diverse as rail transport on the Eastern Front, the political views of Charles de Gaulle, inflation in Burma and the guerrilla campaign in the Philippines – though SWAPO's C-in-C General Douglas MacArthur refused to allow Donovan's people to operate in his theatre.

Some R&A analysts shared the OSS's collective delusions about the potential of guerrilla action to influence grand outcomes. The Central European section asserted that internal political Resistance would contribute as much as external military force to the final collapse of Nazi Germany: 'The record [of Resistance] is a tribute to human endurance and courage, and the revelation of a great hope.' This view reflected the visionary hopes of its German-born authors, rather than representing an evidence-based political judgement. They were on stronger ground in their opposition to the Allied doctrine of unconditional surrender, which they said fostered Nazi claims that the only choices for Germany were victory or annihilation: 'What is wanted is a positive goal for Germany which will dispel this fear and encourage German soldiers and citizens alike to revolt against their Nazi leaders.'

The analysts suggested that the only credible grouping around whom to form a domestic Resistance to Hitler were the communists. They urged telling the German people that if they overthrew the Nazis their country could escape Allied invasion. When the chiefs of staff declared that the Allies should aspire to occupy Germany ahead of any internal revolution, Franz Neumann strongly dissented: 'A revolutionary movement aiming at the eradication of Nazism may be highly desirable.' In August 1944, when SHAEF issued a 'Handbook for Military Government', the content of which was much influenced by R&A, US Treasury secretary Henry Morgenthau was outraged to discover that it included proposals for reviving the German economy – he himself was the principal advocate of pastoralising the entire country. The department was more conscious than any other government body on either side of the Atlantic about what Hitler was doing to the Jews, for many of its staff were themselves Jewish. In October 1943 Leonard Kreiger noted in a widely circulated paper that a visit to Denmark by Adolf Eichmann indicated that 'the Danish pogrom is the beginning of the final campaign to rid Europe of the Jews'.

The OSS team researching the Eastern Front was handicapped by the wall of silence behind which the Soviet Union conducted its war – even copies of *Pravda* and *Izvestia* reached Washington six weeks late. So little data was provided by Moscow that it proved easier to estimate German offensive potential than Soviet defensive capabilities. Averell Harriman, US ambassador in Moscow, refused to accept OSS men on his staff, judging that he had difficulties and embarrassments enough already; only in April 1944 did a young analyst, Robert Tucker, join the embassy to monitor Soviet foreign policy. R&A nonetheless produced some prescient reports on Hitler's predicament and difficulties in Russia, the first of them in 1942. Through many months during which the military leaders of Britain and the US were chronically sceptical about Russia's prospects of survival, Donovan's men emphasised the Germans' huge supply difficulties, and questioned their likelihood of success. The study's methodology was remarkable, including the use of technical information on the efficiency of locomotives at sub-zero temperatures, and the problems of converting European rolling stock to Russian track gauge. In overcrowded Washington back offices, OSS researchers studied the daily forage requirements of the type of horses used by German infantry and computed ammunition expenditure by infantry, panzer and motorised divisions respectively, at different intensities of combat activity. They deployed meteorological data to assess the supply requirements of two hundred divisions fighting across a 1,500-mile front for 167 days. A two-hundred-page study of the Eastern Front produced in the midst of the 1942–43 Stalingrad battle correctly identified the insuperable logistical problems facing Paulus's beleaguered Sixth Army.

R&A's economic sub-division, headed by Emile Despres, at the outset made many of the same mistakes as the British, supposing Hitler's industrial base fully mobilised in 1941; throughout the year that followed, OSS continued to underestimate German production. Later in the war it did better, tearing up British intelligence estimates of German aircraft and tank production in favour of its own 'deductive productive curves'. OSS economists rightly judged that manpower, rather than oil or food, would prove the key bottleneck. Svend Larsen, an economist of Danish origin, decided that British intelligence estimates of enemy battle casualties were too high. He began to extrapolate from the death notices of officers in Germany's press – OSS in Bern forwarded fifty-seven German newspapers – and Larsen's estimates were afterwards found to have been amazingly accurate. Meanwhile R&A became fascinated by the possibilities of tabulating vehicle serial numbers to compute German production. After one of its field researchers checked every wrecked panzer on the Tunisian battlefield in 1943, the department reported – correctly – that while German production was lower than had been thought, it was still increasing. There was an in-house joke that when an R&A man was asked for a phone number he replied, 'Don't know, but I can estimate it.'

R&A's judgement was least impressive, most naïve, about the prospects for future Western relations with the Soviet Union, though this is unsurprising when so many of its leading lights were communists. Their reports adopted an almost uniformly benign view of Stalin's polity. Paul Sweezy warned that the imperialistic British might force America into an unnecessary confrontation with Stalin. The department pressed for US policy to distance itself from that of Britain. Geroid Robinson cabled the London OSS team on 20 May 1944, expressing his conviction 'that everything possible should be done to avoid a clash of interests between the British and the Americans on the one hand, and the Russians on the other', though he admitted: 'It will not be easy to develop a working compromise between an expanding and dynamic power (the Soviet Union), a developing but essentially satisfied power (the United States), and a power that shows symptoms of decline (the British Empire).' He argued that it behoved the West to err on the side of generosity in making concessions to Stalin. Given wisdom and energy in London and Washington, he said, peaceful co-existence was attainable.

Before Yalta, R&A produced a report asserting that at the end of the war 'Russia will have neither the resources nor, as far as economic factors are concerned, the inclination to embark on adventurist foreign policies which, in the opinion of Soviet leaders, might involve the USSR in a conflict or a critical armaments race with the Western Powers.' They were correct, however, in predicting that the USSR could, if it chose, pursue its post-war economic and industrial reconstruction without need for American cash, which the State Department still assumed would prove an invincible force in Washington's dealings with Moscow. R&A was right also to acknowledge the need for the US to treat the USSR as an equal in the new world.

R&A came nearer than any other organisation in the world to fulfilling the British naval officer Donald McLachlan's vision that properly conducted intelligence work should be a scholarly process. Some of its reports were fanciful, but others reflected the remarkable gifts of their authors. R&A produced material more impressive than anything issued by MI6, the Abwehr or – so far as we know – the NKVD and GRU. Unless intelligence services achieve extraordinary access to the high places of enemies or prospective enemies, as did Richard Sorge, in Hugh Trevor-Roper's words 'more can be deduced from an intelligent study of public sources than by any number of "reliable" but unintelligent "agents" listening at keyholes or swapping drinks at bars'. A significant part of R&A's achievement was its exploitation of open sources alongside, and indeed more intensively than, secret ones.

How much did this terrific concentration of brainpower influence the war effort? OSS's reports were routinely circulated across the administration. Unfortunately, however, and like all intelligence material, few of them got read by decision-makers. America's generals in the field were chronically sceptical about OSS-generated data. One of the complaints about R&A's output was that operations staffs found it hard to persuade the scholars to produce quick briefs in real time about issues that commanders were obliged to address within hours or days. The division's intellectuals preferred instead to labour for weeks or even months on 'big-picture' themes. Barry Katz, the historian of R&A, acknowledges that its activities had 'at best a limited influence on the prosecution of the war', though he is consoled by the reflection that it represented 'an indisputably brilliant episode in the history of ideas, of intellectuals, and of intelligence'.

The British intelligence machine benefited in the second half of the war from retaining a leavening of professional soldiers among its clever civilians, who imposed a minimum of discipline and emphasised operational imperatives. The uniformed contingent understood how to secure an audience for their wares among the chiefs of staff and – on the whole – contributed some common sense to the heady deliberations of the academics. OSS's R&A might have made more impact on the war had it pursued the same personnel policy, rather than leaving its eggheads to plough their furrows in isolation from the armed forces' hierarchy.

One of the NKVD's highly placed American informants, identified only as 'Z', reported in late July 1944: 'The main principle of the entire OSS is the principle of amateurism ... poorly trained ... the Cinderella of the American secret services ... The OSS owes its existence only to General Donovan's personal popularity and not to its work.' Donovan and his station heads occasionally caught the attention of Allied warlords with a remark, signal or report. But no national leader or chief of staff had time or inclination routinely to study the cerebrations of R&A, and most of OSS's output was ignored by its intended consumers. America's military leaders, like their British counterparts, focused overwhelmingly on enemy wireless intercepts as their principal source of intelligence, and it is hard to argue that they were wrong to do so.

No one individual, not even Roosevelt or Marshall, exercised the same authority over the US war effort as did Churchill in Britain, and thus there was nobody in Washington to impose overarching discipline on the intelligence community, to curb the rivalry and indeed animosity between the US Army and Navy, and tame the excesses of Donovan's organisation in a fashion that might have helped it to secure more respect. Because America is a much larger country, its intellectual community is less intimate and more diffuse. During the war years its codebreakers recorded extraordinary achievements, but they never mobilised and deployed their nation's civilian brains as effectively as Britain used its Oxbridge villages.

The mindset and conduct of OSS reflected that of America at large. Its men and women exuded a confidence unharrowed by the horrors of Blitzkrieg and of defeats such as Russia, Britain and many other wartorn nations had known. They took for granted a wealth of resources no other belligerent could match. Arthur Schlesinger, one of the many academics on the OSS payroll, made the case for its chief's defence: 'Donovan was in his eccentric way a remarkable man, a winning combination of charm, audacity, imagination, optimism and energy – above all energy. He was a disorderly administrator and an impetuous policymaker, racing from here to there with ideas and initiatives and then cheerfully moving on to something else ... He was exasperating but adorable.'

Stewart Alsop and Thomas Braden, who served as field agents, declared, 'he ran OSS like a country editor'. Most of Donovan's officers reached active theatres only when the darkest days of the conflict were over, and victory was not in doubt. Their belief that nothing was impossible was in many ways admirable. But their impatience with the cautious and sceptical British reflected a lack of understanding of what Churchill's people had been through, and of the constraints which Britain's relative poverty imposed on its war-making. Moreover, if some of the political difficulties and dilemmas identified by the British became excuses for inertia, the OSS's lunges into action were not infrequently ill-judged. The organisation's most impressive contribution was that of its economic analysts, who did better than anyone else in the Allied camp, British or American, in probing the realities and vulnerabilities of Hitler's war economy. By 1945 Donovan's men had learned a lot. Bickham Sweet-Escott of SOE wrote: '[OSS's] bitterest detractors would be forced to admit that they had become quite as good as the British at getting secret intelligence and carrying out special operations, and I personally thought they were doing it better.'

It is easy to lavish scepticism, even scorn, on the excesses of both American and British wartime special forces, OSS and SOE foremost among them. The Germans made little use of irregular units, though the Nazi leadership sometimes fantasised about them: Himmler was sufficiently impressed by Russia's partisans that in 1942 he ordered Walter Schellenberg to set up a similar organisation, codenamed 'Zeppelin', which trained and dispatched reconnaissance groups behind the Russian lines, though not to much purpose. In 1943 the SS chief instructed Schellenberg to contact a famous pre-war mountaineer, Max Schaefer, and instruct him to organise a new Himalayan expedition, to include agents who could operate inside India. In reality, however, only the Brandenburg Regiment and such buccaneers as the SS's Otto Skorzeny carried out significant special operations; the Wehrmacht remained institutionally sceptical about them.

Yet it is interesting to speculate about the consequences had the Germans done more sooner, when they had both means and opportunities. If Britain had been raided in 1940–41, large resources would have had to be diverted to domestic security: the Home Guard – 'Dad's Army' – would not have sufficed. A paratroop assault on Churchill, most plausibly at Chequers, could have paid enormous dividends. Likewise, a few U-boat-launched commando raids on the United States's shoreline could have wreaked havoc and panic, however slight the material damage they inflicted. The Allied approach to secret war may often have been wasteful and misguided, but it was more imaginative than that of the Wehrmacht, and delivered some real successes, especially during the long years before D-Day in June 1944, when only relatively small British and American ground forces were engaging the Axis. As Winston Churchill brilliantly understood, special operations sustained a sense of momentum in the war effort which was partly spurious, but morally important. The activities of SOE, OSS and the armed forces' 'private armies' consumed extravagant resources and sometimes degenerated into juvenile theatricals. But they made a propaganda contribution larger and more useful than their military one.

3 ALLEN DULLES: TALKING TO GERMANS

One American gained more personal credit from the secret war than any other. Allen Dulles, 'Mr Burns', OSS code number 110, a future chief of the

CIA, was hailed in 1945 as the nearest thing to a masterspy his nation had produced. He was a New Yorker, son of a liberal Presbyterian minister with influential family connections in Washington, who attended Princeton and travelled widely in Europe, including a diplomatic posting in Switzerland. He served with the US delegation to the 1919 Versailles peace conference, and thereafter spent some years at the State Department before taking up a career as a corporate and international-relations lawyer. In that role he met politicians including Neville Chamberlain, Ramsay MacDonald, Léon Blum – and Adolf Hitler. A prominent interventionist long before Pearl Harbor, for some months in 1941–42 he served as New York bureau chief of the COI, forerunner of OSS, located in the Rockefeller Center alongside 'Little Bill' Stephenson's British Security Coordination.

In November 1942 Donovan posted Dulles, then aged forty-nine, to become OSS's man in Bern, under diplomatic cover as special assistant to the US minister, Leland Harrison. He accepted no salary, but received $1,000 a month in expenses to sustain a modestly luxurious lifestyle. His wife Clover stayed at home, probably no great sorrow to the embryo spymaster, whose infidelities were many and various: in Switzerland he formed a close relationship with Countess Wally Toscanini, wife of an Italian politician who spent the war there, supposedly engaged on relief work.

Dulles was a smart man, whose benign, avuncular, pipe-smoking manner inspired confidence. He established himself in a flat at 23 Herrengrasse, assisted by Gero von Gaevernitz, a resident German businessman with a US passport. Until the August 1944 liberation of France, the OSS staff in Switzerland was restricted to five officers and twelve cipherenes and secretaries, because of the logistical problems of transporting Americans into the landlocked country. Beyond order-of-battle reports, a dominant theme in Dulles' cables to Washington was funding. Getting cash into Bern was complicated, and the OSS team spent plenty: by 1944, the station had forty informants on generous salaries. Dulles complained bitterly about the shortage of credible Swiss sources, claiming that he had to pay the price of being a Johnny-come-lately; between 1939 and 1942 other Allied secret services had swept up all the available local informants – indeed many, including Rudolf Rössler, multi-tasked for several nations. The OSS station chief had many American friends in common with Frederick 'Fanny' vanden Heuvel, his MI6 counterpart, but their relationship was characterised by rivalry rather than collaboration.

Dulles became an important semi-overt diplomatic figure, rather than a man of the shadows like Alexander Radó. He was a high-profile American, readily accessible to influential Germans. It was evident to all those with an eye to the future that the United States would be arbitrating this, and rumour asserted that Dulles was a secret representative of the White House. Far from him needing painstakingly to build networks of informants, everybody who knew anything – together with a generous quota of fraudsters who pretended to – beat a path to his door. He became friendly with Roger Masson, the Swiss intelligence chief, and met Hans Hausamann, founder of the Buro Ha, at the home of Zürich publisher Emil Oprecht. He held conversations with Major Max Waibel, who ran Swiss intelligence's Lucerne station, though Waibel did not disclose his 'Viking' intelligence line into Germany. An intermediary acting on behalf of Walter Schellenberg also conducted an inconclusive dalliance with the American. All the parties exchanged a good deal of information, the usual blend of truth and falsehood.

Dulles was nothing like a traditional officer of any nation's secret service; he had ambitions for his own role, far beyond mere espionage. Neal Petersen, editor of the Dulles papers, has written: 'He was not just a semi-autonomous intelligence proconsul within the OSS, but a would-be grand strategist for the West.' It is worth considering Dulles' reports in some detail, because they vividly illustrate the virtues and vices of America's most prominent overseas intelligence officer. He recognised from the outset that nobody in Washington had a coherent vision of how Europe should emerge from the war, and himself set about filling that vacuum. In December 1942 he was touting Count Carlo Sforza as Italy's most respected non-fascist politician, and urging that the Allies should feed unrest in that country rather than invade it, with the prospect of fighting a campaign 'against a united German and Italian military opposition'. To the very end of the war he argued against the Allied policy of insistence upon unconditional surrender: 'Whatever our final policy towards Germany, we should today try to convince the German people that there is hope for them in defeat, that the innocent will be protected, while the punishment of the guilty will be through legal process.'

Many of Dulles' dispatches read like the reports of a newspaper foreign correspondent, such as one of 14 December 1942: 'Italy is full of German troops, and total estimated strength is between 150 and 200 thousand … Naples: Everyone criticizes Mussolini. There is unbelievable confusion. It is important to note that people understand that bombing raids are necessary. Rome: Government offices are all going to Frosinone, Avezzano,

Chaeti, Aguila and Rieti; and hotels are being requisitioned for war purposes ... Pistoia: main connection between Bologna and Florence ... railroad bridges. Novi Ligure: two important railroad bridges. Verona: should be bombed immediately since it is an extremely important railroad center ... Modena: At the end of January a special school for flame-throwing units will graduate 780 candidates as lieutenants.'

Dulles provided an ongoing stream of reports about the German domestic opposition – 'the Breakers', as he called them – whose spokesmen visited him with a frequency that suggested remarkable carelessness about their own security. The foremost of these was the enormous Hans Gisevius, the Abwehr's Zürich agent, whom the OSS man dubbed 'Tiny'. Dulles' cook reported these visits to the German embassy, but until February 1944 Gisevius was able to cover himself in Berlin by asserting that he met the American on Canaris's instructions. Among much else, he provided a list of allegedly trustworthy anti-Nazis who might serve in a post-war German government. Dulles eagerly forwarded this to Washington, and cabled in January 1943: 'I am of the impression that this is the moment for a drive of vigor to effect a separation of the Nazis and Hitler from the balance of the German people, and hold out at the same time hope to the German people that surrender on their part does not mean that destruction will befall the individual and the state.' On 3 February he described a meeting with 'the prominent psychologist Professor CG Jung': 'his opinions on the reactions of German leaders, especially Hitler in view of his psychopathic characteristics, should not be disregarded'.

He dispatched many reports on enemy secret weapons, not all fanciful, for they had been supplied by his German visitors: robot tanks; 'offensive preparations for warfare by gas. There are now available in quantities, large-calibre gas bombs'; test flights of fleets of flying-boats designed to be crashed on London laden with explosives. On 8 August 1943 he announced that 'Gotham, and other points on our Atlantic seaboard, will be subjected to bombing by planes that are now being installed in several U-boats.' On 25 April 1944 he suggested that 'in Paris dogs are being requisitioned in large numbers', and that German and Japanese scientists were exploring biological warfare. On 2 May Dulles reported the Germans experimenting with a weapon to freeze the atmosphere to 250 degrees below zero by tubes connected to the undersides of their fighters, which would then fly over Allied bombers and precipitate icing. 'The Nazis regard the results as definitive.'

Fritz Kolbe, a minor diplomat born in 1900 who was serving as a

German Foreign Office courier, arrived in Bern during the summer of 1943 with a briefcase bulging with secret documents, which he initially offered to the British. Morbid fears about trafficking with supposedly disaffected Germans – memories of Venlo – caused MI6 to rebuff him. He turned instead to Dulles, who welcomed him with open arms and gave him a source codename as 'George Wood'. Thereafter, the courier smuggled more than 1,600 classified documents to the Americans, including information on the locations of V-1 and V-2 plants; about 'Cicero's' raids on the briefcase of the British ambassador in Ankara; genocide in Hungary; together with a mound of Japanese material. The British, and especially Claude Dansey, continued to insist that Kolbe was a double agent. In truth, he was merely a drab civil servant who attracted little notice from his masters, but was motivated to defy and betray them by a profound decency.

Dulles was unloved by MI6, whose chiefs claimed that he 'lends himself easily to any striking proposal which looks like notoriety'. Dansey included the OSS's Bern chief in a broader dismissal: 'Americans everywhere "swallow easily and are not critical"'. Both Broadway and Hans Gisevius alerted Dulles that some US codes were compromised, though the Americans were slow to heed the warning and change them. Dansey was entirely wrong in questioning the authenticity of Gisevius and Kolbe as sources, but he was justified in suggesting that Dulles was naïve, especially about the German Resistance. Though its members opposed the Nazis, most were conservatives and nationalists who cherished extraordinary delusions that in a negotiation with the Allies following the fall of the regime they might successfully uphold Germany's claims on the swollen frontiers Hitler had seized.

Dulles told Washington little about the grotesque Swiss profiteering from the conflict, notably by trafficking with the Nazis for a share of the spoils of the slaughter of Europe's Jews. He must have known something at least about this, but was probably reluctant to expose dirty linen that might threaten his amicable relationship with the Swiss authorities and the security of his base of operations – neither MI6 nor the OSS station ever incurred the sort of harassment by Roger Masson's intelligence service that fell upon the Soviet 'Lucy' Ring.

The American had plenty to say about German secret weapons, which confirmed reports reaching the Western Allies from other sources. On 24 June 1943 he sent a reasonably accurate report on German rocket-testing at Peenemünde, saying that quantity production was expected to begin in

September or October, with larger models at an experimental stage. He also mentioned long-range giant cannon, but said that he lacked the technical knowledge to evaluate their potential. On 9 September 1943 he warned that the 'rocket bomb should be taken very seriously', and in December identified 'Professor [Wernher von] Braun' as a key figure in its evolution. On 10 December he reported work on new advanced German submarines fitted with *Schnorkel* underwater breathing devices. He provided information on the German nuclear research programme, though he could not offer any clues to the only question that mattered: how close were Hitler's scientists to building a Bomb?

As for the plight of Europe's Jews, on 10 March 1943 Dulles told Washington that thus far in the year, 15,000 German Jews had been arrested. On 12 June he described Hitler's anger towards the Budapest regime for declining to hand over Hungary's Jewish minority. In general, however, neither from Bern nor from other Allied intelligence sources was there was much traffic about the Holocaust, even in the latter stages of the war. This reflected not a conspiracy of silence, but rather a pervasive consciousness that the Nazis were killing large numbers of people all over occupied Europe – Poles, Greeks, French, Russian prisoners, Yugoslavs, Italians – together with a failure to recognise that the scale and nature of the Jewish genocide transcended all other manifestations of mass murder. Allied intelligence-gatherers focused overwhelmingly on transmitting and analysing information that seemed relevant to winning the war, rather than to illuminating the plight of Hitler's victims.

On 12 June 1943, Dulles forwarded to Washington a brief from Gisevius about Hitler's personal dominance of military operations; the fact that the Stalingrad disaster derived from the Führer's acceptance of Göring's assurance that he could supply the garrison by air; that Berlin's decision to reinforce North Africa reflected defiance of his generals' advice. Dulles described Kluge and Manstein as the ablest German commanders, but said that neither they nor any of their peers had the courage to resist the Führer's will. This was useful and reasonably accurate background for US strategy-makers.

All the intelligence reaching Allied commanders before the Anglo-American landings in Sicily on 9 July 1943 and at Salerno on 3 September confirmed Hitler's intention to abandon southern Italy. On 7 July Dulles cabled from Bern, reporting his German informants' view that Berlin intended to treat the Italian people ruthlessly, but that the Wehrmacht would offer no serious resistance in the south, staking everything on a defence of the Po valley. On 29 July he went further, saying, 'We have reports that southern Italy is being vacated by Nazi troops' – the same message as was reaching the joint chiefs of staff through Ultra. They had no means of guessing that Hitler would change his mind when Kesselring, after tangling with the Anglo-American armies at Salerno, reported that he was confident of being able to contain them in the south for many months.

The dominant theme of Dulles' reporting to Washington for the last two years of the war was that if the US threw its support behind the German opposition movement, Hitler could be overthrown and a peace negotiated with a new moderate regime. On 23 August 1943 he sent an emotional message suggesting that the domestic mood in Germany had become desperate: 'There are no politically strong Generals in view, but Falkenhausen and Rundstedt are both known to be anti-Nazis. Göring is in eclipse and rumor in Berlin has it that he made an attempt to get to Sweden. Bormann and Himmler are in controversy.' Next day, he waxed even more optimistic: 'anything might happen in Germany … If we keep applying pressure [Hitler's overthrow] most likely will happen before the end of the year.' On 19 August he pleaded: 'Can we not do something during or after the Quebec [Roosevelt–Churchill summit] conference in the way of appealing to the masses in the Axis countries? … If we take concerted measures in both the psychological and military fields of warfare, we can crack Germany and end the war this year.'

For months, Washington remained sceptical about Allen Dulles' material from Fritz Kolbe, which seemed too good to be true. The OSS man was correct to emphasise that only the German army had the power to remove Hitler, and that fear of the Soviets dominated all German perceptions, reporting on 6 December 1943: 'It is possibly difficult for you in Washington to realize the extent of the real apprehension of Russia in this part of the world.' Much of his information about the tensions and power shifts within the Nazi hierarchy was accurate, for instance a November 1943 report that Himmler no longer thought the war militarily winnable, and that Speer was now economic supremo. In January 1944 he began to tell Washington about German Resistance groups' hopes of killing Hitler. For the most part, Bern OSS's political reporting about conditions in Germany was reasonably sound, but Dulles revealed a shaky grasp of military matters – scarcely surprising in a lawyer. Like many other secret warriors, he wildly overrated the capacity of guerrilla movements, and especially of the French Resistance, to make a strategic contribution to the advance of the Allied armies, though he was correct in his bitter criticisms of the Roosevelt administration for rejecting de Gaulle as the legitimate standard-bearer of Free France.

In the later war years there was surely a strand of envy in the attitude of MI6 and SOE, which were faced with the embarrassment that a host of Europeans of all political hues who were peddling information or striving for influence sought out Dulles, now the local American grandee, in preference to British agents. He cabled Washington on 30 July 1944, deploring British attempts to claim ownership of French and Italian partisans: 'Am sorry to state that the Bern Zulu-SOE Chief's general attitude is to try to monopolize relations with Resistance.' He devoted much effort to compiling and dispatching material on the Wehrmacht's order of battle, though this was far less accurate and comprehensive than was derived from Ultra. On one occasion he reported *Tirpitz* set to sail in nine days, though the giant battleship was then unfit for sea. On 29 April 1944 he urged parachuting OSS agents, arms and equipment into PoW camps, to empower their inmates to rise: 'A few such outbreaks by prisoners would have a grave psychological effect in Germany.' Here was an example of the sort of silliness that sometimes overtook OSS and SOE – implementation of such a plan would have provoked wholesale Nazi massacres of Allied PoWs, for no military advantage whatever.

On 19 February 1944, Dulles sent a long dispatch once more urging the importance of building foundations for a defeated Germany: 'The only real question today is whether constructive regenerating forces will control and direct the fate of Europe, or whether forces of disintegration and anarchy will prevail.' He urged that the Western Allies should immediately embark on a collaboration with the German Resistance to create a left-of-centre Berlin government-in-waiting that offered a credible alternative to communism. The flaw in all this was that it ignored towering realities on the ground: the Russians were storming westwards, and doing most of the hard fighting to destroy Nazism. The policy adopted by the British and American governments, of focusing on military victory followed by an occupation of Germany, was the only realistic course when any political design embracing German factions must open a disastrous breach with Moscow.

On 7 April 1944 Dulles reported that the German opposition, led by Gen. Ludwig Beck, was ready to move against Hitler. He added ten days later: 'I do not believe that any able Nazi military officials are prepared as yet to throw open the western front to us. I do believe, however, that the collapse of Germany might follow a very few months afterwards, if we could get a solid toehold in the West.' He constantly pleaded with Washington to authorise him to offer political incentives to anti-Hitler Germans – and was rebuffed. On 10 July 1944, ten days before Stauffenberg's bomb exploded, he reported by radiophone to Washington: 'A revolution [inside Germany] is not to be expected; the people are too apathetic and too closely supervised by the police. A collapse can only come as the Allied troops arrive. Further, no Badoglio development is likely here. The opposition movements are not in any position to take such a step.' Three days later, however, he belatedly warned Washington that some big German development might be looming, though 'I am not making any forecasts of success'.

In the same month he speculated about whether the passivity of the U-boat fleet indicated that it was being held in readiness to evacuate the Nazi leadership to Japan. On 9 August he claimed that Gen. Stülpnagel in Paris had attempted suicide. He reported realistically on the mood inside Germany following the failure of the Hitler bomb plot, saying on 19 August that Germans were too preoccupied with coping with the miseries and privations of daily life to become politically interested or to concern themselves with anything much beyond their personal horizons. He wrote likewise of their attitude to Allied air bombardment: 'Their reaction to the repeated raids is rather like that of an injured animal held at bay without any obvious means of escape … The Germans can see no way out except to continue the battle.'

He reported on 18 January 1945: 'Norway and Italy may well be the first theaters from which German [troop] withdrawals start.' He was an enthusiastic believer in a Nazi last-ditch 'redoubt' in southern Germany in the spring of 1945, and was less than perceptive when he reported in a radiophone dispatch on 21 March 1945: 'The Russians are treating the Germans in the occupied territory on the whole very fairly … The Germans feel that the Russians are making a success of their occupation, and there is a growing feeling that they will make a greater success than the English and Americans will of theirs.' Dulles led the US crusade for Austria and its people to be treated as Hitler's victims rather than accomplices, which helps to explain why most of Austria's many war criminals escaped indictment.

In defence of Dulles, he got no more wrong than did most intelligence officers of all nationalities. He provided a useful conduit for anti-Nazi Germans to communicate with Washington, even if the exchanges did them no practical good. Perhaps the most significant consequence of his contacts with the Resistance was to fuel Soviet paranoia about the possibility that the Western Allies would make a secret peace with Germany. The Russians' American agents in high places kept them apprised of Dulles' contacts with Germans – and of some meetings that were products of the traitors' over-fertile imaginations. On 14 June 1944, for instance, the Washington NKVD station reported to Moscow that Dulles had told the State Department of a personal visit to himself in Bern by Gen. Walter von Brauchitsch of the German general staff, offering peace terms on behalf of the Wehrmacht on condition that no Soviet troops should enter German territory. Cordell Hull, the US secretary of state, had responded to Dulles that 'the Americans are not going to conduct any negotiations with the Germans without other allies'. The same signal also described Dulles receiving overtures from prominent Germans who offered to evacuate Western Allied-occupied territories, if they were left free to continue the war against the USSR.

The record suggests that Dulles' emergence from the war as a supposed prince among spies was undeserved. He got some things right, because informed Germans approached him, as a prominent and accessible American, rather than because he performed any notable feat of agent recruitment, or displayed notable judgement as an analyst. Good diplomatic reporting often achieved as much as, or more than, spies in the enemy's camp. Pavel Sudoplatov wrote: 'Some 80 per cent of intelligence information on political matters comes not from agents but from confidential contacts.' These are more likely to be made in embassies or chancelleries than at secret rendezvous on street corners, and it is interesting to compare the tone of Dulles' reporting with some of the dispatches from Allied ambassadors in neutral capitals. On 30 November 1942, for instance, the British ambassador in Stockholm wrote to London, reporting a conversation with a well-connected Swede who had just returned from Berlin. One of Moscow's men in Whitehall, probably Donald Maclean, obligingly passed this to the NKVD, so that it was also read by Beria.

Sir Victor Mallet, the ambassador, asserted that all important German strategic decisions were now being made by Hitler, often against the strong opinion of the army's general staff. Opponents of the regime within the army 'could under certain circumstances become leader of an uprising', but Himmler and the SS were immensely strong and 'very dangerous'. In the view of Mallet's informant, a long series of major military defeats would be required before the Nazi regime became vulnerable. Intelligent

Germans were thoroughly aware that the Wehrmacht faced a crisis on the Eastern Front (at Stalingrad): 'Civilians in Berlin can imagine the horrors of the Russian massacres in Germany if Germany loses the war. It is these fears more than anything else that restrain opposition to the Nazis from active demarches ... Military and civilian leaders of the opposition fully realize that any truce between the Allies and Hitler or anyone from his clique is impossible.'

This was a sound assessment of the mood inside Germany, written by an accredited diplomat, and it is hard to imagine how any secret agent or signal decrypt could have improved upon it. Mallet's remarks closely matched those of the OSS from Bern. Allen Dulles could have functioned just as effectively had he been US ambassador – his principal source on Hungary, for instance, was no spy but instead the local Hungarian minister, Baron Bakách-Bessenyey. The OSS station chief was a clever New York lawyer with less understanding of international affairs, intelligence, war-making or Europe than he supposed. It was fortunate that the administration in Washington ignored his pleas that it should negotiate with the German opposition: there was pathetically little of this, and its political expectations were entirely at odds with reality. If the Americans had opened bilateral talks with Germans of any hue, the Russians would have become even more impossible to deal with than they were already. As it was, they whipped up a storm when without Soviet consent Dulles arranged terms for the surrender of German troops in Italy with Lt. Gen. Karl Wolff on 2 May 1945, three days before the general capitulation. Perhaps the most remarkable aspect of those negotiations was that Dulles was able to place an uncommonly courageous OSS wireless-operator – a Czech named Václav Hradecký, 'Little Wally' – in Wolff's north Italian headquarters, from which he transmitted to Bern for several weeks, and lived to tell the tale.

After completing an exhaustive study of the OSS wartime reports from Bern, Neal Petersen wrote: 'One is hard-pressed to identify a single example of a Dulles report of itself having direct impact on a top-level policy decision.' Like so much other OSS material, most of Dulles' dispatches disappeared into the maw of wartime Washington bureaucracy, without changing hearts and minds either among the US chiefs of staff or at the White House – which were, like Winston Churchill, much more receptive to their daily dose of Ultra.

12

Russia's Partisans: Terrorising Both Sides

On 3 July 1941, Stalin's first broadcast appeal to the Soviet peoples echoed Churchill's earlier clarion calls to the occupied nations of Europe: 'Conditions must be made unbearable for the enemy and his collaborators; they must be pursued and annihilated wherever they are.' What followed across vast tracts of the Soviet empire in the next three years became part of the heroic legend of Russia's war, a tale of its peoples united in resisting the barbarous invader. Contemporary evidence now available, however, tells a more complicated story. From 1943 onwards, guerrilla operations influenced the struggle on the Eastern Front more significantly than any other theatre of war. Partisans could operate more readily in Russia's forests, mountains and such wildernesses as the Pripyat marshes, than across most of Western Europe. Stalin suffered no bourgeois squeamishness about casualties, nor about collateral damage to civilians. The testimony of many wartime partisans shows that they conducted dual campaigns of terror: against the Axis, and also against millions of their own people who felt neither loyalty to Stalin's polity, nor willingness to risk all to restore it. In this, as in so much else, the struggle in the East attained an extraordinary ferocity, and the participants suffered experiences far bloodier than those of Western Europe.

In the early war years, Stalin's partisans faced the same difficulties as their counterparts elsewhere: they lacked organisation, arms, supply aircraft and wirelesses. Pavel Sudoplatov claimed in his memoirs that the NKVD had made elaborate preparations for stay-behind operations in the wake of German advances. This is false. In the 1930s, Stalin had dismantled the entire existing network of partisan bases and cadres across the country, as a threat to his own authority. Many veteran guerrilla leaders of the civil war were shot in the Purges. Throughout the later months of 1941 Sudoplatov and his comrades were obliged to strive and scrabble to improvise intelligence-gathering and partisan groups. Their early operations were shambolic, costly, futile. Almost all the men conscripted were untrained, and many were also unwilling. They were often deployed in regions – notably Ukraine – whose inhabitants had celebrated liberation by the Germans from Stalin's hated tyranny. Partisans were regarded by local people as Moscow's creatures rather than as patriots, as threats to their homes and competitors for desperately scarce food. Moreover, until Stalingrad the Germans were seen as winners, the Soviets as losers. In the Baltic states, during the months before 'Barbarossa' Beria had conducted purges in which tens of thousands of people were executed or shipped to the gulag, which explains why so many Lithuanians, Estonians and Letts garlanded the men of the Wehrmacht. While Britain's SOE made no attempt to stimulate full-scale revolt in occupied Europe between 1940 and 1944, in the desperate circumstances of embattled Russia thousands of men were thrust into operations in the immediate wake of 'Barbarossa'. Russia was paying so dreadful a forfeit that the partisans' murderous losses vanished unnoticed into the great cauldron of blood set bubbling by Hitler and Stalin.

Guerrillas can only swim in a sea of local sympathisers, to paraphrase Mao Zhedong. In Ukraine, focus of Moscow's first clumsy efforts to promote guerrilla war, there were few such people. The local Communist Party's secretary received a report from Commissar Vasily Sergienko, detailing partisan operations in the first year of war on Soviet soil. The NKVD, this stated, claimed to have established 1,874 groups, with a total strength of 29,307; it had dispatched 776 agents and couriers to work with these bands. Yet on 1 May 1942 Moscow Centre acknowledged just thirty-seven groups as operational in Ukraine, with a combined strength of 1,918 men. What had happened to the rest? Some surrendered to the Germans at the first opportunity, while others were captured or killed. Many simply faded back into local communities, abandoning their missions. There was no coordination between rival Party bodies and intelligence organisations, each of which created its own local forces. Sergienko complained in his 1942 report: 'Responsibility for infiltrating partisan groups through the enemy's front is often entrusted to people who have absolutely no experience ... Partisan groups are given contradictory instructions and tasks.'

The NKVD and GRU struggled to gain access to scarce aircraft. Matters began to improve only in May 1942, when a central staff for all partisan operations was created, followed soon afterwards by a partisan air-transport organisation, both under direct Party control. NKVD cells were attached to all the groups, most of which numbered between fifty and a hundred men. Arms and supplies remained chronically short. The worst that Gen. Franz Halder, Hitler's commander in the East, could say about partisans in 1942 was that they constituted 'rather a nuisance'. Only in two areas of north-eastern Ukraine were guerrillas then operating effectively, and even later in the war the survival of such bands demanded forest bases, where the Germans struggled to locate and destroy them.

The leader of one group, a comrade named Kovpak, dispatched to Ukrainian commissar Nikita Khrushchev on 5 May 1942 a report, countersigned by his own band's commissar, which asserted baldly that civilians 'were demoralized by the retreat of the Red Army and the German reign of terror, while certain strata of the population and a number of Ukrainian villages were happy about the arrival of occupation troops and hostile towards partisans and the Soviet regime'. On 21 August 1941 Mikhailov Kartashev, an NKVD agent in Kiev, wrote to Sudoplatov in Moscow, painting a bleak picture of the chaos of partisan operations: 'Dear Pavel Anatolievich! This letter is a private one since the issues below are not within my direct competence. I don't take part in the operation of our organs in Kiev ... All the information below has been obtained without reference to officials of the People's Commissariat, and is thus strictly truthful ... It is hard to say who is performing worst, but it is clear that the work of our organisations is less than brilliant.' Kartashev went on to describe the fate of one 150-strong group established in Kharkov, which was ordered to cross the front in Bessarabia. Its men set forth without guides or maps, dressed in civilian city clothes, carrying only pistols or rifles, and enough of those to arm just half the band. They had no orders, no radios, no passwords by which to re-enter Soviet-held territory. Like most such parties, they were never heard from again. Kartashev continued: 'information about the fate of partisan groups only becomes available if survivors make it back through the lines'. They lacked briefings about enemy deployments: 'You have probably read reports about instances where partisans attempting to cross the line were "driven back". This phrase is inherently false because there is no continuous front, only German concentrations, and of course line-crossers bump into them if they have no idea where they are.'

There was a black-comic episode of this sort when a certain Sergeant Bondarenko was guiding a party in trucks to a rendezvous where its men were to dismount and cross the enemy lines on foot. A Red Army sentry waved down the convoy to warn that only Germans lay in front – and was ignored. The partisans drove blithely on until they met a hail of fire, which killed their commander and most of the party. Thirty survivors fled back to the Soviet lines, without their weapons or vehicles. Another party walked into a German mortar barrage which accounted for several men; the survivors spent five days hiding in a swamp before trickling back to the Soviet lines.

The NKVD's Kartashev catalogued the partisans' deficiencies of arms and equipment: they had rifles for only 50 per cent of their strength, and forty rounds a man, which they were obliged to carry in their pockets or boots for lack of bandoliers and packs. Some had no ammunition at all. One group arrived from Kharkov, composed of highly motivated and well-armed Party cadres, who were promptly deployed to guard the local NKVD headquarters rather than to fight. Kartashev observed witheringly that official reports to Moscow not merely failed to admit these fiascos, but pretended that partisan operations were being successfully carried out. The institutionalised mendacity of the Soviet system was unshakeable.

A few official reports did tell the truth, however, such as one dated 21 November 1941, addressed to Nikita Khrushchev. This recorded the experiences of a battalion of the NKVD's 1st Partisan Regiment in August, when it was surprised by the Germans while resting in the village of Osintsy, near Zhitomir. A two-hour battle took place in which the battalion commander, his chief of staff and commissar were killed. Just two men survived out of a hundred, to return to the Soviet lines with the sorry tale. The report to Moscow concluded: 'We may assume that the 1st Battalion's failure was caused by the following: an unsuitable spot chosen for a halt; lack of necessary reconnaissance and poor security which allowed the Germans to approach unnoticed to within 50 metres; and, finally, possible betrayal of the unit by two partisans who had deserted on the evening before the battle (Levkovets does not know their names). Deputy People's Commissar of Internal Affairs of UkrSSR, Savchenko. 21 November 1941.'

Yet another report to Khrushchev, dated 24 November 1941 and marked 'TOP SECRET', detailed the fate of a group commanded by one Khalyava, who returned from a mission. He had set forth with twenty-four men, hand-picked as supposed keen Party activists, albeit lacking military experience. Most of them, he said, surrendered to the local German Kommandatur in Krasnoarmeisk within hours of that town's occupation, and became drivers for the Wehrmacht. He himself returned alone to the Russian lines on 18 November. A group of forty-seven men sent to Kiev, then still in Russian hands, was ordered to cross the front and make for Vinnitsa and Berdichev, headed by a commander named Rudchenko, who – unusually – was given a wireless transmitter. Within days, Kiev was overrun by the Germans. The next the NKVD heard of Rudchenko, he had been spotted surrendering to the occupiers, along with most of his men. The eyewitness, a young lieutenant who later reached Red Army positions further east, said that he warned the supposed partisan leader that he was committing treason, but was ignored. The report concluded darkly: 'Measures have been taken to verify this information. Deputy People's Commissar of Internal Affairs of UkrSSR, Savchenko. 24 November 1941.'

In the aftermath of the war, the Soviet Union identified for glorification several groups which survived for months in the catacombs beneath the Black Sea city of Odessa, which was occupied by Axis forces for 907 days: in 1969 the tunnels were opened as a museum dubbed 'The Memorial to Partisan Glory'. The official narrative described how, before Odessa fell in October 1941, local Komsomol meetings were held to plan stay-behind Resistance. Later veterans' testimony, however, told instead of an orgy of despairing drunkenness, followed by fist-fights between Moscow and Odessa NKVD men. In the long months that followed, competing secret service groups fought each other much more energetically than they engaged the Germans. One Moscow officer, Captain Vladimir Molodtsov, a former miner captured and executed by the Germans in July 1942, was later made a Hero of the Soviet Union. Following his capture, however, a rival named Lt. Kuznetsov, a member of the Odessa NKVD, disarmed and then killed all but one of Molodtsov's men, claiming that they had been plotting against him.

On 28 August Kuznetsov shot another man for stealing a piece of bread. A month later, he killed two more for taking food and 'lack of sexual discipline', whatever that meant. A month later, Kuznetsov himself – who, if not unhinged, was obviously a brute – was shot by one of his own men in an underground refuge known as 'the Mirror Factory'. Only three NKVD officers thereafter survived, and their mental condition must have been dire. Abramov, the man who had killed Kuznetsov, urged surrender. Another officer chose instead to leave the catacombs, and spent the remaining months of Odessa's occupation hiding in his wife's apartment. After the city's liberation he claimed to have killed Abramov, but that officer somehow survived. The last of the three, named Glushenko, also lived to see Odessa overrun by the Red Army, but then returned to the catacombs for some ill-defined purpose, and perished when a grenade exploded in his hands. This account is riddled with inconsistencies and unconvincing testimony. The only certainty is that the 'partisan group' accomplished nothing save to endure a subterranean ordeal that killed most of them.

The same fate befell another similar party, whose story is known only through an intelligence report to the prime minister of Romania, Hitler's ally Ion Antonescu, compiled on 18 April 1942. It was based on interrogations of captured survivors from the catacombs, and has a ring of authenticity. This Russian group, forty men nominated by the local Party hierarchy, was commanded by two captains, Frolov and Lemichik. On 10 September 1941 they were ordered to penetrate the Romanian sector of the Axis front, but were spotted and returned in disarray to Odessa, reduced to a strength of eighteen. As the enemy swept towards the city, twelve took refuge in its catacombs, which were hastily provisioned, where they were supposedly to await opportunities to carry out espionage and sabotage operations. One day in October this group, which now included two wives and was commanded by Aleksandr Soldatenko, descended into their secret refuge through an entrance at 47 Dalnitskaya Street.

It is easy to imagine the tension, uncertainties and terrors of the days and nights that followed, entombed beneath a city in the hands of the enemy. The party was heavily armed, but to what purpose? Three times in early November one partisan, Leonid Cherney, risked venturing above ground by night, in an attempt to contact a woman courier. He failed, and returned to report merely that the occupiers were everywhere. On 13 November Romanian security police, who had been warned of the party far beneath their feet, sought to penetrate the catacombs. A firefight followed in the darkness, which persuaded the Romanians that it would be easier to imprison their foes by sealing the catacombs' entrances. Thereafter, not a word was heard of Soldatenko's party until February 1942. Their experience in the interlude was among the more dreadful of the war.

Several partisans, succumbing to despair and hunger when their provisions ran out, demanded that the group should ascend into the city and surrender. This proposition was rejected out of hand by Soldatenko. A man named Byalik and his wife Zhenya, prominent among those clamouring for surrender and anyway vulnerable as non-Party members, were shot. During the days and weeks that followed, they were also eaten. Disputes and resentments persisted among the survivors. On 1 February 1942, four men successfully escaped through an imperfectly sealed exit, and were then rash enough to make for their own homes. Three were promptly denounced by neighbours and seized by the Romanians, while one made good his escape.

Odessa's occupiers now pumped gas and smoke into the catacombs to flush out the remaining partisans. This prompted a panic underground, and a new revolt in which Soldatenko and his wife Elena were shot dead. When escape proved impossible the three survivors returned to their underground lair, and subsisted for several days by eating portions of the Soldatenkos. Then, at last, all hope gone, these desperate men made their way to the surface and surrendered. A Romanian patrol ventured below and explored the partisans' refuge. They found the bones of the Byaliks, together with the half-eaten corpses of the Soldatenkos.

In the annals of Western Europe's experience of the war, the massacre of the population of the village of Oradour-sur-Glane by German troops in June 1944 holds a special place, because although thousands of French Resistants and hostages were killed by the Nazis, the extinction of an entire community was a unique occurrence. In the East, however, such things were done constantly by Hitler's forces. From the earliest days of 'Barbarossa' he decreed dreadful reprisals for any act of civilian Resistance. On 23 July 1941 he instructed his commanders that they should create such a reign of terror as would 'cause the population to lose all interest in insubordination'. On 16 September his chief of staff quantified this, decreeing a tariff of fifty to a hundred executions of hostages for every German death at the hands of partisans. The policy was enthusiastically implemented by Erich von dem Bach-Zelewski, who would achieve special notoriety for his blood-drenched 1944 suppression of the Warsaw Rising. Nazi repression was for some time successful: across two-thirds of occupied Soviet territory there was no significant partisan activity. Rear areas in the southern USSR, where the major German operations of 1942 took place, were notably tranquil: the steppes offered no refuges to guerrillas. Here, once again, experience in Russia mirrored that of France, where Resistance was strongest in the central and southern wildernesses, least strategically important to Hitler.

In Belorussia, in a month following the killing of just two Germans, the 707th Infantry Division shot 10,431 people, most of them women and children. In June and July 1942, Second Panzer Army conducted two anti-partisan sweeps, codenamed 'Birdsong' and 'Green Woodpecker', against partisans in the Bryansk area. The first operation involved 5,500 German troops and ended with claims of 3,000 partisans killed, wounded or captured. Most of these were, however, merely local civilians, and Birdsong cost the Germans fifty-eight killed and 130 wounded. Green Woodpecker fared no better. There were dead Russians in plenty, to be sure, but most partisans survived. In Army Group Centre's rear areas, covering some 90,000 square kilometres, in the first eleven months of 'Barbarossa' 8,000 alleged partisans were killed – a number far in excess of the total then operating in the region, and only explicable by assuming most victims to have been civilians – in exchange for 1,094 German fatalities up to 10 May 1943. In January 1943, AG Centre claimed to have killed an astounding total of 100,000 'bandits'. Such reports make nonsense of the Wehrmacht's denials of complicity in Nazi war crimes.

One manifestation of escalating partisan activity was reported by Maj. Gen. Nagel, inspector-general of operations for Economic Staff East, the institution responsible for plundering the occupied regions of food and livestock. During the summer of 1942 he told Berlin that it had become too dangerous to send parties into forests in Army Group Centre's sector to cut timber for railway sleepers. Moreover, local German commanders were unwilling to continue wholesale seizures of livestock, for fear of increasing partisan support in local communities. Millions who had initially acquiesced in German occupation, then become cowed by repression, had now begun to believe that only Soviet victory might deliver them from starvation and destitution. Sixteenth Army HQ reported that between May and July 1942, thirty attacks had been made on bridges and eighty-four on railways in its area, involving destruction of twenty locomotives and 130 wagons. In Army Group Centre's sector, between June and December 1942 there were 1,183 attacks on railways, an average of six a day.

The existence of the partisan bands was brutish in the extreme. Like the French *maquis*, they practised banditry to support their own existences with at least as much zeal as they fought the Germans. One day in September 1942, a group of starving men crawled into a potato field, and began frantically scrabbling in the earth. One of them, named Kovpak, heard a noise behind him and turned to see a woman gazing contemptuously down at them. She said, 'My God! My God! Here you are, big healthy guys – and reduced to stealing potatoes from us!' Many men froze, starved, were shot in clashes with rival bands or faced summary execution for some alleged breach of discipline. 'We shot Kozhedub for firing his gun twice while he was drunk, causing panic in the camp,' wrote a partisan named Popudrenko in February 1942. 'This was a good decision. In the

evening we had an amateur concert, sang to an accordion, danced, and
told funny stories ... Comrade Balabai [killed] one bastard, a forester who
was working for the Germans.' The story was the same everywhere. 'In the
morning I received a report that a former [Soviet] prisoner of war who
served in the 2nd Company had deserted,' scrawled a partisan group
leader named Balitsky on 3 August 1943. 'He was captured in the village
of Lipno ... Having little to discuss with this spy, I merely pulled out my
Mauser and ended this nobody's existence with a single shot.'

A large proportion of the Soviet fighters were mere fugitives, more than
a few of them Jews seeking a refuge from Nazi persecution, rather than
Soviet patriots committed to armed struggle against the Axis. Around half
of all partisans were local peasants, forced into service at gunpoint. Every
band lived in dread of betrayal, and collaborators revealed their locations
to the enemy as often as happened to the *maquisards* of France. Casualties
were appalling: when the Germans located and surrounded a partisan
sanctuary, it was not unusual for every man in a group to perish. But when
Moscow's will was served, it was the partisans who did the attacking.
Popudrenko recorded on 27 February 1942: 'We learned last night that
grain was being assembled for the Germans in Klyusy. We sent thirty men
who brought back more than 100 poods, the rest was distributed among
collective farmers.' A fortnight later: 'We attacked a Hungarian battalion
stationed in Ivanovka village ... First Company attacked frontally, Second
held the flank, Third and Fourth gave fire support. Results of the battle:
killed 92 Hungarians among them 4 officers, 64 policemen. Captured one
heavy machine-gun and 2 light, 15,000 cartridges, an anti-aircraft gun,
103 blankets, seven rifles, one transmitter etc. We have lost ten men killed
and seven wounded.' It is reasonable to guess that many of the Hungarian
dead were shot after being taken prisoner, the custom on both sides of
partisan war.

On 18 August 1942 Hitler issued a new Directive, No. 46, giving
'Guidelines for an intensified fight against the plague of banditry in the
East'. For the first time, this proposed carrots as well as sticks in the
management of the occupied territories: collaborationist communities
would receive enhanced rations, and be excused from forced labour. In
reality, however, this belated concession was seldom observed. And only
two months later Hitler issued a new order, stating that the Eastern partisan war must now be recognised as 'a struggle for the total extirpation of
one side or the other'. A subsequent general order of 11 November 1942
stated that 'captured bandits, unless exceptionally ... enlisted in our fight

against the bands, are to be hanged or shot'. Germany's modern Potsdam historians have written: 'The occupying power was neither willing to create the political framework for pacification nor able to enforce such a condition by military might.'

The Germans ultimately deployed a quarter of a million men for anti-partisan operations and rear-area security in the East, which represented a real achievement for Stalin, Moscow Centre and Pavel Sudoplatov, who provided the NKVD agents and wireless-operators who served with the partisans. Most of the German troops engaged in security duties were men unfit for front-line service, but they had to be armed and fed, and thus became a significant drain on Hitler's war effort. During 1943 the partisans' field strength increased from 130,000 to a quarter of a million. On 28 July Allen Dulles in Bern signalled Washington, reporting his Berlin sources saying that partisans were now making a major impact behind the Eastern Front, seriously disrupting the Wehrmacht's lines of communication. German sigint officers considered the radio discipline of the partisans better than that of Soviet regular units, probably because every group knew that its survival depended on outwitting German locators. In the autumn of 1943 a monthly average of 2,000 telephone poles and three hundred cables were cut by guerrillas behind Army Group Centre's front alone. Its headquarters introduced a special 'partisan warning' radio channel, broadcasting to all units.

Wehrmacht 'special intelligence groups' handled security and interrogation in the German rear areas, among the ugliest aspects of the anti-partisan war. A British file on some of the personalities involved, mostly based on Ultra material, included such figures as Vladimir Bedrov: 'Formerly employed by the NKVD in Leningrad. Deserted to the Germans. Employed as an interpreter and translator. Extremely brutal towards prisoners. Deserted in February 1944 and arrested in Estonia. Sent to a concentration camp in Eastern Germany for people who know too much.' Another man, Sergeant Bohme, came from Riga, had lived in Vienna, spoke fluent Russian and English, 'ran an agent network recruited from Russia PW and three or four women'. Field Police Inspector Karl Brenker was described in his British dossier as 'guilty of every conceivable crime against the Russian population. A veritable beast. Carried out executions himself. Particularly brutal towards women. Decorated with the golden anti-partisan badge.'

The NKVD's Fourth Directorate was responsible for directing what became known as 'the Railway War' because of its emphasis on hitting

German communications. 'An enemy train was blown up at 1 a.m.,' a partisan leader named Balitsky wrote in his diary for 25 August 1943. 'It consisted of thirty-eight wagons and was heading towards the front. We took part of its load and burned the rest. [Most of] the train's escort were killed and five captured, after putting up heavy resistance in which fifteen partisans were wounded.' The attack on German Eastern Front communications during the Russians' huge summer 1944 'Bagration' offensive made more impact on the main battlefront than did that of the Resistance in France in support of D-Day. The Soviets at last had the resources to orchestrate major operations behind the lines as well as against the German armies. They deployed 'strategic intelligence sections', eight to twelve strong, operating ten to sixty miles beyond the front, and were also able to sustain reasonably regular airdrops to hundreds of partisan groups. No reliable balance sheet is possible, though it seems reasonable to assume that – as in every other aspect of the war in the East – the partisan campaign cost the Russians far more people than the Germans. But in the last two years of the war they made a difference. In the words of a German general, partisans became 'formidable, well-trained units … a plague with which all rear-area headquarters, supply, transportation and signal units had to contend every day'.

Between 1941 and 1945, Sudoplatov claimed in his memoirs that the NKVD dispatched a total of 212 teams to lead guerrilla groups, and 7,316 agents and wireless-operators to work behind enemy lines. Its sabotage schools trained a thousand men for the Red Army, and another 3,500 for its own operations. He suggested that 2,222 'operational combat groups' served behind the front in the course of the war. The Soviet official history professed that partisans were responsible for killing 137,000 Germans – which must be an absurdly exaggerated figure – including 2,045 alleged collaborators and eighty-seven senior Nazi officials explicitly targeted for assassination. The Soviet Union after the war produced a roll of honour of heroes of partisan operations, led by such names as Kuznetsov, Medvedev, Prokupuk, Vaopshashov, Karasyov, Mirkovsky. Kuznetsov – even less appropriately codenamed than most wartime agents as 'Fluff' – was an NKVD man of striking blond good looks. Born in 1911, before the war he had served the Lubyanka by sharing with foreign diplomats several Bolshoi ballet stars as lovers. He had grown up in German-speaking Siberia, and thus was able to pass himself off as a Wehrmacht officer, 'Oberleutnant Paul Zibert', operating behind enemy lines. In this role he assassinated several prominent Germans. He was named a Hero of the

Soviet Union after being killed by Ukrainian nationalists while trying to cross back to the Red Army's lines in 1944.

From Stalin's perspective, the most important achievement of Russia's guerrillas was to sustain a semblance of Soviet authority in regions far behind the front, and to create a propaganda legend of national unity against the invader. In reality, the occupied areas of the Soviet Union spawned as many different responses to Hitler – a similar quotient of Resisters, a matching proportion of collaborators – as did Western Europe. The consequence was that Moscow exacted a terrible retribution from those who, following the German retreat, were deemed to have done less than their duty to the Motherland. In 1943 Beria reported that the NKVD had arrested and detained for interrogation 931,549 suspects in territories liberated by the Red Army. Of these, he said, 80,296 had been 'unmasked as spies, traitors, deserters, bandits and criminal elements'.

Many partisan groups killed more Russian people than Germans, with the deliberate purpose of making them more fearful of the wrath of Stalin than that of Hitler. A February 1942 report by the commander of the Kopenkin group, operating in Poltava *oblast*, merits quotation at length, not because it is unusual, but because there are many others like it in declassified archives, marked 'TOP SECRET':

I discovered by interviewing local [Party] activists in Ostanovki that three villagers, including the collective farm foreman, were loyal towards the Germans and betrayed our people. These three persons were arrested and taken to the forest 3–4 km from Postanovki where we shot them. At dawn on 30 October 1941, the detachment reached Khoroshki settlement, and spent the daylight hours in a school. New members of the detachment took the oath. We restocked with supplies from the collective farm's reserves, and one cart was taken to carry the machine-guns. I learned from local activists that the Germans had appointed the former local schoolteacher *starosta* [village head] in Khoroshki. We took him with us when leaving the village and shot him after driving for 3 km ... In Cherevki we arrested the newly appointed *starosta* and another man sympathetic to the Germans. We shot both.

In Bolshaya Obukhovka ... we arrested and shot two *starostas*, five persons recruited by the German intelligence, seventeen people associated with the church, and three deserters. All five persons recruited by Gestapo were 14–19 years old. According to the commander of the Mirgorod partisan detachment comrade Andreev, six locals from

Obukhovka were supporting the Germans. I sent a group to arrest these six persons, who were afterwards shot.

According to the information of comrades Ivashchenko and Andreev, a family with four sons living in Bolshaya Obukhovka were producing and distributing a religious leaflet [which stated]: 'Everyone who finds this should write ten more and give them to people. Pray for the Germans, our liberators. God has saved us from Jews and communists.' A group of six partisans were sent to [the village] led by comrade Tereshchenko. They came to the [evangelists'] house and asked them to open the door, but the occupants did not obey, instead barring the doors and windows with wooden beams. After waiting for two hours, Tereshchenko asked for permission to break down the door ... In the morning, the father and four sons were taken and shot in the forest. I have established by questioning the locals that three [Red] Army men have been living in Bolshaya Obukhovka for over a month. I arrested them with help from local partisans. Questioning them revealed that they had got married and had no intention of returning to the front. I shot these three men as deserters and traitors to their motherland.

According to the information from comrades Ivashchenko, Andreev and local activists in the village Panasovka, a former *kulak* was appointed the *starosta* there. I sent a group to shoot him and his family, as we knew that his wife, daughter and mother were active in spreading unpatriotic rumours, such as that the Soviet regime is gone forever, and that German authority is the only authentic one ... Their property was confiscated for partisan use. According to information received from local people in Olefirovka, the collective farm's agronomist, who had been appointed village chief, refused to issue grain, saying that the Soviet regime was no more, and the Germans needed it. I sent comrade Kaminyar to shoot [the man and his wife] and distribute around sixty tons of grain among the collective farmers.

This report covered three months' activity by a single group, and such campaigns of terror were taking place across the entire western Soviet Union occupied by the Germans, in competition with those of the Nazis, and likewise responsible for a host of deaths.

The NKVD sought to exercise far more rigorous control of partisan operations than did SOE or OSS, because it was conducting a struggle in what then passed for its own homeland. In one important respect, the Soviets enjoyed an advantage over the British and Americans in promoting guerrilla war. If Churchill was sometimes callous about the human cost of 'setting Europe ablaze', Stalin was unfailingly so. His indifference to losses among the fighters, and to consequences for the civilian population, rendered the partisan campaign one of the darkest manifestations of the Kremlin's commitment to 'absolute war'.

13

Islands in the Storm

1 THE ABWEHR'S IRISH JIG

Many of the nations involved in the war were riven by internal factional struggles, sometimes to the death, which persisted throughout the years in which the Allies grappled with the Axis. This was true of China, France, Italy, Greece, Yugoslavia, Burma, India, South Africa, Canada, French Indochina and the Dutch East Indies, to name only a few. The major belligerents thus found themselves striving to induce local activists to direct their fire – sometimes literally – at the other side in the global struggle, rather than at their own compatriots. This often proved more difficult than calming rival wolf packs.

Ireland occupied a marginal place in the global struggle, but both sides cherished mirror apprehensions lest it should become a haven for their foes. The Irish Free State, or Eire, had achieved a qualified independence from Britain less than twenty years before war broke out. To the chagrin of nationalists, six counties of predominantly Protestant Ulster remained part of the United Kingdom. Memories of the ugly 1916–21 struggle to expel the British remained raw. Though Eire was still in name part of the British Commonwealth, throughout the war prime minister Éamon de Valera espoused a stubborn neutrality, resisting all blandishments to join the Allied cause even when America, Ireland's warmest friend, became a belligerent. Yet while de Valera defied the wrath of Winston Churchill, on whom the Irish depended for their subsistence, he was also obliged to combat domestic foes. The rump of the so-called Irish Republican Army, made illegal in Eire in 1936, remained fanatically opposed to the island's partition, and to the settlement with Britain. IRA terrorists sustained a campaign of sabotage and murder against the British – in 1939 there were extensive bombings on the mainland – and also defied the Dublin government.

At the outbreak of war, the Germans identified Ireland as fertile soil, and the British agreed. Late in September 1939 MI6 delivered a luridly sensationalist report on conditions in Eire, claiming that 'an attempt at revolution by the IRA does not appear to be out of the question'. A German-owned hotel at Inver in Donegal became a focus of British concern, because Hitler's embassy staff sometimes stayed there – though so did British officers, including young Lt. Philip Mountbatten, RN. From Berlin's viewpoint there was little merit in intelligence-gathering, because Ireland harboured no significant military secrets, and there were only 318 German and 149 Italian residents in the whole island to provide expatriate support. The Abwehr remained nonetheless convinced that if the underground IRA could be persuaded to resume its campaign of sabotage against military targets in the British North and on the main-land, Berlin would profit. Thus, between 1939 and 1943 a procession of Abwehr emissaries strove to link arms with the terrorists against their common foe.

A pervasive strand in all Germany's Irish operations was an awesome ignorance of the country, much greater than that of the British about say, Albania. Berlin's first agent, dispatched in February 1939 before hostili-ties began, was one Oscar Pfaus, who was briefed ahead of his departure by a Celtic folklore enthusiast named Franz Fromme, who bored the agent half to death. Pfaus, having travelled to Dublin via Harwich, presented himself to the hard-drinking 'General' Eoin O'Duffy, leader of Ireland's fascist Blueshirts, spiritual allies of the Nazis. Could O'Duffy put him in touch with the IRA? Since the Blueshirts and the Republicans represented bitterly opposed interests, this suggestion outraged the 'general'. But Pfaus eventually contrived to meet the IRA Army Council, and in the best tradition of stage spies tore up a pound note and presented one half to the Republicans, so that when they sent a representative to Germany to discuss arms shipments, he might identify himself. Then Pfaus went home.

The IRA decided to pursue the German offer, and dispatched as its negotiator Jim O'Donovan, who took a boat to Hamburg accompanied by his wife. On their arrival, German customs discovered that Mrs O'Donovan had concealed about her person several cartons of cigarettes, and subjected her to a robust strip-search. The high-minded O'Donovan exploded with rage: the couple departed home in dudgeon, without any guns. During the months that followed, the Abwehr became increasingly exasperated by what it considered the irresponsible behaviour of the

IRA, which attacked English cinemas, phone kiosks and letterboxes in a fashion that contributed nothing to German victory, nor to Irish unification. In January 1940, when the Republicans staged a spectacular arms raid on the Irish army's magazine at Phoenix Park, the exasperated de Valera rounded up every IRA man his policemen could catch, and introduced internment without trial. If the prime minister hated the British, he now disliked his erstwhile fellow-freedom fighters almost as much. The Phoenix Park raid was a turning point, because it made Ireland's government explicit foes of Germany's Republican allies.

The Abwehr now dispatched a new agent, to instil some Teutonic discipline into IRA operations. Ernst Weber-Drohl was a diminutive Austrian, already over sixty, who had forged an incongruous career as a circus strongman. His sole qualification to represent Hitler was that he had fathered two children by an Irish girl. Just before he set out by U-boat for the Emerald Isle, his intended wireless-operator avowed such a violent dislike for Drohl that he refused to accompany him. In March 1940 the little strongman thus found himself alone as he paddled a dinghy through darkness and heavy surf to the shore, clutching a wireless transmitter and a bundle of money. The rubber boat capsized, the set was lost, and a bedraggled spy floundered ashore and made his way to Dublin.

There he presented himself at the house of Jim O'Donovan, who waived the memory of the Hamburg customs humiliation and became his temporary host. Drohl delivered a message addressed to the IRA Council and signed by himself, of which the most significant passage read: 'The Pfalzgraf Section very urgently requests its Irish friends and IRA members to be so good as to make considerably better efforts to carry out the [Abwehr's] S-plan ... and to be more effectual against military as opposed to civilian objectives.' The Austrian added an apology: instead of handing over to the secret army US$15,100 entrusted to him by Berlin, the amount was $600 short, because he needed cash himself. Shortly afterwards, while staying in a Dublin hotel he was arrested by the police and charged with entering Ireland illegally. In court the agent claimed that he had come to Ireland merely to seek out his children – his wife was in Nuremberg. The *Irish Times* reported: 'Weber-Drohl's lawyer said that the accused had had no evil intentions when he stepped on to Irish soil. Rather, the motives which had occasioned his course of action were extremely praiseworthy.' Although discharged after paying a £3 fine, he was almost immediately re-arrested and interned. When eventually released the Abwehr's agent stayed in Ireland, eking a living in his old circus role, having lost interest in serving the Fatherland.

The German embassy now urged Berlin that Nazi agents should have no further traffic with the IRA, which merely worsened relations with the Irish government. Yet the Abwehr's fascination with exploiting Germany's enemies' enemies as friends remained undimmed. A thirty-five-year-old political science lecturer and ardent Nazi, Dr Edmund Veesenmayer, was appointed 'Special Adviser Ireland'. The Abwehr consulted with Francis Stuart, an intellectual fanatically committed to the nationalist cause, who turned up in Berlin in the midst of a world war to lecture on Anglo-Irish literature. An IRA man named Stephen Held also arrived via Belgium in April 1940, and presented the Irish half of Oscar Pfaus's torn pound note. Held advanced an imaginative proposal that the German army should effect an amphibious landing near Derry, to occupy British Ulster, though he offered no advice about how the Royal Navy's objections to such a venture might be overcome. In the following month, IRA chief of staff Sean Russell also reached the Nazi capital, having travelled from New York via Genoa. All these men urged the Germans to seize a historic opportunity.

The Abwehr's next emissary was Hermann Görtz – the biker who had spied his way into Brixton prison back in 1936. It seemed an extraordinary choice, to dispatch to Ireland a middle-aged lawyer who had never seen the place in his life, but witnesses at the airfield from which his Heinkel III bomber set forth on the evening of 4 May 1940 were impressed by his cheerfulness and even insouciance. He had trained with No. 800 Construction Demonstration Battalion, the commando unit which later became the Brandenburg Regiment, and nurtured heroic aspirations. Görtz parachuted from the night sky without accident but landed near Ballivor, Co. Meath, seventy miles from his intended drop zone. During the descent he lost both his wireless set and the spade with which he intended to bury his parachute.

He dumped his flying suit, tore up his maps and threw the fragments in a river, then started walking south in search of Mrs Iseult Stuart, wife of the Republican literary lecturer in Berlin. He was now clad in breeches, riding boots, pullover and a beret, and also carried his World War I campaign medals, a somewhat indiscreet gesture for a secret agent. After a long, hard trek he reached Mrs Stuart's door at Laragh Castle, just west of Dublin. She summoned Jim O'Donovan, who drove to collect the visitor. Görtz wrote later: 'Then I came to Dublin where I met some pleasant people who neither knew nor wanted to know anything about me and I moved around freely.' But the spy was brought face to face with the chaotic loyalties of Ireland when he met four young Republicans who demanded the cash he had brought from Germany, and menaced him for half an hour before he was taken to the house of the IRA's Stephen Held.

On 7 May 1940, in the midst of Dublin an IRA gang sought to seize a courier carrying correspondence to Sir John Maffey, Britain's representative in Ireland. This prompted a shoot-out between the gunmen and the police, and infuriated the Irish government. Hermann Görtz vented on his hosts a passionate harangue about the irresponsibility of such conduct; it was obvious that the Irish authorities would now harry the terrorists. The German was fearful of being imprisoned and convicted as a mere spy, rather than – as he saw himself – a colour-bearer for his nation's all conquering armed forces. He bullied the IRA into mounting a search for the Luftwaffe uniform he had dumped. When they unsurprisingly failed to find this, he demanded that a tailor should be found who could make him another.

On the night of 22 May the inevitable happened: police raided the Helds' house. They missed Görtz but found his parachute, together with codebooks, information on Irish military installations, and a thick wad of currency. They arrested Stephen Held and Iseult Stuart, though the latter was swiftly released. Görtz's next movements remain uncertain. He later claimed to have escaped the police dragnet and taken refuge in the Wicklow mountains, where he suffered much from hunger and rain, but this version is disputed. All that is assured is that through the months that followed several women, impassioned Republicans, sheltered him in Dublin, under an alias as 'Mr Robinson'. He dispatched reports to his employers through seamen sailing to the Continent, none of which ever reached Berlin, and which would have done little good to the Abwehr if they had. This lonely, unhappy, cultured and frankly pitiable figure became so desperate to get home that he strove in vain to buy a boat in which to sail there.

The German ambassador in Dublin, Dr Hempel, said crossly that he assumed the Görtz saga was a British plot, designed to drag Ireland into the war on the Allied side; the Dublin government was furious that Berlin was collaborating with its terrorist enemies of the IRA. Yet still the Abwehr refused to give up. As planning advanced for Operation 'Sealion', an invasion of Britain, Berlin became desperate to deploy agents in Ireland, in case the island became strategically important. In June 1940, two more agents of Abwehr 1's Hamburg section were dispatched. Walter Simon was another remarkably elderly candidate for partisan war, fifty-eight, a German seaman who had spent the First World War in an Australian internment camp. Like Görtz, he was a veteran of an earlier unsuccessful espionage mission: in 1938, while reconnoitring British armament factories and airfields, he met some Welsh nationalists who claimed a willingness to serve Germany, and gave each £20 and a Rotterdam mailing address. In February 1939 he was arrested at Tonbridge, imprisoned, and in August summarily deported. It might be expected that this experience would have dimmed Simon's enthusiasm for secret war, but now he accepted the identity documents of Carl Anderson, a Swedish-born Australian, and set forth for Ireland. He was told to stay away from the IRA and communicate with Berlin through a code based on the first verse of Schiller's 'Das Liede von der Glocke', which he had learned by heart.

On the night of 12 June, a U-boat stole into Dingle Bay and landed Simon, who buried his wireless set and headed for Dublin. He was quickly spotted, trailed from Tralee and arrested. His possession of a large wad of cash was incriminating enough, but he knew his fate was sealed when his wireless set was also produced in court. Committed to Mountjoy prison, he was promptly accosted by a startled prisoner who exclaimed, 'Are you here too?' Simon riposted angrily, 'Idiot!' The two men were not supposed to know each other, but 'Paddy Mitchell' was Willy Preetz, the Abwehr's second agent, who had been landed separately on the same mission. The British tipped off Dublin that Simon was a known German agent, and the two men settled down for a long war behind bars.

In the autumn of 1940 Hermann Görtz found himself receiving discreet visits in his secret havens from all manner of Irishmen, prominent politicians among them, who were eager to forge links with a representative of the nation that looked set to secure mastery of Europe. The German agent implored his IRA hosts to make their peace with de Valera, though he had by now realised that statesmanship was not among their skills. He wrote bitterly: 'Nothing more than weakening intrigues and exchanges of fire with the police were achieved instead of battle with the enemy, which they had promised.' Stephen Hayes had succeeded Russell as IRA chief of staff, and Görtz rebuked Jack McNeela, his ADC: 'You know how to die for Ireland, but how to fight for it you have not the slightest idea!'

A grumpy Irish governess named Mrs Daly was persuaded in November 1940 to become a passenger on the neutral Japanese ship *Fushimi Maru*, sent from Spain to evacuate a handful of Japanese nationals from Dublin. In addition to carrying a codebook for Hermann Görtz hidden in an alarm clock and messages secreted in her underwear, she was also nominated official courier for the Irish ambassador in Madrid. Görtz eventually received Mrs Daly's messages, which revealed the Abwehr's confusion about how best to act in the winter of 1940–41, when a threat of British invasion seemed to loom over Ireland. In December, the Irish army's General Hugo MacNeill held talks with Henning Thomsen, the 'strutting Nazi' who served as counsellor at the German embassy, about such a contingency. The Blueshirts' O'Duffy was also present – a fervent hater of the British who asked that if Churchill did invade, the Germans should parachute weapons captured on the Continent to arm Irish Resistance.

Berlin offered a promise that Irish ports were safe from Luftwaffe bombs unless or until the British seized them. Görtz somehow got hold of a wireless set, and persuaded Anthony Deery, an IRA member who had a day job as a Dundalk post office radio technician, to dispatch his messages. This Deery did, until caught by the police early in 1942 and sentenced to five years' imprisonment. In the interval, Görtz's dispatches did little service to the Nazi war effort, for most merely lamented his own troubles.

Hermann Görtz was arrested on 27 November 1941, during a police raid in Dublin's Blackheath Park district, launched in search of IRA men, not German spies. The Abwehr's final bid to put agents into Ireland ended as swiftly and absurdly as all the others. On 16 December 1943 a young Irishman named John Francis O'Reilly was parachuted into Co. Clare, near Morveen. Three days later he was followed by a second man, thirty-five-year-old John Kenny, who had offered his services to the Germans after being detained in the occupied Channel Islands and interned near Brunswick. On landing in Ireland, both men were swiftly picked up by the police – O'Reilly had accepted his assignment merely to secure a passage home from the Luftwaffe. Soon after the war ended, all the Abwehr men in Athlone camp were freed, but Hermann Görtz was informed that he was to be deported to the British Zone of occupied Germany. On 23 May 1947, on receiving this news he immediately took poison in the Aliens' Registration Office at Dublin Castle. He was fifty-seven, a pathetic and in some ways sympathetic figure, tormented by self-pity and almost insanely miscast as a foreign agent of the Third Reich.

Yet if Görtz's story ended with a death, the Germans who landed in Ireland knew that whatever hardships they might suffer in Athlone camp, nobody was going to kill them. Operating in a neutral state, they enjoyed the comfortable assurance that the price of failure would be mere imprisonment, not a rendezvous with the executioner. And before laughing too loudly at the absurdity of the Abwehr's operations, it should be recalled that if Hitler had conquered Britain, Ireland would have shared its fate. Irish jokes would have stopped as assuredly as Irish neutrality would have been forfeit.

2 NO MAN'S LAND

Other neutral states which opted out of their neighbours' existential struggle provided theatres much more important than Ireland for the two sides' secret operations. In cities where lights burned brightly and a semblance of tranquillity persisted, the rival belligerents sustained their contest for mastery, but with buttoned foils. There was childish jostling for advantage: German attachés in Ankara flaunted before their British counterparts tins of Gold Flake cigarettes captured by the *Fallschirmjäger* in Crete. In Lourenço Marques, where the local British, German and Italian agents shared quarters in the Polana hotel, there were spats about which nation's radio news bulletins should be aired in the hotel lounge, resolved only when the management banned all of them.

Bern, Lisbon, Madrid, Stockholm became intelligence street markets, where agent-handlers rendezvoused with the men and women who devilled for them at mortal risk in enemy territory. In the Press Room of Stockholm's Grand hotel, British and American correspondents and spies mingled daily with Germans. Gold and cash were passed – sometimes huge sums in many currencies – stolen documents received. Local policemen gave aid to favoured clients: Portugal's security chief Agothino Lourenço, an ardent pro-Nazi and close acolyte of President Salazar, ensured that the local Abwehr received copies of every passenger list for BOAC's Clipper flights to England. The Spanish until 1944 indulged a huge German espionage operation. A search at British Bermuda of two Spanish liners, the *Cabo de Hornos* and *Cabo de Buena Esperanza*, homebound from the US, revealed them to be carrying Axis agents with dispatches written in secret ink.

The jungle of allegiances became especially intricate in Afghanistan, where almost every senior military and political figure was in the pay of one belligerent or another, and often of several. Axis intelligence chiefs convinced themselves that Indian nationalism was the product of their subtle machinations – though in truth, of course, it derived entirely from domestic sentiment. Bhagat Ram Gumassat was the brother of a nationalist hanged by the British for murdering the governor of the Punjab. He became a frequent guest at the German embassy in Kabul, where he helped to arrange the journey to Berlin of his leader, Subhas Chandra Bose. (The Russians, obscurely, convinced themselves that even when Bose later recruited an 'Indian National Army' to fight against the British, he was in the pay of MI6. In the NKVD's words: 'He maintained personal contacts with Hitler which allowed British secret services to be informed of the Germans' plans with regard to India and the Middle East.') Gumassat arrived one morning at the Soviet embassy in Kabul to explain that, though the Germans supposed him to be their man, he wished instead to serve Moscow. Centre took him on its books as agent 'Rom'. In February 1942 the Abwehr gave him some weapons and a handsome sum of cash, to promote sabotage in India. In a final dizzying twist, Rom gave most of the money to the USSR's Defence Fund.

In every neutral capital, intelligence officers puzzled over the perennial enigma of their trade: which side was this or that source really serving? Often the answer was both or neither, merely their own pockets. In Istanbul, an Armenian Turkish informer named Shamli received 650 Turkish pounds a month from the Japanese, 350 from the Germans, the same again from the Hungarians and a similar sum from Europa Press, a news organisation. A large Italian colony in the same city gossiped in the Casa d'Italia, the former Savoyard embassy now a social centre. Rome's intelligence operations were controlled by its military attaché, Lt. Col. Stefano Zavatarri, whom nobody held in much regard. A Turkish secret policeman said contemptuously: 'The Italians are Hitler's "*petits chiens*" – "lapdogs" – they make use of the lowest type of agent – mongrel Greeks, Armenians, moslems, Jews from the slums. The Turks get whatever they want from this type of agent and then, when they deem the time propitious, lock him up.' The Italians did no better in Rio de Janeiro, where in October 1941 they persuaded Edmond di Robilant, a senior executive of the Lati airline, to start a secret shipping-movement monitoring service. He was given a wireless and $2,600, some of which he used to rent a rabbit farm in Jacarepaguá from which to transmit. The fact that he failed to provide a single report did not spare him from a fourteen-year sentence for espionage after Brazilian police arrested him in September 1942.

No.	Name and Address	Nationality	Birthplace and Date	Occupation
41	DILLINGSHAUSEN, Nicolaus Eduard von Rio de Janeiro.	Esthonian	Katentach, 1904	Engineer

Nicolaus Eduard von Dillingshausen.

Arrived in Brazil from Germany before the war as representative of Stahl-Union. In 1941, by arrangement with Stahl-Union, he became Managing Director of Cia Ferro e Carvão. DILLINGSHAUSEN allowed Schlegel's transmitter to be transferred to his fazenda in Minas, for which participation in Axis espionage activities he was tried on 19.11.1942 and sentenced to 8 years imprisonment.

| 42 | DIAS, Jose Ferreira, (Alias "Jose da Burra") Rio de Janeiro. | Portuguese | Santo Tirso, Portugal, 1888 | Dock Checker. |

Employee of Hermann Stoltz in charge of stevedores. Made regular trips around Guanabara Bay in the Company's launch "Hansa" listing Allied ships which were photographed by Walter Augustin, who accompanied him. Tried on 6.10.1943 and sentenced to 20 years imprisonment. Retrial 29.10.1943, when sentence was reduced to 7 years. A further trial of the Hermann Stoltz group is due to take place shortly.

Suspected enemy agents operating in Brazil, from SIS's files

SS Sturmbannführer Hans Eggen travelled regularly to Switzerland to collect information, notably from two businessmen, Paul Holzach and Paul Meyer-Schwertenbach. Each, however, briefed Swiss intelligence about the meetings, and nobody was confident about their allegiance, even after OSS's Allen Dulles received reports based on Ultra decrypts specifying the information they had given to Berlin. Meanwhile in Stockholm

Col. Makoto Onodera, the Japanese military attaché, who was esteemed in Tokyo, relied heavily on information from a Polish officer named Peter Ivanov – who also reported to the Poles in London.

Foreigners arriving in Portugal's capital from the battered and dark-ened cities of Europe were enthralled by the jangling white trams, café orchestras, flowers everywhere. Malcolm Muggeridge wrote: 'Lisbon, with all its lights, seemed after two years of blackout like a celestial vision … For the first day or so I just wandered about the streets, marvelling at the shops, the restaurants with their interminable menus, the smart women and cafés sprawling over the pavements … By night the cabarets, the dancing lights, the bursts of jazz music coming through half opened doors – Pleasure stalking the streets, with many trailing it.' German oper-ations in Lisbon were based on their five-storey consulate, most of it occu-pied by the Abwehr and SD, though MI5 also held a list of 135 local addresses used by their staff, often for private purposes. In the spring of 1942 the Abwehr's Major Brede, a Luftwaffe officer unwillingly posted into intelligence, informed Canaris that his Lisbon station was corrupt from top to bottom. The admiral dismissed the charge out of hand, but of course it was true.

Most meetings and transactions on neutral turf were conducted discreetly and uneventfully, because it suited everybody to preserve the tranquillity of the international brokerage houses. In September 1940 the MI6 officer 'Biffy' Dunderdale used Lisbon's San Geronimo church as a rendezvous to deliver a wireless set and codes to a French intelligence man who bore them back to Vichy, from which some of the Deuxième Bureau's men, prominent among them the French codebreaking chief Gustave Bertrand, sustained contact with London until November 1942. He then went on the run until he was extracted from the Massif Central by an RAF aircraft in June 1944.

Amid all the indulgent wining and dining in neutral capitals, however, at intervals there were dramas and spasms of violence when deals went wrong, suspected traitors were silenced, or the local authorities checked spies' perceived excesses. On 20 April 1940 MI6's man in Stockholm was arrested and charged with seeking to sabotage Swedish iron ore exports to Germany. This provoked one among many explosions from the British ambassador, Sir Victor Mallet, who wrote to London: 'I do not want you to think that I am blind to the fact that it may sometimes be necessary to employ methods of this kind when we are waging a war against an enemy who hits persistently below the belt. But my complaints are, firstly, that our sleuths seem to be thoroughly bad at their job: so far they have achieved little in Sweden beyond putting me and themselves in an awkward position. Secondly, I am inclined to doubt whether the game is worth the candle in a country where not only are the police and the military very much on the alert ... but where a policy of mutual confidence has shown itself repeatedly to be the one which pays best.' Broadway's man in Stockholm received an eight-year jail sentence, its severity reflecting the perceived might of Germany and weakness of Britain in the summer of 1940.

Stalin demanded the deaths of foreign enemies even more whimsically than did Hitler. When the Soviet warlord heard that the former German chancellor Franz von Papen, now serving as Hitler's ambassador to neutral Turkey, had held a meeting with the Pope, and was being touted as a possible head of government if the Nazis could be ousted, he was so angry that he ordered von Papen killed. An NKVD attempt took place in Ankara on 24 February 1942 which failed when Moscow's Bulgarian assassin blew himself up with his own bomb, leaving von Papen only slightly injured. Meanwhile the Kremlin convinced itself that Argentina, home to a quarter of a million German-speakers, was a major Nazi base, and on Stalin's personal orders the NKVD burned down the German bookshop in Buenos Aires and arranged scores of other incendiary attacks on enemy property. Charges were planted in warehouses holding goods bound for Hitler's empire, and aboard ships that carried them. The FBI and OSS shared Russian paranoia about Argentina, and were disgusted by its government's interpretation of neutrality, whereby when a given number of alleged Nazi agents were arrested and jailed, the same number of Allied sympathisers was also rounded up. Similar even-handedness was displayed over releases: when Argentina's military government belatedly broke off relations with Germany in January 1944, 116 known or suspected Axis agents were arrested. Most, however, were soon set free, and in the FBI's bitter words 'are undoubtedly once again active on behalf of the Reich'.

The Western Allied secret services seldom murdered anyone; assassination was seen as a dangerous game to start, as was confirmed by the reprisals following the 1942 killing of Reinhard Heydrich in Czechoslovakia. In 1944 MI6 considered, then rejected, a scheme for targeted killings of Abwehr personnel in France. Bill Bentinck agreed, saying that while he was not squeamish, this seemed 'the type of bright idea which in the end produces a good deal of trouble and does little good'. An episode in Spain became one of MI6's uglier legends. Paul Claire was a French naval officer employed to help run agents into France by sea. In July 1941 the British embassy in Madrid reported in acute alarm that Claire had visited the Vichy French naval attaché, confessed his secret war role, and demanded help to escape into France. What was to be done? If he crossed the frontier, he would be free to tell the Germans whatever he chose. Alan Hillgarth, the buccaneering naval attaché, was given a dramatic mandate by Broadway: 'liquidate Claire' or seize a member of his family as a hostage to secure his silence.

At 1 a.m. on 25 July, MI6 officer Hamilton Stokes reported that he and Hillgarth had successfully lured Claire to the British embassy and 'drugged him into unconsciousness'. The pair then set out by car for Gibraltar with Claire prostrate on the back seat. 'C' drafted a personal signal to the Rock, ordering that the traitor should be seized on arrival, charged with treason and held incommunicado. This order became redundant, however, when MI6's Morocco representative, who chanced to be in Gibraltar, signalled: 'Consignment arrived ... completely destroyed ... owing to over-attention in transit ... Damage regretted but I submit it is for best.' A later report explained that Claire had suddenly recovered consciousness while the car passed through a village in Andalusia, and started shrieking at passers-by for help. His captors silenced him by a crack over the head with a revolver which proved fatal.

Sir Samuel Hoare, the Madrid ambassador, was furious about the potential scandal. Menzies admitted that Claire should never have been posted to Spain, and there was indeed embarrassing fallout. Vichy French diplomats in Madrid protested to the Spanish Foreign Ministry, and on 12 August Radio France broadcast a more or less accurate report of the affair, describing how Claire's captors had silenced local villagers who heard his screams by saying, 'Don't get upset, it's only a member of the embassy gone mad and we are taking him to a Sanatorium.' On 14 August the London *Daily Telegraph* carried a mocking story headed 'Nazis Invent a Kidnapping'. As is often the case with such sagas, the report seemed so fantastic, and Berlin so chronically mendacious, that few readers at home or abroad gave it credence. In July 1942 Commander Ian Fleming of naval intelligence informed the Red Cross that Claire was 'missing believed drowned' en route to Britain on the SS *Empire Hurst*, which had been sunk by enemy aircraft on 11 August 1941, a fortnight after the Frenchman's actual death. MI6 felt obliged to pay Claire's widow a pension to sustain this fiction, 'however repugnant it may be to reward the dependants of a traitor'.

Stockholm was a key observation post for every intelligence service, though in the early war years British ship-watching operations were hampered by some strongly pro-Nazi Swedish naval officers. The Norwegians maintained an intelligence mission led by Col. Rosher Lund, which did useful work among its fellow-Scandinavians. The local MI6 station generated seven hundred reports a month, mostly fragments of information about German forces in the region, collected by travelling businessmen. Among the many charlatans who offered information was a Russian émigré who, late in 1943, offered MI6 a source in the Japanese legation, together with an economist in Berlin who could provide gossip from Göring's housekeeper. More profitable was a Dane codenamed 'Elgar' who, for more than a year starting in December 1942, delivered sheaves of material about Nazi industry, including some V-weapon intelligence. On one occasion in the autumn of 1943, 'Elgar' arrived in Stockholm with a consignment of industrial acid brought from Germany, in which were hidden glass bottles containing three hundred filmed reports. In January 1944 'Elgar' was caught by the Gestapo and told everything he knew about his MI6 contacts in Stockholm. For good measure, he threw in some fantasies about British spy groups in Berlin, Hamburg, Bonn, Königsberg and Vienna. These revelations may have saved the Dane's neck, since he survived the war in German captivity.

The NKVD's Colonel Boris Rybkin, under cover as embassy first secretary, played a key role in Soviet covert operations in Stockholm, many of which were concerned with securing supplies of commodities. A popular Swedish actor, Karl Earhardt, became an intermediary for purchasing high-tensile steel for aircraft construction. The Wallenberg family, which controlled the Enskilda Bank, profited handsomely from exchanging Russian platinum for scarce industrial metals. Rybkin's wife Zoya, his fellow-NKVD officer, described how one day she saw several ingots on her husband's desk. 'Tin?' she asked curiously. 'Try lifting one,' said the colonel, and she found herself barely able to do so. Nonetheless, whatever the successes of the NKVD's Stockholm as a commercial conduit, the modern official historians of Soviet intelligence frankly admit that it failed to establish networks in neighbouring Scandinavian countries, and especially in its attempts to explore German nuclear research, heavy water production in Norway and suchlike. The principal intelligence value of Sweden to the Russians, as to all the Allies, was as a window on Germany.

Malcolm Muggeridge, MI6's man in Portuguese Mozambique, lodged at the Polana hotel in Lourenço Marques alongside Dr Leopold Werz, the

German vice-consul and Abwehr representative – 'youthful, blond, pink and earnest'. Werz had escaped from internment in South Africa. His history was well known, because lurid articles about his Nazi intelligence connections had appeared in newspapers on both sides of the Atlantic. Also living at the Polana was Mussolini's standard-bearer, an Italian named Campini who strutted in emulation of his Duce and even likewise affected a cloak. Much of Campini's traffic was intercepted at Bletchley, for instance a signal of 13 January 1943, reporting: 'A convoy of ten American ships with troops, war and aviation material left Capetown on 11/1 for? Sydney.' In the weeks that followed, Campini also wirelessed: '6 Loaded tankers from Persian Gulf reached Durban on 11/1'; 'The English have raised the salaries of sailors to £27 a month'; '28.1.43 a large American convoy bound for Australia passed through Capetown'; '4 tankers have left Durban for Persian Gulf.' On 29 March 1943 an MI5 officer noted on these intercepts: 'Assume this material comes from LEO. Sending same stuff as Werz. If LEO is Doctor WERZ in Lourenco Marques, he would seem an admirable creature to have stuff planted on him, as his little items, which so far seem to be wholly inaccurate, reach the three Axis capitals in a matter of days.'

Muggeridge enjoyed access to some facilities denied to his Axis rivals, such as summaries of their outgoing material, forwarded by Kim Philby. The embryo spy learned his trade by experience: when he first attempted to bribe a local police inspector, the man spurned his largesse with contempt, saying that the Germans paid three times as much, the Japanese and Italians even more. The most interesting revelation to come Muggeridge's way during his early months was that Dr Werz went to bed in a hairnet. More serious tasks included the kidnapping, and transfer to British-administered Swaziland, of an Italian-paid ship-watcher, who was reporting Allied convoy movements. The MI6 agent's most exciting assignment was to organise the hijacking of a Greek merchant ship, whose captain was discovered by Bletchley to be planning a rendezvous with a U-boat in the Mozambique channel. The arrangements for this coup were made in Marie's Place, a local brothel. Members of the crew, suborned by large bribes, duly seized their captain and sailed the ship to Durban.

Muggeridge formed an acquaintance with a glamorous enemy agent, the half-estranged wife of a local German, and with Johann, her lover, who had worked for Himmler and reminisced entertainingly about him. The MI6 man also screened a group of Polish Jews whom the Japanese had released from internment, and who were thereafter dispatched to British Tanganyika. These small encounters and events were the highlights of a two-year sojourn in Lourenço Marques, though like all agents he dispatched copious reports, dominated by trivia. In one sense, and as the cynical spy himself declared, his activities were fatuous. But in the midst of a world at war, it was indispensable for every nation to be represented in such places as Mozambique, if only to ensure that the other side was not left free to make mischief there.

Neighbouring South Africa was a hotbed of Nazi sympathisers, eager to assist the Reich. Paul Trompke, the German consul-general in Lourenço Marques, a portly fifty-year-old, ran an Afrikaner agent network out of Mozambique. One of these was Sydney Robey Leibbrandt, a former South African heavyweight boxing champion who spent three years in Germany, joined the Wehrmacht and was trained as a paratrooper and saboteur by the Brandenburg Regiment before returning home secretly in June 1941, equipped with a wireless set and ardent Nazi convictions, in a schooner captained by the astonishing Heinrich Garbers. Leibbrandt found friends and sympathisers happy to hide him, but few who wished to join a revolt. On Christmas Eve 1942 he was arrested while driving between Johannesburg and Pretoria, and sentenced to death by a court to which he testified only by giving a Nazi salute.

Recognising the vulnerability of Afrikaner opinion, prime minister Jan Smuts commuted the sentence on this national sporting hero. Likewise, when Malcolm Muggeridge tried to get Johannesburg police to pick up a courier driving to the city carrying messages from the Lourenço Marques Abwehr station, he was crisply informed that there was not an Afrikaner homestead in the Transvaal which would not be proud to feed Berlin's man and speed him on his way. Bletchley intercepted a steady stream of wireless messages from Afrikaner pro-Nazis, which prompted occasional round-ups, such as one in July 1942 which resulted in ten arrests and the discovery of some weapons and dynamite intended to be used for sabotage in Durban. But the signal traffic made it plain that most enemy sympathisers were content to await a German victory rather than precipitate an immediate uprising. Two coded messages were found in a pro-Nazi house in East London. The first read: 'Everything alright work somewhat sluggish people also poor ... not much sabotage here in East London.' The second wailed: 'It is damned hopeless to work alone.' It was fortunate for the Allies that the Afrikaners lacked both access to information of value to Hitler and scope for raising much mayhem.

Switzerland, at the hub of Europe between Germany, France and Italy, was the most important of all intelligence junctions, a teeming souk of spies, refugees, diplomats and crooks of all nationalities. In a single morning, a man might visit the Bern offices of MI6, OSS, the Abwehr and SD, all within a few hundred yards of each other. The city played host to many exiled politicians, some of them prominent and well connected in Germany, Austria, France. Secret wireless communications enabled the British, Americans and Russians to transmit a mass of information and fabrication derived from sources inside Germany. The Nazis likewise sought to use the country as a window on the world. In Bern, the Abwehr picked up information from Professor Keller, head of the Swiss commercial delegation to London; from the manager of the Bank of International Settlements; and from a few seamen home on leave. One agent codenamed 'Ober' brought back from Gibraltar details of football matches being played between British unit teams, which supposedly contributed to order-of-battle intelligence. The Germans' most valued agent was 'Jakob', otherwise Walter Bosshard of Swiss intelligence. The Abwehr claimed in all to have a thousand informants in Switzerland, while it had its own Gestapo branch office, 'Bureau F', attached to the Bern embassy.

The local espionage industry, which involved representatives of the Chinese, Poles and Czechs as well as the major belligerents, posed a constant dilemma for the Bern government about how far to indulge it. Swiss intelligence had been headed since 1937 by the energetic Lt. Col. Roger Masson. František Moravec held Masson in high respect, not least because the Swiss never troubled the Czech intelligence cell in Zürich. The colonel's responsibility was to preserve Switzerland's independence by ensuring that no belligerent, above all neighbouring Germany, felt sufficiently threatened or provoked to bomb or occupy the cantons. Among the nation's population of six million, a small but vociferous minority lobbied and demonstrated for the privilege of incorporation in the Third Reich. Bankers and industrialists made large profits by exporting commodities to Germany, providing financial services for the Nazi leadership collectively and severally, and exploiting the murder of rich Jews. Yet most Swiss, as democrats, preferred that the Allies should win the war. The Germans knew this: following their 1940 occupation of France, they laid hands on documents which revealed discussions between Bern and Paris about joint resistance in the event of a German invasion of Switzerland.

Masson intervened against foreign agents and made arrests only when a hubbub among the spies of one nation or another became too conspicuous to be ignored. He also strove to prevent Swiss citizens from causing embarrassment by taking sides. In the course of the war, 1,389 people were arrested in Switzerland for betraying secrets. Military courts passed 478 sentences, 283 on Swiss nationals and 195 on foreigners. Life was by no means always tranquil for the local security forces. GRU operator Alexander Foote reported consternation in the international espionage community when a Swiss policeman was blown up by an infernal machine he chanced upon, and attempted to defuse. The Englishman wrote: 'We never knew whose bomb it was.'

In most capitals, diplomats were better informed than any spy. The German ambassador in Lisbon, Baron Oswald von Hoyningen-Huene, was sharp, energetic and well liked; he was on close terms with the intimates of Portuguese dictator António Salazar, and ran a special unit for purchasing foreign newspapers, which every warring nation mined as intelligence sources. MI5 became concerned about sensitive material being passed to Madrid – and thence to Berlin – by the Duke of Alba, the Spanish ambassador in London, who was caressed in British aristocratic circles as an impeccably mannered grandee. His acquaintances, including such members of the government as Sir John Anderson, were content to overlook Alba's role as the representative of Franco's murderous tyranny: his dispatches – secretly intercepted and read by Anthony Blunt – revealed him as beneficiary of more than a few well-sourced indiscretions. Guy Liddell wrote: 'Probably a good deal of information goes west over the second glass of port.' Alba, like many other diplomats around the world, almost certainly provided more reliable intelligence than his nation's secret agents.

14

A Little Help from Their Friends

1 'IT STINKS, BUT SOMEBODY HAS TO DO IT'

Guy Liddell of MI5 wrote in June 1943, following the discovery of a communist cell in the Air Ministry: 'Unfortunately the law is somewhat inadequate in the case of a man who is spying on behalf of an ally.' The principal link in the ring, International Brigade veteran Douglas Springhall, was attempting to pass to the Russians details of 'Window', Bomber Command's top secret – and then still unused – radar baffler. Springhall eventually served four and a half years of a seven-year prison sentence. In the course of MI5's investigation, it was discovered that he was also in contact with an MI6 officer, Ray Milne, who was promptly sacked, and with Captain Desmond Uren of SOE's Hungarian section, who received a seven-year prison sentence. Liddell wrote: 'Penetration of the services by the Communist Party is becoming rather serious.'

The Second World War was never a simple two-sided contest between the Allies and the Axis, conveniently definable as the causes of Good and Evil. All manner of forces were in play. Currents swirled ceaselessly within societies, as supporters of left and right, of imperialism and anti-imperialism, or of rival factional interests, vied for primacy in the post-war world. Churchill created the necessary rhetorical myth of the 'Grand Alliance', a noble partnership of Britain, Russia and the United States. Yet the three Powers cherished entirely different visions of the new universe they wished to emerge from victory. Stalin was the most clear-sighted warlord: his accommodation with Roosevelt and Churchill to secure the destruction of Hitler did not abate by a jot or tittle his desire thereafter to pull down the edifice of bourgeois capitalism about their heads. Whereas neither the British nor the Americans spied on the Soviet Union during the war years, Stalin's agents conducted hugely ambitious espionage operations against the democracies. Heedless of Nazi interruptions, the Kremlin never allowed the Revolution to sleep.

It was hard for Western counter-intelligence services to assess the risk posed by left-wing sympathisers in the tumultuous political climate of the mid-twentieth century. There was mockery then, and has been more since, about MI5 suspicions focused upon such communist journalists as Claud Cockburn. Paranoia is an occupational hazard of intelligence officers: Lord Cherwell's office once showed R.V. Jones a list of British scientists and engineers whose loyalty was considered doubtful. Among thirty-odd names, Jones saw several whom it was ridiculous to mistrust, foremost among them that of Barnes Wallis, creator of the RAF's dambusting mines. It transpired that a security officer had compiled most of the list from his own fanciful imagination.

Yet hundreds of impeccably middle-class British and American men and women – including Ivor Montagu, brother of Ewen, the naval officer who ran the 'Mincemeat' deception – did indeed betray their country to the Soviet Union, while a handful of British fascist sympathisers, and many more European ones, lent their services to the Nazis. MI5 initially recommended rejecting the art historian Anthony Blunt for employment in military intelligence, because he had visited Russia and once offered a contribution to a leftist magazine. Posterity would deride the use of such criteria to cast doubt on a man's trustworthiness, had not Blunt been later exposed as a traitor. Noel Annan, an academic who spent the war in the secret world, wrote about the recruitment of such figures as Kim Philby and Guy Burgess: 'The intelligence services were staffed in peacetime with men who regarded Stalin as the first enemy, and Hitler a disagreeable fellow but a potential ally; [civilised people] rejoiced to see intelligent men of the left being recruited to redress the balance.'

It was hard to balance the rival claims of personal freedom and national security in the midst of a war. MI5 had achieved notable successes against Soviet spy rings in Britain during the 1920s and 1930s. Its officers displayed imagination, indeed brilliance, in handling and 'turning' Nazi spies. The security service nonetheless failed to identify the most important of the British communist traitors who penetrated Whitehall and the secret community. Anthony Blunt, by then serving in MI5, told his NKVD handler that he found it personally reassuring to discover that the pre-war Soviet informant Captain John King was exposed only when a defector denounced him.

From June 1941 until 1945 the Western Allied governments, and espe-cially the British, were cautious about how much they told the Russians, above all because they feared leakage of the Ultra secret. They constantly forwarded operational information that might assist the Red Army, but sourced it to non-existent Allied agents in Germany. Even on those terms, the traffic made Broadway uneasy, partly because it went exclusively one way. In the first weeks of 'Barbarossa', Bletchley intercepted an order directing Fourth Panzer Army to support the encirclement of Smolensk, while the Luftwaffe bombed rail links behind the Red Army's positions. On the evening of 15 July 1941 Churchill, after reading this decrypt, scrib-bled below the text in his red ink: 'Surely it is right to give them warning of this. Please report before action.'

Stewart Menzies took strong exception, minuting the prime minister: 'I am of the opinion that the source [Broadway's term for Ultra] would definitely be imperilled if this information was passed to Moscow in its present form, as it would be impossible for any agent to have secured such information regarding operations for the 16th July. I have, however, arranged with the War Office for the gist to be incorporated with other material.' Menzies added: 'I would point out that General [Mason-] MacFarlane [British military attaché in Moscow] was instructed to inform the Russians that we possess a well-placed source in Berlin who has occa-sional access to operational plans and documents. This explanation has been accepted by the Russians. I have, however, refused to furnish them with detailed [unit] identifications, which might well arouse their suspi-cions as to the real origin of the information.'

Such precautions were confounded by the fact that the NKVD and GRU were receiving a steady stream of documents and Ultra intercepts from highly placed British informants. Among the most notable of these, John Cairncross worked early in the war as private secretary to Lord Hankey, a cabinet minister, and thereafter at Bletchley and elsewhere for MI6. There is also alleged to have been another Soviet informant at the Park earlier in the war, never identified, and codenamed 'Baron'. Anthony Blunt worked for MI5. Kim Philby became a senior officer of MI6. Guy Burgess was successively employed by MI6, the BBC and the Foreign Office. Donald Maclean worked in the upper reaches of the Foreign Office. Other British sources provided technical intelligence, above all about the atomic bomb programme.

Guy Liddell of MI5 wrote in November 1942, amid reflections on the saga of Richard Sorge, which had been reported to London by informants in Tokyo: 'There is no doubt that the Russians are far better in the matter of espionage than any other country in the world. I am perfectly certain that they are well bedded down here and that we should be making more active investigations. They will be a great source of trouble to us when the war is over.' Liddell did not know the half of it. Soviet penetration of the British government, scientific institutions and intelligence machine was already more extensive than he could have imagined in his nightmares. Once the Soviet Union became an ally, however, Churchill was insistent that no intelligence operations should be conducted against Stalin's regime. The Foreign Office formally instructed the secret services that even scrutiny of British communists should be circumspect, and that no informants should be recruited inside the Soviet Union. Very little was done by MI5 even to monitor NKVD and GRU activities in Britain, and Bletchley's small Russian section was shut down in December 1941. These honourable scruples were not credited by Moscow, of course, far less reciprocated.

British folk legend treats the so-called Cambridge Five as a unique gallery of scoundrels, exemplars of the rottenness within the class system, a knot of gilded young men who systematically betrayed their country as no others did. It seems more appropriate, however, to consider them alongside Moscow's British agents from less privileged backgrounds – the likes of the lethally effective nuclear spy Melita Norwood – together with hundreds of Americans who likewise betrayed national secrets to Stalin's tyranny. Communism as a creed enjoyed widespread support across the Western world, in that era when many people on the left chose to blind their consciousness to the institutionalised inhumanity of the Soviet Union. In their eyes capitalism, whether represented by Republican corporate interests in the United States or by the Conservative Party in Britain, sustained the oppression of the working class. 'Looking around us at our own hells,' said Philip Toynbee, the historian who became a communist at Cambridge, 'we had to invent an earthly paradise somewhere else.'

Moscow Centre's recruiters profited mightily from the Soviet Union's status as principal standard-bearer for communism as a creed. Many NKVD and GRU sources around the world embraced the fiction that by giving secrets to the Comintern, they were aiding an international ideal rather than any narrowly national cause. Zbigniew Brzezinski defines ideology as combining theory and action with a 'consciousness of purpose and of the general thrust of history. It gives its adherents a sense of consistency and certainty that is too often absent among those ... brought up in

the tradition of short-term pragmatism.' Even before the enormity of the
fascist menace in Germany, Italy and Spain became apparent, left-wing
socialism attracted many enlightened and compassionate people. The
creed came dressed in many guises. Explicitly to avow communist sympathies was no barrier to admission to cultured London, Paris or Washington
society, because communism was not then universally identified with the
barbarities laid bare in the second half of the twentieth century. James
Klugmann, a Moscow informant who worked for SOE, said later: 'We
simply knew, all of us, that the revolution was at hand. If anyone had
suggested it wouldn't happen in Britain for say thirty years, I'd have
laughed myself sick.'

In the 1930s communists seemed to be the only people who were chal-
lenging fascism with any conviction, and the 1936 outbreak of the Spanish
Civil War dramatically enhanced the credibility of the Soviet Union in
intellectuals' eyes. They became obsessed with Spain in an even more
profound sense than a later generation embraced Vietnam. No Westerners
in the 1960s, however hostile to American policy, took up arms for Ho Chi
Minh. Yet thousands of Europeans and Americans fought for the
Republicans in Spain, or worked to assist them. Millions of people around
the world identified with the cause with an almost religious fervour. In this
febrile climate, perhaps more intensely politicised than at any time before
or since, Moscow recruited young idealists of all nationalities to serve as
covert warriors for communism.

Centre's British and American informants were diverse characters,
united by a messianic belief in their own rightness, indispensable to enable
them systematically to betray their employers, colleagues and country.
Hugh Trevor-Roper reflected long afterwards that he and many others of
his generation had underestimated the perils posed by communists within
British and other democratic societies, because they had mistakenly
perceived adherents to the creed as 'merely the most radical of our allies
against fascism, the militants on the extreme left of a coalition in which
men agreed to differ with mutual respect. Educated liberal Englishmen
and Americans failed to understand that communism is a religion ...
[which] can totally paralyse the mental and moral faculties of its converts
and cause them to commit any turpitude and to suffer any indignity, for
its sake.'

Yet many of those who called themselves communists throughout the
1930s felt obliged to recant in the face of the supreme cynicism of the
August 1939 deal between the Nazis and the Soviets. Trevor-Roper wrote:

'Many of our friends had been, or thought themselves, communists in the 1930s, and we were shocked that such persons should be debarred from public service on account of mere juvenile illusions which anyway they had now shed; for such illusions could not survive the shattering impact of Stalin's pact with Hitler.' Thus, as the high tide of enthusiasm for communism receded in the Western democracies, all but the most doctrinaire conservatives became reluctant to hold it against young men and women that they had avowed enthusiasm for Moscow before the Nazi–Soviet Pact exposed its turpitude.

It remains nonetheless remarkable that the Cambridge Five, and others of their kind, sustained for so many years parallel roles in the secret services of Britain and Russia. The spies had in common dysfunctional personalities, together with an anger against family, class or society which impelled their treachery and, in their own minds, justified it. All had intellectual gifts and varying degrees of charm. John Cairncross was the outsider, born the son of a Lanarkshire ironmonger in 1913. He became a scholarship boy first at Glasgow University, then at Trinity, Cambridge. Frail and untidy in appearance, adorned with a shock of red hair, his earnestness and gaucherie caused him to be dismissed by Churchill's private secretary Jock Colville as 'very brilliant, very boring'. The latter handicap set him apart from the other, famously personable Cambridge spies, though brains secured him a government job. In 1936 Cairncross passed top of his year into the civil service.

Like the others, he was recruited to the NKVD by Arnold Deutsch, a Viennese Jew and enthusiastic sexual liberationist who since 1934 had occupied a flat in Lawn Road, Hampstead, next door to Agatha Christie. Deutsch pursued a strategy of wooing young high fliers who seemed to be in transit towards the corridors of power. Kim Philby later described him as 'a marvellous man', funny and brilliant, who treated the Five as comrades rather than subordinates. He later asserted that he never hesitated for a moment before embracing Deutsch's proposal: 'One does not look twice at an offer of enrolment in an elite force.' Donald Maclean, after his 1951 flight to Moscow, justified his own treason in more disdainful terms: 'It's like being a lavatory attendant. It stinks, but somebody has to do it.'

Cairncross was introduced to Deutsch by James Klugmann in Regent's Park in May 1937. A few months later, the NKVD man was recalled to Moscow during the Purges. His successors as the Cambridge spies' handlers never, in their eyes, matched Deutsch's charm and professionalism. Though he narrowly preserved his own life, he remained suspected by his employers, and the Five's association with him sustained the NKVD's wariness of them. A winter 1938 assessment by Moscow Centre warned that the London intelligence operation 'was based on doubtful sources, on an agent network acquired at a time when it was controlled by enemies of the people and therefore extremely dangerous'. Although Centre for a time kept open its links with the Five, their material was treated with the utmost caution.

Early in 1940, Russian suspicions mounted. Lavrenti Beria became convinced that the Cambridge spies were serving either the British or the Germans, and not the cause of socialism. He recalled to Moscow Anatoly Gorsky, sole remaining member of the NKVD's London legal residency. For several months, while the greatest war in human history unfolded, Soviet intelligence conducted no significant operations in Britain; Stalin made it plain to his spymasters that he was more interested in killing Trotsky than in discovering what Hitler – or, for that matter, Churchill – was doing. Only late in 1940 did the intelligence policy of the Kremlin shift with its accustomed abruptness. The word went forth that Centre was to rebuild its foreign agent networks, which had been allowed to atrophy.

When relations with the Five were resumed, the new NKVD resident agent arranged meetings with them in Kensington Gardens, because the rendezvous was handy for the nearby Soviet embassy. The spies resumed their covert crusade for socialism, even though at this time Stalin was supposedly the associate of Hitler. Cairncross's absence of social skills caused him to be transferred from the Foreign Office to the Treasury, and then in 1940 to become private secretary to Lord Hankey. If there was anything Moscow Centre did not know about the structure and activities of Britain's intelligence services, Hankey now filled the gaps through the agency of Cairncross. The minister had conducted an exhaustive inquiry into MI6 and Bletchley. Cairncross slipped his NKVD handler a copy of Hankey's interim report, which had been first circulated within Whitehall in March 1940.

Thereafter, he spent a year as a codebreaker in Bletchley's Hut 3 before his health failed, prompting a transfer to MI6. Between 1941 and 1945 he passed 5,832 documents to the Russians, including many decrypted German signals. Cairncross was so technically incompetent that he was incapable of photographing material: he could only copy extracts by hand, or temporarily filch them for his handler to film. The NKVD resident often found himself unable to cope with enciphering all the material his informant supplied, but he was sufficiently appreciative to give Cairncross cash to buy a car to make it easier for him to deliver stolen secrets. The spy's personal unpopularity with colleagues proved no barrier to his continued employment by MI6, and Moscow eventually presented him with the Order of the Red Banner in recognition of his contribution to its own interests.

Guy Burgess was a naval officer's son, born in 1911, who attended Eton and Trinity College, Cambridge, then began to scrape a living from the BBC, while partying on the fringes of London intellectual and political circles. Even in an era of hard drinking, Burgess's consumption of alcohol amazed his acquaintance. His favourite tipple was a large port, which became known to waiters at the Reform Club in Pall Mall as 'a double Burgess'. Amid the defiant squalor of his flat in Bond Street, he sometimes cooked a stew of porridge, kippers, bacon, garlic, onions 'and anything else lying about in the kitchen' to sustain him through a weekend. In December 1938 his wit and social connections caused him to be recruited into MI6's propaganda department. After some months he transferred to the BBC, where he produced the radio programme *The Week in Westminster*, a passport to useful political contacts.

Thereafter he enjoyed a rackety existence, commuting between Broadcasting House and the Fitzrovia intellectual world, the wilder shores of homosexual London and the darker corridors of its secret world, both British and Russian, while excused from military call-up through the good offices of Blunt at MI5. How he avoided disaster mystified all those who encountered his reckless indiscretion long before he was exposed as an agent of Moscow. A characteristic 1942 Burgess contribution to the war effort was to recruit as an MI5 source Andrew Revoi, leader of the so-called Free Hungarians in London – whom he himself had put on the NKVD payroll back in 1938. During the early war years Burgess contributed less to Centre's interests than the other Cambridge spies, but in 1944 Sir Alexander Cadogan incomprehensibly appointed him to the Foreign Office News Department. Between January and July 1945 Burgess passed 389 top secret files to his Soviet handler.

Donald Maclean provided Moscow with its most important secret political intelligence. His family were Highland Scots, oppressively Presbyterian and committed to temperance; his father was a lawyer who eventually became a Liberal cabinet minister. Young Donald, born in 1913, was educated at Gresham's, a harsh Norfolk public school where boys had their trouser pockets sewn up to discourage putting hands in them. Maclean, tall and handsome, was once described by an admiring

Nazi as having 'perfect Aryan good looks'. From an early age, with his Balkan cigarettes and lounging charm, he cultivated a pose of mandarin ease. Philip Toynbee wrote of his friend's 'lazy wit and sophisticated good humour'. Maclean and the others recruited by Moscow at Cambridge professed to believe – and perhaps initially did so – that they were working for the Comintern rather than explicitly for the Soviet Union. Maclean joined the Foreign Office and began to pass documents to his NKVD controller. In 1937 Kitty Harris, born to poor Russian parents in London's East End and briefly bigamously married to American communist leader Earl Browder, assumed this role. She and Maclean concluded their first meeting in bed together, and thereafter for some months conducted an affair. The following year he was posted to Paris. Robert Cecil, who had known Maclean in his younger days and was now an embassy colleague, thought his demeanour had become uneasy and hesitant, in contrast to his earlier self-assurance. At the time Cecil was bemused by the change, but much later he identified it as reflecting guilt about Maclean's double life. The handsome young diplomat was by no means universally liked: typists referred to him disdainfully as 'smarty-pants'.

Nonetheless Melinda Marling, an American girl whom Maclean met in Paris, gave a glowing account of him to her mother: 'He is six foot tall, blonde with beautiful blue eyes … He is the soul of honour, responsible, a sense of humour, imagination, cultured, broadminded (and sweet), etc.' In June 1940 she found herself pregnant amid the chaos of France being overrun by the Germans. These twin shocks caused her to brush aside earlier reservations about marrying Maclean. After a hasty wedding, they were evacuated to Britain. Melinda then sailed for New York, where their first child was born – and swiftly died. Only in the autumn of 1941 did she return to live with Donald in London. It seems almost certain that from an early stage the left-leaning Melinda was aware both of her husband's work for Moscow, and of his bisexuality.

The enforced accession of the Soviet Union to the struggle against Hitler lifted the spirits of the Western spies serving Moscow. Now that Britain and Russia, and soon afterwards also the United States, were fighting the same fascist foes, such people as Maclean could persuade themselves that passing information to 'Uncle Joe' was no betrayal, but instead merely a means of assisting a common cause. In 1942 alone, the documents he stole or copied from the Foreign Office filled forty-five files in the NKVD's Moscow archives. Maclean's rich crop included much material about Britain's relations with the Soviet Union and details of British positions in negotiations and before summit meetings. In April 1944 he was posted to the British embassy in Washington as first secretary, where he played tennis with Lord Halifax, and raised his game as a purveyor of Anglo-American secrets. The strain of life as a spy and bisexual showed in Maclean's increasing consumption of alcohol and lapses into ugly scenes under its influence. But his intelligence and charm, leavened with Foreign Office and class solidarity, enabled him to keep both his job and his role as the Soviet Union's most important source on Western foreign policy.

Anthony Blunt, a vicar's son born in 1907 and educated at Marlborough, won a mathematics scholarship to Cambridge and later took a First in foreign languages. Thereafter he became a don and an embryo art historian. Both his homosexuality and his left-wing sympathies were well known – his friend Guy Burgess may have been responsible for recruiting him to the NKVD. But in 1939 neither politics nor sexuality proved a bar to his joining the Intelligence Corps, with which he served for some months in France. Finding himself homeless after Dunkirk, he became a temporary London lodger of Victor Rothschild of MI5, through whom Guy Liddell recruited him to the security service.

Blunt won immediate plaudits as an intelligence officer, especially for his dexterity in examining the contents of neutral diplomatic bags. An MI5 secretary of the time later recalled: 'My God, he was a charmer! Poor Anthony! We were all a bit in love with Anthony, you know ... He used to wander around with his cod-liver oil and malt, saying "That's what Tiggers like for breakfast." He knew *Winnie the Pooh* very well. He had a Leslie Howard face – a matinee idol – a rather thin and drawn-looking face but it was the face of Leslie Howard. Everyone was in love with Leslie Howard at that time.' On several occasions Blunt was sent to represent MI5 at meetings of the Joint Intelligence Committee, and in 1944 he was seconded to SHAEF to work on deception planning. In his parallel NKVD role he recruited and ran as a sub-agent Leo Long, who worked in military intelligence. Blunt provided a stream of MI5 documents and some Ultra decrypts, including signals relating to the 1943 battle for Kursk, the substance of which had been conveyed to Moscow through British military channels. He also briefed the Russians about the activities of the Twenty Committee, which ran 'turned' Nazi agents in its masterly wireless game with the Abwehr.

Harold 'Kim' Philby, most notorious of the Cambridge group because he gained access to the most sensitive secrets and his treachery ultimately cost most lives, was the son of the Arabist scholar St John Philby, an obsessive personality who tottered on the edge of insanity. The elderly sage declared, for instance, that Hitler was 'a very fine man', and in 1940 became convinced of the inevitability of British defeat, which caused him to be briefly interned in India. After Westminster and Cambridge, the NKVD gave Philby career counselling: get into newspapers, said Arnold Deutsch, which would provide an ideal platform for his Moscow work. During the later 1930s Philby became a well-regarded journalist, serving in Spain during its civil war as a correspondent for *The Times* as well as an agent of the NKVD, who doubled his newspaper income. Philby's personal extravagance made Russia's cash as important to him as the pleasure of assuaging his closet contempt for Britain by serving its enemies. People of power and influence loved him as the most congenial of companions: he was sponsored for membership of London's august Athenaeum Club by the military theorist Basil Liddell Hart. A joke that pleased Philby mightily was that Franco the fascist awarded him Spain's Red Cross of Military Merit, though in 1937 the Russians briefed him to gather intelligence to facilitate Franco's assassination.

Thereafter, however, during the Purges and the period of the Nazi–Soviet Pact he found himself dropped as abruptly as were many other NKVD informants. His offers of new material, forwarded to Moscow through Donald Maclean, were spurned. He was obliged instead to busy himself as a *Times* war correspondent with the British Expeditionary Force in France. Philby was appointed to MI6 in 1940, after expressing an interest in an intelligence career to one of the service's talent-spotters, Harriet Marsden-Smedley. One of MI6's deputy chiefs, Valentine Vivian, was a friend of St John Philby, and cheerfully accepted the old man's assurance that his son had forsworn dalliance with the left. Kim started his career with British intelligence by lecturing on techniques of subversive propaganda to foreign exiles recruited to SOE. He often opened his flamboyant talks by urging his audiences, many of whom recognised Stalin and Hitler as matching monsters: 'Gentlemen, I have no wish to prevent you blowing up the Russians, but I would beg you, for the sake of the Allied war effort, to blow up the Germans first.' Philby won the affection as well as the warm approval of Broadway colleagues and chiefs, and in October 1941 was promoted to head the Iberian section of MI6.

The Russians had renewed contact with him nine months earlier, but his initial reports about life at Broadway earned their scorn. He asserted that the Soviet Union stood only tenth on MI6's penetration target list, an incredible proposition to Centre, which was convinced that the exis-

tential purpose of the British secret service was to achieve the destruction of the Soviet Union. Russia's leaders inhabited a society in which
nobility of conduct was alien, indeed dangerous to the state. They were
thus unable to credit the fact that for the war's duration even the most
impassioned anti-communists, including Churchill, had set aside their
hostility to throw everything into the struggle against the Axis. This was
emphasised in 1940 when Walter Krivitsky, the former NKVD resident
in Holland, defected to the Americans. On 23 January, MI5 debriefed
him at London's Langham hotel. Krivitsky described almost a hundred
Soviet agents in Europe, sixty of them working against British interests,
including sixteen who were British subjects. Yet MI5, overwhelmingly
preoccupied with the Nazi menace, felt able to commit only a single
officer to investigate Soviet penetration, and it is thus unsurprising that
he failed to identify an unnamed British journalist, mentioned by
Krivitsky as having helped the NKVD in Spain to plan Franco's assassination, as Kim Philby.

Moscow's interest was reawakened by Philby's appointment to head the
Iberian section. Thereafter he provided Centre with almost a thousand
wartime secret documents, channelled through Anatoly Gorsky, now
reappointed as NKVD resident at the Soviets' London embassy. Short and
fat, Gorsky was a caricature Stalinist whose merciless chill roused the
repugnance of the Cambridge spies, though insufficiently so to put them
off their work. At this stage, Philby's most significant contribution was to
fuel Soviet paranoia about the prospect that Britain would make a compromise peace with Hitler, through the agency of Deputy Führer Rudolf Hess.
This was pure mischief-making, presumably designed to raise its agent's
standing with Centre. In the same spirit, Philby reported that his MI6
masters had abandoned a plan to kill Admiral Canaris on one of his
frequent visits to Spain, allegedly because the British anticipated that he
might become the intermediary in bilateral negotiations.

Inside Broadway Buildings, Philby affected an old 1914–18 army tunic
of his father's. With his stammer, shabby clothes and diffident manner he
seemed, in Robert Cecil's words 'like one of Graham Greene's seedy
anti-heroes'. Yet Malcolm Muggeridge warmed to an apparent fellow-free
spirit: 'His romantic veneration for buccaneers and buccaneering, whatever the ideological basis – if any – might be. Boozers, womanisers,
violence in all its manifestations, recklessness however directed he found
irresistible.' Philby once told Muggeridge, in a familiar half-self-mocking
key, that Göbbels was a man he felt he could have worked with.

Philby's qualities commanded an extravagant premium inside Broadway: Hugh Trevor-Roper found him 'an agreeable and effective person ... intelligent, sophisticated and even real'. The historian was hated by many of his career colleagues because he never concealed his contempt for them, but Philby flattered and caressed them. The consequence was that Trevor-Roper the patriot was mistrusted – repeatedly threatened with dismissal and once with a prosecution for treason, for conveying details of Broadway's failings to Lord Cherwell – while Philby the betrayer secured his masters' absolute confidence.

Common to all the Cambridge Five was a disdain for loyalty not merely to country, but also to family and friends. In 1935 Philby rifled his own father's papers on NKVD orders. He made much of his relationship with an old Westminster schoolfriend, Tom Wylie, in hopes of exploiting Wylie's role as a War Office official. Goronwy Rees broke contact with Centre following the Nazi–Soviet Pact, an ideological bridge too far for him. Donald Maclean spat at Rees: 'You used to be one of us, but you ratted!' The writer promised the other traitors that their secret remained safe with him, and kept his word, an unedifying moral compromise. Burgess, however, remained fearful of Rees's knowledge. In the spring of 1943 he urged his Soviet handler that his friend should be murdered. When Moscow dismissed this suggestion as a clumsy British provocation, at a meeting with Gorsky on 20 July Burgess offered to kill Rees himself, which was also thought superfluous.

Centre often sought to press money on its British agents. Most professed scruples, declaring themselves enthusiasts for an ideal rather than mercenaries. Anthony Blunt once surprised his handler by demanding, and receiving, £200 for some undisclosed personal purpose. He signed a receipt for the cash which thereafter reposed in the NKVD's files, much to the satisfaction of Centre: the long, lean, boundlessly devious art historian was thus chained to its oar. Meanwhile, Philby's lifestyle could only be sustained by an income from Mother Russia as well as from MI6.

As is often the case with double agents, both sides had moments of doubt about his loyalty. In November 1942 Stuart Hampshire, one of the Radio Intelligence Bureau's Oxford dons, produced an important report on the power struggle taking place in Germany between Himmler and Canaris. Philby secured a ban on its circulation, without giving a reason. This caused Hampshire to say thoughtfully, 'There's something wrong with Philby,' though neither he nor his colleagues could figure out what. Long afterwards, they concluded that Kim was probably under orders from Moscow to stifle any information that might encourage the British to talk to German opposition groups. At the time, Hugh Trevor-Roper was so annoyed by Philby's behaviour that he gave a copy of Hampshire's document to Lord Cherwell, which earned him yet another formal reprimand from Menzies and Valentine Vivian. He was ordered to write a formal apology for communicating with the prime minister's adviser, rather in the spirit of a schoolmaster punishing an errant child by imposing 'lines'.

Meanwhile in Moscow, at exactly the same time Elena Modrzhinskaya, one of the NKVD's most respected analysts and an obsessive conspiracy theorist, urged that all the Cambridge Five were part of a British plot, 'an insultingly crude capitalist provocation'. This seemed the more credible since three of the group's early handlers – Deutsch, Theodore Maly and Alexander Orlov – had already been branded as traitors. Modrzhinskaya complained that the content of the copies of MI6's signals to the British embassy in Moscow, passed to Centre by Philby, were far too banal to be authentic. The Russians never abandoned their conviction that their own country teemed with British spies. An NKVD report of 30 October 1945 stated: 'The English intelligence organs took advantage of improved opportunities during the war and intensified the espionage against the Soviet Union. A total of around 200 British agents worked in the USSR during the war, of which 110 were in Moscow, 30 in Murmansk and over 20 among various delegations.' This was an exquisite fantasy. MI6 had lacked any Moscow station since 1936, and the British ambassador vetoed a proposal to establish one.

By contrast, in the course of 1941 the NKVD's London station forwarded to Moscow 7,867 British classified documents, 715 on military matters, fifty-one on intelligence, 127 on economics, and the rest on political or other topics. A similar traffic flow was sustained through the later war years. To preserve the security blanket over sources, inside Centre almost all original material was destroyed after being translated and paraphrased by desk staff. Such was the bulk, however, and so severe the shortage of English linguists, that thousands of pages were dispatched to the incinerators unexamined. Yuri Modin, one of seven Moscow desk staff charged with handling this mountain of material, later reflected sardonically: 'What would [the spies] have thought if they had known that their telegrams and reports had barely a 50 per cent chance of being read?' When Philby provided an address book of British agents in far-flung places, the NKVD brushed it aside: its chiefs wanted only material about MI6 activity in countries where Moscow had explicit interests.

But some of the British spies' reports, true and false, found their way into the Kremlin. A typical missive from Centre to the USSR's State Defence Committee was dated 21 April 1942: 'This is to pass on to you the information from an agent, which NKVD of the USSR has received from London as a result of conversations between the sources and an official from the American embassy ("Gilbert") and a number of MPs. 1. On The Second Front. It has become clear that ... apart from active opponents of Churchill who think he is sabotaging the opening of the Second Front from his hostility towards the USSR, the delay is being viewed from two angles: Political aspect: there is disagreement among members of the government as to when offensive operations [an invasion of the Continent] should start ... Many of those who know Churchill, including Lloyd George, say that he remains haunted by the failure of the Dardanelles campaign [in 1915] when he was blamed for the Gallipoli disaster ... According to "Gilbert" ... only 4 British divisions have had specialised amphibious training.' This report, which continues at length, is not much different in style, accuracy and usefulness from routine diplomatic and for that matter newspaper reporting.

A similar NKVD report from London, dated 28 July 1942, was broadly sound in substance, but quoted some risible sources: 'Our fixed agent in London sent the following information, obtained by an agent. Most officials have recently been asserting that the Second Front will not be opened this year. Such people as Lady Colefax – the agent-informant of the Conservative Party's executive committee ... are now declaring with almost complete assurance that the Second Front will not happen.' Sibyl Colefax was, in reality, a mere social alpinist and conspicuously foolish woman, of whom a contemporary joke suggested that she scrawled on one of her luncheon invitations 'to meet the mother of the Unknown Soldier'.

Meanwhile Donald Maclean told Moscow that Poland's General Władysław Sikorski dismissed talk that the Katyn massacres of Polish officers were Nazi work, saying he was confident that they had been carried out by the NKVD, as of course they were. Anthony Blunt warned that the Polish government in London would never accept the proposed redrawing of its country's borders. This was one of the British messages that appears to have had some influence on the Kremlin, confirming Stalin in his determination to spurn the 'London Poles' and create his own puppet regime. The MI5 officer also provided Moscow with a useful list of British sources recruited among the personnel of exile European governments in London.

The Russians received much information that was plain wrong, and reflected only their obsession with supposed conspiracies against themselves. For instance, on 12 May 1942 'a reliable source' reported to Moscow that an official from the German embassy in Stockholm had arrived in London aboard a Swedish aircraft bearing peace proposals whereby: 'England will stay intact as an empire. The Germans will withdraw troops from Czechoslovakia and restore its old borders. All Eastern Europe will be restored to its previous borders. The Baltic states will also remain independent. After England accepts these conditions Germany will reach an agreement with the USSR.' The Russians assumed the worst about admittedly muddled Anglo-American policy in Yugoslavia. On 28 March 1943 an NKVD source in Algiers – possibly an OSS informant – messaged almost hysterically: 'In collaboration with the Americans the English have instructed [General] Mihailović not to join any active operations [against the Germans], but instead to build strength and materiel and make his army as capable as possible [for operations against Tito and his communist partisans]. The English and Americans are helping Mihailović despite being well aware of his links with the Germans ... In parallel with this the English have decided to exploit all opportunities to compromise Marshal Tito. Among other things they are using the neutral Swiss media for this purpose.'

Moscow nursed a running grievance about the British refusal to forward to them raw Ultra recrypts. The modern Russian intelligence official website asserts as fact in 2015: 'Although the British intelligence service was getting reliable information of the plans of German army leadership at the Eastern Front, the English preferred to keep this information secret from their Soviet ally. It was through agents among the British secret service that the Soviet foreign intelligence service did acquire this information.' Yet Yuri Modin admitted that London had reason on its side. The Russians were themselves haunted by fears of Nazi agents inside Soviet headquarters – including the NKVD – which were probably unjustified, but cost two suspect generals their lives.

In May 1943, MI6 created a new Section IX, tasked to study communism and Soviet espionage, though its staff was authorised to work only with such material as could be gathered outside the Soviet Union. In accordance with Churchill's stern *diktat*, no penetration activities were carried out – not that these could have achieved much anyway. When an Estonian named Richard Maasing was debriefed by MI6, Philby displayed a keen interest, unsurprising to posterity: he wanted to discover who were

Maasing's contacts in territories claimed by the Soviet Union. Early in July 1944, MI6's Lisbon station received some warning of the Hitler bomb plot from Otto John of the Abwehr. Philby was insistent that this report had no significance and should be 'spiked' – almost certainly for the familiar reason that his Moscow orders obliged him to do everything possible to frustrate Allied intercourse with the German Resistance. After the Abwehr officer Paul Vehmehren's 1944 defection in Istanbul and subsequent debriefing, Philby passed to the Russians Vehmehren's long list of Catholic conservative contacts in Germany: all those in the East were liquidated by the Russians in 1945–46, as actual or potential anti-communists.

Moscow's suspicions of Philby nonetheless persisted, intensified by an episode in the autumn of 1943. He supplied to his handlers a copy of a supremely sensitive Ultra decrypt of a signal to Tokyo from the Japanese embassy in Berlin, detailing Baron Ōshima's 4 October conversations with Hitler and Ribbentrop. The version wirelessed to Moscow omitted the concluding paragraph, because Bletchley had only a corrupted text. When the NKVD secured from another source a copy of the same signal, but including the missing section which discussed a possible separate peace, Fitin, the chief of the First Directorate, assumed that Philby had deliberately omitted it from his delivery on Broadway's orders. Moreover, all the Cambridge Five were damned by their continuing failure to provide details of the non-existent British spy rings in the Soviet Union. On 25 October 1943 Centre told its London residency that it was plain Philby and his friends were double agents. It dispatched eight men to London with an explicit brief to secure confirmation of this, by shadowing their movements. Since none of the newcomers spoke English, the 'tailing' operation against the NKVD's own sources was less than successful.

Only in August 1944 was there a change of heart in Moscow, a renewal of belief that the Cambridge spies were serving Soviet rather than British interests. Centre wrote to its London station that new evidence about Philby 'obliges us to review our attitude towards him and the entire group', who were 'of great value'. In Moscow and London alike, rival employers now clamoured for his services. His old newspaper *The Times* strove to persuade him to return to journalism; one of its senior executives characterised him as 'steady, experienced and wise'. Philby did indeed consider such a career change, but instead continued on his path of secret devastation at Broadway, facilitated by the disastrous decision of Stewart Menzies to appoint him to head MI6's anti-communist espionage section. 'C's' protégé rewarded him in his own inimitable fashion, by spending many hours at MI6's St Albans out-station, photographing the files of its agents for Moscow's edification.

Long afterwards, following the exposure of Philby, Burgess and Maclean, and amid a tidal wave of recriminations against the intelligence community for admitting such men to their councils, Hugh Trevor-Roper reflected upon both their recruitment and its cost to British interests: 'If [Philby] had been turned down as an ex-communist, and never afterwards exposed, our fashionable left-wingers would have denounced his exclusion, just as they now denounce his appointment, as an infamous example of social and intellectual discrimination ... Until 1944 I do not believe that Philby had much opportunity, or much need, to do harm. His work was against the Germans, in Spain, where Russia was powerless and, by now, uninterested. He had no access to political secrets. Anyway the interest of the Russians was, at that time, the same as ours: the defeat of Germany.'

Philby then wrote from his Moscow refuge, commenting on Trevor-Roper's remarks, and bitter strictures against him: 'I note that you abhor treason. So do I. But what is treason? We could spend many days motoring around Iraq and discussing this without getting much nearer agreement.' Trevor Roper responded, '"What is treason?" You gaily ask, and, like jesting Pilate, do not wait for answer ... To serve a foreign power, even to spy for a foreign power, does not seem to me necessarily treason. It depends on the foreign power, and the conditions of service ... But to serve unconditionally, to equate truth with the reason of state of any power, that to me is treason of the mind; and to make this surrender to a form of power that is cynical, inhuman, murderous, that to me is treason of the heart also.'

Some of Moscow Centre's officers retained doubts to the bitter end about the loyalties of the Cambridge spies. Elena Modrzhinskaya attended Philby's 1988 funeral, in order to view his open casket. She was haunted by suspicions that even in death the British traitor might somehow have achieved a last deceit. Whatever the defiant claims of Philby and his kin to have taken pride in serving Moscow, the alcoholism and premature decay which overtook all save Blunt suggest that they found little contentment in treason. On Philby's arrival in Moscow he was crestfallen to discover that he lacked any NKVD rank – no mere foreign informant was granted one. Trevor-Roper said he believed that Philby had enjoyed his supposed triumph over bourgeois capitalism less than he pretended: 'Did Judas enjoy the Last Supper? I doubt it.'

Sir Dick White, later head of both MI5 and MI6, wrote to a friend after the Cambridge spies were exposed: 'On balance it was not such a bad bet to fight the war on a united front. The cost was to have had Blunt in [MI]5, Philby in [MI]6 and B[urgess] and M[aclean] in the F.O. On the other side of the equation a massive intake of brain and abilities from the Universities which set entirely new standards of intellectual achievement.' This was an extreme *post-facto* rationalisation of a disaster for the reputation of Britain's secret services. Yet White was thus far right: that Britain's war effort, not to mention its standing as a bastion of freedom, would have been much the poorer had every officer with a left-wing history been excluded from its inner councils.

How much damage did the traitors do to British interests? Until the late wartime years, the likely answer is: not much. For long periods Moscow refused to believe that the British were so stupid as to allow avowed communists – albeit supposed apostates – access to their deepest secrets. Probably the most significant contribution of the Cambridge Five, and explicitly of Donald Maclean, was to keep Stalin informed about British political and diplomatic intentions; an immense volume of cable traffic concerning – for instance – Anglo-American weapons and supply deliveries to the USSR was also passed to Moscow. The Russians' default diplomatic posture towards the Western Allies of stone-faced indignation successfully concealed from Washington and London the fact that, at summit meetings, the Soviet delegation was fully informed in advance of intended British and American positions. Churchill especially, who often awaited apprehensively Stalin's response to unwelcome surprises, especially about delays to D-Day, might have spared himself discomfort. The 'surprises' were nothing of the sort: the Soviet dictator merely brilliantly simulated amazement, then unleashed anger to order. It was impossible for Churchill and Roosevelt to play poker with the Kremlin, because Stalin knew their hands. Meanwhile, it is known that Anthony Blunt at MI5 handled many Japanese Purple decrypts, and it is likely that he gave some to the Russians, even if Izumi Kozo's material did not enable them to break the cipher on their own account.

Apologists for the Cambridge spies cite some of the above in defence of their men. Philby and the rest, they argue, gave aid not to Britain's enemies, but to its foremost ally in the struggle against Nazism. Was it not shameful – a cause for righteous anger to people of conscience, today as in the 1940s – that Britain did so little to aid Russia in its desperate hour, and even denied Moscow access to Ultra, the foremost weapon in Churchill's hands? The first answer to such a defence is that the traitors provided information to Moscow long before Russia became an ally, indeed while the Soviet

Union was coupled to Nazi Germany, from August 1939 to June 1941, a period that embraced such triumphs for Moscow Centre as the Katyn massacres. Even after 'Barbarossa', when Britain, Russia and later the US were joined in the struggle against Hitler, Stalin never wavered in his perception of the Western Allies as ultimate foes. The treachery of Philby and his friends later cost the lives of many good men and women, executed for the mere crime of resisting tyranny.

Meanwhile, Bletchley Park was the most secret organ of British war-making. The danger was enormous that once its doings were known in Moscow, a leak – perhaps through a compromised Russian code – would alert the Germans to Enigma's vulnerability. The fact that this did not happen in no way excuses the conduct of those who revealed the Ultra secret to the Kremlin. The Russians were careless, or worse, with the secrets of others; it should be remembered that, while Stalin was still Hitler's friend, the Soviet ambassador in Washington told his German counterpart that the Japanese Purple cipher was broken. The most that can be said about Philby and his kin is that it was fortunate all of Britain's significant wartime traitors gave their allegiance to the Soviet Union, the looming menace to freedom and democracy, rather than to Nazi Germany, its present danger.

2 AMERICAN TRAITORS

The United States is a temple of freedom, and thus also of indiscretion. Even after Pearl Harbor, Americans found it hard to adjust to the imperatives of security, to shake off habits acquired over centuries. Operational pilots gossiped over voice links; politicians and service officers discussed plans over cocktails; newspapermen and broadcasters chafed against censorship, and published information of value to the enemy – most notoriously the *Chicago Tribune*'s 1942 revelation, reprised by Walter Winchell, that US triumph at Midway had been gained by breaking Japanese codes – whenever they thought they could get away with it. The eastern seaboard's blazing illuminations, which persisted for weeks after the 'Day of Infamy', much to the advantage of U-boat captains who sank scores of merchantmen silhouetted against their glare, were symbolic of much else that might be magnificent, but were also perilous, in a nation at war.

Fortunately for the Allied struggle against the Axis, German spies who landed on US soil were rounded up with little difficulty by police and the FBI. The Japanese enjoyed as little success intelligence-gathering in

America as they did nearer home. The Soviet Union, however, exploited the open society to sponsor espionage inside the United States on a scale unmatched by any other nation. The 1950s allegations of Senator Joseph McCarthy, who promoted a witch-hunt in a climate of hysteria and paranoia, were unfounded against many individuals, but had substance in the generality. Hundreds of Americans of left-wing sympathies, and a smaller number who worked for cash, systematically betrayed their country's secrets to Moscow. The atomic traitors, to be discussed later, have been the focus of much historical attention, while the Russians' host of other wartime informants have received less notice than they deserve. NKVD and GRU sources in Washington were privy to some of the nation's most sensitive policy debates.

Until the post-war era, the FBI had negligible success in identifying American traitors, and the guilt or innocence of some high-profile suspects remains unproven to this day. As early as 15 July 1941 a State Department official wrote: 'Ample evidence exists that American communists are taking advantage of the present situation to attempt to ingratiate themselves in high government circles as advocates of democracy under the guise of advocating all-out aid to the Soviet Union.' FBI attention, however, focused more closely on the US Communist Party than on Soviet agent-runners. There are sheaves of reports in the Washington archives concerning American communist sympathisers, but until the later 1940s the FBI's surveillance targets were almost all people at the lower end of society – dock workers, trades union activists and suchlike. The FBI breathed heavily upon such bodies as the National Council of Soviet–American Friendship and East European expatriate and nationalist groups. It held a bulging file on the National Maritime Union's alleged subversive activities. It had one success against the Soviet Union in April 1941, when it secured the recall of the NKVD's New York station chief after FBI agents arrested him at a meeting with an informant, but this was the tip of a huge iceberg, invisible to J. Edgar Hoover.

The wartime FBI claimed knowledge of just five American citizens spying for Russia, while subsequent revelations and confessions identified at least another eighty. The 1948 Venona decrypts provided codenames for two hundred Russian sources in the US, of whom half remain unidentified in the twenty-first century. Since the Venona material covered only a part of Moscow's operations, it is reasonable to assume that in the 1930s and 1940s there were many more American traitors, a view supported by the memoirs of contemporary NKVD and GRU officers who served in the US.

In the FBI's defence, Hoover could plead that the nation's declared enemies – Germany, Italy and Japan – enjoyed no significant espionage success within the continental United States. After June 1941 the Russians were America's professed allies rather than foes, and President Roosevelt himself treated them with trust and respect. Apologists for the Bureau's failure against the NKVD might say that this merely reflected a wider naïveté, extending to the summit of US government, about the scale of the menace posed by the Soviet Union. The FBI also faced some of the same problems as did Abwehr and Gestapo men hunting the Red Orchestra: most of the significant players inhabited upper-middle-class social and professional circles, where law enforcement agencies were unaccustomed to tread.

As elsewhere in the world, the NKVD's American operations became almost moribund between 1939 and 1941, and most of its US sources became perforce sleepers. The first attempt to reactivate networks failed when Arnold Deutsch, rehabilitated and dispatched to become US station chief, appears to have drowned when his ship was sunk in the mid-Atlantic. In December 1941, Itzhak Akhmerov was appointed in his stead. He had served in the US since arriving there in 1934 under cover as a student, and as he told an audience of KGB trainees twenty years later, 'switching from the status of a foreign student to the status of an American in such a large city as New York was not difficult'. After a time he moved to Baltimore, which was handier for managing his Washington sources. He and another NKVD officer settled down to run a furrier's shop, which proved successful in its own right, turning a good profit as well as providing cover; but he had indifferent success recruiting new informants, a role that others filled better.

The NKVD's three acknowledged stations – at the Soviets' AMTORG trade organisation in New York, the Washington embassy and the San Francisco consulate – were each manned by thirteen intelligence officers, supported by others at sub-stations in Los Angeles, Portland, Seattle and elsewhere. Scores more agents worked under cover of Soviet front organisations – the TASS news agency, Sovfilmexport, the Russian Red Cross and suchlike; some American material was also channelled through the NKVD's Mexico City station. It might be supposed that Soviet spies, arriving from the most repressive and austere society on earth at their usual first port of call, New York City's Taft hotel, would be dazzled by American wealth, glitz, glamour, inexhaustible energy. Yet remarkably few 'went private' – defected – and even those who wrote memoirs long after the

Terror ended say little or nothing in praise of the US. Most seem to have lived and worked in a grey cocoon of Russianness and socialist rectitude.

Soviet espionage was often a family business. When Alexander Feklisov left Moscow for an NKVD posting in New York, he had the customary farewell meeting with foreign minister Molotov, who expressed dismay that he was a bachelor: 'We don't send single men abroad, especially to the USA. They will immediately foist a beautiful blonde or brunette on you, and a honeytrap will be ready.' Feklisov's boss reassured Molotov that there were some good Russian girls serving at Soviet institutions in New York, and a bride could be found among them for the novice agent. In 1944 the dutiful Feklisov indeed married a Russian student sent to study at Columbia.

Itzhak Akhmerov did wed an American – but she was Helen Lowry, niece of US Communist Party leader Earl Browder. When Vasily Zarubin, fresh from participation in the Katyn massacres of 25,000 Poles, left Moscow to become Washington station chief in December 1941, he took with him his wife Elizabeth, herself an NKVD captain, who played an important role as recruiter for her husband's network, and who often travelled to California to meet Robert Oppenheimer and other useful contacts. She passed easily as a sophisticated, cosmopolitan European woman, equally fluent in English, German, French and Hebrew. She came from a family of revolutionaries, and was one of Centre's most ruthless operatives. Having cut her teeth working as a case officer for the terrible Felix Dzerzhinsky after the Revolution, she was posted to Turkey. There she gave impressive proof of loyalty to Bolshevism by betraying her then husband, Yakov Blumkin, another Soviet agent. He had been entrusted with the sale of Moscow's Hasidic Library, and rashly gave some of the proceeds to Trotsky, who was then exiled in Turkey. Almost before the echo of the shots from Blumkin's firing squad had died away, his widow married Zarubin. For thirteen years thereafter the two travelled and spied together across Europe. In America, Elizabeth played her role so skilfully that the FBI identified her as a career intelligence officer only in 1946, after her return to Moscow. She and her husband meanwhile played a pivotal role in Centre's global espionage programme. Before October 1941, Stalin had taken little personal interest in the US – though always eager to steal its technology – because there was no direct clash between Soviet and American interests. Now, however, its policies became a top priority: Stalin met personally with Zarubin before he departed for his American posting, to urge its importance.

The new NKVD resident was forty-seven when he arrived in New York. His subordinate Alexander Feklisov, who idolised Zarubin as a giant among Soviet spies, described him thus: 'He was of medium height, slightly overweight, with thin fair hair which he brushed back. He wore glasses in a white metal frame, and his eyes were forever inflamed from overwork. He was immensely strong, very good at tennis, full of life and an obvious leader in any company. He loved singing and played several musical instruments ... He spoke quickly and his voice was somehow trumpet-like, though he was also a good listener, easy and friendly with subordinates. He demanded they should show initiative, boldness, even recklessness. He derived his strength from his immense experience and professionalism, though he could sometimes be indiscreet. He had all kind of connections among foreigners, and was a great recruiter. He handled our most important agents personally.' Feklisov omitted to mention that Zarubin, a secret servant of the Soviet state since 1925, was also a ruthless killer, though this did not spare him from himself once feeling the warmth of the executioner's breath. At a meeting Beria invited him to stand, then said, 'Tell us about your links to the Fascist intelligence services.' Zarubin sternly rejected the slander – and suffered no consequences. But those who witnessed the scene left the room trembling. Zarubin dominated Soviet espionage in the United States until his expulsion in 1944.

In the US as in Britain, the Comintern provided a figleaf to spare informants from the discomfort of acknowledging that they were giving secrets to a foreign power. Those involved, said the Iowan-born Marxist writer Josephine Herbst, 'took great pride in their sense of conspiracy'. Among early recruits was Harold Ware, a radical New Dealer in the Agriculture Department, killed in a 1935 car crash. At the State Department the GRU secured the services of Alger Hiss, while the NKVD from the mid-1930s received a steady stream of information from Noel Field and Laurence Duggan. The latter was a political romantic, much influenced by his formidable wife Helen Boyd, whom a Russian described as 'an extraordinarily beautiful woman: a typical American, tall, blonde, reserved, well-read, goes in for sports, independent'. Hedda Gumpertz, a German exile and passionate anti-Nazi working for the NKVD, had cultivated Duggan as a friend of Field. Duggan was once handed a birthday present by his Soviet handler: a monogrammed crocodile toiletries case. He rejected it in the same spirit that some of the British traitors declined money, 'stating that he was working for our common ideas and making it understood that he was not helping us for any material interest'.

The Russians profited from thinking long. Since the Soviet Union saw itself in a historic adversarial relationship to the Western Powers, its rulers were content for agents to spend years in training and orientation for their roles. Semyon Semyonov, for instance, was a short, stocky figure with a duck nose and big eyes, who rubbed along easily with people and could pass for a middle-rank corporate executive. In January 1938, aged twenty-six, he was sent at Moscow's expense to do advanced studies at the Massachusetts Institute of Technology – the NKVD intended him to become a scientific-technological intelligence officer. At MIT there were complaints that Semyonov was lazy and conceited, but he proved an adept when he started his career as an agent. By 1943 he was running twenty-eight American sources, eleven of whom provided material on chemistry and bacteriology, six on radio, five on aviation. Among the more notable was thirty-three-year-old Harry Gold, born in Switzerland to Russian refugee parents. Gold came to America as an infant, and started spying for the Soviets in his first job, where he stole a dry-ice process that stopped ice cream melting. In 1942 he abandoned his day job as a chemist to manage his own agent-running operation, meeting Semyonov once a week to arrange assignments.

Centre was uneasy that so many of its key Washington sources knew each other, mostly through links to left-wing groups, but could do little about it. One man who might have exposed the extent of its penetration in the US was Ignatz Reiss, an NKVD officer who quit and fled for his life during the Purges. His employers caught up with him, however, in a Lausanne restaurant on 4 September 1937. He was shot nearby, his body dumped by the roadside. This proved a useful execution, for other spies who considered withdrawing their services tended to drop the idea when they remembered Reiss's well-publicised fate. Maybe they also knew about Juliet Poyntz, an American informant who decided to leave the Soviets' employ, but instead vanished from the New York Women's Club on 3 June 1937 and also appears to have been liquidated.

Though some American leftists' faith in the socialist dream was shaken by the Nazi–Soviet Pact, it was renewed in full measure by 'Barbarossa', which threw upon Russia the chief burden of defeating Hitler. When Alfred Slack, an informant working at Eastman Kodak, was offered a $150 bonus for an unusually useful piece of information, he told his handler to send the money to Moscow for the 'Joseph Stalin tank column', a popular fund of the time. Semyon Semyonov, the agent in question, solemnly gave Slack a receipt, to keep alive the flame of his illusions.

Others, however, shamelessly sold secrets for the money. Semyonov liked to tell the story of an American chemist at DuPont who passed the Russians material on nylon and explosives, without any pretence of ideological motive. 'Democrats, Republicans, fascists, communists, they are all the same to me,' the man said. 'I meet you because I need cash. I need to build a house, educate my daughter, dress her nicely and make sure she marries well.' At every rendezvous there was protracted haggling between the Russian and the American about the value of his wares, which customarily started with the seller demanding $1,000, then taking home two or three hundred, together with a burning indignation. Semyonov told his colleague Alexander Feklisov that he always felt exhausted after meeting 'Hustler', as the DuPont man was codenamed. It took the Russian hours to recover his sangfroid, as he debated whether the angry American would see him again. Feklisov asked, 'Why not pay the guy more?' Semyonov answered, 'Because if he buys his house and saves enough money, he will stop working for us.' As it was, their exchanges continued for years.

By contrast Laurence Duggan of the State Department, who was handled by Itzhak Akhmerov, did the business for love. In October 1939, State's security officers warned him that his loyalty was being questioned, but they had no inkling of the magnitude of his treachery, and after a cursory investigation he was allowed to keep his job, becoming a personal adviser on Latin America to Cordell Hull. In July 1944 Duggan resigned from State and joined the UN relief agency UNRRA. Four years later, after being questioned by the FBI he jumped from the sixteenth floor of his office building, but even then the authorities were oblivious of the importance of his NKVD role, revealed only by the 1990 opening of a Moscow archive. Arthur Schlesinger, who knew and liked Duggan, wrote long after: 'One wonders what impulses of idealism may have inextricably entangled this decent man with the harsh machinations of Stalinist tyranny.' Some of those who spied for Moscow remained unidentified. 'C-11', a woman source in the Navy Department, ceased providing information in the summer of 1940, when threatened with exposure. Another American woman, codenamed 'Zero', who worked for a Senate committee and passed on reports from the US commercial attaché in Berlin, sought work in the State Department but was rejected, partly because it was reluctant to employ Jews. She nonetheless secured transcripts of Cordell Hull's conversations with foreign ambassadors.

The Soviets also had plenty of duds on their payroll. Martha Dodd, daughter of America's 1933–38 Berlin ambassador, was recruited by the NKVD's Boris Vinogradov, with whom she fell desperately in love. Even by Soviet standards, Centre's manipulation of their relationship touched extremes: hours before his execution during the Purges, Vinogradov was persuaded to write a letter to Dodd, urging her to keep spying in expectation of being reunited with him. His death was concealed from her, and she sustained contact with her handlers through the war years. An NKVD report asserted contemptuously: 'She considers herself a Communist and claims to accept the Party's program. In reality, however, "Liza" is a typical representative of American Bohemia, a sexually decayed woman ready to sleep with any handsome man.' Moscow was in exceptionally credulous mood when it gave Dodd's brother William $3,000 to help him buy a small newspaper, the *Blue Ridge Herald*. By 1945 he was working in the New York office of the TASS news agency, run by the NKVD station chief, and was under unsurprisingly close FBI surveillance. Moscow gained nothing from the Dodds after their father left the Berlin embassy.

Michael Straight was another Russian failure, a rich young American recruited by the NKVD's London station chief Theodore Maly, supposedly acting for the Comintern. His subsequent handler, Arnold Deutsch, dismissed Straight as a dilettante with more money than sense, who once wrote a cheque for £500 to help fund the communist newspaper the *Daily Worker*. On the young idealist's return to the US, he secured a job with the State Department. When the NKVD's Washington station expressed scepticism about his value, Moscow Centre cautioned sternly: 'Straight is prospectively a big agent, and burning him ... is not our intention.' The Nazi–Soviet Pact caused Straight to resign from the State Department – and from the NKVD. He never, however, revealed the knowledge he had acquired in London about the treachery of Blunt and Burgess. The Russians, cynically and perhaps correctly, believed that this was not out of loyalty to the renegades, but because the fate of Ignatz Reiss showed what happened to those who betrayed Centre or its agents.

Since the United States is a nation of immigrants, it was impossible to monitor a host of such citizens as Boris Morros, born in St Petersburg in 1891, who became a minor-league Hollywood director-producer. The NKVD recruited him in 1934, chiefly to provide cover for other agents rather than as a source of information. Morros had three brothers still in the Soviet Union: one was executed after incurring the displeasure of the Party, but his own NKVD role enabled him to save the lives of the other two. In 1944 Vasily Zarubin drove Morros to meet Martha Dodd and her rich husband Alfred Stern, whom he persuaded to invest $130,000 in the producer's music publishing business. This not only proved a poor investment for Stern, but also a waste of effort for the NKVD, who got little or nothing of value from Morros before he was belatedly 'turned' by the FBI in 1945. Likewise 'Leo', a freelance journalist, proved a conman who invented intelligence for cash, as did New York congressman Samuel Dickstein, born a Lithuanian and contemptuously codenamed 'Crook', who nonetheless received $12,000 of Soviet funds before Moscow decided he was not worth any more money. The only significant service Dickstein performed was to secure a US passport for an Austrian NKVD agent. He died in 1954, aged seventy, a justice of the New York Supreme Court whose work for the Soviets was unrevealed.

Moscow was as vulnerable to such unrewarding sources as every other intelligence service, but it could also boast superb ones. Alger Hiss of the State Department, recruited by the GRU in 1935, was born in 1904 into a prominent Baltimore family. He suffered a childhood tragedy when his father committed suicide, but became a brilliant student at Johns Hopkins and Harvard Law School. His wife, New York writer Priscilla Fansler, was an eager accomplice in his espionage activities. In August 1939 Hiss was denounced to assistant secretary of state Adolph Berle by Whittaker Chambers, a former fellow-comrade. The spy nonetheless kept his nerve, and his job. The Comintern's resident hitman Otto Katz explored the merits of killing Chambers, and was deflected only by the intended victim's warning that he had concealed documents which would critically damage Soviet interests in the US if anything happened to him. In 1941, both Hiss's friend Dean Acheson and his mentor Felix Frankfurter assured the young man they had complete faith in him. Such was the reluctance to believe ill of this brilliant diplomat that he rose onward and upward in the State Department, serving with the US delegation at the 1945 Yalta conference.

Before every major Allied summit of the war, the NKVD briefed the Soviet politburo about the members of the American and British delegations and – in Pavel Sudoplatov's smug words – 'indicated whether they were under our control as agents'. This was a gross implicit exaggeration: only three or four senior American and British diplomats were Soviet sources. But it was indisputably true that, thanks to Stalin's wellwishers in Washington and London, he entered every summit comprehensively informed about the policy positions of his fellow-warlords. If this helped little towards achieving victory over the Axis, it contributed significantly to securing Russia's objectives in the post-war settlement.

Sudoplatov believed that when Hiss briefed the Russians, he was acting at the behest of Roosevelt's aide Harry Hopkins. Hopkins certainly provided important information to Moscow. He warned the Soviet embassy that the FBI had bugged a meeting at which an NKVD officer passed cash to an American communist. He almost certainly briefed Centre's agents about the substance of the Roosevelt–Churchill bilateral summits, and probably about much more. This should not imply, however, that the prominent New Dealer was consciously betraying America's secrets to an enemy; rather, he was committed to seeking a working collaboration between the US and the Soviet Union. He thought, as did his master Franklin Roosevelt, that a parade of trust was an important tool towards achieving this. Hopkins said without embarrassment: 'Since Russia is the decisive factor in the war she must be given every assistance and every effort must be made to obtain her friendship.' The relatively confiding attitude of himself and some other prominent administration figures towards the Russians helped to make subordinates feel justified in going much further, betraying undoubted secrets.

Russian-born William Weisband, a known post-war Soviet source, served in wartime US Army signals intelligence, latterly at Arlington Hall, and is believed to have passed information from an early stage. The OSS was awash with Moscow informants. Karl Marzani worked in the graphics department, Julius Joseph in the Far East section. Other staffers serving two masters included Bella Joseph, Donald Wheeler, Jane Zlatowsky, Horst Berensprung, Helen Tennei, George Wuchinich, Leonard Mintz. The NKVD's OSS informants provided far more material than Centre's five-man US desk could translate. The Latin American division was headed by a former University of Oklahoma professor named Maurice Halperin, who kept a copy of the *Daily Worker* conspicuously on his desk, submitted reports in strict accordance with the Party's line, and worked tirelessly to promote its interests in the countries within his sphere. He was less successful, however, in winning plaudits from Centre, who thought little of his material. Franz Neumann, an economist in the German section, received higher marks for passing on a voluminous American study of the Soviet economy. Noel Field, who provided some assistance to Allen Dulles in Bern while Europe was occupied, in 1945 sought to promote a Party agenda through OSS. Arthur Schlesinger wrote: 'Field was a Quaker Communist, filled with idealism, smugness and sacrifice. What struck me most was his self-righteous evasiveness ... He sought nothing more than a life of pious devotion on the other side of the Iron Curtain.'

Julius Joseph and his wife Bella became prime Moscow sources on US policy towards China, Japan and Korea. Even following the couple's acrimonious divorce, so strong was her loyalty to the Soviets that she did not expose Julius. Donald Wheeler's NKVD handler wrote that 'he treats his OSS colleagues very critically, and considers all empty-headed'. Wheeler took pride in his own contempt for the risk of exposure, saying, 'It makes no sense to be afraid: a man dies only once.' He passed to the Soviets all OSS analytical material on Germany, and – far more dangerously – identified Donovan's agents in Europe, including some who were operating undercover. After the German defeat, Wheeler fingered a US Airborne officer who was engaged on a secret mission in the Soviet Zone of occupation, to report on the Russians' removals of industrial plant.

Arthur Schlesinger said: 'Donovan knew about some OSS communists but not perhaps about others.' The general shrugged: 'I'd put Stalin on the OSS payroll, if I thought it would help us defeat Hitler.' It is nonetheless hard to believe he was aware that his own personal assistant was a Soviet informant. Duncan Lee provided a stream of strategic insights, though the US government would have given some of these to the Russians through open channels, for example Lee's March 1944 warning that D-Day had been delayed until June. He did better service for Centre by warning its agents about security probes, including one on Donald Wheeler. Late in 1944 Lee started a love affair with his ex-NKVD courier Mary Wolfe Price, secretary to the great journalist Walter Lippmann and thus herself a conduit for many privileged confidences. This thoroughly annoyed Centre, because it shifted his priorities. On 3 February 1945 the NKVD's Joseph Katz reported to Moscow: 'Saw Lee last night. After beating his chest about what a coward he is, how sorry he feels about it, etc., he told me he must stick to his decision to quit ... In my opinion there is no sense in using him. He is totally frightened and depressed. He suffers from nightmares where he sees his name on lists.' Katz had two more meetings with Lee, whose nerves were so shredded that his hands shook. They would have shaken even more had he known that his Soviet visitor – not to be confused with his namesake Otto, also a killer – had personally liquidated several informants whose loyalty was suspect. Lee, however, was allowed to survive. In April 1945 the NKVD simply broke off contact with him.

* * *

On 25 November 1943, a fifty-four-year-old Russian Jew named Jacob Golos died of a heart attack in his New York apartment. This caused passionate grief to his lover of five years' standing, Elizabeth Bentley – and to Moscow Centre, whose foremost American network-runner he then was. Golos had fled his homeland as a Bolshevik back in 1910, joined the US Communist Party, then gone home to share the heady joys of Revolution. Later, however, he abandoned a wife and son in the Soviet Union to return to America as an intelligence officer. He became a US citizen, and in 1938 took up with Bentley, a strapping thirty-year-old ex-Vassar girl with a weakness for left-wing causes and unusual foreign men. Golos was busy training her in the arts of intelligence work when he himself was arrested as a spy – hardly surprising, since he was a close friend of Party leader Earl Browder. But he escaped with a short sentence, and – amazingly – felt able to resume his activities.

Golos recruited his friend Nathan Silvermaster, a veteran communist who became Moscow's most important American connection, and in turn secured the services of Harry Dexter White – 'Lawyer' – and other key Washington sources. Julius Rosenberg, much later sent to the electric chair, first gave information to Golos. Cedric Belfrage, a British journalist working for Sir William Stephenson in New York, was another useful contact. Joseph Gregg, an official who moved to the State Department in 1944, provided information about the US Army and Navy, and also forwarded FBI reports on communist activity in Central and South America. A significant number of the network's informants have never been identified. In 1943 a communist codenamed 'Buck' and working in UNRRA, who reported first to Golos then to Silvermaster, passed on a sixty-five-page report on the US machinery industry, then in late June 1945 provided an agenda for US positions at Potsdam. 'Arena' had access to information from the Pentagon's military intelligence department, where his wife worked.

From 1940 onwards, Golos was obliged to subject himself to the Foreign Agents Registration Act, and soon thereafter to FBI surveillance. None of this inhibited him in sustaining his NKVD career, using Elizabeth Bentley – 'Umnitsa' – to make his contacts. His employers were highly nervous about him, however, and made repeated attempts to persuade him to return home, very likely for execution. Golos not merely refused these demands, shrugging that he could not get a passport, but made sure Centre knew that he had taken out, or rather hidden, a life insurance policy: a sealed envelope containing details of Moscow's operations in the US. The Soviets were equally unsuccessful in persuading him to turn over his sources to other US NKVD stations. Golos told Bentley that no other Russian in the US understood Americans as he did. Then he heard that back home his son had joined the Red Army, and talked of wanting to join him. He took the considerable risk of travelling to Washington to meet Vasily Zarubin, to whom he complained bitterly about being asked to transfer his sources.

Then, suddenly, he was dead. Amidst her grief, Elizabeth Bentley remained cool enough to destroy the sealed envelope in a safe deposit, which contained the secrets with which Golos had shielded himself against a visit from Moscow's executioners. Itzhak Akhmerov assumed responsibility for handling her, and assured Centre that Bentley, whom he liked, was 'one hundred per cent our woman'. But Moscow remained uneasy, especially as her alcohol consumption rose. She showed growing signs of strain, and wailed that she needed a man in her life. Eventually, under pressure from Akhmerov, she turned over to him Nathan Silvermaster and thus his group.

Silvermaster was born in Odessa in 1898, emigrated to the West Coast in 1914, and was for years an active US Communist Party member before taking a job at the US Treasury. There, in Moscow's interests he forged links with a string of fellow-sympathisers, some of whom became black-comically muddled about their allegiances. Frank Coe, for instance, complained that his workload as a Soviet agent was hampering his career at the Treasury. Silvermaster's sources produced material from all over Washington. There was data on military-equipment procurement programmes and the views of policy-makers, which probably came from Harry Dexter White, a senior economist at the Treasury. June 1941 brought reports on the Wehrmacht from the office of the US military attaché in London. Moscow learned on 5 August that at a 31 July Washington lunch, navy secretary Frank Knox bet against Morgenthau of the Treasury that Hitler would have Moscow and Leningrad inside a month. Harry Hopkins's report to the White House on his summer 1941 visit to Moscow was also passed to Centre, together with a note on the US cabinet's discussion of Averell Harriman's mission to the Soviet Union.

Intriguing though all this gossip was – and Stalin himself read some of the Silvermaster material – the NKVD wanted more. In 1942 the Washington station was told to brief its man to discover whether the US was fulfilling its Lend-Lease promises, and if not to identify those members of the administration who blocked progress. What were American intentions about opening a second front? What were the administration's views about post-war frontiers, especially those of the Soviet Union? Was there any evidence of fifth-column sabotage in the US? Centre also sought more detail on policy discussions. Its highest priority was to penetrate the White House and to secure information from Hopkins and Morgenthau, because of their intimacy with the president.

Meanwhile, Centre was receiving government material from Robert Miller, Charles Flato, Harold Glasser, Victor Perlo, Charles Kramer, John Abt. Harry Magdoff, a statistician at the Department of War Production, delivered a stream of data on weapons output. It is surprising that Moscow did not run out of codenames for its American sources; there were so many that it became not unusual for them to run into each other in the course of their official duties, sometimes with knowledge of shared disloyalties. Field, Duggan and Straight crossed paths. Accredited diplomat and covert NKVD handler Anatoly Gorsky found himself in the US Treasury Department one day in December 1944, to receive a trivial briefing about German postage stamps. He was directed first to the office of Harry Dexter White, and then – in White's absence – to that of Harold Glasser. Both men were Soviet agents: White protected Glasser from a security inquiry about his communist links, though the two men's personal relationship became strained when their wives quarrelled. Glasser considered it prudent to reject an offered post on the top deck of the State Department, because he would be unlikely to survive the security checks the appointment required. He was nonetheless able to provide Moscow with important cables about US post-war policy planning, including details of Washington's views on financial aid to Russia. In an ambitious moment, Vasily Zarubin sought to target Ernest Hemingway as an informant, though he suspected him of being a Trotskyite rather than a Stalinist. In any event, the wayward writer showed no enthusiasm.

Just as at home in Russia, within the extended Soviet secret family in America denunciations were a way of life, and of death. In August 1944 the NKVD's new resident in San Francisco, Grigori Kasparov, signalled to Moscow a blistering critique of his counterpart in Mexico City. Kasparov accused him of bungling efforts to liberate Trotsky's assassin, Ramón Mercader, and of adopting a 'grand lifestyle', which included breeding poultry and parrots. Similarly, the New York deputy chief claimed that his own boss, twenty-eight-year-old Stepan Apresyan, was 'utterly without the knack of dealing with people, frequently showing himself excessively abrupt and inclined to nag … A worker who has no experience of work abroad and cannot cope on his own.' Apresyan was demoted to the San Francisco residence in March 1945.

The Zarubins were undone not by the artifice of the FBI, but by a disgruntled subordinate colonel named Vasilii Mironov. Mironov's first shot at his chief was to write to Stalin, asserting that Zarubin was doubling for the Axis. When this got him nowhere, he dispatched an anonymous letter to J. Edgar Hoover's office, fingering Zarubin as a Soviet spy, and also naming ten other agents, including Hollywood producer Boris Morros. During the war years the British were too fearful of straining their difficult relationship with the Soviets to expel even identified Soviet 'illegals', but in 1944 the Americans insisted on the Zarubins' departure; both they and their accuser went home. The husband-and-wife team received a heroes' welcome in Moscow; he was loaded with medals, and ended his career as deputy chief of foreign intelligence. Meanwhile Mironov, surprisingly, was allowed to live – for a time. Back in Moscow, he was diagnosed as schizophrenic and dispatched to an asylum. While such Soviet institutions were scarcely havens of compassion, given the damage the errant colonel had inflicted, it is astonishing he was not shot. He was less fortunate in 1945, however, when he attempted to inform the US embassy about Soviet massacres in Poland; this time he was silenced by a firing squad.

In the spring of 1942, as a known communist Nathan Silvermaster was investigated by the House Un-American Activities Committee. This proved nothing against him, though in June the US Navy's intelligence department insisted on his dismissal from the Treasury. Further inquiries into his political activities were quashed – it is thought that Harry Dexter White and another friend, Lauchlin Currie, a Canadian-born senior economic adviser to the White House, intervened on his behalf. Although nothing was ever proved against Currie, it seems almost certain that he too was a Soviet informant. Silvermaster stayed in Washington, with a new job in the Farm Security Administration. Though this had no access to sensitive defence information, he promptly became a member of the War Production Board, which did.

Moscow's American sources were not highly trained intelligence professionals, but instead enthusiastic amateurs. Over half of the hundreds of US government documents photographed by William Ullmann in 1944, for instance, proved unreadable when Centre's men pored over his films, forwarded by Elizabeth Bentley. What could be deciphered was impressive, however; Ullmann was a former Treasury man drafted to the

Pentagon, who supplied a mass of technical data on US combat aircraft and industrial production. In March 1945 the important nuclear spy Ted Hall passed information out of Santa Fe on the design of America's atomic bomb which he had copied onto a newspaper, using milk as ink. The Russians fumed at such hamfistedness.

Much material reached Moscow out of real time. An exasperated memo from Fitin to Merkulov in July 1944 complained that documents such as a copy of an Anglo-American Lend-Lease agreement arrived months late, as did a forty-one-page Treasury memorandum on post-war trade relations between Washington and Moscow, and a draft by Harry Dexter White of a new US-USSR Lend-Lease deal. Fitin sought authority to shift a man from Los Angeles to New York to handle the groaning caseload. The Soviets were even more exasperated by emotional complications: William Ullmann started an affair with Nathan Silvermaster's wife. Akhmerov complained to Moscow: 'Surely these unhealthy relations between them cannot help but influence their behaviour and work for us negatively.' He also reported that Silvermaster bullied his sources. Vladimir Pravdin, now the NKVD's New York station chief, urged Akhmerov to rein in the wayward spy. Akhmerov responded bluntly: 'The main thing is to get results. For twenty-five years, we couldn't get information about the politics of this country. Now [Silvermaster] is doing a tremendous job and giving our government a complete picture of [US] politics on all questions.' In August 1944, Fitin at Centre recorded that since January the Washington network had handed over 386 important US government documents. He was sufficiently impressed by the Silvermasters' work to contribute a $6,000 down-payment on a farm the couple wanted to buy. Nathan was awarded a Soviet decoration, which he was permitted to glimpse before his handler returned it to secret safekeeping. The volume of information passed to Moscow by all its American networks rose spectacularly in the course of the war, from fifty-nine reels of microfilm in 1942, to 211 in 1943, six hundred in 1944 and 1,896 in 1945, with the Silvermasters among the major contributors.

How did the Russians get away with so much for so long? Most citizens of democracies accept that part of the tariff imposed for freedom is that their defences against subversion and treachery are less comprehensive and effective than those of a totalitarian state, and such a price usually seems worth paying. Yet the FBI's incompetence was astonishing. Its agents charged with monitoring Soviet activities showed themselves less than astute. Alexander Feklisov wrote in his memoirs: 'There were many green young men in the [FBI's] foot surveillance teams ... and our officers exposed them by using simple tricks. Tails were probably selected from young men reared in small towns, who would start working against us after two or three months' training. One could see straight away that they were provincials – by their clothes, the guilty, larcenous look in their eyes; their clumsiness. They felt lost when they realised that they had been spotted, and didn't know what to do. They would turn away, or walk quickly into the first building they saw.'

Feklisov sometimes walked straight towards his tail, for the fun of seeing the man flee before him in embarrassment. Surveillance is highly labour-intensive, requiring back-up cars in case a suspect grabs a bus or taxi. 'I often spotted followers when getting into the subway or standing on the platform. They were so scared they would lose me when I boarded a train that they almost ran down the stairs. Once on the platform, I normally chose a spot where it was hard to see me: behind a pillar, by the wall, in the crowd. There were occasions when the only people in a quiet subway station were myself and the tail. In such cases I normally tried to think about something nice, smiled and hummed a popular American tune while pacing along the platform with a carefree look, to show that I paid no attention to the surveillance. The tails dressed modestly, mostly in dark dull suits and overcoats. In summer they mostly wore their shirts hanging out, with no tie. On one occasion I was watched by a team of four. One of them wore army uniform for half the day. I saw him on the escalator in the metro, then he followed me into the Cunard White Star office where I booked steamship tickets for Soviet citizens travelling to London. I saw this "soldier" yet again when lunching at a cafeteria.' Hoover could fire only one counter-charge against his more skilful and subtle British counterparts: his own Bureau was never infiltrated by a Soviet agent, as was MI5.

The Roosevelt administration apparently agreed about the FBI's limitations. In July 1941 the Soviets' Washington ambassador, Konstantin Umansky, reported to Moscow an emotional appeal by Henry Morgenthau. The treasury secretary said that he was asking 'not on behalf of the American government, but on my personal behalf' that if the Russians knew the identities of key German agents in the US, they should provide them to himself and the president, 'since the FBI works poorly today ... leaving the core of Nazi leaders free and still carrying on their undermining work'. A Moscow Centre hand scrawled exclamation and question marks on this cable. Morgenthau repeated the same demand to Umansky's successor, Maxim Litvinov. Early in March 1942 Moscow ordered the ambassador to reject any requests for intelligence cooperation: 'The NKVD of the USSR is not interested in establishing this liaison.' In the summer of 1944, and partly in response to concern about the security of the Manhattan Project, the FBI planted wiretaps in all known Soviet head-quarters buildings, through which they learned a good many codenames, together with indisputable evidence of Itzhak Akhmerov's intelligence role. He was declared *persona non grata*, and went home to receive a hero's welcome in Moscow. He was presented with the Order of the Red Banner, and his wife Helen with the Red Star.

By the end of the war Centre was convinced that Elizabeth Bentley was chronically unstable and a menace to their US operations, especially after she formed a friendship with a man who was plainly an agent of either 'the Hut' – the FBI – or 'the Arsenal' – the US War Department; in reality, it was the former. Centre decided upon her kidnapping and extraction to Moscow for liquidation. It was too late: she was already singing a long aria to Hoover's men, news that was conveyed to her employers by Kim Philby. In a post-mortem on the Golos–Bentley saga, Centre concluded that it was a serious mistake to have allowed its agent to forge links with members of the American Communist Party, and to become 'the main pillar of our intelligence work in the US'. It was extraordinary that a spy so careless as to meet informants in their own apartments – as did Bentley – escaped exposure for so long. Following her surrender, she gave evidence at several trials and to congressional committees but became increasingly unstable and weakened by alcoholism. She died in 1963, aged 55.

The same arguments are advanced to excuse America's communist traitors as their British counterparts: that it is scarcely surprising so many liberals sought to assist the Soviet Union, when the institutional barbarity of Stalin's regime was inadequately understood, and Russians bore the over-whelming burden of the struggle to defeat fascism. As the East German spy chief Markus Wolf later put it, Moscow's informants considered them-selves members of an elite secret club, fighting for a noble ideal. Pierre Cot, a former minister in several French governments living in exile in the US, undertook a long 1944 mission to Moscow for de Gaulle. He concluded his subsequent report: 'Liberty declines unceasingly under capitalism and rises unceasingly under socialism.' A remarkable number of American and British intellectuals likewise embraced this idiot judgement. From 1941 to 1945, Russians were the allies of the United States in the greatest conflict in history.

In response, however, it may be argued that few informed people – which included almost all the American spies – could have failed to be aware of the horrors of the Soviet system, had they chosen to make themselves so. Apologists also argue that the traitors' actions had no adverse impact upon the Allied cause in the Second World War. That is only narrowly true: recall the Soviet leak to the Germans about the American penetration of Purple. Those were still the days of the Nazi–Soviet Pact: Hitler's emissary passed on this momentous warning to the Japanese. Baron Ōshima messaged Japan's foreign minister from Berlin on 3 May 1941 – a dispatch subsequently broken by the Americans – saying that 'it is quite reliably established [by the Germans] that the U.S. government is reading Ambassador Nomura's code messages [from Washington] ... drastic steps should be taken regarding this matter'. The fact that Tokyo was foolish enough to take no heed does not alter the gravity of the threat to US interests. It is also virtually certain that the Russians acquired this vital secret from one of their American informants in the upper reaches of the administration. This man may have supposed that by briefing Moscow he was merely aiding the international socialist cause. It was only by a miracle, however, that his action did not cause the US to lose its access to Purple.

Arthur Schlesinger wrote in his memoirs: 'There is no evidence that the information OSS moles gave the Kremlin did much damage to the United States. The discovery that OSS was not planning subversive operations against the Soviet Union may well have soothed Stalin and reduced any chance of his making a separate peace with Hitler.' Here, the historian makes a valid point: Soviet penetration of the organisation would have inflicted serious damage at the time only if Moscow's agents had been passing intelligence that showed the United States double-crossing its supposed ally – which was not the case. Yet at no time during the Second World War did Stalin entertain any notion of sustaining peaceful co-existence with the Western Powers once it was ended. The American and British traitors did substantial harm to their own nations' interests, by ensuring that Washington bargained with Moscow – for instance at Yalta and at the United Nations' founding conference in San Francisco – at a serious disadvantage: Soviet delegations knew precisely where American and British final positions lay.

The Americans who gave technological and scientific data to the Soviets, of whom more below, did greater harm to their own nation's interests than those who merely peddled political, diplomatic and strategic information during the war years. Most of the Russians' immense invest-ment in espionage in the US achieved little. The best that can be said of the Americans who served their cause is that they were monumentally naïve – the Russians certainly thought so. The US informants who worked so enthusiastically with Vasily and Elizabeth Zarubin might have supped less eagerly had they seen the bloodstained footprints that marked every step of their paths from Moscow to Washington, DC.

15

The Knowledge Factories

Britain's intelligence services employed hundreds of impressively determined and courageous young field agents, of whom the Norwegian Oluf Reed-Olsen may stand as an exemplar. In September 1940, aged twenty-two, he escaped to Britain from his own occupied country by crossing the North Sea in an eighteen-foot boat, surviving extraordinary hazards and tempests during the two-week passage. Thereafter he spent two years as a pilot trainee in Canada, and flew several operations for RAF Coastal Command before accepting a transfer to agent training, in the course of which he broke both legs parachuting. In April 1943 the plane carrying him to Norway twice turned back, because wind speeds were deemed too high for a jump. The third time, he insisted on making the descent, landed in a treetop and badly dislocated his knee. This caused him to spend a month in a Norwegian hospital, constantly exposed to betrayal, having fluid drained from the injury. On belatedly starting intelligence work, he brushed disaster at every turn. Carelessness prompted him to use English phrases in public places. His British briefers had known nothing about new regulations which required him to carry a travel permit. He found it hard to create a network from scratch: 'Most of the people who at that time were capable of doing a job efficiently were already up to their necks in illegal activity elsewhere ... I would not let any man work for me and in other organizations at the same time. This was a mistake to which far too many fell victims.'

He wasted a month bivouacked in a wilderness with two companions, wirelessing his AKY callsign into nothingness, before his signals to Whaddon Hall received an acknowledgement: 'PBO ... PBO.' He then spent thirty minutes transmitting a situation report: 'The difference it made to our spirits – after our weeks of toil and increasing setbacks – cannot be described. It was like a breeze of encouragement blowing through all the blackness.' Olsen and his companions lived for some time on semi-starvation rations – three boiled potatoes a day with a little bread, mackerel or herring. Poor diet goes far to explain how injured men in the field often proved vulnerable to septicaemia. Only after many months did Olsen's team receive their first parachute drop, of which the most valued ingredients were not weapons or explosives, but 270 pounds of chocolate, 5,000 cigarettes, dried plums, apricots, apples. Although temporarily driven from the area by a German sweep, they were fortunate enough to return later to find the supply cache undisturbed, in a cave amid thick woodland.

Secret warriors spent much of their time preoccupied with humdrum subsistence activities, rather than with collecting intelligence or blowing up bridges. Reed-Olsen sometimes found himself toiling across a mountainside carrying an eighty-pound load – an MI6 transmitter weighed almost half of that, with its batteries. For agents obliged to live in rural areas, it helped to be countrywise: the young Norwegian was often alerted to interlopers by the cross call of a stonechat or blackbird. His main job was to monitor and report shipping movements and German troop deployments. In October 1943, after weeks of playing catch-as-catch-can with Abwehr director-finders monitoring his wireless transmissions, he was obliged to flee to neighbouring Sweden. Flown to London in January 1944, he took two months' leave in Canada to get married, before being parachuted back into Norway in May. Thereafter he transmitted local weather reports several times a day, and answered such questionnaires as this late-July example from Broadway:

1. Is there a divisional staff in Arendal? Give number, HQ and name of CO.
2. Is there a Grenadier regiment's HQ in Kristiansand South and/or Lyngdal? Give number, location of HQ and name of CO.
3. Are the army troops in Mandal subordinated to Lyngdal or Kristiansand?

This continued through six more questions with multiple sub-headings.

In the last months of the war Reed-Olsen was able to recruit two German deserters, abandoning the sinking Reich, to assist in addressing such requests from London. He was latterly successful in evading German DF units, though these often taunted him across the ether to repeat code groups, and finally sent 'HEIL HITLER!' in plain language.

Reed-Olsen, like hundreds of his comrades around the world, lived for years in peril of capture and a ghastly death. Attrition was especially high in the Low Countries, where the terrain was ill-suited to covert activity, informers were many and the Abwehr's counter-intelligence branch notably efficient. Of eighty-nine MI6 agents dispatched to occupied Belgium and Holland during the war years, thirty-nine were captured, of whom just eleven survived the war. By 1945, only thirteen MI6 wirelesses remained operational in the region.

Meanwhile in the mountains of Greece, by July 1944 Nigel Clive was using two radio-operators to process a constant flow of military, political and economic material: 'The good intelligence we were receiving was a reflection of the skill and determination of our agents. They had the advantage, however, that almost everyone believed that the Germans would soon be gone. In these circumstances open opportunities were offered to our agents to approach those who wished to hedge their bets.' Clive was conscious of the triviality of much of the information: 'I would be told that Andreas had just been conscripted by the Germans into a labour force for building an airstrip; that Evangelos had a cousin whose brother-in-law was now serving in [the communist] ELAS against his will and wanted to defect to Zervas; that Macros's uncle in Ioannina had heard that the Germans would definitely be out of Greece before the summer; that Leftheris had heard from his sister in Arta that EDES was planning an attack on the town in the following week ... I always listened patiently to everything that was told me and naturally assured Costakis and others who approached me directly that every scrap of information was of great value. This was the only deception I practised and it helped me to be accepted as a member of their community.'

After the Germans quit, Clive suffered a succession of unwelcome revelations. First, his labours on the enemy's order of battle had served no useful purpose. The Wehrmacht evacuated Greece of its own volition, without fighting a battle for which his jigsaw-building might have become relevant. He also discovered that German knowledge mirrored his own: the local enemy commander Lt. Gen. Hubert Lanz 'knew about us what we knew about him', from informers and interception. It was even more bewildering for the British agent to learn that Zervas, the guerrilla leader to whose group he was attached, had been conducting parleys with the Germans, aimed at achieving a common front against the communists. A signal from Lanz to higher headquarters, dated 7 August 1944 and eventually passed to Clive, spoke of Zervas's 'up to now loyal attitude' – towards the occupiers.

Finally, the spy found that he had been the victim of cynicism, incompetence or treachery higher up the intelligence food chain: the head of MI6's political section told him in January 1945 that not one of his long and often perceptive political reports had reached Broadway. It will never be known whether these were suppressed for ideological reasons by communist sympathisers inside the Service, especially in Cairo, or – equally plausible – lost amid the morass of unread paper generated by tens of thousands of intelligence officers of all nations, at risk of their lives. That is not to say that field agent activity was wasted: Donald McLachlan of NID paid generous tribute to the value of the reports of Norwegian ship-watchers such as Reed-Olsen, who warned of some enemy movements and especially U-boat sailings that escaped Ultra's net, although it was another matter to put the information to practical use: throughout the war the Royal Navy and the Fleet Air Arm had little success in interdicting Scandinavian coastal traffic. As for German troop deployments, whether in Norway, Greece or elsewhere in occupied Europe, while Ultra provided a good picture, this was never comprehensive, and it was everywhere useful for its coverage to be supplemented by men on the ground.

British intelligence never achieved significant humint penetration inside the Reich. Plenty of anti-Nazi Germans were eager to escape to Allied territory, but not many were interested in returning to Hitler's empire thereafter as spies or saboteurs. John Bruce Lockhart of MI6 – nephew of the old spy Robert – wrote ruefully in 1944 that there were 'plenty of rats that leave the sinking ship, and we shall get more, but precious few are prepared to go back to gnaw another hole in her bottom'. In Italy, Broadway abandoned attempts to recruit agents from among Italian PoWs, because the human material available proved so poor. Only when the Allies began to fight inside the country, and partisan groups provided relatively safe rustic havens behind enemy lines, did British and American officers operate there in numbers. Moreover, not all MI6 agents overseas were as conscientious as Reed-Olsen and Clive: the novelist Graham Greene treated espionage, and indeed the whole war, as an absurdity. He signalled Broadway from Freetown, Sierra Leone, in 1942, proposing that the service should open a brothel for Vichy French sailors from the *Richelieu* on a Portuguese island off the battleship's base at Dakar. Following his recall to Britain, Greene joined MI6's sub-section at St Albans, run by Kim Philby. Though the novelist personally disliked Philby while he worked with him, he treated him with indulgence when he was revealed as a traitor, as merely another trader in a ridiculous secrets bazaar.

The Russians provided the Western Allies with scarcely any information about their own operations, far less those of the Axis. For a time they grudgingly supplied copies of decrypts of low-level Wehrmacht codes they had broken, but on 1 December 1942 this service stopped abruptly, and was never resumed. In the spring of 1944 a Royal Navy mine and sabotage expert, Lt. Shirley, was sent to the Black Sea to survey German demolitions in recaptured Russian ports before the Allies faced the problem of clearing captured French harbours after D-Day. When 6 June came, however, Shirley was still kicking his heels in Sevastopol, vainly awaiting Russian consent to be allowed to inspect harbour installations.

The need to sustain a semblance of collaboration created other dilemmas in London. Back in December 1941, when British hopes of an intelligence partnership with the Soviets ran much higher than they stood eighteen months later, the NKVD dispatched four Austrians to Britain, whom the RAF were supposed to drop back into their native land. The spies arrived only after long delays and adventures – one man's ship was sunk en route, with the loss of his wireless. All complained bitterly about the poor quality of their forged identity documents, and a second set sent from Moscow proved no better. The NKVD's agents flatly refused to undertake their mission with such papers, and also rejected return to Russia on the not unreasonable grounds that they would be executed. The Austrians, who were plainly eager to secure permanent billets in Britain, told their hosts that their mission had little to do with defeating Hitler: they were briefed instead to form a Comintern 'sleeper' cell, to promote post-war communist interests. Whether or not this was true, the British felt unable to frogmarch the men aboard an RAF aircraft bound for enemy territory. Yet they also flinched from the diplomatic storm that must follow, if the spies were granted asylum. In April 1943, MI5's ingenious and humane solution was to dispatch them back to Russia via Panama, where they were allowed to jump ship and disappear.

Broadway's activities and staffing expanded dramatically in the course of the war, with departments spilling over into a network of out-stations. Section V, for instance, grew from a strength of eight in 1940 to 250 five years later. MI6's senior officers, however, remained little changed, and Hugh Trevor-Roper thought no better of them: 'A colony of coots in an unventilated backwater of bureaucracy ... A bunch of dependent bumsuckers held together by neglect, like a cluster of bats in an unswept barn ... The high priests of an effete religion mumbling their meaningless rituals to avert a famine or stay a cataclysm.' An officer who served in MI6 noted that its top brass, who regarded themselves with unflagging seriousness, never arrived on time for a meeting: they excused their unpunctuality by implying that they had been held up attending a cabinet committee. An intelligent and not unsympathetic observer told one of MI6's officers that in recruiting personnel, 'we are too ready to be satisfied with good second-raters'. Even at the height of a world war, the Foreign Office treated the Service as 'poor and rather disreputable relations'. A diplomat complained about the 'low social status' of MI6's representatives on his patch, though this reflected more upon Foreign Office snobbery than on the agents concerned. Waste was prodigious: Broadway purchased an aircraft to scour the coast of Argentina for German shipping, an impossible task given the distances involved, and anyway directed against a non-existent threat.

An obsession with securing advantage in Whitehall's wars persisted at Broadway, as in Tirpitzüfer and Moscow Centre. MI6's official historian writes of Claude Dansey's attitude, manifested in his role supervising the escape organisation MI9: 'He frequently gave the impression that his engagement was as much to deny any other government department the opportunity to meddle on the Continent as it was to rescue British personnel.' One day Dansey strode into the office of Patrick Reilly, the brilliant young diplomat who served for a time as Stewart Menzies' personal assistant. 'Great news,' he said. 'Great news.' His exultation was caused by the collapse of a major French agent network run by SOE, whom Dansey hated even more than the Americans. Reilly wrote: 'Misery, torture and death for many brave men and women, British and French: and Dansey gloated.' Reilly recorded that he himself felt sick.

Menzies' personal sanctum was guarded by two venerable ladies who addressed each other, even after years of shared service, as 'Miss Jones' and 'Miss Pettigrew'. The former was the milder and better-looking, while the latter was large and formidable. Both were drawn from the same extensive stable of female servants of Broadway – genteel, loyal, discreet, tireless. Malcolm Muggeridge observed, surely rightly, that a common characteristic of people who serve intelligence services is a delight in opacity for its own sake, a conceit derived from access to knowledge denied to others: 'This sense of importance, of cherishing secrets beyond the ken of ordinary mortals, was characteristic of SIS personnel at all levels, particularly the females, who, however careless they might be about their chastity, guarded their security with implacable resolution.'

In 1943, Robert Cecil succeeded Reilly as Menzies' personal assistant, and thereafter became a sturdy defender of his chief. 'C's' most important contribution, he argued years later, was to ensure that the Ultra secret was preserved. The Special Liaison Units which served with commanders in the field, created by Broadway's Fred Winterbotham, were a brilliant security device, said Cecil. Every Allied commander-in-chief had his personal SLU, living apart from the rest of the headquarters, and charged with filtering decrypts securely into the intelligence process. 'C' also retained a clear sense of the purpose of his organisation's existence. In a memorandum to his staff on 10 November 1942, he expressed its rationale: 'all Intelligence about the enemy, whether collected by secret means, or by open field Intelligence, should be based on the old dictum that "Intelligence is the mainspring of Action" ... SIS's prime function is to obtain information by secret means which may admit of or promote action ... Information on which no action can be taken may be of interest, it may be useful for records or for the future, but it is of secondary importance.'

Life at MI6's headquarters was no more free from hazard than in that of any other central London office: on Sunday, 18 June 1944 Cecil and Menzies were working in Broadway Building when a V-1 flying bomb descended, one wing touching Queen Anne's Mansions next door before the projectile slewed into the Guards Chapel and exploded during a service, killing 120 of the congregation. Cecil argued that a wartime 'C' needed to be a man of 'cool courage and high integrity, seeking only how best to apply the ingenuity of others in the common cause. Menzies was the right man in the right place at the right time.' Cecil's case for the defence deserves notice. It has been a source of exasperation to British intelligence officers since 1945 that their service's best-known chroniclers of its wartime experience were Hugh Trevor-Roper, Graham Greene and Malcolm Muggeridge, all notoriously erratic personalities. Of the three, only Trevor-Roper distinguished himself as an intelligence officer, and even he seemed to recognise in his post-war writing that blander qualities than his own were needed in the managers of a secret service: 'Apparently miraculous achievements are the results not of miraculous organisations, but of efficient routines. The head of an intelligence service is not a superspy but a bureaucrat.' Bill Bentinck of the JIC was once canvassed as a candidate to supplant Menzies, but there was no appetite to change jockeys relatively late in the race, when Bletchley's achievement was being celebrated throughout the councils of the Allied warlords.

In all the belligerent camps there was fierce debate about the merits of centralisation versus dispersal of intelligence effort. Empire-building and rivalry by Britain's MI5, MI6 and SOE, especially, caused duplication and wasted resources. But this also enabled disparate groups of men and women, some of the highest intellect, to pursue their own ideas and courses, to the advantage of the Allied cause: a thousand seeds were sown. Though many proved sterile, some produced wondrous blooms, the Radio Security Service and Radio Analysis Bureau notable among them. If intelligence-gathering and sabotage had been centralised under MI6's control, the weaknesses of Broadway would merely have become more deeply embedded. And even the notorious feuds between MI6 and SOE did less injury to the Allied war effort than did the glacial relationship between the US Army and US Navy.

The most plausible defence of Broadway's wartime record is to pose the question: which other nation's secret service performed better? Stewart Menzies was a limited man, but he showed himself a stabler personality than Donovan, Canaris, Schellenberg, Fitin – his counterparts in the other warring capitals. On the debit side, MI6 created nothing comparable with OSS's Research & Analysis division. It never forged links with anti-Hitler Germans, especially in the army, as did the Russians and latterly the Americans. But there was a constraint here: the prime minister had imposed draconian restrictions upon any contacts with Germany which might feed Stalin's morbid fears that the Western Allies wanted a separate peace. It was this that caused the Foreign Office repeatedly to spurn approaches from anglophile members of the German Resistance such as Helmuth von Moltke and Adam von Trott. Only on technological issues, such as the V-weapons discussed below, can it be argued that well-placed humint sources in Germany could have exercised important influence. Ultra provided such peerless insights into the enemy's camp that it is hard to imagine what spies might have done better.

2 THE JEWEL OF SOURCES

The triumph of the US Signals Intelligence Service in securing access to the Japanese Purple diplomatic cipher contributed little to winning the war, because it was not a military channel, but notable among its achievements was recruitment of the Japanese ambassador in Berlin as a source. It was a drollery of the time that the strivings and sacrifices of Allied secret agents secured no humint as interesting as that unconsciously contributed by Baron Hiroshi Ōshima. His dispatches, decrypted by Arlington Hall and Bletchley Park, provided a window on the Nazi high command, and occasionally on Hitler's intentions. Ōshima was not a clever man – indeed, his military and political judgement was terrible. Until the end of 1942 he remained an unswerving believer in Hitler's impending triumph, and impatient for Japan to share the spoils. From 1939 onwards, he repeatedly urged his countrymen: 'Don't miss the bus!' His short, chunky figure was often photographed gazing admiringly up at the Führer. In 1942 Göbbels wrote in his diary: 'Oshima really is one of the most effective champions of Axis policies. A monument ought in due course to be erected in his honour.' This sentiment would have been echoed, for different reasons, in Washington and London, because the Nazi leadership confided more freely in the Japanese ambassador than in any other foreigner, and the Allies became privy to everything he learned. He sent to Tokyo seventy-five dispatches in 1941, a hundred in 1942, four hundred in 1943, six hundred in 1944 and three hundred in the last months of the war, some of them voluminous, and all read by the Allies within a week or so of their transmission.

Ōshima was born in 1886, son of a politician who served as war minister in two 1916–18 Tokyo cabinets. He knew Germany intimately, having been first posted there as military attaché in 1934, and became a popular figure on the Berlin diplomatic circuit, a music-lover and keen party-goer who sometimes consumed an entire bottle of kirsch without visible ill-effects. In 1938 he was elevated to ambassador and lieutenant-general. Though recalled to Tokyo in the autumn of 1939, he was reappointed in December 1940, by which time Washington was reading Purple, and soon provided the British with the means to do likewise. Thereafter until the end of the war some 2,000 of Ōshima's dispatches and messages were decrypted, translated and circulated to Roosevelt, Marshall, Churchill and senior intelligence officers on both sides of the Atlantic. If his assessments and predictions were often poor, his accounts of conversations with top Nazis appear to have been accurate, and he was an intermediary for important exchanges between Tokyo and Berlin.

For instance, on 10 May 1941 foreign minister Yōsuke Matsuoka sent a letter to the ambassador for onward passage to Ribbentrop, urging restraint in the German government's public remarks about the United States: 'Our mutual loyalty makes me deeply anxious to cause the American

President to reflect and check his reckless plans, and ... I have been working night and day to this end. By preventing the staging of Armageddon
and the consequent downfall of modern civilization (if an act of man can
make that possible) I shall thereby discharge my dual responsibility to
God and man.' On 24 May Ōshima reported a conversation with Ciano,
Mussolini's foreign minister, in which the latter said: 'Do you not think
that outbreak of war between Germany and Soviet Union is virtually
inevitable?'

On 4 June 1941 Ōshima reported to Tokyo, and thus to Washington
and London, the views of Hitler and Ribbentrop that 'in every probability
war with Russia cannot be avoided'. A few days later he expressed the view
that Germany would secure victory too quickly for the Americans and
British to be able to offer Stalin useful help; it was the decrypt of this
dispatch that belatedly convinced the Joint Intelligence Committee in
London that Hitler was indeed determined on war. At the end of July
Ōshima told Tokyo of his conviction that the US would soon come into
the war; the only doubt in his mind was how far the Americans would be
able to give meaningful assistance to Britain. Tokyo, however, told him
nothing about its hardening commitment to striking first. Throughout
1941 the Allies remained uncertain about Japanese intentions towards the
Soviet Union – as was Berlin. The Tokyo government asserted its intention
to join the Germans in attacking the Russians, but refused to specify a
time scale. Ōshima sent home full and frequent dispatches about the
progress of 'Barbarossa', which reinforced American and British perceptions that the Russians were on the ropes. When Ōshima reported on 25
August that the Red Army was estimated to have suffered between five and
six million casualties – no great exaggeration – how could Western
governments fail to be impressed? By late November, however, Tokyo was
telling the baron that it would welcome a peace deal between Hitler and
Stalin.

From 1942 onwards Ōshima reported the sailings to Japan of block-
ade-running vessels, and later submarines. The combination of intercepts
from his Berlin embassy and Kriegsmarine signals snared by Bletchley and
Op-20-G enabled the Allies to wreak havoc with attempts by the Japanese
to break the Allied blockade and carry either commodities to Europe or
technological prizes homeward. Once surface blockade-runners had been
disposed of, and the Axis was reduced to underwater communication,
from 1942 onwards fifty-six load-carrying submarines were dispatched, of
which twenty-nine were sunk, three abandoned their missions and one

was interned. Of twenty-three which completed a one-way passage, only five succeeded in returning home intact, survivors of devastation by sigint.

Churchill was prompted to launch a pre-emptive British invasion of French Madagascar by a 17 March dispatch from the ambassador asserting that Japan would receive Germany's full support in attempting to secure the island for itself. On 27 July Tokyo told the baron that all his urgings had been in vain: there would be no Japanese attack on the Soviet Union – on 5 August Franklin Roosevelt forwarded these tidings to Stalin in a personal message. The Soviet warlord may have remained sceptical nonetheless, since only six weeks earlier the US president had given him a contrary warning.

On 21 September 1942, Ōshima reported the serious depletion of German oil stocks, which could only be remedied by the capture of the Caucasus – then deemed imminent – 'after which the situation will not be as discouraging as it now looks'. The ambassador urged Ribbentrop that the Wehrmacht should use poison gas to ensure the successful invasion of England, which the Japanese still considered should be a priority objective long after Hitler had abandoned it. On 23 September Ōshima renewed his pleas to Tokyo that Japan should attack Russia: 'Let us join forces with the Germans and be in on the kill.'

On 28 November, Japan's foreign minister wrote to Ōshima dismissing his optimistic forecasts and highlighting German weakness, especially in oil, along with failure to take Stalingrad: 'You say that Germany has weakened Russia. Well, what about Russia weakening Germany? … I think you would be very wrong if you supposed that it is impossible for the Soviets to come back with a swift blow, and that right soon. I think you had better wait a while before judging Soviet forces to be so weak … However you view it, Germany cannot easily get into the Middle and Near East. Now what we want is for Germany to ready itself for a long war.' Ōshima passed back explicit assurances from Hitler and Ribbentrop that Germany would make no separate peace with Russia, though in Washington and London doubts persisted that the Nazis might change their minds, as the strategic tide turned against them. In December 1942 Ribbentrop confided Berlin's serious alarm about the North African situation following the Allied 'Torch' landings.

Slowly but surely, Anglo-American intelligence analysts, who had been initially wary about the authority of Ōshima's communications, realised how much trust he commanded among the top Nazis. Never in history had belligerents been empowered to eavesdrop on the conversation of their enemies' policy-makers, as now they were. On 15 December 1942 the ambassador reported Ribbentrop acknowledging that 'the war with Russia is not progressing as expected'. After spending two hours with Hitler on 21 January 1943, Ōshima quoted him as saying: 'I don't want you to think that I am weakening in my conviction that we shall win, but … it is clear that if, in order to destroy the striking power of Russia, you Japanese would, from the East, take a hand and help us out, it would be very advantageous in getting this job off our hands.' On 2 February the Japanese diplomat reported with startling bluntness that the defeat suffered by the German army at Stalingrad was 'the greatest disaster to have overtaken it since Napoleon crushed the Prussians at Jena [in 1806]'. At a time when the Soviets were telling Washington and London almost nothing credible about the course of the war, here was authoritative intelligence about the transformation of the Eastern Front.

Ōshima continued: 'Since Germany has been fighting Russia, Hitler and the generals have been at odds over the conduct of the war, and now is the time for [him] to stop and think … The military say that it is not that they want to quarrel with Hitler, but that winning the war is the first consideration. [He] understands this and will, in all probability, willingly give in. It is rumoured that a number of the generals who have been in disgrace will soon be brought onto the staff again and that Field-Marshal Keitel will be moved [from his position as chief of the high command]; however, so far there seems no certainty as to these matters.'

In May 1943 another Japanese general, Kiyotomi Okamoto, was a member of a large delegation that travelled by rail across the Soviet Union, with which his country was not yet at war. The visitors compiled exhaustive notes on everything they saw from their train, counting boxcars, oil tankers, aircraft on airfields, for a fat dossier they proudly presented to Hitler, and which was afterwards read by Tokyo, Arlington Hall and Bletchley. All these audiences may have questioned the value of such nuggets as '2nd field (about 4 kilometres north of Alma Ata station). One Douglas passenger plane and about 40 single-seater, slow training planes of uncertain type, a wireless station and three two-storey barracks. One plane taking off, landing and taking off again.' There were pages of such stuff, characteristic of intelligence flannel of all nationalities.

In justice to the Japanese, however, their overall estimate of the Soviet Union's combat power, compiled in Tokyo, was both honest and reasonably sound, given that it was drafted for a partly Nazi readership: 'The Stalin regime, through able management and careful mobilization, has rallied all resources of the state to combat Germany. The army and people are firmly behind Stalin and war consciousness is running high.' The foreign minister, now Mamoru Shigemitsu, wrote to Ōshima on the same date – 28 April 1943 – saying that the Tokyo government feared that 'Germany may lose all her self-reliance and that in the meantime America and England will be left free to strengthen their striking power and finally to launch a great offensive.' Ōshima was urged to exert his influence and pass on to the Nazis Japan's strategic assessments, to encourage Germany to pursue a separate peace with the Soviets.

It was three months before the ambassador had another personal meeting with Hitler, but on 30 July, following the disaster at Kursk, the Japanese did indeed urge peace. Germany's Führer dismissed this fantasy, saying, 'Don't you know that if I did [the Soviets] would beyond any peradventure of doubt reach out, clasp hands with the United States, and squeeze you Japanese to death between them!' Hitler lamented Italy's collapse, saying, 'What an ally! If we had only had you Japanese in the [geographical] position of Italy we would assuredly already have won this struggle.' Following a further meeting at the Wolf's Lair on 9 October 1943, Ōshima told Tokyo that Hitler had told him that he was 'inclined to believe' the Allies would land in the Balkans instead of moving north in Italy. On Russia, Hitler said, 'we are making our stand … but, depending on whether or not the Soviet forces resume the offensive, we may fall back to the line which we have prepared on the Dnieper. In the north, if the worst comes to the worst, we can retire to a second defence line which we have prepared across the narrow strip of land adjoining Lake Peipus … I think it the best policy first to strike at the American and British forces as soon as we get the chance, and then to turn on the Soviets.'

In November 1943 Ōshima wirelessed a sixteen-page report to Tokyo, describing a tour he had just made of the Atlantic Wall, and detailing the locations of sixteen German coastal defence divisions. He emphasised the ability of strongpoints to fight independently, and made plain the German expectation that the Allies would land in the Pas de Calais. An American codebreaker bore witness to the thrill that ran through him as he worked on reading the Japanese dispatch, and understood its momentous significance: 'Within a few hours the magnitude of what was at hand was apparent … I was too electrified to sleep.'

Ōshima suggested to Ribbentrop that the British and Americans might make a preliminary descent on Normandy or Brittany. On 23 January 1944 Hitler told his Japanese friend, 'beyond any doubt the most effective area [for the main landing] would be the [Pas de Calais]'. The ambassador's February, April and early May reports on the invasion prospects ignored Normandy, and it was obvious that Ōshima's confusion of mind reflected that of the entire Axis high command. On 19 May he told Tokyo that an Allied landing might be staged in Dalmatia, Norway or southern France. The following day, he suggested that it could take place in Sweden, 'however Jodl [operations chief of OKW] told me that he does not think as I do'.

A second Allied source within the Japanese embassy also deserves mention. It came on stream in March 1944 when Op-20-G, with assistance from Hugh Alexander's team at Bletchley, broke the 'Coral' naval attaché cipher. Vice-Admiral Katsuo Abe, chief of the naval mission to Germany, was a more intelligent and certainly much more sceptical observer than his ambassador – Op-20-G referred to him gratefully as 'Honest Abe'. He too sent copious reports to Tokyo, especially informative about Dönitz's new Type XXI and Type XXIII U-boats, both with very high underwater speeds, and fitted with *Schnorkel* breathing devices. Abe gave detailed technical specifications for the submarines and reported regularly on their production schedules, especially after personal briefings by Dönitz and his constructors in April and August 1944. By that stage of the war, Abe – unlike Ōshima – was in no doubt of the inevitability of German defeat, asserting on 21 August: 'I regret to say that it is hard to see what the Germans can do that will suffice to bridge the yawning gap between the material and military strength of themselves and their opponents.' He reported on the serious impact of American bombing on German oil production – a crisis about which Albert Speer also briefed Ōshima on 18 August.

Allied commanders had by now become as eager as the ambassador himself for his meetings with Nazi leaders, which were as useful as holding such conversations on their own account. George Marshall acknowledged later that the Japanese envoy had become 'our main basis of information regarding Hitler's intentions in Europe'. On 27 May Ōshima reported on his latest session with the Führer at the Burghof: 'Judging from relatively ominous portents, I think that diversionary actions will take place against Norway, Denmark, the southern part of western France, and the coasts of the French Mediterranean – various places. After that, when they have established beachheads on the Norman and Brittany Peninsulas and [have] seen how the prospects appear, they will come forward with the establishment of an all-out Second Front in the area of the Straits of Dover.'

Eisenhower read this message on 30 May. Here, for the Allied high command, was the most authoritative possible confirmation of German confusion of mind, intensified by Allied deceptions. And the gusher of priceless insights, of precious reassurance, continued to pour forth after D-Day. On 8 June Ōshima reported the Germans saying that the Normandy invasion still left them uncertain whether the Allies 'will later attempt a landing in the Calais–Dunkirk area'. Next day he added that the Germans 'are now on their guard against landings in the Calais and Saint Malo directions'. On 6 July he messaged Tokyo: 'Germany is still waiting for Patton's [army] group to engage in a second landing operation in the Channel area'; a month after D-Day, the 'Fortitude' deception was still working its spell.

On 20 July, within seven hours of the bomb explosion in Hitler's head-quarters Ōshima was one of the first to confirm the Führer's survival. On the 23rd, after a long talk with Ribbentrop he told Tokyo: 'The attempt on Hitler's life is the most serious occurrence for Germany since the outbreak of the war.' It was always known that there were anti-Nazis among the old Prussian general staff, he said, but they had remained mute as long as the war was going well. However, 'more recently, the war situation has deteri-orated to the point of producing such an event as that which has just taken place. Judging from the information which has ... so far been made avail-able, the group of rebels was not very large ... However, in my opinion it will almost inevitably have unpleasant domestic and foreign repercussions ... Although Germany has received hard blows both within and without, the fighting spirit of the German leaders is high, and they continue to exert their best efforts to bring the present war to an end with a clear-cut victory.'

In the spring of 1945 Ōshima sent detailed reports on living conditions in Berlin, because there was nothing more useful to be said about strategy. In March, Ribbentrop informed the baron of the outcome of the Yalta conference, giving details derived from an OKW/Chi decrypt of a message from the Polish government in exile. Ōshima conducted a last phone conversation with the Nazi foreign minister before himself leaving the capital for southern Germany on 14 April, telling Tokyo that 'it was planned to transfer the high command and government to the south after they have watched developments a little longer'. Though Eisenhower's headquarters had neglected Ōshima's warnings before 'Autumn Mist' – the December 1944 Ardennes offensive – they readily succumbed to his talk of a Nazi fortress in the south, which skewed Anglo-American strategy in the closing days of the war.

Ōshima provided the Allies with their most important insider glimpses of attitudes within Hitler's circle. If his reports were often mistaken – because Nazi leaders told him falsehoods, some of which they believed themselves, especially about their own military prospects – they provided everything that could be asked of any informant: the truth as it seemed at the time to a privileged spectator. He was more useful to Washington and London than would have been any Nazi or Japanese renegade, better placed than the Red Orchestra or 'Lucy' Ring. He was the spy who never knew that he spied, the unknowing betrayer. Ōshima was convicted at a 1948 US Tokyo war crimes trial of conspiring to wage aggressive war and remained imprisoned until 1955. He died in 1975.

3 PRODUCTION LINES

Peter Calvocoressi, one of Bletchley's codebreakers and later chroniclers, wrote that from late 1942 onwards, if the globe had been combed to identify the people who knew most about – for instance – every operational and organisational aspect of the Luftwaffe, these would have been found not in Germany, but in Britain and America. The same was true of the Abwehr, and indeed of every other branch of the enemy's armed forces and institutions – though emphatically not of the German economy. Signals intelligence became so central to the Allied war effort that from 1944 onwards the Americans became reluctant to bomb identified Japanese wireless communications centres, because their output seemed more useful to Allied military operations than to those of Nippon. Between 1942 and 1945 the United States spent half a billion dollars a year on sigint, and this has been justly described as its most cost-effective investment of the conflict.

After Pearl Harbor, Henry Stimson recognised that beyond the tiny team of SIS cryptanalysts who had broken Purple, its wireless intelligence apparatus was weak: only four officers were working on Japanese army traffic, and the Signal Corps leased just thirteen tabulating machines – IBM would never sell them – against four hundred in 1945. On 19 January 1942 Stimson appointed as a special assistant Brooklyn-born lawyer Alfred McCormack, with a brief to examine the whole field of sigint. Thereafter events moved swiftly. The Signals Intelligence Service moved from Washington's Munitions Building to a former girls' school, Arlington Hall – 'the salt mines' – thereafter the hub of military decrypt activities, which soon occupied several dozen brick and wood-frame buildings in the grounds, and eventually employed 7,000 people, many of them civilians and women. A Section handled diplomatic and clandestine material. B Section studied the Japanese army; its card index eventually identified 46,000 enemy officers. C – 'Bunker Hill' – addressed German material forwarded from Bletchley Park. The army also assumed sole responsibility for handling Japanese diplomatic traffic. Despite repeated protests, however, until June 1944 Arlington Hall had no control over interception, which remained the jealously guarded bailiwick of the Signal Corps, whose intercept arm and cryptographic school took over Vint Hill Farms at Warrenton, Virginia. The need to create a network of interception stations almost from scratch was a serious handicap for the army cryptanalysts until the last stage of the war.

Col. Carter Clarke was appointed to direct a new and highly secret 'Special Branch' based at the Pentagon, with McCormack as his assistant, to analyse Ultra material from both Arlington Hall and Bletchley Park. McCormack recognised the army's dire shortage of trained intelligence officers. Some senior generals, including George Marshall, were slow to correct a weakness they shared with many professional soldiers of all nationalities – they thought too much about what they themselves might do, not enough about the enemy's capabilities and intentions. Colonel McCormack, as he became, hired and put into uniform hundreds of lawyers, whom he believed had the appropriate training and skills to analyse complex data. He visited Bletchley in April 1943 with Lt. Col. Telford Taylor and William Friedman, and thereafter adopted many British procedures for handling Ultra material and ensuring its security – though never British rates of pay. A woman graduate serving at Bletchley started on £2 a week, while her American counterpart earned five times as much. Special Branch grew to an eventual strength of four hundred, with Taylor heading its most important out-station at GC&CS; this had a direct teleprinter link to the Pentagon, and eventually a cluster of British-built bombes under its own control. Most of the American contingent proved to be exceptionally able people, who made a notable contribution. Stuart Milner-Barry said that their coming was 'one of the luckiest things that happened to Hut 6'.

In the spring of 1943 an agreement was signed which became known as BRUSA, and was justly described as the closest intelligence-sharing pact in history between any two nations. Though not always immaculately observed on either side, its success was astonishing. In mid-August a scrambler was installed on the Washington–London phone line, enabling intelligence officers of the two nations to converse when an issue was important enough. A series of major conferences was held, at which British and American officers exchanged information and techniques.

Cryptanalysis was a world of its own, using a language incomprehensible to those outside it, but American and British practitioners came to understand intimately each other's doings and difficulties. In October 1943, for instance, the JIC in London noted that US forces signalled some weather reports in plain language, while the British encrypted the same information. This posed a danger that enemy codebreakers could exploit the match, and the Americans duly started to encrypt all meteorological information. Likewise a memorandum from the British SLU in Washington to Bletchley Park on 16 February 1945 offered practical advice of a kind which flew to and fro daily across the Atlantic in the latter part of the war: 'noted ref JN-11 Ransuuban. For recovery of strip digits a straight additive attack has proved to be superior; with particular emphasis on the heavy use of Hatsu and related groups in the first position. Speed of recovery is dependent upon the condition of the code once the strips are identified and completed, recovery of the daily key on a complete day's traffic proceeds rapidly by stripping.'

It was agreed at an early stage that the Americans should major on Japanese traffic, while Bletchley Park maintained the lead role on German material, and trawled neutral states' messages. An OSS officer who urged burgling safes in Vichy to secure its codes was politely informed that this was unnecessary – they had long since been given to the Allies by sympathetic French intelligence officers. London also gave a dusty answer in 1943 when Arlington Hall requested help with its discreet monitoring of some Soviet traffic: this would have breached Churchill's prohibition on espionage against an ally. The British were always cautious, perhaps extravagantly so, about adopting any course of military or naval action that might betray the Ultra secret, while US forces were more willing to take the security risk involved in exploiting prospective targeting information.

For the most part, however, the US displayed considerable sophistication in protecting Ultra. When a Japanese Purple signal was broken on 28 December 1942, requesting Spanish diplomats in Washington to retrieve on their behalf half a million dollars in cash left in their abandoned embassy safe, the Americans made no attempt to seize the money, in case the signal was a coat-trailing ruse to discover whether Tokyo's traffic was being monitored. On 18 April 1943, after US fighters shot down the aircraft carrying Admiral Isoroku Yamamoto, the official American bulletin merely routinely reported the destruction of four Japanese planes in the North Solomons. No hint was given that the attackers knew the supreme importance of one passenger, an act of forbearance that proved decisive in lulling Japanese suspicions of a communications breach. It was left to Tokyo to announce Yamamoto's death.

In the spring of 1944 the Americans went even further to reassure the Japanese about their own security. On 1 April, two Imperial Japanese Navy flying-boats were damaged in a tropical storm, en route from Palau to Davao. One of them carried Admiral Mineichi Koga, commander-in-chief of the Combined Fleet. In the second was Vice-Admiral Shigeru Fukudome. When this plane ditched off Cebu island, Fukudome floundered ashore without his attaché case, containing Japanese codes and important strategy documents in plain language. Guerrillas on Cebu alerted the Americans, who got to the plane. A US submarine rushed the attaché case to the Australian Army's intelligence department, where Fukudome's codes and documents were photographed. Then the case was hastened back to the crash area for local people to hand over to the Japanese, claiming that they had chanced upon it. Fukudome himself eventually got home, to be forgiven and promoted. The Japanese navy never suspected that its haul of secrets had passed through American hands.

There was a 1945 debate between Bletchley and Arlington about whether to commit Allied bombers in Europe to attack key German land-line telephone exchanges, whose locations and importance Ultra had identified. An eventual decision was made to go ahead, but subject to consultation between the targeting officers and Bletchley's Hut 6 – with a cut-out through SHAEF intelligence – before each such attack was launched. The security system within the armed forces protecting Ultra worked remarkably well: the most significant threats to it proved to be not Axis intelligence officers, but instead recklessly indiscreet American journalists.

It would be wrong entirely to idealise the conduct of the vast Allied interception and codebreaking staffs, most of them very young men and women performing monotonous and repetitive tasks. In 1944–45 the British teleprinter intercept centre at Knockholt in Kent suffered severe problems from staff discontent: its six hundred staffers resented their low pay and poor working conditions; absenteeism rose sharply at weekends, and no manager bothered to explain to the girls why their work mattered. Meanwhile Lt. Ed Parks of the dissemination unit at Arlington Hall scrawled an earnest little note on 16 October 1944: 'In the last few days our work has tailed off considerably ... We turned out a total of 15,739 messages in the 15 days ... But now that the work is not too pressing, we should make a special effort to keep all the messages going through promptly. I noticed last week a tendency to leave early, and to play around when there were messages waiting to be typed. I think the impression given is bad ... It seems to me essential to remember that the work we are doing is of vital importance to the conduct of the war ... [and] deserves our best efforts.'

From late 1942 onwards, the British and Americans were processing enemy decrypts in industrial quantities, though inter-service rivalries and jealousies continued to hamper US activity. The ambitious and expensive bombes designed and built for the US Army were a failure, but the navy models attained higher technical standards than the British ones, and were produced in numbers unimaginable in Churchill's straitened island: for a period National Cash Register of Dayton, Ohio, was completing three or four each *day*. Op-20-G bombes, twice the size of their British counterparts, began to achieve operational effectiveness only in August 1943, but by April the following year eighty-seven were in service, which proved subject to fewer technical failures than their Bletchley counterparts. Thus, they took over from Hut 8 an increasing share of the burden of reading Kriegsmarine traffic. Bletchley Park's staff held Op-20-G and its cryptanalysts in the highest respect.

Until 17 September 1941, when GC&CS made its first significant breaks into Wehrmacht traffic, most Ultra information came from the army-Luftwaffe keys, and from reading traffic dispatched through the Italians' Hagelin-C38m machines. Between December 1941 and May 1942, some thirty to forty Ultra messages a day were transmitted to overseas commands by Hut 3. Thereafter, however, there was a rapid increase – to eighty a day between June and October, then to a hundred by April 1943, a level which it sustained thereafter, to achieve a cumulative wartime total of 100,000 decrypts circulated to operational headquarters. This, in turn, was only the small proportion deemed useful or relevant to commanders, among 90,000 decrypts a month processed at Bletchley in 1944–45.

The physical and mental strain on the codebreakers never eased. While machines aided their labours, the foremost weapons in the battles waged by Bletchley, Op-20-G and Arlington Hall were always human brains.

Reading enemy signals seldom became an easy or routine task – during the last two years of the war, Stuart Milner-Barry said it was impossible to aspire to read more than half of all incoming German intercepts, even under the most favourable circumstances. 'There was a perpetual excitement about each day's breaks, at whatever time of day or night they might come. To the chess-player' – he himself had represented England before the war – 'it was rather like a long-running tournament with several rounds being played each day, and never any certainty that the luck would continue to hold.'

Efforts to read the Italian navy's higher traffic, encrypted through book codes, were abandoned as a failure, a decision influenced in part by the fact that Italian warships had ceased to be a threat to Allied operations. Many of those engaged in codebreaking were obliged to take sick leave at intervals to obtain a respite. In July 1943 John Tiltman of Bletchley and William Friedman of Arlington Hall exchanged letters, in which beyond discussing the difficulties of breaking Japanese army traffic, both acknowledged the stresses of their role. There were never enough qualified staff available on either side of the Atlantic. Friedman mentioned that Commander Joseph Wenger, now chief of Op-20-G, had missed a scheduled meeting with him because 'he was out at the Naval hospital. I suspect that he will have to take a rest for several weeks. As a matter of fact, I had been wondering how long he would be able to stand up under the strain … for a number of months now I have watched him go down noticeably.' Never should it be thought that freedom from physical danger provided the codebreakers with a passport to a 'cushy' war.

As for the impact of this huge effort on the battlefield, until the summer of 1942 the British Eighth Army's commanders-in-chief and their staffs in North Africa were sceptical, even contemptuous, about intelligence. They could assert in self-justification how patchy was the service they received – for instance, Bletchley warned that Rommel would launch an attack in May, but did not give any clue where. Both the Park and senior officers in the Middle East were slow to grasp the scale of the Afrika Korps' logistical problems. The appointment of Gen. Sir Bernard Montgomery as C-in-C in June coincided with an important increase in the Ultra flow. A Luftwaffe signal, for instance, stated that Axis day-bombing of Malta was to be abandoned. The theatre air intelligence chief, Group-Captain Harry Humphreys, immediately recognised this meant the Germans would transfer their Messerschmitt Bf109 fighters from escort duties to North Africa, and thus felt able to get Spitfires shifted from defending Malta to securing air supremacy over Egypt and Libya. Breaks in Italian traffic empowered the Royal Navy and the RAF to devastate the Germans' Mediterranean supply line, sinking forty-seven ships totalling 169,000 tons between July and October, while German messages famously warned the British of the impending Axis thrust at Alam Halfa in August. This was among the most important intelligence breakthroughs of the war, and enabled Montgomery to achieve his first victory.

Before the British launched their own Alamein offensive on 23 October 1942, on the 7th Gen. Georg Stumme, Rommel's deputy, told his officers that the main axis of the forthcoming British attack would be between Ruweisat and Himeimat, confirmed on 20 October as 'the northern part of our southern sector', together with an advance along the coast road. This view was strongly influenced by elaborate British deception operations in the south, and Montgomery's officers thereafter congratulated themselves on the cleverness of their scheme involving dummy tanks and pipelines; but it deserves notice that the Germans were able to switch 21st Panzer Division to the north three days later, before the British achieved their breakthrough. Deceptions were only serviceable until an attacker showed his real hand.

After Montgomery's victory his critics – prominently including Ralph Bennett of Bletchley's Hut 3 – argued that the sluggish British pursuit was inexcusable when decrypts flagged in real time almost every movement the retreating Germans made. Bennett wrote of 'the fierce indignation and dismay felt throughout the Hut at Montgomery's painfully slow advance from Alamein to Tripoli, incomprehensible in the light of the mass of Ultra intelligence showing that throughout his retreat Rommel was too weak to withstand serious pressure … [Montgomery's] delay seemed to cast doubt on the whole point of our work.' From the beginning of 1943 onwards, matters got better: Eighth Army's commander and his staff developed complete confidence in Ultra, and became more proficient about exploiting it on the battlefield.

For months after the Americans arrived in North Africa in November 1942, they made the same mistakes that the British had done a year or two earlier. One of Rommel's intelligence officers paid tribute to the value of German voice-monitoring of US Army channels: 'they were still happy-go-lucky and careless of their signals procedure'. As for Ultra, a young British intelligence officer who visited Allied headquarters in Algiers lamented that Eisenhower's staff 'did not know what they ought to be doing and had learned a whole lot of wrong things they ought not to have been doing'. Bletchley's input was scrappy in the early part of the Tunisian campaign, but more skilled and experienced intelligence officers in Algiers could have anticipated Rommel's punishing February 1943 assault on the Kasserine Pass. The sacking of Brigadier Eric Mockler-Ferryman, Eisenhower's British intelligence chief, was a just penalty for his failure. Thereafter in North Africa, Sicily and Italy, the Allies usually had an extensive knowledge of the Germans' strengths and deployments.

Bletchley Park became marginally less uncomfortable in 1942, when four steel and concrete blocks, designated 'A' to 'D', replaced some of the wooden hutments. A pneumatic tube system used in London department stores was introduced for shifting messages between sections, replacing the earlier tray-and-pulley operation – this was a brainchild of Hugh Alexander, who in his earlier life had been head of research for the John Lewis store chain. Alexander supplanted Turing as head of Hut 8, not because the latter was the victim of any persecution or palace coup, but because he was too disorganised a human being to administer anything. It was recognised that his astounding intellect was best left to roam free.

Ralph Bennett has painted a vivid portrait of the daily routine of the team in Hut 3, which kept its name even when moved into a brick building. It was its inmates' function to translate and render coherent broken or part-broken signals, with increasing input from officers of the US Special Branch who were now attached to several Bletchley sections. The codebreakers knew almost nothing about Allied operations – the context of campaigns – and thus saw the war through a peculiarly narrow, enemy prism. 'We knew much more about most German divisions and some German generals,' wrote Bennett, 'than we did about any on our own side … [Rommel's] 90th Light Division became so daily an acquaintance during the African campaign that there was even a sort of temptation to rejoice when it scored a success.' He also emphasised an important constraint on Ultra's practical utility: 'No message had more authority than that of the officer who sent it, nor more reliability as a guide to his superiors' intentions than the extent of the knowledge they allowed him to have.' Again and again – for instance when decrypts caused the Allies to expect a German evacuation of southern Italy in September 1943, when instead Kesselring stood and fought – regular access to enemy traffic ended in a misreading of Hitler's intentions, often because he changed his mind.

In the second half of the war, however, the Allies could plan most of their operations with remarkable confidence that the enemy had no unpleasant surprises in store. Over three hundred Allied ships passed through the Straits of Gibraltar in the thirty-three hours before the 'Torch' landings, knowing that they were most unlikely to face enemy air interference. The January 1944 Anzio landings were launched with the assurance that Kesselring had no hint of them, and Ultra also flagged his big February counterattack against the beachhead, which belatedly convinced the US Army's Gen. Mark Clark that Ultra was a reliable source of intelligence. The Allies knew before the August 1944 'Anvil' invasion of the south of France that Hitler anyway intended to evacuate the region, which caused Gen. Sir Harold Alexander, commanding in Italy, to urge that it would make more sense to leave the invasion force fighting with his own army. Once the Americans were ashore in southern France, they could pursue the retreating Germans with unusual exuberance, because they knew they need fear no counterattack. Bletchley was breaking a substantial portion of traffic transmitted in some fifty different Wehrmacht and Luftwaffe Enigma keys, and was forwarding the fruits to forty subscribers in Allied headquarters everywhere that the Germans were being fought.

Ultra never told all, however. A popular modern delusion holds sway that GC&CS, through the agency of Turing's bombes and those of the US Navy, made the Allies privy to the enemy's communications throughout the war, and that all German messages of significance were transmitted by Enigma. None of this is so. The Wehrmacht's Enigma traffic posed ongoing difficulties, and until a late stage of the war Bletchley remained vulnerable to delays and blackouts in its decryption. In September 1944, Hut 6 solved only 15 per cent of army messages; in October 18 per cent; in November 24 per cent. By contrast, in September 64 per cent of Luftwaffe intercepts were read, and 77 per cent in October and November. Many decodes of all kinds were achieved too slowly to influence events on the battlefield.

Moreover, from 1941 onwards the German high command transmitted an ever-growing proportion of its most sensitive traffic by teleprinter, of which there were several models. The most widely used were the Lorenz *Schlüsselzusatz* SZ40/42 'Tunny', in Bletchley parlance, and the Siemens & Halske *Geheimschreiber* T-52 – 'Sturgeon'. These systems worked on-line, in contrast to Enigma's off-line operation, and employed the so-called Vernam cipher, a non-Morse language. When British interceptors recorded its incomprehensible stutter across the ether, in August 1941 a Bletchley team led by Col. John Tiltman began to probe its significance. They managed to break a single message from Athens to Vienna for which an obliging German signaller repeated a corrupt text, but this took them little nearer to reading the traffic. Tiltman, a decorated First World War soldier, was a cryptographic veteran who showed that not all the Park's wizards were civilian eggheads. He was an unusual colonel: when a newly arrived private soldier recruited to Tiltman's section stamped to attention before him and saluted, the officer set the tone for their subsequent association by his pained response: 'I say, old boy, must you wear those damned boots?' Thereafter the young man adopted plimsolls.

Piece by piece, though painfully slowly, the codebreakers at Bletchley groped towards a solution to a riddle even more dense than that of Enigma, partly because they lacked a physical example of the transmitting machine. In the early months of 1942, by sheer intellectual endeavour the Park's research section created a theoretical model of the Lorenz SZ40/42. Most credit for this went to a chemistry student turned mathematician named Bill Tutte, who deserves to be almost as well known as Turing and Welchman. He was born in 1917, the son of a gardener and a cook-housekeeper at a Newmarket racing stable. He won a scholarship to the Cambridge and County Day School, then progressed to Trinity College. In October 1941 he was assigned to study the Tunny traffic, and spent the months that followed performing the extraordinary cerebral feat of deducing what kind of machine the Germans must be employing to produce the noises recorded by the interceptors. Tutte established that the teleprinter would have two sets of five wheels, one of these 'stepping' irregularly, with 501 settable pins and a further two motor wheels, between them creating a range of combinations much greater than that produced by Enigma. His astounding feat, a triumph of intellectual effort unassisted by technology, caused his senior colleagues to support his later successful application for a prize fellowship at Trinity, based entirely on his doings at Bletchley, though their nature was not disclosed to the college. Nigel de Grey hailed his contribution as 'one of the outstanding successes of the war', and so it was.

Establishing the character of the machine was an important beginning, but one that brought the British only a little closer to reading its traffic. Edward Travis, BP's chief, observed that the German teleprinter's output was 'as analogous to the other machine ciphers as a Maori and an Eskimo'. In May 1942, Tiltman acknowledged that 'the *Geheimschreiber* [Siemens teleprinter] is a great worry to us'. A young Oxford mathematician, Michael Crum, modelled the T-52, and his findings led the codebreakers to conclude that it presented too great a challenge to be pursued. Instead, they must concentrate all possible resources on the Lorenz – and quickly. The more the Germans used their fast-expanding WANDA-Netz Continental teleprinter system for top secret communications, the less they would use Enigma to encrypt them. It is remarkable that Berlin's enthusiasm for the teleprinter was so great, because its vulnerability had already been exposed – back in 1940, by the Swedish codebreaker Arne Beurling, who tapped into the Stockholm exchange link connecting Berlin to its forces in Norway, and broke T-52 messages by a methodology never disclosed. The Swedish company Ericsson built a machine it called 'the App', to assist Beurling's operations, and he read considerable traffic until May 1943, when the Germans, warned by the Finns of what was happening, introduced new keys and security measures. Berlin did not, however, question the integrity of the whole system, and the British knew nothing of Beurling's activities.

Between July and October 1942, by endeavours which owed little to mechanical assistance, a group working within Major Ralph Tester's new section, 'the Testery', read some Lorenz SZ40 traffic, using a higher mathematical method known at Bletchley as 'Turingery', after its inventor. Those responsible included eighteen-year-old Donald Michie, who later taught the Baudot code, through which messages were transmitted after Vernam encryption, to the future statesman Roy Jenkins; Peter Hilton, a twenty-one-year-old Oxford mathematician; and Peter Berenson, who much later founded Amnesty International. Increasingly disciplined German procedures made the flow of decrypts irregular: different keys were allocated names of fish and marine creatures – 'Bream', 'Grilse', 'Octopus' and so on; 'Jellyfish' later proved to include some of the most momentous German high command messages.

Human brainpower remained the main engine of the teleprinter codebreakers until the middle of 1943. In June the Park broke 114 Lorenz signals out of 575 dispatched to Berlin by the German high command in Italy. Bletchley reported in August: 'the quality of the intelligence derived from Fish is of the highest order'. Though Lorenz traffic was never broken in anything like the same volume as Enigma, it was of exceptional importance, because it addressed the enemy's most sensitive exchanges. Moreover, Bletchley's difficulties and delays in breaking German army Enigma persisted until the end of the war, and Tunny offered a priceless alternative route into military traffic.

The transformative development for the codebreakers came, inevitably, from the enlistment of machines. These were even more innovative than Turing's bombes, and were created by other minds and hands. Max Newman was born in 1897. His father was a German named Neumann, and like the Saxe-Coburgs his son changed his name during the First World War, in which he served briefly and reluctantly as a British Army paymaster. Between the wars Newman gained a formidable reputation as a mathematician at Cambridge, where he came to know Turing. Professor Pat Blackett drew him to Bletchley's attention, describing him as a fine chess-player and musician. Newman was initially unwilling to join the Park, because he feared that the work would be insufficiently interesting. When he grudgingly accepted an appointment at the end of 1942, he did so on condition that he retained an option to leave after a year if he became unhappy. Few men, however distinguished, dared to make such a stipulation in the midst of a world war – and even fewer found it accepted.

Newman's first months at Bletchley proved so frustrating that it looked as if he would indeed quit; he was not a success as a codebreaker. But he initiated a critical breakthrough by studying Tutte's analysis of the teleprinter's workings, and urged that a machine could and should be constructed to test the 1.6 x 1,019 possible start positions for its wheel settings. Alan Turing, newly returned from a long trip to the US, was now exploring the science of electronic circuitry, as was Charles Wynn-Williams, a circuit specialist transferred to Bletchley from radar research at Malvern. Turing urged Newman to discuss his project with Tommy Flowers, a senior engineer at the Post Office's Dollis Hill research station in north-west London, who had played a modest role in the creation of the bombes.

Newman was a gifted organiser of considerable diplomatic as well as intellectual skills. An American who served at Bletchley, Sgt George Vergine, described him as 'a marvellous fellow', always open to new ideas: 'We used to have tea parties which were mathematical discussions of problems, developments, techniques ... a topic would be written on the blackboard and all of the analysts, including Newman, would come tea in hand and chew it around, and see whether it would be useful in cracking codes.' He assumed direction of a new Bletchley section, dubbed 'the Newmanry', charged with identifying more advanced mechanical and electronic aids to codebreaking. He could claim credit for recognising the practicability of a machine to assist in breaking Fish messages, and for securing approval and resources for the first relatively primitive such device to be built. This version, dubbed 'the Robinson', was inspired by the design of Wynn-

Williams, and built at Dollis Hill under the direction of engineer Francis Morell. The collaboration of Newman and Wynn-Williams – assisted by others of almost equal gifts such as mathematician Jack Good, who had worked with Turing on the bombes – produced a succession of technological marvels which outclassed any other codebreaking aid created on either side of the Atlantic in the course of the war. The first Robinson was delivered to Bletchley in June 1943, followed by a dozen stablemates by the end of the year, and more thereafter. The Robinson operated as a super-fast bombe, attacking the output of the German teleprinters by exploring punched tapes photo-electrically at the then fantastic speed of a thousand characters a second. It enabled the Park to read some Lorenz messages in the autumn of 1943, and hundreds by the following spring. Its limitation was mechanical – the difficulty of synchronising two tapes which had to run simultaneously; preventing breaks; dealing with repeated valve failures.

Tommy Flowers was impatient with the Robinson and its weaknesses. This senior telephone engineer nursed a far more ambitious, all-electronic vision. He was a builder's son from the East End of London, born in 1905, who won a scholarship to a technical college where he displayed a precocious talent for mechanics and science. Having joined the Post Office, he spent a decade working on the evolution of automated telephone systems. For much of the war, though he held a title as head of the telephone switching department, he played a leading role in manufacturing technology for Bletchley. But while he forged a close working relationship with Turing, who often visited Dollis Hill, the formidable and influential Gordon Welchman took against the engineer, who was certainly no 'gentleman' in the parlance of those days. Welchman treated him with disdain, as a mere artisan with ideas above his station. Flowers is nonetheless considered to have made a brilliant contribution to realising and improving upon the concepts of Newman and Wynn-Williams, by creating the new wonder of 'Colossus', which may be considered the first computer in the world.

It is a measure of Bletchley's difficulties with the German teleprinters that while the output of 'Fish' messages from the enemy's high command doubled in the course of 1943, the volume of decrypts fell, from 330 in January to 244 in December, albeit many of high value to Allied intelligence officers. Flowers grasped the improvement in reliability that could be achieved if hard valves were used in place of gas-filled ones, and were never switched off. He initiated production of the first Colossus without an explicit directive from the Bletchley authorities, who urged focusing on delivery of Robinsons, which required only a hundred relatively scarce valves, while Colossus used 1,500, and a more advanced 1945 version 2,500. Max Newman was always supportive of Flowers, but others were less so. The engineer, in his own field an obsessive like so many of those involved with Bletchley, was obliged to use some of his own money to purchase scarce components. Within ten months Dollis Hill, using fifteen of its own engineers and forty technicians at a Post Office factory in Birmingham, had brought into being a huge machine which processed data at five times the speed of the Robinson. It was first tested on 25 November 1943, and entered service at Bletchley in January 1944. Flowers after the war received an *ex-gratia* payment of £1,000, together with an MBE, a shamefully condescending recognition of his role as begetter of Colossus. Most Bletchley hands testify that he was the practical brain who played a pivotal role in translating the concepts of Turing, Newman and Wynn-Williams into reality, and indeed for advancing them to a new level of sophistication. The most advanced codebreaking technology of the war was devised at Bletchley, though when the Americans built their own variants they often improved upon the originals, as with the US Navy's bombes. Arlington Hall's 'autoscritchers' performed some of the same functions as Colossus, though they operated against Enigma traffic, and each cost as much as a fighter.

An unnamed Bletchley staffer penned a description of his own fascination with the spectacle of Colossus at work, a machine of a complexity and energy such as no previous generation had ever seen: 'the fantastic speed of thin paper tape round the glittering pulleys; the childish pleasure of not-not, span, print main headings and other gadgets; the wizardry of purely mechanical decoding letter by letter (one novice thought she was being hoaxed); the uncanny action of the typewriter in printing scores without and beyond human aid … periods of eager expectation culminating in the sudden appearance of the longed-for score … the frantic chatter of a motor run, even the ludicrous frenzy of hosts of bogus scores'.

By 1945 six hundred staff were working around the clock at the Knockholt interception station to record Germany's teleprinter traffic. Bletchley Park expanded from 3,800 personnel in 1943 to 5,600 in 1944, then to 9,000 in 1945. Though Enigma remained by far the most productive source of intelligence by volume, the teleprinter decrypts conveyed the most important messages. The Newmanry alone employed twenty-six cryptanalysts, twenty-eight engineers and 273 Wrens to service ten

Colossi, three Robinsons and scores of lesser machines. Dollis Hill was building one new Colossus a month. A total of 476 Tunny teleprinter decrypts were recorded in May 1944, 339 in July, 404 in August, then a flood in the last months of the war, for a grand total of 13,500 Tunny decrypts out of 168,000 German transmissions intercepted since November 1942. The cryptographic historian Ralph Erskine has described the breaking of the teleprinter traffic as 'the greatest code-breaking feat of the war ... finding Tunny's wheel patterns and settings required the highest cryptanalytic skills and involved advanced statistical techniques and some of the most complex electronic equipment of the war'.

Although it is right to marvel at Bletchley's achievement, it is also essential to recognise its limitations, even in the last eighteen months of the war. In February 1944, just 17 per cent of the German army's traffic was being broken. Around half the US Navy's high-powered bombes at Mount Vernon were handling Kriegsmarine traffic for Hut 6, because Bletchley's resources could not alone bear the strain, and sometimes American aid was also needed to address German army-Luftwaffe material. A significant portion of Enigma traffic was being read within ten to twenty hours, but teleprinted Fish messages often took a week to read. Each Robinson was able to process an average of one signal a day, Colossus fifteen. The Lorenz Tunny was the goldmine in quality terms, providing a stream of intelligence about German high command thinking, most importantly in advance of D-Day.

Consumers at Allied military headquarters received all such material without distinction as 'Ultra'. Only those serving at the Park were aware of the infinite variations and nuances in its cryptographic operations. Even within the Enigma traffic, there was never enough bombe capacity to attempt the breaking of all the enemy's messages, and thus daily choices had to be made about allocation of resources. In the last year of the war American and British air intelligence officers grew progressively less interested in Luftwaffe decrypts, because what the enemy was doing had little influence on their operational decisions. At sea, Ultra had played its critical part in securing Allied dominance both in the Pacific and in the West, and by 1944 this had been achieved. Bletchley once again lost much of the U-boat traffic in November that year, when the Germans introduced 'one boat' ciphers – unique encryption of a message for a single recipient. Moreover, a significant number of Kriegsmarine Enigma keys, such as 'Pike', were never broken.

By 1944–45, however, the Allies were so strong, and Dönitz's force so weak, that this no longer mattered. Moreover, the US Navy's Op-20-G had assumed the lead role in handling U-boat intercepts, because of its greater resources. On land, Ultra's contribution was far more often strategic than tactical, because so much material reached commanders out of real time: Ralph Bennett of Hut 3 wrote of 'the frequently recalcitrant army keys'. Even more fundamental, while knowledge of the enemy's strength and deployments was immensely reassuring to commanders, it provided no assured passport to victory. From the late summer of 1943 onwards, for instance, Ultra thoroughly informed the Allies about the opinions and intentions of Kesselring, commanding Hitler's considerably inferior forces in Italy. But it told them nothing that enabled British and American troops to defeat Kesselring's army until the very last weeks of the war.

4 INFERNAL MACHINES

Intelligence about enemy weapons systems often yielded more practical value to the Allied war effort than insights into Hitler's thinking. The five-year grapple in the sky between the Allies and the Luftwaffe – the challenge being to overcome Germany's invisible electronic defences as well as its fighters – persisted until 1945, and prompted endeavours almost as dramatic as the Bruneval raid. A thirty-year-old Belgian doctor named André Mathe of '*Service Marc*' was one of several Resistance workers who took extraordinary risks to explore local German night-fighter direction stations. In the summer of 1942 he dispatched a moving message to London pleading for more effective support, and better guidance about what the British would like to know. Mathe – whose real identity was then unknown to MI6 – suggested that the seriousness with which the Germans guarded certain installations in his area implied their importance. He and his comrades had several times been fired upon by sentries while reconnoitring them, 'fortunately with more zeal than accuracy ... As far as our work is concerned, it would be helpful if we knew to what extent you and the British services are interested. We have been working so long in the dark that any reaction from London about our work would be welcome to such obscure workers as ourselves. We hope this will not be resented since, whatever may happen you can rely on our entire devotion and on the sacrifice of our lives.' One of Mathe's network, a local jeweller named Willi Badart, made detailed sketches of a Seeburg bomber-plotting table, after bribing a Belgian SS guard to give him access to the fighter direction tower while its Luftwaffe controllers were off-duty, which gave useful aid to Reg

Jones and his colleagues at the Air Ministry. Mathe proved that there was nothing vacuously histrionic about his message pointing out the risks of such men's efforts for the Allied cause: he himself was arrested on 31 March 1943 and executed in the following year.

Some such intelligence could only be assembled by men and women who could physically examine relevant German equipment. Other information, however, had to be gathered by probing the enemy's defences in the air, at mortal peril. One of the most heroic flying missions of the war took place on the night of 2–3 December 1943. The British established the key role of the Germans' Lichtenstein airborne radar in guiding their night-fighters. For some time thereafter, efforts were made to provoke an encounter with a night-fighter by sending lone Ferret aircraft to roam the night skies over France, Belgium and Holland – comparatively close to home for the RAF – but the enemy ignored these. It became plain that data could only be obtained by dispatching an investigatory mission deep into enemy airspace. Thus, the decision was made to send a twin-engined Wellington of Bomber Command's 1473 Wireless Investigation Flight to join the 'stream' on a night raid over Germany.

The plane was piloted by Ted Paulton, a former car worker from Ontario, who set forth with the almost suicidal purpose of inviting fighter attack, in order that electronic specialist Harold Jordan – the only Englishman among a crew of Canadians – could monitor a radar frequency of 490 megacycles and record what happened – for as long as he lived. At 4.30 a.m., just west of Mainz, 'Lichtenstein' emissions were indeed detected. Through the ten minutes that followed, minutes of appalling tension and apprehension for the Wellington crew, Jordan monitored the strengthening signals as the German fighter edged closer, closer, closer. Flt Sgt. Bigoray, the wireless-operator, transmitted a brief coded message drafted by the radar expert, reporting what was happening. Then, as German radar signals swamped his own headphones, the Englishman shouted down the intercom that they would be attacked at any second. Almost instantly a stream of 20mm cannon shells hammered into the bomber, which Paulton flung into a diving turn as the rear-gunner identified a Ju-88 on their tail. Jordan, though hit in the shoulder, scribbled another message for England while the rear-gunner kept firing at the German until an incoming burst wounded him and disabled the turret. Attacks came again and again, inflicting further fragment wounds on Jordan's jaw and eye.

Then, suddenly, they were alone. The fighter had vanished, leaving four of the Wellington's crew seriously wounded, the plane crippled, its fuselage riddled. In the cockpit, for the next three and a half hours Paulton nursed his airborne wreck towards home. The port engine throttle was shot away, while its starboard counterpart was jammed at full power; an aileron and most of the instruments were wrecked; the hydraulics were unserviceable. Only the Wellington's geodetic construction, based on a weave of mutually supporting duralumin strips – a brainchild of Barnes Wallis – enabled it to stay in the air. Jordan and Bigoray felt a sense of despair, because after enduring their ordeal and repeatedly signalling details of the German fighter's electronic emissions, no acknowledgement was transmitted from base until 4.55 a.m., and by that time the Wellington's receiver was dead.

At 6.45 a.m. they crossed the French coast near Dunkirk, and thirty minutes later made an English landfall. Paulton decided that the aircraft was too badly damaged to risk an airfield landing: they must ditch in the sea. Bigoray, his legs bleeding from multiple fragment wounds, was obviously incapable of making an escape from a sinking hulk, so instead buckled on his parachute and dragged himself to the rear escape hatch. Over Ramsgate, the pilot gave him the word to jump. The wireless-operator descended safely, carrying a copy of Jordan's report. Then Paulton bounced the doomed Wellington onto the sea two hundred yards off Deal. It ploughed to a waterlogged standstill, and the crew struggled out through the hatches. To their dismay, they found their dinghy shot to ribbons, and instead had to cling to the sinking wreckage until rescued by local boatmen. This was a rare case in which heroism and devotion to duty were suitably recognised: Jordan, who lost an eye, received a DSO, Paulton a DFC and Bigoray the DFM. The Wellington's mission provided RAF scientific intelligence with one more among a thousand pieces for its jigsaw of information about Germany's air defences, secured by airmen who accepted an encounter against odds such as few secret agents would have cared to face.

Yet the outcomes of other technological intelligence campaigns were more equivocal, including one of the highest importance. On 15 May 1942 Flt Lt. Donald Steventon, among the RAF's most skilled reconnaissance pilots, was on his way to photograph the German Baltic port of Swinemünde when he spotted unusual construction activity below him, at a German airfield on Usedom island. He banked his twin-engined Mosquito and made a short run over Peenemünde, then a name of no special significance to the Allies. When Steventon's images were examined under the magnifiers of the RAF Medmenham photographic interpretation centre, they could make nothing of three large circular embankments: the Peenemünde photographs were filed. It was only eleven months later, at the end of April 1943, after three more reconnaissance sorties had been flown over the site, that a committee codenamed 'Bodyline', appointed by Churchill to study a suspected German rocket programme, concluded that Peenemünde was the hub and heart of whatever diabolic project the Nazis were fomenting.

The V-weapon saga remains one of the most fascinating intelligence studies of the war. German scientific ingenuity commanded well-deserved British respect. As soon as it became plain, and was reflected in Nazi public rhetoric, that Berlin was developing long-range weapons with which to exact retribution for the Anglo-American bomber offensive, immense efforts began in London to identify the nature of the threat. By 1943 the tide of war had swung decisively towards the Allies, who were now vastly strong, especially in the air. Bletchley Park was reading a substantial proportion of the enemy's secret wireless traffic. Yet despite these advantages, until the Germans began to fire V-1s and V-2s at Britain, Churchill's intelligence machine remained confused and uncertain about the exact nature of Hitler's 'revenge weapon' programme. The story offers a powerful corrective for those who suppose that Ultra laid bare all the enemy's secrets: here was an important one, which largely defied penetration.

The Wehrmacht had been experimenting for years with rockets, and the Luftwaffe with pilotless planes. The 1939 'Oslo Report' to MI6 mentioned the significance of Peenemünde as a test station. Only in July 1943, however, did Hitler, exasperated by the Luftwaffe's inability to retaliate for RAF and USAAF attacks on Germany, decide to commit massive resources to manufacturing new weapons, then still at the experimental stage, that might achieve what his manned aircraft could not by wreaking havoc on Britain. At that stage the British had already been debating for some months the significance of clues that reached them about German rocketry. R.V. Jones read of a conversation between German scientists, overheard in a Berlin restaurant by the Danish chemical engineer codenamed 'Elgar', mentioned above, who reported regularly to Broadway. On 22 March 1943, eavesdroppers at the celebrity PoW camp at Trent Park heard two captured Afrika Korps generals, Cruwell and von Thoma, discuss prospects for the rocket programme. A week later, Broadway received a message from a Luxembourg Resistance group, providing scruffy sketches and fragments of information supplied by its own people serving as forced labourers at Peenemünde. This was forwarded via Bern by junior officers, in the absence of the head of station, 'Fanny' vanden Heuvel. He returned to the office to rebuke his staff for wasting cipher groups on such nonsense – then received a signal from London saying that the information was of the utmost value, and urging every effort to secure more of the same. On 12 April the British vice-chiefs of staff reported the gist of all this to the prime minister, who decided to take the threat seriously. He appointed his own son-in-law Duncan Sandys, a junior supply minister, to head an ongoing investigation. Its initial report, on 17 May, stated that 'such scant evidence as exists suggests that [a German rocket programme] may be far advanced'.

Sandys was widely disliked – Alan Brooke promised that he would resign if, as was widely feared though it did not come to pass in the war years, the ambitious young upstart was made secretary for war. Sandys' appointment transferred management of the Bodyline investigation from the hands of the professional intelligence analysts into those of a politician, and this was no accident: from start to finish, V-weapons were viewed in Downing Street as intensely political. Nothing the Nazis contrived at this late stage could alter the outcome of the war, and thus the military threat from 'secret weapons' must be limited, given that German atomic research seemed to have made little progress. But it seemed alarmingly plausible that a revolutionary form of conventional attack could damage 'Overlord' – the looming invasion of the Continent – and inflict pain and misery on the weary British people of a kind that might sour the sweetness of victory. An estimate by the Ministry of Home Security, directed by the Labour politician Herbert Morrison, suggested that each rocket which exploded on London might kill six hundred people and seriously injure a further 1,200, and that the Germans might be able to launch one such weapon an hour. Here was crystal-gazing of a fevered kind that sustained alarm in Whitehall through many months of 1943 and 1944.

The error that dogged British intelligence activity for over a year was that the Bodyline group supposed the Germans to be working on a single secret weapon, whereas in reality they were testing several different technologies, including a giant gun. A Polish intelligence group based in Paris reported in April on plans for a 'bomb with wings' that was evolving at Peenemünde. In August a Danish naval officer provided details of a crashed V-1 that he had inspected, which appeared to have no engine; this prompted speculation in London that it might be a new variant of the glider bombs the Germans were known to be building, for stand-off release from Luftwaffe manned aircraft. There were some harsh exchanges between Medmenham's photographic interpreters and R.V. Jones, who for all his brilliance was not universally beloved. He often made snap judgements that were inspired but also disputed, and delivered with a rudeness Hugh Trevor-Roper would have respected. Today, when ballistic missiles have been etched on the world's consciousness for seventy years, the aerial images of what was taking shape at Peenemünde would be recognised by a child. But in 1943, interpreters peering through their fine lenses acknowledged them only as 'objects', or 'vertical columns'. And who can blame them?

Again and again that summer and through the months that followed, the Bodyline group – rechristened 'Crossbow' on 15 November – stumbled in its analysis, because of the irreconcilability of the reported characteristics of the artefacts seen at Peenemünde and other sites in Poland and France. On 29 June 1943, MI6 reported that the Germans were building a giant gun with a range of 230 miles. There was also speculation about a rocket that might deliver a ten-ton warhead, a devastating punch. The British were baffled by suggestions that such a missile might be liquid-fuelled, because their own scientists doubted the feasibility of such technology. London asked the Americans and Russians to contribute whatever information they had, and drew blank. Washington said it had nothing to tell. Moscow Centre could have passed on some clues collected by the 'Lucy' Ring, but was not much interested in assisting the British with their puny war effort – as Stalin viewed it. Allen Dulles transmitted several 1943 OSS reports about Peenemünde and the German secret weapons programme, which at least provided independent confirmation of British speculations, but R.V. Jones's lengthy narrative makes no mention of either the Bern station chief or OSS, and it may be that the American cables were never passed to the British.

In the late summer of 1943, the only common ground among the interested parties in London was that Peenemünde was the focus of highly dangerous German activities. Thus, on the night of 17 August its airfield complex, factories and workshops were devastated by 596 Lancasters, Halifaxes and Stirlings of the RAF's Bomber Command. As a coastal target, the island was easily pinpointed. The raid was highly successful, save that German night-fighters were able to destroy forty of the bombers, 6.7 per cent of those committed, which were operating at extreme range from their home airfields. On the ground, many installations were wrecked and 180 German scientists and engineers, as well as more than five

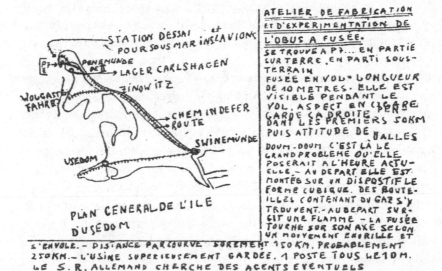

Hand-drawn map by an agent in the field of the German
V-weapon site at Peenemünde received by SIS in June 1943

hundred mostly Polish slave labourers, were killed. Wernher von Braun, the V-2 programme's chief scientist, had hoped to initiate attacks on Britain by November 1943. This deadline would anyway probably not have been met, but Bomber Command's assault retarded it by several months.

On 27 August a new report signed by Duncan Sandys at last recognised that the Germans were developing two different weapons, but fierce argument persisted about the weight of explosive either might deliver. Dr Jones was among those who pointed out that any credible projection showed that the enemy could create only a small fraction of the devastation the RAF and USAAF were wreaking daily in Germany. There nonetheless seemed something profoundly sinister about the notion that the

Nazis, by employing infernal machines, might slaughter tens of thousands of British people without risking the lives of their own aircrew; such an assault appeared spiteful and unfair, when the outcome of the war was decided.

American bombers were committed to two attacks against new secret weapon bunkers identified at Watten, in France. These caused the site to be abandoned by the Germans, although Resistance reports showed other, apparently related, construction activity elsewhere in the north of the country. An MI6 informant named Michel Hollard, a travelling salesman for the *gazogène* engines that powered most French cars of the time, collected extensive information about the V-1 sites through his 'Agir' network. Hollard inspected one site himself, disguised as a labourer; in the course of the war he crossed the Swiss frontier ninety-eight times to deliver his material for Broadway before being betrayed and captured, though mercifully he survived.

The Peenemünde raid also prompted the Nazis to shift secret weapon production to underground sites almost impervious to Allied air attack. Some intelligence reports about this development, compiled at enormous risk by Allied informants in enemy territory, failed to complete the tortuous passage to London: in December 1943 a former officer of the French Deuxième Bureau acquired details of the design of V-2 rockets being built at the RAX works near Wiener-Neustadt. He dispatched a message via Madrid, but this never reached British scientific investigators, to whom at that time it would have been invaluable.

On 7 October an Ultra decrypt of one of Baron Ōshima's reports to Tokyo, dispatched a week earlier, described German plans to start firing long-range guns, accurate up to 250 miles, as early as mid-December. But while the German high command told Ōshima much that was true, it was also feeding him some fanciful information, merely to sustain Tokyo's stomach for the fight. Doubts persisted within the Sandys group about how far both the Nazis' public threats to the world and their private promises to allies were mere propaganda. The Joint Intelligence Committee in London remained sceptical, as did Lord Cherwell, Churchill's influential scientific adviser. In the weeks that followed, Ultra picked up only two relevant military signals, which concerned the flak defences at various secret weapon sites. Almost all German exchanges about the technical aspects of V-weapons were conducted on paper or by landline, and thus remained impenetrable by Bletchley Park.

During the winter of 1943 debate in London about V-weapons became fierce and anxious, because there were so few certainties. On 24 October Duncan Sandys suggested that the Germans might soon be able to start firing rockets at Britain in large numbers, delivering by Christmas a possible total of anything up to 10,000 tons of explosives. This was nonsense, never credited by the likes of Reg Jones, but it nonetheless alarmed the prime minister. Bletchley Park was ordered to maintain a special watch on the signals of the 14th and 15th Companies of the Luftwaffe's Signals Experimental Regiment, which were known to be involved in the pilotless aircraft programme. At the end of November, new decrypts suggested that what later became known to British people as the 'doodlebug' could fly at between 200 and 300mph, for 120 miles.

On 4 December, the Crossbow committee agreed that scores of mysterious 'ski sites' which the Germans had been building in the Pas de Calais and other parts of northern France – Hollard's Agir network identified a hundred – were designed for launching the pilotless aircraft. It was agreed that ski sites, so called for their resemblance to ski-jump launching ramps, should become priority targets for the RAF's and USAAF's bombers, though they proved resistant to effective air attack. Urgent studies also began on a defensive response to the V-1, based on the use of fighters, balloon barrages and flak guns. In March 1944 a new Ultra fragment showed that the Germans had improved the weapon's accuracy. Two months later, the British naval attaché in Stockholm was able to study wreckage from two V-1s which crashed in Sweden. At about the same time, a Wehrmacht chemical warfare specialist captured by the British in Italy told his interrogators he had attended a rocket course at Peenemünde, and gave details – some accurate, others fanciful – of what he had learned about the V-2. In May 1944 also, Bletchley broke an obscure Wehrmacht cipher being used to communicate between Peenemünde and the V-2 test site at Blizna in Poland. The Park was instructed as a top priority to monitor transmissions in this key, even at the cost of diverting staff and bombes from other important work.

On 13 June 1944, a week after D Day, the first V-1 flying bombs, primitive Cruise missiles, began to land on Britain. Until the day of their arrival, as both R.V. Jones and the official intelligence history readily concede, the British had scant idea either of the precise nature of the weapon, or of how serious a peril it represented. The last pre-attack estimate by the Air Ministry – on 12 June – suggested that the Germans might be able to drop four hundred tons of explosive in the first ten hours, a wild exaggeration. It came as a relief to the British and Americans that the offensive opened too late to disrupt 'Overlord', the Normandy invasion, as had been feared. And it soon became apparent that balloons, fighters and the inherent limitations of the V-1 could contain the assault, deeply unwelcome though 'doodlebugs' were to the battered British people.

Britain's rulers, particularly the home secretary Herbert Morrison, remained deeply concerned about the threat posed by the Germans' as yet uncommitted rocket, the V-2. It was Morrison who attempted to frustrate one of R.V. Jones's inspired strokes – using Double Cross Abwehr agents to inform the Germans that the V-1s were overshooting London, so that they shifted their aiming point southwards: the home secretary objected, absurdly and fortunately in vain, that this would represent a malign interference in the workings of Providence. In July, at his behest the war cabinet considered a proposal for evacuating two million Londoners and removing the government from the capital if a bombardment proved sufficiently devastating. There was still speculation that the V-2's warhead might be as heavy as ten tons. A July estimate from Air Ministry experts, who travelled to Sweden to inspect prototype crash wreckage, suggested five tons. On that basis, the Germans could rain eight hundred tons of explosives a month on Britain, though this would still be only a fraction of the volume descending upon Germany. Reg Jones conceded on 16 July that the Germans had brought a technically impressive missile to a stage where it could probably mount 'at least a desultory bombardment of London', but he thought the warhead unlikely to weigh much more than a ton – as indeed it did not.

On the night of 25 July 1944 an unarmed RAF C-47, piloted by a young New Zealander, Flt Lt. Guy Culliford, undertook an extraordinary long-haul flight from Italy to the remotenesses of Nazi-occupied Poland, accompanied by a Polish navigator, F/O Szrajer. In deep darkness, Culliford descended near the village of Zaborow, twelve miles north-west of Tarnow. Four hundred Germans were bivouacked a mile away, and the airstrip on which the Dakota landed was used by the Luftwaffe during the daylight hours. At night, however, it was sometimes exploited by the Poles: Culliford was guided in by UHF S-Phone, and safely met by a reception committee of partisans arranged by SOE. They manhandled through the aircraft doors nineteen suitcases containing wreckage from a V-2 which had landed beside the river Bug, together with scores of photographs and drawings, and five members of the Polish Resistance. After just five minutes on the ground, Culliford revved his engines for take-off. And stuck. The Dakota's brakes jammed, and its wheels sank into the soft earth.

Only after an hour of frenzied digging by the ground party, and by cutting the plane's hydraulic lines, did Culliford manage to stagger into the air at his fourth attempt. The Dakota droned away southwards with agonising sluggishness, slowed by its undercarriage, which remained partially extended. As dawn was coming up, the plane and its exhausted crew and passengers made a clumsy landing at Brindisi; the V-2 parts were flown to London, reaching R.V. Jones and his colleagues two days later. Culliford received the Virtuti Militari, Poland's highest air decoration, which was assuredly richly deserved. It would be satisfying to record that this remarkable episode solved the riddle of the German rocket. It did not, however. The British remained as puzzled as ever about the technical specifications of the V-2.

In the course of the summer and autumn, just over 10,000 flying bombs were launched against England, of which 7,488 crossed the coast; but only 2,419 reached London, and most of the balance were shot down. They inflicted 6,184 deaths, cause for grief enough, but nothing like the devastating campaign Hitler had intended and the British feared. The consequence was a surge of premature euphoria. Early in September the vice-chiefs of staff delivered a remarkably reckless report: 'All those areas from which the flying bomb or the rocket might be launched against London have been, or are about to be, occupied by Allied troops. There should thus shortly be no further danger to this country from either of these causes.' At a press conference on 7 September, Sandys stated publicly: 'Except possibly for a few last shots, the Battle of London is over.' Yet the very next day the first V-2 rockets, fired from Holland, landed on Paris and Chiswick, and soon three or four a day were exploding around the British capital. The scale of attack rose until an average of fourteen a day were landing – albeit with wild imprecision – on Holland and south-east England.

The official historians of wartime intelligence note frankly that British information about the V-2 had been sketchy for many months, and 'it was long to remain insufficient for all practical purposes'. R.V. Jones made a pretty good estimate of the weapon's size and warhead weight on the eve of its first firing in anger, but only in December 1944 did it become understood in London that the weapon was not radio-controlled, and thus could not be jammed. The Crossbow committee and the JIC lacked any significant knowledge about the location of the V-2's factories, depots or fuel plants in Germany. No defence against the rocket was practicable save to overrun its launch sites in Holland, which did not happen until the end of the war. It is a measure of the extravagant alarm provoked by the V-2 campaign that Herbert Morrison called for all-out Allied bomber attacks on its launchers around The Hague, heedless of the cost to Dutch civilians. The air chiefs invoked humanitarian considerations to resist saturation attacks, but Allied bombing of ski sites and other V-weapon installations in France, and of V-2 sites in Holland, nonetheless killed more French and Dutch people than Hitler's secret weapons killed British civilians. Between 8 September 1944 and 27 March 1945, 1,054 rockets fell on England and 2,700 Londoners perished.

Since the summer of 1943, Lord Cherwell had been a consistent sceptic about the plausibility of Hitler's rocket programme. Late in that year he said: 'At the end of the war, when we know the full story, we shall find that the rocket was a mare's nest.' He has been mocked ever since for making that statement, and it is certainly true that Cherwell overstated his case, as he often did. But he was fundamentally correct that the Nazis in 1944–45 created two weapons that were remarkable within the limits of the technology of that time, but quite incapable of changing the strategic balance of the war. After the V-weapons began to explode on Britain, Cherwell reiterated his scorn: 'The mountain hath groaned and brought forth a mouse.' He was right that Hitler made one of his many huge errors, by diverting to V-weapons manpower and raw materials that he could have used much more profitably elsewhere – to increase tank production, or to hasten and expand the Me-262 jet fighter programme. Seven German fighters could have been built with the resources expended on each V-2.

The Nazi leadership failed to see that the only issue that mattered was not the innovatory brilliance of a gyro-stabilised ballistic missile, nor that of the flying bomb, but merely what weight of explosives either was capable of delivering to Britain. A warhead of rather less than a ton in the case of the V-1, and somewhat more in that of the V-2, was smaller than the bombload of a Heinkel or Ju-88 bomber. The moral impact of V-weapons on the British was considerable: it was a terrifying experience to go about one's daily business beneath the 'doodlebugs', whose buzzing motors cut seconds before they plunged in murderous silence to earth, or the V-2s, which delivered devastation with awesome abruptness. But even had the programme created more weapons sooner, they were capable only of distressing Hitler's enemies, not of seriously injuring their war effort. It would have been more relevant to direct them against Eisenhower's forces in France, though neither system was sufficiently accurate to inflict serious damage upon armies in the field. It is no more useful to speculate, as do some historians to this day, about the possible effect had the Germans built and launched tens of thousands of V-weapons against Britain, than to try to compute the impact on the war of a dramatically larger Luftwaffe or U-boat fleet. Both, as Cherwell and R.V. Jones correctly surmised, were beyond Hitler's means.

The V-weapons intelligence failure was certainly not absolute. The British discovered that there was a threat. They delayed the German programme by months through bombing Peenemünde and the French ski sites, which they correctly identified as important elements in the V-weapon project. The Crossbow group learned enough about the V-1 to prepare some moderately effective countermeasures before it began; and no Allied weapons system existed that could have destroyed V-2s in flight. It was nonetheless remarkable that, in the last months of the war, Hitler could launch a campaign against the Allies which they could no more precisely define than they could monitor the German atomic bomb programme, such as it was. There were good reasons for this. The RAF's photographic interpreters were highly skilled, but could nonetheless be baffled by the unfamiliar – artefacts such as they had never seen before. Resistance groups in Poland and Western Europe, which provided reports, sketches and crash fragments, displayed extraordinary bravery and determination, but their efforts yielded insufficient evidence to enable scientists and agents in London to reach firm conclusions. Finally and most important, the British intelligence machine was so Ultra-weighted that it struggled when confronted with an issue about which Bletchley Park could reveal little: the Germans were not so obliging as to dispatch wireless signals describing the exact nature of their Führer's revenge weapons.

In the grand scheme of the war, none of this mattered much. As Lord Cherwell said, the Nazi mountain produced a mouse. But it remains striking that, for all the Ultra-driven triumphs of Allied intelligence in the latter years of the war, there was a remarkable amount the high command yearned to know, yet failed to discover.

'Blunderhead': The English Patient

Many spies of all nationalities adopted muddled or multiple loyalties, as the behaviour of a host of characters in this book illustrates. Yet few Englishmen who served in the war experienced such an odyssey as that of Ronald Seth, who is scarcely known to posterity, or even to most historians of the secret war. His doings did not influence the struggle in the smallest degree, but they nonetheless absorbed countless man-hours among the senior officers of SOE, MI5, MI6 and MI9 – and of the Abwehr and RSHA. What makes Seth even more unusual is that the documents about his case survive almost in their entirety in Britain's National Archives. It is thus possible to recount in detail the story of one of the few wartime agents 'turned' by the Germans, a man who baffled both sides' secret services in a fashion that relegates Eddie Chapman – 'ZigZag' – to amateur status.

Seth was born in eastern England in 1911, a metal merchant's son who attended King's School, Ely, and read English at Cambridge before embarking on a career as a teacher. Having considered, and finally rejected, ordination as a priest, in 1936 he accepted a post at the English College in Tallinn, Estonia, and from there graduated to become assistant professor of English at the local university. He wrote a little book on Estonia entitled *Baltic Corner*, which was published in Britain in 1938. At the outbreak of war he returned home and spent a year as an announcer for the BBC's Estonian Service before falling out with the Corporation and being called up for service in the RAF, becoming an administrative officer at an airfield in Wiltshire.

Although Seth was married with two small children, he hankered for a more dramatic personal role in the conflict. On 26 October 1941 he wrote a long letter to the Air Ministry, suggesting that he was just the man to raise the standard of revolt against Nazism in the Baltic states: 'Because of my activities I became well-known to the ordinary Estonian man-in-the-street and, if I may say so, held in high esteem and admiration throughout the country. It cannot be denied that I am the best-known Englishman in Estonia. In addition to this I made friends with a very large circle of prominent and influential Estonians who included the president [and] most members of the government. All the Estonians ever wanted, and I am positive still want, is political independence ... I wish to place before you the following proposal: that I should be permitted to go to Estonia and attempt to organise a [Resistance] movement ... I realise the difficulties and the risks. I realise that if I am caught I shall be "a gonner". If I succeed I shall have done a fair spot of work ... In any events, I should be happier attempting it than I am now, in more or less enforced inactivity ... at an Operational Training Unit.'

Many such wartime appeals from bored or unfulfilled men and women with romantic ambitions were dismissed unheeded. However, Seth's remarkable letter was passed to SOE, which responded enthusiastically. Russia's survival hung by a thread; the British were eager to do everything in their limited power to provide aid. The Germans were extracting hundreds of tons of shale oil from Estonia, which were fuelling Wehrmacht formations besieging Leningrad. Baker Street put the question to Ronald Seth: how would he like to be parachuted into the country, blow up the oil plants and start a local Resistance movement behind the Eastern Front? The aspiring hero embraced the scheme and completed SOE's application form, answering a question about his political views by writing 'vaguely socialist'. He stated that he had written 'two novels of no consequence' and was unable to drive a car. None of this was held against him, nor was a complaint from his former RAF station that a cheque he left behind in settlement of his final officers' mess bill had bounced. He spent most of 1942 attending the usual schools in sabotage, tradecraft, unarmed combat and wireless transmission.

Seth performed reasonably well as an embryo secret agent. He was uncomfortable with weapon training, and weak wrists made him a poor shot, but he improved after some fitness classes. Following an exercise in Newcastle, his examiner reported: 'This student's work was of an unusually high quality. He is exceptionally keen and competent ... Under a rigorous interrogation on his identity, his life, his past and present activities, his presence in Newcastle and his future plans, the student was superbly self-confident. He was completely unperturbable, his story was convincing.' The parachute school at Ringway, where he jumped in his spectacles, described him as 'a talkative but pleasant type who seemed sincere and determined … a nervous type of officer. Likeable.' His finishing report said: 'intelligent, but an erratic type of brain. Mentally immature. He is intensely enthusiastic, bordering on the fanatic. He appears to possess abundant self-confidence … He has a charming personality and is a good mixer but his great weakness is that he is inclined to dramatise nearly everything he does. He requires a far greater degree of security-minded-ness and self-discipline if he is to succeed. It is his determination rather than his character which inspires a degree of confidence.' The final verdict on Seth, in September 1942, was that 'although his sublime self-confidence is … possibly somewhat excessive, it is at the same time one of his strong-est weapons'.

He provided a clue to his own eccentricity, if not mental instability, by suggesting to SOE that before he jumped into Estonia he should be subjected to some bodily mutilation, such as would render him unfit for forced labour in Germany. His handlers rejected this proposal, on the somewhat cynical grounds that if they fulfilled his proposal the British government would become liable for paying him a disability pension after the war. One sensitive planner in Baker Street was troubled at the prospect of dispatching an agent on a mission which, the political runes already indicated, would raise hopes among local people that must go unfulfilled: 'If Estonia is to be handed over to Russia at the end of the war,' wrote an unnamed officer on 1 May 1942, 'and the Estonians get to know Britain's acquiescence, I do not see how R[onald] can in good faith get the Estonians to rally round him in sabotaging their way to a non-existent freedom!'

Doubts might have also have been raised about the plausibility of send-ing such an immediately noticeable figure as Seth – six feet two inches tall – to blend into Baltic society as a spy. But all scruples were brushed aside by SOE's chieftains, and in October the decision was taken to dispatch him on the first suitable night an RAF aircraft was available. There was one small hitch: an Estonian seaman named Arnold Tedrekin had been selected to drop with him, but Seth baulked at undertaking the mission with a comrade who, he pointed out, seldom drew a sober breath. It was agreed that the Englishman should jump alone. The SOE operational order noted bleakly if ungrammatically: 'there is little hope of withdraw-ing this personnel'.

Winston Churchill delivered a stern injunction to his service chiefs, warning them against allocating frivolous codenames. It was intolerable, said the prime minister, that a wife or mother should be obliged to learn

<u>MOST SECRET</u>

MPO/PD/2002   31.8.42.   80A

To: MO
Copy to: S

From: MPO

   I am dealing with OPERATION BLUNDERHEAD
for S.   The operation consists of dropping two
operators, one or two large "A"s and containers
in Estonia and in order that the operation may be
carried out before next Spring, it seems to me that it
will have to take place in the end of October moon
period, this for two reasons:

 (a) the relatively long night available
 (b) on any later date, the operators would be
   in danger of starvation after landing
   owing to the climatic conditions in
   that country.

   The matter has been discussed with the
Air Ministry before but I should be obliged if you would
now take the matter up again in order to settle details.
There will be no Reception Committee and the question
of the dropping point therefore depends upon finding
a spot which would be most convenient both from an
air point of view and from the point of view of the agents
At the moment, I should suggest somewhere near RAKWERE
but this is subject to revision as I hope to have the
Estonian operator in my hands towards the end of the
week and he may be able to suggest somewhere more
suitable from a cover point of view.

Ronald Seth made meticulous preparations
for Operation 'Blunderhead'

that her husband or son had perished to fulfil a mission with such a code-name as 'Bunnyhug' or 'Ballyhoo'. SOE breached this injunction in the case of Ronald Seth, by dubbing the agent and his Baltic mission 'Blunderhead'. Its start was inauspicious, because the take-off was three times scheduled and cancelled because of bad weather. Seth's morale understandably plummeted, according to the RAF officer responsible for the Special Duties Squadron. But shortly before 6 o'clock on the evening of Saturday, 24 October 1942, a Polish-piloted Halifax bomber took off from Linton-on-Ouse in Yorkshire for the six-hour flight to Estonia. It carried the newly minted agent, dressed in a camouflaged jumpsuit, together with a wireless set, some rations and explosives.

Seth would be dropping 'blind', with no reception committee to meet him, because there was no known local Resistance. He had opted to land near a coastal farmhouse whose owner, Martin Saarne, he knew and trusted, having taught his son English. The pilot afterwards described how his passenger came and stood beside him in the cockpit, peering down through the clear night at the Baltic coastline until he was sure they were in the right place, above a clearing in forests at the western base of the Kolga peninsula. Seth vanished into the darkness with remarkable good cheer, followed on a second circuit by three containers that bore his equip-ment. He flashed a torch from the ground to confirm a safe descent, then the big bomber banked and turned for home, landing safely at 7 o'clock next morning after thirteen hours in the air. The pilot reported Seth's delivery: 'Agent jumped without hesitation after selecting the point with the captain of the aircraft.'

Thereafter, however, a deafening silence descended upon 'Blunderhead'. Weeks passed, then months. A report reached SOE that a source in Tallinn had heard of a British parachutist answering its man's description, who had been captured by the Germans, then committed suicide. The agent's handler, Major Ronald Hazell, a former shipbroker who was head of SOE's Polish Section, was asked if 'Blunderhead' had been provided with poison. Yes, of course: all agents were issued with an 'L' for lethal potassium cyanide pill for optional use in the event of their capture, though most promptly flushed it down the nearest toilet. Hazell felt obliged to write to Josephine Seth, reporting that her husband was missing, and that it might be necessary to assume the worst. She responded with a moving letter, in which she explained that successive postings to different RAF stations meant she saw her children at schools in the West Country only every three months, so she was experiencing a difficult time. She acknowledged

SOE's interpretation of her husband's silence, but said, 'I shall always go on believing that Ronnie is alive' – a phrase used by many, many wartime wives who were eventually obliged to admit themselves widows.

The next development in this saga derived from a fluke. In April 1943 two Luftwaffe aircraft forced-landed in neutral Switzerland. They proved to contain large quantities of German documents, which were impounded by the Swiss. The local MI6 station gained access to photograph them, and when the haul was examined in London, on 30 April an SOE officer reported gloomily to colleagues, 'the following, I am afraid, concerns us'. The file to which he referred was a translation of a Luftwaffe report on the interrogation of a British spy, Ronald Seth, at Dulag Luft, Oberursel, on 6 February. Baker Street's man, it appeared, fell into German hands within days of landing in Estonia. He had since told his captors everything about his SOE experiences – with a protective gloss. He claimed that he had been forced to accept his espionage mission by a Jew at the Air Ministry who had threatened him with a revolver.

SOE commented after studying the Abwehr interrogation: 'This report is factually correct so far as the individual, his training with us and his delivery in Estonia are concerned. It is difficult to credit, however, the statement that SETH makes in regard to a pistol held to his head by a WING-COMMANDER in the AIR MINISTRY ... There is some possibility of his being alive ... It may be, however, that in the process of time we shall hear more as to the further treatment meted out to him. Until then, it is impossible to say whether he has remained a prisoner in enemy hands, or has been executed.' Another SOE officer took a harsher view: 'I am sorry to have to do so, but I feel that I can put no other construction on this unfortunate operation than that SETH got cold feet on his arrival. I never met him, so far as I know, but all the reports I have heard of him pointed to his being somewhat nervy and likely to break down under any strain of loneliness or opposition.'

On 5 May 1943 SOE's Signals Office was instructed to abandon its listening watch for wireless transmissions from 'Blunderhead'. A month later, a memorandum reported that Seth's handler, Major Hazell, 'has seen Mrs Blunderhead who says she would be very glad to have some approved story to tell her friends – for example, that her husband is missing. [Hazell] has not told her anything about our information as to Blunderhead, and says that his wife will be reconciled to waiting until the end of the war for news ... In all the circumstances I would suggest that the Personnel department of the Air Ministry should ... send the wife a letter saying that

Blunderhead is missing from operations.' Josephine Seth was delicately informed that although her husband was not dead, his circumstances were extremely precarious. The strain on the poor woman must have been appalling.

Thereafter, for more than a year not another word was heard of Seth. It was reasonable to assume that, like almost all captured Allied agents, he was being held in a concentration camp or – more likely – was dead. A few weeks after D-Day, on 29 July 1944 SOE minuted: 'Information has now been received that Flight-Lieutenant Ronald Seth must now be reclassified "Killed on active service 24.10.42" … Mrs Seth has already been informed unofficially of her husband's death.' Less than a month later, however, the liberation of Paris produced a new and sensational twist in the Seth story, which thereafter engaged the serious attention of MI5, MI6 and MI9. A man who called himself Émile Rivière approached an RAF officer in the French capital and handed him an envelope addressed to the War Office in London. This was duly forwarded to its destination. On examination it proved to contain a densely pencilled seventy-six-page narrative headed 'Paris, August 7th, 1944', and addressed to 'the GOC S[pecial] T[raining] S[ervices] HQ, Room 98 Horse Guards. From BLUNDERHEAD. In The Field.'

A covering letter began, 'Dear Sir, I hope you will forgive my asking this very great favour, but if my operation has so far been successful in your opinion, please could you possibly apply for my promotion to the rank of: ACTING GROUP-CAPTAIN (unpaid), with seniority *retrospective twelve months* from the date of this letter? I ask for this favour, Sir, because should anything happen to me in the months that are to come, my wife and children would at least have a suitable pension on which to live. This has worried me considerably throughout the whole of my operation, although Major Hazel assured me that he thought that in the event of my death the Organisation [SOE] would provide £1000 for my children. But £1000 will not provide the education for my son and daughter that I could give them were I there to provide for them. And education is going to count more than ever in post-war England, I am sure.'

If this was a somewhat humdrum opening gambit, the rest of Seth's report to SOE was page-turning stuff: a lurid, highly coloured narrative in which it is no easier today to distinguish truth from invention that it was for Britain's secret services to do so in 1944. The only incontrovertible fact was that, in the course of almost two years in occupied Europe, in the hands of a ruthless enemy, SOE's man had known experiences fantastic even by the standards of world war. He claimed that he had made his original parachute landing on top of a group of Germans, from whom he managed to flee, at the cost of abandoning his arms and equipment, then suffered adventures which included being fired upon by Estonian militia-men: 'one shot whizzed through the undergrowth in which I was hiding, narrowly missing my head'. He described how he had blown up several German aircraft and an artillery position, but had been obliged to spend days living in the wilderness without food, sustained only by opium tablets and a flask he had brought from England: 'I could find no chickens. For shooting deer, even if I could stalk them successfully I had only my Colt .32 and thirty rounds. The outlook was bleak, as my whiskey was getting low. Having sampled the temper of the natives, I decided to adhere to my plan to make no contacts until I had seen [his old friend] Saarne.'

Seth met the farmer at last on 5 November, and during a tense, bleak conversation was told that his mission was hopeless: 'Those older people remaining after the Russian occupation of 1939–40 were lethargic, the young Estonians were whole-heartedly with the Germans, who had very cleverly exploited the disgusting Russian excesses during the Red occupa-tion.' Seth said he thereupon decided to go to Tallinn, and was walking through the nearby village when he was arrested by militia, who handed him over to the Germans. He was promptly incarcerated in Cell 13 of Tallinn Central prison, and interrogated by a Major Vogl. Asked if he would make wireless transmissions to England, this agent weakened by hunger and privation tearfully agreed to do so. He was questioned for eight days, and invented the tale of a Jew at the Air Ministry named Goldmann who had forced him to accept the SOE assignment. He length-ily described to his London readership experiences of first being tortured, then informed that on 21 December he would be publicly hanged. He said that on the appointed day he was indeed led out onto a gallows, and placed before the trap: 'I refused a handkerchief for my eyes with as heroic a shake of my head that I could manage.' After a long and circumstantial account of this ordeal, he claimed he was told that his execution would be postponed until after the Christmas holiday. He told the Germans that he would be happy to work for them against the Russians. This persuaded them in January 1943 to put him on a train from Riga to Berlin, thence to Frankfurt am Main.

Seth spun his jailers a series of fantastic yarns, describing himself as a group-captain with a knighthood and close connections with the royal family. He told SOE he had informed the Germans that in 1941 he was initiated into a secret society called the Windsor League, seeking the restoration of King Edward VIII, and had attended meetings at which Sir Stafford Cripps and several other MPs had been present. He urged the Gestapo – who held him for a time – that his experience as a BBC announcer could be immensely helpful to them. He was eventually told that he was being transferred to the custody of the Abwehr, who proposed to train him to carry out an espionage mission in Britain.

In November 1943 he was taken by his Abwehr handler Major Emile Kliemann to Paris, where he was lodged with a French family of well-known German collaborators named Delidaise, and granted liberty to move freely around the city carrying an *Ausweis* – official pass – in the name of Sven Passikiwi, a Finn. Here his narrative for SOE assumed Baron Munchhausen proportions: he claimed to have shot dead two German soldiers in the Metro. He confessed that he had formed an easy relationship with Richard Delidaise and his family, and especially with Liliane, his host's sister-in law. He told SOE: 'I was known by everybody as "M. Ronnie" ... It was inevitable, I am afraid, Sir, that Mlle. Liliane would become my mistress. The present report is no place to enter into pathological or psychological details, but I feel I must justify this somewhat unagentlike behaviour on my part, by saying that for me "practical love" is a PHYSICAL NECESSITY; but also, at this time, I was mentally desperately in need of some mundane contact to make my world seem real ... I ask you if you will, Sir, to imagine yourself in my place. I was playing a role, not like the ordinary actor, for two or three hours a day, but for twenty-four.'

For six months he underwent Abwehr training as an agent, including instruction in wireless technique and coding, about which he provided SOE with copious detail, including charts and numerical expositions. He appears sometimes to have worn a Luftwaffe uniform on the streets of Paris. Shortly after D-Day, he was told that within a fortnight he would be dispatched to England. On 20 June, however, he was abruptly informed that his new employers had lost confidence in him; Berlin now refused to approve his mission. He was removed from his comfortable quarters and from his lover and lodged in the Cherche-Midi prison, where he endured sufferings that he described extensively, including finding lice 'as big as a fingernail' and developing scabies. His Abwehr handler 'Kilburg' – Major Kliemann – visited him to report that a debate was taking place about whether to send him back to Berlin. After six weeks in a cell, he was suddenly informed that it had been decided to use him as a stool-pigeon in British PoW camps.

He was thereupon released from the Cherche-Midi, restored to semi-liberty, and – in those days when it was obvious that the Allies would soon be in Paris – occupied himself in composing his voluminous report, which he entrusted to Richard Delidaise – who also used the name Émile Rivière. The Frenchman must have believed, not wrongly, that by assisting Seth to make contact with the British he could save his own unattractive neck, together with those of his relations. Seth included in all his subsequent messages to London passionate pleas to protect Delidaise – and, of course, his beloved Liliane. He assured SOE that although they might think he was now working for the Germans, in reality he was still a loyal British agent. In the valediction of his report addressed to the War Office, he wrote histrionically: 'I do not yet know whether I shall go to camps in Germany or France, or indeed if I shall yet come out alive. But if you do not receive reports of my death when the armistice is signed, please will you look for me in P.O.W. camps, and if I am not there, in German civil prisons and concentration camps ... I beg to remain, Sir, your obedient servant BLUNDERHEAD August 7th 1944.'

When this astonishing document reached London it prompted a new surge of memoranda and commentaries, thickening files on Seth in Broadway, Baker Street and at MI5 that already ran to hundreds of pages. A dozen overworked senior intelligence officers, from Stewart Menzies and Felix Cowgill at MI6 to Lt. Col. 'Tar' Robertson of MI5 and Lt. Col. James Langley of MI9, found themselves attending meetings to discuss the past doings and future prospects of 'Blunderhead'. SOE, reasonably enough, sought to make the best possible case for its man, but was obliged to admit that his narrative was impossible to swallow: 'Seth is extremely prolific on paper, of a highly-strung temperament, very vainglorious, but possesses initiative, imagination and quickness of mind ... It would appear that, in the spirit, SETH is very much under the domination of the Germans ... he would have had many opportunities to escape in PARIS which he did not embrace. If the Germans decide that they have no further use for SETH, it is likely he may be executed. He has, however, shown himself very astute by putting the Germans off with promises and he may succeed in continuing to do so ... It would appear to be the case that he is genuine in his assertions that he intends to double-cross the Germans, and if he were sent back to ENGLAND, would certainly not carry out any mission for them.'

On 25 September Commander John Senter of SOE wrote to 'Tar' Robertson, emphasising Baker Street's 'responsibility in this matter, first of all to Seth who undertook a mission calling for great personal courage ... I understand that you are in full agreement that he should not be treated on his return to this country as a felon, but as a British officer who must be invited to explain what happened.' RAF administrators joined the Seth paperchase, expressing concern that some months earlier they had paid a gratuity to his wife on the assumption of her husband's death, and were even now paying her a pension. It had now become plain that she was not entitled to either. Should she be made to pay back the money?

On 5 October an initial report from counter-intelligence in Paris expressed bewilderment that Seth's document addressed to SOE had been handed over to an RAF officer by Richard Delidaise – under his alias as Rivière – a known creature of the Abwehr. The CI team had interviewed the family, and emerged with scant enthusiasm for any of them. They described 'Liliane', Seth's acknowledged mistress – full name Lucie Beucherie of 3, Rue Lincoln, Paris 8 – as 'a woman of loose morals, one lover succeeding another', some of them German. She was up to her neck in the black market, and Seth was merely one among a multitude of her men. He had spent some of his time in Paris under an assumed German identity as 'Lt. Haid', but she told her interrogator that 'Blunderhead' had confessed to her that he was only pretending to work for the Germans in the hope of facilitating his escape. The author of the Paris counter-intelligence report concluded with a list of 'questions to which I should like the answers', which started with that of 'When and where did SETH find time to write his 76-page report?'

On 10 October there was another flurry of excitement in London following receipt of a new emotional outburst, scribbled by Seth in Belgium and given to a local man who passed it on to an American officer when the liberators arrived a week later. This letter, dated 2 September, explained that he had left Paris with the retreating Germans on 17 August, having agreed to work for the SD in PoW camps. 'Having found out what they wanted me to do, I decided that this work would be so important from the British side and although I have had many chances to escape in the last two weeks I am carrying through. I have got so much important political information that it is absolutely essential I should be released immediately war is over. I shall be in the Oflag at Limburg under the name of CAPTAIN JOHN DE WITT.' An MI5 officer wrote to John Senter of SOE, saying that the latest message from Seth 'only deepens the mystery of his case, and I must say I find it difficult to understand his argument that, having as he says so much important political information for this country, he should consider it even more important not to escape but to stay behind and work for the Sicherheitspolitzei in P/W camps'.

The British PoW 'Captain John de Witt' made his debut in a letter from the officers' camp at Limburg, dated 15 September 1944. He wrote to a supposed sister – in fact his wife Josephine – saying among much else: 'There is one thing worrying me. Will you get in touch with Hazel? He knows I have been nursing the Ely constituency, and I am afraid that after this is all over, there may be some delay in getting released, and I may miss the General Election. Ask Hazel to pull every string he can – see Anthony [presumably Eden, the foreign secretary] if necessary – and get me out of here *immediately* peace is signed. I must get home at once, otherwise all my work will have been wasted.' In case this letter failed to get through, Seth persuaded a fellow-officer writing home to include some remarks which reached SOE and MI5: 'by the way Ronnie is here, as blunderheaded as usual. It's good to have him.' The copy in SOE's file is marked 'original with MI9'.

Other British prisoners in the camp sent coded messages to London, demanding to know what they should make of 'Captain de Witt', who seemed to spend much of his time talking to Germans outside the compound on the pretext of arranging musical entertainments, and who occasionally confided that he was really SOE agent Ronald Seth. The senior officer at Limburg later testified that the newcomer had 'started behaving in a most peculiar manner. He drew attention to himself in no uncertain fashion by telling all and sundry incredible and diverging stories.' Another bulletin reached MI9 in an officer's letter dated 10 October from Oflag 79. It said: 'DE WITT claims joined RAF bomber 1940 promoted Group-Captain and made KCB. Seconded SOE dropped Esthonia 24 October 1942.' MI5 discussed the 'de Witt' letters with SOE. Obviously the 'Hazel' to whom the writer referred was his own former handler, now a lieutenant-colonel working in France, where he was dispatching agents into Germany. But the MI5 officer commented wearily: 'I must say I cannot find any satisfactory hypothesis to explain why SETH should be given a false name and then permitted to write to his wife under the false name as if he was her brother.'

And what was all this stuff about the Ely constituency? Did Seth have political ambitions? After more messages from Germany referred to Ely and the prospect of a post-war election, on 5 December 1944 SOE wrote to Felix Cowgill of MI6, saying, 'As Seth continues to harp on the Ely topic, we are still racking our brains for some explanation.' The most pathetic victim of this farrago was Josephine Seth, still serving at an RAF station in the north of England, and utterly bewildered about the correspondence from her husband. She appealed repeatedly to SOE for guidance on how to handle Ronald's messages, especially one asking her to open a bank account with £150. SOE minuted: 'Mrs SETH states that in fact she has not the necessary money to open an account for £150.'

Seth persuaded inmates to send more secret messages on his behalf in their letters home, for instance: '5th October. From THUNDERHEAD [sic] FOR STS 98 HORSE GUARDS. FAILED TO BLOW ESTONIAN MINE. 8th October VON KLUGER SHOT HIMSELF. HUNS HAVE GOT THE FULL DETAILS OF OUR ROCKET BOMB TRIALS IN AFRICA. 9th October RUSSIANS INFILTRATING MANY FIFTH COLUMNISTS INTO NORWAY.' On 15 December, in another long memorandum, Baker Street suggested to MI5: 'we cannot help wondering whether his reason has not been to some extent affected'. MI9 eventually dispatched a general coded warning to all British PoW camps, instructing their inmates to have nothing to do with anybody calling himself either de Witt or Seth, who was 'gravely suspect … [his actions] have rendered him suspect of collaboration with the enemy'. He spent his last months in Limburg in 'protective custody' by his fellow-prisoners – unable to move in the compound unless escorted by a British officer – until he was 'arrested' by the Germans and vanished on 11 March 1945.

With hindsight at least, it is not difficult to understand that Seth was playing the accustomed roles of every double agent, striving to keep two employers happy. Despite the comic aspects of his story, he was at the mercy of the Nazis, who would shoot him the moment his usefulness seemed to have expired, or his loyalty to them was in doubt: captured British, American and Soviet agents continued to be executed by German firing squads until the last day of the war. Seth's only chance of survival was to convince the Abwehr and RSHA that he was an important person, hence all the references to his fictitious high rank, knighthood and parliamentary prospects. He displayed amazing ingenuity and thespian skill in sustaining this delusion. There was nothing noble, heroic or admirable about his behaviour. But who is to say what a man may do to save his skin under such circumstances?

Seth saved his best trick for last: on 16 April 1945, three weeks before the war in Europe ended, he presented himself at the door of the British legation in Bern, and demanded to see the minister. Ushered into the august presence, he said that he must be flown to London immediately, to report to Winston Churchill on a matter of the utmost gravity: he was carrying peace proposals from Himmler, whom he had met personally only days before, while staying in Munich as a guest of the SS, under a Dutch alias as 'Jan de Fries'. MI6's Bern station signalled this news to London, where it precipitated a new ferment. What was to be done with Seth? Broadway's Bern officers said that he appeared to be sane. He was plainly acting with the complicity of the Nazi hierarchy, or some part of it, otherwise he could never have secured a passage to the Swiss frontier, and licence to cross it. No possible message from Himmler could hold any interest for the Allied governments at this stage, and indeed urgent instructions were signalled to Bern, to ensure that Seth was unable to discuss his 'peace proposals' with anybody, nor be questioned about them; but even the world-weary, or rather war-weary, senior intelligence officers in London felt an urgent curiosity to interrogate Seth.

He was flown home on 20 April in his persona as Captain John de Witt, and permitted to see his wife and children. He claimed to have expected to be received as a returning hero, having survived the most harrowing experiences. He maintained a persistent, manic clamour about SOE's failure to produce a suitcase containing civilian clothes that he claimed to have left in its charge. He showed dismay, even disgust, when his handlers made plain that unless he could produce some plausible answers to their questions, there was every prospect that he would face a trial for high treason, such as would soon dispatch William Joyce and John Amery to the gallows.

Guy Liddell of MI5 felt that he and his colleagues must agree a position about Seth before people in high places learned anything of his activities, which could inflict grievous embarrassment – 'disastrous results' – upon the secret community. How could such a man have been recruited and deployed as a spy? On 22 April 1945 'Blunderhead' reported for his first session of questioning by the security service bearing a medical certificate stating that he was subject to paranoiac tendencies. Liddell commented acidly in his diary: 'from the sensational nature of his story this indeed seems likely'. Seth told MI5 that the Germans were still holding back some terrifying secret weapons for their last-ditch resistance, including germ warfare.

During the months that followed, he was questioned by some of the most skilled officers of MI5, including 'Tar' Robertson. They emerged from the process emotionally exhausted, in no doubt that Seth was a fantasist who seemed incapable of distinguishing truth from falsehood. On 16

May 1945 Captain E. Milton of MI5 produced a twenty-five-page report, half of which was taken up with cataloguing the obvious inconsistencies and falsehoods in the spy's account of himself. Milton believed Seth had surrendered to the Germans almost immediately after landing; had never fulfilled any acts of sabotage; and had never been subjected to torture or a mock execution: 'I think this information was invented by SETH as an excuse for many of his subsequent actions with which we might reproach him and also perhaps to justify to his own enormous vanity why he humiliated himself by offering to work for the Germans ... I feel personally that Seth was badly frightened and willing to work for the Germans, even to the prejudice of this country ... Seth was not maltreated by the Germans, because he told them all they asked.' He had latterly been controlled by an officer named Graf Christopher von Dönhoff, who had lived in Kenya for ten years, but who now made a wise career decision to relocate himself to Zürich. The report concluded that Seth was 'undoubtedly suffering from megalomania and would seem to be of long-term interest to the security services'. Uncertainty persisted, however, about whether he should be branded a full-blooded traitor, and indicted for treason.

Trouble was never far from 'Blunderhead'. He was permitted to travel to the north of England to see his wife at the RAF station where she was serving. This compassionate outing prompted a baffled letter to MI5 from the chief constable of Lancashire, who wrote to say that while in his county, Seth had given all and sundry a wildly fanciful account of his adventures abroad, which seemed to constitute an industrial-scale breach of national security. Meanwhile, a passionate letter addressed by Seth to Liliane and written in French was intercepted and confiscated; it seemed undesirable for the SOE man to have any further contact with his lover, especially when her brother-in-law Richard was in the security service's custody as a collaborator, and was under interrogation – not least about Seth. MI5's final conclusion about SOE's would-be Resistance chief in Estonia was that, while there was no doubt he had given the Germans far more active assistance than he would admit, there was insufficient evidence to send him for trial. It is easy to deduce that none of the secret services wanted this sample of their dirty laundry exposed in public at a time when the British people simply sought to celebrate the triumph of British virtue over Nazi evil. In August 1945 Seth was discharged from the RAF, in which he had held the nominal rank of flight-lieutenant during his service with SOE.

Even in the surreal world of intelligence, Seth's doings were remarkable. He must have embarked on his Estonian adventure in good faith – why else would a man of thirty-one, with a young family, have volunteered to become a saboteur parachuted into enemy-held territory? Most of his own account of his experiences in German hands seems as absurd as MI5 judged it to be. It is most likely that, having set forth from Britain with high ambitions to make himself a hero, once on the ground in Estonia a collision with terrifying reality dispelled such illusions, and focused his attentions exclusively upon dissuading the Germans from killing him. The shock must have been devastating, of meeting Estonians whom he expected to greet him as the harbinger of their freedom, a symbol of their future deliverance, and finding instead that they merely wished him to go away. The most persistent enigma is why Seth went back to Germany from Paris with his Abwehr hosts in August 1944, instead of making a break for the Allied lines, as he himself admitted that he easily could have done. The likely answer is that, by that stage, he was painfully conscious that if the Germans did not shoot him, his own countrymen might do so. It seems to the credit of Britain's intelligence services that they treated Seth, on his return, with an understanding not far short of compassion. It was, after all, SOE which had dispatched him into a place of utmost danger, as it dispatched so many others.

17

Eclipse of the Abwehr

1 HITLER'S BLETCHLEYS

It remains one of the most fascinating puzzles of the Second World War, how a society as advanced as Germany failed to match the Allies as code-makers and breakers. Its hubs of civil and military power employed at least as many people as the British on signals intelligence – some 30,000, working in six separate and rival organisations. After VE-Day, interrogators quizzed their captured personnel exhaustively. A dramatic moment came at Flensburg, when one of the most senior officers of the high command's *Chiffrierabteilung* – OKW/Chi, as it was known – was asked to identify his service's most important achievement. There was a protracted silence. The Allied questioner wrote: 'It became apparent that OKW/Chi had not achieved an outstanding success.'

They tried, however. They tried. Nazi Germany had clever men who strove mightily to match the prowess of Turing and Welchman, Friedman and Rowlett, of which mercifully they knew nothing. Those who know only the history of Bletchley suppose that Allied sigint success and Axis failure were absolutes. This they certainly were not. The B-Dienst achieved important penetration of British naval codes during the Battle of the Atlantic, described earlier. The Luftwaffe's eavesdroppers acquired an immense amount of information about RAF and USAAF operations over Europe by monitoring voice traffic – aircrew talking to each other amid the stress of combat operations were notoriously insecure – through electronic observation and PoW interrogation. On the Eastern Front, the Germans acquired much useful order-of-battle data through traffic analysis and breaking field codes – the army radio intelligence service deployed six regiments in Russia. As late as March 1943, a Bletchley report on German 'Y Service' operations on the Eastern Front revealed them reading most Red Air Force traffic from their station W40 at Wildpark,

Potsdam, partly because the Russians seldom troubled to change callsigns. The Luftwaffe accessed their two-, three- and four-figure cipher messages. An American pen commented: 'What, if anything, the British have done to jack up the Russians, I don't know.' The Germans also claimed to have made occasional breaks into higher ciphers, because of Soviet wireless-operators' shortage of, and thus careless reuse of, one-time pads. In North Africa, until July 1942 the Afrika Korps exploited sigint more effectively than did the British. Beyond the Germans' access to the War Office's W Code, captured in Norway in 1940, which thereafter rendered some low-level British Army traffic accessible, they also had the US Military Attachés' code until June 1942, and later claimed to have broken into US Army M-209 field ciphers. Both Western Allied armies used radio voice communication carelessly, to the advantage of their enemies' excellent intercept stations.

Never, however, did the Germans remotely match the achievement of Bletchley, Arlington Hall and Op-20-G in regularly reading higher ciphers in real time. It was their misfortune that the American Sigaba was a critical step smarter than Enigma. Experts believe traffic from the British Type-X machine might have been broken had the Germans laid hands on the appropriate rotors, but they never did. Berlin's efforts also suffered severely from the division of its cryptographic efforts between rival armed forces and Nazi empires. The smallest establishment was that of Ribbentrop's Foreign Ministry, Pers ZS, which had its own intercept station at Landhaus, as well as receiving some messages from OKW/Chi. Its leading personalities included Dr Adolf Pashke, a Russian and Italian linguist who had worked for the Foreign Ministry since 1919 and by 1945 had become Pers ZS's *de facto* chief. Dr Werner Kunze, another veteran since World War I, was the senior mathematical cryptanalyst, who ran the department's IBM machinery. Dr Ursula Hagen was one of the few women working in her field, supervising a group of twelve cryptanalysts studying England, Ireland and Spain. The post-war American report on the department suggests a group of reasonably proficient but relatively elderly specialists who 'seemed overly preoccupied with cryptanalysis as a science, and apparently not ... as a prime source of intelligence'. Pers ZS's greatest triumph was to read the Japanese 'Red' diplomatic cipher until February 1939, when it was replaced by Purple. During the war its codebreakers broke some Allied and neutral medium-grade diplomatic traffic, but there is no evidence that its content was much heeded by policymakers, or even subjected to serious analysis.

German military sigint organisation changed so much and so frequently in the course of the war that it is meaningless to detail the variations, save to say that they did nothing to help codebreaking. At the outset Wilhelm Fenner of OKW/Chi, which was charged with creating Germany's own diplomatic ciphers as well as breaking the enemy's, was his country's most influential cryptanalyst. Though Fenner was experienced and competent, his department suffered from his own delusion that he was brilliant. He was born in 1891 in St Petersburg, where his father ran a little newspaper for the German community, and he himself became fluent in Russian and English. After working for some time as an engineer, and then as a wartime army interpreter, in 1921 he joined the army cryptographic bureau, and scored an early success by breaking the Russian military attachés' code. He introduced into the department an exotic figure whom he considered his mentor, a White Russian ex-naval captain named Professor Peter Novopasakenny. The two were soon reading most French and Polish codes, which perhaps persuaded them that cryptanalysis was not too difficult. Fenner later complained stiffly about the problems of 'Haltung' – 'attitude' – that were created by the Nazis' ascent to power: 'The restless times were not favourable for scientific cryptanalysis.' Loyalty was esteemed far more highly than intellectual integrity.

The tips of Chi's sigint tentacles lay in its receiving stations at Treuenbrietzen, south-west of Berlin, and at Lauf, south of Baden-Baden. The former was composed of two single-storey stone buildings surrounded by wire and sentries, the compound dominated by a forest of sixty-foot aerials. Inside, banks of operators manned sixty receivers in six-hour shifts around the clock, assisted by Morse-recording machines. The Wehrmacht employed some blind operators, recruited for the acuteness of their hearing, of whom Fenner noted approvingly, 'the precision of their work was highly esteemed'. Most of the incoming material was composed in five-letter or -number code groups, and a good operator handled 3,000 to 4,000 in a shift, maybe two hundred messages a day.

The same routines were observed at Lauf, and there were subsidiary intercept stations at Breslau, Munster, Königsberg, Sofia and Madrid: in the Spanish capital operators occupied the extensive premises of the former Florida nightclub in the north-eastern suburb of Castellana. In 1941 Chi established a further out-station staffed by some fifty men on a German-owned cattle ranch north of Seville. This ran until 1944, when the Spanish authorities belatedly acknowledged the tilt of the war and enforced its closure. Further afield, a former Luftwaffe radio-operator serviced a one-man operation in the Canaries. All these stations teleprinted *Geheime Kommandosache* – Top Secret – material to Berlin, where it was sorted according to source, for discard or attack by the codebreakers. As at Bletchley and Arlington, only a proportion of intercepts could be addressed, and some broken foreign signals had to be left untranslated.

During the pre-war years the Germans read much of France's diplomatic traffic. A September 1939 decrypt provided OKW with the critical information that the French army's incursion into the Saarland was only a gesture which required no transfer of German forces from the Polish front. For much of the rest of the war, Chi accessed the traffic from London of the Free French and the Polish exile government, together with some Swiss Enigma, and allegedly some Soviet messages, though there is no evidence of anything important. The German attack on the traffic of the Allied armies was complicated and weakened by the division between OKW/Chi's role and that of the army's radio intelligence branch, which eventually became OKH/GdNA, or Inspectorate 7/VI, to which a steady stream of Chi specialists were seconded. This ultimately deployed 12,000 personnel including its field regiments on the battlefields, though Eastern Front activities were separately managed, under an organisation named HLS/Ost.

Until Allied bombing of Berlin achieved devastating proportions in the winter of 1943, both the army's cryptographic headquarters and OKW/Chi's various 'nation' departments were located in the same district of the capital as Canaris's offices, with the American *Referat* and Chi's main HQ situated on Matthaeikirchplatz, the Balkan and English *Referaten* at 9 Schellingstrasse, and so on. Some 320 crypto-linguists were employed, together with several hundred clerical and administrative staff, many of them women. The evaluation department was housed on Bendlerstrasse, where officers created the same sort of card indexes of enemy officers, callsigns, units and warships as Bletchley's. Chi's codebreakers worked behind locked office doors, and none of the female clerical staff had access to safe keys. Ongoing rivalry with Göring's Forschungsamt, chiefly a Nazi Party instrument dismissed by Walter Schellenberg as the minister's 'private plaything', was a handicap. The latter's 2,000 codebreaking personnel might have achieved more under a common roof with Chi and OKH/GdNA.

Chi used the same staff selection methods as the British and Americans – testing recruits with crossword puzzles and mathematical problems. Successful candidates were assigned to a four-week induction course, learning the substitution and transposition methods, and suchlike. They were also urged to read a French history of cryptanalysis, and Herbert Yardley's account of the old 'Black Chamber'. In Chi's 1941 heyday it employed around 3,000 people, but thereafter this strength fell, as rear-area organisations were combed for personnel who might become *Frontsoldaten*, or shifted to OKH/GdNA. Whereas Bletchley's success secured ever more resources, Chi's lack of it earned ever more scepticism. Moreover, from July 1944 it became a focus of hostile scrutiny, following the execution of its two most senior officers, signals corps generals, as plotters against Hitler. Fenner, Chi's veteran cryptanalyst, found himself under investigation, accused by an SD officer of plotting to sabotage the Wehrmacht's communications by recommending an inferior cipher system. Fenner said later, 'the whole cryptographic service came under political suspicion'. Though he was eventually cleared, in Nazi eyes the department's reputation was irretrievably tarnished.

Britain's Turing and Welchman, America's Friedman and Rowlett, had no equals in the enemy's camp. Recruitment was not assisted by the fact that many of Germany's most brilliant brains were exiled, imprisoned or slaughtered, because they were Jews. It bears notice that three of the four members of Friedman's original US Army codebreaking team were Jewish, together with some of the highest intellects at Bletchley. The names of Hitler's codebreakers are almost unknown to posterity, even in their own country, while their British and American counterparts have belatedly become famous. Nonetheless, some of Chi's men were talented by any standard save that of its enemies. Among the foremost was Dr Erich Hüttenhain, born in 1905 in Westphalia, a brilliant student who professed a passion for Mayan chronology. He left university in 1932 laden with laurels in astronomy, mathematics and physics. Thereafter he served for five years as an astronomical research assistant in Munster before being recruited as a cryptanalyst. He was quickly appointed to head a division, and set about recruiting the best brains he could identify, and ensuring that they were kept away from the front when war came. His assistant, Walther Fricke, produced a doctorate on the dynamics of the stellar system, and in 1939 had been due to take up a research post at Edinburgh University. Fricke joined Chi in 1941 knowing nothing of cryptanalysis, but proved an adept. Lt. Schubert became an expert on Russian traffic, assisted by a codebook captured by the Finns during their 1939–40 war with the Soviet Union; he was later transferred to OKH/GdNA, where he read some Red Army four-figure code material. Fenner also thought highly of Bernert, a Viennese who worked on British messages, and

Döring, who was 'always called in for difficult jobs'. There was an engineer who built 'phase decoders' – Willi Jensen, the nearest the organisation had to Tommy Flowers at Dollis Hill.

Other notable personalities included Wolfgang Franz, Ernst Witt, Karl Stein and Gisbert Hasenjaeger, the last the youngest in the team, aged twenty-four. Hüttenhain recruited five professors of mathematics, including Georg Aumann, Werner Weber and Johann Schultze – together with a physician of mathematical leanings. While the British allowed most of Bletchley's codebreakers to retain their civilian status, the Germans inducted theirs into the Wehrmacht as *Gefreiters* – privates first class – a loss of status which these relatively distinguished academics resented. Erich Hüttenhain had his first significant success cracking French field codes in 1938; the Germans continued to read these through 1940 and indeed thereafter, even though monthly changes were made. During the Blitzkrieg in France, army sigint decrypted relatively few important British signals, but was nonetheless able to provide German commanders with a full picture of their order of battle; to track their advance into Belgium; to read the order to their Calais garrison to hold out to the last.

In a prominent position in Chi's Tirpitzüfer headquarters stood a British Type-X cipher machine captured at Dunkirk, albeit without its rotors. Hüttenhain told interrogators in 1945 that 'since Enigma was similar to Type-X, and we believe that the Enigma cannot be broken, no great effort was made to break Type-X … Enigma might be broken if a vast Hollerith complex [tabulator] was used, but this is scarcely feasible.' The Germans created a range of intermediate technology to assist their labours, including a *Roellchengerät*, a 10 x 10 cylinder device built by the Foreign Ministry's cipher department, which performed a primitive calculating function. Chi also had an electric typewriter that could handle simple letter substitution. Fenner complained after the war: 'Mechanical scanning of perforated tapes [by Bigram devices] was always much too slow. The future belongs to photo-electric scanning.' The British, however, had achieved miracles with intermediate technology, and in comparison with the bombes and Colossus working their marvels at Bletchley, the machinery employed by Chi and OKH/GdNA resembled a 1914 biplane alongside a 1945 jet fighter.

The Germans relied overwhelmingly on human ingenuity to access lower Allied systems. Groups of men were assigned to work together on a given signal, cross-fertilising ideas just as at Bletchley and Arlington Hall. Fenner testified that during the early war years, when the Germans were reading America's strip-cipher military attaché code, 80 per cent of the breaks were achieved through user errors, especially when identical messages were repeated in different codes – the familiar vulnerability that assisted the Allies. Fenner said that Soviet ciphers were secure if properly employed, 'but if the cryptanalysts in Moscow could only see how they were used, they would be very unhappy'. This smug little observation should be judged, however, in the context of the fact that Berlin seems to have learned little of any significance to its war effort from whatever breaks it achieved.

In 1941 the Germans transferred from France to North Africa wireless eavesdroppers with experience of monitoring British traffic, and reaped handsome dividends. On 26 June, a long report from Bletchley drew War Office attention to British operational signals decrypted by the Germans during the Cretan débâcle, some of them detailing aircraft and warship movements. The Afrika Korps considered Eighth Army's wireless discipline very slack, and attributed many of Rommel's 1941–42 successes to his foreknowledge of British deployments. Some of the interceptors were highly qualified linguists. One, an NCO named Schwartze, was the twenty-six-year-old son of an English mother and a half-Jewish German father. He had been educated at Cheltenham College and Merton College, Oxford, where he read law, though debarred later from practising in Germany because of his ancestry. He worked in North Africa alongside a friend named Graupe, a Berliner a few years older, who had studied in Louisiana and worked in a US factory until the authorities declined to renew his visa.

After the war, Lt. Gen. Albert Praun described how spasms of Anglo-American carelessness enabled his officers to piece together enemy orders of battle, just as the Allies did. The sigint out-station in Athens, for instance, read a message from a British paymaster in Palestine, instructing a division being transferred to Egypt to leave behind its filing cabinets – which enabled a big red pin to be shifted on the map of British deployments in the Middle East. Later, the Germans discovered that the US 82nd Airborne Division had moved from the Mediterranean to Britain because they broke an administrative message about one of the formation's paratroopers who was facing a paternity suit. They received warning of an impending attack in Italy by decrypting a signal about an issue of rum to the assault units. Italian codebreaking of British traffic played an important role in empowering Axis intelligence.

Hans-Otto Behrendt, one of Rommel's officers, wrote gleefully that in 1941–42 his chief 'often had a clearer picture of what the British C-in-C planned than some of the British subordinate formation commanders'. The German general called 621 Radio Interception Company his 'circus'. Until El Alamein, he boasted that no major British formation entered a battle without having been previously identified by his sigint team. The overrunning of 621 Company by New Zealand troops on 10 July 1942, with the loss of almost all its personnel by death or capture, was deemed a major disaster for the Afrika Korps. When Bletchley decrypted traffic that revealed the German break into the US military attaché traffic, it achieved an important success by persuading Washington to change ciphers. Thus, on 29 June 1942 Rommel lost access to the traffic, which he himself had described affectionately as his 'little Fellers' – the name of the US attaché in Egypt. A German staff officer described this development as 'a catastrophe'. The trauma felt by the codebreakers of Chi and army radio intelligence in Berlin was as great as that imposed on Bletchley by Dönitz's introduction of the fourth rotor to U-boat Enigma. GC&CS had warned the Americans about the lethal threat posed by the Cairo traffic early in May, but bureaucratic bungling caused more Fellers signals to be sent, including highly sensitive material about defence of the Nile Delta, for almost another two months before the breach was finally closed. Colonel McCormack wrote to Washington from Bletchley, where he was visiting: 'The mishaps … have produced in a high quarter here (and you must admit with some justification) a somewhat unfortunate impression of our own security procedures.'

Until the summer of 1942, the Germans and the Allies were in about the same place in the struggle for intelligence in the Mediterranean: Rommel and his British counterparts knew approximately the same amount about each other. Moreover, in northern France the disaster that befell the August Dieppe raid was partly attributable to the fact that the defenders were on high alert, thanks to plentiful German sigint and humint about British preparations. Thereafter, however, the Wehrmacht lagged increasingly far behind. It became the turn of the Germans to suffer from the deficiency that had dogged British operations for the past three years: lack of hard power to exploit information. By 1943, one of Rommel's intelligence officers noted that while they were still acquiring some good material from the Y Service and PoW interrogation, they could do little useful with it: 'tactical intelligence was not of much use. We were just too weak.' The Germans never secured another Allied military source as good as Bonner Fellers. Operation 'Torch', the November 1942 North African invasion, came as a complete surprise to Berlin because Allied wireless discipline was strict, special new naval cipher tables had been introduced, and the Abwehr supposed the 'Torch' convoys, though reported by its watchers in Spain, to be destined for Malta, or else for landings further east. In 1943 they were sometimes alerted to impending Mediterranean landings by references in British or American field-ciphered signals or voice traffic to colours – beaches designated 'Green', 'Blue', 'White' and suchlike. In the first hours of Operation 'Husky' in July, however, they were slow to respond partly because a fortnight earlier radio intelligence had rung false alarm bells about just such an Allied invasion of Sicily. Investigation showed that German eavesdroppers had picked up transmissions from a landing exercise in North Africa, which happened to take place on the same compass bearing as Sicily from one of their direction-finders, but a hundred miles further south.

As for the Eastern Front's HLS/Ost, in February 1943 the intelligence officer of XXXth Panzer Corps paid lavish tribute to the 'outstanding' sigint service being maintained on his formation's front. But about that time the Russians captured a German interception company at Stalingrad, and belatedly awoke to the sophistication of its activities: thereafter, Soviet officers often broke off a voice conversation if their other parties violated security. After Stalingrad, said Albert Praun, the Red Army maintained the best radio discipline of any of Hitler's adversaries, 'and posed a greater problem to German direction-finders than did their Western Allies', who became ever more careless. In the year beginning 1 May 1943, Army Group North, for instance, intercepted 46,342 Russian signals, but read only 13,312 – all at low level and many out of real time. Gen. Kurt von Tippelskirch said after the war: 'As time went on [the eavesdroppers] had more and more difficulty coping with Russian deception measures, consisting of constant simulated troop movements'. The Wehrmacht's spirits were not improved by breaking an enemy signal in which a Red Army intelligence officer urged units that killed German prisoners to spare at least one for questioning. This appears to have prompted another Soviet message: '20 Fritzes captured, one sent back for interrogation, remainder shot'. Praun wrote disdainfully after the war that this gave 'a truly shocking picture of the Asiatic combat methods used by the Russians' – he had evidently forgotten that his own army killed or allowed to starve to death two million Soviet prisoners in 1941–42, and plenty more thereafter.

In the early summer of 1944, before the Red Army launched 'Bagration', greatest offensive of the war, Pavel Sudoplatov was summoned to the

Kremlin with his boss Merkulov, Abakumov of SMERSh and the GRU's chief to discuss a new twist to the long-running deception operation 'Monastery'. Reinhard Gehlen and the Abwehr were still enthusing about the steady flow of information they received from Agent 'Max'. The Germans' Eastern Front intelligence chief was rash enough to tell his own high command that it might expect 'a calm summer'. The Stavka in Moscow thus decided that the time was ripe to use Alexander Demyanov and his network to build a new edifice of disinformation to support 'Bagration'.

The intelligence chiefs entered Stalin's suite in cocky mood, inspired by the tide of success attending Russian arms – Sudoplatov had recently received the Order of Suvorov for his own role. Stalin, however, with characteristic perversity, received the visitors coldly. Traditional deception ideas were played out, he said; he wanted to try something new, of immediate assistance to the Red Army. Sudoplatov, at a loss, kept cautiously silent. Abakumov simply urged placing 'Monastery' under his own control. Stalin then called in the deputy chief of the general staff, Gen. Sergey Shtemenko, who read an order already drafted. The 'Monastery' team was to pass intelligence to OKH to persuade the Germans that one of their brigades in Belorussia was cut off, but still fighting. The objective was to goad the Germans into launching an operation to break through to relieve it.

Sudoplatov was excited by the boldness and originality of the plan. In July 1944 his deputy Leonid Eitingon, along with 'Fisher' the radio specialist and an NKVD team, were dispatched to Belorussia to implement it. Alexander Demyanov – 'Max' – informed the Germans that he had been transferred to a new assignment, in the communications department of the Red Army on the Belorussian front. On 19 August Gehlen informed his commanders, on the authority of 'Max', that a Wehrmacht brigade of 2,500 men commanded by Lt. Col. Heinrich Scherhorn, with some guns and a few tanks, was struggling desperately in an encirclement near the Berezina river. The size of the bait was finely crafted by the Russians: small enough to be credible, large enough to be worth an effort to save. In reality, of course, Scherhorn and 1,500 survivors of his shattered command had been disarmed and were in the hands of the Red Army; their wireless-operators were now transmitting with Eitingon and his comrades holding pistols to their heads, figuratively and perhaps literally.

Amazingly, this deception was successfully sustained from 19 August 1944 to 5 May 1945. Although the Wehrmacht's circumstances were too desperate to launch a ground-force operation to relieve Scherhorn, during those months a procession of transport planes parachuted to the colonel supplies, ammunition, radio equipment, cash and Polish guides tasked to lead the brigade across country towards the German lines. All this material was recovered, including thirteen wirelesses and ten million roubles, together with twenty-five Abwehr personnel. Some of the German aircraft carrying out the drops were allowed to fly safely home, to sustain the deception. To the special delight of the NKVD, on 28 March 1945 Scherhorn received a personal signal from Gen. Heinz Guderian, announcing his promotion to full colonel and the award of the Knight's Cross. Although the Scherhorn deception was superbly ingenious, from the Kremlin's viewpoint the results were modest, not remotely matching the contribution of 'Monastery' to the Stalingrad envelopment.

Amid the Wehrmacht's dire shortage of sources, its intelligence officers devoted increasing effort to determining where the Red Army was massing artillery, but this became problematic as ever more guns proved to be dummies. Gen. von Tippelskirsch said, 'PoW interrogation was the most profitable source [of information], with the Y service second.' The Germans had despaired of cracking high-level Allied codes, and now focused exclusively on humbler traffic. Moreover, it was always necessary for knowledge to be matched by capability. In the latter war years on the Eastern Front, Albert Praun noted gloomily that it became fruitless to locate Soviet concentrations, because the Wehrmacht and Luftwaffe could act on such intelligence only 'inasmuch as the Germans had the means for appropriate counter-measures in this theatre'. Which was not often.

In 1944–45, after the Germans lost the capability to carry out significant air reconnaissance, the *Nachrichtenarmaufklärung* voice-interception service became ever more important. Its stations abandoned interception of low-priority traffic in such places as Ireland and Spain, to concentrate on the Allied armies. They tracked many US formations through the movements of their APOs – Army Post Office numbers. The German interception station at Bergen in Norway had 150 receivers, and monitored a wealth of traffic as far afield as the continental United States. Albert Praun praised British radio discipline, but expressed bafflement that its units customarily transmitted callsigns and signatures in plain language. Voice chatter during Allied exercises proved a fertile source of intelligence.

Erich Hüttenhain of Chi regarded cipher-making and cipher-breaking as processes that should fertilise each other, and was exasperated that the

Wehrmacht ignored his warnings about the vulnerability of some of its codes, and of its teleprinter links – though not, until a late stage, of the Enigma machine. Even after a special Chi cipher security department headed by Karl Stein was created in 1942, OKW's hubris persisted. Wilhelm Fenner said sourly after the war: 'The high command's view was that "Germany had won all her battles so far by using the system [it had got], and there was no need to overload the troops with new methods."' In August 1944, when Stein's team belatedly urged abandonment of Enigma, the army's resistance persisted. Fenner again: 'There was a storm of protest whenever the army was asked to change a system.' Compare and contrast the attitude of the US Army, which lost a cipher machine in France, and accepted the immense logistical burden of rewiring every other Sigaba in the theatre, just in case the Germans had captured the lost example – which it was eventually found that they had not. In November, Hüttenhain lectured to a military signals symposium, highlighting the vulnerabilities of Wehrmacht communications, but nothing was done to assuage his fears. Chi's cryptanalysts had no hard evidence of British success in breaking Enigma, and in its absence were forced to make their case simply by demonstrating its theoretical vulnerability. This was not enough for Germany's generals. Meanwhile, manufacturers dallied for years with the development of a new and more advanced Enigma rotor, the *Luckenfüllerwalze*, but this became fit for introduction to service only on 1 May 1945.

The Germans never concentrated their codebreaking talents and resources in the fashion that was essential if they were to accomplish big things. An American analyst observed after interrogating the chief German codebreakers in 1945: 'Neither the Abwehr nor the head of OKW/ Chi seems to have had an adequate idea of the difficulties faced by the cryptanalysts … Directions always came too late.' The British genius lay in creating a partnership between the free spirits of the civilian academic codebreakers and a highly disciplined system of analysis and dissemination. Germany, among the most organised societies on earth, failed first in making best use of its cleverest minds, and second in devising innovative technology to provide the support indispensable to breaking machine ciphers in real time. Wehrmacht intelligence officers asserted that their most useful sources in the second half of the war, when aerial reconnaissance ceased to be feasible in the face of Allied air superiority, were – in descending order – captured documents; human observation on the battlefield; sigint traffic analysis; and material derived from open sources – reading Allied newspapers and listening to the BBC.

At Bletchley, Britain's codebreakers had to perform tasks which called for supreme concentration in conditions of relative discomfort, especially winter cold. The plight of Chi's people and the German army's cryptographic headquarters was much worse, however. In November 1943 British bombing destroyed or severely damaged most of the Tirpitzüfer houses in which they worked, and the B-Dienst lost a large part of its filing system. It was hard to focus on complex mathematical problems while shivering in dust-shrouded offices that lacked windows and doors. Moreover, almost nightly attacks deprived staff of much chance of sleep. Fenner reckoned that the codebreakers' output – the number of signals they broke – diminished by two-thirds in the winter of 1943–44, and never recovered thereafter, amid repeated evacuations and transfers to temporary quarters. He himself was married to a Prussian army officer's daughter, Elise, and the couple's spirit was crushed by the death of their only son on the Russian Front. From 1944 to the end of the war, Chi became almost entirely preoccupied with German cipher security – a role in which, of course, it also failed. The struggle to crack higher Allied wireless traffic was almost abandoned. It was left to the tactical eavesdroppers of army radio intelligence in the field to do what they could with lower codes and traffic analysis.

Each month between January and June 1944, Chi logged 3,000 decrypted messages – 'VNs', as they were tagged, 'Verlässliche Nachrichten', reliable reports – the German equivalent of the British 'most secret sources'. The vast majority, however, addressed Allied housekeeping issues, or the affairs of such neutrals as the Turks. Fenner and his comrades read a hundred diplomatic signals a day dispatched by twenty-nine secondary powers, which generated hectares of paper and helped to convey to themselves, and in some degree also to their superiors, an illusion of useful activity. They wasted much effort cracking messages out of 'real time': an extreme example was a report from Japan's Moscow ambassador about the economic and military condition of the Soviet Union, dispatched to Tokyo on 10 December 1943. This was finally broken on 11 October 1944; a copy fell into American hands after the war, annotated by a Chi clerk 'solved after delay'.

Germany's finest cryptanalysts also cracked a 23 August 1944 Argentine message from Rio de Janeiro to London which read: 'The Economic Office for Sugar and Alcohol approves the extension of the intermediate agreement for 2 years and deems it suitable to ask for an increase of the quota.' If this seems banal, in 1945 the Allies captured thousands of painstakingly filed 'VNs' that made even less exciting reading. Until 1943 the Germans could claim some useful, though never decisive, codebreaking successes. For the rest of the war, however, Chi illuminated little more than sugar quotas. Bletchley, Arlington Hall and Op-20-G mined plenty of dross, but in its midst were seams of gold. Berlin could boast no such assaying triumph.

2 'CICERO'

It is a scene from some 1920s Hollywood espionage drama: in a sumptuous diplomatic drawing-room, a mustachioed aristocrat with a name that defies parody plays Beethoven on a grand piano, while upstairs a villainous little Balkan servant photographs his secret papers for sale to the enemy. The British take just pride in their intelligence triumphs in World War II, but the staff problems of Sir Hughe Knatchbull-Hugessen, ambassador to Turkey, represent a sorrier aspect of the record. It was one of the German secret service's last successes, if it can be dignified as such, for it did scant service to Hitler's cause.

Knatchbull-Hugessen had served in Ankara since 1938, living with his wife Mary at the British residence beside the embassy in the hills of Cancaya, above the capital. It is well known to history that in 1943–44 he employed a valet who sold his secrets to the Germans. It is less familiar, and almost defies credibility, that as early as 1941 the Abwehr was receiving material from his safe, lifted by other hands. In October and November of that year Dr Viktor Friede, Canaris's local station chief, boasted that he had accessed Hugessen's papers. Moreover, in a second January 1943 incident, the ambassador's then valet Andrea Marovic telephoned the German embassy to report his master's departure for Adana to meet Winston Churchill. When the Foreign Office in London got wind of this and instructed Hugessen to dismiss Marovic, he prevaricated. He said that he could scarcely be expected to fulfil his duties without a valet, and would do nothing until a substitute was recruited. The Foreign Office scolded Hugessen, saying the matter was 'a serious one which admits of no delay'. Marovic was belatedly dismissed on 15 May, and temporarily replaced by a footman. Two months later, Hugessen hired Elyesa Bazna to fill the role, despite being warned against the man by the Turkish authorities.

Bazna was a self-confessed rogue, greedy and always in trouble. The son of a Muslim religious teacher, born in southern Yugoslavia when it was still part of the Ottoman Empire, he drifted through a series of chauffeuring jobs from which he was sacked for incompetence, and once served a sentence in a French penal camp where he acquired some lockpicking skill. On his release, in his own words, 'I became what everybody becomes who has never learned a job and has nothing behind him but his wits – a *kavass*.' As a domestic servant and chauffeur he worked successively for American, Yugoslav, German and finally British employers. Fancying his own voice, in off-duty hours he trained to become a professional singer. By 1943, however, this cocky little man found himself depressed by his own condition: he was thirty-eight, and a self-avowed failure. While working at the German embassy he idly photographed a few letters, which prompted an inspiration: 'I was a person of no consequence … Why not set up as a spy?'

He secured a domestic post with the first secretary at the British embassy in Ankara, and began reading his employer's private papers between leisurely baths in the residence bathroom. He also embarked on an affair with the secretary's teenage nanny Mara: 'her arms were entwined around my neck more often than my fourteen ties'. Their relationship continued when Bazna became the ambassador's valet, and she was a wide-eyed witness to his transition from casual villain to committed spy. After his luncheon, the ambassador invariably played the piano in the drawing-room, leaving his keys within reach of Bazna, who made a wax impression of those which opened the dispatch box and safe. Hugessen always took the most important papers into his bedroom, offering the valet and his camera further opportunities. 'I am doing all this for my country,' Bazna told Mara solemnly as he set forth for the marketplace – or rather, for the German embassy. He said that he was working to keep Turkey out of the war, while the British and Americans were conspiring to drag her into it.

The wife of German counsellor Albert Jenke – who chanced to be Ribbentrop's brother-in-law – gave Bazna a frosty reception when he arrived with his first wares late on the night of 26 October 1943: he had once been her own least favourite servant. Bazna announced that he had fifty-six photographed documents to sell for £20,000. Jenke viewed the caller as he might have examined a beetle in the bath, but duty compelled him to pass Bazna on to a case officer, an Austrian SD man named Ludwig Moyzich who served Schellenberg's Department VI of the RSHA, under cover as commercial attaché.

Moyzich thought the valet 'looked like a clown without his make-up'. He was initially disbelieving about both the material and the means by which it had been acquired, which reeked of cheap melodrama – or, more plausibly, of an enemy deception. Bazna claimed that he was motivated by his own father's killing by the British, but it was obvious that he was a mere mercenary. Berlin duly paid up, and Bazna set about photographing his employer's papers day after day, then week after week. One stolen memorandum summarised quantities of war material being delivered to Russia by the Western Allies; there was much correspondence about Britain's efforts to drag Turkey into the war; most appetising of all, in German eyes, was a summary of exchanges between Churchill, Roosevelt and Stalin at their November 1943 summit meeting in Tehran. Properly analysed in Berlin, the latter material could have told the Germans a good deal about the Allies' most closely guarded secret, Operation 'Overlord', the planned invasion of France. But this document, like others from the same source, never received the sort of imaginative scrutiny it deserved. Within a few months Bazna – whom the Germans codenamed 'Cicero' – had secreted a fortune, £300,000 in sterling. It was enough. He was rich, and he was losing his nerve.

In January 1944, Roosevelt informed Churchill of an OSS report that a German agent had secured details of diplomatic negotiations between Britain and Turkey. The British assumed a leak from Turkish sources, but this was of course the work of Bazna. Fritz Kolbe of the German Foreign Ministry had tipped off Allen Dulles in Switzerland, who in turn informed Washington. A month later, with British intelligence increasingly convinced that the leak came from the ambassador's staff, Bill Cavendish-Bentinck prepared deception documents – supposed war cabinet papers relating to peace feelers from Bulgaria to the Allies – which were placed in Knatchbull-Hugessen's briefcase.

Nobody touched the bait. Bazna had downed tools as both a spy and a valet. Abandoning both his British and his German employers, in April 1944 he set off on a riotous spending spree, and indulged this for some weeks before both he and the hotels he patronised discovered that the Germans had paid him in forged British banknotes. He should have guessed as much when they so readily surrendered such huge sums. Despite a spasm of dubious fame when his story became public after the war, he died broke in 1970, his vainglorious dreams shattered. Given the game Bazna played, however, he might consider himself fortunate to have preserved his life and freedom.

When the Foreign Office learned of the 'Cicero' affair, Knatchbull-Hugessen merely mumbled that he had found Bazna 'a good servant'.

Incredibly, although recalled from Ankara, he was given another posting in Brussels. When captured German files revealed the full facts in 1945, the permanent under-secretary Sir Alexander Cadogan wrote in his diary: '"Snatch", of course, ought to be court-martialled, but I must think over this.' Cadogan's eventual decision was predictable: the foremost imperative must be to protect the Foreign Office's reputation, which meant shielding this booby to whom an ambassadorship had been entrusted. Though Knatchbull-Hugessen received a 'severe' formal reprimand in August 1945, he was allowed to retire on full pension two years later, and published a complacent memoir of his diplomatic career before the Ankara débâcle became public knowledge.

Stewart Menzies fulminated over the 'Cicero' case, calling it 'an appalling national disaster'. It was certainly true that it reflected deplorably upon the Foreign Office. Though it became the most notorious example of diplomatic insecurity, it was by no means the only one. When the story was revealed to the world by Bazna himself in the 1950s, many people expressed amazement that, with such figures as Knatchbull-Hugessen in positions of influence, the Allies had won the war. It defied imagination that a British ambassador in a sensitive neutral capital should have exposed his personal papers to the attentions of a newly employed Yugoslav valet – to three successive ones, had the full facts been known. The cover-up after the event, protecting from disgrace an Old Etonian schoolfriend of Anthony Eden, reflected the worst traditions of the British Establishment.

How much, however, did the coup profit the Nazi war effort? Hugh Trevor-Roper, in his May 1945 assessment of German intelligence, mused about Berlin's failure to exploit the Hugessen papers. Broadway knew that Walter Schellenberg's exaggerated respect for MI6 caused him to assume that 'Cicero' was a British plant. Trevor-Roper wrote: 'Thus the most successful scoop of [the RSHA's] Amt VI, being the capture of genuine documents from which the nature and incidence of "Overlord" might have been inferred, was never acted upon.' For months after 'Cicero's' material started to reach Berlin, it was dismissed as an Allied deception. When it was belatedly acknowledged as authentic in the spring of 1944, OKW did make the significant deduction that the Allies would launch no major operation in the Mediterranean while they addressed the liberation of France, which was obviously imminent. But Hitler dissented. The only decision-maker who mattered continued to believe that some Balkan initiative by the Allies was still plausible. As for the spy himself, when Bazna quit there is no evidence that anybody in Berlin cared. By that stage of the war, the glimpses he provided of Allied motions seemed of little practical value to the Nazi cause, even had they been credited.

An overriding handicap to exploitation of the 'Cicero' documents, like all other German intelligence product, was that by the winter of 1943–44 the initiative in the war had passed irretrievably to the Allies. Intelligence must inform action, and there was now no course available to Germany to counter Anglo-American initiatives, even granted secret knowledge of them. In August 1944 Turkey broke off diplomatic relations with Germany, though wisely declining to become a full belligerent. With or without the insights on British diplomacy provided by 'Cicero', nothing could change the overarching reality, plain to the Ankara government, that the Germans were losers.

3 THE FANTASISTS

Admiral Wilhelm Canaris insisted to the end of his life that the Abwehr produced sound information, which Germany's high command failed to use. This was nonsense. The Wehrmacht acquired some good operational intelligence through codebreaking, direct observation, eavesdropping, staff analysis and air reconnaissance while the Luftwaffe was able to fly, but the Abwehr could scarcely blame on Hitler's interference the fact that its foreign informants were contemptible, most much less impressive than 'Cicero'. Countess Freda Douglas, for instance, was the wife of a well-known German agent, Albrecht Archibald Douglas. She left Romania in 1940 following an arrest on espionage charges, then after falling out with her husband travelled to America, where she was arrested by the FBI after Allied decrypts from Chile mentioned a 'Countess D'. She told her interrogators that she had agreed to provide information after being threatened by the Nazis' Santiago embassy.

In 1942 Prince Charles de Ligne was arrested by the Abwehr and sentenced to death after confessing to aiding the Belgian Resistance. He was reprieved, however, after 'giving his word of honour as an officer and a prince' that he would switch sides and work loyally for Germany. He was thereafter sent to Spain, but promptly abandoned his employers and made his way to Britain. Major Brede, his handler, later told Allied interrogators that he had always doubted the sincerity of de Ligne's change of allegiance, but 'ran the risk because the Abwehr was at that time very short of useful contacts'.

Werner Waltemath, born in Germany in 1909, emigrated to Brazil in 1930. A decade later he returned to visit his sick mother, was conscripted into the Wehrmacht and trained as a wireless-operator. In July 1941 the Abwehr sent him back to Brazil, where he built his own radio transmitter. As soon as he tapped out his MNT callsign, however, this was pinpointed by US direction-finders. Similarly, Brazilian police alerted by the Americans intercepted secret letters he dispatched to Madrid, containing microdots and reports written in phenol invisible ink. On 1 June 1943 Waltemath's house was raided by police, who found his radio, microfilm and other paraphernalia concealed in a cavity under the living-room floor. He received a twenty-five-year jail sentence, while a fellow-expatriate whom he had recruited to his network, Hans-Christian von Kitze, became a double agent for the British.

Three barely literate Moroccans, stranded in France, were trained at the Abwehr spy school in Angers, then dispatched to report back from their own country. The only communication the Germans received thereafter was a letter, written in Aspro invisible ink, thanking them for their kindly treatment, and for the invaluable assistance in getting home. A French Abwehr spy named du Chaffault, twenty-six years old and from Tours, recruited in 1942, proposed himself for a posting to Montevideo, which he may have considered a safe distance from the war. He was trained for a mission to the United States, and lacking wireless skills was provided with invisible inks. In July 1943, OKW sanctioned his move to America. To travel first into Spain, he was provided with a German passport in the name of Wenzel, several hundred dollars and some pesetas, with the promise of more if he produced results. He reached Bilbao, where he acquired a local girlfriend. When he left the city, he told her that he would be sending her letters from America for onward transmission to the Abwehr. Thereafter, the Germans and the Spanish girl alike lost track of him. Most likely, and in common with the rest of the above, he vanished into the mass of human flotsam clinging to a fugitive existence in every community in Europe.

A Canadian-born source, thirty-four-year-old Grace Buchanan-Dineen, was trained in secret writing before leaving Europe for the US late in 1941, provided with $2,500 together with Budapest and Stockholm mail drops. She was briefed that if she ran into trouble, she should cable the Abwehr's Lisbon station 'Ill. Require Operation' – but this proved no help when the FBI arrested her in December 1942, following a British tip-off derived from a decrypt. She appears to have joined the Nazi payroll for the money – she was promised $500 a month. After a spell as a somewhat unconvincing FBI double, Buchanan-Dineen served almost four years of a twelve-year jail sentence before being paroled in 1948. The Germans learned nothing of value from her.

Twenty-four-year-old Robert Rousseau, 'Rodolphe', from Nantes, deserted from the French to the Germans in North Africa. In August 1943 he was sent for wireless training, then posted to Saint-Brieuc, with cover as head of a local recruiting office for the Todt Organisation. Late in October Rousseau told his handler he had joined the Resistance in order to acquire information. A few weeks later, however, some captured Gaullists under interrogation told the local SD that Rousseau had offered to sell them his wireless and codes. He was promptly arrested and dispatched to Germany – presumably to a concentration camp. Several Frenchmen at Vichy's Washington embassy sought to serve the Abwehr, notably Lt. Col. Bertrand-Vigne, the assistant military attaché, and Charles Emmanuel Brousse, the press attaché. Another diplomat, Jean Musa, acted as a courier and as a conduit to sympathetic New Yorkers. Xavier Guichard of Vichy's *milice* contacted a number of Frenchmen living in the US and invited them to provide intelligence, on pain of unpleasant consequences for their families still in France should they refuse. Guichard was eventually exposed and obliged to leave America.

There were large expanses of the globe where spying, or even a pretence of it, seemed an unproductive activity because they were strategically irrelevant. When a question was raised in London about running some double agents out of Canada, the responsible MI5 officer – Cyril Mills, of the well-known British circus-owning family – demurred. Even the Abwehr, he said, could see that nothing of much importance happened in Canada. Canaris disagreed. On 9 November 1942 a U-boat landed his man Werner Janowsky on the Gaspe peninsula. Following his subsequent arrest he was found to be carrying a Quebec driving licence taken from a Canadian PoW captured at Dieppe, but with an Ontario personal identification and address. Most of the $5,000 in Canadian currency with which Janowsky was supplied was time-expired – a mistake which prompted his capture after he used it to pay a New Carlisle hotel bill. He had already roused the proprietor's suspicions by smoking German cigarettes and taking a bath at mid-morning. Among the possessions appropriated by the Canadian police were a Wehrmacht travel *pro forma* and diary, a .25 automatic pistol, radio, knuckle-duster, five US$20 gold pieces, a microfilm copy of coding instructions and a copy of *Mary Poppins* as a code crib. Janowsky was a thirty-eight-year-old former

French Foreign Legionnaire who had a wife living in Canada, and knew the country. But no Allied secret service, even on a bad day, would have dispatched an agent into the field – at the cost of a substantial investment of Nazi resources, including the U-boat – so absurdly ill-equipped. Janowsky was fortunate to survive the war in British captivity.

Some Abwehr recruits were amazingly credulous about accepting post-dated cheques, for encashment following a Nazi victory. One, named Franz Stigler, was promised an estate in South Africa. Jorge Mosquera, a Chilean who had built up a substantial fortune in Germany, was told that if he did some spying for Berlin in the US, his Reichsmark holdings would be released. It is equally puzzling how the Germans supposed that an untrained civilian informant such as Mosquera, living on the US East Coast, could secure answers to questions posted by Berlin such as: 'Since when has Curtiss delivered types P40 and P46 instead of P36A? Have there already been deliveries of B-17s?'

The personalities mentioned above, far from being unusual, were typical of those through whom the Abwehr professed to gather foreign intelligence for OKW. The consequence was that its overseas stations felt obliged to invent material to compensate for lack of the real thing. A striking example of the circularity of espionage was provided by Dr Karl-Heinz Kramer, a flamboyant Abwehr officer based in Stockholm and tasked with running penetration agents into Britain and the US. MI5 became alarmed when both Ultra and OSS in Switzerland revealed Kramer transmitting material from British sources. In April 1943, MI6 assigned Peter Falk of its Stockholm station to monitor the Abwehr officer and identify his informants – the German repeatedly cited a British agent codenamed 'Josephine'. Who could this be? Once on the trail, Falk discovered that Kramer shared Richard Sorge's manic appetite for fast living – it was hard to keep pace with either his sports car or his partying. Moreover, the German was constantly importuned for cash by the Japanese military attaché, Col. Onodera, whose remittances from Tokyo failed to arrive: Kramer loaned his ally $20,000 of Hitler's money.

In December, MI6 got a break. An anti-Nazi Austrian woman in Stockholm offered her services to the British legation, along with those of a friend who was working as Kramer's maid. Throughout 1944 she provided material lifted from Kramer's wastepaper basket and desk – the latter opened with a key copied by impressing it in a butter dish. British alarm grew when inspection of the Abwehr man's old passport showed that he had visited England before the war. Here was a hint that he might have established a real network, and MI6 received it during the tense weeks before D-Day. Could Kramer secure intelligence from Britain that discredited the 'Fortitude' deception plan, blew open the Double Cross operation?

Peter Falk gathered increasing evidence that Kramer was living way beyond his means, presumably by pocketing Berlin's expenses money. Might not MI6 – the intelligence officer now suggested – blackmail and 'turn' the German, putting him on their own payroll? But D-Day was by then history: the moment of maximum danger for the Allied cause was past. Thus, Broadway sternly rejected such a sordid proposal: 'We cannot do business with war criminals to save their necks. There is surely nothing very important that this peculiarly unpleasant rat could give us if he was allowed to leave the sinking ship.' Only after the war's end did Allied interrogations reveal the truth: Kramer had made fools of the British as well as the Abwehr. His 'agent network' was the figment of a fertile imagination; his reports to Berlin were founded in fantasy. MI6's counterattack, the maid's little melodrama with the desk key in the butter dish, had been pointless. All the players save Kramer himself, who enjoyed an unusually safe and comfortable wartime existence, accomplished no more than caged hamsters scrambling up their wheels.

The Abwehr cherished as gold dust all reports from its agents that seemed authoritative – which meant those provided by the British Twenty Committee, controlling 120 double agents, of whom thirty-nine were used more or less seriously to transmit false information, much of it drafted, or at least monitored, by Bentinck of the JIC. Oversight of the system by Col. Johnny Bevan, the peacetime stockbroker who ran the London Controlling Section in charge of Allied deceptions, required nice calculation to achieve a tempting blend of fact and fiction. When the Germans in February 1943 asked 'Garbo' to send them some current British railway timetables, Guy Liddell of MI5 was consulted. Hand them over, he said – they could do little harm when there were so many trains, most of which ran late. Contrarily Peter Loxley, Sir Alexander Cadogan's private secretary, once rang Liddell to report that the Germans had condemned to death five Polish agents. Was there a chance that an exchange could be offered, for Nazi agents in British hands? Absolutely not, responded the MI5 officer: every surviving Abwehr man knew far too much about Double Cross.

In 1943–44 Germany's intelligence service atrophied to the point of near-impotence. MI6 reports in May and June 1943 adopted a tone of condescension towards the enemy: 'we have evidence from our signals of the disappointment felt in Berlin about the failure to predict the North African campaign or the Casablanca conference ... From the beginning of 1943 the Abwehr has been briskly, if amateurishly, wielding the weapon of deception. The Deception office has sponsored the issue of a considerable number of strategic lies or half-truths for ultimate consumption by us ... The Abwehr relies on a very small number of pipes to carry the lie-stream to us and our Russian, American and, recently, French allies. But though the technique is elementary, the intention is obvious – to strengthen their guard on the Balkan flank by tricking us into over-estimating its strength.' The British took for granted their mastery of Abwehr postings and over-seas intelligence operations: 'Since the fall of Tunis,' reported the Radio Analysis Bureau, 'several members of Abwehr Group Africa have been transferred after only a very short spell of leave to the Balkans. Obst. Lt. Seubert, at one time [chief] of the Abwehr group, has been visiting Sofia. Obst. Lt. Strojil, who has conducted operations in Greece, the Crimea and Tunisia, has been made Leiter II at Salonika, etc.'

Nazi self-deception had become institutionalised. In the summer of 1943, Himmler and Göbbels agreed that Hitler should no longer be shown the SD's monthly reports on the German public's mood, morale and responses to press and radio broadcasts. Thereafter, these went no further than their own desks. Meanwhile many neutral states, seeing Allied victory looming, adopted harsher policies towards Nazi residents and visitors. Under pressure from the British, in 1943 the government in Madrid insisted on closure of the *Unternehmen Bodden* – the Abwehr's important ship-watching service – and in the following year Canaris himself was denied admission to Spain. The best sources by now available to the German military attaché in Chile, Major von Bohlen, were American avia-tion magazines, whose contents were prized in Berlin because hard to procure elsewhere. There was no longer any rational intelligence-handling process inside Germany, only – as Hugh Trevor-Roper put it – 'a vortex of personal ambitions'.

From the summer of 1943 onwards, Trevor-Roper attended the monthly meetings of the London Controlling Section in the war cabinet offices. He told its chiefs that the atmosphere within German intelligence had become so paranoid that its officers no longer dared to filter and analyse material; instead, they merely passed on to the high command a mass of undigested and unassessed reports, most of them fanciful or composed by British hands. At the end of April 1943, so straitened were the circumstances of the Abwehr's Sarajevo station that it begged Vienna for a delivery of 250 kilos of birdseed to feed its 150 carrier pigeons, while both Zagreb and Sarajevo were demanding more manpower to manage the birds' lofts. There were also repeated bizarre requests from local Abwehr officers in Yugoslavia for supplies of shoe leather, which caused Trevor-Roper to suggest caustically that when the Allies entered the country they should be wary of well-shod men.

On 5 June 1943, Berlin asked its Tangier and Madrid stations to secure Allied order-of-battle information from North Africa. This request received a whimpering response: 'The assignment cannot be carried out, as there are no agents in Africa.' On 4 August Trevor-Roper reported on the chaos of Abwehr operations. In the three weeks preceding 'Husky', the Allied invasion of Sicily, he noted that reports were forwarded to Berlin making forecasts of Allied attacks as enumerated: Norway 3, Channel coast 4, Azores 1, Spanish Morocco 1, Southern France 6, Italy 8, Corsica 7, Sardinia 4, Sicily 6, Dalmatia 9, Greece 7, Crete 8, Dodecanese 8, Cyclades 1, Romania 2: 'Evaluation at Abwehr HQ doubtless reduced this variety, but it can hardly have supplied any valuable positive conclusions.' Trevor-Roper observed that the only exception to the pervasive vagueness of Abwehr analysis concerned the material submitted by the British through the 'Mincemeat' deception – the stranding on the Spanish coast of the corpse of a 'Royal Marine officer' carrying top secret papers about British plans – which was considered entirely reliable.

Canaris himself was in a state of chronic bewilderment. When his agent 'Melilla', hitherto little regarded, sent a 9 August message reporting Allied convoys en route for Sicily (after the landings there had started), the admiral signalled back personally, enquiring plaintively what the man thought would happen next. 'Melilla', a British-controlled double, told Berlin that he believed 100,000 men would land in south-west France. He followed up by reporting Allied forces heading for Corsica and Sardinia.

Trevor-Roper expressed bafflement that the Abwehr forwarded a mass of raw material to OKW 'without distinguishing between the valuable local tactical information and the mass of general and particular strategic tripe'. His conclusion was that the Abwehr was 'confessedly unable to evaluate its own reports … Berlin has no knowledge or solid opinion about the strategic future and therefore has to let the local generals and admirals make up their own minds by giving them prompt access to all the reports that come in. It dare not winnow, lest the generals should complain later that they had not been allowed to see the straws which in fact showed which way the wind was blowing.' Admiral von der Marwitz, the German naval attaché in Istanbul, agreed: he was a prominent critic of Abwehr reports, in language echoing that of Trevor-Roper, as the MI6 officer noted with glee when he read the naval officer's decrypted commentary.

Perversely, the weakness of German intelligence sometimes made it more difficult for the Allies to conduct deceptions ahead of their own big operations: it is hard to catch trout if baskets of crumbs are being emptied into the river around a fisherman's fly. 'The carefully orchestrated "signals" that the deception authorities were feeding into the enemy intelligence systems were usually swamped,' in the words of official historian Sir Michael Howard, 'by the "noise" generated by the mass of rumours, gossip, diplomatic indiscretions and garbled reports that the Abwehr collected and forwarded, largely unfiltered, to their head offices ... The overworked officers at FHW [German high command intelligence in the West] learned to pay little attention to anything emanating from that source unless it was backed by more solid evidence such as air reconnaissance or Sigint.' Allied deceptions became more successful from 1943 onwards, when air recon-naissance became impossible and some German officers, at least, felt obliged to take double agents' reports reasonably seriously, for lack of information from anybody else.

Nevertheless, the Germans never became wholly gullible about everything, all the time: large Allied deception operations were staged in August 1943 off the French coast, involving the movement of scores of ships and hundreds of aircraft, designed to deflect attention from the impending landings in Italy. Von Rundstedt, commanding in the West, unhesitatingly rejected any notion that these Channel operations were serious, saying there was no doubt that anything big the Allies intended in 1943 would take place in the Mediterranean. OKW accordingly reduced German strength in France from forty-five divisions to thirty-five, and only began to increase it again in October, when it was obvious that an Anglo-American landing in France was becoming a practicable prospect.

The fall of Canaris as Hitler's intelligence chief was precipitated by a Broadway coup: in January 1944, MI6 officer Nicholas Elliott stage-man-aged the defection of the Abwehr's deputy station chief in Istanbul, Dr Erich Vermehren, together with his wife Elizabeth and later two of his subordinates. Vermehren gave the British a vivid personal account of conditions in the German intelligence community. The German wailed that the SD's influence dominated, because its reports went straight to

Hitler via Himmler. 'The Abwehr is the Cinderella of the OKW,' he said, 'and has to accept officers who have no experience of foreign countries … The Abwehr in Turkey is ludicrously understaffed, and cannot hope to compete effectively with the British and American I.S., whose members outnumber the Abwehr by nearly 10–1. Officers at Abwehr HQ do not understand and are not interested in political or semi-political reports, preferring minutiae about divisional signs and numbers.' Vermehren described Col. Georg Hansen, from March 1943 chief of Canaris's intelligence branch, as 'a great man', the most efficient officer in the organisation, honest, cultivated, intelligent, energetic and determined to get results. Nonetheless, said Vermehren, 'there was no centralised grading office responsible for assessing the bona-fides or acumen of agents'. Just so, Trevor-Roper would have said.

On 16 February 1944, Allen Dulles commented somewhat priggishly to Washington on the sensational Vermehren defections in Turkey, saying that he himself had never encouraged such open switches of allegiance, because such people were more useful in place. He was assuredly mistaken in this case, because the Turkish affair completed the destruction of the Abwehr's reputation in the eyes of the Nazi leadership, and plunged its stations into a condition of chaos and demoralisation from which they never recovered. A Broadway memorandum dated 24 March 1944, and marked 'TOP SECRET', bore the pencilled annotation 'source is MI6's man in Stockholm'. Five pages thereafter detailed the troubles of the Abwehr's chieftain: 'In the middle of February Admiral Canaris was summoned to the Führer's HQ in Bavaria … He was warned that his stay there would probably last not less than 8 days so that it would be advisable for him to nominate somebody to replace him during his absence … [He chose] Col. Bentevigni, the chief of Section III. On arrival at the Führer's HQ he got a very sour reception and was informed by [Field-]Marshal KEITEL that the Führer had seen all the material incriminating him and had decided that under the circumstances it was impossible for the Admiral to remain in office. CANARIS was ordered to take three months leave … The future organisation of the Abwehr was then to be decided in agreement with the chief of the SD (KALTEN-BRUNNER) and the chief of the Foreign Intelligence Service (SCHELLENBERG).'

This was a broadly accurate version of events: Walter Schellenberg served for the rest of the war as Hitler's foreign intelligence chief, and the RSHA progressively absorbed the Abwehr. Following the July 1944 plot against Hitler, some of its most senior officers and ex-officers were imprisoned and sooner or later executed, including Canaris, Oster, Hansen, Freytag von Loringhoven – the former head of sabotage section, who killed himself – and Graf Marogna-Redwitz, the able head of the Vienna station. Wilhelm Kuebart was arrested and tried, but miraculously escaped the hangman.

4 THE 'GOOD' NAZI

Walter Schellenberg was a notably handsome man with sensitive features who presented himself to the outside world, with some success, as the acceptable face of the SS: mild-mannered, courteous, rendered vulnerable by chronic liver trouble. Unlike the thugs around him, the RSHA's foreign intelligence chief could talk sensitively about music and the arts. He was successful in convincing some of those with whom he trafficked, notably the Swede Count Bernadotte, that he was 'a decent and humane person'. Posterity should not doubt, however, that Schellenberg was a committed Nazi, fully complicit in the regime's crimes; he was merely intelligent enough to discern from an early stage that Hitler could lose the war, and thereafter to hedge his bets with serpentine intent, if not success.

He was a builder's son from Saarbrucken, born in 1910. After some legal training he joined the National Socialist Party in April 1933. Less than a year later, seized by the glamour of the black uniform, he became a member of the SS. Schellenberg showed himself an ingenious secret policeman, who won the special approval of his superiors after the 1939 occupation of Poland: rifling Warsaw's intelligence records, he identified 430 Germans who were acting as Polish informants, conveniently indexed for removal by the SD to the gallows or concentration camps. He became a protégé of Heydrich and Himmler, though his relationship with the former was damaged for some time by rumours that he was having an affair with Lena, Frau Heydrich. In October 1940, following a divorce of his own, Schellenberg married Irene Grosse-Schönepauck. He seems to have had few, if any, friendships outside his work. An ambitious and boundlessly devious loner, he was less clever than he supposed himself. An American analyst of German intelligence wrote after the war: 'He tends to confuse his magnificent schemes with actual accomplishments.'

There were plenty of schemes. In 1940 Schellenberg was dispatched to Lisbon with Hitler's personal mandate to snatch the Duke of Windsor, the former King Edward VIII. He declined to execute a crude kidnapping, preferring instead to attempt a seduction, and before this could take place he was obliged to watch from the German embassy balcony in August, as the duke and his wife sailed away towards the governorship of British Bermuda. Thereafter, he spent some time compiling a 'Wanted G.B.' roster of high-profile figures to be detained following a German occupation of Britain. Though Schellenberg often expressed a respect for Churchill's nation, his list revealed an epic ignorance and naïveté about who was who among its elite. He was sent back to Lisbon with orders to poison a German émigré, Otto Strasse, using a substance provided by a Munich bacteriologist. Strasse survived because he failed to turn up as scheduled in the Portuguese capital. Schellenberg was next appointed by Himmler to head Section VI, the RSHA's foreign intelligence branch, despite having a poor relationship with Ernst Kaltenbrunner, the Reich security chief. He exploited this role to indulge more foreign travel than most men, even spies, contrived in the midst of a world war. Schellenberg cultivated the Swedish minister in Berlin, Arvid Richert, securing his goodwill by arranging the release of some Nordic prisoners in whom Sweden had an interest – Danish policemen and Norwegian students.

In 1941 the RSHA officer flew to Stockholm for a meeting with Martin Lindquist, chief of the Swedish security police; the two men got on well, partly because they shared a deep hostility to communism. The friendship became important in the following year, when the Gestapo charged with espionage five top managers of the Polish arm of a big Swedish company. Two were acquitted, but one was sentenced to life imprisonment and four were condemned to death. Schellenberg intervened, first to secure better conditions for the captives, and eventually to secure their release, the last before Christmas 1944. He conducted personal negotiations about the case with Swedish business leaders Axel Brandin, Jacob Wallenberg and Alvar Moeller.

Schellenberg's ascent to high office was founded upon his skills as an intriguer at home and abroad, rather than upon any conspicuous skills as an intelligence officer. He was perceptive enough to understand the damage being done by rivalry between the Nazi empires, but himself became a prominent part of it. A few months before Reinhard Heydrich's killing in June 1942, Hitler's Czech proconsul invited Canaris and Schellenberg to a grand shooting party. The two men argued so heatedly about the responsibilities and boundaries of their respective services that they failed to notice the pheasants streaming unscathed over their heads.

The SS officer used Switzerland in the same fashion as did the Allies – partly as a battlefield on which to duel against enemy intelligence services, and partly as a rendezvous for making contacts that would be treasonable inside Germany. Himmler said dismissively about Section VI's Swiss dalliances: 'Well, I don't wish to know all the details – that's your responsibility.' From an early stage, it is likely that Schellenberg was looking ahead to Switzerland as a prospective refuge for himself if the Nazi cause foundered, and his chief may have shared his aspirations. Never the type to relish participation in a Berlin *Götterdämmerung*, Schellenberg opened lines of communication that might enable him to survive a day of reckoning for the Third Reich.

He was thus a natural intermediary when, in the autumn of 1942, Swiss intelligence chief Roger Masson became apprehensive that the Nazis were considering an invasion of his country. After a negotiation conducted by Otto Kocher, the German minister in Bern, the two men met on 8 September near Waldshut, just inside Hitler's territory. SS Sturmbannführer Hans Eggen escorted the colonel to the frontier, then watched him cross the Rhine bridge alone and on foot. Masson was desperately nervous, as well he might be, about both his personal safety and that of his country. He and Schellenberg met at a nearby hotel, then walked and talked by the Rhine, where they felt safe from eavesdroppers.

Masson sought to wheedle back from the Section VI chief documents that revealed Swiss intelligence's pre-war collaboration with the Czechs, which Hitler might exploit to justify an invasion. The colonel also asked for the release of Ernst Morgeli, one of the Swiss consulate's Stuttgart staff, sentenced to death for espionage. He requested Schellenberg to curb the activities of a Vienna press agency run by two Swiss Nazis, who sustained a propaganda bombardment against their own country, and especially its army commander-in-chief, Gen. Henri Guisan. The Nazi spy chief agreed to all these requests, but needled Masson by showing him a copy of a 1940 cable from the US military attaché in Bern, who had reported to Washington that his Swiss sources said that twenty-five German divisions were poised to invade Switzerland. Surely, the SS man enquired mildly, this proved that the Swiss were working with the Allies? As Masson immediately realised, it also showed off the reach of German intelligence, which in those days was reading such American cipher traffic.

Schellenberg and Masson achieved a better understanding at a second meeting, held on 16 October 1942 inside Switzerland, at the Lake Constance estate of businessman Wolfsberg Meyer-Schertenbach. The two men wore civilian clothes, and Schellenberg gossiped freely about his own life and early career, extolling the joys of marriage. He spoke warmly of

Switzerland, and expressed sympathy with its difficulties and dilemmas, isolated amid a warring Europe. Masson briefly pondered whether Schellenberg was probing for the possibility of Swiss mediation in opening negotiations with the Allies. Then the German revealed that Berlin had decrypted two of the 'Lucy' Ring's December 1941 messages to Moscow: Schellenberg was convinced that there was a serious leak inside OKW. This caused Masson to decide that his visitor was not a peace envoy, but simply an intelligence chief seeking clues to assist in identifying traitors. The two spent three days together before the SS man departed for Germany under cover of darkness.

What did Schellenberg get out of the meetings? He made significant concessions to Swiss interests, and it is impossible to believe that he did so without getting a return – both officers were traders. Masson never revealed what he himself told the SD chief, but it is likely that he fed him titbits about Allied intelligence activities in Switzerland. The colonel sought to show sufficient friendliness towards Germany to deter an invasion. Schellenberg was surely reconnoitring a line of retreat for himself if his Führer's vision collapsed. Moreover, he was able to cover his back in Berlin by reporting that his exchanges with the colonel provided important intelligence material. On 6 January 1943 he passed a note to Hitler warning – on the authority of his Swiss sources – that the RAF was planning a bombing campaign to close the Brenner Pass linking Austria and Italy. He also said that the Swiss were considering a new mobilisation of their army, prompted by nervousness about Nazi intentions.

On 30 January 1943 the Swiss 'Viking' intelligence line, controlled from Lucerne by Major Max Waibel, reported to Masson that Hitler and his high command had held a meeting the previous October to discuss an invasion of Switzerland. The colonel decided that he must meet Schellenberg again, this time accompanied by the Swiss army's C-in-C. On 3 March the SD chief flew by Lufthansa to Zürich, accompanied by two security men. Hans Eggen met them at the airport. They were initially booked into the Bellevue hotel, but Schellenberg preferred to stay at the Schweizerhof, before driving to Biglen, twelve miles from Bern, for his meeting with Masson and Gen. Guisan at the Baran hotel. Himmler had given his man explicit instructions: he was to press the Swiss publicly to emphasise their commitment to strict neutrality. On 4 March a statement declaring Switzerland's determination to resist any incursion by any foreign army was drawn up on Swiss army notepaper, and signed by the commander-in-chief. The Baran's proprietor, much excited by his exalted visitors, persuaded them all to sign the hotel's visitors' book, but a Swiss RSHA contact afterwards prudently tore out the page.

Although Guisan left at this stage, Schellenberg stayed for a further week, and held several more meetings with Masson. He pressed the intelligence officer for details of the German traitors who were feeding the 'Lucy' Ring, but Masson was sincere in pleading ignorance. The Swiss, in his turn, asked the visitor to secure the release of the family of Gen. Henri Giraud, who had been seized by the Gestapo following the French officer's escape from fortress captivity. Schellenberg assented – and again fulfilled his promise. Masson told the German he was much concerned that Hitler still appeared to be considering an invasion of his country. This was tactically inept, because it alerted Schellenberg to the fact that Bern, too, had secret sources within the Nazi high command. But on 27 March the Viking Line's sources changed tack completely, and said there was no longer any danger at all of an invasion of Switzerland. The whole exercise by the Germans, orchestrated by Schellenberg, had been designed to intimidate the Swiss, to galvanise them to take harsher countermeasures against Allied intelligence agents in their country, especially the Soviet networks – which Masson eventually did, rounding up much of the 'Lucy' Ring. Meanwhile, the head of the Swiss government's military affairs department exploded in fury at the disclosure of Gen. Guisan's unauthorised negotiations with the Nazis.

When Allen Dulles told Washington – many months later – about the contacts between Schellenberg and Masson, he commented that he himself remained confident that the Swiss government favoured an Allied victory. However, some of the country's military men were so morbidly fearful of Soviet communism that they hoped for a compromise peace, which would leave some bastion between Stalin's empire and the West. It was this threat, Dulles suggested, that induced them to traffic with the likes of Schellenberg, and he was probably right. There is no evidence about which unnamed Swiss intelligence officer tipped off the Abwehr in August 1943 – allegedly on the basis of information received from a Swiss-American source – that the Allies had broken German U-boat codes. But it is not impossible that it could have been Masson, as a gambit in his continuing horse-trading with the Nazis.

Schellenberg's other foreign plots were ingenious, fanciful, and no more successful than those of Canaris. In 1941 he wasted thousands of Reichsmarks on two communists, worknamed 'George and Joanna Wilmer', who were turned in Plötzensee jail, then dispatched to Switzerland to try to break into the 'Lucy' Ring. They spent the RSHA's cash enthusi-astically, but Alexander Foote rejected their advances with contempt. During a July 1942 visit to Portugal and Spain, Schellenberg conducted negotiations with a Brazilian exile, Plínio Salgado, who promised great things for the German cause, but delivered nothing. The spy chief also trafficked with Dr Felix Kersten, a German masseur with Finnish nation-ality, one of the legion of charlatans who extracted large sums of cash from Himmler, whom he introduced to the prominent Swedish lawyer Dr Carl Langbehn. Langbehn was one of many neutrals eager to exploit the war for his personal enrichment: he demanded 80,000 kronor from the Stockholm government as a fee for helping to negotiate the release of several Swedish citizens held by the Germans in Poland. Dr Wilhelm Bitter, a psychoanalyst at a Berlin hospital, was sent abroad by the RSHA with a mission to find a channel through which Germany might negotiate with the Allies. Having got himself a safe distance from Germany, Bitter sent just one hysterical message home, saying that the only answer was to overthrow Hitler, then vanished forever.

With the encouragement of Himmler, Schellenberg gave the wife of Ribbentrop's former foreign press chief 'Putzi' Hanfstacngl a wad of cash to start an art shop in Paris, with the implausible purpose of opening a line to the British prime minister's son Randolph, whom she had known in London. A chronically overwrought woman, she duly visited Paris in July and September and spent the money, but made no contact with any Churchill. In April 1944 one of Albert Speer's officials suggested that Schellenberg contact Coco Chanel, who he said was violently anti-Soviet, and on sufficiently friendly terms with Churchill to make her a credible intermediary for peace negotiations. Chanel, then sixty and living at the Paris Ritz with her Abwehr friend Hans-Gunther von Dincklage, was duly brought to Berlin. The couturier told the Germans she had just the right friend to make a connection with the British – Vera Bate, an Englishwoman married to an Italian named Lombardi, currently interned because of her links to the Badoglio government. Schellenberg acceded at once: Signora Lombardi was released, and just a week later was sent by air to Madrid, carrying a letter addressed to Churchill for presentation at the British embassy; Dincklage was appointed as her go-between, to convey the British response to Schellenberg. Once arrived in Madrid, however, the ungrateful Signora Lombardi told all, denouncing Chanel as the Nazi stooge she was.

Schellenberg heard no more from Vera Bate, yet he was adept at evad-ing blame for such failures. In November 1942, when Hitler and Göbbels raged at Canaris and the Abwehr for their failure to predict the Anglo-American 'Torch' landings in North Africa, the chief of the RSHA's Department VI merely shrugged that military intelligence was not his responsibility. Two months later, he invited a delegation of top Turkish police and intelligence officers to tour Germany, for what was intended to be a display of the Reich's might. Schellenberg strove to woo Pepyli, the police president, a staunch anti-communist who was indeed responsive, and gave a lavish party on the Golden Horn when the SS officer visited Turkey later in the year – the Turk shared the Nazis' loathing of communists and Russians. But for all his hosts' elaborate courtesy, Schellenberg got nowhere in securing greater latitude for his officers in their country. The Ankara government, conscious of the way the war was going, was so dismayed by the hospitality Pepyli extended to the Nazi foreign intelligence chief that it sacked him from the police presidency.

In May 1943 Schellenberg and Ribbentrop agreed that a Nazi propaganda team should be dispatched to the US to influence the 1944 presidential election against Roosevelt. They were duly trained and dispatched, but the U-boat carrying them vanished without trace, presumed sunk. Two other men who did get ashore north of New York in July were soon arrested by the Americans, who assumed them to be saboteurs. In truth, they had been sent on an absurd political intelligence mission. Meanwhile, when the Allies invaded Italy Schellenberg went to elaborate lengths to rescue the exiled grand mufti of Jerusalem. He was successful in transporting this violently anti-British, anti-Semitic Muslim leader from Rome to Berlin, but quickly tired of the mufti's company and despaired of his usefulness.

He recruited for the SD Irna, Baroness von Rothkirch, a former singer and the widow of an industrialist, now in her forties and serving as mistress to the Portuguese ambassador in Berlin. After a stint gathering gossip on the German capital's diplomatic circuit, she was dispatched to Lisbon on a fishing expedition. She ran up some impressive bills there before securing a transfer to Switzerland, where her son was attending school. Here too she squandered the SD's money until Schellenberg recognised her worthlessness, common to most 'social spies'. In October 1943 he paid a personal visit to Stockholm, supposedly in pursuit of medical advice about his own liver troubles, but chiefly to put out a cautious feeler to the Allies. The Swedish mood had shifted dramatically now that Allied victory loomed: British and American intelligence officers operated with a freedom denied to them earlier in the war, while Nazi visitors had become much less popular dining companions. Schellenberg called on the hotel of a notable rich American guest, one Abram Stevens Hewitt, who held some vague status as a 'European observer' for President Roosevelt. The SD chief advanced a proposal astoundingly crass and naïve: that the Germans should negotiate a compromise peace with the Western Allies, while continuing the war on the Eastern Front. At a second meeting Hewitt agreed that if this proposal found favour in Washington he would insert a personal advertisement in the *Svenska Dagbladet*: 'For sale, valuable goldfish aquarium for 1,524 Kr.' Hewitt returned to the US and appears to have passed on Schellenberg's message, but unsurprisingly the aquarium remained unadvertised. In November 1943 the Swedish government was emboldened to break off economic relations with Germany: the Nazis were running out of neutral friends.

In February 1944 this would-be 'good Nazi' inherited from Canaris control of the Abwehr, in a condition of decay which it was too late to reverse. Germany had lost the power to attract foreign informants because it was plainly destined to lose the war, and also lacked the military and naval capability to exploit good strategic intelligence even if it secured this. Thus Schellenberg spent ever more time in dalliances with foreign intermediaries, of a kind that would have caused him to be shot had he not enjoyed the backing of Heinrich Himmler. RSHA chief Ernst Kaltenbrunner, who disliked Schellenberg, wielded more power, but the latter retained the ear of the SS overlord, while playing a perilous game amid the crumbling Third Reich. Schellenberg was skilled in providing reassurance – his soothing bedside manner sustained Himmler's trust in him.

In August 1944, following the Hitler bomb plot, the RSHA officer was commissioned to drive to the house in the Betazielestrasse at Zehlendorf where Wilhelm Canaris lived in enforced retirement. He found the admiral entertaining two visitors, to whom he bade farewell before accompanying Schellenberg to meet his jailers at the Sipo school in Fürstenberg. Canaris seemed untroubled, perhaps sincerely so, since he lacked the courage of his convictions, and had not participated in the failed coup. Before he was handed over to the SS he merely asked Schellenberg to arrange an interview with Himmler for him. The Reichsführer-SS initially promised to help with the admiral's case, but a subsequent discussion with Kaltenbrunner persuaded him to let injustice take its course: Canaris remained imprisoned until he was hanged at Flossenburg concentration camp in April 1945. Schellenberg did intervene, however, to save the life of another plotter, Count Gottfried von Bismarck, who had once urged him to assassinate Göring.

In the last months of the war, under Schellenberg's direction the German intelligence-gathering machine adopted ever more desperate expedients. Its officers recruited hundreds of Russian PoWs as expendable line-crossers, to be herded into Soviet-held territory to discover whatever they could before their inevitable capture – this was designated as Operation 'Zeppelin'. Rough-and-ready, indeed barbaric, methods were employed to insure against their defection: many were photographed by the Germans executing fellow-countrymen. Schellenberg's officers also recruited prostitutes. The RSHA's Section V, responsible for licensing the girls, issued a directive to its regional offices: 'I ask that you look around in your areas … for suitable women … very good-looking … who have flawless manners, intelligence, and tact and if possible knowledge of foreign languages … Report them … to Department VI.' The project's outcome is unrecorded, but it seems unlikely that many such dazzlingly qualified women were to be found in brothels.

In September 1944, among the mass of fanciful intelligence material that crossed Schellenberg's desk came a warning via Sweden that the Allies planned an airborne landing in Holland, to seize a Rhine bridge. He took no action, perhaps because he mistrusted the source. The message came from a supposed British informant, but was in truth an inspired guess by Dr Kramer, the Abwehr's resident fantasist in Stockholm. Schellenberg was anyway now devoting almost all his energies to intrigues that might serve himself or his master in the wake of a German defeat. In October, he introduced to Himmler Jean-Marie Musy, an elderly Swiss Catholic conservative, to discuss an exchange of trucks for Jews. The upshot of these negotiations was that in February 1945 Schellenberg personally handled the departure of 1,200 Jews for Switzerland; a second exodus of 1,800 was agreed, but never took place. When Himmler was given an army command on the Eastern Front in February 1945, Schellenberg urged him to throw all the military resources left to Germany into holding back the Russians, and effectively to open the Western Front to the Anglo-Americans.

He sustained a friendly dialogue with the Swiss, who at his behest agreed to destroy an Me-110 which forced-landed at one of their airfields, thus pre-empting Otto Skorzeny, who was eager to lead a commando raid to recapture it. Schellenberg's adjutant Franz Göring played a role in countermanding an order for the liquidation of Ravensbrück's prisoners in the last weeks of the war – 10,000 of its inmates were instead shipped to Denmark.

On 20 April 1945 Schellenberg had breakfast with Norbert Masur, a representative of the World Jewish Congress, an action for which Hitler would almost certainly have had him shot, had he become aware of it. The RHSA officer's belated good deeds towards Jews might have merited respect had they been carried out in 1942 or 1943; as it was, they seem to represent mere gestures in support of his claims upon Allied clemency. On 1 May Kaltenbrunner sacked Schellenberg, but now his Swedish connections paid off: Count Folke Bernadotte, whom he had first met at Gottfried Bismarck's home, assisted the Abwehr boss to fly to Sweden on a Red Cross plane.

The story of the Abwehr, of Canaris and Schellenberg, may be viewed as a mere marginal scribble on the vast canvas of world war, as in considerable degree it was. Even if Hitler's strategic intelligence had been better, and if he had been willing to heed it, it is unlikely that he could have altered the course of history – for instance, by repelling the vast Russian and Anglo-American offensives of 1943–45 – though he could have made their victories much more costly. The fundamental lesson of the Abwehr experience was that the democracies handled intelligence better than the dictatorships – including that of Stalin – because they understood the merit of truth, objective assessment of evidence, not as a virtue, but as a weapon of war. Moreover, few prospective Abwehr agents of any nationality were attracted to Hitler's service by ideological enthusiasm: in the early war years they served because they supposed Germany likely to win. Once this belief faded, as it did from 1942 onwards, it became implausible that any intelligent man or woman with a choice would espouse the Nazi cause. Only human dross was available for recruitment.

Not for a moment should posterity be deluded into thinking Walter Schellenberg a 'good' Nazi, far less a competent intelligence officer, because he boasted some manners and a charm lacking in most of the gangsters who managed Hitler's Germany. He was merely one who weighed the odds more carefully and cynically than most. Not for Schellenberg, at the end, a cyanide capsule or a bullet from his own gun; given his relative youth, he might have become one of the rare survivors from Hitler's high priesthood, had not his liver betrayed him. His conceit would have been pricked by the verdict of Allied interrogators on Hitler's last intelligence chief, after he returned from Sweden in 1945 to face captivity: they reported that he did not seem very intelligent.

18

Battlefields

1 WIELDING THE ULTRA WAND

In advance of D-Day in Normandy on 6 June 1944, some rational German commanders believed that the Allied invasion of the Continent offered them a final opportunity to avoid losing the war, by repelling the Anglo-American invaders then committing the entire strength of the Wehrmacht against the Red Army. Forecasting the time and place of the Anglo-American landings thus represented the supreme challenge for their intelligence officers. Every casual reader of the world's press in 1944 knew that an invasion of the Continent was almost certain to come during the summer. But when, exactly? The codebreakers of OKH/GdNA said 4 June. Col. Alexis von Rönne, who headed the thirty officers and 110 other ranks of Fremde Heer West, or FHW, the intelligence department of von Rundstedt's armies manning the Atlantic Wall, was the only important soldier who took this prediction seriously. Most German commanders in the theatre, including Rommel, their judgement heavily influenced by lack of Atlantic weather stations, chose instead to believe that no landing was likely before 10 June. They were thus absent from their headquarters when the invasion started.

Yet forecasting the date was far less useful to the defenders than guessing where the invaders would strike. The Allies' deception operation 'Fortitude' made an important contribution to creating and sustaining enemy confusion. This should be set in context, however. The defenders' uncertainty before D-Day was hardly a unique wartime phenomenon. Throughout the summer and autumn of 1940 the British were in a state of chronic bewilderment about when or whether Hitler might invade them; during the Mediterranean campaigns they were often surprised. The Russians were wrongfooted not merely by 'Barbarossa', but repeatedly thereafter, likewise the Americans and British in the Far East. 'Fortitude', like other 1943–44 deceptions, could only work its spell because the Western Allies owned the hard power – absolute command of sea and air – to provide them with a genuine variety of invasion options along hundreds of miles of coastline.

Given the erratic influence of Hitler, if an Abwehr intelligence officer had announced a week before D-Day that he was assured by agents that Normandy was the target, it is unlikely that the Germans would have altered their deployments. By June 1944 trust in the Abwehr, OKW/Chi and OKH/GdNA was low, at least as far as the Western war was concerned. Germany's field commanders were increasingly willing to accept only what they and their staffs could see before their eyes in their own operational areas; to believe only in what their troops and tanks could achieve by the expenditure of blood and iron.

Hitler was far from the only one who thought the Pas de Calais the obvious place to attack: there had been forceful advocates in the Allied camp for making the landings there rather than in Normandy. It was not merely in Berlin that some strategists believed the British and Americans could also make a second thrust, perhaps in Brittany: until the last moment Churchill was urging Roosevelt to do just that. Far from the Germans displaying bullet-headed stupidity by questioning whether the Allies would attack solely or at all in Normandy, they would have been foolish not to acknowledge several alternatives. It was as necessary for the Wehrmacht in 1944 to fortify and defend a great swathe of northern France as it had been for the British in 1940 to build pillboxes behind their own beaches from Devon to Norfolk.

None of this is to say that 'Fortitude' was unsuccessful. Some people in the German camp – though certainly not all – took seriously the signals of 'Garbo' and other double agents controlled by the British Twenty Committee. Allied deception fed an enemy uncertainty that was anyway inevitable. It is merely necessary yet again to cite Churchill's dictum: 'All things are always on the move simultaneously.' What was of decisive importance to the success of D-Day was not that the Germans believed the Allies might land in the Pas de Calais, but that Berlin was denied assured knowledge that they would do so in Normandy. Protection of the secrecy of Operation 'Overlord' mattered more than promotion of Operation 'Fortitude' – at least until the Allies had got ashore. Britain's island status, the peerless moat provided by the Channel, was the most important factor here.

Allied radio deception, which was brilliantly sophisticated, probably played a larger role in deceiving the Germans about Allied plans before and after D-Day than did double agents, because Germany's generals had more faith in its reliability. On 16 May 1944, after studying the latest Ultra, 'Tar' Robertson of MI5 told Guy Liddell that the Germans seemed to have exploited wireless traffic analysis to build up a reasonable assessment of the disposition of Allied formations in Britain, some of them fictional: 'the whole picture is built up from a number of details. Agents' reports do not appear to play a very big part.' Liddell commented: 'I cannot help feeling that the enemy, as is the case of ourselves, are more likely to depend on Y information and wireless intelligence than on anything they may receive from other sources, when formulating their plans. All that agents can really do is to fill in the picture.' This was so. The Allied wireless deception element of 'Fortitude', its simulation of the fictitious First US Army Group in south-east England, almost certainly influenced the Germans' thinking, their massive overestimate of Allied strength, more than did material transmitted by the Abwehr's informants controlled by MI5, though the latter excite more twenty-first-century imaginations.

Exceptionally, in June 1944 Hut 8 placed a temporary interception station inside Bletchley Park, to hasten the flow of decrypts to operational commanders. Through those vital days, the codebreakers provided a drastically accelerated intelligence feed to commanders: decrypted Kriegsmarine traffic reached the Admiralty within an average of thirty minutes of interception – the record for one signal was nineteen minutes for reception, registration, deciphering, translation and teleprint dispatch to the Royal Navy. On the other side, the Wehrmacht's Albert Praun later paid rueful tribute to the excellence of Allied signals discipline: 'The radio picture did not change noticeably until the last day before the invasion … No radio deception was recognised. No kind of radio alert was observed before the landing.' The German intelligence apparatus never swallowed Allied deception plans suggesting an impending descent on Norway – but Hitler was morbidly protective of his northern fastness, which was what mattered in determining deployments. Praun asserted that after 6 June his own organisation was sceptical about the notion of a second Allied landing in the Pas de Calais because most of the available Allied forces seemed committed to Normandy, but he acknowledged that OKW remained for weeks sold on the second landing scenario, especially after chance washed ashore an Allied landing-craft at Boulogne.

Ultra in the latter part of the war fortified the confidence – latterly over-confidence – of the Allies' ground commanders. They believed that they could launch their own operations without fear that the enemy was about to unleash some fearsome surprise of his own. While tension in the Allied camp before D-Day was acute, because the stakes were so high, all the odds were on the invaders' side. Never before in history had armies gone into battle as well briefed as were those of Britain and the United States before 6 June. Beyond bulging files prepared by the War Office's MI14 on the German units identified in the invasion area, among tons of intelligence material distributed to the invaders was a breakdown of all known German facilities across the whole of northern France. In Amiens, for instance, were listed 'Hôtel du Commerce, Rue du Jacobins – food store; 164, Rue Jeanne d'Arc – German police; 219, Rue Jules Barni – hospital.' Similar inventories, partly compiled from agent reports, partly from Ultra, covered scores of major towns and cities. MI6 informants in Belgium and northern France made a significant contribution by mapping, photographing and drawing, at mortal risk, hundreds of installations along the Atlantic Wall, though such humint was weakest about positions on the immediate Normandy invasion front.

Bletchley supplied to Allied commanders a reasonably comprehensive German order of battle. The invaders knew most about the paratroop formations, because these signalled in the ever-vulnerable Luftwaffe ciphers. The roster was incomplete: little was known about the army's 352nd Division, which wreaked some havoc among the Americans landing on Omaha beach, nor about the 711th and 716th divisions further east, but it is absurd to make much of this, as have a few historians: no army can expect to know everything about its foe. What mattered was that all Hitler's 'heavy' formations were accurately pinpointed, and their movements towards the beachhead could be tracked. Once the Allies were ashore, Ultra was able to give real-time warning of – for instance – the 12 June German counterattack on Carentan, and of most impending Luftwaffe raids. Nonetheless, it deserves notice that on 10 June Bletchley lost Fish teleprinter decrypts for some days, when the Germans tweaked their encryption system; it was fortunate for Allied peace of mind that no such blackout had occurred a week or two earlier.

On the other side of the hill, even though German intelligence got the big things wrong in June 1944, once battle was joined local commanders and staffs in Normandy displayed their usual competence in exploiting information gained from patrolling, prisoner interrogation, interception of radio voice traffic. The Wehrmacht's Albert Praun thought that overweening confidence in their own strength made the Americans and British lazy about preserving wireless silence before they launched operations: 'This carelessness was possibly due to a feeling of absolute superiority ... [that] offered the weaker defenders much information which cost the attackers losses which could have been avoided ... Many attacks of division strength and greater could be predicted one to five days in advance.'

Some American messages sent by the M-209 field cipher machine were broken, said the German, and the RAF 'continued to be careless' in its voice chatter, especially its air liaison officers attached to ground units. Allied reconnaissance aircraft often reported sightings in plain language, including map references, sometimes in time for the Germans to bolt, and especially to move out artillery batteries. Patton's army had the worst radio discipline, said Praun, Gen. Alexander Patch's the best. French communications continued to be easily read, as they had been since 1940 – the Germans followed Gen. Leclerc's advance on Paris kilometre by kilometre. Meanwhile the Wehrmacht became morbidly sensitive to Allied monitoring of its own communications: 'A radio psychosis developed among German troops,' said Praun. 'They became most reluctant to signal' – to avoid precipitating a storm of bombs and shells. Moreover, a fundamental problem now beset the Germans, which would dog them for the rest of the war: it was fruitless to garner enemy secrets if military strength was lacking to exploit them. On 7 June in Normandy German troops captured a detailed American operational order, but were quite unable to do anything with it, because all their available forces were fighting desperately to stave off an Allied breakthrough. Likewise sigint operators identified Chicksands as a key RAF transmission and interception station, but the Luftwaffe was incapable of bombing it.

The Allied intelligence mosaic became ever more dominated by Enigma and Tunny decrypts. For British and American generals in the later stages of the war Ultra became an addictive drug, requiring a twice- or thrice-daily 'fix' before any operational decision was taken. In camouflaged trucks and tents high on windswept Italian mountains or deep in muddy French fields, bespectacled young staff officers in British battledress or US Army combat fatigues huddled over the latest signals from Bletchley. The Allied high command faced a constant dilemma about how much Ultra material to disclose to those who must fight the Germans at the sharp end. If it was claimed that a given piece of intelligence came from agent reports or – less convincing still – from line-crossers, nobody much credited it. But if they knew that it bore the authority of the enemy's own words, they could hardly fail to do so.

A wardrobe specialist at OSS's London station dresses an American agent for a mission in the latest Continental fashion.

TRAITORS
Above left: The young Anthony Blunt, before he became an officer of MI5 and an informant of the NKVD. *Above right*: A Russian stamp celebrating Kim Philby's contribution to the Revolution. *Below*: Donald and Melinda Maclean with their children on a transatlantic liner.

Above: Alger Hiss successfully bluffing out his evidence to the House Committee on Un-American Activities in 1948 – he was long dead before his treason was confirmed. *Below*: John Maynard Keynes in amicable converse with Harry Dexter White, one of Moscow's most important US secret sources.

GERMANS
Above: Hitler, the Allies' best friend in frustrating intelligence analysis, with courtiers including Keitel, Göring and Ribbentrop. *Below*: A general staff officer extends himself to explore Soviet deployments. *Opposite*: The V-2, which alarmed the Allies and set them one of the most intractable intelligence puzzles of the war.

RESISTANCE

Left: One of the seminal images of the secret war – Frenchmen use a bren gun supplied by the British to harass Germans fleeing France in August 1944. *Below left and centre*: SOE trainees set charges on a railway line and wireless London. *Below right*: Three SAS officers of the 'Bulbasket' mission to France, June 1944. Lt. Twm Stephens wears the civilian disguise in which he rode a bicycle to Châtellerault to reconnoitre petrol trains, intended to fuel the Das Reich 2nd SS Armoured Division, for attack by RAF Mosquitoes. Only John Tonkin, on the left with the pipe, survived the operation.

Baron Ōshima, pictured here with Nazi foreign minister Ribbentrop, Japan's ambassador in Berlin, and through Purple decrypts the Allies' best secret agent of the war.

ONSLAUGHT IN THE ARDENNES
Hitler's last throw in December 1944, which ranks as one of the Allies' great intelligence failures of the war.

SPIES AND COUNTERSPIES
Above: 'Wild Bill' Donovan in 1941 doing what he liked best, talking to reporters. *Above right*: Donovan's OSS station chief in Bern, Allen Dulles. *Right*: FBI director J. Edgar Hoover. *Below*: A priest gives solace to a hapless German 'line-crosser' before he is shot by an American firing squad in November 1944. *Opposite*: Ilya Tolstoy *(centre)* and companions on their fantastic OSS mission to Tibet.

THE EASTERN FRONT

Left: Alexander Demyanov, key figure in 'Monastery', the most astounding Russian deception operation of the war, photographed in 1943. *Opposite*: Col. Reinhard Gehlen, at the extreme right of the photo, the German intelligence chief who became a dupe of the NKVD.

The occupied peoples of Russia were equally liable to be shot by either side. *Below*: Peasants lead out a supposed traitor for execution, while (*opposite below*) the Germans prepare to inflict Nazi justice on a peasant.

BLETCHLEY'S FINEST HOUR
Above: Colossus, the world's first computer, created by Cambridge mathematician Max Newman (*right*) and Post Office engineer Tommy Flowers (*below right*). Their creation enabled GC&CS to read some top secret traffic of the German Lorenz teleprinter (*below*), which employed an entirely different encryption system from Enigma.
Opposite: The young mathematician Bill Tutte, who by sheer brainpower identified the characteristics of the Lorenz, and deserves to be almost as celebrated as Alan Turing.

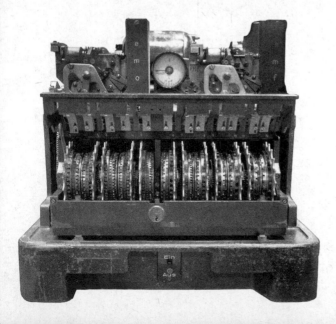

R.V. Jones, the great British scientific intelligence officer, with his family at a 1945 Buckingham Palace investiture.

Bill Williams, Montgomery's intelligence chief, said that officers who had been indoctrinated about codebreaking became pathologically discreet: 'What an agent says becomes gossip. To explain the nature of Ultra was to slam the door on this approach ... The vast number of its recipients were so frightened of losing what ... was obviously an immense strategic asset that we got away without its loss.' The US Army in Italy had a half-solemn, half-mocking phrase for its Ultra-indoctrinated officers, who were said to be 'steeped in the blood of the lamb'. Ultra product was known as 'Black Market'. Rumour among headquarters officers not privy to the secret suggested that it was a channel through which Allied commanders conducted arguments or issued reprimands unfit for the eyes of junior personnel.

Knowledge of the wizardry of Bletchley was restricted to intelligence officers at army level and above. No one who might fall into enemy hands should be capable of betraying its story; thus, past service at the Park formed a permanent bar to a combat role, even if a few men aspired to one – Keith Batey alone achieved it. Corps and divisional commanders who were not Ultra-indoctrinated were simply informed of a clear distinction between what Army HQ stated as fact about German deployments or intentions, and what it merely suspected. Much lighter security attended the activities of the Y Service – eavesdroppers on enemy voice traffic – because the Germans were obviously aware of its existence, and them-selves played the same game. 'Y' often provided a cloak for intelligence secured through decrypts. Bill Williams believed that even the highest commanders should merely receive briefs based on sigint, rather than being allowed to see decrypts as they came in: 'No senior officer should ever read naked Ultra unless he is trained in Intelligence ... They are given a weapon often too big for their hand.' In the view of Britain's chiefs of staff this applied especially to their prime minister, who often used a decrypted report from an enemy commander as a club with which to belabour his own generals about their alleged pusillanimity.

Special operations and Resistance contributed something, though less than romantics wish to believe, to eventual Allied triumph in Normandy. In the first days after the Allied landings, parties of the British Special Air Service, together with SOE and OSS teams, were dropped all over France to foment trouble for the Germans by any means to hand. On 10 June a party of local Resistance fighters visited the camp of a British Special Air Service group in the forest of Verrières in the Vienne, bearing important news. The SAS, fifty strong, had been parachuted into France on 7 June for an operation codenamed 'Bulbasket', intended to promote sabotage attacks far behind the German front in collaboration with Resisters. Now the visitors urged the English to address an important rail junction at Châtellerault some thirty-five miles northwards, where German petrol stocks were being held. The SAS team's commanding officer, Captain John Tonkin, deputed Lt. Twm Stephens to accompany two Frenchmen on a cycle ride to reconnoitre the junction. Stephens, a mustachioed little Welshman who looked plausibly French, donned an ill-fitting civilian suit and beret and set forth on what was a highly dangerous journey – in the wake of D-Day the region teemed with alert and fearful Germans. He and his companions nonetheless reached Châtellerault, where the British officer found that the locals had not exaggerated. In the marshalling yards stood line upon line of tanker wagons, enveloped in heavy camouflage netting, and thus far unscathed by Allied air attack.

Stephens and the others rode back to the camp at Verrières, which they reached the following night, after an absence of thirty-six hours. Tonkin's wireless-operator signalled to the SAS Brigade's British base the map reference of eleven petrol trains halted in sidings a thousand yards east of the junction. An Ultra intercept the same day showed that the Germans intended the fuel for the Das Reich 2nd SS Armoured Division, incongruously designated in the British decrypt '2 Sugar Sugar Panzer', which was en route to Normandy. Within three hours, twenty-four twin-engined Mosquitoes of the RAF's 487, 646 and 107 squadrons strafed and bombed the junction, destroying the trains and their precious fuel. 2nd SS Panzer reached Normandy in the end, but its arrival on the battlefield was significantly delayed by the air attack, prompted by the SAS's signal from France.

Here was a textbook example of coordination between intelligence, special forces, Resistance and air power to achieve an outcome which – as Ultra revealed – materially assisted the Allied battle for Normandy. Few such operations ended as successfully as Lt. Stephens's reconnaissance – for which he paid with his life when he and most of his comrades were captured and executed following a German assault on their forest base a few days after the bicycle ride to Châtellerault. But the summer of 1944 witnessed a dramatic and bloody fulfilment of Churchill's vision for Resistance and special forces back in July 1940, when he enthused about setting Europe ablaze.

*   *   *

In the first three weeks of July, Bletchley broke remarkably few army messages – the Wehrmacht's Enigma key was going through one of its intractable periods – and the Allies were obliged merely to fight and die as best they could, with no significant Ultra assistance. In any event, this would have been unlikely to provide details of practical value about enemy deployments to meet the British assaults on Caen, which caused them much grief and successive failures before achieving belated success. For Bletchley, much the most important moment of the Normandy campaign came on the evening of 6 August, when a broken signal – once more from Luftwaffe traffic – revealed the German intention to strike in force west-wards, with almost all their remaining panzers, towards the sea at Avranches. Thus forewarned, an overwhelming concentration of Allied air power and artillery, together with a gallant stand by the US 30th Division, wrecked the so-called Mortain counterattack.

Ultra also flagged Hitler's determination to persevere with this assault, even as American troops burst out of their perimeter and surged south and east, bypassing the struggling panzers. Allied forces could advance to close the 'Falaise Gap', knowing that much of the Germans' surviving strength was trapped to the west of it, still battering vainly at the American holding force between themselves and Avranches. This represented Ultra's last intervention in the north-west Europe campaign which significantly influenced battlefield events, as distinct from merely keeping Allied commanders informed of their enemies' condition. Stuart Milner-Barry of Hut 6 never forgot breaking 'the desperate message from the German commander in Normandy, which heralded the collapse of the German resistance … This kind of message, shown to us maybe in the middle of the night, gave one an extraordinary sensation of living with history.'

Since 1939 the codebreakers had been told pathetically little about the impact of their herculean labours upon the course of the war. Only in the final months, with the tide running irresistibly in favour of the Allies, did field commanders belatedly recognise that morale at Bletchley might be boosted by a little feedback. Montgomery's intelligence staff began to dispatch daily briefs from 21st Army Group headquarters. 'One felt one was talking to friends,' wrote Bill Williams, 'and from that feeling of grat-itude which we hoped was reflected in the words sent to the Park emerged a belief that because of them [we] were getting a better service.'

Only a few score British and American officers in the field knew how great was the armies' debt to GC&CS. The codebreakers did not provide Allied soldiers, sailors and airmen with a key to victory; only hard fighting could achieve that. But they waved a magic wand which swept aside the shroud of secrecy behind which the enemy moved and had his being. This was a boon never before conferred on any nation at war in history. It was no fault of BP's that generals on the battlefield sometimes ignored, misinterpreted or failed to take advantage of its bounty – as they did in northwest Europe in the closing months of the war.

2 SUICIDE SPIES

The most ruthless and cynical operations run by all intelligence services were those involving short-range spies – locally recruited civilians dispatched to report what they could see behind the enemy's front line. Their prospects of success or even survival were slight, but this did not deter either the Axis or the Allies from thrusting a small army of them into the fray. In the months before D-Day, the Germans recruited three hundred French 'stay-behind' agents for deployment when the Allies had gained a beachhead. They were trained at the Abwehr's spy school at Angers on the Loire, run by a fifty-three-year-old languages professor from Hamm, Hauptmann Clören, a Nazi Party member with a Swiss wife. His students, he told Allied interrogators later, were 'of a very poor standard ... unemployed men who accepted the work "for the sake of earning some money"'.

The habitual gloom of one of Clören's pupils, dark, bespectacled twenty-three-year-old 'Bardou', may have been explained by his day job as assistant to Rouen's municipal undertaker. The Germans paid him 3,000 francs a month, and got nothing for their money. 'Beccassino', a young Norman, was wanted by Saint-Malo police for theft, and proved so conspicuously incompetent as an agent that the Abwehr employed him as its station cook in Angers to justify his 2,000 francs a month. After D-Day he was dispatched through the Allied lines and never heard from again. The same silence descended upon 'Berthelot', a former Paris art student given 20,000 francs to report from American-occupied Cherbourg. 'Beru', another young Parisian, allegedly sent some useful messages from Allied territory before announcing in August that he was ill, and being allowed to go home.

After the Allied landings thirty-five-year-old Bigault de Casanove – 'Calvert' – was left in western France, from which he sent two wireless messages in October. The first said that 250 Resistance men planned to attack the German garrison of Saint-Nazaire. The second read: 'I have no money left and need new orders. Please send money and orders.' Most of the agents committed in the summer of 1944 were paid 500–800 francs a month and issued with half a dozen carrier pigeons and a supply of feed. In advance of D-Day the Abwehr kept a hundred birds at its Angers station, which were trucked out into the countryside once a month to practise flying home. A German intelligence officer told Allied interrogators sourly: 'No messages were ever received from agents with pigeons.'

Other Abwehr stay-behinds included twenty-three-year-old Parisian Geneviève Mouquet, 'Girot', an idealist who professed to believe that Vichy and the Nazis represented a 'New Europe'. Far from being the glamorous woman spy of fiction, she was decidedly stout, but after training as a wireless-operator, in June 1944 she was sent to American-occupied Saint-Lô. Several times she returned to her base at Angers, saying that Allied bombing made it too difficult to get across the Vire to her objective. She was instead deployed to the estate of a racehorse trainer named Devoy, west of Villedieu in Normandy, who had ingratiated himself with the Germans by keeping pigeons for them during the Occupation. Mouquet lasted a month with him before fleeing east, having abandoned her wireless, saying that the place had become too dangerous. The Germans eventually allowed her to decamp to Württemberg, recording in her file that she was 'unfit for any further intelligence work'. She had backed losers, and by August 1944 must have known it.

The Allies fared no better than the Axis in recruiting stay-behinds. In the worst days of the Ardennes battle in December 1944, the Americans became sufficiently alarmed that they made their own frantic efforts to identify some local agents in Belgium, in case the panzers thrust onwards beyond the Meuse. A US Ninth Army officer reported gloomily: 'The problem is not a simple one; radio-operators, at once willing and able, must be discreetly concealed in places where they have some chance of remaining even if the enemy moves in and evacuates most of the populace and searches the houses. The neighbors cannot be let in on the secret. The agent must be kept in a reasonably good frame of mind during a dull and nervous waiting period.' It was fortunate the Bulge stay-behinds were never needed.

In those days the Germans launched a new surge of their own line-crossers. Among enemy agents detained by the US Ninth Army during the Bulge battle were Bernard Piolot, who was allegedly caught cutting an American field telephone line; Betsy Coenegrachts, *née*

Stratemans, of Vroenhoven, Belgium, 'a proven smuggler and informant of the Gestapo who was responsible for the arrest of two Belgian underground espionage agents during the occupation'; Philip Staab, who allegedly admitted having worked for the Gestapo; Joseph Bernard, of Kerkrade, Holland, who confessed to being an SD agent. In all in January 1945 Ninth Army – whose G-2 records alone survive – arrested 156 people suspected of being enemy agents, of whom twenty-one were soldiers in civilian clothes, a further eleven were handed over to the Belgian authorities, twenty-eight were detained, fifty-six held for further interrogation and just twelve released. It is no more possible to guess whether such people were guilty or innocent, given the hysteria of those days, than it is to discover their eventual fate.

As the Wehrmacht retreated, in the last months of the war hundreds of line-crossers recruited by the Allies were thrust forward into Germany. Almost all vanished, and were presumed dead. One day in March 1945, for instance, an SOE officer herded a batch of Poles up a road towards the German lines, with orders to push forward as far as they could in pursuit of information. He wrote after watching one man go: 'I cannot say I was altogether hopeful about his chances.' The other Poles displayed last-minute reluctance, but eventually disappeared towards Osnabrück, 'three rather forlorn-looking figures disappearing into the blue'. Nothing is known of their later stories.

The Americans enlisted the services of the Belgian Sûreté to identify local men willing to risk their lives by plunging into the maelstrom of a collapsing Reich. A report on an operation launched on 1 March 1945 by an OSS officer named Josendale described a farcical attempt to parachute agent 'Peter' behind the German front. During the flight to the dropping zone 'the operation was brought to an unfortunate end when the agent shot himself in the leg … Had this incident not occurred, the mission would have failed in any event as the plane was recalled, due to quite heavy enemy action on the ground and in the air in the vicinity of the proposed pinpoint drop.' Other such operations fared no better: 'Agent "Bert" became difficult to manage and developed into a troublemaker … Agents "George" and "Hank" lost their value as the area with which they were familiar and in which they were due to operate was overrun.' 'Hans returned on 23 March after swimming across the Rhine, but Joseph was captured and his fate is a foregone conclusion. On the night of 23 March missions "Peter" and "Mac" were mounted. This was an airdrop operation. Agent "Peter" refused to go through with the mission at the last moment and agent "Fred" was substituted in his place. For security reasons agent "Peter" has been placed in custody for the duration of the war. Agent "Fred" was dropped in the Hamm area and one testing W/T contact was made with him on 24 March, since then no contact has been established with him.'

Soviet line-crossers suffered equally devastating attrition. In July 1944 Stalin decreed the creation of networks up to three hundred miles beyond the front, in German, Hungarian, Romanian, Czech and Polish territory, for the promotion of sabotage and intelligence-gathering, with the same purposes for which SOE and OSS dropped hundreds of agents into France after D-Day. An officer named Nikolsky, who ran such Soviet groups from Brest and Kobrin, frankly admitted their failure: 'We learned even before the end of the war that almost all of our intelligence and sabotage groups had been eliminated by the enemy soon after they landed.' An Abwehr officer in Norway, Hauptmann Pardon, picked up one GRU team and thereafter persuaded its controllers in Murmansk to parachute several supply drops into German hands.

Few GRU agents even spoke a local language, and most were dropped blind. Every German within miles closed in on the site of a reported parachute landing, to begin a '*Hasenjagdt*' – a hare hunt – which was usually successful. Nikolsky reported that only a dozen of 120 trained intelligence officers that he himself dispatched survived, 'by a miracle', until they were overrun by the Red Army. One of those who perished was a veteran of underground operations in German-occupied territory named Anna Morozova. A trained wireless-operator, she was eventually trapped and wounded on 11 November 1944 while serving with a Polish partisan group in East Prussia, and blew herself up with one of her own grenades.

Even the Russians became dismayed by the losses of their own nationals in such operations, and in the winter of 1944 adopted a new policy – dispatching German deserters, or double agents, to fulfil Stalin's demands. The GRU infiltrated 'turned' PoWs at the rate of up to thirty a week, though most promptly surrendered to the Wehrmacht on arrival. Scarcely any of the eighteen teams Nikolsky dropped behind the German lines between August 1944 and March 1945 were heard from again, including one deliberately parachuted into the midst of a battle. Such agents as did transmit later proved to have been under German control. Nikolsky commented dryly, 'The results were far from encouraging.'

It is possible to detail the fortunes of one such mission, because a survivor later fell into the hands of British interrogators. What follows seems fantastic even by the standards of wartime special operations, but there must be significant portions of truth in it. Waldemar Bartsch was born in Ukraine to German parents, and was studying in Odessa when the Wehrmacht occupied the city in 1942. The British report describes him as 'intelligent, has a good memory and is an opportunist. He appears to have no national loyalty', a verdict justified by his chequered experiences. Bartsch worked as an interpreter with the Luftwaffe until March 1944, when the Russians overran the area and dispatched him to become a forced labourer with an engineer battalion. A counterattack restored him to the custody of the Germans, who charged him with desertion. He was handed over to the Abwehr, who decided to use him as handler for a double agent, Mihail Kotschesche, a fellow-Ukrainian born in 1919.

Kotschesche had served with the Hungarian army until captured by the Russians near Kharkov in 1942. After some months as a prisoner, he was one of a group of twenty-seven chosen for training as a Soviet agent and dispatched to a spy school at Detskoe Selo, twenty-five miles east of Moscow. There he underwent fifteen months of training in the Russian language, photography, wireless-operation and political indoctrination. He then spent a further three months in Moscow before being dispatched on a mission, with the codename 'Dodi'. On 24 May 1944 he was flown to Kursk, and briefed for a drop in Hungary. He was provided with the uniform of a Hungarian sergeant, a large sum of cash, an American Tensor wireless set with a ten-metre wire aerial, and a table of frequencies to which he was told to add 3,000 kc on even days, and subtract 2,000 on odd ones. He also received a Hungarian prayer book, not for spiritual solace but as a coding key.

Kotschesche was dropped from a US-built Boston bomber, and it was scarcely surprising that he twisted his ankle on landing, since he had received no parachute training. He managed to hobble to a railway station, from which he travelled to his mother's home near Svalava. He spent two weeks there, and hid his money, before obeying the instructions of his Russian handlers: to surrender himself to the police, admitting that he had been sent by Moscow, and thereafter play a double radio game in the enemy's hands. The Hungarians spent three hours debating his fate, then gave him to the Germans, who allocated him an Abwehr codename as 'Adam', and Waldemar Bartsch as his handler. Kotschesche duly began messaging Moscow, first from Debrecen and then, as the Red Army advanced, from Budapest. He allegedly sent some material at the behest of the Germans, some on his own initiative to his Soviet customers. His

Moscow orders required him to transmit only once a week. He signalled information on troop and vehicle movements, but was reprimanded by Centre when he mentioned American bombing: 'American bombing of no interest. Stick to your instructions. Where are you living?'

On 22 August the GRU demanded to know what he had done with the money he had been given. Kotschesche replied: 'Have spent 2,000 pengo on car hire. 2,000 left with mother to buy a horse.' On 2 September he told Moscow: 'The poor are waiting for the Red Army, the rich make for the west in a hurry. I saw in a restaurant three Hungarian and six German generals.' On 19 October he messaged: 'I have no clear picture yet of Budapest. There is unrest in city. Arrow Cross [fascist movement] supported by Germans have seized power.' This brought a furious response from his Russian masters: 'Stop sending unclear messages or you will be held responsible. Observe the political situation ... Do not listen to rumours. They are fascist lies.'

It seems remarkable that the Germans, at such a late stage of the war, persisted with intelligence activities that could not be of the smallest practical use to their cause, but all institutions, including intelligence services, retain a zombie momentum even in the face of catastrophe: at the same period the Abwehr was still parachuting line-crossers behind the Russian front. Bartsch later told the British that he never doubted that Kotschesche was working for Moscow, but thought his own interests best served by keeping his mouth shut and appearing to collaborate with the Germans. Kotschesche frequently mocked his fellow-Ukrainian that he would not dare tell the Germans about his treachery, and boasted that he himself would be a big man when the Red Army arrived.

In December 1944, both men fled from Budapest to Vienna, where nervous local policemen arrested Kotschesche as a suspicious person – which, heavens knows, he was – and Bartsch had some difficulty securing his release. At the end of January 1945 they moved on to Graz, where the spy resumed transmissions to Moscow. He also acquired a twenty-year-old blonde lover named Ilse Killer, and passed the last months of the war in relative tranquillity. The Red Army arrived in Graz to find Kotschesche strutting as a self-appointed commissar, interrogating Austrian civilians. The ungrateful spy denounced Ilse, his girlfriend, as a German stool-pigeon, and she swiftly vanished, presumably into the maw of SMERSh. Bartsch escaped westwards, while Kotschesche's ultimate fate is unknown.

What conclusions can be drawn from his tortuous story, as told to the British? The most obvious is that it would be unwise to accept a word of it at face value, though much of the narrative seems too circumstantial and fanciful to be untrue. Both Bartsch and Kotschesche displayed remarkable talents as intriguers, matching those of Ronald Seth, merely by dissuading two of the most ruthless regimes in history from shooting them. It seems unlikely that the doings of the two Ukrainians, which absorbed substantial Russian and German resources, yielded the smallest advantage to either side. They were flotsam, swept into the intelligence game for a season, who played a few hands before being swept away on the tide of war.

3 TARNISHED TRIUMPH

In the last months of the war in Europe, the Allied march to victory was sullied by repeated intelligence failures that cost many lives, wasted opportunities and granted the Germans entirely gratuitous successes, albeit afterwards reversed. Ralph Bennett of Bletchley's Hut 3 believed that after achieving victory in the Normandy campaign at the Falaise Gap in August, euphoria distorted the judgement of Allied commanders, blinding them to both intelligence and prudence. In the early autumn of 1944 the codebreakers read a stream of desperate signals from German commanders in the West, describing their own forces as at the last gasp. For some days Eisenhower and his subordinates, as well as the British JIC – though emphatically not Winston Churchill – were convinced that the war was as good as won. Bennett notes that Ultra flagged Hitler's acute concern about the vulnerability of the Moselle–Saar sector of the front, which Eisenhower ignored in favour of supporting Montgomery's northern thrust. It remains highly doubtful, however, whether Patton – who commanded in the south – could have made a decisive breakthrough, even had he been given logistic support. Unfavourable terrain told heavily against attackers who took that road into Germany.

Bennett is surely right, however, to emphasise Montgomery's culpability for failure to secure the Scheldt approaches to Antwerp at the beginning of September, when they stood open for the taking. Ultra repeatedly emphasised German determination to defend the estuary and thus deny use of the vital port to the Allies, together with details of shipments of German troops and guns to fortify positions on the east bank. Incomprehensibly, the British failed to interdict the German crossings, even after Admiral Sir Bertram Ramsay warned Montgomery of this danger. In the face of the German stand on the Scheldt, Antwerp remained unusable for almost three months after its intact capture, with crippling consequences for Allied logistics. The little British field-marshal's neglect of crystal-clear intelligence, and of an important strategic opportunity, became a major cause of the Western Allied failure to break into the heart of Germany in 1944.

The same overconfidence was responsible for the launch of the doomed airborne assault in Holland on 17 September, despite Ultra's flagging of the presence near the drop zone of 9th and 10th SS Panzer Divisions, together with Field-Marshal Walter Model's headquarters at Oosterbeek. Had 'victory fever' not blinded Allied commanders, common sense dictated that even drastically depleted SS panzers posed a mortal threat to lightly armed and mostly inexperienced British airborne units. Ultra on 14–15 September also showed the Germans alert to the danger of an airborne landing in Holland. It was obvious that it would be very hard to drive the British relief force eighty miles up a single Dutch road, with the surrounding countryside impassable for armour, unless the Germans failed to offer resistance. The decision to launch Operation 'Market Garden' against this background was recklessly irresponsible, and its defeat remains a deserved blot on Montgomery's reputation.

The greatest Allied intelligence disaster of the campaign was, of course, failure to anticipate Hitler's 16 December 1944 Operation 'Autumn Mist', when two German armies smashed into the weakest sector of the US First Army's front in the Ardennes. After the event, every senior American and British intelligence officer gazed ruefully upon the stack of Ultra decrypts that should have alerted Eisenhower and his generals. On 4 September the Japanese ambassador, Baron Ōshima, had met Hitler in East Prussia. The Führer asserted that as soon as his new reinforcement army was ready, he intended 'to take the offensive in the West on a large scale', exploiting poor seasonal weather to mask redeployment of his forces from the Allied air forces; the attack would come 'after the beginning of November'. Yet although British and American intelligence officers read Ōshima's report of that conversation, on 11 November the British Joint Intelligence Committee wrote: 'The Germans may be planning a limited spoiling attack designed to upset Allied preparations and thus postpone the major Allied offensive, possibly even until the spring of 1945 … We do not think that the evidence warrants the conclusion that the Germans are planning a spoiling offensive.'

The official historians of intelligence say: 'It is not a misuse of hindsight to hazard the judgement that the British chiefs of staff and the JIC made a fundamental mistake' in failing to take this warning, together with other Ultra about the formation of Sixth Panzer Army and redeployment westwards of substantial Luftwaffe elements, with the seriousness they merited. Ōshima repeatedly restated his forecast of an offensive in the West, mentioning the prospect twenty-eight times in dispatches between 16 August and 15 December 1944. His messages, matched by other clues about German redeployments and concentrations, and the disappearance of panzer formations from the Eastern Front, should have rung bells at Allied headquarters. Ralph Bennett of Hut 3 noted later the other unheeded clues about the looming onslaught that Bletchley provided: massive train movements flagged in decrypts of messages in the German State Railways code; forward concentrations of Luftwaffe aircraft on a scale unseen for years; requests for intensive air reconnaissance of key sectors of the American front – 'It was extraordinary that Ultra did not arouse more forebodings.'

The British bore much of the responsibility for the failure of analysis, because they led the Allied intelligence effort against the Germans, and SHAEF's intelligence chief was their own Maj. Gen. Kenneth Strong. The British officer had been flown to reinforce Eisenhower's team in North Africa following the February 1943 Kasserine Pass fiasco, and had been with the Supreme Commander ever since. He now directed a staff a thousand strong, and thus as bloated as every other element of that Anglo-American headquarters. He asserted in a 16 September SHAEF strategic assessment of the German condition: 'No force can be built up in the West sufficient for a counter-offensive or even a successive defensive,' and he never wavered from that view during the three months that followed.

A lifelong bachelor, Strong was an odd-looking figure, with bulbous cheeks and protruding ears. Bill Williams, Montgomery's intelligence chief, included among his own multiple charges against Ike's G-2 the accusation that he 'wouldn't go near the front if he could help it'. The Oxford don dismissed the career soldier in the top intelligence job as a 'headless horror and a faceless wonder ... Strong worried about everything.' It should also be noted that intensive activity by OSS, MI6 and SOE in dispatching line-crossing agents into Germany failed to produce a single report about preparations for 'Autumn Mist'. Enemy wireless silence prevented the Y Service from detecting anything amiss, and some important clues from PoW interrogations in the days before 16 December went unnoticed. The SHAEF intelligence chief was neither clever nor imaginative, and was indeed unfit to hold the top post on Eisenhower's staff. But

Williams at 21st Army Group did no better than his superior in anticipating 'Autumn Mist'. The US Army was always sceptical about British willingness to allow amateur soldiers such as this thirty-two-year-old academic to rise to the highest ranks in intelligence departments. Gen. Omar Bradley wrote of Williams after the war: 'He is brilliant but inclined to be erratic like most brilliant men ... frequently wrong because he lacks the military background that we demand.' Bradley cited a typical Williams remark: 'My digestion is bad this morning – I've been eating my words for a week.' Presumably this was said in the wake of the Battle of the Bulge.

In December 1944 both Strong and Williams were guilty of the same blunder as the JIC: they dismissed a scenario because it did not conform to their own logic. Strong wrote in his own post-war apologia for the Ardennes failure: 'Members of the Intelligence staffs ... were considered to be defeatists if they predicted anything but continued Allied success; if they expressed doubts about the future they were accused of being out of touch with the realities of the war.' He said that the US First Army's senior intelligence officer emerged from the battle with most credit, having warned that he believed the Germans were up to something. 'Of all the officers concerned with Order of Battle intelligence,' said Strong, 'it was Col. "Monk" Dickson who came nearest to getting the correct answer to the riddle about the whereabouts of unlocated German divisions.'

The US Army throughout the war remained short of trained intelligence officers, but Dickson was one of its better practitioners – others included John Petito, Richard Collins and James O. Curtis. Strong admitted, however, that the American's pre-Ardennes credibility was weakened by the fact that he had acquired a reputation for pessimism, indeed alarmism, 'and we had therefore developed a habit of discounting some of the things he reported'. It should also be noticed that Dickson departed on leave for Paris on the eve of the Ardennes offensive. The historian Peter Caddick-Adams observes that if the colonel had been sure the Germans were about to attack, he would certainly not have quit First Army's headquarters at such a moment, even though he was encouraged to take a break.

MI6's report on the Ardennes surprise was circulated on 28 December 1944. 'It can be stated at once,' this said, 'that Source [Ultra] gave clear warning that a counter-offensive was coming. He also gave warning, though at rather short notice, of *when* it was coming. He did not give by any means unmistakable indications of where it was coming, nor ... of its full scale. This was largely due to new and elaborate deceptions staged by

German security. German planning ... must have been greatly helped by
the insecurity of certain Allied signals ... It is a little startling to find that
the Germans had a better knowledge of US Order of Battle from their
Signals Intelligence than we had of German order of battle from [Ultra].

'There does exist in Intelligence, of which the present is a serious example, the tendency to become too wedded to one view of enemy intentions.
It had grown to be generally believed that the Germans would counter-at-
tack, head on, when we had pushed them hard enough, probably in the
Roer sector with its dams. This idea died hard ... Unless Intelligence is
perpetually ready to entertain all the alternatives, it seems only the
evidence that favours the chosen view ... There is a risk of relying too
much on [Ultra]. His very successes in the past constitute a danger, if they
lead to waiting for further information because "Source will tell us that",
or to doubting the likelihood of something happening because "Source
would have told us that" ... The Germans have this time prevented us from
knowing enough about them; but we have not prevented them from
knowing far too much about us.'

This was an impressively candid document – a tribute to the objectivity
with which the Allied intelligence community and high command did
most of their business. It is hard to improve on its judgements seventy
years later, though it would have been graceful if Broadway had acknowledged that, in the absence of any useful material from agents of its own,
the Allied armies' commanders had little choice save to rely upon Ultra for
their assessments. Bill Williams wrote a few months after the Ardennes,
acknowledging that he shared with Strong and the JIC responsibility for
an egregious lapse: 'The record is not impressive ... On the Ardennes
offensive we were wrong ... We gave a lead, but the wrong lead ... The
error did not lie with the Park [Bletchley], but rather in our attitude to the
Park.'

Yet if the Battle of the Bulge gave the Allies a devastating shock, what
mattered in the end was that the Germans lost it. During the months that
followed, Wehrmacht intelligence atrophied in step with everything else
in Hitler's armies. Col. Alexis von Rönne of FHW had been arrested and
executed for his role in the failed July bomb plot against Hitler. He was
succeeded as German intelligence chief in the West by Col. Willi Burklein.
In the absence of high-level decrypts, captured documents became the
most prized German sources, of which the September 'Market Garden'
plan, taken from a dead US officer on a Dutch landing zone in the first
hours of the operation, was the most notable, and exercised an important

influence in making possible that German victory. This was a rare success, however. FHW became so starved of resources, as well as of intelligence, that when tons of American documents fell into Burklein's hands during the Bulge battle, most of them never even got translated.

German intelligence continued wildly to overestimate Anglo-American strength, as it had been doing for at least two years. In October 1944, FHW estimated that fourteen divisions of the British Army were still poised at home, awaiting commitment to the European campaign. In truth there were none; existing British formations were being cannibalised to maintain the shrinking strengths of Montgomery's units. But the Germans were haunted by a belief in Churchill's hidden reserve, which caused them to fear an amphibious landing behind their flank, perhaps in Heligoland Bight – evidence of 'Fortitude's' lingering influence. Finally, of course, the Germans were crippled by battlefield weakness. During the Ardennes battle, Albert Praun's eavesdroppers broke into the US Military Police net. They knew that the white helmets were stationed at important road junctions – ideal targets for Luftwaffe assault. Yet the airmen shrugged that not a plane could be spared for such missions. The Germans lacked means to act, even when they discovered things.

In the last months of the struggle against Hitler, Ultra delivered an unprecedented volume of decrypts to Allied commanders – 25,000 were dispatched from Bletchley to British and American Special Liaison Units between January 1944 and May 1945, many of these during the final stages of the campaign. Copious strength and casualty reports, documents recording fuel states and tank serviceability were intercepted, but few made much impact on the battlefield when German capacity to take the initiative was spent. The challenge for Eisenhower's armies was merely to drive small forces of weary but stubborn enemy soldiers out of fixed positions. Moreover, in the mood of hubris prevailing as victory loomed, Allied commanders lost interest in studying the enemy's motions, and in attempting to deceive him about their own. 'Deception during these closing months seems to have been an unsatisfactory and largely unsuccessful affair,' wrote the British official historian, Michael Howard. 'Few of the commanders of the huge new forces committed to battle fully understood what their deception staffs could be expected to do … Most important of all, Allied strategy itself was so opportunistic … that no serious cover plans could be made … The Allies were so strong that they effectively dispensed with strategy altogether and simply attacked all along the line, much as they had done in the closing months of 1918.'

Bletchley suffered one last alarm call: in the course of 1944 the Luftwaffe, whose traffic had been the easiest to break since 1940, introduced a new rewirable reflector on its Enigma – *UmkehrwalzeD*, christened 'Uncle Dick' by Bletchley – which threatened to render the bombes incapable of reading its wheel settings until the changed wirings were identified and applied. The flurry of alarm this development provoked among the code-breakers caused the Americans to embark on a crash effort to produce technology to overcome it, but the war ended before it became necessary. The Luftwaffe innovation emphasised that the Germans might at any stage have made modest changes to the Enigma and its manner of use which would have rendered its signals impervious to Allied penetration. It was a miracle that they had not done so.

The final significant intelligence issue of the war in the West was a chimera: Eisenhower's headquarters were disturbed for weeks by the possibility that the Nazis would stage a last-ditch stand in an 'Alpine redoubt'. It was a measure of the Allies' profound respect for the fighting power of Hitler's legions that, even as their survivors bled to death amid the ashes of the Third Reich, they could still inspire fear in their conquerors.

19

Black Widows, Few White Knights

1 FIGHTING JAPAN

The war in Asia and the Pacific embraced four vast theatres, wherein the only common factor was the participation of the Japanese. In the central Pacific, Nimitz's patch, during the year following Joe Rochefort's triumph at Midway, codebreaking played only a marginal role, because the Japanese navy's higher ciphers mostly defied penetration in real time. While Ultra in Europe became from 1943 onwards plentiful, if never comprehensive, progress with breaking Japan's codes was slower and more erratic, partly because some manually encrypted enemy army traffic proved less vulnerable than Enigma. It has been suggested that Arlington Hall made a strategic mistake by focusing too many resources on reading Purple traffic, which had been broken and offered little intelligence directly relevant to the battlefield, and insufficient skilled manpower on the huge problem of Japanese military communications.

Sigint contributed to some 1942–43 naval battles, but achieved maturity only in 1944–45, and even then never influenced a single action as dramatically as it had done at Midway. During the Solomons and New Hebrides campaigns, for instance, coast-watchers played a more important role than Hypo at Pearl Harbor: the heroic Australian Paul Mason, a plantation manager on Bougainville, provided wireless warning of incoming Japanese air attacks during the long struggle for Guadalcanal. The Allied naval disaster at Savo in August 1942 reflected continuing American difficulties with the enemy's JN-25 cipher. Better information became available later that month for the Battle of the East Solomons, but all through the savage, costly naval actions the rest of that year and into 1943, Nimitz's squadrons often groped for their enemies. No major US strategic decision in the Pacific during 1943 was significantly influenced by Ultra.

Bletchley Park had a small Japanese section, a Cinderella whose staff were frequently frustrated to discover that they had spent hours or days breaking signals already read in Washington – GC&CS's communications and intercept facilities were much inferior to those of the US Navy. BP's branches outside Delhi, and at the Colombo headquarters of South-East Asia Command, addressed themselves almost entirely to studying Japanese traffic in British operational areas. In March 1943, Arlington Hall made the first break into a higher Japanese army system – the so-called Water Transport Code, which soon yielded fifty to a hundred decrypts a day. The British in Delhi achieved their own entry to it at about the same time, but thereafter – not without considerable hand-wringing – they relinquished the lead on Japanese material to the Americans. John Hurt, one of SIS's veteran Japanese linguists at Arlington Hall, asserted after the war that even as late as 1944 and early 1945 codebreaking was 'performed rather inefficiently'. It is a fundamental reality of the Pacific and Asian war that the Allies never enjoyed anything like the strength of sigint coverage they achieved in Europe.

From 1942 onwards the US Navy's cryptographic operations expanded on a similar scale to those of the US Army, and likewise shifted out of Washington – to Mount Vernon Academy in Virginia. An eleven-month crash Japanese language course was established at Boulder, Colorado, which by 1945 had processed a thousand students. Much codebreaking activity took place in the US rather than abroad, because Mount Vernon, like Arlington Hall, possessed batteries of machines – in addition to bombes, it had two hundred IBM tabulators by 1945, up from sixteen in December 1941 – that were unavailable in such quantity in overseas theatres. Increasing numbers of women WAVES were recruited to operate the machines, after solemn inaugural briefings in the Navy Chapel, warning them that if they spoke of their work outside the Annex, they were liable to be shot. The egregious Captain Joseph Redman continued as director of naval communications, with a few months' break in 1942, while his brother John filled an influential role in the office of the chief of naval operations; both contributed unhelpfully to the Allied war effort.

Nimitz ran his own intelligence operation at Pearl Harbor as an almost independent fiefdom, much expanded from Rochefort's original Hypo, renamed FRUPAC – Fleet Radio Unit Pacific – supposedly working with Commander Rudolph Fabian's Cast station at Melbourne, though collaboration was never Fabian's forte. In April 1943 FRUPAC's staff were transferred from the Dungeon to a new building, sunnier and healthier, with an air-conditioned machine room, close to the rim of the Makalapa Crater, and also to Nimitz's headquarters. The labours of the codebreakers and translators remained as relentless as ever, entrusted exclusively to service personnel, albeit often civilians in uniform. Shortages of qualified staff bedevilled all Allied sigint activities, and Jasper Holmes felt that the Pearl operation suffered from the C-in-C's ban on women. Nimitz considered their presence a breach of naval custom and discipline, even ashore, yet when women belatedly joined FRUPAC in the last weeks of the war they made a significant contribution.

The challenge posed by the successive variations of the Japanese navy's main code, JN-25, was enormous. From August 1942 onwards, the additive books for most of the ciphers contained 100,000 entries, changed every sixty days. In all there were ten codebooks and at least seventy-seven ciphers. Until the cryptanalysts had seen a significant volume of messages at the beginning of each new period, showing the most used additives, it was impossible to make much of a start on reading traffic. It is less surprising that it took so long to achieve ongoing penetration of Japanese communications than that this happened at all. Some early fruits were seen in January 1944, when almost all of Nimitz's subordinate commanders expected and advocated progressive assaults on the outer islands of the Marshall group. Instead, the admiral decreed that his forces would drive headlong for the key atoll of Kwajalein, because he knew from Ultra that the Japanese were weakening its garrison to strengthen the outer islands. The subsequent 30 January invasion was a brilliant success. Thereafter, Nimitz was generally aware of his enemies' deployments, except when wireless silence was imposed on their warship sailings.

More Japanese language specialists slowly became available – eighty-four were deployed in the field with the Okinawa invasion force in April 1945, and FRUPAC produced 127 tons of intelligence material about every known topographical feature and defensive position on the island, for distribution afloat and ashore. No quantity of such information, however, could spare the Americans from desperate fighting in the 1944–45 campaigns. The US Army and Marine Corps found themselves battering at Japanese defensive positions, the locations and subtleties of which they were ignorant, because these were neither visible to reconnaissance aircraft and photographic interpreters, nor revealed by enemy signal traffic.

The most important achievement of Ultra in the Pacific in 1943–44 was to empower Nimitz's submarine flotillas to launch the most devastating assault in maritime history against Japan's overseas commerce, lifeblood of its home industries. The 'Maru' cipher, by which the merchant service communicated, was broken in 1943, and ever more warship traffic was read. A direct telephone link from FRUPAC to the submarine operational headquarters enabled the codebreakers instantly to forward intelligence on Japanese convoy movements – and to receive news of consequent sinkings, which helped the intelligence staff to feel in touch with the outcomes of their travails. FRUPAC made possible such a signal as that dispatched at 8 a.m. on 9 June 1943 to the submarines *Trigger* and *Salmon* patrolling the Japanese Inland Sea:

ANOTHER HOT ULTRA COMSUBPAC SERIAL 27 LARGEST AND NEWEST NIP CARRIER WITH TWO DESTROYERS DEPARTS YOKOSUKA AT 5 HOURS GMT 10 JUNE AND CRUISES AT 22 KNOTS ON COURSE 155 DEGREES UNTIL REACHING 33.55 NORTH 140 EAST WHERE THEY REDUCE SPEED TO 18 KNOTS AND CHANGE COURSE TO 230 DEGREES X SALMON AND TRIGGER INTERCEPT IF POSSIBLE AND WATCHING FOR EACH OTHER. WE HAVE ADDITIONAL DOPE ON THIS CARRIER FOR THE BOYS NEAR TRUK WHICH WE HOPE WE WONT NEED SO LET US KNOW IF YOU GET HIM.

The British would have considered such a signal a reckless breach of Ultra security, because it was sent to low-level personnel in an operational area, but the Americans got away with this one, and many more like it. Commander John Cromwell refused the chance of escape from his own doomed boat *Sculpin*, to join his crew in Japanese captivity, because as he said laconically, 'I can't go with you. I know too much.' About Ultra was what he meant, of course. *Trigger* indeed attacked on the night of 10 June at point-blank range, badly damaging the Japanese carrier *Hiyo*, but torpedo failures, the blight of the US Navy in 1943, prevented its sinking. Only when this deficiency was belatedly made good did it become possible for Nimitz's submarines to strangle enemy supply lines, as well as sink many warships. In 1942 the Japanese lost a million tons of merchant shipping to all causes. By 1945 ten times that tonnage was gone. Between January and April 1944, US submarines sent to the bottom 179 ships totalling 799,000 tons, and by the end of August a further 219 vessels. When the Japanese sought to dispatch two army divisions from Shanghai to New Guinea in April, the so-called 'Bamboo 1' convoy carrying the troops was almost wiped out at sea, and eventually abandoned the attempt to reinforce New Guinea. Even before the USAAF launched its intensive sea-mining campaign in the last months of the war, the Japanese merchant fleet had been largely destroyed by submarine attack.

It was often difficult to judge how, or whether at all, to exploit sensitive information. In April 1944, FRUPAC learned that the trawler *Tajina Maru*, a vessel deliberately chosen by the enemy for its insignificance, was carrying the Japanese navy's new codes to Wake Island. Two US submarines were dispatched to capture *Tajina Maru* – but instead blew it to pieces. Jasper Holmes and his colleagues fumed, regretting that an intelligence officer had not been put aboard one of the submarines to supervise the operation and ensure the trawler's seizure intact. An American intelligence officer, Commander Kenneth Knowles, said after the war, "The British were more clever in use [of Ultra], we more daring.' Jasper Holmes wrote: 'Intelligence, like money, may be secure when it is unused and locked up in a safe, but it yields no dividends until it is invested.' It was this conviction that led the Americans to override British security scruples and launch a ferocious assault on U-boat refuelling rendezvous in the summer of 1943, which inflicted dramatic losses on Dönitz's fleet. Likewise in the Pacific, one of the more dramatic US Navy coups was prompted by a May 1944 decrypt forwarded from FRUPAC, allocating new patrol positions to all Japanese submarines off the Solomons. Armed with this information, a destroyer escort group led by the USS *England* sank six enemy vessels in twelve days. Kenneth Knowles was gracious enough to add to his post-war remarks about British caution in exploiting Ultra: 'But they had more to lose.' Which was true.

Nimitz was a wise man, MacArthur was not. This helps to explain why Ultra exercised only marginal influence on America's South-West Pacific campaign against Japan. The general rejected the War Department's intelligence system and instead established his own 'Central Bureau', first in Melbourne, later at Hollandia and Leyte. MacArthur banned all OSS personnel from his theatre, though he backed guerrilla activity in the Philippines, provoking predictably brutal Japanese reprisals. His intelligence chief Maj. Gen. Charles Willoughby, whose pomposity caused him to be known to subordinates as 'Sir Charles', was no cleverer than the supremo's other courtiers, and held sigint in some contempt. Instead of the Special Liaison Units the US Army adopted in the European theatre for handling and protecting Ultra, MacArthur instead allowed his staff to handle decrypts with a casualness that would have appalled Allied officers anywhere else in the world. Documents, personnel and even office furniture were openly addressed to 'The Ultra Section', and officers freely discussed codebreaking.

Sigint influenced three important events in the South-West Pacific campaign: the 1943 Kokoda Trail battles in Papua-New Guinea; the March 1944 decision to leapfrog six hundred miles forward to Hollandia; and the July defeat of the Japanese assault down the Driniumor river, which cost the enemy 9,000 dead. In each of these actions Ultra – in 1944 assisted by 9th Australian Division's capture of a pile of the Japanese 20th Division's buried codebooks in New Guinea – flagged the enemy's intentions and vulnerabilities, though MacArthur, in the same fashion as Montgomery, afterwards attributed the Allied victories to his own clairvoyance. His USAAF officers adopted a more enlightened view. Maj. Gen. George Kenney, who commanded 5th Air Force, was an exceptionally able airman who used sigint to good effect, especially for attacking Japanese reinforcement convoys, and most notably in the March 1943 Battle of the Bismarck Sea. Familiar inter-service feuding caused the US Navy to refuse to provide Ultra material to Gen. Claire Chennault, commanding the USAAF's 14th Air Force in China. The British eventually forwarded such material to him via SEAC headquarters in Colombo, which improved air targeting of Japanese shipping in the last phase of the war.

The Burma campaign was of marginal relevance to the defeat of Japan, but mattered immensely to the self-esteem of the British, and especially to the struggle to regain possession of their South-East Asian empire. Britain's generals in the theatre complained loudly and often about the weakness of battlefield intelligence, both humint and sigint. Beyond the many Anglo–American tensions and disputes, the officers of SOE and MI6 were barely on speaking terms with each other, and intelligence-gathering was poor. In the summer of 1943 Lt. Col. Gerald Wilkinson, MI6's liaison officer on MacArthur's staff, wrote in his diary: 'Far East intelligence from [Britain's secret service] has now dwindled to a trickle from a few Chinese coolies.' Admiral Lord Louis Mountbatten, the Supreme Commander, urged MI6 to abandon its fumbling efforts to secure intelligence about the Japanese, and instead concentrate on studying the various regional nationalist movements, which would obviously play a critical role in determining post-war outcomes.

Latterly SOE had 1,250 personnel in Asia and MI6 175, but few of them commanded much confidence. The local MI6 chief, a soldier named Lt. Col. Leo Steveni, was a typical Broadway placeman, who became a laughing stock at SEAC meetings and ran his operations out of Delhi because he knew that Mountbatten in Colombo had no time for him. Steveni was finally sacked in July 1944, but his replacement was no improvement – a 16th Lancers officer named Brigadier 'Bogey' Bowden-Smith, who took the job after a chance meeting in Boodle's Club, where he mentioned that he was out of a job because he was thought too old to command troops in the field. Mountbatten's intelligence coordinator, a Royal Navy captain, deplored the chaos that stemmed from lack of unified control: 'Two characteristics are always present in personnel of Clandestine Services. The first is jealousy and the second is what I would describe as scoop-mindedness.'

Operational commanders felt severely hampered by shortage of intelligence, and above all sigint. Esler Dening, Mountbatten's influential political adviser, wrote to the JIC in London on 29 September 1944: 'Do we know, or am I just not being told, what the Japanese intentions are in Burma, bearing in mind that they upset the whole of our offensive-defensive plans earlier this year and that a good deal of their movement passed unnoticed?' – Dening here referred to the ferocious Japanese thrusts against Kohima and Imphal. 'If we do not know, then if I were the Army Group commander I should be very unhappy to go into battle with an enemy disposed I know not how, and of whose full intentions I am equally ignorant. No doubt there is a limit to what the Japanese can do today with the land forces available to them in Burma, but past experience has shown that it is both inconvenient and decidedly unpleasant when they do the unexpected. You will remember my saying the other day that it was never wise to assume that the Japanese will not do a thing because it seems stupid to us.'

Maj. Gen. Lamplough, Mountbatten's director of intelligence, summarised his own view in a signal to the JIC in London on 1 October 1944: 'What we know and what we don't know: We know the total strength of the Japanese Army, Air Force and Navy in SEAC. We also know the composition of these forces in sufficient detail. We also know the location of the more important H.Q.'s ... We can usually tell if and when reinforcements are likely to come into SEAC. All the above is from SIGINT. We do not know Japanese intentions.' Bill Slim, commanding Fourteenth Army, complained about the shortage of battlefield information at the end of 1943, and renewed his protests in November 1944. He said that OSS seemed to be doing a better job than MI6 in securing information about the enemy. He urged ending the interminable wrangling among clandestine organisations by merging them – a proposal that prompted a closing of ranks among them all, for rejection. Gen. Sir Oliver Leese delivered a similar broadside a month later, messaging Mountbatten's headquarters: 'As you know I am most disturbed by the lack of intelligence.' He told his own senior intelligence officer that he was 'exceedingly dissatisfied with [Intelligence] … very dissatisfied with the Sigint side, which compares most unfavourably with the situation in Europe'. He also complained that the various intelligence organisations refused to accept briefs from the army about what it needed to know.

Some of the problems derived from the fact that the Japanese used wireless much less than the Germans; their forward elements communicated sparingly with rear headquarters. Moreover, even in Europe the Germans did not always oblige Bletchley Park by telling the Allies through Enigma or Tunny what they intended to do next. Beyond this, the Americans led the codebreaking campaign against the Japanese, and thus the Pacific was inevitably the focus of their interest, while the British struggled to read relevant South-East Asian traffic. The British and Americans each ran an industrial-scale intercept station outside Delhi, and the Royal Navy had a Colombo facility, HMS *Anderson*, where by March 1944 1,300 staff handled two hundred enemy messages a day. The Japanese Water Transport Code yielded a steady flow of order-of-battle intelligence. But the British codebreakers' labours were hampered by a chronic shortage of language specialists, and Royal Navy intelligence officers suffered the same problem as their American counterparts: cryptanalysis was a career dead-end. Colombo received only grudging cooperation from the US Navy's Cmdr Rudy Fabian in Melbourne, and never really recovered its balance after successive 1942 evacuations first from Singapore to Ceylon, then briefly to East Africa, and back to Ceylon again.

Leese's denunciation of the shortage of sigint prompted a response from Bletchley Park on 22 December 1944 which frankly acknowledged the difficulties the British faced in reading Japanese wireless traffic. Edward Travis, GC&CS's chief, said that nothing like the same number of staff, and especially linguists, were available to address Japanese signals as German ones. While Britain was well endowed with fluent German-speakers, there were precious few familiar with Japanese. Although cooperation with the Americans was excellent, 'there is no question that it is not so rapid and effective to deal with problems between parties 3,000 miles apart, with a front which stretches half across the globe, as it has been with the compact

European theatre, which has been an all-British effort, at least in the vital early stages'.

Travis then addressed the technical problems, which, he said, were entirely different from those posed by the German systems: 'The Japanese do not at present use machines for ciphering military or air force signals. They use code books and then extremely tough enciphering methods to conceal the coded text ... The upshot is that the work of producing a Japanese text is long and laborious, that only a percentage of messages ever become readable.' He admitted that only fragments of a small proportion of traffic became available in real time: 'Even their divisional systems are very difficult and such as can never be handled in the field as we have handled German field ciphers. On the Army side nothing is intercepted below division for nothing is audible [by the Y Service], even to units pushed right up into the line.' Finally, and significantly, he said that the taciturn Japanese were nothing like as accommodating as the Germans, who frequently transmitted comprehensive situation reports: 'The Japanese do not as a rule pass high-level appreciations and future intentions by signal. Their intentions strategically have to be assessed therefore from indirect evidence.' Here was an authoritative statement of the weakness of Allied sigint operations against the Japanese. The British were receiving even less Ultra than the Americans of a kind which provided direct assistance to their troops on the battlefield. Both Allied armies were usually well informed about overall Japanese strengths. But – given that prisoner interrogation was usually an unprofitable activity – by comparison with the European theatre commanders depended for much of their intelligence on pre-sigint methods: patrolling, air reconnaissance, and painful experience in contact with the enemy.

The British in Burma, when their Fourteenth Army began its 1944–45 campaign to recapture the colony, expended considerable efforts on deception, run by Col. Peter Fleming, brother of journalist Ian and himself at that time much more famous, as a pre-war adventurer and travel writer, and husband of the hugely popular actress Celia Johnson. Fleming wrote gleefully on 9 October 1944, reflecting on the exaggerated notions of Japanese army headquarters in Burma about Allied strengths: 'Their margin of error, until recently slightly in excess of 100 per cent, is likely to increase during the coming months.' He reported that his own team had a large imaginary British army, ready for deployment: 'Experience has shown that the mere existence of these forces in our back areas has little influence on [the Japanese].' He suggested moving these fictional forces onto the battlefield, to intimidate the enemy into a belief that they faced overwhelming odds.

Such games as these gave pleasure to the officers involved, but there is little evidence that they influenced the battlefield, save at one important moment when Slim successfully deceived the Japanese about his February 1945 crossing of the Irrawaddy, feinting in the north while making his big move in the south. It was almost impossible to run useful deceptions against an enemy high command which conducted military operations with almost no heed for its own intelligence department, and which deemed it an affront to the Japanese warrior code to allow its own strategic decisions to be influenced by what the Allies might or might not be doing.

2 FIGHTING EACH OTHER

Throughout the Asian war, a parallel internecine struggle took place between officers of the rival secret services of Britain and America. Much British intelligence material was marked 'Guard' – not to be shown to Americans – and many US documents were stamped 'Control' – to be hidden from British eyes. Esler Dening, Mountbatten's political adviser, wrote in June 1944: 'It is a melancholy and disquieting fact that the brotherhood in arms of the United States and ourselves in the Far Eastern war has been accompanied by a steady deterioration in … collaboration … which is adversely affecting the prosecution of the war.' In February 1945 Lt. Gen. Frederick 'Boy' Browning, Mountbatten's chief of staff, wrote savagely: 'I have yet to meet the senior officer who can bear with equanimity the trials and tribulations inflicted on a suffering world by the clandestine organisations.'

Unpalatable local realities made SOE's task almost impossibly difficult. Whereas in the countries of occupied Europe Allied agents could expect assistance from at least enthusiastic minorities among local populations, this was not the case in South-East Asia. British defeats in 1941–42 had shattered imperial prestige, a centuries-old myth of Western invincibility. Attempts to conduct covert operations in Japanese-occupied Burma and Malaya laid bare the colonial rulers' unpopularity: many inhabitants betrayed the British agents and special operations teams thrust into their midst. Thoughtful officers understood that it was a mockery to talk of 'liberating' South-East Asia when its peoples might have learned to hate and fear the Japanese for their brutality, yet wanted no resumption of British, French or Dutch rule. Freddy Spencer Chapman of SOE, who survived for three years in occupied Malaya, vividly described the embarrassment of living among, and relying for his survival upon, people who had lost all confidence in Britain.

SOE's headquarters in the subcontinent was located in a rambling cluster of bungalows outside Colombo known as Mount Lavinia, guarded by New Zealand Maoris. A report on the prospects for stay-behind operations in India, compiled in the dark days of March 1942 when enemy invasion seemed imminent, asserted gloomily: 'The effect of Japanese successes has been enormous in this country. Any operations carried out by the Army, or by ourselves [SOE] in the great bulk of Bengal, will be carried out in an essentially hostile country ... There is no conviction so strongly fixed in the Oriental mind as that he must choose the winning side, and if he can choose it slightly earlier than his fellow-man, so much the better for him.' Gen. Sir Archibald Wavell, as commander-in-chief, took a bleak view of SOE. He said that he had thought little of its performance in the Middle East, and was even less impressed in Asia: 'Insofar as SOE is known out here, its reputation does not stand high. It is considered to have been an expensive and substantial failure.'

Matters looked no more promising in August, when Baker Street's formidable local chieftain Colin Mackenzie, who commanded useful backing through his friendship with the viceroy Lord Linlithgow, set about training 150 Indian communist students as stay-behind agents. The police insisted that the loyalty of these young men should be tested, by briefing them on the whereabouts of secret British arms dumps, with instructions not to go near these unless or until the Japanese were at hand. The students responded by staging an immediate rush for the weapons, which caused the programme to be shut down. This was only the beginning, however. The historian Richard Aldrich has written: 'The ambitions of Mackenzie and SOE in the Far East were without limit.' Once the British and American secret services realised that they could contribute little to the defeat of Japan, both focused their energies on the advancement of rival post-war commercial, political and strategic interests. Aldrich suggests, on good evidence, that SOE's men saw themselves as 'shock troops for reasserting control of the empire'.

So did OSS. Its Research & Analysis division contained a British Empire section which was virulently anti-colonialist. William Donovan wrote scathingly on 27 October 1944 that Britain's strategy was to recover South-East Asia 'making the fullest possible use of American resources, but foreclosing the Americans from any voice in policy matters'. Many of

Donovan's men, together with some senior officers of the US Army, strove to prevent the British, French or Dutch from regaining control of their Asian empires. Less moralistically, and as the British were keenly aware, the Americans sought to use their resources and clout to carve out post-war commercial advantage for the US, and wherever possible to diminish that of Britain.

The two allies incessantly lied to each other. Colonel John Coughlin, Donovan's chieftain first in India then at SEAC, told his boss that its operations were 'not only important in defeating the Japs but may also be considered in part as cover for an opportunity to serve as a listening post for American interests in Asia' – and to monitor the activities of British secret organisations, which Coughlin did with a will. Meanwhile the British ambassador in China blandly assured his US counterpart that Britain had no interest in the future of Thailand, when of course it did – with an especially keen appetite for appropriating the Kra isthmus. Donovan sought to use his own officers to secure an opening in Thailand for US post-war commercial penetration. The supposedly neutral Thais arrested both OSS and SOE officers indiscriminately and collected them in jails until June 1944, when Bangkok deemed it politic to allow them to make contact with their respective headquarters.

With fourteen British and American clandestine organisations represented in South-East Asia, competition to recruit agents in Japanese-occupied territory resulted in what one officer deplored fastidiously as 'an undignified scramble for indigenous personnel'. In the Dutch East Indies there were allegations that some locals had been enlisted at gunpoint. After the Japanese occupied Malaya, during 1942 they rounded up and executed several thousand real or supposed British stay-behind agents and sympathisers. Thereafter Allied covert operations in the country became overwhelmingly dependent on Chinese communists, including Lai Tek, their pre-war party secretary general, who was almost certainly a double agent serving Tokyo.

Local support for British activities in occupied territory did not much increase even when Allied fortunes improved. An SOE party parachuted into the Kokang area of Burma in December 1943, and reinforced in June 1944, succeeded in staying alive and patrolling west of the Salween river, but failed absolutely to rouse the local population to participate in a resistance movement. Its report concluded: 'Local opposition restricted the party in carrying out the original tasks of arming and training guerrillas,' and it was evacuated in October 1944. Two British officers dropped into

Karen territory in October 1943 were killed, whereupon Major Hugh Seagrim, an almost saintly figure who had stayed behind in the area since the 1942 retreat, gave himself up to the Japanese in an attempt to spare the local people from reprisals. The towering, bearded Seagrim, six feet four inches tall and dressed in the rags of the Karen costume he had worn for so long, stood erect as he addressed a Japanese court-martial at Insein, north of Rangoon. 'I obey the orders of my country, as a British officer,' he said, 'and I have merely carried out my duty. I have no complaints at being sentenced to death. But the men with me merely carried out my orders, and I ask you to declare them not guilty.' His plea failed. When he was shot on 2 September 1944, his seven Karen companions were also executed.

Even as late in the war as January 1945, when yet another team – 'Group Burglar' – parachuted into Burma east of Pyminama, 'the party was hampered by the hostility of the local population and had continually to keep on the move'. The commander of SOE's Force 136 minuted with authentic imperial condescension on 2 April 1945: 'The local inhabitant has neither the patriotic motive nor in most cases the education and intelligence to make him an adequate secret agent ... Europeans cannot mingle with the local population in the same way as infiltrated secret agents in Europe. A much larger local proportion of the population has been neutral or even hostile, so that chance of survival of secret agents is thereby made more difficult.' MI6 reported at the same period that in Malaya locals would provide no help with intelligence-gathering, nor assist any organisation they could not themselves control. A post-war report on SOE operations in the Dutch East Indies noted: 'No contact with resistance movements in Sumatra was made by Force 136 ... Intelligence indicated that the population was collaborating with the Japanese and the prospect of successful clandestine operations was small.' The dominant reality of British covert operations across the areas of South-East Asia occupied by the Japanese was that few local people were willing to risk ghastly reprisals to aid representatives of discredited, disliked and apparently defeated imperial powers, and this changed little even in the last months of the war. SOE achieved its only important successes in paramilitary operations against the Japanese in the wild tribal regions of northern Burma, whose inhabitants were chronically alienated from their fellow-countrymen of the plains.

Even as SOE strove to justify its existence in Britain's Japanese-occupied colonies, its officers sustained their wider struggle with the Americans. In June 1942, OSS and SOE had apportioned the globe into regions acknowledged respectively as predominantly British or American for the purpose of special operations, with equal rights for both in Spain, Portugal and Switzerland. China was defined as chiefly American, and Donovan's men fought like tigers to make it exclusively so. SOE and OSS waged a continuous turf war there, and neither contributed much to the defeat of the Japanese, beyond rescuing some downed aircrew and escaped PoWs. In Washington, however, OSS exercised more political influence on Far East matters than on most others. For about a year from the spring of 1944, Donovan's officers attached to the so-called 'Dixie Mission' in Yenan province became the Roosevelt administration's principal source of information about Mao Zhedong's communists, though thereafter the OSS China group lost its clout in high places. Allied intelligence activity in the Nationalist regions was not assisted by the need for obsessive caution in preventing Ultra material, and indeed anything sensitive, from reaching Chongqing, because the Japanese read almost all the Chiang regime's cipher traffic, despite repeated warnings about its insecurity. Before D-Day in 1944 the British felt obliged to withdraw the cipher privileges of the Chinese embassy in London, even though Chiang was supposedly a formal ally, because it was well known that whenever the ambassador saw a British general or politician, within days a transcript of their conversation was on desks in Tokyo as well as Chongqing.

French Indochina witnessed the most intense Anglo–American conflict of all. OSS officers were determined to prevent France from regaining control of its cherished colony, while the British strove to assist the French cause. The clash plunged to a symbolic nadir on the night of 23 January 1945, when P-61 Black Widow night-fighters of the US 14th Air Force appear to have shot down two RAF Liberators carrying French agents into Indochina, with the loss of all on board. The Americans hoped that the episode would prove a salutary warning, deterring the British from providing any further help to France, but in the first two months of 1945 the RAF flew seventy-one Special Duties sorties to Indochina, some of them carrying French officers in defiance of an explicit veto from the White House. Churchill, probably wisely, decided to avoid a direct confrontation with FDR about the issue, and a British investigation into the loss of the Liberators was abandoned. In the last months of the war, both London and Washington despaired of imposing order on their nations' clandestine operations in South-East Asia, and left the officers on the ground to fight it out – which they did, to no conclusive outcome.

By 1945 there were few delusions among intelligence chiefs about the failure of SOE's mission in the old Asian colonies as standard-bearers for the restoration of British rule. The depth of the divide between the European imperial powers and the Americans was also plain. On 26 April the Political Warfare Executive discussed the prospects at a meeting in London. It recommended that spokesmen 'should admit frankly the loss of prestige in empire: this grave situation must be repaired by implanting the conviction in the oriental mind that the people of the British Commonwealth of Nations have in fact contributed decisively to the defeat of Japan ... Unfortunately this task is one of considerable difficulty, since our American Allies are playing the major and the spectacular role ... Successfully emancipated colonials themselves, Americans itch to free others from the yoke under which, they feel, they once groaned ... We are thought to be returning [to liberated colonies in South-East Asia] under the aegis of our American Allies who are known to orientals to be funda-mentally opposed to a great deal for which we, as an Asiatic power, neces-sarily stand ... Only by skilful manipulation ... can we hope to regain our lost prestige.' In another similar paper, the authors urged with shameless cynicism that Britain's liberators should be less than explicit about acknowledging their commitment to restore imperial rule: 'we should make as much capital as possible out of not defining precisely the details of the future set-up'. By the summer of 1945, the Japanese had become the least formidable of Britain's foes in South-East Asia.

3 THE ENEMY: GROPING IN THE DARK

Bizarre though it seems to Westerners, for much of the Second World War the Soviet Union and China – where most of the Japanese army was deployed – loomed larger than the United States and Britain in the minds of Tokyo's decision-makers. They sought to conduct the war they wanted, rather than the one they had got. The army originally planned for the Pacific struggle to end in the spring of 1942, with the Americans accepting peace terms, whereupon Japan would fall upon the carcass of the Soviet Union. On 14 January that year, the Operations Department in Tokyo told the Kwantung army in Manchuria to expect to receive major reinforce-ments by March, in time for the intended assault on Russia. Only in October 1944, after suffering crushing naval defeat at Leyte Gulf, did the Japanese formally recognise the US, rather than the Soviet Union, as its foremost intelligence target. They left their generals to collect whatever information they needed in their own operational areas, with whatever means were to hand. They never exploited clever civilians in anything like the fashion the British and Americans did. The military's hubris was undiminished by early setbacks. Maj. Gen. Kenryo Sato, chief of the Bureau of Military Affairs, made a speech to the Diet in Tokyo in March 1943, after Japan suffered defeat at Guadalcanal, asserting that American troops were undisciplined and amateurish: 'They are good at shooting, but their fighting spirit and morale are very poor ... Most US soldiers do not understand why they are fighting.'

The Japanese were slow to understand the importance of attacking British and American codes – the ease with which they read Chinese Nationalist wireless traffic had perhaps made them slothful. In any event, only in 1943–44 were Japanese officers dispatched to Germany, Hungary and Finland to study codebreaking. In 1943, when Japan's defeat was already looming, the army created the *Tokushu Joho-bu* – Central Special Intelligence Section – to gather sigint, belatedly acknowledging that 'codebreaking activities against the United States and United Kingdom are extremely inadequate, with few qualified staff'. This initially employed three hundred personnel, which swelled to over a thousand by 1945. Several hundred additional intelligence and codebreaking staff served in Manchuria with the Kwantung army, the air forces and field armies. In May 1944 its chief started to recruit graduates in maths and languages, and acquired a few IBM machines. A Military Cryptographical Research Association was created, with some help from Tokyo's Imperial University.

Yet all this was much too little, far too late. Even the emperor expressed bewilderment that the army spent so much time talking about a prospective war against the Russians, when it was fighting an actual one against the Americans. The Japanese claimed for a time to have broken into some US codes in MacArthur's theatre, but these were soon changed. One of the Special Intelligence Section's officers claimed after the war that on 11 August 1945 it had decrypted the word 'nuclear' in a signal sent by an American M-209 cipher machine. Even if this was true, however, it contributed precious little to the Japanese cause, any more than did their intermittent breaks into Soviet traffic.

The Imperial Japanese Navy's intelligence department logged the statistics for its incoming reports from different sources between 1 October 1944 and 19 July 1945, a fair representation of the balance throughout the war: 393 sigint, almost all based on traffic analysis; 102 attaché reports from neutral foreign embassies; twenty-seven from PoW information; two captured documents; seven foreign-agent reports; 110 open-source radio broadcast items; 769 newspaper items. The Japanese had always placed more faith in information acquired through espionage than from sigint, yet they never showed much skill in recruiting and running foreign agents. Commander Nobuiko Imai wrote sourly: 'In New Guinea we hired native Chinese and Australians, but they eventually double-crossed [us].' Tokyo paid substantial sums to informants in Mexico, Chile and Argentina, though it is hard to imagine how these could have contributed to its war effort. The Japanese had no greater luck running agents in British India. Forty-five – the bulk of the crop – were captured in 1942, most of whom proved to have been seconded from Tokyo's Indian National Army, recruited from PoWs in their hands. In 1944 Japanese intelligence started taking a keen interest in Islam as a potential focus for anti-Allied activities. A large party of Muslim saboteurs was landed on the coast of Baluchistan early in 1945 – but promptly surrendered to the British.

Japan's intelligence service tried hard in the continental United States. On 3 May 1944, Tokyo's minister in Madrid sent a melodramatic report to his Foreign Ministry about a Spanish agent who had supposedly been serving Japanese interests in America, and had now returned to Spain to report, since he lacked wireless or a courier: 'I have secretly warned him that since he came home with the woman early in April not only the British and Americans but the Spanish also have been keeping him under close observation. He is therefore acting outwardly as though he had no connection with me at all ... Since it would be as good as signing his death warrant if we were to meet direct, I have instructed him to furnish me with a written report ... [He] is due to return to his duties in America on 17th May and he is going ahead (as matters stand at present the Americans see no objection to his re-entry).'

The attached agent's report was written in the manner of a period thriller: 'Living in an enemy country and collecting information while facing all manner of danger, it was unavoidable that I should have to depend to a great extent on my memory. To ensure accuracy I naturally used special ink and small photographs on every occasion when matters of importance were involved.' Since what followed represented a summary of fourteen months' alleged observation, it was scarcely being delivered in real time. The spy reported, among much else, the fabulous fiction that four US battleships had been sunk in the November 1942 Solomons battles, and devoted several hundred words to listing America's senior commanders and their posts, information readily available in the

Washington Post. There was a final twist: the Japanese agent's dispatch survives only because it was decrypted by Arlington and Bletchley, and has reposed since May 1944 in American and British files.

From 1944 onwards Japanese commanders showed themselves chronically reluctant to consider evidence, preferring instead decision-making by instinct, with a growing appetite for fantasy. The navy devoted even fewer resources to codebreaking than the army, and focused most of its sigint activities on direction-finding and traffic analysis. A Japanese admiral, Rear-Admiral Yokoi Tishiyuji, observed despairingly after the war: 'Our navy was being defeated in the battle of the radio waves. Our cards were bad, and the enemy could read our hand. No wonder we could not win in this poker game.' The IJN nonetheless had some modest code-breaking successes, by monitoring lower-grade American logistics communications. Intelligence officers read about half the 1944–45 BAMS traffic – Broadcast For Allied Merchant Shipping – which enabled them to forecast major US amphibious assaults through tracking the huge support 'tail' that accompanied each one. They anticipated the January 1944 Marshalls operations, the Marianas in June and Iwo Jima in February. Yet the high command chose instead to believe that, rather than go for the Marianas, the Americans would target the Philippines, northern New Guinea and the West Carolines. And even when Japan's admirals and generals correctly anticipated American intentions, they were repeatedly and decisively outfought on land, at sea and in the air. Hard power was lacking.

During the summer and autumn of 1944, the climate of fantasy at imperial headquarters became feverish. US deception activities convinced them that the Americans were building up forces in Alaska with a view to invading the Kuriles. Thus, in June Japanese intelligence estimated that the US had 400,000 men and seven hundred aircraft in Alaska, whereas the true figures were 64,000 and 373. Tokyo increased its own forces in the Kuriles from 25,000 men and thirty-eight aircraft in January to 70,000 and 589 in June. Japan's senior officers chose to believe that the 12–16 October air battles off Taiwan, which devastated their own air force, had cost the US nineteen carriers and four battleships. Japanese radio monitors correctly reported that traffic analysis showed all the elements of Halsey's Third Fleet still afloat – but their views were dismissed as unacceptable. Captain Kaoru Takeuchi of the Intelligence Department raved: 'The staff of the Operations Department are inexcusable ... They are insane! It's unbelievable that the mad officers have their own way.' It was the surge of optimism about American losses off Taiwan that persuaded Japan's admirals to launch the Combined Fleet's Operation 'Ichi-Gō', which ended in disaster at Leyte Gulf.

Yet Leyte prompted an even more frenzied Japanese flight from reality. The Navy Intelligence Department's broadly accurate assessments were ignored, while wildly inflated claims were accepted for the success of kamikaze attacks on US warships. On six occasions the navy's Operations Department declared the carrier *Lexington* sunk, and four times wrote off *Saratoga*. The emperor noticed these reports, and suggested that they might be a trifle fanciful. The army high command relied increasingly for intelligence about the Pacific theatre on its 'Special Information' staff in Harbin, north China, which had a source in the Soviet consular office. Unfortunately, this was controlled by the NKVD. When the intelligence staff realised this, its officers warned the high command, but the generals preferred to believe what Moscow wanted to tell them, rather than any portion of unacceptable truth.

The army's intelligence chief, Gen. Seizo Arisue, deplored the Operations Department's hubris, saying that its officers 'disliked even listening to the opinions of others'. He cited the March 1944 assault on British and Indian forces at Imphal. For once, Arisue had been consulted in advance, but as soon as he expressed strong opposition to the plan he was expelled from imperial headquarters' debate on the operation. The Japanese as a race, according to the 2nd Department's Kiichiro Higuchi, prefer a subjective approach to problem-solving to objective analysis of evidence: 'The affairs of individuals may be determined by subjective criteria, but it is most dangerous to use these to determine the fate of nations.' The most conspicuous example of this came in April 1945, when intelligence warned of a dramatic increase in Soviet military traffic towards the Manchurian border and concluded: 'The 2nd Department concludes that the USSR has already started to prepare for a war against Japan.' Because this represented the worst nightmare of Japan's generals, they dismissed the reports out of hand, and continued to do so until the Red Army launched its overwhelming offensive in Manchuria in August. All Japanese military planning in 1945 assumed an American invasion of their homeland, upon which they believed they could inflict intolerable losses. It is a fine irony that the Western Allies could most plausibly have confounded their enemy's high command by announcing publicly that they did *not* intend to invade Japan, but instead to bomb and starve it into submission.

Whatever difficulties the British and Americans faced in working with each other, these were as nothing compared with the lack of trust, the cultural chasm, dividing the Germans and Japanese. Though the two nations had an intelligence-sharing agreement, little was done to implement it. Senior Wehrmacht intelligence specialists despised their Japanese counterparts. One German officer described them as 'very poor', noting that they often identified an American division as opposing them in the Pacific when Berlin knew that it was in France. Col. Ohletz of the RSHA said after the war that his service had 'an uneasy and unprofitable partnership with the Japanese I[ntelligence] S[ervice]'. Canaris, while he ran the Abwehr, maintained tenuous links with Tokyo. An officer named Hauptmann Plage was retained as Berlin's supposed resident expert on Japan. The Germans passed on to Tokyo fragments – for instance, a report supposedly from a British source (one of MI5's double agents) – about the US landings at Leyte Gulf in September 1944.

As the war situation deteriorated, so too did the relationship between the two allies. Each regarded the cause of the other as doomed, but the Germans strove to keep the Japanese in the fight. OKW urged the RSHA's chiefs to tell their Oriental brethren anything that might stiffen their resolve – for instance, about prospects for the December 1944 Ardennes offensive. One night just after Operation 'Autumn Mist' had been launched, Ernst Kaltenbrunner and Walter Schellenberg hosted a big Japanese party for dinner in a villa on the Wannsee. This was not a success. Col. Ohletz got the impression that the Japanese 'wanted nothing to do with the SD'. Kaltenbrunner emerged asserting contemptuously that 'the Japanese had become so "soft" that, if the [Ardennes] offensive did not succeed, they would probably "rat"'. The Germans nodded contemptuously to each other when, soon afterwards, the Japanese began to evacuate their Berlin embassy archives to Switzerland, Sweden and Spain.

In the spring of 1945 Makoto Onodera, the Stockholm-based head of Japanese intelligence in Europe, made an offer to take over control of the Abwehr's stations in neutral capitals. Seeing the Nazi ship foundering, he observed that the Japanese wanted to take over its intelligence apparatus as a going concern. Yet when Japan had been unwilling or unable to use intelligence effectively since at least 1942, it is hard to imagine what service the Nazis' sclerotic European spy networks could have done for imperial headquarters, as Hirohito's commanders gazed upon the ruin of their own ambitions, and of their empire.

20

'Enormoz'

In 1944, when the young American physicist Ted Hall, working on the atomic bomb project at Santa Fe's Camp 2, told all that he knew to Moscow Centre, he justified himself by saying fervently to his NKVD handler, 'There is no country except for the Soviet Union that could be entrusted with such a terrible thing.' Perhaps fifty of those on both sides of the Atlantic who were privy to the atomic bomb programme surrendered portions of its secrets to the Soviet Union. The betrayal of the Manhattan Project by British and American informants was the most important espionage story of the war. It had no effect on the outcome of the struggle against the Nazis, of course, but a major influence on what happened thereafter: when the first Soviet bomb was exploded in 1949, it proved to be an exact copy of the July 1945 Alamogordo test device. Apologists for Moscow's informants have ever since made two points: first, that with or without the traitors, the Soviet Union would have built its own bomb soon enough, because that is how science and technology evolve around the world; second, that the NKVD's informants performed a service to the cause of peace, because they ensured the creation of a balance of terror, making it impossible for America's right-wing fanatics credibly to advocate a nuclear first strike against the Soviet Union. Both arguments merit consideration. All that seems certain, however, is that the atomic spies dramatically strengthened Stalin's strategic hand, and provided the NKVD with one of the biggest coups in its history.

In 1940 Soviet scientists asserted that the creation of an atomic bomb from uranium was a theoretical, but not a practical, possibility. Moscow allocated no funds to atomic espionage, though the NKVD's scientific desk alerted all foreign stations to be watchful for indications of activity in this field. In the following year the Russians received a series of reports from British informants, John Cairncross notable among them, about work on uranium-based weapons, based on clues from meetings of the British chiefs of staff and the Uranium Committee. An NKVD officer in London, Vladimir Barkovsky, was assigned to address the issue. On 16 September 1940, Donald Maclean forwarded a sixty-page report on the project the British had codenamed 'Tube Alloys'. This suggested that Churchill's government was taking seriously the nuclear possibilities, though another British source, in the laboratories of ICI, contradictorily asserted that it had decided a Bomb was impracticable. Moscow next learned of a decision by the British chiefs of staff to undertake a feasibility study. In August 1941 the German-born physicist Klaus Fuchs, a passionate communist, was recruited in Britain by the GRU's Jurgen Kuczynski – brother of Ursula Hamburger. When he went to work with Rudolf Pierls soon afterwards, Fuchs became a key Moscow source, providing early information that autumn. On 24 November the NKVD's New York station chief reported that three American scientists were on their way to Britain to do work on 'an explosive of enormous power'. The London station promptly questioned Cairncross, in Lord Hankey's office, about the truth of this. He responded that it must relate to Uranium 235. Cairncross's handler Anatoly Gorsky remained sceptical, however, because his other informants learned nothing about the visit, which proved most influential in persuading the United States that a Bomb might be built.

Then came Pearl Harbor. Soon afterwards secret tidings reached Moscow that the British had abandoned their own nuclear aspirations, leaving the US to pursue a Bomb through the Manhattan Project, naïvely regarded in Whitehall as a shared Anglo-American venture. In March 1942 Beria sent Stalin a summary of Soviet knowledge of British atomic research, chiefly based on information from Cairncross. About the same time one of the NKVD New York station's sources, Franklin Zelman, met an acquaintance named Clarence Hiskey, a Columbia chemistry professor and fellow-communist, who told him that he was working on an American radioactive bomb project; that this was making progress, but that the Germans were far ahead. Hiskey was mistaken on both counts, but his remarks caused alarm in Moscow. Leonid Kvasnikov, a scientist on the NKVD payroll, sought to reassure his masters: after examining the available information from British, American and German sources, he suggested that nobody had yet made much headway. Nonetheless, he urged intensive further enquiries.

Gregory Kheifetz, Centre's San Francisco resident who worked undercover as Soviet vice-consul, met Robert Oppenheimer, now secretly charged with the scientific direction of the 'Manhattan Project' to build a

Bomb, at a fundraising reception for Spanish Civil War refugees, and learned that he was engaged in a large-scale new research operation. Kheifetz was an espionage veteran: he had previously served as deputy resident in Rome, where he targeted Enrico Fermi and Bruno Pontecorvo as prospective sources. Even earlier, he worked as a secretary to Lenin's widow Nadezhda Krupskaya, then played a major part in establishing the Comintern in the United States. With such a background, he commanded both interest and respect in San Francisco's left-wing social circles. Oppenheimer seems to have given Kheifetz some important hints, possibly including mention of the fears of Washington and London that the Nazis might be building a Bomb. He also revealed Einstein's secret 1939 letter to Roosevelt, drafted by Leó Szilárd, urging him to explore the possibilities of harnessing nuclear energy.

Oppenheimer was assigned the NKVD codename 'Star'. Some of his closest friends, including Steve Nelson, born in Croatia as Stefan Mesarosh, were communists and active Soviet informants. Oppenheimer's formidable and somewhat sinister wife Kitty had once been married to a communist. At the end of 1942, under orders from the Soviet consulate in San Francisco, a communist British chemist instructed the literary academic Professor Haakon Chevalier to approach his old friend Robert Oppenheimer and invite him to share the Manhattan Project's secrets with the Russians. The scientist, however, after a time – a suspiciously long time in the view of Oppenheimer's post-war accusers – reported this approach to Gen. Leslie Groves, Manhattan's overseer, and Chevalier found himself consigned to outer darkness. In the following year a succession of further approaches were made, one of them by Solomon Mikhoels, the famous Moscow actor with the Yiddish State Art Theatre, who was on a US tour sponsored by the Jewish Anti-Fascist Committee, along with his comrade the Yiddish poet Itzik Feffer. Beria had personally briefed the two men to assure Oppenheimer that anti-Semitism in the USSR was now a dead letter.

Pavel Sudoplatov asserts in his memoirs that Oppenheimer, Fermi and Szilárd knowingly assisted the NKVD to place moles in Manhattan's laboratories. Even more startling, he suggests that Oppenheimer requested the services of Klaus Fuchs, knowing that he was a Soviet agent. Both propositions seem wildly implausible – Oppenheimer's most recent biographer Ray Monk calls the notion 'risible'. Because Oppenheimer indisputably lied to congressional hearings in 1954 about some of his old communist associations, there has been controversy about his loyalty ever since. Yet the most plausible verdict is that, not unlike Harry Hopkins, he was guilty of indiscretions to some communist friends and contacts, rather than of making a conscious commitment to betray his vast responsibility for the most ambitious military project in history.

Moscow was impressed and alarmed by the revelation that the Americans had begun to commit huge resources to the creation of a Bomb. In this matter as in so much else, Stalin looked far beyond mere victory over Hitler, towards a post-war world in which no aspiring superpower without an atomic bomb could hope to challenge another which owned one. The Soviet warlord seems to have grasped much earlier than Churchill or Roosevelt the game-changing nature of such a weapon. Sudoplatov cites Oppenheimer, Fermi, Szilárd and Szilárd's secretary as Russia's most important American atomic sources, but whether or not he told the truth about these individuals, it is undisputed that there were plenty of others. Lise Meitner was a physicist who had fled from Germany to Sweden, where she now worked at the Physical Institute of the Academy of Sciences. Soviet agents run by Zoya Rybkina approached and quizzed her about what she had learned from the international fraternity of scientists about a Bomb; it could be built, she said. In March 1942 Donald Maclean sent a new report from London, emphasising the high priority being given to the Western Allies' atomic research. On the 10th, Beria wrote to Stalin endorsing this view, which was echoed by Soviet physicist Professor George Florev, who in May declared to the Kremlin his conviction that a Bomb was feasible.

The NKVD progressively intensified its efforts to penetrate the research plants of the Manhattan Project. Semyon Semyonov – 'Twain' – the long-serving science specialist in Centre's US operation, was assigned to recruit sources. The Russians recognised that they had little prospect of securing the help of the top atomic scientists through bribery or coercion; instead, they must appeal to their finer instincts, to a supposed community of interest and culture with the Soviets, America's allies against Hitler, who were bearing the lion's share of the struggle and of the sacrifice. Semyonov quickly identified most of the key Manhattan scientists, but had limited success in recruiting them. He supervised the NKVD veteran Harry Gold, who worked with Fuchs, but failed in the wooing of Ukrainian explosives expert George Kistiakowsky.

The Russians meanwhile puzzled endlessly about what Germany was, or was not, doing about atomic research. The evidence was thin and confusing. For instance, if heavy water was an important element of the process, why was Berlin not taking far more serious steps to guard its

Norwegian production? The British obviously took heavy water seriously: the NKVD's Norwegian agents told Moscow about the November 1942 Combined Operations attempt to destroy the Rjukan hydro-electric plant, which failed with the loss of the entire assault party of glider-borne engineers. Kim Philby also forwarded a report on the fiasco, which was followed by the successful February 1943 operation conducted by six SOE-trained Norwegian saboteurs. Soviet paranoia about Anglo-American deceitfulness was intensified by the fact that the Allies neither sought Russian help in launching the raid, nor informed Moscow about it afterwards; this, though the history of British attempts to collaborate on secret operations was one of unyielding Soviet intransigence.

Beria now controlled a Special Committee on Atomic Energy, under the nominal chairmanship of two deputy prime ministers, with Sudoplatov attached as director of intelligence. A Soviet academician, V.I. Vernadsky, suggested that Moscow should formally invite the Western Allies to exchange knowledge on nuclear research. Stalin responded contemptuously: 'You are politically naïve if you think that they would share information about the weapons that will dominate the world in the future.' *Hozyain* agreed that Russia's intelligence agencies should intensify covert efforts to prise information out of Western scientists. They got nowhere with Niels Bohr, though the great Danish physicist did urge upon Churchill and Roosevelt that they should voluntarily share atomic secrets with the Soviet Union. In January 1943, Semyonov took delivery of Bruno Pontecorvo's report on the first nuclear chain reaction.

In February 1943, Sudoplatov was authorised to show Soviet scientists nuclear intelligence from America, without disclosing the sources. Such ring-fencing was unsuccessful, however. The physicist I.K. Kikoin took one look at a translated report in Sudoplatov's office at the Lubyanka and said, 'This is Fermi's work. He is the only one capable of producing such a miracle.' Sudoplatov displayed other documents in English, with the authors' names masked. The scientists guessed most of their identities, and told him not to be naïve: the nature of such supremely sophisticated research findings enabled them almost instinctively to divine the authorship. Thereafter the NKVD officer secured Beria's authority to show the Soviet group most incoming material from the US. By July 1943 Moscow Centre had received 286 US classified documents on Manhattan, and with the guidance of Russian scientists began to brief American agents about specific technical questions that needed answers.

The importance of Bomb intelligence was emphasised in February

1944, when Beria added to Sudoplatov's responsibilities the direction of a new, autonomous 'Department S', to handle atomic espionage and disseminate its fruits to Soviet scientists. The Russians gave their own penetration programme the uncharacteristically appropriate codename '*Enormoz*'. Sudoplatov later claimed that he had not wanted the job, because he preferred to focus on his main responsibility – providing support for partisan operations behind the German lines. No Soviet official, however, refused either an increase in his power or an order from Beria. Sudoplatov wrote later that he derived comfort from his faith in Semyon Semyonov, together with his longstanding friendship with Vasily and Elizabeth Zarubin. Klaus Fuchs, who had become a critical technical source, was transferred from GRU handlers to the care of Department S.

Its new director was instructed to forge close working relationships with Russia's top scientists. This was easier said than done: like all Soviet citizens, they lived in terror of any contact with the NKVD. The dinner parties that the spymaster initiated in the sitting-room behind his office in the Lubyanka must have been appalling ordeals for these wretched men. At a time when much of Russia's population subsisted on the verge of starvation, in the Lubyanka sumptuous meals were served by maids. Tensions cannot have been eased by the fact that, while the guests were urged to drink deep of Sudoplatov's Armenian brandy, he himself was teetotal. He told the scientists that he was empowered to provide further inducements for them to give of their best for Stalin's Bomb programme, through access to extra rations and shops accessible only to the Party's chosen few. He did not record what matching threats were offered, in case of failure.

In 1943 the Russians were still learning more about the Manhattan Project from their British sources than their American ones. Fifty-six years later, when eighty-seven-year-old Mrs Melita Norwood was exposed as a former Soviet agent, the British media treated the revelation as comic: 'the suburban granny who spied for Moscow'. Norwood issued an impenitent statement, justifying her actions: 'I did what I did not to make money, but to help prevent the defeat of a new [Soviet] system which had, at great cost, given ordinary people food and fares which they could afford, given them education and a health service.' Not only was she spared from criminal trial and punishment, but her fellow-countrymen treated her past treachery with good-natured indulgence. Yet other than Klaus Fuchs, Mrs Norwood – 'Tina' – was Moscow's most important wartime and post-war

source of nuclear intelligence in Britain, through her role as a secretary at
the British Non-Ferrous Metals Research Association.

The daughter of a Latvian father and a British mother, she was a lifelong
secret communist, recruited by Centre in 1937. MI5 failed to notice her
involvement in the Soviets' Woolwich Arsenal spy ring, exposed in 1938.
Moscow's files categorised her as 'a committed, reliable and disciplined
agent, striving to be of the utmost assistance'. She provided a mass of data
on American and British nuclear activities from their beginnings into the
1950s. These were forwarded by her courier, none other than Ursula
Hamburger, once a key figure in the 'Lucy' Ring, who now operated a
wireless link to Moscow from cottages in a succession of idyllically rural
Oxfordshire villages such as Great Rollright, Glympton and Kidlington.
Centre described Norwood's reports as 'of great interest and a valuable
contribution to the development of work in this field'. Soviet scientists said
later that the technical detail provided by herself and Fuchs contributed
more than any other informants to the creation of their own first bomb.

Beyond Norwood and Cairncross, another important British source
was 'Eric', a young communist physicist who has never been identified.
This man asserted that the Americans were making big strides, and his
reports caused Moscow to urge its New York station to strain every sinew
to find out more. Five times in 1942 Klaus Fuchs supplied further batches
of material about his team's theoretical calculations on atomic fission.
Fuchs' courier in Britain from that autumn onwards was a supposed
German Jewish refugee living in Britain, a 'Mrs Brewer' – once again
Ursula Hamburger. For her contributions to Russia's secret war in
Switzerland and Britain, she later became the first woman to be made an
honorary colonel in the Red Army.

The first significant American breakthrough came from 'Mar', a scientist working for DuPont, who forwarded material through his sister-in-
law. In April 1943 she delivered a letter to the Soviet consulate in New
York, detailing the plutonium route towards a nuclear explosion. 'Mar'
asserted that his motive was to defeat the 'criminal' efforts of the US military to conceal the construction of a bomb. On 1 July the NKVD New
York station reported that five hundred people were now working on the
Manhattan Project – an underestimate: by that date some 200,000, including construction workers, were engaged, a total that ultimately reached
600,000, if sub-contractors are included. Penetration of its most secret
plants had thus far proved impossible. The Russians reviewed their strategy. First, they made the sensible decision to end the GRU–NKVD contest

for nuclear information, by transferring all the GRU's sources to NKVD handlers. Pavel Sudoplatov was given overall responsibility for directing *Enormoz*. Centre then reviewed prominent names known to be associated with the bomb project, with a view to identifying recruitment targets. Enrico Fermi? Clarence Hiskey? Robert Oppenheimer? Moscow asserted that Oppenheimer was a secret Party member, but this was never proved, and seems unlikely. One NKVD source, a Senate staffer named Charles Kramer, met the Manhattan director several times, but reported back that he was a visionary, rather than a prospective Moscow agent.

In December 'Mar' passed documents on the construction of a nuclear reactor; its cooling system; the extraction of plutonium from irradiated uranium; and radiation protection. Another source, 'Kvant', or 'Hustler', about whose greed Semyon Semyonov had complained, as usual merely wanted money. In June he received $300 for a report on uranium isotope separation through gaseous diffusion. Moscow enthused. By Christmas 1943 its scientists had received a mass of relevant British and American material, some of the latter from a 'progressive professor' in the radiation laboratory at Berkeley. Still, however, the NKVD had failed to secure the services of any informant inside the Los Alamos development centre.

In the winter of 1943 Klaus Fuchs was posted to the United States, where Harry Gold became his courier, though the two men disliked each other. Through the early months of 1944, on the first and third Saturdays of each month Fuchs presented himself at 4 p.m. at the entrance of the Henry Street settlement on New York City's Lower East Side, initially with a green book and a tennis ball in his hands, meeting a man wearing gloves who asked directions to Chinatown. After the first meetings this elaborate performance was simplified, at Moscow's insistence. Later, Gold travelled to the Cambridge, Mass., home of Fuchs' sister, an American Party member. The visitor presented his credentials by saying, 'I bring you regards from Max.' Ms Fuchs responded, 'Oh, I heard he had twins.' 'Yes, seven days ago.' All the parties had been reading bad thrillers. Nonetheless, the material Fuchs provided was eminently serviceable, mostly about his own work on the separation of isotopes. Moscow expressed frustration that Gold's reports did not tell them enough about Fuchs as a man. From mid-1944 onwards the NKVD's Anatoly Yatskov controlled him through Gold, because Semyon Semyonov had become so closely watched by the FBI that he could no longer meet agents, and indeed had to be recalled home. Moreover, in October Fuchs returned abruptly to Britain, causing an interruption of his reporting.

At the beginning of 1944 San Francisco station chief Gregory Kheifetz returned to Moscow, if not in disgrace for his own failure to break into Los Alamos, at least in hopes that a successor might prove able to do so. Centre thereafter focused extraordinary effort on the US atomic programme – more, indeed, than upon espionage in Germany. The struggle against Hitler might be the present, reasoned the Kremlin, but the confrontation with the bourgeois capitalist democracies would be the future. The chief clearing-house for information dispatched from the western USA was a drugstore in Santa Fe. Moscow mobilised West Coast sleepers, some of them inactive for a decade, including a Polish Jewish dentist codenamed 'Chess-Player', who had been subsidised by the old OGPU to secure a French medical degree, and whose wife now befriended the Oppenheimers. Sudoplatov claims that beyond orally delivered progress reports, 'Chess-Player' passed on five classified documents acquired from Oppenheimer and his friends. It seems rash to credit these assertions unsceptically. It is possible to acknowledge that many scientists who worked on the Manhattan Project held left-wing convictions, and were especially sympathetic to the Soviet Union in the circumstances of its death struggle against Hitler, without accepting that they were committed NKVD sources.

Even inside America, terror could occasionally play as useful a recruitment role as ideology. George Gamow was a Russian-born physicist who had defected to the US back in 1933. Elizabeth Zarubin approached Gamow's wife Rho, also a physicist, and warned her that the safety of their relatives still in the Soviet Union depended on the couple providing assistance to Moscow. There was a carrot as well as a knout: spy well, said Mrs Zarubin encouragingly, and your family will eat better; refuse, and there is the gulag. Gamow acceded, and was able to exploit a wide network of sources in the scientific community. Trickles of material arrived from unexpected people: in the summer of 1944 an unknown stranger delivered a package of top secret material to the Soviet consulate in New York. Its technical content fascinated Moscow's analysts, making them all the more furious that the supplier left the building without revealing his identity – and was never heard of again.

Meanwhile, a young US Communist Party member named Fogel was working for Kellogg Construction on the Manhattan Project, though to Moscow's frustration he declined the company's offer of a transfer to Los Alamos early in 1945, and stopped providing information. When Ted Hall decided that he wanted to tell everything he knew to the Russians, he had trouble finding an appropriate conduit. In the end a journalist for the propaganda newspaper *Russian Voice*, Sergei Kurnakov, who was also on Centre's payroll, became his courier. Kurnakov sent Moscow a description of Hall: 'rather tall, slender, brown-haired and a bit pimply-faced, dressed carelessly, shoes appear not cleaned for a long time, fallen-down socks … He is witty and somewhat sarcastic … comes from a Jewish family, though doesn't look like a Jew.' Hall later became the first American informant to reveal the implosion method of detonation, backed up by a more detailed report from Fuchs on 6 April 1945. Yet another atomic spy, David Greenglass, an army sergeant working as a mechanic at Los Alamos, was able to pass out information from autumn of 1944 when he received visits from his wife Ruth. She later told Julius Rosenberg that 'socialism was the sole hope of the world and the Soviet Union commanded her deepest admiration'. Moscow Centre was dismissive about the quality of Greenglass's material, but every little helped.

Like all Soviet operations, *Enormoz* was fortified by an impregnable self-righteousness. In 1944 the Russians professed to be affronted when the most prominent scientists of Britain and America declined *en masse* – at their governments' insistence – invitations to attend a Moscow conference to celebrate the 220th anniversary of the Russian Academy of Sciences. Yet this was planned explicitly as a festival of secrets-gathering and informant recruitment. The Soviet Union was now conducting technological intelligence operations in the US on an industrial scale. The output of the illegal residency in Washington increased from 211 rolls of film of classified documents in 1943 to six hundred in the following year, and 1,896 in 1945. The information related to much else beyond nuclear research: stolen American secrets made a large contribution to advances in Russian radar, wireless technology, jet propulsion and synthetic rubber. There were those who argued that an ally deserved no less, but this was the same ally who had declined to admit to the British in 1941 that the Red Army used 57mm anti-tank guns, and who refused to give London and Washington technical details of the *Katyusha* rocket-launcher, among its few relatively sophisticated weapons systems.

A.E. Ioffe, director of the Soviet Union's Academy of Sciences and Physics, offered warm praise for the contribution of the atomic informants: 'The information always turns out to be accurate and for the most part very complete … I have not encountered a single false finding.' Yet some recipients in Moscow were troubled by the very ease with which America's most sensitive secrets had begun to flow onto their desks. Beria questioned the authenticity of the flood of material from the atomic spies.

Anatoly Iatskov, one of his aides, said later that the intelligence chief thought the Western Allies 'were trying to draw us into huge expenditure of resources and effort on work which had no future'. Beria persisted in this belief even after the Soviet Union had started its own atomic programme, and changed his mind only after the destruction of Hiroshima. Even during the period of his scepticism, however, he did not dare to allow his conspiracy mania to shut off the long, rich intelligence pipeline running to Moscow from the US and Britain.

In November 1944 Department 5 learned that Klaus Fuchs was back in the US – better still, working in New Mexico. Centre urged New York to identify a woman courier who could travel there under cover as his lover, but this idea got nowhere. Instead, in February 1945 Harry Gold met Fuchs in Cambridge, Mass., and was briefed by him about the huge expansion of Los Alamos. Gold asked this priceless source if he would like some cash. No, said Fuchs; all he wanted was that when the Red Army occupied Kiel and Berlin, they should locate and destroy the files the Gestapo held on him.

By the spring of 1945, from both the US and Britain Moscow was receiving a steady flow of atomic intelligence, which enabled Soviet scientists to monitor the progress of the Manhattan Project. Slowly and belatedly, however, American security was improving; it became more difficult for NKVD handlers to meet agents. Julius Rosenberg was sacked from the plant where he was working on the nuclear programme because of his Communist Party membership, though had the US Army G-2 branch that handled internal security but known it, he was among the less dangerous Soviet agents. His sub-sources were transferred to other handlers.

The NKVD's officers were acutely conscious of the importance of the atomic spies to their own country. Lev Vasilevsky, Centre's resident in Mexico City, became uneasy about allegedly careless security at the Soviet embassy in Washington, and began himself to wireless New Mexico material to Moscow. By August 1944, MI5 in London was aware of communist penetration of the Manhattan Project. Guy Liddell noted that 'details ... are almost certain to be known to the Russians'. Neither the British nor the Americans, however, recognised the scale of Soviet nuclear espionage until after the end of the war. Anatoli Yatkov, the Russians' science and technology specialist in New York, said later that the FBI uncovered 'perhaps less than half' of his own network.

In January 1945, Moscow claimed a triumph – the acquisition of details of the design of the first atomic bomb. But its American agents were far from perfectly informed: they reported that, while a test explosion was expected within a few months, it would take at least one year and possibly as long as five to produce a usable weapon. Inside the Soviet Union, a frantic search began for supplies of uranium. That which was available within its own borders was of low quality, but in February captured German documents revealed that the mineral was to be found at Bukovo, in the Rodopi mountains of Bulgaria, forty miles from Sofia. This site had now been overrun by the Red Army, and mining began there immediately. Meanwhile there was a big intelligence sweep of Czechoslovakia for possible uranium sources, though only low-grade material was found.

Probably the most important atomic secret had been the 1940 establishment of the proposition hitherto deemed untenable: that a man-made nuclear explosion was feasible. Once this great leap of faith was made, Stalin's scientists were almost assured of success in building a Bomb within a few years, though their American and British informants significantly accelerated the process. Twelve days before the first atomic bomb was assembled at Los Alamos, the NKVD secured descriptions of the Bomb via both their New York and Washington stations, from Fuchs and Pontecorvo respectively. Four years of frenzied striving lay ahead before Stalin's scientists produced their own weapon, but the Russians had triumphed in the intelligence war; not against the fascist enemy, whose defeat was supposedly the common objective of the Second World War, but against their supposed ally, the United States. Some of the tales told in this book about the secret war seem comic or grotesque. Here was one, however, that was deadly earnest, and in which the stakes were as high as the world has ever known.

21

Decoding Victory

When the war ended, most of the West's temporary intelligence officers abandoned secret service and returned to their civilian lives, as did many of their former spies. SOE's Ronald Seth applied for a passport, in order to take up a British Council post in Istanbul. This prompted an explosion at MI5, which observed that although there had been insufficient evidence to try Seth for treason, he certainly could not be considered a loyal British subject. In the end the Foreign Office conceded a passport to the ex-agent, but the British Council job failed to materialise. The last document in 'Blunderhead's' security service file is a copy of a 1946 application that he made, apparently in earnest though without success, to become chief constable of Wiltshire. Seth spent his later life writing books, a mixture of sex manuals and espionage stories; he once attempted to patent a penis enlarger. His own 1950 account of his wartime role was entitled *A Spy Has No Friends*, and bears little relationship to the facts of the case as determined by MI5. He died in 1985, a symbol of the ceaseless tension between comedy and tragedy, absurdity and deadly earnest, which characterised the secret war. Nigel Clive served for a further decade as an MI6 agent abroad, then in retirement published a vivid reminiscence of his service in Greece. Oluf Reed-Olsen worked as a pilot for some years before turning businessman. His memoir *Two Eggs on My Plate* is regarded as a minor classic. He died in 2002.

Some OSS officers in the field cherished into 1945 delusions about communist goodwill towards the United States, and were thus shocked when, for instance, Tito's partisans expelled Americans from Belgrade alongside the British, while the Red Army was welcomed. In the winter of 1944, OSS's Frank Wisner acted as impromptu US ambassador in Bucharest, where he was once seen scurrying around a dance floor attempting to persuade Romanian socialites to dance with Red Army officers; the ungrateful Russians deported him anyway. 'Wild Bill'

Donovan, now a major-general, still did not despair of a working partnership with his NKVD companions in arms: on 23 July 1945 he made an offer to turn over to Centre an entire German intelligence unit commanded by the deputy foreign chief of the Gestapo, Dr William Höttl. Höttl had volunteered his services to the Americans, but Donovan suggested share-and-share-alike. His office wrote to Pavel Fitin: 'General Donovan not only feels that you should have this information but that it would be most desirable for American and Soviet representatives on the spot [in Germany] to discuss ways and means of eliminating Höttl's entire organization.'

Marshall and Eisenhower fumed when they heard about this unilateral gesture, having themselves despaired of cooperation with Moscow. Meanwhile Donovan's men in Manchuria were seized by the NKVD as they photographed Russian engineers dismantling and removing Japanese industrial plant. In the autumn of 1945 the first revelations became public about Soviet intelligence penetration of the United States. Arrests and trials followed, although years elapsed before the FBI and the American people became aware of the scale of treason within their own camp.

In 1943 Sir William Stephenson observed to Lt. Col. Gerald Wilkinson: 'MI6 is old and rather obsolete compared with SOE [which] … is likely to survive after the war because of its younger and abler organisation; it may in fact alternatively take over MI6.' Following victory, however, in both Britain and the US the old guard prevailed in intelligence power struggles. Though Bill Bentinck, chairman of the Joint Intelligence Committee, was a critic of MI6, he strongly opposed a continuing division of responsibilities for espionage and sabotage. He concluded a 1945 official report on Britain's wartime intelligence experience: 'Despite the real contribution that SOE has made, we cannot believe that the experiment of running special operations as a separate military function outside the direct control of the chiefs of staff and under the direction of a non-Service minister, will be repeated.' In 1946 the Foreign Office, War Office and Broadway between them secured the extinction of SOE, though it had recruited abler people, and could identify more achievements in the field. MI6's influence and prestige had soared through its feudal suzerainty over Bletchley Park, and the upstart sabotage organisation was wound up. Menzies kept his job as 'C' until 1952, despite the betrayal to Moscow by Kim Philby of MI6's most sensitive early Cold War operations and informants, with the loss of many lives, and lived in retirement until his death in 1968.

In the US, J. Edgar Hoover's voice proved decisive in securing the demise of OSS, assisted by the fact that the armed forces chiefs of staff had never liked Donovan, and thought nothing of his costly operation's contribution to the war effort. Late in 1945 Lt. Col. Richard Parke, the US Army representative in the White House map room, compiled an unsolicited indictment of OSS for President Harry Truman. It is tempting to conclude from the organisation's excesses that the critics were right – that Donovan and his organisation merely squandered a not insignificant portion of America's vast wealth. But OSS's excesses were not much worse than those of SOE, and its Research & Analysis division was superior to any other such body in the world. In 1947 the rising menace from the Soviet Union persuaded Truman to authorise the creation of the Central Intelligence Agency, employing many ex-OSS personnel such as Richard Helms, William Colby, William Casey and Frank Wisner, by then an ardent Cold Warrior, of whom Arthur Schlesinger said wryly: 'He had seen the Communist future at first hand and not liked it at all.'

In 1944 Sterling Hayden parachuted into Croatia on a mission for which he was awarded the Silver Star, saw a little shooting and ended his service seconded to the US First Army in north-west Europe. He enjoyed his part in the secret war, which suited his character and talents, but cherished a suspicion that the sceptical army intelligence officer's verdict cited above – that OSS had contributed little to defeating Germany – held more than a grain of truth. Madeleine Carroll and Hayden were divorced, and he became briefly a communist. He returned reluctantly to Hollywood for the money, but finished his career where he had started it, sailing boats to the far shores of the world.

The NKVD's Pavel Sudoplatov wrote: 'The end of the war is still vivid in my memory as a glorious event that washed away all my doubts about the wisdom of Stalin's leadership. All heroic and tragic events, losses and even purges, seemed to be justified by the triumph over Hitler.' Christopher Andrew has observed that many of the Soviet secret service personnel decorated by Moscow for their wartime services received medals not for valour, but for crimes against humanity: at Stalingrad, for instance, the NKVD had executed in cold blood some 13,500 alleged deserters and 'defeatists'. The most conspicuous consequence of peace was to unleash a new wave of Kremlin paranoia, which extended to the intelligence community. Many Soviet agents who flew home in 1945 were shot or sentenced to long terms of imprisonment. By 1953 the roll-call of those who had faced firing squads included Lavrenti Beria and Vsevolod

Merkulov, while Sudoplatov spent fifteen years behind bars as an 'enemy of the people'.

In embittered old age, the former Special Tasks chief raged against this injustice at the hands of the Soviet Union, 'to which I devoted every fibre of my being and for which I was willing to die; for which I averted my eyes from every brutality, finding justification in its transformation from a backward nation into a superpower'. Yet Sudoplatov's loyalty to Stalin and Beria caused him to become the instrument of many dreadful deeds. His only defence might have been that such ruthless men as himself played a larger part in the destruction of Nazism than did the more squeamish Western Allies. Vladimir Putin assuredly acknowledges such a figure as a hero.

Ursula Hamburger retired to East Germany in 1950, and spent her later years writing modestly successful stories for children, together with suit-ably sanitised spy books, some of them about herself. She went to her grave in 2000 an impenitent Stalinist. Leopold Trepper informed Moscow Centre that his network had been betrayed to the Germans by 'Monsieur Kent', Anatoli Gourevitch, but this did not save him from a subsequent decade of imprisonment for his own collaboration with the Nazis. Gourevitch reached Paris from Germany in May 1945 with a train of followers that included the senior officer Heinz Pannwitz, together with the latter's secretary-mistress Henne Kempe. On 7 June they flew together to Moscow, where all were immediately shown into cells. Pannwitz spent the next nine years assisting Centre with identification of Gestapo inform-ants, real and imagined, before being allowed to leave for the West in 1955. He died in 1975, aged sixty-four. Gourevitch faced treason charges; he was damned by SMERSh's discovery of a document dated 1 February 1944, in which Gestapo chief Heinrich Muller told Pannwitz that the Soviet agent must be brought to Germany with his wife and son, and looked after: 'It goes without saying that I regard it as my duty to defend and protect "Kent" following the fulfilment of the tasks which had been assigned to him.' In January 1947 the Special Council of the Ministry of State Security sentenced 'Kent' to fifteen years' imprisonment. 'Prisons are the same everywhere,' Gourevitch wrote morosely, after experiencing those of both Hitler and Stalin. He was released on parole in 1960, but secured formal rehabilitation and a tiny pension only in 1991, when a post-Soviet exam-ination of wartime GRU documents showed that his first 1943 radio messages to Moscow included the agreed warning that he was transmit-ting under enemy control. He died in 2009.

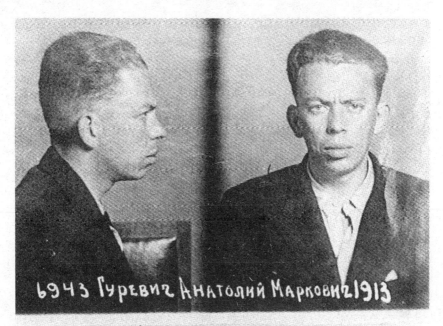

(от одной кромки ногтя до другой)

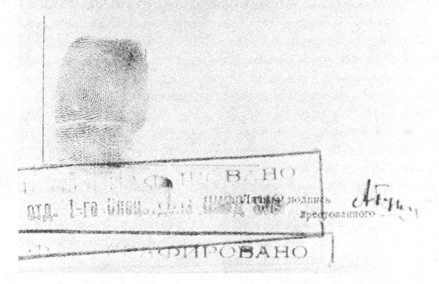

Mug-shot and fingerprint of Anatoli Gourevitch taken by the
NKVD on his return to Moscow

While Gourevitch reposed in his Moscow cell, in London an army officer, Brigadier Tristram Lyon-Smith, appeared one morning late in 1945 at MI5's St James's Street headquarters to complain that a Gestapo officer kept writing unwelcome letters to his daughter from Germany, claiming that she had promised to marry him. This was of course Tonia Lyon-Smith, the English girl last seen at Gestapo headquarters in Paris, who was suspected of giving information to the Germans about Leopold Trepper and Georgie de Winter. She had returned to England following the French liberation. An MI5 officer who saw the brigadier and discussed his daughter's year-long sojourn as a guest of the Nazis on not uncomfortable terms reported sardonically: 'I did not think it advisable or necessary to ask for details of the precise quid pro quo.'

A subsequent interrogation of the girl concluded: 'The story is a little complicated, and she herself has been far from candid. She certainly became Karl Gagl's mistress and almost certainly disclosed to the Germans all her knowledge of the SPAAK [French Resistance] organisation, which I believe to have been considerably greater than she admits.' MI5 nonetheless concluded, with what seems compassionate good sense, that although she could probably be prosecuted for treason, given her age and her unhappy story – she had been fourteen when marooned in France in 1940, and was still just nineteen – it seemed that it would have been mistaken to take the case further. The Gestapo officer was nonetheless told there would be no wedding bells – in 1946 Lyon-Smith briefly married a young naval officer – and that he should abandon his passionate letter-writing. She died in 2010.

As for Gourevitch, he never saw Margaret Barcza again, and after his release married a Russian woman. Only in 1992 was he reunited with his son by Barcza at Sacha's home in Spain. There will never be a conclusive answer to the question of who gave away what in the matter of the Red Orchestra and the Trepper network; none of the protagonists' accounts are remotely trustworthy. But if SMERSh and the GRU, instruments of the least merciful regime on earth, were insufficiently sure of Gourevitch's culpability to shoot him, he seems to deserve the benefit of doubt. He died in 2009, aged ninety-five.

Alexander Radó, sensing the way the wind was blowing, made a break from a Soviet flight in transit to Moscow during a Cairo stopover in September 1944. His appeal to the British for asylum was rejected, however, and in August 1945 he reached Moscow under guard. He remained imprisoned without trial until 1954, but was then rehabilitated and allowed to retire to Hungary. The Lausanne wireless-operator Alexander Foote spent two years in Moscow before defecting back to Britain through Berlin in 1947. Conspiracists cherish a theory that Foote was always an agent of MI6, at whose behest he supposedly channelled some Bletchley material about the Eastern Front to Moscow, under the pretence that it derived from the 'Lucy' Ring. Such a narrative wildly over-rates the subtlety of Broadway. Moreover, it would assuredly have been known to Kim Philby, who would have tipped off the Russians. Foote could scarcely have risked flying to Moscow in 1945, nor would the GRU have allowed him later to leave the city alive, had he served Britain during the war years. It is most plausible that the Englishman was what he seemed – a communist adventurer who enjoyed the game for its own sake.

Rachel Dübendorfer was released from compulsory treatment in a Soviet prison's mental hospital only in 1956, when she was allowed to retire to East Germany. In 1969 she and several members of the anti-Hitler Resistance were awarded the Order of the Red Banner. Rudolf Rössler was bailed from his Swiss cell in September 1944, but remained subject to Swiss police scrutiny. He made several further court appearances for alleged foreign espionage activities before his death in Lucerne in 1958, aged only sixty-one. Though he had received large sums from Moscow, Rössler died broke. Nothing ever came of a proposal inside Centre that he should be decorated for his services, on the reasonable grounds that he served the 'Lucy' Ring as a mere mercenary, rather than as a true believer. Meanwhile Alexander Demyanov, 'Agent Max' or 'Heine', returned to work as an electrical engineer. The NKVD in the 1950s sought once more to exploit his White Russian connections, by dispatching him with his wife to penetrate the émigré community in Paris. But its members rebuffed him, and after months of inactivity the couple were recalled to Moscow. Demyanov died of a heart attack in 1975, aged sixty-four.

In Tokyo in 1949, Hanako Ishii prompted the exhumation of Richard Sorge's skeleton, still clearly identifiable beneath the yard of the prison in which he had been hanged five years before. She arranged his cremation and reinterment in the Tama cemetery, preserving for herself his spectacles and belt. Pathetically or grotesquely, she had the gold bridgework from his teeth reset as a ring which she wore for the rest of her life. She composed an epitaph for his grave, which would have aroused mixed feelings among others with whom he lived – spies, friends and lovers alike: 'Here lies a hero who sacrificed his life fighting against war and for world peace.' She died in 2000.

Any student of the wartime era who explores the conduct of the Soviet Union, and especially of its intelligence services, is likely to emerge bewildered that the word 'ally' could ever have been used to describe Russia's wartime status alongside the democracies. Stalin accepted their assistance to secure the destruction of Hitler, an association that was inescapable for embattled Britain in June 1941, and thereafter saved countless British and American lives, because the Red Army accepted most of the human sacrifice necessary to defeat Germany. It is difficult, however, to perceive the smallest moral superiority in the Soviet system over that of the Nazis, though the West has always seemed willing to accept in mitigation the considerations that Stalin confined his programme of mass murder to his own people and those of Soviet satellite nations, and did not commit a Jewish genocide.

The failure of both the British and American security services to catch the multitude of Soviet spies and informants in their midst incurred criticism and indeed scorn in the Cold War era. Amid the climate of paranoia which overtook British intelligence, Guy Liddell of MI5 was denounced as a possible traitor, partly because of his friendships with Guy Burgess and Anthony Blunt. In truth, it is wildly implausible that Liddell, a first-class intelligence officer who became deputy director of the security service, betrayed his country; but he gave his confidence to some men who were undeserving of it. He died in 1958.

Although the West's intelligence services appeared foolish when the British and American betrayers were exposed, there is nonetheless a powerful, surely overriding argument that the presumption of trust which was and is the default mindset within Western democracies, and which made treason relatively easy for the likes of Blunt and Maclean, Hiss and Harry Dexter White, was vastly preferable to the climate of oppression, suspicion, denunciation and near-madness which prevailed in the Soviet Union throughout the communist era. The Russians were more successful in identifying their own traitors, with a few notable exceptions, but at what cost to the humanity of their society?

Although Joseph McCarthy had a point when he asserted the scale of treachery in high places, the senator went on to conduct a witch-hunt of such gross extravagance that in the eyes of the world, as well as of his own people, the reputation of American justice was besmirched for a generation. The moral and historic stature of Britain and the United States was better served by indulging a certain naïveté about their traitors than it would have been by instilling into the FBI and MI5 the thought processes of Moscow Centre. That assertion holds good even after acknowledging that post-war revelations of treason in secret places created within the Anglo-American intelligence community a distrust of colleagues which sometimes approached Soviet paranoia, and persisted for a generation.

The final triumph of Hugh Trevor-Roper was to interrogate Walter Schellenberg, who returned from Sweden to face Allied captivity. This experience enabled the MI6 officer to demonstrate that he knew far more about the German intelligence service than did the Nazi high functionary. Trevor-Roper asserted in his April 1945 valedictory report that in 1939–41, British knowledge of the Abwehr was 'very imperfect', while in 1943 it became 'adequately representative', and from then until the end was 'probably complete'. He exaggerated only a little in asserting that all the Abwehr's agents deployed overseas were either fictional – such as those created by Dr Kramer in Stockholm – or controlled by London, as were 'Garbo' and his kin. In Trevor-Roper's contemptuous words, 'Those officers of the GIS who were intelligent enough to see the necessity of central evaluation were corrupt enough to see the necessity of preventing it.' He was probably right to suggest that the Germans secured better intelligence about the Allied war effort by purchasing it from open sources than by running incompetent spies.

In the autumn of 1945, at the instigation of the senior MI6 officer Dick White, Trevor-Roper was commissioned to travel to Berlin and explore the circumstances of the Führer's death, which enabled him to translate his subsequent report into a best-selling book, *The Last Days of Hitler*. Thereafter he resumed his career as an Oxford historian, unflaggingly controversial, cantankerous, snobbish and brilliant, his last years tarnished by a foolish endorsement of the authenticity of the 1983 'Hitler diaries'. He died in 2003. Dr R.V. Jones also returned to academic life, as professor of natural philosophy at Aberdeen University, having been driven out of the intelligence community by its time-servers, who found him too clever by half. Jones received appropriate recognition of his wartime contribution only in 1994, when he was made a Companion of Honour. He died in 1997.

Walter Schellenberg served a remarkably brief term of imprisonment, given that he had held senior posts in the Nazi hierarchy: he was released on compassionate grounds in 1951, the year before his death at forty two from liver failure, and spent his last months in Switzerland, writing a memoir with the assistance of his favourite secretary, Marie-Luise Schienke. When Germany's intelligence services were wound up, Reinhard Gehlen's self-promotional skills enabled him to achieve a coup. Long before the end of the war, in anticipation of Germany's defeat he prepared his military intelligence apparatus to exploit the looming new struggle between the Soviet Union and the West. In 1945 he offered the Americans his services, complete with personnel and files. They accepted enthusiastically, and the Gehlen Bureau later became an important arm of the CIA's activities in Europe, proving the only branch of the Wehrmacht general staff which survived virtually intact into the Cold War.

Gehlen's new role was warmly welcomed by his old adversaries of the NKVD and GRU, since almost all his sources in the East were either controlled by or known to Centre. Erich Hüttenhain, principal brain of OKW/Chi, joined the Gehlen organisation as its chief cipher expert, and later ran the German government's codemaking and codebreaking operations, dedicated to improving upon its wartime performance. Arthur Schlesinger was among the Allies who recoiled from the spectacle of the OSS's Frank Wisner enlisting such men as Gehlen and Hüttenhain: 'There was something aesthetically displeasing about Americans plotting with Nazis, who had recently been killing us, against Russians, whose sacrifices had made the Allied victory possible.'

On 28 June 1945, the British chiefs of staff drove to Bletchley Park, where Sir Alan Brooke addressed four hundred of its staff, thanking and congratulating them for their extraordinary contribution to the Allied war effort. The new mood of the time was illustrated by the fact that, soon after VE-Day, traffic analysts at the Park who had been monitoring German transmissions were ordered to switch to French and Russian wavelengths; this caused some to down tools in impassioned protest, and indeed to resign from GC&CS. Almost all the codebreakers soon returned to academic life. Max Newman, the mathematician who had joined Bletchley reluctantly because he feared that the work would bore him, told his section: 'One of the prices of peace must be the losing of the most interesting job we've ever had.' It was fortunate that he had derived such satisfaction from his work, because a grateful nation offered him only a lowly OBE, which he rejected with scorn. Gordon Welchman accepted his own OBE. Alan Turing and John Tiltman became OBEs, at a time when scores of indifferently competent generals, admirals and air-marshals were being awarded knighthoods. Bill Tutte, who had led the way towards breaking the German teleprinter traffic, got nothing at all save his prize fellowship at Trinity College, Cambridge. He emigrated to Canada in 1948, and spent the rest of a distinguished working career as a mathematician at Waterloo University, Ontario, among people who knew nothing about his dazzling wartime contribution but admired the energy of himself and his wife Dorothea as leisure hikers. He died in 2002.

The men and women of Bletchley left behind a formidable technological legacy, which enabled GC&CS's successor, the Government Communications Headquarters or GCHQ, to become Britain's foremost contribution to the Atlantic alliance from 1945 to the present day, the nuclear deterrent not excluded. It was not by chance that GCHQ became an institution independent of MI6: never again would Broadway's bureaucrats wax fat on the achievements of the codebreakers. In the United States, the National Security Agency exercises the codebreaking responsibilities once fulfilled by Arlington Hall and Op-20-G, while the CIA conducts US intelligence operations abroad on a scale that would gladden the heart of 'Wild Bill' Donovan, who died in 1959.

Although Bletchley was supremely a team achievement by one of the most remarkable groups of human beings ever assembled within a single organisation, there is no doubt of Alan Turing's primacy. In twenty-first-century Britain it has become a source of national shame that Turing killed himself in 1954, aged only forty-one, following a criminal conviction for gross indecency. The 2014 Hollywood film about Turing, *The Imitation Game*, offered a version of his experience at Bletchley Park that was a travesty of the reality: far from suffering persecution, he was treated there with a respect verging on reverence, albeit tinged with bewilderment at his eccentricities. Alastair Denniston, in the movie Turing's sinister nemesis, was in reality an enlightened administrator notable for his kindness. It is nonetheless rightful cause for amazement that when the great mathematician and pioneer of computing faced prosecution and ruin only seven years after the war ended, nobody in Britain's secret community, knowing of Turing's personal contribution to victory, intervened to save him from chemical castration.

MI6 today still declines to open its archive, to establish whether Turing's case attracted the notice or sympathy of its senior officers – most plausibly that of Stewart Menzies – in 1952, but it seems reasonable to assume that it did not.* There are grounds for dismay at the British government's populist 2013 decision to grant Turing a posthumous pardon, since his conviction was perfectly proper by the inhumane legislation of the day,

---

* The author made such a request for information to today's 'C' in December 2014, and was told, albeit in the most courteous terms, that there can be no breach of the principle that MI6's post-1949 archive remains closed.

which imposed similarly harsh punishments on thousands of other homo-
sexuals, no less deserving of rehabilitation, if such gestures are to be made.
It seems much more significant that the British public today salutes
Turing's supremely lonely genius. It is ironic, but also right and fitting, that
this man known to scarcely anyone outside BP and the Royal Society
during the war years and for half a century thereafter is today the most
celebrated 1939–45 secret warrior in the world.

The Second World War witnessed a huge expansion of the intelligence
services of every belligerent nation, so that in Richard Aldrich's words,
'secret service became the struggle's growth industry'. Never in the history
of conflict had such vast resources been deployed by all belligerents to
compile and assess so much information about their enemies. The overwhelming bulk was wasted, of course. As late as January 1943, in the
heyday of Bletchley Park, Lord Beaverbrook expressed scepticism about
intelligence, telling Bruce Lockhart that in cabinet he heard 'very little
secret information which was of real value. Secret Intelligence Service
reports were of doubtful quality, and their quantity made it difficult for
anyone to sift the good from the bad.' Beaverbrook even expressed caution
about Ultra intercepts, saying that 'The enemy could put out deception
messages in a code they knew we had just as easily as we could.' Today we
know this did not happen, but it deserves notice that, at such a relatively
advanced stage of the conflict, a grandee privy to the affairs of the Allied
intelligence community, albeit also a professional cynic, could speak in
such terms; contemporary witnesses did not always regard Allied secret
war operations with the reverence conferred on them by a twenty-first-century generation.

The historian Paul Kennedy argues that an objective assessment of
wartime intelligence should highlight its preponderance of failures: the
Russians' underestimate of Finnish defensive capability in 1939–40; British
misjudgement of the Norway campaign; the confounding of French
expectations by the German thrust through the Ardennes in May 1940;
Stalin's rejection of predictions of the German invasion of Russia in June
1941; American blindness about the threat to Pearl Harbor; German
failure to anticipate the Russian envelopment at Stalingrad, the reverse
pincer movement at Kursk, or the central thrust of Operation 'Bagration'
in 1944. The Western Allies misjudged German responses to their landings
at Salerno in 1943 and Anzio in 1944, and to the Arnhem airdrop. The
Americans were surprised in the Ardennes in December 1944. The

Japanese began by grossly underrating America's moral strength as well as industrial capability, and were then blindsided by almost every US initiative of the later Pacific war. Kennedy concludes his catalogue of failures: 'even if one can readily concede that the Allied record on intelligence was far better than that of the Axis, it is easier to demonstrate where smooth logistics helped win the war than to show where intelligence led to victory'.

There is a scintilla of truth in this, but the evidence shows that knowledge of the enemy's motions made a more important contribution to the Western Allied war effort than Kennedy allows, especially at sea, both in the Pacific and Atlantic theatres. Ironically, Hitler's spies achieved more for the Allied cause than did those of MI6, OSS, the NKVD or GRU. The Abwehr agents dispatched to Britain and Russia who were 'turned' did better service thereafter to Allied deception operations than did most of the men and women paid by their secret services to operate abroad. Much overseas intelligence work was a zero-sum game: every belligerent needed to be represented by its secret service even in such far-flung places as Lourenço Marques and Santiago, but their foremost aspiration was merely to frustrate the machinations of the other side, whatever those might be.

The information provided by the Sorge ring and the Red Orchestra might have been invaluable to Moscow in preparing to meet 'Barbarossa', had Stalin been willing to heed it – but he was not. No British humint source remotely matched the quality of intelligence supplied by the Berlin networks of Harnack, Schulze-Boysen and the Swiss 'Lucy' Ring. Allen Dulles of OSS forwarded to Washington useful and reasonably accurate material about conditions in Germany between 1943 and 1945, but there is little evidence that this influenced US policy- or strategy-making.

The towering reality about Western Allied intelligence is that it became dominated by Ultra, which bore an inherent authority no spy's reports could match. Hugh Trevor-Roper noted that all the important achievements in his field were the product of sigint, not humint: 'Of the great intelligence triumphs of the war not one was directly or exclusively due to the Secret Service proper ... MI6 was marginal, very marginal.' Noel Annan said: 'The cryptanalysts did not win the war, but they stopped Britain losing it.' This is too glib a verdict, but there is something in it: Ultra was a critical force in protecting Allied commanders from making egregious blunders. Even while acknowledging the failures at Arnhem and in the Ardennes, in the second half of the war it became much harder for them to walk blindly into German or Japanese traps.

The practical military value of Allied access to the Japanese diplomatic ciphers was limited, but Gen. Ōshima's wirelessed dispatches to Tokyo from Berlin provided more useful insights than did any Allied agent into the Nazi hierarchy's thinking, just as Admiral Abe provided some superb information on German naval technology. The price of having gained such access was that it distorted the wider process of intelligence assessment in London and Washington, and in the field with the armies. If a threat was not flagged through Ultra, it was assumed not to exist. Donald McLachlan of naval intelligence wrote: 'Experience on both sides in two world wars … has shown that an intelligence organisation which lived on cryptographical expectations alone became spoiled. It lost the skill and application to make the fullest use of other sources such as air photography, prisoner-of-war statements, neutral observers and even press and radio indiscretions. One might say that easy knowledge corrupts and entire knowledge corrupts absolutely.' Major Lewis Powell, a future US Supreme Court justice, warned in an early 1944 army report on exploitation of sigint in the Mediterranean: 'There seems to be a tendency to rely too heavily upon ULTRA to the exclusion of all else.'

In October 1945, Montgomery's intelligence chief Brigadier Bill Williams penned 'MOST SECRET' reflections on the wartime uses and abuses of Ultra, in which he espoused the same view as McLachlan and Powell. 'The material was dangerously valuable,' he wrote, 'not only because we might lose it, but because it seemed the answer to an intelligence officer's prayer … It was liable to save the recipient from doing Intelligence. Instead of being the best, it tended to become the only source. There was a tendency at all times to await the next message and, often, to be fascinated by the authenticity of the information into failing to think whether it was significant … Probably essential wood was ignored, because of the variety of interesting trees on offer … The information purveyed was so remarkable that it tended, particularly if one were tired or overbusy, to engulf not only all other sources, but that very common sense which forms the basis of intelligence.'

Trevor-Roper again: 'Secret intelligence must always be relevant to real political or military purposes; it must always be contiguous with "open" intelligence' – information derived from diplomats and published sources – 'and it must always be verifiable, for if it is not verifiable it is, in the strict sense of the word, worthless; it cannot be believed or used.' It is striking to notice that the US State Department's regular bulletins on the world at war, circulated throughout the Roosevelt administration and derived chiefly from open sources, were as informative as and often more sensible than the output of the Allies' secret services, and the same endorsement might be given to some British ambassadors' dispatches from overseas.

It was important, noted Bill Williams, for officers constantly to remind themselves that, though the German commander dispatching a given message told the truth as he saw it, 'it was not necessarily true in relation to the situation as a whole'. There were many gaps, and – especially in the middle war years – much material reached Allied field commanders out of real time. Williams tried to tell himself that he was not doing his job properly unless he evaluated the battlefield situation correctly before the Ultra signals came in, but he admitted that he was no more successful in this than most of his fellow-tradesmen in the Allied camp. Intelligence officers recognised by 1945 that the wartime work of British and American codebreakers had changed the very nature of their business. Henceforward 'the old cloak and dagger', as Guy Liddell and a Bletchley friend described pre-war espionage in a fit of nostalgia, was not quite redundant: highly placed agents in the enemy's corridors of power, such as Col. Oleg Penkovsky, remained important assets during the Cold War. As influences upon strategy and policy, however, they were recognised as entirely secondary to signals intelligence.

Since 1945, historians of some other nations have made large claims for what their own codebreakers allegedly achieved – for instance, Russian assertions that they read Japanese Purple traffic or even broke Enigma. Given what we now know about Izumi Kozo, the former proposition is not incredible. But to credit such successes, documentary evidence is necessary, which is still almost entirely absent in Moscow's case. Where Russian archives hold copies of decrypts of higher German and Japanese wartime messages – it is undisputed that Centre broke pre-war cyphers – it is more likely these were passed to Moscow by British or American traitors than decrypted by its own codebreakers. Even the triumphs of the British and Americans need to be qualified by studying exact dates on which decrypts became available to commanders – sometimes well beyond 'real time'. The most important issue about all intelligence is whether it empowered commanders in the field and at sea to take action. Unless this can be proven, all claims to codebreaking prowess become suspect or meaningless.

This book has sought to show that the radio intelligence war between the Allies and Germany was not as one-sided as popular mythology supposes. Hitler's codebreakers, especially in the first half of the war, could claim some important successes. In North Africa until June 1942, Rommel knew as much about the British Eighth Army as his enemies knew about the Afrika Korps, and the latter's commander used his information better. Dönitz's B-Dienst provided the U-boat command with an ongoing stream of intelligence about British convoy operations. Even when Allied ciphers could not be broken, traffic analysis and voice interception gave Berlin ongoing information about Allied operations in both East and West, on the ground and in the air, throughout the conflict.

But not as much as the Allies possessed. Many things about the 1939–45 era remain disputable, but few informed people would question the proposition that Bletchley was one of the most remarkable institutions the world has ever known, and one of the greatest achievements in Britain's history, towering over any narrative of the nation's part in the conflict. It does not diminish the codebreakers' achievement to emphasise how extraordinary it was that the Germans never recognised the vulnerability of Enigma and Lorenz. Berlin garnered plentiful clues, and received warnings from its own experts – yet carried on regardless. A most unGermanic laziness of mind persisted. While the Third Reich executed wholesale spies, traitors and saboteurs who threatened its security, its functionaries remained insistently oblivious of the most deadly threat of all – a few hundred tweedy, bespectacled young English academics labouring in drab suburban Bedfordshire. The only credible explanation is hubris: an institutional unwillingness to believe that their Anglo-Saxon enemies, whom they so often humbled on the battlefield, could be so clever.

Granted the brilliance of the American achievements in breaking Purple and forecasting the Japanese strike at Midway, the most innovative codebreaking technology of the war was devised at BP. The United States became in some degree a prisoner of its early success with Japan's diplomatic cipher: it might have better served its armed forces in the struggle with Japan had Arlington Hall focused more intensively upon breaking the enemy military codes it could not read, rather than Purple, which it could. Its efforts were also handicapped by division of effort – the crippling army–navy rivalry. Painful experience showed that it was more difficult to break Japanese book codes than machine-generated ciphers. Op-20-G and Arlington Hall could boast remarkable achievements, and eventually succeeded where the British had failed with some Japanese communications, but they never fully mastered them.

Allied intelligence made its greatest impact on the war at sea, both in the Atlantic and the Pacific. Nimitz's FRUPAC at Pearl Harbor achieved more than did Arlington Hall, partly because of the difficulties of reading the Japanese army's traffic in real time, and partly because decrypts were of limited value to land campaigns in which the enemy manoeuvred little, but instead fought stubbornly from fixed positions. In naval operations, by contrast, the foremost challenge was always to locate the enemy's warships at sea and concentrate force against them, for which Ultra provided the Royal Navy and US Navy with unprecedented opportunities. If the Allies had not been able to exercise almost unchallenged control of the Atlantic sea route in the spring of 1944, the D-Day invasion of Normandy could not have taken place – and such dominance owed much to Ultra. Nimitz's triumphs in the Pacific, with both his surface fleets and submarine flotillas, were immensely assisted by Ultra, and sometimes altogether made possible by it.

In 1944–45 the USAAF used economic intelligence more effectively and imaginatively than did the RAF to inform its bomber operations. Nonetheless, no Allied nation achieved a complete understanding of Hitler's industrial machine, even though some of the best brains in Britain and the US engaged in the attempt. On land, it was of immense value to the Allies to possess a vivid picture of deployments, but only on rare occasions – the most conspicuous being at Alam Halfa in August 1942 and at Mortain in July 1944 – was Ultra directly responsible for enabling Allied forces to frustrate major German attacks. It is impossible and almost irrelevant to judge the rival claims of the Russians and Germans to sigint superiority on the Eastern Front; what is indisputable is that, from the summer of 1942 onwards, the Red Army decisively won the overall intelligence contest.

There was a debate at Bletchley Park in February 1945 about what steps, if any, should be taken to create a historical record of its achievement. Edward Travis, its chief, minuted his own view that unless this was done immediately after the cessation of hostilities, no later historian would be able to make sense of BP's records and intercepts, in the absence of technical knowledge and context which he believed only a contemporary witness could have. Meanwhile, sustaining secrecy was deemed paramount when so many nations around the world continued to employ in the post-war era communications technology vulnerable to Anglo-American penetration – the Red Army enlisted in its own service many captured Lorenz teleprinters.

When war crimes trials began in 1946, intelligence officers expressed horror at the notion that they might have to give evidence, which would expose the use of stool-pigeons, electronic eavesdropping – and Ultra decryption. These methods, said the War Office, would be indispensable in future wars, and must on no account be mentioned in open court, nor indeed anywhere else. It was a notable irony that some tens of thousands of American and British men and women who shared knowledge of the Ultra secret preserved it through the subsequent three decades with almost religious fervour, while the Soviets – the only enemies who mattered – were privy to it from the outset, thanks to Western traitors. When Bletchley's story began to be publicly revealed in 1974, enough veterans survived to pen dozens of authoritative accounts of their own roles, while Professor Harry Hinsley led the team which produced the official history of wartime intelligence.

Ideological enthusiasm for communism was the principal force in enabling the Soviet Union's intelligence services to recruit a host of informants in both the Axis and Allied nations with better access to secrets than the human sources of MI6 and OSS achieved. Much technical intelligence generated from the US and Britain, especially about aircraft design and above all about the Bomb, was of value to the Russians. This bore fruit, however, not during the struggle against Hitler, but in strengthening Moscow's hand in the Cold War that followed; it not merely influenced the nuclear arms race, but also empowered the Soviet Union to build jet aircraft and much else beyond its native competence. The record of the NKVD and GRU, working under the dead hand of Stalin, shows that their chiefs were no more sensible or skilled, and infinitely more barbarous, than their Western counterparts.

The Soviets profited from the honourable policies of the Western warlords, who sought to treat them as genuine allies, and deployed scarcely any intelligence or counter-intelligence resources against them. Stalin's paranoia rendered sterile the labours of his admirers in Nazi Germany, who sacrificed so much to influence Soviet actions so little. The master of the Kremlin was able to make formidable use of material secured from American and British traitors to arm himself against Roosevelt and Churchill in the political struggle to shape the post-war world. But probably the most influential wartime elements of Soviet intelligence activities against the Axis were their deception operations, the foremost being that of Agent 'Max' through 'Monastery', at the time of Stalingrad.

The NKVD and GRU tied up the Abwehr in as many knots as did MI5 through the Double Cross system. The German and Japanese leaderships made their decisions shrouded in bewilderment and ignorance about their enemies, partly because of an institutionalised resistance to the objective examination of evidence, emphasised by Hitler's refusal to explore the economic potential of the Soviet Union and the United States before he declared war on them. From 1942 onwards the Axis conducted its campaigns with only meagre, or wildly mistaken, ideas of what was happening in the enemy's camp. In considerable measure, of course, this was due to the madness of Hitler and the wilful blindness of Japan's generals. In Trevor-Roper's words, written in the last days of the war: 'All strategy, and indeed all decisions of policy and interpretations of acts, became increasingly dependent on the arbitrary whims of a group of ignorant maniacs.' In lesser degree German bewilderment was attributable to the fog of misinformation generated by Allied counter-intelligence and deception staffs.

By far the most important reality about the impact of intelligence on the Second World War – on all wars – is that knowledge of the enemy's motions does not alter or diminish the requirement for soldiers, sailors and airmen to defeat him on the battlefield. There were some delusions in 1918, wrote Stewart Menzies in a 1942 circular to his officers, that Germany had been defeated 'by means of the spoken, written word, or some other ancillary war activity'. Not so, he said. 'Germany was defeated because the German Armies were beaten.' MI6 would have failed in its primary function, the spy chief wrote, if it did not materially contribute to such another outcome in Britain's latest conflict with Germany.

A British general once lectured to Allied students at the Haifa staff college on the principles of war. When he sat down and invited comments, a Polish officer sprang to his feet and said, 'Sir! You have left out the most important: Be stronger!' The Pole was right. Sir Alan Brooke, as head of the British Army, complained at a chiefs of staff meeting in November 1943 that the Joint Intelligence Committee consistently underestimated the enemy's military capabilities in all theatres. This was only half-true. Brooke should instead have acknowledged that the chronic problem for the Allies was not that their intelligence staffs misjudged Axis paper strengths, though they sometimes did, but that the enemy consistently displayed superior combat skills to those of the Anglo-American armies, even when the latter had more troops, overwhelming air power – and sometimes foreknowledge conferred by Ultra.

Decrypted signals provided the Allied warlords with a knowledge of their enemies' strengths and deployments unparalleled in history. 'Few armies,' acknowledged Bill Williams, 'ever went to battle better informed of their enemy.' But Ultra seldom told Churchill, Roosevelt and their generals much about German intentions, and especially about Hitler's intended response to a given Allied course of action. The achievements of Bletchley Park, Arlington Hall and the US Navy's Op-20-G were very great. They elevated intelligence, hitherto a little-respected branch of staffwork, to an unprecedented importance in operational planning. They did not, however, provide Anglo-American forces with magic keys to victory on the ground, in the air and at sea. The Germans, Italians and Japanese always had to be fought. It is unsurprising that good intelligence seldom proved decisive in altering battlefield outcomes in the first half of the war, when Allied forces were weak. Especially in land campaigns, knowing where a blow was to fall did little to improve the prospects of countering it, in the absence of competent commanders and sufficient armed strength. In December 1941, for instance, the British had extensive forewarning about Japanese intentions in the Far East, especially towards Malaya, but their local forces were too feeble and too incompetently led to profit from it.

Ultra came fully into its own, serving up to Allied warlords a daily feast of secret knowledge, only between late 1942 and 1945, when the recipients knew that they were anyway certain to win the war. It is impossible credibly to quantify its contribution to final victory, to foreshortening the conflict, because it was a Western Allied tool, while the Red Army bore the principal burden of destroying Nazism. What can be said, however, is that Bletchley Park and its brilliant civilian brains, together with their American counterparts, went far to compensate for deficiencies in the fighting qualities of the British and US armies against the Wehrmacht and the Imperial Japanese Army. As I asserted in *All Hell Let Loose*, for all the genius of the German soldier and courage of the Japanese one on the battlefield, the Allies made better war than did the Axis nations. The superiority of their strategic, if not always tactical, intelligence apparatus was a key element in this achievement. Despite the criticisms of Western Allied secret services in the narrative above, they were much more effective than those of their foes, and of the Soviet Union. Winston Churchill deserves credit for his personal engagement with the secret services in general and with Bletchley Park in particular, upon which he conferred a benign patronage unmatched by any other war leader. The indispensable element in making all intelligence useful, in peace or war, is that it should pass into the hands of a wise and effective leader; if such a person is absent, whether general, admiral or statesman, then even the most privileged information is worthless.

It is sometimes argued that certain nations display a genius for intelligence which others lack. Although the Japanese conducted meticulous tactical reconnaissance of the targets for their initial 1941–42 assaults on the Western Powers, thereafter their mindset proved ill-suited to the collection or objective analysis of intelligence. The Russians sustained their historic gift for conspiracy, but made little effective use of what they learned. The Americans' wartime intelligence activities were dominated by successes in breaking Japanese codes, though they also developed – through the Research & Analysis division of OSS – a more effective arm for economic and political assessment than MI6 possessed, or even recognised a need for. Rather than distinguishing relative intelligence skills by nationality, it seems more appropriate to do so by culture. Many of the finest intelligence officers of all nations were Jews. The Third Reich paid heavily for excluding them from its secret services, as also did the Soviet Union when it purged them in the early 1950s: Semyon Semyonov, Moscow's brilliant agent-runner in America, was among those then dismissed. The nations that gathered and used information best in the Second World War were those committed to intellectual honesty and the pursuit of truth, while those that failed were the dictatorships to which truth was inherently alien, unacceptable, antipathetic – which included the Soviet Union. While democracies do not always trade in frankness, as the modern experience of the 2003 Iraq War vividly demonstrates, at least most of their citizens are reared to regard truth as a virtue, while those of dictatorships are not.

As for the guerrilla campaigns conducted in Axis-occupied nations, only in Yugoslavia and Russia between 1943 and 1945 did partisans make a significant contribution to the final outcome, and even there all the big things had to be done by the Red Army. In the Far East, SOE and OSS could achieve nothing that mattered in societies overwhelmingly preoccupied with ridding themselves of their colonial masters, as well as of the Japanese. In Western Europe, the Anglo-American secret services performed a useful function by sustaining an Allied presence, and marginal military activity, in advance of D-Day, when the process of liberation began in earnest. Their foremost contribution, however, which justified their existence, was to raise banners throughout the occupied countries beneath which fighters for freedom could rally. The Allied agents who went forth into occupied Europe offered a symbolic sacrifice which many of their inhabitants – the non-communist ones, at least – never forgot.

Most of the supposed military achievements of guerrillas, especially in connection with D-Day, were negligible: for instance, the story that the Resistance 'liberated' parts of France in August 1944 is a fairy tale – the German army retired because it had suffered defeat in Normandy, with mobs of *maquisards* snapping at its heels. 'Resistance is small business,' said a shrewd OSS officer, Macdonald Austin, who served in occupied France. 'Any attempt to make it more than that is bound to go wrong.' Yet the moral contribution of secret war, which would have been impossible without the sponsorship of SOE and OSS, was beyond price. It made possible the resurrection of self-respect in occupied societies which would otherwise have been obliged to look back on the successive chapters of their experience of the conflict through a dark prism: military humilia-tion, followed by enforced collaboration with the enemy, then by belated deliverance at the hands of foreign armies. As it was, and entirely thanks to Resistance, all European nations could cherish their cadres of heroes and martyrs, enabling the mass of their citizens who did nothing, or who served the enemy, to be painted over on the grand canvas cherished in the perception of their descendants.

Finally, a hindsight and a foresight. This book has trafficked little in romance, much in harsh realities. Yet no account of the secret war would be complete without acknowledging that for many agents serving their countries abroad, especially when they were winning, the experience was irresistibly thrilling, even when their own lives were imperilled. A wartime SOE officer posted to the Levant described the impact on local listeners when he used the French word '*intelligence*' to describe his mission: 'The sharp intake of breath by Arabs who had read their *romans policiers*, and knew the omnipotence, omniscience and ruthlessness of the British Secret Service, was flatteringly audible. Some instantly asked me if I was a lord.' He loved it. So, too, did many other spies of many nations. Why else would they have taken the work?

Between 1939 and 1945, secret war was still in its infancy. The victories that decided outcomes were secured by great armies, fleets, air forces. In the twenty-first century, however, it seems ever less plausible that mass uniformed forces of the Great Powers, numbered in millions, will again clash in arms. By contrast the importance to national security of intelli-gence, eavesdropping, codebreaking and counter-insurgency has never been greater. Cyber-warfare is a logical evolution of the process that began in Room 40 during World War I, and expanded vastly at Bletchley Park and OKH/GdNA, Arlington Hall and Op-20-G during World War II. It would be extravagant to suggest that conventional strife has become redundant: in Ukraine, Vladimir Putin finds main battle tanks highly serviceable. But he also employs tactics of subversion backed by Moscow's secret soldiers that would command the immediate sympathy and applause of Pavel Sudoplatov.

Electronic surveillance of communications has become the foremost weapon of both Britain and the United States in identifying and monitoring terrorists within their own frontiers and abroad, to the dismay of some civil libertarians. The 2013–15 revelations of Edward Snowden, the former NSA employee who has seen fit to disclose the scale of Western eavesdropping, from the awesomely inappropriate sanctuary of Moscow, has done important damage to American and British security, and invites a stab of relief that he did not serve at wartime Bletchley or Arlington Hall. He inhabits a new universe, in which old definitions of conflict, and also of patriotism, are no longer universally acknowledged. The balance of tactics and methodology in struggles between nations has changed, is changing, and will continue to change. Secret war, as it was practised by the nations that fought the conflict of 1939–45, may well prove to be future war.

Acknowledgements

Because this is my first book explicitly about intelligence, my foremost debts are to historians with specialist knowledge, who have been kind enough to give me assistance at various stages. Professor Sir Michael Howard OM CH MC, the official historian of British wartime deception, read and commented upon my draft manuscript, as he has done so often and importantly for other books of mine in the past. I also received valuable guidance from my old friend Antony Beevor, who copied for me Albert Praun's important German sigint report, a real labour of love for a fellow historian; Richard Aldrich, David Kahn, Alan Petty, Christopher Andrew, Chris Bellamy and two of the secret world's archivists, who in keeping with tradition wish to remain anonymous. None, of course, bears the slightest responsibility for my judgements and errors. My obligation is immense to Ralph Erskine, a fount of information about every aspect of wartime cryptanalysis, which is both a maze and a minefield for the uninitiated. He corrected a host of mistakes in my original draft, some of them egregious, and provided me with many source references and pointers; my text is immeasurably improved by his attentions. William Spencer at the British National Archives and Tim Nenninger at the US National Archives were wonderfully helpful, as ever, as was my dear friend Rick Atkinson, a peerless historian of the US Army. Like almost every author in the land, I give daily thanks for the London Library and its peerless staff. I must reprise my gratitude to Dr Lyuba Vinogradovna for researching and translating a mass of Russian material, and to Susanne Schmidt for doing likewise with German documents, notably from the Freiburg Archive. My old friend and colleague Don Berry read the manuscript as an expert editor who brought a non-specialist's eye to my text.

Virtually all the wartime generation of intelligence officers are now gone, but in decades gone by I was fortunate enough to interview many men and women who served with SOE, OSS and MI6, together with some of their Continental agents and informants. Those encounters were significant, I think, in helping me to understand the nature of the secret war, the extraordinary challenges faced by those who waged it, together with the sacrifices made by those who became its casualties.

I never cease to thank my stars for the support of Michael Sissons and Peter Matson, my agents in London and New York respectively. My relationship with HarperCollins in Britain, and especially with Arabella Pike, Robert Lacey and Helen Ellis, has been unfailingly happy. It is a new delight to work with Jonathan Jao of HarperCollins in the US. My secretary Rachel Lawrence has endured my frailties and saved me from my follies for almost thirty years now. My wife Penny has served nearly as long a sentence in my company; I am fearful that she will soon demand parole, as a just reward for saintly behaviour.

Notes and Sources

It deserves renewed emphasis that scepticism is essential about all accounts related to intelligence in every nation, and thus to the memoirs of agents, official reports, published histories and even contemporary documents. Almost everyone who participated in the secret war lied, and sometimes it was their job to do so. This book represents an attempt to describe and explain what happened, but it would be absurd to pretend to vouch for its authenticity. The memoirs of Pavel Sudoplatov, for instance, make fascinating reading, and constitute almost the only available testimony about some Russian aspects of the wartime story. Parts of his narrative are undoubtedly true, but it is impossible to be sure which. The same applies to accounts given by many other former intelligence officers, Russian, German, British, American and Japanese alike. A mass of documentary material is available not only in the US National Archives in Maryland, but now also online: the post-war American TICOM studies of the radio intelligence struggle are especially relevant and useful.

A large body of material relating to British intelligence is accessible in the National Archives at Kew. This includes some MI6 papers, but the service's own files have never been opened to any historian save its official chronicler, Keith Jeffery, a decade ago, and he was debarred from naming informants, even long-dead ones, in his published narrative. Because the available material suggests that MI6 – other than its subordinate branch, GC&CS – played a marginal role in wartime intelligence, defenders of the service make the point that only a limited proportion of its own contemporary archive has survived for scrutiny, by Keith Jeffery or anyone else. Thus, loyal secret servants argue, it is plausible that details of many good deeds performed by Broadway's men have been lost. This is possible, but doubtful. My own scepticism about MI6's performance is influenced by the number of informed contemporary witnesses who thought poorly of Stewart Menzies and his senior officers, not all of them as jaundiced as

Hugh Trevor-Roper or Malcolm Muggeridge. The likes of Bill Bentinck, Alexander Cadogan and Nigel Clive had no axes to grind.

An estimated 13 per cent of SOE's files survive, and have been available for some years to historians and students in the National Archives. Christopher Andrew's authorised history of MI5 contains much fascinating information, and quotes some important internal documents. The Soviet intelligence archives have never been opened to researchers, but substantial quantities of material derived from them have been published in collections over the past two decades. We may assume that most of these papers are authentic, and they are certainly fascinating to historians. But there is an important caveat: Moscow has released documents on a highly selective basis, designed to show its wartime intelligence services in the best possible light. Thus, it is no more possible to achieve a rounded assessment of the GRU's and NKVD's activities from what modern Russia chooses to reveal than by studying a list of a racing tipster's winners without reference to the also-rans. Moscow makes some ambitious claims for the achievements of its wartime codebreakers, but has thus far produced little documentary evidence to support them, beyond some decrypts of which the origins are unspecified; until it does so, it seems reasonable to attribute to nationalistic exuberance its professions to have matched Bletchley and Arlington Hall. Meanwhile a substantial body of Abwehr and German army staff intelligence assessments is held by the Military Archive in Freiburg, where – for instance – it is possible to read almost the entire output of 'Agent Max', composed by Moscow Centre for the delectation of Reinhard Gehlen.

In the notes below, the British National Archives are designated as UKNA; their US counterpart as USNA; Germany's military archive is given as Freiburg.

Introduction
xv 'All aspects of' Praun MS p.15 Friedman online archive, see Bibliography for access details
xviii 'His transportation expenses' Kahn, David *Hitler's Spies* Hodder & Stoughton 1978 p.198
xix 'There has never been' Jones, Dr R.V. *Most Secret War* Heinemann 1978 p.7

Chapter 1 – Before the Deluge
3 'The Abwehr somehow' Jones, Dr R.V. *Reflections on Intelligence* London 1984 pp.69–70
4 '[MI6] values information' Stewart Hampshire in Trevor-Roper, Hugh *The Wartime Journals* ed. Richard Davenport-Hines I.B. Tauris 2012 p.149 Apr 1943
6 'Under our system' Liddell, Guy *The Guy Liddell Diaries* ed. Nigel West two vols Routledge 2005 vol. I p.86
9 'Practically every officer' Usborne, Richard *Clubland Heroes* Constable 1953 p.1
9 'Foreign intelligence services envied' Sisman, Adam *Hugh Trevor-Roper* Weidenfeld & Nicolson 2010 p.90

11 'The Air Ministry complained' Jeffery, Keith *MI6: The History of the Secret Intelligence Service* Bloomsbury 2010 p.287
12 'On 25 July, a British delegation ...' This account is based upon that given in Ralph Erskine's 'The Poles Reveal their Secrets: Alastair Denniston's Account of the July 1939 Meeting at Pyry' *Cryptologia* 22.11.2006
16 'We were daily inundated' Cadogan, Alexander *The Diaries of Sir Alexander Cadogan 1938–45* ed. David Dilks Cassell 1971 p.158
17 'Instead, however, Sinclair's' UKNA FO1093/127
21 'I accepted the brutality' Sudoplatov, Pavel *Special Tasks* Little, Brown 1994 p.62
24 'at an ironmonger's shop' Foote, Alexander *A Handbook for Spies* Museum Press 1949 p.22
25 'I think that from that time' ibid. p.38

Chapter 2 – The Storm Breaks

42 'instead of starting' Jones *Intelligence* p.274
43 'casual sources should not' ibid. p.275
45 'The Venlo incident' UKNA FO1093/200-202
45 'I think they [the German' Cadogan p. 226
45 'the permanent under-secretary ordered' Cadogan p.231 10.11.39
46 'the real nigger in the woodpile' Liddell vol. I p.51
46 'we had a continuous stream' Strong, Kenneth *Intelligence at the Top* Giniger 1968 p.55
47 'Reg Jones cited' Jones *Intelligence* p.216
47 'can to some extent be' Liddell vol. I p.32
48 'Perfect intelligence in war' Bill Williams in USNA RG457 Entry 9002 SRH 037
49 'A German aeroplane came down' Liddell p.57
49 'complete plan of German invasion' Cadogan p.245 13.1.40
49 'So often I have' Strong p.61
49 'but he's rather mercurial' Cadogan p.248
50 'Col. Handeeming' Praun MS p.53; Friedman online archive, see Bibliography for access details
50 'brilliant in every respect' Behrendt, Hans-Otto *Rommel's Intelligence in the Desert Campaign* Kimber 1980 p.59
50 'carrying important lists' ibid. p.219
50 'Guidelines for the interrogation' Freiburg Archive R606055 1/2 & 2/2
51 'The officers (and most of the men)' Lockhart, Bruce *Diaries* p.47 16.1.40
52 'Like all South Africans' Freiburg archive RW4/320-84 June 1941
52 'MI6's Major Monty Chidson' Jeffery p.386
52 'MI5 spurned torture' Liddell p.98
53 'Naval Intelligence Division interrogators' McLachlan, Donald *Room 39: Naval Intelligence in Action 1939–45* Weidenfeld & Nicolson 1968 p.176
53 'the War Office's director' Strong p.69
54 'our "intelligence" gives nothing' Cadogan p.318
54 'Little or no reliance' Aldrich, Richard *Intelligence and the War Against Japan* Cambridge 2000 p.37 6.1.41
54 'In other circumstances' Sukolov-Gourevitch, Anatoli *Un Certain Monsieur Kent* Grasset 1995 p.117
55 'was composed almost entirely' ibid. p.129
55 'Writers of thrillers' Muggeridge, Malcolm *The Infernal Grove* Collins 1973 p.117
57 'following the interrogations' Strong p.94
57 'I am forever discovering' Trevor-Roper *Journals* p.33
59 'mind of a mounted spectator' Sisman p.107
59 'In the world of neurotic' ibid. p.88
59 'irreverent thoughts' ibid. p.89

60 'a team of a brilliance' ibid. p.96

60 'With the finest feel' Kahn *Spies* p.228

62 'The writer Cyril Connolly' Langhorne, Richard ed. *Diplomacy and Intelligence During the Second World War: Essays in Honour of F.H. Hinsley* Cambridge 1985 Andrew essay p.31

63 'He returned safely to Europe' UKNAWO208/5542 SIR 1595, 1598

63 'We soon became aware that' Sisman p.119

64 'on 28 March 1941 he told Szymańska' Jeffery pp.381–2

65 'This cannot be' Kahn *Spies* p.187

65 'Himmler in 1944 declared' ibid. p.270

65 'Leaders in a democratic system' Handel, Michael ed. *Strategic and Operational Deception in the Second World War* Frank Cass 1987 p.119

66 'The Y Service was the best' Behrendt p.49

66 'this incomparable source' ibid. p.167

67 'a mirror image of [MI6]' Sisman p.117

Chapter 3 – Miracles Take a Little Longer: Bletchley

68 'Stewart Menzies, knowing' Jeffery p.332

68 'whether or not Cryptanalysis' ibid. p.335

69 'Within a week I was' Annan, Noel *Our Age* Weidenfeld & Nicolson 1990 p.223

69 'It is the lawyer' McLachlan p.343

69 'It must be made' UKNA WO208/3575

70 'A neutral traveller' UKNA WO169/18

70 'It is piteous to find ourselves' Jeffery p.401

70 'My impression is' Howarth, Patrick *Intelligence Chief Extraordinary* Bodley Head 1986 p.144

70 'We no longer depend' Strong p.98

72 'The achievements of German' Praun MS p.129

72 'gave German commanders' ibid. p.3

73 'If he is to stay' Hodges, Andrew *Alan Turing: The Enigma of Intelligence* Allen & Unwin 1983 p.26

74 'I liked his sly' Annan p.237

74 'Do you have religious' Hinsley, F.H. & Stripp, Alan *Codebreakers: The Inside Story of Bletchley Park* OUP 1993 Hugh Denham p.264

74 'You've travelled a bit' quoted Andrew essay in Langhorne p.31

75 'On a snowy' Lucas, F.L. in *Enigma: The Battle for the Code* Weidenfeld & Nicolson 1980 p.36

75 'By Jove' Jones, R.V. *Intelligence and National Security* 9 1994 p.2

76 'It's amazing how' Budiansky, Stephen *Battle of Wits* Penguin 2000 p.114

77 'almost total inability' Budiansky p.159

78 'The ideal cryptanalyst' ibid. p.135

78 'patience, accuracy, stamina' Christopher Morris in Hinsley & Stripp p.243

78 'When a new word' Skillen, Hugh *Enigma and its Achilles Heel* Pinner 1992 p.48

78 'I was about to return' Baring, Sarah *The Road to Station X* Wilton 65 2000 p.93

79 'William Millward recalled' Millward in Hinsley & Stripp p.28

79 'If not satisfied' Calvocoressi, Peter *Top Secret Ultra* Cassell 1980

79 'DOC NOTE, I DISSENT' Jack Good in Hinsley & Stripp p.160

80 'entirely dependent on Herivel' Welchman, Gordon *The Hut Six Story* McGraw-Hill 1982 p.101

80 'some Eastern goddess' Winterbotham, F.W. *The Ultra Secret* Futura 1975 p.33

80 'Built by the British Tabulating Machine' Welchman p.140

81 'It was like a lot of knitting' McKay, Sinclair *The Secret Life of Bletchley Park* Aurum 2010 p.106

84 'probable date of ending preparations' UKNA HW1/3

84 'the greatest disappointment' Stuart Milner-Barry in Hinsley & Stripp p.98

85 'CAS [Chief of Air Staff] How many hours' ibid.

86 'Many of the cryptanalysts' Annan p.236

86 'Cryptanalysts have to be handled' UKNA HW14/13

86 'It is a serious charge' Ralph Erskine to the author 27.4.15

86 'Despite the high tension' Thomas in Hinsley & Stripp p.45

87 'Its files record details' UKNA HW14/43 15.7.42

87 'There was much snapping' UKNA HW14/11 Jan 1941

87 'Although an excellent linguist' UKNA HW14/13

87 'Wren Kenwick is inaccurate' McKay p.151

87 'nineteen-year-old mathematician' Smith, Michael and Erskine, Ralph eds *Action This Day* p.104

88 'It was acknowledged that' Grey, Christopher *Intelligence and National Security* 28 no. 6 Dec 2013 pp.705–807

89 'I had left as one of' Bennett essay in Hinsley & Stripp p.38

90 'devoted to the task' Taunt, Derek in *Action This Day* p.82

90 'exemplary leadership' ibid. p.207

90 'My touchiness is probably' UKNA HW14/37

91 'MI5 bought up and pulped' Liddell vol. I p.33

92 'highly commendable' McKay p.104

92 'New faces are being' UKNA HW14/13

92 'There have been recent' UKNA HW14/37 11.5.42

93 'A wonderful set of professors' Brooke, Alan *War Diaries 1939–45* ed. Alex Danchev and Daniel Todman Weidenfeld & Nicolson 2001 p.250

93 'the whole Enigma is garbage!' Kahn *Kahn On Codes* p.113

96 'In March 1943, two such' Budiansky p.241

97 'running a mistress' Liddell vol. I p.264

98 'Donovan ... is extremely friendly' Kennedy, Sir John MS, King's College London, Liddell Hart Archive 7.3.41

99 'What will they think' Jeffery p.44

100 'a very good fellow' Liddell vol. I p.116 11.12.40

100 'might win the war' USNA RG65 Box 124

100 'In January 1941, when an American' This account is based on Ralph Erskine 'What Did the Sinkov Mission Receive from Bletchley Park?' *Cryptologia* 22.9.2007

101 'that for Britain Ultra' Budiansky in *Action This Day* p.222

101 'the general policy is to be' UKNA WO193/306

101 'still reveal instances of gross' UKNA CAB120/768

Chapter 4 – The Dogs That Barked

103 'As early as July 1940' Sotskov, L.F. ed. *Aggressiya. Rassekrechennye dokumenty sluzhby razvedki RF, 1939–41* (Aggression: Declassified Documents of the Foreign Intelligence Service of the Russian Federation) Moscow 2001 p.222

104 'The Germans have raised' Gorodetsky, Gabriel *Grand Delusion: Stalin and the German Invasion of Russia* Yale 1999 p.58

104 'Pressure was to be exerted' ibid. p.57

105 'Vsevolod Merkulov, Beria's deputy' ibid. p.114

105 'remained the decisive focus' ibid. p.122

106 'We have completely altered' ibid. p.133

106 'The majority of the intelligence' ibid. p.135

108 'What news from "the village"?' Gourevitch p.87

112 'I am lonely' Prange, Gordon *Target Tokyo: The Story of the Sorge Spy Ring* McGraw-Hill 1984 p.342

113 'Berlin has informed' Sorge dispatches p.277, document 150 TsAMO RF f.23, op.24127, d.2,l.422
113 'I think that one can never' Gorodetsky p.53
115 'No special assignments' Peshchersky, Vladimir Krasnaya *Kapella: Sovetskaya razvedka protiv abvera i Gestapo* (Rote Kapelle: The Soviet Intelligence Service Against the Abwehr and Gestapo) Moscow 2000 p.70
115 'Most significantly, he told' Sotskov p.141
117 'The NKVD Fifth Department's' ibid. p.234
118 'on 7 February 1941' ibid. p.256
118 'Next day came another' ibid. p.258
118 'This was followed by' ibid. p.262 et seq.
119 '"Breitenbach" reported that the British' ibid. p.271 19.3.41
119 'Kuckhoff strikes one' ibid. pp.165–6
120 'rumours about Germany's attack' ibid. p.391
120 'We can pump whatever information' Gorodetsky p.53
121 'Behrens was anyway' ibid. p.176
122 'Moreover, on 20 June' Sotskov p.490
123 'anti-Soviet elements' Gorodetsky p.301
123 'A visiting American' John Deane in Waller, Douglas *Wild Bill Donovan* Simon & Schuster 2012 p.223
123 'a nervous Fitin scribbled' Sotskov p.461
123 'the usual contradictory rumours' UKNA FO371/29479 N1390/78
123 'German plan is as follows' UKNA FO371/26518 C2919/19/18
125 'In early April the JIC's' UKNA FO371/29479 N1364/78/38 and 29465 N1713/3/38
125 'As late as 23 May' UKNA WO208/1761 jic 41/218
125 'Cripps told the American ambassador' US State Department 740.0011 EW/39/8919 7.3.41
126 'The NKVD also suggested' Gorodetsky p.185
126 'They responded that Berlin' ibid. p.187
126 'On 24 May, when' ibid. p.222
130 'But he also stated' Sudoplatov p.123
130 'The only certain thing' Gorodetsky p.306
131 'Misinformation! You may go' ibid. p.206

Chapter 5 – Divine Winds
140 'The saga vividly illustrates' This account is principally based upon Seki Eiji's *Mrs Ferguson's Tea Set: Japan and the Second World War* Global Oriental 2000
143 'like searching for very fine' Kotani, Ken *Japanese Intelligence in World War II* Osprey 2009 p.32
143 'The [US] Army and Navy' ibid. p.83
144 'characteristic impertinence' Liddell vol. I p.161
148 'In Japan we are in' Kotani p.20
151 'It is expected that the Germans' ibid. p.101
154 'I became aware of' ibid. p.71
155 'He was recruited by Tokyo' see Elphick & Smith *Odd Man Out* Hodder & Stoughton 1993
155 'He reported three times' John Hurt MS in Friedman Papers Box 212 'The Japanese Problem in the Signals Intelligence Service' 1930–45 p.28
158 'Rochefort was born' The principal source for the biographical information that follows is Elliot Carlson's *Joe Rochefort's War* Naval Institute Press Annapolis 2011
158 'makes you feel' ibid. p.35
159 'The few persons who' ibid. p.39
161 'the results they achieved' ibid. p.21

165 'Forget Pearl Harbor' Holmes, W.J. *Double-Edged Secrets: US Naval Intelligence Operations in the Pacific During World War II* Naval Institute Press 1979 p.43

166 'Now, there goes' ibid. p.96

173 'In the defensive stages' USNA RG457 Box 78 SRH264

173 'the enemy had grasped' Kotani p.87

Chapter 6 – Muddling and Groping: The Russians at War

174 'Are you sure' Sudoplatov p.127

175 'The newly liberated officers' ibid. p.128

175 'It is hard to suppose' Andrew, Christopher & Mitrokhin, Vasili *The Mitrokhin Archive* Allen Lane 1999 p.106

175 'Since 1939 Sudoplatov' Sudoplatov p.112

176 'He was a man who' ibid. p.113

177 'We did not go home' Voskresenskaya, Zoya *Teper ya mogu skazat pravdu* (Now I Can Tell the Truth) Moscow 1993

178 'He appeared to me' Sudoplatov p.150

179 'A modern Russian' *Velikaya Otechestvennaya Voina 1941–1945 Godov* (The Great Patriotic War of 1941–1945) vol. VI (Intelligence and Counter Intelligence During the Great Patriotic War) Moscow 2013 p.196

180 'It is a mistake' Masterman, Jack *The Double-Cross System* Granada 1979 p.32

183 'Sergei Tolstoy' L.A. Kuzmin, in an essay entitled 'Ne zabyvat svoikh geroev' (We Must Not Forget Our Heroes), claims that Tolstoy's team broke the Japanese Orange, Red and Purple ciphers

183 'All that seems certain' *Velikaya Otechestvennaya Voina 1941–1945 Godov* (The Great Patriotic War of 1941–1945) vol. VI p.196

184 'Western cryptographic experts' Ralph Erskine made this point to the author 5.4.2015

184 'He was an unusually gifted' This narrative is based on the account in Degtyarev, Klim & Kolpakidi, Aleksandr *Vneshnyaya Razvedka SSSR* (Soviet Foreign Intelligence) Moscow 2009 p.130 et seq.

187 'Almost every offensive' Franz Halder in a 1967 interview with *Der Spiegel*

188 'Radó revealed after the war' By endorsing a published version of his story, *Moscow's Eye* by German journalist Bernd Ruland

188 'By this means the spy' Peshchersky p.235

191 'a big, imposing house' Gourevitch p.159 et seq.

192 'I'm thrilled to see you' ibid. p.164

192 'I could not rid myself' ibid. p.165

193 'Army Group B, said the *Rote Kapelle*' Korovin V.V. *Sovetskaya Razvedka i Kontrrazvedka v Gody Velikoi Otechestvennoi Voiny* (Soviet Intelligence and Counter-Intelligence During the Great Patriotic War) Moscow 2003 p.48

193 'This summer the Germans' ibid. p.49

194 'Germany's counter-intelligence agencies' Echterkampf *Second World War* vol. IX/1 p.821 et seq.

Chapter 7 – Britain's Secret War Machine

195 'the results of which' There is an exemplary account of this and related Mediterranean naval actions in Richard Woodman's *Malta Convoys* John Murray 2000 p.244 et seq.

198 'Admiral Ciliax's squadron' This account is chiefly based on Hinsley et al. *British Intelligence* vol. II pp.179–88

199 'a tactical victory' Roskill, S.W. *The War at Sea* HMSO 1956 vol. II p.159

200 'The best arrangement' Cradock, Percy *Know Your Enemy: How the JIC Saw the World* John Murray 2002

202 'It was like a French farce' Howarth p.113

202 'very impressive … He had a temperament' ibid. p.171

202 'An advance by the Axis' UKNA CAB81/103
202 'leading my choir' Howarth p.143
203 'rather as an army commander' Jones *Intelligence* p.91
203 'The British armies and the new' Howarth p.171
203 'to use the Soviet [front]' UKNA CAB81/103
204 'Assuming that the campaign' UKNA CAB81/103
204 'We think her inclination' UKNA CAB81/103
204 'a German in touch with' UKNA CAB81/103
206 'If Elizabeth had taken' Trevelyan, G.M. *A Short History of England* Pelican 1959 p.256
206 'I think, Captain' McLachlan p.264
207 'When I looked coolly' Sisman p.90
207 'I do not think he ever' Trevor-Roper *Secret World* p.103
208 'Is it necessary to argue' Sisman p.107
208 'Trevor-Roper found himself' ibid. pp.109–10
208 'If good work results in' Jones *Intelligence* p.158
208 'Only Bletchley kept' Howarth p.115
208 'Intelligence is only' Schlesinger, Arthur M. *A Life in the Twentieth Century* Mariner 2000 p.328
209 'It's hopeless conducting' Cadogan p.405 6.9.41
209 'They are to be regarded' UKNA HW14/13
209 'The British service' see Hastings, Max *Bomber Command* Michael Joseph 1979 p.98
210 'The science of destroying' UKNA CAB163/6
211 'It is striking' Bonsall, A. *An Uphill Struggle: The Provision of Tactical Sigint Support to the Allied Air Forces in Europe in WWII* and Stubbington, John *Kept in the Dark* p.205
212 'Like the driver' McLachlan p.2
212 'if not the wisest' ibid. p.2
213 'On 11 March 1942 C-in-C' UKNA ADM205/23
214 'So reliable was' McLachlan p.38
215 'entertaining at the Ritz' ibid. p.174
219 'The enemy possessed' TICOM files online, German Naval Communications Intelligence SRH-024, p.21
219 'The most complete single' ibid. p.25
219 'The convoys then at sea' ibid. p.22
219 'the more important ciphers' Erskine *Action This Day* pp.374–5
220 'Whether and to what' Dönitz *Memoirs: Ten Years and Twenty Days* p.143
221 'After the war Donald McLachlan' McLachlan p.340

Chapter 8 – 'Mars': The Bloodiest Deception

223 'In the winter of 1941' Praun MS p.98
223 'The British were alarmed' UKNA HW14/62 Dec.1942, HW14/33, HW14/60, HW14/19, HW14/17. There is further detail on UK monitoring of German intercepts of the Eastern Front in HW14/27, HW14/29, HW14/62, HW14/28 and HW14/33. There are useful insights into the 'Mars' deception in the *Information Bulletin of the Russian Association of Second World War Historians* no.6 200 p.16 et seq.
223 'the Germans can read' UKNA HW14/19
224 'FHO's chief offered' Freiburg Archives RH2/1981, sheet 46–51 Foreign Armies East
227 'Early in 1942, during' Damaskin, Igor *Stalin i Razvedka* (Stalin and the Intelligence Service) Moscow 2004 p.284 et seq.
227 'The chaos in the GRU' ibid. p.285
227 'Even as late as 19 June' Damaskin p.287
232 'The 6 November report should' Freiburg Archive RH2/1957, sheets 180, 183
233 'very highly valued' UKNA CAB154/105

233 'He and his section puzzled' UKNA HW19/347
234 'MAX must be regarded' Liddell vol. II p.99
236 'Pavel Sudoplatov is too' see David Glanz writing in Handel et al. p.188
236 'Bishop Vasily Ratmirov' Sudoplatov p.160
236 'The bishop asked for' Rybkina p.321

Chapter 9 – The Orchestra's Last Concert
243 'Centre kept sending' Zoya Rybkina memoirs p.239
248 'I did not know that he' Gourevitch p.213
249 'After the break-up' Praun MS p.185
250 'it gave me moral' Foote p.119
250 'For the first time' ibid. p.143
251 'a motherly old soul' ibid. p.110

Chapter 10 – Guerrilla
259 'set Europe ablaze' Dalton diary p.62 22.7.40
259 'You should never be' ibid. p.52 1.7.40
259 'The time is not' Howarth p.138
259 'tended to give Churchill' Beevor p.15
260 'Robert Bruce Lockhart' Lockhart p.168–9
261 'Sometimes they would' Hastings, Max *Das Reich: The 2nd SS Panzer Division's March to Normandy June 1944* Michael Joseph 1981 p.137
261 'You could never make' To the author 10.3.80
262 'The only good point' Bennett *Churchill's Man of Mystery* Routledge 2009 p.261
262 'several of its training schools' Jeffery p.629
262 'The man who is' Sweet-Escott, Bickham *Baker Street Irregular* Methuen 1965 p.24
264 'nothing more than a wicked' ibid. p.12
264 'The Abwehr was bemused' see UKNA CAB301/51 Hanbury-William/Playfair June 1942 report on shortcomings of SOE
265 'A January 1942 Baker Street' UKNA HI5/203 21.1.42
265 'He tells me that' UKNA HI5/203 December 1942
265 'action for action's sake' Sweet-Escott p.60
265 'The sacrifice might' ibid. p.197
266 'What matters most' Clive, Nigel *A Greek Experience 1943–48* Michael Russell 1985 p.85
266 'the Germans were infuriated' Praun MS p.121
266 'Could nothing be done' Lockhart p.222
266 'They never achieved' See UKNA FO1093/155 for attempts by MI6 to stifle SOE
267 'Lack of unity' Liddell vol. II p.61
267 'The Greek Alphabet' Jeffery p.355
268 'Those were exceptions' UKNA WO208/3629 Weigel interrogation
269 'WHENEVER YOU WILL COME' This account is taken from Foot, M.R.D. *The Special Operations Executive 1940–46* BBC 1984 pp.130–4
270 'displayed an enthusiasm' *Times Literary Supplement* 18.3.53
270 'good people, very good' Howarth p.175
270 'There were a lot of' ibid. p.174
270 'to frontal assault' ibid.
271 'One was most afraid' Reed-Olsen, Oluf *Two Eggs on My Plate* Allen & Unwin 1952 p.234
273 'like trying to live' Jeffery p.434
273 'Carlton Gardens was indifferent' Liddell p.206
274 'it was not exclusively' Reed-Olsen p.45
274 'Escapers and evaders' Foot, M.R.D & Langley, J.M. *MI9: Escape and Evasion 1939–45* Bodley Head 1979 p.65

275 'James Langley' Langley, James *Fight Another Day* Magnum 1974 p.242
275 'Your trouble, Jimmy' ibid. p.193
276 'one colonel tried' Sweet-Escott p.73
276 'all his energies' Clive p.45
276 'Political rather than' ibid. p.123
277 'of carrying out two' Haukelid, Knut *Skis Against the Atom* North American Heritage 1989 p.13
277 'there were many more' Sweet-Escott p.154
278 'Our effort in Greece' Clive p.128
278 'Wallace was quite wrong' Unpublished Hiller MS, see Hastings *Das Reich* p.48
278 'I enjoyed one of' Clive p.134
279 '20 per cent for Liberation' Harris Smith, R. *OSS: The History of America's First Central Intelligence Agency* University of California Press 1972 p.112
279 'for instance, the 2nd SS' see Hastings *Das Reich* passim
279 'It was only just worth it' ibid. p.218

Chapter 11 – Hoover's G-Men, Donovan's Wild Men

281 'Gentlemen, I am' Hayden, Sterling *The Wanderer* Sheridan House 2000 p.330
282 'An SOE man visiting' Sweet-Escott p.126
282 'Reader's Digest, Twentieth Century-Fox' USNA RG65 Box 125 FBI Narrative
282 'What he did when' ibid.
283 'inability to fit into' USNA RG65 Box 122
283 'The British MI6 displayed' ibid.
284 'On March 17' USNA RG65 Box 125
284 'Consideration is being' USNA RG65 Box 126
284 '"skulduggery" and intelligence-gathering' Howarth p.148
285 'calculatingly reckless' Harris Smith p.35
285 'Everyone was working up' Hayden p.310
285 'When Arthur Schlesinger joined' Schlesinger p.296
286 'The chiefs of the various' Hayden p.310
286 'Major William Holohan' Smith p.111
286 'The colonel has aged' Lockhart p.175 17.6.42
287 'The training I have' USNA RG59 Box 151 103.91802
288 'He feels very *strongly*' RG59 Box 150 103.91802 July 1944
288 'The US ambassador in Chonqing' USNA RG59 Box148 103.91802/14 14.10.43
288 'The US consul in Tangier' ibid. Box 149 103.91802/1921 Apr 1944
288 'Gollys, young feller' Hayden p.236
289 'My duty was to' Stafford, David *Roosevelt and Churchill* p.213
290 'in intelligence, the British' Tompkins, Peter *Italy Betrayed* Simon & Schuster 1966 p.253
290 'these callow, touchy' Trevor-Roper *Journals* January 1943 p.128
290 'British imperialism' Sweet-Escott p.150
291 '"great value", and authorised' USNA RG59 Box 151 103.91802 November 1944
291 'SOE and MI6 agreed' UKNA HIS/210
291 'We are shortly coming to' UKNA HS1/103
291 'The overland journey took' Smith p.254
292 'were not interested in' ibid. p.128
292 'Here, I was' Seitz, Albert *Mihailovitch* Columbus 1953 p.49
292 'We established a' Hayden 1951 Testimony to the House US Committee pp.152–3
293 'found himself committed' Hayden p.314
293 'I told you in earlier' ibid. p.315
293 'unusual methods of interrogation' Katz, Barry M. *Foreign Intelligence: Research and Analysis in the Office of Strategic Services 1942–45* Harvard 1989 p.185
294 'Please turn over to' USNA RG59 Box144 103.91810-2144 23.10.44

294 'If [Robert] Murphy' Smith p.43

295 'We learn that King' USNA RG59 Box 144 103.91810-344

295 'a swell bunch' Smith p.246

295 'Woe to the officer' Bruce writing in the *New York Times* 15.2.59

295 'The US ambassador to Spain' See UKNA CAB301/91 for British embassy correspondence on bribing Spaniards to stay out of the war

296 'In the summer of 1943' Waller pp.201–2

296 'In that kind of game' *New York Times* 31.8.48

296 'We were very much' *Wedermeyer Reports* New York 1958 p.107

297 'more or less like' Katz p.9

298 'The record [of Resistance]' ibid. p.40

298 'The analysts suggested' ibid. p.41

300 'Don't know, but I can' ibid. p.115

301 'at best a limited' ibid. p.29

301 'The main principle of' Weinstein, Allen & Vassiliev, Alexander *The Haunted Wood: Soviet Espionage in America – The Stalin Era* Random House 1999 p.245

302 'Donovan was in his' Schlesinger p.305

302 '[OSS's] bitterest detractors' Sweet-Escott p.126

303 'he ordered Walter Schellenberg' Doerries, Reinhard R. *Hitler's Last Chief of Foreign Intelligence: Allied Interrogations of Walter Schellenberg* Frank Cass 2003 p.102

305 'He was not just a' Petersen, Neal *From Hitler's Doorstep* Penn State University Press 1996 p.20

306 'I am of the impression' ibid. p.33

306 'offensive preparations' Dulles signal 4.3.43

306 'test flights of fleets' Dulles signal 10.4.43

307 'Americans everywhere' Jeffery p.509

308 'how close were Hitler's' Dulles report 24.3.44

310 'On one occasion he' Dulles signal 17.2.44

311 'Their reaction to the' Dulles signal 15.3.44

312 'the Americans are not' Korovin p.617

312 'One of Moscow's men' ibid. p.593

313 'One is hard-pressed' Petersen p.16

Chapter 12 – Russia's Partisans: Terrorising Both Sides

315 'The NKVD, this stated' see *Krasnye Partizany Ukrainy* (Red Partisans of the Ukraine) Gogun, Kentiy eds Kiev, 2006

317 'The NKVD's Kartashev' This account is taken from Glebov V. *Voina bez pravil. Predannyi rezident* (A War With No Rules. The Agent Who Was Betrayed) Moscow 2005 c.54–6

317 'We may assume' No3272/SV TsDAGO Ukragni F.1 Op.22 Spr.62 Ark.40–1 quoted Gogun

317 'Most of them' 24.11.41. No 3292/sp.TsDAGO Ukragni F.1 Op.22. Spr.62. Ark.45–6 quoted Gogun

318 'Measures have been' No 3290/SVTsDAGO Ukragni F.1 Op.22 Spr.62. Ark.49–50 quoted Gogun

320 'They found the bones' Report compiled by Chief of Romanian Special Intelligence, Director General Eujen Kristescu. DAOO (Derzhavniy arkhiv Odeskoi oblasti) F.492(st.) Op.1(st.) Spr.13(st.) Ark.20–4(st.) quoted Gogun & Kentiy

321 'During the summer of 1942' Potsdam history vol. VI p.1010

321 'My God! My God' Kovpak diary p.30 quoted Gogun

321 'This was a good decision' N. Popudrenko diary p.165 1.2.42 quoted Gogun

322 'He was captured in the village' G.V. Balitsky diary p.522 3.8.43 quoted Gogun

322 'We attacked a Hungarian' N. Popudrenko diary pp.175, 179

323 'The occupying power was' *Potsdam Germany and the Second World War* vol. VI p.1020
323 'Formerly employed by' UKNA WO208/5543 serial 1675
324 'An enemy train was' G.V. Balitsky diary p.543
324 'Born in 1911' Sudoplatov p.131
325 'unmasked as spies' Andrew *Mitrokhin Archive* p.xxx
325 'I discovered by' TsDAGO Ukragni F.130 Op.1 Spr. 231 Ark.5–39. P.111–11449. From the
       report of Partisan Detachment Kopenkin on the Raid in the Poltava Oblast in Oct–Dec
       1941 26.2.42

Chapter 13 – Islands in the Storm

329 'the British agreed' Much of this account is based on the narratives by Robert Fisk *In Time
       of War* André Deutsch 1983 and Enno Stephan *Spies in Ireland* London 1963
329 'an attempt at revolution' Liddell vol. I p.29
332 'Then I came to Dublin' Stephan p.119
333 'Nothing more than' ibid. p.195
334 'In December, the Irish' Fisk p.217
336 'In Istanbul, an Armenian' UKNA HW19/333
336 'the Italians are Hitler's' ibid.
338 'Lisbon, with all its lights' Muggeridge p.135
338 'The admiral dismissed' UKNA WO208/5545 Brede interrogation
338 'prominent among them' Jeffery pp.393–4
338 'I do not want you to' Bennett *Churchill's Man of Mystery* p.220
339 'but where a policy' See UKNA FO1093/138 for Foreign Office attempts to control MI6
       sabotage schemes
339 'are undoubtedly once again' USNA RG65 Box 122 FBI record
339 'Bill Bentinck agreed' Jeffery p.539–40
339 'the type of bright idea' UKNA FO1093/292
339 'Paul Claire was a' UKNA1093/225
340 'however repugnant' Jeffery pp.404–6
341 'Russian émigré who' Jeffery p.513
342 'Assume this material' UKNA KV2/757
343 'Likewise, when Malcolm' Muggeridge p.167
344 'František Moravec held Masson' Moravec p.57
345 'We never knew' Foote p.42
345 'Probably a good deal' Liddell vol. II p.22 and passim

Chapter 14 – A Little Help from Their Friends

346 'Unfortunately the law' Liddell vol. II p.77
346 'Penetration of the services' ibid. p.117 29.9.43
347 'It transpired that' Jones, *Intelligence* pp.70–1
347 'The intelligence services were' Annan p.233
348 'In the first weeks' UKNA HW1/14
349 'There is no doubt' Liddell vol. II p.24
349 'Looking around us' Toynbee, Philip *Friends Apart* Sidgwick & Jackson 1980 p.71
350 'We simply knew' Boyle, Andrew *Climate of Treason* p.52
350 'merely the most radical' Trevor-Roper *Secret World* p.80
351 'Many of our friends' ibid.
351 'a marvellous man' Borovik, Genrikh *The Philby Files* ed. Philip Knightley London 1994
       p.29
351 'One does not' ibid. p.28
351 'It's like being' Cecil, Robert *A Divided Life* Bodley Head 1988 p.77
352 'was based on doubtful' Andrew *Mitrokhin* p.109
353 'and anything else' Annan p.226

354 'smarty-pants' Howarth p.163

354 'He is six foot tall' Cecil p.60

355 'My God, he was' Andrew, Christopher *The Defence of the Realm: The Authorized History of MI5* Allen Lane 2009 p.270

356 'Gentlemen, I have' Harrison, E. *The Young Kim Philby* Exeter University Press 2012 p.96

357 'Yet MI5, overwhelmingly' Andrew *The Defence of the Realm* pp.263–8

357 'Philby reported that' Modin, Yuri *My Five Cambridge Friends* Headline 1994 p.63

357 'like one of Graham Greene's' Andrew, Christopher & Dilks, David eds *The Missing Dimension: Governments and Intelligence Communities in the Twentieth Century* Macmillan 1984 p.173

357 'His romantic veneration' Muggeridge p.126

358 'an agreeable and effective' Sisman p.93

358 'There's something wrong' ibid. p.113

359 'an insultingly crude' Harrison p.156

360 'This is to pass on' Korovin p.566

360 'London Poles' Modin p.92

361 'England will stay' Korovin p.566

361 'In collaboration with' ibid. p.599

361 'The Russians were themselves' Modin p.113

361 'In accordance with Churchill's' Jeffery p.486

361 'he wanted to discover' ibid. p.554

362 'obliges us to review' Andrew *Mitrokhin* p.165

363 'What is treason?' Sisman p.396

363 'Did Judas enjoy' ibid. p.397

363 'On balance it was not' White to Trevor-Roper 10.2.80

366 'Ample evidence exists' USNA RG59 Box 3471 81100B/7–1541

367 'switching from the status' Weinstein p.36

368 'We don't send' Feklisov memoir p.41

369 'He was of medium height' ibid. p.57

369 'took great pride in' Weinstein p.39

369 'an extraordinarily beautiful' ibid. p.4

369 'stating that he was' ibid. p.12

371 'Why not pay' Feklisov memoir p.137

371 'One wonders what' Schlesinger p.304

372 'She considers herself' Weinstein p.62

372 'Straight is a prospectively big agent' ibid. p.81

373 'indicated whether they' Sudoplatov p.227

374 'Sudoplatov believed that' ibid. p.227

375 'he treats his' Weinstein p.252

375 'Donovan knew about' Schlesinger p.305

375 'Saw Lee last night' Weinstein p.260

378 'Its highest priority' ibid. p.160

380 'Surely these unhealthy' ibid. p.164

380 'There were many green' Feklisov p.121

381 'not on behalf of' Weinstein pp.238–9

382 'the main pillar' ibid. p.94

383 'it is quite reliably' https://www.nsa.gov/public_info/declass/friedman_documents/

383 'There is no evidence' Schlesinger p.305

Chapter 15 – The Knowledge Factories

385 'Most of the people' Reed-Olsen p.126

385 'The difference it made' ibid. p.136

386 '1. Is there a divisional staff' ibid. p.254

387 'The good intelligence' Clive p.73
387 'I would be told that' ibid. p.69
387 'The Wehrmacht evacuated' ibid. p.136
387 'knew about us what' ibid. p.133
388 'the head of MI6's political section' ibid. p.146
388 'plenty of rats' Jeffery p.501
388 'Broadway abandoned attempts' ibid. p.425
388 'Though the novelist' Private information to the author from Alan Judd 2.3.2015
389 'When 6 June came' McLachlan p.321
389 'The need to sustain' Liddell vol. II pp.66–8
389 'In April 1943, MI5's ingenious' ibid. p.70 et seq.
389 'A colony of coots' Trevor-Roper *Journals* p.63 Mar 1942
390 'An officer who served' Sweet-Escott p.19
390 'we are too ready' Jeffery p.419
390 'Broadway purchased' ibid. p.457
390 'He frequently gave' ibid. p.410
390 'Misery, torture and death' Harrison p.109
390 'This sense of importance' Muggeridge p.128
391 'all Intelligence about' Jeffery p.369
391 'Cecil's case for' Cecil, Robert 'C's War' *Intelligence and National Security* May 1986
    pp.171–83
393 'His dispatches, decrypted' Except where otherwise specified, the quotations below are
    taken from Carl Boyd's *Hitler's Japanese Confidant* Kansas University Press 1993
393 'Ōshima really is' Goebbels, Joseph *The Goebbels Diaries* ed. Louis Lochner Doubleday
    1948 p.181
393 'Our mutual loyalty' UKNA HW12/264 serial 090774
394 'Do you not think' UKNA HW12/264 serial 091401
398 'I regret to say' Hinsley *British Intelligence* vol. III pt. ii p.366
398 'He reported on' ibid. p.511
398 'our main basis' Marshall 27.9.44 quoted Kahn *Codebreakers* p.606
400 'Peter Calvocoressi, one of' Howarth p.173
401 'one of the luckiest' *Action This Day* p.78
402 'noted ref JN-11 Ransuuban' UKNA HW14/122
403 'There was a 1945 debate' UKNA HW14/1 22 28.2.45
404 'In the last few days' USNA RG457 P11 201 G23-0108-6
405 'There was a perpetual' Milner-Barry in Hinsley & Stripp p.97
405 'In July 1943 John Tiltman' JT 25.7.43, WF 18.9.43; see Friedman Papers in NSA online
    archive ACC35865/41775129081420.pdf
405 'The theatre air intelligence chief' USNA RG457 SRH-037
406 'Breaks in Italian' Behrendt pp.61, 198 and Howard, Michael *British Intelligence in the
    Second World War* vol. V *Deception* p.66
406 'the fierce indignation' Hinsley & Stripp p.37
406 'they were still happy-go-lucky' Behrendt p.173
406 'did not know what' Hunt, David *A Don at War* Kimber 1966 p.147
407 'Ralph Bennett has painted' Bennett, Ralph *Ultra and Mediterranean Strategy 1941–45*
    Hamish Hamilton 1989 p.408 et seq.
407 'We knew much more' ibid. p.410
407 'No message had more' ibid. p.412
409 'I say, old boy' Smith, Michael *Station X: The Codebreakers of Bletchley Park* Pan 2004 p.77
409 'one of the outstanding' UKNA HW25/4 & 5 'General report on Tunny with emphasis on
    statistical methods' by Jack Good, Donald Michie & Geoffrey Timms
409 'as analogous to' UKNA HW14/67 18.2.43
410 'Between July and October 1942' UKNA HW25/5 p.313 sects 43A and 43B

410 'the quality of the intelligence' UKNA HW13/53 16.8.43

411 'We used to have tea parties' Vergine interview Virtual Jewish Library

413 'An unnamed Bletchley staffer' Gannon p.340

414 'the greatest code-breaking feat' Erskine in *The Times Higher Educational Supplement* 6.10.2006 pp.24–5

415 'the frequently recalcitrant' Bennett *Normandy* p.16

415 'In the summer of 1942' Jones *Intelligence* pp.217–18

417 'The Wellington's mission provided' UKNA 1473 Flight record book in AIR29/870, material on the Luftwaffe radar system in AVIA6/9380 & 14420, AVIA26/540

417 'On 15 May 1942 Flt Lt. Donald' Williams, Allan *Operation Crossbow* Preface 2013 p.113

419 'Its initial report' Much of the account that follows is taken from Hinsley et al. *British Intelligence* vol. III pt. i pp.357–455

422 'in the course of the war' Jeffery p.534

422 'He dispatched a message' Jones *Intelligence* p.223

424 'On the night of 25 July' This account is taken from Allan Williams *Operation Crossbow* pp.274–6

425 'Except possibly for' Hinsley et al. *British Intelligence* vol. III pt. ii p.464

Chapter 16 – 'Blunderhead': The English Patient

428 'Yet few Englishmen' Seth's story, as recounted here, derives from UKNA files HS9/1344, HS9/1345, KV2/377, KV2/378, KV2/379, KV2/380, HS4/240 and Seth's account of himself in *A Spy Has No Friends* Headline Review 2008

432 'Its start was inauspicious' W/Cdr. John Corby, private information to the author

441 'Guy Liddell of MI5 felt' Liddell vol. II p.285

Chapter 17 – Eclipse of the Abwehr

444 'It became apparent' Freiburg archive copy of US Army Security Agency S-3873 Doc. D3422796

444 'As late as March' USNA RG457 Taylor report in GAFY

445 'Its leading personalities' TICOM online archive/II/The Foreign Office

445 'seemed overly preoccupied' TICOM/II p.1

446 'the precision of' TICOM Fenner interrogation

446 'Most of the incoming' UKNA WO208/3612 serial 1446

447 'Chi used the same' UKNA WO208/3609

448 'the whole cryptographic' TICOM Fenner interrogation

449 'Mechanical scanning' Freiburg copy of ASC S-3873 doc. D3422796

450 'On 26 June, a long' UKNA HW13/52

450 'The Afrika Korps considered' UKNA WO208/5544 serial 1704

450 'Later, the Germans' Praun MS p.73

450 'often had a clearer' Behrendt p.165

451 'a catastrophe' ibid. p.169

451 'tactical intelligence was not' Behrendt p.203

452 'Investigation showed that' Praun MS p.65

452 'the Red Army maintained' ibid. MS p.83

452 'intercepted 46,342' Kahn *Spies* p.206

452 'As time went on' UKNA WO208/4178

452 '20 Fritzes captured' UKNA WO208/4178

452 'a truly shocking' Praun MS. p.109

453 'a calm summer' Kahn *Spies* p.440

454 'that it became fruitless' Praun MS p.109

454 'Albert Praun praised' ibid. MS p.19

455 'Neither the Abwehr' ibid.

457 'He said that he could' Baxter, Christopher *Forgeries and Spies: The Foreign Office and the 'Cicero' Case* Intelligence and National Security Dec. 2008 p.811

458 'I became what everybody' Bazna, Elyesa *I Was Cicero* Andre Deutsch 1962 p.13

458 'I was a person of' ibid. p.17

458 'her arms were' ibid. p.34

460 'Thus the most successful' UKNA CAB154/105

461 'ran the risk because' UKNA WO208/5545 Brede interrogation

462 'The only communication' UKNA WO208/35618

462 'Most likely, and in common' ibid.

463 'He was promptly' ibid.

463 'Even the Abwehr' UKNA WO203/367

464 'Jorge Mosquera, a Chilean' USNA RG65 Box 123 FBI narrative

464 'Have there already been' USNA RG65 Box 123 FBI narrative

465 'We cannot do business' Jeffery p.515

465 'they could do little harm' Liddell 10.3.43

465 'every surviving Abwehr' ibid. Jan 1943

465 'we have evidence from' UKNA HW19/347

466 'Since the fall of Tunis' ibid.

466 'Thereafter, these went' UKNA WO208/5544 SS Grup. Ohlendorf interrogation

466 'American aviation magazines' UKNA WO208/5545 Brede interrogation

466 'a vortex of personal' Trevor-Roper *Secret World* p.28

467 'when the Allies entered' UKNA HW19/347

467 'The assignment cannot be' ibid.

467 'He followed up by' ibid.

467 'without distinguishing between' ibid.

468 'The carefully orchestrated' Howard *Deception* p.50

468 'OKW accordingly reduced' ibid. p.79

470 'a decent and humane' Korovin quoting Mallet p.648

470 'He became a protégé' Gerwath, Robert *Hitler's Hangman* Yale 2011 p.113

470 'He tends to confuse' Freiburg archive copy of US Army Security Agency S-3873 Doc. D3422796

474 'When Allen Dulles told' Dulles 1.3.44

476 'Here too she squandered' Kahn *Spies* p.335

477 'For sale, valuable' Doerries p.132

478 'I ask that you' Kahn *Spies* p.274 BA R58/117: 24

Chapter 18 – Battlefields

482 '"Tar" Robertson of MI5 told' Liddell vol. II p.196

482 'the record for one' Alexander, Hugh *Cryptographic History of Work on the German Naval Enigma*

482 'The radio picture did not' Praun MS p.74

482 'his own organisation' ibid. p.76

483 'Similar inventories, partly' UKNA WO208/4312

484 'This carelessness was' Praun MS p.72

485 'What an agent' UKNA WO208/3575

485 'Black Market' USNA RG457 SRH-031

486 'Few such operations' For a fuller account of this extraordinary episode see Hastings *Das Reich* pp.187–209

487 'the desperate message' Milner-Barry in Hinsley & Stripp p.98

487 'One felt one was' UKNA WO208/3575

488 'They were trained at' The personal stories below derive from UKNA WO208/35618

489 'She had backed' This account of the stay-behinds is taken from UKNA WO208/35618 Clören interrogation report
489 'The problem is not' USNA RG407–Entry 427 Box 2410 Ninth Army reports
490 'It is no more possible' ibid.
490 'I cannot say' UKNA HS6/704
490 'the operation was brought' USNA RG407 Box 2411 109.31
491 'We learned even before' V. Nikolsky *Aquarium 2*, quoted in Damaskin p.286 et seq.
491 'An Abwehr officer in Norway' UKNA WO208/3629
491 'The GRU infiltrated' UKNA WO208/5543 serial 1675
491 'What follows seems' UKNA WO208/5556
493 'What conclusions can be' ibid.
495 'It is not a misuse' Hinsley et al. *British Intelligence* vol. III pt. ii p.418
496 'It was extraordinary' Bennett *Normandy* p.185
496 'headless horror and' Forrest Pogue *The Ardennes Campaign: The Impact of Intelligence* Dec 1980 available online through NSA website public_info/_files/cryptologic_spectrum/Ardennes_campaign.pdf
497 'My digestion is' USAMHI Carlisle Chester B. Hansen Collection, Diary, Box 6
497 'Of all the officers' Strong p.178
497 'Peter Caddick-Adams' Caddick-Adams, Peter *Snow and Steel: The Battle of the Bulge 1944–45* Preface 2014 p181
497 'It can be stated' UKNA HW13/45
498 'The record is not' UKNA WO208/3575
499 'existing British formations' Howard *Deception* p.199
499 'During the Ardennes battle' Praun p.85
499 'Deception during these' Howard *British Intelligence in WWII* vol. V p.197

Chapter 19 – Black Widows, Few White Knights
502 'performed rather inefficiently' Hurt MS Friedman Papers pp.31–2
504 'I can't go with you' Hastings, Max *Nemesis: The Battle for Japan 1944–45* HarperCollins 2007 p.297 et seq.
505 'The British were more' Budiansky p.294
505 'Intelligence, like money' Holmes p.129
506 'Far East intelligence from' Aldrich p.233
507 'Two characteristics are' UKNA HIS/304 Captain GA Garron-Williams 28.4.45
507 'Do we know' UKNA WO208/5606
507 'What we know' Aldrich p.254
508 'As you know' UKNA HS1/304 14.12.44
508 'exceedingly dissatisfied' ibid.17.11.44
508 'Leese's denunciation' UKNA WO208/5075
510 'It is a melancholy' UKNA WO203/5606
510 'I have yet to meet' UKNA WO203/6451
510 'Freddy Spencer Chapman' Spencer Chapman, Frederick *The Jungle is Neutral* Chatto & Windus 1949 passim.
511 'Insofar as SOE is' UKNA HI5/203 25.3.42
511 'The ambitions of Mackenzie' Aldrich p.284
511 'making the fullest' ibid. p.176
512 'an undignified scramble' ibid. p.185
513 'When he was shot' Allen, Louis *The Longest War: Burma 1941–45* Dent 1985 pp.577–8
513 'the party was hampered' UKNA HIS/203
513 'MI6 reported at the same' UKNA H51/304
513 'No contact with' UKNA HI5/203
514 'The clash plunged' Aldrich p.xv

515 'should admit frankly' UKNA HIS/210
516 'In 1943, when Japan's' Kotani p.17
517 'In New Guinea we' ibid. p.10
517 'A large party of Muslim' Aldrich p.164
517 'I have secretly warned' UKNA HW12/300
518 'Our navy was being' Friedman Papers in NSA online archive Lecture V, Part II 1/1/1958
   Folder 023 A38400 41699909073923
518 'Tokyo increased its own' See Katherine Herbig in Handel et al. p.274
518 'The staff of the Operations Department' Kotani p.106
519 'disliked even listening' ibid. p.101
519 'The affairs of individuals' ibid. p.104
519 'The most conspicuous example' ibid. p.39
520 'very poor' UKNA WO208/5543 serial 1673
520 'an uneasy and unprofitable' UKNA WO208/5545
520 'Seeing the Nazi ship' ibid.

Chapter 20 – 'Enormoz'

521 'There is no country' Weinstein p.196
521 'In the following year' Antonov, V. 'Moscow Looked Forward to the Information from
   Agent "Dan"' in *Nezavisimoe Voennoe Obozrenie* 17.10.2008
523 'Pavel Sudoplatov asserts' Sudoplatov p.192
523 'Oppenheimer's most recent' Monk, Ray *Inside the Centre: The Life of J. Robert
   Oppenheimer* Cape 2012 p.336
524 'Sudoplatov cites Oppenheimer' Sudoplatov p.172
527 'of great interest' Andrew *Mitrokhin* p.168
527 'On 1 July the NKVD' Weinstein p.182
529 'Elizabeth Zarubin approached' Sudoplatov p.192
530 'The information always' Andrew *Mitrokhin* p.173
531 'details … are almost certain' Liddell vol. II p.222
531 'perhaps less than half' Sudoplatov p.188

Chapter 21 – Decoding Victory

534 'MI6 is old' Wilkinson diary 24.2.43 Churchill College, Cambridge
534 'Despite the real contribution' UKNA CAB163/6
535 'He had seen the Communist' Schlesinger p.349
535 'The end of the war is' Sudoplatov p.170
536 'enemy of the people' ibid. p.431
536 'It goes without saying' Gourevitch p.8
536 'Prisons are the same' ibid. p.79
538 'The story is a little' UKNA KV2/3552
541 'very imperfect' UKNA CAB154/105
542 'There was something' Schlesinger p.350
542 'this caused some' Thirsk, James in *Action This Day* p.277
542 'One of the prices' Gannon p.447
544 'secret service became the struggle's' Aldrich p.xv
544 'very little secret information' Lockhart p.219
544 'Paul Kennedy' Kennedy, Paul *Engineers of Victory* Allen Lane 2012 p.358
545 'The cryptanalysts did not' Annan p.237
546 'Experience on both' McLachlan p.28
546 'There seems to be a tendency' USNA RG 457 SRH-031
546 'The material was dangerously' UKNA WO208/3575
546 'It is striking to notice' USNA RG59 Box 3064
547 'the old cloak and dagger' Liddell vol. II p.237

549 'Edward Travis' UKNA HW14/22
550 'These methods, said' UKNA WO311/632
551 'by means of the spoken' Jeffery p.369
551 'Sir! You have' Anecdote quoted to the author by Gen. Sir David Richardson 22.4.81
551 'Few armies ever' UKNA WO208/3575
554 'Resistance is small' Hastings *Das Reich* p.218

Bibliography

Author's Note

In writing this book I have consulted a huge range of titles, many of them narratives of aspects of the conflict, rather than explicitly intelligence-related: thus, some general works are unmentioned below. Meanwhile 1939–45 espionage, codebreaking and guerrilla war form vast literatures of their own. I have read a significant fraction over the past half-century, but list below only titles explicitly relevant to my text. Their inclusion is not an endorsement of their credibility – often, the reverse is the case; it is instead simply a reflection of the fact that I or Dr Lyuba Vinogradovna have read them while researching this work.

Articles, Online Sources etc.

Aizenshtat, Yakov 'Zapiski sekretarya voennogo tribunala' (Notes of the Secretary of the Military Tribunal) London, Overseas Publ. Interchange 1991

Baxter, Christopher 'Forgeries and Spies: The Foreign Office and the "Cicero" Case' *Intelligence and National Security* Dec 2008 p.807

Bonsall, A. 'An Uphill Struggle: The Provision of Tactical Sigint Support to the Allied Air Forces in Europe in WWII' in Stubbington, John *Bomber Command: Kept in the Dark* p.205

Butirsky, Larin & Shanki http://www.ozon.ru/context/detail,id/23880430

'Chris' http://chris-intel-corner.blogspot.gr/2012/07/japanese-codebreakers-of-wwii.html

Crossland, James 'Operation Kitchenmaid' *Intelligence and National Security* 28 no. 6 Dec 2013 pp.808–23

Erskine, Ralph 'Tunny Reveals B-Dienst Successes against the "Convoy Code"' *Intelligence and National Security* 28 no. 6 2013 pp.868–89

—'Captured Kriegsmarine Enigma Documents at Bletchley Park' *Cryptologia* 32 no. 3 2008 pp.199–219

—'The Admiralty and Cipher Machines During the Second World War: Not So Stupid After All' *Journal of Intelligence History* 2 no. 2 2002 pp.49–68

—'William Friedman's Bletchley Park Diary: A Different View' *Intelligence and National Security* 22 no. 3 Jun 2007 pp.367–79

—(with Peter Freeman) 'Brigadier John Tiltman: One of Britain's Finest Cryptologists' *Cryptologia* 27 no. 4 Oct 2003 pp.289–318

—'Eavesdropping on "Bodden": ISOS v. the Abwehr in the Straits of Gibraltar' *Intelligence and National Security* 12 no. 3 Jul 1997 pp.110–29

—'Ultra and Some U.S. Navy Carrier Operations' *Cryptologia* 19 no. 1 Jan 1995 pp.81–96

—'Ultra Reveals a Late B-Dienst Success in the Atlantic' *Cryptologia* 34 no. 4 Oct 2010
    pp.340–58
—'What Did the Sinkov Mission Receive from Bletchley Park?' *Cryptologia* 24 no. 2 Apr 2000
    pp.97–109
—'Naval Enigma: A Missing Link' *International Journal of Intelligence and Counterintelligence*
    3 no. 4 Winter 1989 pp.493–508
—'The Soviets & Naval Enigma: Some Comments' *Intelligence and National Security* 4 no. 3 Jul
    1989 pp.503–11
—'The Poles Reveal Their Secrets: Alastair Denniston's Account of the July 1939 Meeting at
    Pyry' *Cryptologia* 30 no. 4 Oct 2006 pp.294–305
Ferris, John 'British Estimates of the Imperial Japanese Army' *Canadian Journal of History*
    28 Aug 1993 pp.223–56
Ford, Harold 'The US Government's Experience with Intelligence Analysis' *Intelligence and
    National Security* Dec 1995 p.35
Gildea, Robert 'Resistance, Reprisals and Community in Occupied France' lecture at the
    University of Wales 18.10.2000
Good, Jack, Donald Michie & Geoffrey Timms 'General Report on Tunny' http://www.
    alanturing.net/turing_archive/archive/index/tunnyreportindex.html; or in UKNA
    HW25/4 &5
Grebennkov, Vadim http://www.cryptohistory.ru/book/
Grey, Christopher *Intelligence and National Security* 28 no. 6 Dec 2013 pp.705–807
Hurt, John 'The Japanese Problem in the Signal Intelligence Service 1930–45' Friedman
    Papers Box 212
Ivanov, Ivan *Promyhlennyi kurier* 2 Sept 2005
Jones, R.V. *Intelligence and National Security* 9 1994 p.2
Kedward, H.R. 'Resisting French Resistance' lecture at Sussex University 27 Mar 1998
Kuromiya, Hirokaki & Peplonsky, Andrezej 'Kozo Isumi and the Soviet Breach of Imperial
    Japanese Diplomatic Codes' *Intelligence and National Security* 28 no. 6 Dec 1913
Naftali, Timothy 'Intrepid's Last Deception' *Intelligence and National Security* Jul 1993 p.72
Official website of the Russian Intelligence Service http://www.svr.gov.ru
Pavlov, A. 'Military Intelligence in the USSR in 1941–1945', in Igor Damaskin p.286 et seq.
Pavlov, Vitaly 'Open, Sesame' in *Sezam, otkroisya*
Praun, Albert 'Report on German Wartime Sigint Operations' https://www.nsa.gov/
    publicinfo/files/friedmandocuments/Publication/Folder240/2494174899907819.pdf
Richard, Joseph 'The Breaking of the Japanese Army's Codes' *Cryptologia* 28 Apr 2004
    pp.289–309
Rusbridger, James 'The Sinking of the *Automedon*, the Capture of the *Nankin*: New Light on
    Two Intelligence Disasters in World War II' *Encounter* 64 no. 5 May 1985
Thomas, David 'The Legend of Agent Max' *Foreign Intelligence and Literary Science* 5 1986
TICOM studies of German cryptanalysis, various, in online archive https://www.sites.google.
    com/site/icomarchive/the-targets/okm-chi/relatedreports; also http://www.chris-intel-
    comer.blogspot.co.uk
Weaver, Michael 'International Co-Operation and Bureaucratic Infighting: American and
    British Economic Intelligence Sharing and the Strategic Bombing of Germany' *Intelligence
    and National Security* Feb 2008 p.153

Books

Albertelli, Sebastien *Les Services Secrète de la France Libre* Ministère de Defence & Nouveau
    Monde 2012
Aldrich, Richard *Intelligence and the War Against Japan* CUP 2000
Allen, Louis *The Longest War: Burma 1941–45* Dent 1985
Andrew, Christopher *Secret Service: The Making of the British Intelligence Community*
    Heinemann 1985

—*The Defence of the Realm: The Authorized History of MI5* Allen Lane 2009
—& David Dilks (eds) *The Missing Dimension: Governments and Intelligence Communities in the Twentieth Century* Macmillan 1984
—& Vasili Mitrokhin *The Mitrokhin Archive* Allen Lane 1999
Annan, Noel *Our Age* Weidenfeld & Nicolson 1990
Bailey, Roderick (ed.) *Target Italy: The Secret War Against Mussolini 1940–43* Faber 2014
—*Forgotten Voices of the Secret War* Ebury 2008
—*The Wildest Province* Jonathan Cape 2007
Bamford, James *The Puzzle Palace* Sidgwick & Jackson 1983
Baring, Sarah *The Road to Station X* Wilton 65 2000
Bazna, Elyesa *I Was Cicero* André Deutsch 1962
Beesly, Patrick *Very Special Intelligence* Hamish Hamilton 1977
Beevor, Antony *The Mystery of Olga Chekhova* Viking 2004
Beevor, J.G. *SOE: Recollections and Reflections 1940–45* Bodley Head 1981
Behrendt, Hans-Otto *Rommel's Intelligence in the Desert Campaign* Kimber 1980
Bennett, Gill *Churchill's Man of Mystery* Routledge 2009
Bennett, Ralph *Ultra and Mediterranean Strategy 1941–45* Hamish Hamilton 1989
—*Ultra in the West* Hutchinson 1979
Beus, J.G. de *Tomorrow at Dawn!* Norton 1980
Binney, Marcus *The Women Who Lived for Danger* Hodder & Stoughton 2002
—*Secret War Heroes* Hodder & Stoughton 2005
Borovik, Genrikh *The Philby Files* ed. Philip Knightley London 1994
Bower, Tom *The Perfect English Spy: Sir Dick White and the Secret War 1935–1990* Heinemann 1995
Boyd, Carl *Hitler's Japanese Confidant* Kansas University Press 1993
Boyle, Andrew *Climate of Treason* Hutchinson 1979
Brinkley, David *Washington Goes to War* Knopf 1988
Brooke, Alan *War Diaries 1939–45* ed. Alex Danchev and Daniel Todman Weidenfeld & Nicolson 2001
Bruce Lockhart, Sir Robert *Diaries 1939–65* ed. Kenneth Young Macmillan 1980
Budiansky, Stephen *Battle of Wits* Penguin 2000
Butler, Ewan *Mason-Mac* Macmillan 1972
Caddick-Adams, Peter *Snow and Steel: The Battle of the Bulge 1944–45* Preface 2014
Cadogan, Alexander *The Diaries of Sir Alexander Cadogan 1938–45* ed. David Dilks Cassell 1971
Calvocoressi, Peter *Top Secret Ultra* Cassell 1980
Carlson, Elliot *Joe Rochefort's War* Naval Institute Press 2011
Cecil, Robert *A Divided Life* Bodley Head 1988
Clayton, Eileen *The Enemy Is Listening* Hutchinson 1980
Clive, Nigel *A Greek Experience 1943–48* Michael Russell 1985
Cookridge, E.H. *Inside SOE* Arthur Barker 1966
Copeland, B. Jack (ed.) *The Essential Turing* OUP 2004
—*Colossus: The Secrets of Bletchley Park's Codebreaking Computers* OUP 2006
Cradock, Percy *Know Your Enemy: How the JIC Saw the World* John Murray 2002
Cruickshank, Charles *Deception in World War II* OUP 1979
—*SOE in Scandinavia* OUP 1986
Damaskin, Igor *Stalin i razvedka* (Stalin and the Intelligence Service) Moscow 2004
Deacon, Richard *The Japanese Secret Service* Muller 1982
Debruyne, Emmanuel *La Guerre Secrète des Espions Belges 1940–44* Racine 2000
Degtyarev, Klim & Kolpakidi, Aleksandr *Vneshnyaya Razvedka SSSR* (Soviet Foreign Intelligence) Moscow, Eksmo 2009
Delattre, Lucas *Betraying Hitler: The Story of Fritz Kolbe, the Most Important Spy of the Second World War* Atlantic 2006

Docrrics, Reinhard R. *Hitler's Last Chief of Foreign Intelligence: Allied Interrogations of Walter Schellenberg* Frank Cass 2003

Dulles, Allen *From Hitler's Doorstep: The Wartime Intelligence Reports of Allen Dulles 1942–45* ed. Neal Petersen Penn State University 1996

Elliott-Bateman, Michael (ed.) *The Fourth Dimension of Warfare* Manchester UP 1970

Elphick, Peter & Smith, Michael *Odd Man Out: The Story of the Singapore Traitor* Hodder & Stoughton 1993

Farago, Ladislas *The Game of the Foxes* Hodder 1972

Feklisov, Aleksandr *Za okeanom i na ostrove, zapiski razvedchika* (Across the Ocean and on the Island: Memoirs of an Intelligence Man) Moscow 2001

Fisk, Robert *In Time of War* André Deutsch 1983

Foot, M.R.D. *The Special Operations Executive 1940–46* BBC 1984

—*SOE in France* HMSO 1976

—& Langley, J.M. *MI9: Escape and Evasion 1939–45* Bodley Head 1979

Foote, Alexander *A Handbook for Spies* Museum Press 1949

Fourcade, Marie-Madeleine *Noah's Ark* Allen & Unwin 1973

Gannon, Paul *Colossus: Bletchley Park's Greatest Secret* Atlantic 2006

Garlinski, Josef *The Swiss Corridor* Dent 1981

Gladkov, Teodor *Ego Velichestvo Agent* (His Majesty's Agent) Moscow 2010

Glanz, David *Soviet Military Intelligence in War* Frank Cass 1990

Gogun, Aleksandr & Kentiy, Aleksandr *Krasnye partizany Ukrainy* (Red Partisans of the Ukraine) Ukrainsky Izdatelsky Soyuz 2006

Goodman, Michael S. *The Official History of the Joint Intelligence Committee* vol. I Routledge 2014

Gorodetsky, Gabriel *Grand Delusion: Stalin and the German Invasion of Russia* Yale University Press 1999

Gourevitch, A. *Un Certain Monsieur Kent* Grasset 1995

Handel, Michael (ed.) *Strategic and Operational Deception in the Second World War* Frank Cass 1987

Harris Smith, R. *OSS: The History of America's First Central Intelligence Agency* University of California Press 1972

Harrison, E.D.R. (ed.) *The Secret World: Hugh Trevor-Roper on Wartime Intelligence* I.B. Tauris 2014

—*The Young Kim Philby* Exeter University Press 2012

Hastings, Max *Bomber Command* Michael Joseph 1979

—*Das Reich: The 2nd SS Panzer Division's March to Normandy June 1944* Michael Joseph 1981

—*Overlord: D-Day and the Battle for Normandy* Michael Joseph 1984

—*Armageddon: The Battle for Germany 1944–45* Macmillan 2004

—*Nemesis: The Battle for Japan 1944–45* HarperCollins 2007

—*Finest Years: Churchill as Warlord 1940–45* William Collins 2009

—*All Hell Let Loose: The World at War 1939–45* William Collins 2011

Haukelid, Knut *Skis Against the Atom* North American Heritage 1989

Hayden, Sterling *The Wanderer* Sheridan House 2000

Hinsley, F.H. et al. *British Intelligence in the Second World War* four vols HMSO 1979–90

Hinsley, F.H. & Stripp, Alan *Codebreakers: The Inside Story of Bletchley Park* OUP 1993

Hodges, Andrew *Alan Turing: The Enigma of Intelligence* Allen & Unwin 1983

Hohne, Heinz *Canaris* Secker & Warburg 1979

Holmes, W.J. *Double-Edged Secrets: US Naval Intelligence Operations in the Pacific During World War II* Naval Institute Press 1979

Holt, Thaddeus *The Deceivers* Weidenfeld & Nicolson 2004

Howarth, Patrick *Undercover: The Men and Women of SOE* Routledge, Kegan Paul 1980

—*Intelligence Chief Extraordinary: The Life of the Ninth Duke of Portland* Bodley Head 1986

Hue, Andre *The Next Moon* Viking 2004

Hunt, David *A Don at War* Kimber 1966
Jeffery, Keith *MI6: The History of the Secret Intelligence Service* Bloomsbury 2010
Jones, R.V. *Most Secret War* Hamish Hamilton 1978
—*Reflections on Intelligence* Heinemann 1984
Kahn, David *Hitler's Spies* Hodder & Stoughton 1978
—*Seizing the Enigma* Souvenir 1991
—*How I Discovered World War II's Greatest Spy* CRC Press 2014
Katz, Barry M. *Foreign Intelligence: Research and Analysis in the Office of Strategic Services 1942–45* Harvard University Press 1989
Kemp, Peter *The Thorns of Memory* Sinclair Stevenson 1990
Kennedy, Paul *Engineers of Victory* Allen Lane 2012
Komatsu, Keiichiro *The Importance of Magic* Routledge, Kegan Paul 1999
Korovin, V.V. *Sovetskaya razvedka I kontrrazvedka v gody Velikoi Otechestvennoi voiny* (Soviet Intelligence and Counter-Intelligence During the Great Patriotic War) Moscow 2003
Kotani, Ken *Japanese Intelligence in World War II* Osprey 2009
Langhorne, Richard (ed.) *Diplomacy and Intelligence During the Second World War: Essays in Honour of F.H. Hinsley* Cambridge 1985
Langley, J.M. *Fight Another Day* Magnum 1974
Lewin, Ronald *The American Magic* Farrar, Straus & Giroux 1982
Liddell, Guy *The Guy Liddell Diaries* ed. Nigel West two vols Routledge, Kegan Paul 2005
Lloyd, Mark *The Art of Military Deception* Leo Cooper 1997
Lord, Walter *Lonely Vigil* Viking 1977
Macintyre, Ben *A Spy Among Friends* Bloomsbury 2014
—*Double Cross* Bloomsbury 2012
—*Operation Mincemeat* Bloomsbury 2010
—*Agent ZigZag* Bloomsbury 2007
Mackay, Sinclair *The Secret Life of Bletchley Park* Aurum 2010
Mackenzie, William *The Secret History of SOE* St Ermins 2000
McLachlan, Donald *Room 39: Naval Intelligence in Action 1939–45* Weidenfeld & Nicolson 1968
Martelli, George *Agent Extraordinary* William Collins 1960
Masterman, J.C. *The Double Cross System* Granada 1979
Meyer, Hebert *Real World Intelligence* Weidenfeld & Nicolson 1987
Millar, George *The Bruneval Raid* Cassell 1974
—*Road to Resistance* Bodley Head 1979
Modin, Yuri *My Five Cambridge Friends* Headline 1994
Monk, Ray *Inside the Centre: The Life of J. Robert Oppenheimer* Jonathan Cape 2012
Moss, W. Stanley *A War of Shadows* BFB 2014
Muggeridge, Malcolm *The Infernal Grove* William Collins 1973
Multiple authors *Partizanskaya voina na Ukraine. Dnevniki komandirov partizanskikh otryadov I soedineniy. 1941–1945* (Partisan War in the Ukraine: Diaries of Commanders of Partisan Detachments and Groups. 1941–1945) Moscow 2010
Mure, David *Master of Deception* Kimber 1980
Newby, Eric *Love and War in the Apennines* Picador 1983
Pahl, Magnus *Fremde Heere Ost. Hitlers militärische Feindaufklärung* (Foreign Armies East: Hitler's Military Reconnaissance) Berlin 2012
Perrault, Giles *The Red Orchestra* Arthur Barker 1968
Persico, Joseph *Piercing the Reich* Michael Joseph 1979
Peshchersky, Vladimir *Krasnaya Kapella: Sovetskaya razvedka protiv abvera i Gestapo* (Rote Kapelle: The Soviet Intelligence Service Against the Abwehr and Gestapo) Moscow 2000
Peskett, S. John *Strange Intelligence* Robert Hale 1981
Petersen, Neal H. *From Hitler's Doorstep: The Wartime Intelligence Reports of Allen Dulles 1942–1945* Penn State University Press 1996

Pidgeon, Geoffrey *The Secret Wireless War* UPSO 2003

Porch, Douglas *The French Secret Service* Macmillan 1996

Poznyakov, V. *Sovetskaya razvedka v Amerike 1919–1941* (The Soviet Intelligence Service in America 1919–1941) Moscow 2005

Prange, Gordon *Target Tokyo: The Story of the Sorge Spy Ring* McGraw-Hill 1984

Price, Alfred *Instruments of Darkness* Panther 1979

Prudnikova, E. *Rikhard Zorge, chuzhoi sredi svoikh* (Richard Sorge: An Enemy Within) Moscow 2010

Reed-Olsen, Oluf *Two Eggs on My Plate* Allen & Unwin 1952

Schlesinger, Arthur M. *A Life in the Twentieth Century* Mariner 2000

Seki, Eiji *Mrs Ferguson's Tea Set: Japan and the Second World War* Global Oriental 2000

Seth, Ronald *A Spy Has No Friends* Headline 2008

Sharapov, Eduard & Voskresenskaya, Zoya *Taina Zoi Voskresenskoi* (The Mystery of Zoya Voskresenskaya) Moscow 1998

Sharp, Tony *Stalin's American Spy: Noel Field, Allen Dulles and the Eastern European Show Trials* Hurst 2014

Sisman, Adam *Hugh Trevor-Roper* Weidenfeld & Nicolson 2010

Slowikowsky, Maj. Gen. Rygor *In the Secret Service: The Lighting of the Torch* Windrush 1988

Smiley, David *Albanian Assignment* Chatto & Windus 1984

Smith, Bradley *The Ultra–Magic Deals and the Most Secret Special Relationship 1940–1946* Airlife 1993

Smith, Michael *Station X: The Codebreakers of Bletchley Park* Pan 2004

— with Ralph Erskine (eds) *Action This Day* Bantam 2001

Soboleva, T.A. *Istoriya shifrovalnogo dela v Rossii* (A History of Cryptography in Russia) Moscow

SOE Syllabus Public Record Office 2001

Sotskov, L.F. (ed.) *Aggressiya. Rassekrechennye dokumenty sluzhby razvedki RF, 1939–41* (Aggression. Declassified Documents of the Foreign Intelligence Service of the Russian Federation, 1939–41) Moscow 2001

Spencer Chapman, Frederick *The Jungle Is Neutral* Chatto & Windus 1949

Stephan, Enno *Spies in Ireland* Macdonald 1963

Stirling, Tessa (ed.) *Report of the Anglo-Polish Historical Committee: Intelligence Co-operation Between Poland and Great Britain* London

Strong, Kenneth *Intelligence at the Top* Giniger 1968

Stubbington, John *Bomber Command: Kept in the Dark* Pen & Sword 2010

Sudoplatov, Pavel (with Anatoli Sudoplatov and Jerrold & Leona Schecter) *Special Tasks* Little, Brown 1994

Sweet-Escott, Bickham *Baker Street Irregular* Methuen 1965

Thorne, Christopher *Allies of a Kind* Hamish Hamilton 1978

Tooze, Adam *The Wages of Destruction* Penguin 2005

Trepper, Leopold *The Great Game* Michael Joseph 1977

Trevor-Roper, Hugh *The Wartime Journals* ed. Richard Davenport-Hines I.B. Tauris 2012

— *The Secret World* ed. Edward Harrison I.B. Tauris 2014

Trubnikov (ed.) *Ocherki Istorii Sovietski Vneshei Razvedki* (Essays on the History of the Soviet Foreign Intelligence Service) Moscow 2007

Vinogradov et al. (eds) *Sekrety Gitlera na Stole u Stalina* (Hitler's Secrets on Stalin's Desk) Moscow 1995

Voskresenskaya, Zoya *Teper ya mogu skazat pravdu* (Now I Can Tell the Truth) Moscow 1993

Wake-Walker, Edward *A House for Spies* Robert Hale 2012

Waller, Douglas *Wild Bill Donovan* Simon & Schuster 2012

Webster, Jason *The Spy With 29 Names* Chatto & Windus 2014

Weinstein, Allen & Vassiliev, Alexander *The Haunted Wood: Soviet Espionage in America – The Stalin Era* Random House 1999

Welchman, Gordon *The Hut Six Story* McGraw-Hill 1982

West, Nigel *MI6: British Secret Intelligence Service Operations 1909–45* Weidenfeld & Nicolson 1983

Wheatley, Dennis *The Deception Planners* Hutchinson 1980

Williams, Allan *Operation Crossbow* Preface 2013

Winterbotham, F.W. *The Ultra Secret* Weidenfeld & Nicolson 1974

Woodman, Richard *The Malta Convoys* John Murray 2000

Index

About the Author

MAX HASTINGS is the author of more than twenty books, most recently *Catastrophe: 1914*. He has served as a foreign correspondent and as the editor of Britain's *Evening Standard* and *Daily Telegraph*. He has received numerous British Press Awards, including Journalist of the Year in 1982 and Editor of the Year in 1988. He lives outside London.